BEN JONSON: A LIFE

Ian Donaldson is a General Editor, with David Bevington and Martin Butler, of *The Cambridge Edition of the Works of Ben Jonson* (Print Edition, 7 volumes, 2012; Electronic Edition, 2013). His previous OUP books include *The World Upside-Down: Comedy From Jonson to Fielding* (1970), *The Rapes of Lucretia: A Myth and its Transformations* (1982) *Ben Jonson* (Oxford Authors, 1985), *Jonson's Magic Houses: Essays in Interpretation* (OUP, 1997). He has taught at the Universities of Oxford (tutorial Fellow in English at Wadham College, 1962–9), Edinburgh (Regius Professor of English, 1991–5), and Cambridge (Fellow of King's College, 1995–2005, and Grace 1 Professor of English, 1995–2001), and at the Australian National University, Canberra (Professor of English, 1969–91). He was founding Director of the ANU's Humanities Research Centre (1974–90, 2004–7) and of Cambridge University's Centre for Research in the Arts, Social Sciences, and Humanities (CRASSH, 2001–3) and is now Honorary Professorial Fellow at the University of Melbourne.

Praise for *Ben Jonson: A Life*

Ian Donaldson's 'deep involvement with Jonson scholarship and criticism . . . is apparent on every page of this authoritative, elegantly written, and illuminatingly illustrated new biography.'

Stanley Wells, *New York Review of Books*

'*Ben Jonson: A Life* is a serious, scholarly biography that is the result of years of painstaking labour. It is also a great pleasure to read. Ian Donaldson has an eye for detail, as well as episodes, events and pieces of evidence that can be reproduced to provide insight into the subject's complicated life. His judgements are never made lightly, and the treatment of Jonson's religious views, his fractious relationship with the authorities, and that between his life and his art is exemplary.'

Andrew Hadfield, *PN Review*

'Ian Donaldson has long been a student and editor of Jonson. He has now produced a first-rate academic biography, authoritative, persuasive, a goldmine of information, freshly illuminating, for instance Jonson's famous walk from London to Edinburgh when he was 46 and weighed twenty stone; his education, his recusancy, his learning; his part in the Folio . . . a learned biography, it cuts a revealing section through the Jacobean age.'

Michael Alexander, *The Tablet*

'In this magisterial biography, Donaldson does justice to all aspects of this fascinating figure . . . a splendid life of this extraordinary man, which all claimants to the "tribe of Ben" will savor and prize.'

Edward Short, *The Weekly Standard*

'Ian Donaldson's excellent new biography is the fruit of a lifetime's study . . . It gives the most detailed account we are likely to have of Jonson's life, based on a mastery of primary and secondary sources, with many penetrating comments on his plays, masques and poems . . . He is the first biographer to do justice to the range and complexity of his life, an achievement that will be difficult to surpass.'

Brian Vickers, *The Times Literary Supplement*

'There has been no more authoritative or assured biography of a Renaissance writer, and none that has more successfully brought historical and literary insights together.'

Blair Worden, *London Review of Books*

Frontispiece. 'He was (or rather had been) of a clear and fair skin; his habit was very plain', wrote John Aubrey of Ben Jonson. Aubrey is unlikely ever to have seen Jonson, who died while Aubrey was still a child in Wiltshire. 'A staring Leviathan' with 'a terrible mouth', 'a beard afraid to peep out', 'a parboiled face . . . punched full of oilet holes, like the cover of a warming pan' was Thomas Dekker's less kindly description of Jonson, whom he had observed critically and at close quarters. This portrait of Jonson by the Flemish artist Abraham van Blyenberch, now in the National Portrait Gallery, London, was probably painted around 1617, and may once have been owned by James I's favourite, George Villiers, first Duke of Buckingham.

BEN JONSON
A Life

IAN DONALDSON

OXFORD
UNIVERSITY PRESS

OXFORD
UNIVERSITY PRESS

Great Clarendon Street, Oxford, OX2 6DP,
United Kingdom

Oxford University Press is a department of the University of Oxford.
It furthers the University's objective of excellence in research, scholarship,
and education by publishing worldwide. Oxford is a registered trade mark of
Oxford University Press in the UK and in certain other countries

First Edition published in 2011
First published in paperback 2013

Impression: 1

British Library Cataloguing in Publication Data

Data available

Library of Congress Cataloging in Publication Data

Data available

ISBN 978–0–19–812976–9 (Hbk.)
ISBN 978–0–19–969747–2 (Pbk.)

Printed in Great Britain by
Clays Ltd, St Ives plc

2 4 6 8 10 9 7 5 3 1

FOR GRAZIA

Acknowledgements

THIS book has been greatly delayed but also (I hope) appreciably enhanced by another undertaking with which—together with my friends David Bevington and Martin Butler and an international team of editors—I've been simultaneously engaged over the past decade and a half, and which is also now approaching completion: *The Cambridge Edition of the Works of Ben Jonson*. I've learnt much from this large collaborative exercise, and am grateful to all members of the editorial team for the illumination they have (wittingly or unwittingly) provided for this present study of Jonson's life. Particular debts to these editors are acknowledged in the text or end-notes of this book, but some special acts of kindness must be mentioned here. James Loxley has generously allowed me to quote from a hitherto unknown document which he discovered in the Cheshire and Chester archives relating to Jonson's walk to Scotland, which he and Julie Sanders are currently preparing for publication. He and Tom Cain have commented helpfully on early chapters of the book. David Bevington and Martin Butler have aided and encouraged the present work in more ways than I can easily describe or repay. Professor Butler has read the entire typescript with a sharp eye, making many suggestions for improvement, and rescuing me from errors. I thank him warmly for this help, and both these colleagues for their friendship and support.

I am grateful for the encouragement and advice offered in the earliest stages of my work by Kevin Sharpe, Alvin B. Kernan, the late Jonas A. Barish, the late J. B. Bamborough, and the late Samuel Schoenbaum, as well as by two authors of earlier studies of Jonson's life, David Riggs and David Kay; and by members of a class on 'Ben Jonson in his Age' I was privileged to run at the Folger Shakespeare Library, Washington, DC, in 1988. Ian Britain and Park Honan offered helpful comments on individual chapters, and Peter Rose kindly reviewed a late draft of the entire manuscript. I am indebted to other friends who have offered help, information, and support: Nick Alfieri, Anne Barton, Kate Bennett, Jonquil Bevan, Mark Bland, Michael Brennan, Karen Britland, the late Derek Britton, Christopher Burlinson, Colin Burrow, Graeme W. Clarke, David Colclough, Katherine Craik, Richard Dutton,

Robert C. Evans, John Frow, Ian Gadd, Eugene Giddens, R. D. S. Jack, David Jaffé, Peter Jones, the late Sir Frank Kermode, John Kerrigan, Arthur Kinney, James Knowles, Hester Lees-Jeffries, David Lockie, the late D. F. McKenzie, Rosalind Miles, John Morrill, Lena Cowen Orlin, Michael O'Sullivan, John S. Richardson, the late Tony Tanner, James Tulip, the late Stephen Wall, Henry Woudhuysen, and the late Iain Wright. I owe special thanks to Richard Holmes for his encouragement and good counsel.

My enjoyment and understanding of Jonson's life and writings have been constantly extended by the students I've had the pleasure of teaching at four universities—the Australian National University, the University of Edinburgh, the University of Cambridge, and the University of Melbourne—while writing this book. I thank them warmly and collectively for all I have learnt from our discussions. I am particularly indebted to the work of my former Cambridge doctoral students Gabriel Heaton, Tom Lockwood, and Andrew Lynn, on which I gratefully draw in this book.

This book was originally commissioned by the late Kim Scott Walwyn, an inspirational editor. I am deeply grateful for her initiative and trust, and sad that she is not here to see the book in its final state. Her colleagues and successors at Oxford University Press have been unfailingly helpful and supportive. Sophie Goldsworthy has maintained a close eye on the book's progress; Andrew McNeillie has spurred me forward during critical stages of rewriting; and Jacqueline Baker has offered encouraging guidance throughout the final period of composition. I thank them all most sincerely, as I do the book's assistant editor, Ariane Petit, its copy-editor, Jackie Pritchard, and its picture editor, Sandra Assersohn.

My greatest debt is to my wife, Grazia Gunn, to whom this book is lovingly dedicated.

Contents

List of Plates

Family Trees

Abbreviations

CSPD   *Calendar of State Papers, Domestic Series*

CSPV   *Calendar of State Papers, Venetian Series*

CWBJ   *The Cambridge Edition of the Works of Ben Jonson*, ed. David Bevington, Martin Butler, and Ian Donaldson, Print Edition, 7 vols. (Cambridge, 2012); Electronic Edition (2013)

DNB   *The Dictionary of National Biography*

H&S   *Ben Jonson*, ed. C. H. Herford and Percy and Evelyn Simpson, 11 vols. (Oxford, 1925–52)

ODNB   *The Oxford Dictionary of National Biography*

Note on Texts and Dating

ALL quotations from Ben Jonson are taken from the modernized text of the seven-volume Cambridge University Press Print Edition of *The Cambridge Edition of the Works of Ben Jonson*, general editors David Bevington, Martin Butler, and Ian Donaldson (Cambridge, 2012). The Electronic Edition of *The Cambridge Edition of the Works of Ben Jonson*, representing roughly four times the capacity of the Print Edition, is scheduled for publication by Cambridge University Press in 2013. This contains a range of textual and contextual materials which are cited here prospectively, wherever possible with an additional reference to their original source. In keeping with the conventions of this edition, all other quotations from the early modern period (apart from those to the works of Spenser) are silently modernized, even when taken from old-spelling editions. Manuscript material is cited in its original form only when it seems important to preserve a doubt or ambiguity (e.g. over the identity of a place or person) or other particular quality. Names are elsewhere spelled wherever possible in the preferred style of the *Oxford Dictionary of National Biography*.

Various systems of dating existed within Jonson's lifetime (1572–1637). On 24 February 1582 Pope Gregory XIII introduced a reformed calendar which was adopted by most Catholic countries in Europe by 1583, but resisted in England until 1751. Throughout most of Jonson's lifetime the English calendar consequently lagged ten days behind that of continental Europe. The dual system of dating is indicated here (as often in correspondence in Jonson's time) by a double citation, e.g. 12/22 November 1610. Within England, the new year was sometimes reckoned to begin on 1 January, but sometimes, in accordance with legal practice, on 25 March (Lady Day). In Scotland, the Gregorian calendar was introduced in 1600, and by a simultaneous adjustment the new year was declared to begin on 1 January. All datings given here assume that the British year began on 1 January. Jonson's own varying practice in dating was examined by W. W. Greg, 'The Riddle of Jonson's Chronology', *The Library*, 6 (1926), 340–7. Greg's conclusions have now been significantly challenged by Martin Butler, 'The Riddle of Jonson's Chronology Revisited', *The Library*, 7th series, 4 (2003), 49–63.

I

Prologue
The Biographer's Bones

'HE lies buried in the north aisle in the path of square stone (the rest of lozenge)', noted John Aubrey meticulously in his otherwise haphazard recollections of the life of Ben Jonson:

opposite to the scutcheon of Robertus de Ros, with this inscription only on him, in a pavement square of blue marble about 14 inches square,

O RARE BEN JONSON

which was done at the charge of Jack Young (afterwards knighted) who, walking there when the grave was covering, gave the fellow eighteen pence to cut it.

All details of these final arrangements for Jonson's interment are precisely observed and accounted for: the colour, location, and size of the marble tablet, the laconic wording of this last tribute, the name (and subsequent honouring) of its deviser, the fee paid to the engraver. Many facts relating to the lives of the subjects he attempted to chronicle, as Aubrey well knew, were open to question or wholly irrecoverable, but death delivered the ultimate and (as it seemed) incontrovertible items of biographical evidence. Such details he recorded whenever he could with similar fastidious care. Thus the poet Samuel Butler—so Aubrey carefully noted—lay in the churchyard of Covent Garden 'in the north part next the church at the east end. His feet touch the wall. His grave, two yards distant from the pilaster of the door (by his desire) six foot deep.' The scholar John Hales, he observed, 'lies buried in the churchyard at Eton, under an altar monument of black marble, erected at the sole charge of Mr . . . Curwyn, with too long an epitaph'. Sir William Davenant, Jonson's immediate successor as royal laureate, 'had a coffin of walnut-tree (Sir John Denham said 'twas the finest coffin that ever he saw)', and was buried in Westminster Abbey 'in the south cross aisle, on which, on a paving stone of marble, is writ, in imitation of that on Ben Jonson, "O rare Sir Will Davenant"'. Such details play a central, validating role within Aubrey's *Brief Lives*, furnishing (so it seems) the hard, verifiable evidence on which his large, disorderly, sprawlingly ambitious biographical enterprise ultimately rests.[1]

Occasionally, through astounding good fortune, Aubrey was able to make even closer approaches to the realms and remains of the dead. Writing of Father William Barrow (otherwise known as Harcourt), for example, a Jesuit who was burnt at the stake at Tyburn in the aftermath of the Popish Plot, Aubrey notes that when the priest was disembowelled and his entrails thrown into the blaze,

a butcher's boy standing by was resolved to have a piece of his kidney which was broiling in the fire. He burned his fingers much, but he got it; and one . . . Roydon, a brewer in Southwark, bought it, a kind of Presbyterian. The wonder is, 'tis now absolutely petrified. I have seen it. He much values it.

I have seen it: Aubrey here offers the clinching evidence of his own senses. In another note on this event, he describes the precise feel, the tactility, of the Jesuit's kidney, which is 'now petrified and very hard. But 'twas not so hard when he first had it. It being always carried in the pocket hardened by degrees better than by the fire—like an agate polished.' The Great Fire of London provided further opportunities for biographical verification, its intense heat searing open the monuments in St Paul's to reveal the leaden coffins of Sir Philip Sidney ('which . . . I myself saw') and the former Dean of St Paul's, John Colet. This coffin,

which was lead, was full of a liquor which conserved the body. Mr Wyld and Ralph Greatorex tasted it, and 'twas a kind of insipid taste, something of an ironish taste. The body felt, to the probe of a stick which they thrust into a chink, like brawn. The coffin was of lead and laid in the wall about 2 foot ½ above the surface of the floor.

Probing, prying, thrusting, touching, tasting: Aubrey's biographical enquiries were conducted in the same empirical spirit as the anatomical dissections and archaeological excavations that captured the imagination of contemporary scientific investigators in England. Through systematic application of Baconian method, it seemed possible to penetrate the physical mysteries and limits of human life itself, and to establish legitimate procedures for the enticing and still very new art that was gradually coming to be known as *biography*.[2]

Given Aubrey's abiding interest in such matters, it is safe to assume that his silence about one startling aspect of Jonson's interment was due to lack of knowledge rather than indifference. For according to common and persistent gossip, Jonson was buried in the Abbey in a vertical, not a horizontal position. He did not lie in his grave (it was said), but stood. Peter Cunningham offers an explanatory version of the story in his *Handbook of London* more than two centuries after the event:

One day, being rallied by the Dean of Westminster about being buried in the Poets' Corner, the poet is said to have replied (we tell the story as current in the Abbey): 'I am too poor for that, and no one will lay out funeral charges upon me. No, sir, 6 feet long by 2 feet wide is too much for me: 2 feet by 2 feet will do for all I want.

In a variant of the tale, Jonson asks Charles I to grant him eighteen square inches of ground; the King agrees, then asks where this ground may be: 'In Westminster Abbey', says Jonson; 'Your request is granted,' responds the King. Numerous implausible legends were attached, for convenience' sake, to Ben Jonson's name in the years following his death, and both versions of this anecdote sound suspiciously like late and fanciful inventions.[3] It is the more surprising then to find that the central proposition in these stories, that Jonson had been buried in a vertical position—impatiently dismissed as ludicrous by earlier historians of Westminster Abbey—appears to have been literally true.

In 1919 the American scholar Joseph Quincy Adams—distinguished Shakespearian editor and biographer, later to be appointed as inaugural Director of the Folger Shakespeare Library in Washington DC—published an intriguing study entitled 'The Bones of Ben Jonson', in which he reviewed the evidence revealed during three separate exposures of Jonson's grave during the previous century.[4] The first disruption occurred in 1823, when the grave was opened to allow a new corpse to be buried in the adjacent plot. An eyewitness, writing later as 'J.C.B.' in *The Gentleman's Magazine*, reported that Jonson's body, clearly exposed during this exercise, had indeed been buried in a vertical position, but—somewhat incongruously—with the head downwards and the back turned towards the east, the feet sticking upwards to within a few inches of the Abbey floor. The skeleton was in a state of 'tolerable preservation', with most of the ribs still clinging to the spine. Believing Jonson to have been a small man, J.C.B. was anxious to measure 'the exact depth of the cell which the body occupied', but was evidently restrained while attempting to set about this task. He did nevertheless have the opportunity of examining Jonson's skull, which still had tufts of hair adhering to it when first lifted from the grave, though it was totally bald by the time it was returned, the tufts having been removed as souvenirs, by whom we are not told. J.C.B. trusted the poet's remains would now be 'sheltered, perhaps forever, from further disturbance, or the gaze of the curious'; but more troubles, alas! were to come.

In 1849 Ben Jonson's grave was opened up for a second time during the course of another nearby interment. On this occasion the Dean of Westminster, the geologist William Buckland, knowing the legend surrounding the burial of Ben Jonson, sent his 23-year-old son, the naturalist Francis Buckland, to watch over the excavations. Francis Buckland—a medical student at this time, and a sharp-eyed observer—confirmed that from the appearance of the remains, Jonson's coffin must indeed have been placed originally in an upright position. A gravedigger named Spice handed him a skull that he had identified as Jonson's, which Buckland immediately carried to his father's study. They examined it together, then returned it reverently to the grave, taking only a few fragments of the coffin this time as souvenirs.

Ten years later, in 1859, Jonson's grave was opened for a third time. In the years following the last disturbance, Francis Buckland had succeeded in locating the body of the famous surgeon and anatomist John Hunter, whom he much admired, and had arranged for the body's reburial in the Abbey. As chance would have it, Hunter was reinterred, with great ceremony, in a spot in the Abbey (again) right next to Jonson's grave, which was then broken open once more, its contents being exposed to the curious gaze of several hundred distinguished scientists who had gathered to witness Hunter's reburial. According to *The Times* of London of 29 March 1859, the scientists now eagerly inspected Jonson's skull, passing it freely from hand to hand. Or so they imagined. In fact the loyal Spice, anticipating this rude intrusion, had already removed the skull and conveyed it to Buckland, who had cunningly placed it on John Hunter's coffin, where it remained until Hunter's grave was nearly filled up. The skull that circulated amongst the onlookers on this occasion belonged to someone else. The skull that was placed on Hunter's grave, to be venerated perhaps by the scientific observers as a relic of the great anatomist, was actually that of Ben Jonson. Or so Francis Buckland thought at the time.

Later, however, other stories about this event began to emerge. The London *Times* of 11 November 1865 reported that, shortly before the ceremony in the Abbey six years earlier, a blind gentleman visiting Shakespeare's birthplace at Stratford-upon-Avon, and believing no one but the guide to have been present, was heard to remark that a friend of his had a relic that would be a fine trophy to display in this place: the skull of Ben Jonson. This skull, he went on, the friend had taken from Jonson's grave in Westminster Abbey as the tomb stood open awaiting Hunter's interment, and had smuggled out of the Abbey under his cloak. In consternation at this report, the then-Dean of Westminster, Dr Stanley, sent at once for Francis Buckland, who, equally concerned, looked for the faithful gravedigger, Spice, for confirmation of his own understanding of these events. But Spice unhappily had died in the intervening years. There was however Ovens, who had worked as an assistant to Spice during these interments, and was still alive. Buckland eagerly sought out Ovens. To his dismay he found Ovens to be very old, his memory almost totally gone. Ovens could remember nothing whatever about these events. There was still however Mr Ryde, the former Clerk of Works at the Abbey, who was also alive and living in retirement. Buckland tracked down Mr Ryde, whose memory was fine, though his tale was disconcerting. None of these skulls, he firmly announced, belonged to Ben Jonson. He himself had taken off the real skull many years earlier, when the grave was opened in 1849. Yes, the body had been buried vertically: he had seen the two leg-bones sticking upright through the sand, while the skull itself was at the bottom of the grave. There was still hair adhering to it, and this hair was red in colour. Ryde himself had reburied the skull in Jonson's own grave some twelve or eighteen inches below the triangular tablet in 1849 and was confident it was still there. There were three or four other skulls in the vicinity of John Hunter's grave, to be sure, but none of these (he thought) belonged to Jonson.

The story, with its bizarre twists and turns, now enters the world of *Flaubert's Parrot*, Julian Barnes's brilliantly cautionary tale for intending biographers. What had started as a pre-modern quest for biographical certainty moves into shimmering postmodern confusion. For Jonson's hair, so far as we can tell, was never red. The well-known portrait of Jonson after

Abraham van Blyenberch, now in the National Portrait Gallery in London, shows his hair as black (see frontispiece). Later, by his own account (*The Underwood*, 9.14), Jonson's hair turned partly to grey; later still, James Howell, his next-door neighbour in Westminster, observed that Jonson's 'pericranium' by now was 'snowed' (*CWBJ*, Life Records, 90, Electronic Edition). None of his contemporaries ever refers to Jonson as a redhead, though Jonson gibes at the red-headed John Marston in the character of Rufus Laberius Crispinus in *Poetaster* ('if you can change your hair, pray do', 2.2.80–1). The skull that Mr Ryde retrieved is unlikely therefore to have been that of Ben Jonson. So which skull, exactly, was his, and where is it nowadays lodged? And how exactly—to press the more obvious question—would our knowledge of Jonson be in any way enhanced if we could ever manage to find out? Empirical enquiry here runs, quite literally, into the sand. Joseph Quincy Adams concluded his researches with the hope that the poet's skull may be resting quietly today within John Hunter's grave—as quite possibly it is (though equally possibly, it is not). The larger purpose and value of Adams's quest meanwhile remained unexplained. Beyond the detailed queries concerning the exact positioning of Jonson's bones and the colour of his hair, no further questions were asked. The art of biography here (if such it could be called) seemed doomed to the graveyard in more senses than one.

§§

In 1919, however, the very year in which Joseph Quincy Adams published his report on Ben Jonson's bones, another more enterprising critic was proposing a radically different method of approach to the life of the long-dead poet. What was needed for a true understanding of Ben Jonson, so T. S. Eliot argued that year in an influential essay, was 'not archaeology but knowledge of Jonson'—knowledge which began with 'intelligent saturation in his work as a whole', and a sense of his living force as a writer, and his place 'as a contemporary' in the modern world. Eliot writes with characteristic discernment in this essay about Jonson's writings, yet it is not Jonson's writings alone, the words on the page, that interest him. He is intrigued by a larger and altogether more tantalizing phenomenon, the 'complex and devious' relationship of Jonson's life to his work: what he calls, in a striking phrase, 'the process of transfusion of the personality, or, in a deeper sense, the life, of the author' into the dramatic characters he creates.[5]

Eliot had provided a much better set of questions for biographers to think about: how the life of the poet informs the work, how the life of the past informs the present, the vitality of the entire process—so unlike the dustiness of those graveyard forays—brilliantly conveyed through that simple word *transfusion*. The questions that Eliot posed, however, were far from simple, while others that he failed to ask were equally perplexing: what Jonson's 'personality' might have been like in the first place (for example), before being transfused into his art, or how its nature might ultimately be discovered. In 1919, before Freudian analysis had made much of an impact on literary thinking in England, these were not generally seen—by more conventional scholars, at least, than Eliot—as troublesome matters. Jonson's personality, it was commonly assumed, was plainly evident from his writings. Here is how Gregory Smith, in his study of Jonson in the English Men of Letters series, published in that same year—the book that Eliot was actually reviewing for this famous *TLS* essay—confidently describes the accessibility of his subject:

We know more of Jonson than any of the great writers of his age. There are no mysteries, or at least great mysteries, in his literary career, and the biographer is not driven, with the Shakespearians, to conjectural reconstruction from the shards of record and anecdote. Even his personality stands forth fresh and convincing beside the blurred portrait of Marlowe, or Shakespeare, or Fletcher. For this fuller knowledge we are indebted to Jonson himself.[6]

Half a dozen years later, in the biographical essay that opens the first volume of the Oxford *Ben Jonson*, C. H. Herford was to express an even stronger belief in the immediate legibility of Ben Jonson's character. 'The personality of Jonson', he wrote, 'detaches itself from the crowd of literary contemporaries with a distinctness by no means wholly due to the fact that our knowledge of it happens to be unusually full and clear.' For there was also, so Herford believed, 'something potent and distinctive in the ethos of the man'. 'Almost every sentence he wrote, however derivative in substance, carries an unmistakable relish of the man—is, in a greater or less degree, a document of the Jonsonian temperament and the Jonsonian will.'

Herford saw Jonson as a writer who was remarkably consistent in his ideas, convictions, and impulses from the beginning of his career to the end. The evidence for this view lay in a literary text that was assumed to be at once transparent and homogeneous. Jonson's work, Herford wrote,

is, in a rare degree, of a piece; we can distinguish its phases and its kinds; but the note of Jonsonian personality is singularly continuous; the apprentice challenging the veterans of Spain and the old poet indicting an Ode to Himself are the same; of the extraordinary power of inner growth, which astonishes us in a Dante, a Shakespeare, a Goethe, there is little trace in Jonson.[7]

It is hard to tell here whether a critical verdict has prompted a psychological conclusion, or the other way about, for 'the Jonsonian personality' that is invoked is in every sense a continuum, seamlessly encompassing apprentice-ship and maturity, life and works, raw historical data and literary self-invention. No attempt is made to distinguish between Jonson's own tactical declarations of personal constancy and imperturbability, and the actual shifts, transformations, experiments, back-trackings, and inconsistencies which might be revealed by a closer scrutiny of his work as a whole and the serpentine progress of his professional career. The claim to an easy recogni-tion of 'something distinctive in the *ethos* of the man', though based on an unrivalled knowledge of Jonson's work, was in the final estimate little more than a subjective assertion, an editorial hunch of the kind that prompted similar judgements about the composition and dating of the canon. Those otherwise undatable works which deviated markedly from Herford and Simpson's 'potent and distinctive norm' were explained in terms of authorial senility and dismissively assigned to the period of Jonson's so-called dotage. It is only in more recent times that scholars have begun to query the Oxford editors' view of Jonson's long, coherent, and consistent career that droops inexplicably into dotage some twenty years before the author's death, and to challenge many of their once firmly established datings. The revised Jonson-ian chronology gives an altogether more irregular, various, and interesting view of the canon, and of the imaginative development of the author.[8]

Biography, whatever its methodologies, is never an exact science, and the stories biographers set out to tell must always rely to a high degree upon interpretation, imagination, and guesswork. This will be especially true in the case of a subject who was born more than 400 years ago, whose life—though comparatively well documented in relation to the lives of Shakespeare and other contemporaries—can only be known imperfectly and in part. There are large gaps in our knowledge of most lives from the early modern period, and

Jonson's is no exception. At times one is tempted almost to say that his life is mainly a matter of gaps, interspersed by fragments of knowledge. All of these fragments, moreover, demand interpretation before they can be meaningfully pressed into service.

Reading from work to life, imagining how Jonson's own identity might (in Eliot's suggestive phrase) have been *transfused* into his art, poses particular problems for any biographer. Here, as a brief foretaste of issues to come in this book, are four typical kinds of problems that might be encountered while thinking about this process: moments at which the biographer might pause, like a gravedigger on his shovel, to wonder what object—what subject, what subjectivity—is actually being unearthed.

I CHARACTERIZING

The view of Ben Jonson that Gregory Smith and C. H. Herford offered—that of a man unwavering in temperament, unchanging in creative preferences and capacities, wholly knowable and wholly known—was clearly derived in large measure from Jonson's own writings. 'For this fuller knowledge', as Gregory Smith candidly observed, 'we are indebted to Jonson himself.' At a casual reading, Jonson indeed seems the most self-revealing of poets. He writes verses constantly *to* and *about* himself. His name recurs constantly within his verse ('Ben Jonson his best piece of poetry'; 'The humble petition of poor Ben'; 'Sir, you are sealed of the tribe of Ben') as if to remind us insistently of his very identity. His poems offer frequent glimpses of the poet himself, dining contentedly with Robert Sidney at Penshurst, or preparing for a painter's visit, or tetchily demanding his laureate's ration of wine from an official of the royal household. All of these various self-portraits and allusions are devised, however, for particular rhetorical ends, and in terms of biographical evidence need to be warily regarded. 'A Celebration of Charis', for example (*The Underwood*, 2), often viewed in Victorian times as the chronicle of some doomed real-life love affair in which Jonson himself had been unhappily entangled, might more plausibly be seen as a skilful assemblage of lyrics written on quite separate occasions over many years, lyrics that are mainly (and perhaps, for all one can tell, entirely) fictional in nature.[9] Jonson's various and seemingly forthright odes 'To Himself' may similarly often be understood as idealized rather than naturalistic representations, which—like Jonson's many verse portraits of men and women he admired—show us what the subjects (the poet himself included) were capable at their best of being, rather than what, in their day-to-day lives, they actually might have been like. Poetry of this idealizing kind, as Jonson himself was uneasily aware, might seem open to moral question, but at least gave the recipients a standard to live up to. 'I have too oft preferred | Men past their terms, and praised some names too much,' Jonson confesses in an epistle addressed to his friend the jurist John Selden, 'But 'twas with purpose to have made them such' (*The Underwood*, 14.20–2).

Jonson's 'Epistle Answering to One that Asked to be Sealed of the Tribe of Ben' (*The Underwood*, 47) gives some idea of the general style of these seemingly autobiographical poems, and the interpretative problems they pose. The Epistle was written in August or September of 1623 during an anxious period of negotiation between England, Spain, and the Vatican over the proposed marriage of Prince Charles to the Spanish Infanta, a match deeply unpopular in England and critically dependent upon the still-unknown conditions that Rome might impose before the final arrangements could go forward.[10] Elaborate preparations were in train throughout the summer for the reception of the Infanta at Southampton. The official party of dignitaries to be dispatched from London included a number of privy counsellors, along with the veteran actor Edward Alleyn and Jonson's masquing collaborator and arch-rival Inigo Jones, but not Jonson himself. As the leading poet of the day and outstanding deviser of court masques, Jonson had every reason to feel resentment at his exclusion from this select group, an omission that in these final years of James's reign augured ill for his future at court under the young monarch-to-be. By early October, negotiations for the marriage having collapsed, Charles would be back from Spain without his bride, to the great relief of his loyally rejoicing people. While the Epistle was being composed during the late summer, however, these developments were still unknown. From references within the poem it is clear that Jonson was watching with sharp attention the current progress of events in Madrid and elsewhere, to which he nevertheless professes supreme indifference. The ephemeral activities of the court, 'the late mystery of reception', so the poem insists, are of scant interest to the otherwise-occupied poet. What he prizes rather are the loyalties of those devoted friends, 'the tribe of Ben', who meet regularly in the Apollo Room in Fleet Street, and the pious and stoical state of mind that he himself strives to attain.

Live to that point I will, for which I am man,
And dwell as in my centre as I can,
Still looking to, and ever loving heaven;
With reverence using all the gifts thence given.
(*The Underwood*, 47.59–62)

'*So short you read my character*,' Jonson concludes, as though offering a frank and comprehensive account of his personal condition. The poem tells us much about Jonson, but it is possible also to feel that it holds something back: that as a characterization of himself, this picture is not quite complete.

What is offered here as Jonson's *character* is (moreover) easily misunderstood. That word at this time had not yet acquired its familiar modern sense of 'personality', but more commonly meant simply a mark or sign: something cut or engraved or stamped or otherwise forcibly impressed. By extension, it might refer to qualities valued and worth aspiring to, though not necessarily yet achieved. John Donne in 'A Valediction: Of my Name in the Window' scores the *characters* of his name in the glass as a mark of resolve, a talisman, a perpetual reminder of his wish for constancy, in full knowledge of other temptations and possible eventualities. In his 'Epistle to Katherine, Lady Aubigny' Jonson provides a 'character' or idealized account of his patroness's unwavering virtues, 'Wherein your form you still the same shall find, | Because nor it can change, nor such a mind' (*The Forest*, 13.24, 123–4). The poem offers Lady Aubigny her 'truest glass', not by reflecting faithfully her every feature, but by giving her a standard against which to measure her life. In a similar sense, well-known contemporary handbooks furnished so-called 'mirrors' for princes and magistrates: ideal exemplars or patterns for living, which those in high office might try to live up to.

In this respect, Jonson's poetic 'characters' have something in common with the mottos that routinely accompanied personal emblems and *imprese*, proclaiming the bearer's fixity of judgement, conduct, resolve, and temperament: *semper idem* or *semper eadem,* for example ('always the same'), the personal motto of both Anne Boleyn and Elizabeth I. Sir Philip Sidney, according to Jonson's friend and mentor, William Camden,

to note that he persisted always one, depainted out the Caspian sea surrounded with his shores which neither ebbeth nor floweth, and over it: SINE REFLEXU.[11]

Jonsonian canon; that, practically, the book is not his; or, at least, that the merit and interest of it are for the most part attributable to other men.[15]

Neither Swinburne not Castelain, however, exactly noted the curiously hybrid nature of *Discoveries*, and the peculiar problems of interpretation the work poses for a modern reader, as it shifts almost imperceptibly from faithful transcription of some classical source to personal revelation.

Here is a typical instance of those problems, as Jonson writes about the operation of human memory. It is a passage that Swinburne hailed as 'mental autobiography', lamenting the fact that Shakespeare had never revealed himself with similar openness.

Memory, of all powers of the mind, is the most delicate and frail; it is the first of our faculties that age invades. Seneca the father, the rhetorician, confesseth of himself he had a miraculous one, not only to receive but to hold. I myself could in my youth have repeated all that ever I had made, and so continued till I was past forty; since, it is much decayed in me. Yet I can repeat whole books that I have read, and poems of some selected friends, which I have liked to charge my memory with. It was wont to be faithful to me, but shaken with age now, and sloth (which weakens the strongest abilities), it may perform somewhat but cannot promise much. By exercise it is to be made better and serviceable. Whatsoever I pawned with it while I was young and a boy, it offers me readily and without stops; but what I trust to it now, and have done of later years, it lays up more negligently, and often-times loses; so that I receive mine own (though frequently called for) as if it were new and borrowed. Nor do I always find presently from it, what I do seek; but while I am doing another thing, that I laboured for will come; and what I sought with trouble will offer itself when I am quiet. (346–60)

The piece of personal testimony is closely modelled, often phrase by phrase, on a passage in Seneca the elder's preface to his *Controversiae*, in which Seneca speaks of his own astonishing feats of memory in his youth—how, if 2,000 names were recited, he could repeat them back immediately in the same order; how, when 200 of his pupils each supplied him with a line of verse, he could recite these lines exactly in reverse order. Now age has dimmed his powers, and he can no longer call to mind what he knew when he was young. This is how Seneca then continues:

Ex parte enim bene spero: nam quaecumque apud illam aut puer aut iuvenis deposui, quasi recentia aut modo audita sine cunctatione profert; at si qua illi intra proximos annos commisi, sic perdidt et amisit ut, etiamsi saepius ingerantur, totiens tamen tamquam nova audim.

To some extent I am quite hopeful: whatever I entrusted to it as a boy or young man it brings out again without hesitation as though new and just heard. But things I have deposited with it these last years it has lost so entirely that even if they are repeatedly dinned into me, I hear them each time as new.[16]

This passage from *Discoveries* needs to be read with almost surgical care, for it is neither pure autobiography nor mere translation, but a curious blend of both. Jonson views his personal situation through the historical prism of a figure from the classical past for whom he feels a particular admiration and affinity. He begins by recalling Seneca's exceptional memorial powers, then parallels his own more modest yet still striking gifts, then, in phrases more closely echoing Seneca's own, proceeds to trace their gradual decline. Jonson and Seneca walk pace by pace together in these final sentences, meditating a common fate. Jonson appropriately *remembers*, in the very texture of his language, the author who, above all others in the ancient world, knew what the power of human memory could accomplish, and what its diminishment meant. The verbal echoes, melancholy as they seem, are quietly consoling: though individual powers decline, collective memory lingers. True intellectual distinction, as Jonson hopefully thought, would not be forgotten by posterity.

3 IMPERSONATING

Jonson's comedies often turn on some more or less mischievous act of impersonation, as one character fraudulently assumes the personality of another. Thus Volpone plays by turns the roles of a dying Venetian *magnifico*, of the notorious charlatan Scoto of Mantua, and of a *commendatore* or courtroom attendant at the Venetian Scrutineo. In *The Alchemist*, Subtle and Face similarly assume the roles of alchemist, alchemist's lackey, and military captain. In *The Devil is an Ass*, young Wittipol, in search of amorous conquest, disguises himself as a Spanish lady, while the minor devil Pug takes on the identity and physical form of a cutpurse hanged that very morning at Tyburn. These various acts of role-playing are by turns amusing, sinister, and thrilling.

Yet, as the passage from *Discoveries* just examined testifies, there was another more sober and seemingly more legitimate form of impersonation in which Jonson was also deeply interested, associated with the practices of

Not only does Jonson lack the moral, social, and literary graces of the Roman Horace (Dekker's satire implies), he does not even *look* like Horace. The Roman Horace was famously fat: 'a goodly corpulent gentleman'. Jonson is far too skinny, too 'lean a hollow-cheeked scrag', to pass muster as his English equivalent. Later in life, of course, Jonson would become corpulent indeed, swelling both literally and metaphorically to Horatian proportions, but at this stage of his career he was still perceived as being, in more senses than one, a lightweight.[18] Dekker's scathing description of this upstart Horatian pretender is a caricature, certainly, yet it provides an unusually vivid glimpse of the young Ben Jonson, pushily making his way in the London literary world, with his straggling beard, his pockmarked face, his eager acceptance of favour from those in positions of power.

Yet Jonson's determined efforts of literary impersonation would ultimately be rewarded. Just a year or two after Dekker had publicly ridiculed his Horatian pretensions, the dramatist Henry Chettle was to hail Ben Jonson as 'our English Horace, whose steel pen | Can draw characters which will never die'. In the years that followed, Jonson was to apply himself assiduously to Horatian imitation and translation. In 1640, some three years after Jonson's death, a duodecimo edition of his translation of Horace's *Art of Poetry* was published with an engraved title page showing a bust of Jonson in the guise of Horace himself, a Roman toga about his shoulders, a garland on his brow: the 'copy' and the 'original' now finely merged. Jonson had at last become (at least in the eyes of the portraitist) the 'very he' he sought to imitate. Lord Herbert of Cherbury, a friend of Jonson's during his lifetime, celebrated the transformation with these verses:

> 'Twas not enough, Ben Jonson to be thought
> Of English poets best, but to have brought
> In greater state, to their acquaintance, one
> Made equal to himself, and thee; that none
> Might be thy second: while thy glory is
> To be the Horace of our times, and his.[19]

4 SURROGATES

If Jonson seems in many ways a more visible, more knowable, more coherent figure than Shakespeare (or indeed most other authors from the early modern

Fig. 1. Jonson as Horace. William Marshall's engraved title page of 1640 duodecimo, *Q. Horatius Flaccus, his Art of Poetry, Englished by Ben Jonson*, printed for John Benson, 1640.

period), it is in part perhaps because of his greater readiness to prompt and guide his audiences' responses to his work through prologues, epilogues, choruses, inductions, epistles, and specially inserted or appended scenes; to point out beauties, novelties, precedents, and authorial intentions. In the Apologetical Dialogue presented after an early performance of Jonson's satirical comedy *Poetaster* in 1601, the character of The Author, possibly portrayed by Jonson himself, appears on stage to give a slow-witted audience an extended piece of his mind. In his readiness to act as commentator upon his own work, in his fondness for self-dramatization, Jonson anticipates the practice of Bernard Shaw, who liked to reflect in a similar fashion on his own dramatic craftsmanship in prefaces appended to the printed texts of his plays, and who in a late piece entitled *Shakes versus Shav* would present a version of himself in feisty contention with his greatest rival.

Jonson at other times makes use of characters who seem charged to act as his personal delegates or spokesmen: figures such as Cordatus in *Every Man Out of His Humour*, 'The author's friend; a man inly acquainted with the scope and drift of his plot; of a discreet and understanding judgement', who comments on the action of the play in the role of a 'moderator'; or Master Probee in *The Magnetic Lady*, who together with 'A Boy of the House' speaks admiringly between the acts about Jonson's dramatic work, which he defends against the cruder critiques of the censorious Master Damplay.[20] Readers have at times been tempted to regard such characters as idealized but palpable representations of the author himself, or to identify other figures within the plays which they believe might serve, in some sense or another, as autobiographical portraits or self-projections: as keys to an understanding of Jonson's own psychological state, or of his social aspirations. In one notably over-elaborated piece of analysis inspired by his reading of the works of Freud, the great American critic Edmund Wilson found Jonson to be anally retentive and *morose*, like the central (misogynistic, misanthropic, deeply tormented) character of that name in his own comedy *Epicene or The Silent Woman*.[21]

Such casual elisions and identifications of Jonson's own psychological make-up with that of his own dramatic characters tend however to ignore the more obviously dialogic, multivocal, oppositional nature of all theatrical experience, and of the particular plays in which these characters are to be found. If the judicious figure of Cordatus in *Every Man Out of His Humour* can be thought to 'represent' in some partial manner Ben Jonson himself, then so too (it might be suggested) do other characters in that play: the mild-mannered commentator Mitis; the ranting Asper, 'presenter' of the comedy; and the snarling satirist Carlo Buffone. All of these characters share, to a lesser or greater degree, aspects of what Foucault has taught us to call the authorial function, yet none stands in a simple one-to-one relationship with the actual creator of the play. If Jonson's own idealized character is reflected in part in the dramatic character of Horace in *Poetaster*, it finds further resonance in the characters of Virgil and Ovid. If aspects of Jonson's own personality can be glimpsed, however distantly, in the character of Morose in *Epicene*, then other of his more obviously sociable, high-spirited traits may be embodied in the mischievous figure of Truewit. Like his most famous contemporary, Jonson is (one might say) everywhere and nowhere within his own dramatic work: his personality deeply transfused into his theatrical creations in ways that Eliot recognized, yet seldom clearly recognizable from them.

The puzzles and excitements that confront a biographer of Jonson—despite the confident pronouncements to the contrary by an earlier generation of scholars—are not (in short) so very different from those that are faced by a biographer of Shakespeare, or of any other writer from the early modern period. 'Conjectural reconstruction' must play its part at many moments in the story that follows, as it will in any narrative of the life of Shakespeare. Jonson's life has been less fully examined in recent times than that of Shakespeare. Like the astonishing corpus of his work which makes the telling of its story so enticing—which drives, yet at times defeats, the effort to comprehend it—Jonson's life is familiar to most modern readers only in part. Here, with all its gaps and guesses, is what can be told of the writer who—as many good judges believed throughout his lifetime and the century following his death—was the greatest literary figure that England had ever seen.

2

Scotland 1618–1619

BEN JONSON is often remembered as a great metropolitan writer. Most of his life was spent within the cities of London and Westminster, whose particular localities—Moorfields and Blackfriars and Pimlico, Puddle Wharf, Fish Street, Scalding Alley—are vividly evoked and celebrated within his work. Like Dickens, who so admired his plays, Jonson created a vision of the modern city as a busy, mysterious, and labyrinthine place, teeming with eccentric life. He helped to invent the new genre of city comedy that intriguingly reflected the Jacobean London back to itself. He castigated city vice, and thrived on the stimulus of city living. 'Our delicacies are grown capital,' he wrote in a poem around 1620 urging a friend to leave London and recruit for the continental wars (*The Underwood*, 15.37). 'Capital' at this time could mean 'fatal'. But the word was beginning to acquire two new senses that are glanced at, perhaps, in this compact phrase: it denoted a country's principal city, and also the money-stock needed for commercial enterprise. Jonson's phrase associates the new mercantilism with big city life and also with moral decline.[1]

London in Jonson's day was indisputably the nation's capital. In 1600 it had about 200,000 inhabitants, a number that increased dramatically year by year as migrants swarmed to the already congested metropolis. 'That chief and head city London . . . as an adamant draweth unto it all the other parts,' John Norden observed towards the end of Elizabeth's reign. No other city in England was even a tenth of London's size; Norwich with around 15,000 inhabitants in 1600 was the next biggest settlement, followed by Bristol with a population of about 12,000, and York with 11,500. In the inner areas of

Fig. 2. The cities of London and Westminster: from volume 1 of Georg Braun and Franz Hogenberg's *Civitates Orbis Terrarum*, published in Cologne in the year of Jonson's birth, 1572. This depiction of the two cities may be based on the (now-lost) Copperplate Map prepared a dozen years earlier, for it shows, still intact, the spire of St Paul's Cathedral that had in fact been destroyed by fire in 1561 ('a divine | Loss' as Jonson later called it in his 'Execration upon Vulcan', *The Underwood*, 43.193–6). London's first theatres had not been built at the time this map was published. The amphitheatres shown here in Southwark—on the south side of the river, to the west of London bridge—are for 'Bowll [= bull] baytyng' and 'Beare-baytyng', popular sports throughout Jonson's lifetime. Charing Cross, near which Jonson lived as a boy, is visible near the bend of the river on the Strand, the major arterial road linking the two cities. The principal buildings of Westminster are shown at the extreme left of the picture.

In the character of Ursula the pig-woman in *Bartholomew Fair* Jonson had already vividly suggested the problems of locomotion suffered by the corpulent: 'I do water the ground in knots as I go, like a great garden-pot: you may follow me by the Ss I make' (2.2.44–5). His portraits of such characters as Amorphus in *Cynthia's Revels* and Sir Politic Would-be in *Volpone* suggest that he maintained a healthy scepticism about the benefits of travel. He warmly praised Sir Robert Wroth for choosing to dwell modestly and securely 'at home' on his estate at Durrants (*The Forest*, 3.13), and in verses to his friend William Roe who was setting off on his foreign travels spoke principally about the pleasures that would attend his homecoming (*Epigrams*, 128). Why should this man have undertaken such a remarkable journey at this particular moment in his career?

'He is to write his foot pilgrimage here, and call it *A Discovery*,' noted William Drummond while Ben Jonson was staying with him at Hawthornden (*Informations*, 317). Had Jonson's account of his journey survived, perhaps this episode in his career would seem less mysterious than it does at present, but this work was evidently destroyed by fire in 1623, along with other papers and books from his personal library. Ruefully listing in his 'Execration upon Vulcan' the writings consumed in this catastrophe, Jonson includes

> among
> The rest, my journey into Scotland sung,
> With all th'adventures...
> (*The Underwood*, 43.93–5)[5]

Though one catches in these lines a slight whiff of the burlesque, the journey must also have had a serious dimension. The very name of the lost work is suggestive: Scotland would be for Jonson a *discovery* comparable in some ways to the 'discoveries' he had made in the authors of antiquity. Walking and learning—so Jonson had learnt in an epistle of Seneca that seems to have determined the name of his own commonplace book, *Discoveries*—might indeed be viewed as roughly analogous activities. For truth, Seneca wrote,

will never be discovered if we rest contented with discoveries already made. Besides, he who follows another not only discovers nothing, but is not even investigating. What then? Shall I not follow in the footsteps of my predecessors? I shall indeed use the old road, but if I find one that makes a shorter cut and is smoother to travel, I shall open the new road. Men who have made these discoveries before us are not our masters, but our guides. Truth lies open for all; it has not yet been monopolized. And there is plenty of it left even for posterity to discover.[6]

Walking at this time could indeed be a serious business. William Camden, Jonson's old friend and former teacher at Westminster School, methodically perambulated the counties of England over several decades to conduct his own antiquarian researches, zigzagging the country with a similar zeal to that shown in a later age by Sir Niklaus Pevsner in his ancient Volkswagen. During his years at Westminster, Camden sometimes took a present or former pupil on these expeditions; it is known that the young Robert Cotton, for example, went along with him on one occasion. These walks were undertaken in the name of chorography, a then fashionable branch of academic study combining geography, topography, folklore, and antiquarianism. In the preface to *Britannia* Camden proudly reveals how he has worked at this art:

I have attained to some skill of the most ancient, and English-Saxon tongues; I have travailed over all England for the most part, and I have conferred with most skilful observers in each country. I have studiously read over our own country writers, old and new, all Greek and Latin writers which have once made mention of Britain. I have had conference with learned men in other parts of Christendom; I have become diligent in records of the realm.

Jonson would have been very familiar with these walks, might conceivably have accompanied Camden on one of them, and would in all likelihood have prepared himself for the expedition to Scotland in a manner befitting Camden's best pupil. We know that one of Jonson's intentions was to write 'a fisher or pastoral play' set on Loch Lomond, and that he also pestered William Drummond for useful titbits of historical and geographical information, including some seemingly intractable details of Edinburgh borough laws.[7]

The extent to which Jonson shared Camden's passion for local antiquarian knowledge is evident in the detailed allusions to rural lore, custom, and topography that are to be found in such pieces as *A Tale of a Tub*, *The Gypsies Metamorphosed*, and *The Entertainment at Welbeck*.[8] Interestingly enough, most of Jonson's works with a rural setting post-date his walk to Scotland, and many post-date the stroke that incapacitated him in 1628, and largely confined him to his house in Westminster. Is there a touch of autobiography in the lines which the Host utters in the final act of Jonson's comedy *The New Inn* (1629) as he at last reveals his true identity?

> I am Lord Frampul,
> The cause of all this trouble. I am he
> Have measured all the shires of England over,
> Wales and her mountains, seen those wilder nations
> Of people in the Peak and Lancashire;
> Their pipers, fiddlers, rushers, puppet-masters,
> Jugglers, and gypsies, all the sorts of canters,
> And colonies of beggars, tumblers, ape-carriers,
> For to these savages I was addicted,
> To search their natures and make odd discoveries!
>
> (5.5.91–100)

Since the accession of James VI of Scotland to the throne of England in 1603, Jonson had been attracted by his monarch's vision of a single kingdom uniting under the ancient name—Britain, or Britannia—that Camden's historical scholarship had conveniently helped to popularize. It was Camden, as Jonson proudly wrote, 'to whom my country owes | The great renown and name wherewith she goes' (*Epigrams*, 14.3–4), and it was to Camden's work that Jonson had turned in welcoming James to London on the occasion of his Coronation as 'MONARCHIA BRITANNICA'. For Camden, the relationship of London to the rest of the kingdom resembled that of Rome to its imperium. London was 'the epitome and breviary of all Britain, the seat of the British Empire, and the King of England's chamber', a city which, like Virgil's Rome, 'has reared her head as high among all other cities as cypresses oft do among the bending osiers'. In his welcome to James, Jonson was content to echo Camden's very words: London was indeed

the King's Chamber, and therefore here placed as in the proper seat of empire, for so the glory and light of our kingdom, Master Camden, speaking of London, sayeth she is: *totius Britanniae epitome, Britannicique imperii sedes, regumque Angliae camera, tantum inter omneis eminet, quantum, ut ait ille, inter viburna cupressus.* (*The King's Entertainment*, 20–4)

Now, in 1618, that 'empire' about which Jonson had written imaginatively for many years could be quite literally observed, walked from end to end.[9]

Jonson had not always been affably disposed towards Scotland and the Scots. In 1605 he and two collaborators, George Chapman and John Marston, had made passing fun in their comedy *Eastward Ho!* of King James's Scottish accent and his freedom in conferring knighthoods upon those Scots who had accompanied him south in 1603. The authors were promptly impeached by one of those same Scottish knights, Sir James Murray, and, as Jonson later reported to Drummond, were in danger of having their ears and noses cut (*Informations*, 207–15, and Ch. 10 below). Jonson was now on friendlier terms with some, at least, of these powerful and sensitive Scots. The poet Sir Robert Aytoun, who 'loved him dearly', was one such; a Gentleman of King James's Bedchamber, he belonged to the innermost group of the King's Scottish advisers. He had succeeded William Drummond's brother-in-law William Fowler in the post of private secretary to Queen Anne. Jonson would have had close dealings with both men over the performance of masques at court.[10]

In the summer of 1617, the year before Jonson undertook his walk to Scotland, James himself had journeyed back to Scotland, on his first return visit since 1603. Accompanied by a huge retinue—Edinburgh was instructed to find billets for no fewer than 5,000 persons and stabling for the same number of horses—James had trundled majestically up the Great North Road and down again in an elaborate seven-month progress that was skilfully presented as a nostalgic homecoming. 'We are not ashamed to confess that we have had these many years a great and natural longing to see our native soil and place of our birth and breeding,' James had written to his Scottish Privy Council in December 1616,

and this salmon-like instinct of ours has restlessly, both when we were awake, and many times in our sleep, so stirred up our thoughts and bended our desires to make a journey thither that we can never rest satisfied till it shall please God that we shall accomplish it.

A more central motive for James's journey was, less sentimentally, to impose Anglican ritual on the Scottish Kirk, a feat he was ultimately to perform through the Five Articles of Perth.[11] Jonson's patron William Herbert, Earl of Pembroke, travelled in the royal entourage, as did the King's cousin the Duke of Lennox, brother to Esmé Stuart, Lord d'Aubigny, in whose house Jonson had lodged for several years. Jonson was on good terms with both men, and would undoubtedly have heard much about their Scottish expedition.

Jonson's walk to Scotland was also in all likelihood a piece of fun. One pictures some rowdiness at the Mermaid tavern at his setting out. Bacon seems to have caught the spirit of the journey when he gravely remarked that 'he loved not to see poesy go on other feet than poetical *dactylus* and *spondaius*'.[12] Jonson himself in the past had been amused by others who

The
High and mighty
Prince, IAMES
KING of great
Britane, Fraunce
and Ireland. &c.

Fig. 4. James VI and I on horseback: engraving by Francis Delaram in *Forth Feasting: A Panegyric to the King's Most Excellent Majesty* (Edinburgh, 1617), William Drummond's poem of welcome to the King on his arrival in Edinburgh a year before Jonson's visit to Scotland. Drummond noted that Jonson's 'censure of my verses was that they were all good ... save that they smelled too much of the schools, and were not after the fancy of the time ... yet that he wished, to please the King, that piece of Forth Feasting had been his own' (*Informations*, 75–9). London and the Thames are depicted in the background of this engraving, with the Bear-garden and the Globe and Swan theatres visible below the horse's front hooves.

had undertaken epic journeys of this sort. He had been especially intrigued by the performance of Thomas Coryate of Odcombe in Somerset, a laborious buffoon who in 1608 had journeyed almost 2,000 miles across Europe, mainly on foot, hanging up his shoes proudly in the church at Odcombe for parishioners and pilgrims to wonder at. (The shoes remained there until the following century.) Failing at first to find a publisher for *Crudities*, his undigested account of his travels, Coryate had the inspired idea of appealing to the best-known poets of the day to write commendatory verses upon himself and his undertaking. The response was tremendous, and in 1611 there appeared a handsome folio edition of Coryate's *Crudities*, with engraved frontispiece and a large and distinguished gathering of facetious commendatory verses. The outstanding contributions came from Jonson himself, who was once thought to have acted as editor of the volume.[13] Jonson was later jocularly to compare his own great walk with that of Coryate, observing to William Drummond that his shoes 'were appearing like Coryate's. The first two days he was all excoriate' (*Informations*, 515–16).

Jonson had responded with similar mock-heroic enthusiasm to a small boat journey that was taken along Fleet Ditch—at that time little more than an open sewer issuing into the Thames—by two enterprising travellers named Heydon and Sheldon. In his poem 'The Famous Voyage' Jonson compared these two adventurers with others of recent times; with

> those that put out moneys on return
> From Venice, Paris, or some inland passage
> Of six times to and fro without embassage,
> Or him that backward went to Berwick, or which
> Did dance the famous Morris, unto Norwich)
> At Bread's Street Mermaid, having dined, and merry,
> Proposed to go to Holborne in a wherry:
> A harder task than either his to Bristo',
> Or his to Antwerp. Therefore, once more, list ho!
>
> (*Epigrams*, 133.32–40)

The journeys to Norwich, Bristol, and Antwerp mentioned here are authenticated exploits of the day. It was the actor Will Kemp who danced the 130 miles from London to Norwich in February 1600, and published the account of his footwork, *Kemp's Nine Days' Wonder*, later the same year. (Danced at least some of the way—danced for three days out of the twenty-three that it

Fig. 5. Title page of *Crudities* (1611), Thomas Coryate's account of travels by foot across Europe in 1608; engraved by William Hole. Jonson knew Coryate well as a fellow-member of the Mermaid Club, and wrote humorous verses about each of the adventures illustrated on this title page.

finally took him to complete the journey, slowed down by bad weather and physical exhaustion.[14]) The wherry journey to Bristol had been undertaken by Richard Ferris and two companions in 1590. It is not known who walked backwards to Berwick, but in 1589 Sir Robert Carey won £2,000 for walking from London to Berwick—face forwards, presumably—in twelve days. Those who 'put out moneys on return | From Venice, Paris, or some inland passage' were wagering on their chances of successfully completing their journey within a given period of time. This was a popular sport of the day,

Fig. 6. Title page of *Kemp's Nine-Days' Wonder*, 1600.

but not without its hazards. Will Kemp had put out money on his marathon dance to Norwich in the expectation of a threefold return, but found to his annoyance that many with whom he had laid his bets refused to pay him when he got back to London.[15]

Jonson too may have wagered on his chances of walking successfully from London to Edinburgh and back. 'Ben Jonson is going on foot to Edinburgh and back, for his profit,' George Gerrard informed Sir Dudley Carleton on 4 June 1617.[16] This is the summer before Jonson actually set out on his travels. James and his entourage were comfortably stationed at Edinburgh, and reports of their Scottish welcome were already reaching London.[17] It was evidently at this moment, under such a stimulus, that Jonson resolved to visit Scotland by more strenuous means and *for his profit*. Some doggerel verses entitled 'To Mr Ben Jonson in his Journey. By Mr Craven' seem to confirm the suspicion that the 'profit' was financial.

> When wit and learning are so hardly set
> That from their needful means they must be barred,
> Unless by going hard they maintenance get,
> Well may Ben Jonson say the world goes hard.

> *This was Mr Ben Jonson's Answer Of The Sudden*
> Ill may Ben Jonson slander so his feet,
> For when the profit with the pain doth meet,
> Although the gate were hard, the gain is sweet.

The identity of 'Mr Craven' and the 'gain', if any, Jonson made from his journey are quite unknown. A series of playful references to the Scottish expedition in Jonson's masque of the following year, *News from the New World Discovered in the Moon*, suggests however that, like Will Kemp, Jonson might have found it difficult in the end to collect his hard-earned winnings.[18]

§§

Until now it has always been assumed that Jonson undertook this long walk alone, or perhaps in the company of a servant who carried his bags and helped him along the way. But an astonishing recent find by the Edinburgh scholar James Loxley has now provided a vivid new perspective on Jonson's expedition up into Scotland. For amongst the papers of the Aldersey family, now

housed in the Cheshire and Chester Archives, Loxley has come across evidence that on his journey northward Jonson was accompanied by a fellow-walker. What he has discovered is a manuscript account covering some eighteen leaves entitled 'My Gossip Joh[n]son his foot voyage and mine into Scotland', which records in compelling detail the daily incidents on the walk from London to Edinburgh that Jonson and his hitherto unsuspected companion undertook together in the summer of 1618.[19] Though the identity of this fellow-walker is still unknown, both the provenance and general nature of this account suggest he might possibly have been a junior member of the Aldersey family, still perhaps in his teens, and perhaps an actual godson, if the phrase he habitually uses of Jonson, 'my gossip', is taken in its most literal sense ('gossip' at this stage meaning either 'godparent' or, more casually, 'friend' or 'companion').[20] Two facts suggest that this diarist is a young and, as yet, quite undistinguished person. First, there is his relative invisibility in the record. None of the existing accounts of Jonson's journey to Scotland has hinted at the possibility of the poet having walked with a companion, who, as the new manuscript reveals, seems generally treated not quite as a servant, but as a person of decisively lesser status than the celebrated public figure on whom he attends. Then there is the nature of the journal itself, which methodically records the names of the towns and places of interest through which the two men journeyed and the people they encountered along the way, but shows little interest in the responses, observations, or anecdotes of Jonson himself. To have walked the entire length of the country in the company of Britain's most famous, spirited, and opinionated writer without attempting to record any of his utterances is in itself remarkable, suggesting exceptional restraint or deference on the part of the diarist. This is compatible with his having been a much younger man, but might also suggest—a further possibility, to which we shall return—a specifically defined purpose for which the journal was maintained.

Yet what the diarist does choose to record about the journey is of absorbing interest none the less, prompting in turn further questions about the nature of the expedition as a whole. The two walkers left London (so his notes reveal) on Wednesday 8 July 1618, arriving that night at Tottenham High Cross, and moving on next morning to Waltham near Cheshunt, where 'my Lady Wroth' came out to greet them with a small group of friends. Sir Robert Wroth, to whom Jonson had addressed a poem in *The Forest* some years earlier, had died in 1614, bequeathing massive debts to his widow Mary, Lady

Wroth (daughter of Robert Sidney), who was now living at Loughton Hall, just a little further up what is now the A10, near the Wroth estate of Durrants. Jonson was devoted to Lady Mary, and the encounter would have been warm. She had danced in his masques of *Blackness* and *Beauty*, and been flatteringly addressed by him both in verse and in prose; his comedy *The Alchemist* was affectionately dedicated to her. Jonson had been altogether less taken with her late husband, who had evidently resented his intimacy with Lady Mary; Jonson darkly reported to William Drummond that she had been 'unworthily married on a jealous husband' (*Informations*, 275–5). The walkers then pressed on, pursued by 'a lunatic woman' who went dancing before them and 'a humorous tinker, of whom we could not be rid', and three minstrels wanting to sing a merry song about the life and death of the Earl of Essex. They continued up into Hertfordshire, passing through Ware and Royston, where 'the maids and young men came out of town to meet us', and then came 'weary to Huntington'. They journeyed next to Stanford, a major coaching stop and trading centre at that time on the Great North Road, over ninety miles from London. At the invitation of Francis Manners, the sixth Earl of Rutland—a Catholic peer who, along with his elder brother Roger, had been heavily fined and imprisoned for his part in Essex's rising of 1601—the two walkers now veered westward away from the Great North Road in order to visit Belvoir Castle, near Grantham. King James had also stopped at Belvoir Castle the previous year, and had persuaded Manners to accompany him north to Edinburgh. Belvoir was a favourite spot of James's, which he visited half-a-dozen times throughout his reign. Jonson's foot journey, it seems, was beginning now to shadow the grander progress of the royal party.

Francis Manners was Warden of Sherwood Forest, towards which the travellers were now heading: a region that was to feature, with its romantic local legends, in Jonson's late pastoral play *The Sad Shepherd*. Ben Jonson, the great city dramatist, was by now encountering rural sights and stories that would (perhaps unexpectedly) inspire the next phase of his creative work. 'The scene is Sherwood,' he was to write with a touch of fancifulness as well as faithful recall at the outset of *The Sad Shepherd*, 'consisting of a land-shape of forest, hills, valleys, cottages, a castle, a river, pastures, herds, flocks, all full of country simplicity. Robin Hood's bower, his well, the witch's dimble, the swineherd's oak, the hermit's cell.' At Rufford Abbey Jonson and his companion received 'extraordinary grace and entertainment' from Lady Jane Talbot, née Ogle, Countess of Shrewsbury, before heading for Welbeck

Abbey near Worksop in Nottinghamshire, the estate of the Countess's nephew Sir William Cavendish, the future Duke of Newcastle. Some years later Jonson would write a respectful elegy on the Countess at her interment in Westminster Abbey ('a noble countess, great | In blood, in birth, by match, and by her seat'). His relationship with William Cavendish, a generous patron throughout the last two decades of Jonson's life, was to grow even more devoted as time went by.[21] The two men had probably known each other for about four years at the time of this encounter. Cavendish however had only recently inherited Welbeck Abbey, along with Bolsover Castle in Derbyshire, at the death of his father Sir Charles Cavendish in April 1617. He took evident pride in now escorting Jonson and his companion around these two estates, each of which was to serve, years later, as the location for a Jonsonian entertainment. Cavendish was a passionate horseman, and at Bolsover Jonson watched in fascination as their host—as the diarist notes, in a rare moment of reported speech—'rid his great horse, which he did with that readiness and steadiness as my gossip say they were both one piece'. Jonson was to repeat this last phrase in an epigram on Newcastle's horseman-ship, *The Underwood*, 53:

> When first, My Lord, I saw you back your horse,
>   Provoke his mettle, and command his force
> To all the uses of the field and race,
>   Methought I read the ancient art of Thrace,
> And saw a centaur, past those tales of Greece;
>   So seemed your horse and you both of a piece! (1–6)

Jonson and his companion passed on through York into north Yorkshire, at Sherburn enjoying the taste of 'cherries in the midst of August'. By now they had been going for about five weeks, and the wear and tear of travel were beginning to show. At Darlington, Jonson bought himself a new pair of shoes, 'which he minded to take back that far again' (*Informations*, 514–15). At Durham they were lavishly entertained by Bishop Richard Neile, a former Dean of Westminster and (like Jonson) former student of Westminster School. Neile was a protégé of the Cecils, father and son, and a special favourite of James, whom Neile had accompanied the previous year on his northward journey to Scotland: a diligent act of service which may well have earned him his present bishopric.[22] Jonson once more may have felt he was treading in the rut-marks of his monarch's carriages. The walkers pushed on

37

Fig. 7. 'So seemed your horse and you both of a piece!' wrote Jonson admiringly of William Cavendish in 1618 (*The Underwood*, 53.6), as he watched his future patron riding at Bolsover Castle, Derbyshire. Copper engraving (1743) after Abraham van Diepenbeeck.

through Newcastle upon Tyne, then moved away from the Great North Road to take a less travelled, more easterly, route along the Northumberland coast past Bamburgh, thence to Berwick, and so at last into Scotland. Jonson was fighting illness as the pair passed through Musselburgh on the final lap of their long walk, but groups of welcoming dignitaries, headed by the Lord Provost, Sir William Nisbet, were by now coming out from Edinburgh to escort them to their destination, along with milling crowds of curious spectators: 'The women in throngs ran to see us, some bringing sack and sugar, others acquavita and sugar.' The walkers entered the city on Thursday 17 September, having taken two months and ten days to complete their journey.

This was hardly record-breaking speed, but then there had been no need to hasten: the pair had been pleasurably detained along the way, and must have been tempted often to pause and to digress. Writing about rhetoric in *Discoveries*, Jonson was later to ask, 'why do men depart at all from the right and natural ways of speaking?', and answered by analogy: sometimes

they may do so 'for pleasure and variety, as travellers turn out of the highway, drawn either by the commodity of a footpath, or the delicacy or freshness of the fields'.[23] On his walk, as in his writing, Jonson probably did just this. A foot journey from London to Edinburgh in those days usually took about a month. Sir Robert Carey's twelve-day walk from London to Berwick had been good going, but then Carey was something of an athlete. It was he who in 1603 had brought the news of Queen Elizabeth's death to King James by riding non-stop from Westminster to Holyrood in less than three days, being slowed to 'a soft pace' in the latter stages of his journey by a kick in the head from his horse's heel after one of his numerous falls.[24] Very early in his reign, James had realized the political importance of establishing good communi-cation between London and Edinburgh, and introduced, with an elaborate system of fines for neglectful postmasters, an efficient system for the delivery of royal mail, which travelled between the two kingdoms in an average time of seven days.[25] This was quite rapid, for as late as 1750 it would take an average of ten days to journey by coach from London to Edinburgh.[26] These reliable mails were crucial to the smooth governance of the two kingdoms.

Yet however leisurely Jonson's walk to Edinburgh had been, it was still regarded (as the newly discovered manuscript reveals) as an extraordinary feat, worthy of formal celebration and commemoration. On the day follow-ing the walkers' arrival in Edinburgh, they were escorted by the city fathers to the 'High Cross'—the Mercat Cross in Parliament Square, the traditional centre of the city, from which Royal Proclamations are read by the Lord Lyon, King of Arms. The civic party

there on their knees drank the King's health, testifying that in that place he had performed his journey. My gossip also drank to the bailiff and aldermen and the whole people their health, they being so thick in the street that we could scarce pass by them that ran in throngs to have a sight of my gossip. The windows also being full, everyone peeping out of a round hole like a head out of a pillory.

The ceremony was evidently designed to serve as an official verification that Jonson's long journey by foot from London to Edinburgh had indeed been truly 'performed', strengthening the notion that his walk had been under-taken as part of a formal and publicly known wager. This theory is further confirmed by an incidental fact that James Loxley has alertly noted. In the seventeenth century travellers from York to Darlington customarily crossed the River Tees by ferry at Neasham, an option that Jonson and his companion on this occasion chose to forgo, taking instead a two-mile detour in order to cross the river instead on foot by the bridge at Croft-on-Tees. Their reluctance to board the ferry suggests that Jonson was anxious to avoid the pedantic objection that he had not literally walked every inch of the way from London to Edinburgh.

If Jonson's walk to Scotland was indeed undertaken partly to fulfil a wager, then one might venture a further guess about the role of his companion, and the purpose of the journal he kept. If the terms of this undertaking were to be precisely fulfilled, it was essential there be a witness: someone to vouch for the fact that Jonson had indeed walked every part of the journey, avoiding all temptation to ride even briefly on horseback or in a mail-coach or in a farmer's cart heading for market, or to jump aboard a ferry rather than cross a river by foot. For the 'foot voyage' to be seen as fully authentic, it needed, in short, to be observed and recorded. Was Jonson's companion then the witness; the keeper of the log? If the journal was maintained with this principal aim, there would have been no need also to include Jonson's incidental observations and anecdotes, however much these might have been treasured by later generations. The journal would have been much as we find it to be: a simple recording of dates and of places through which the travellers passed, together with the names of their hosts and of others whom they encountered along the way.[27]

On his famous dance from London to Norwich, Will Kemp was similarly accompanied not only by Thomas Sly, his tabourer, and William Bee, his servant, but by 'George Sprat, appointed for my overseer, that I should take no other ease but my prescribed order'. Sprat's job was to ensure that Kemp fulfilled precisely the terms of his contract to dance all the way from the one city to the other. An episode towards the end of his journey nicely illustrates the manner in which Sprat fulfilled this role. Dancing vigorously past the market place as he entered the city of Norwich, Kemp accidentally set his foot on the skirts of a young woman in the crowd, whose petticoat fell embarrass-ingly to the ground. Feeling sorry for the girl, but deciding suddenly to take advantage of the diversion caused by this event, Kemp

went towards the Mayor's, and deceived the people by leaping over the church-yard wall at St John's, getting so into Mr Mayor's gates a nearer way; but at last I found it the further way about, being forced on the Tuesday following to renew my former dance, because George Sprat, my overseer, having lost me in the throng, would not be deposed that I had danced it, since he saw me not...[28]

Did Jonson's unknown companion play a similar verifying role on the walk to Scotland, serving as the distinguished poet's witness or 'overseer', deposing for the fact that he had walked the entire journey from London to Edinburgh?

The crowded scene at Mercat Cross as Jonson finally completed his travels strikingly testifies to another, perhaps more surprising, aspect of this adventure. Here in Edinburgh, as throughout the journey, Jonson is greeted and fêted as a person whose fame, while enhanced by his present act of athleticism, is in a sense already known. Along the road, local dignitaries, emissaries from the great houses, young people and old turn out to welcome him. That those with court connections were aware of his approach and of his standing and were anxious to receive him is only to be expected. More remarkable is the interest shown by humbler people in more remote parts of the kingdom. Outside Berwick-upon-Tweed, church bells are rung and volleys of shot are fired in Jonson's honour. At North Berwick a local landowner arrives with an unusual request, telling 'my gossip that his shearers had made a great suit to him to have a sight of him. So we walked up into the fields where was a number of them with a bagpipe, who no sooner saw my gossip, but they circled him and danced round about him.' 'Shearers' is a generic word at this time for farm workers, those that harvested the crops, and those that tended the sheep.[29] Most of these men would in all likelihood have been illiterate, and here in the Scottish borders (one supposes) would generally have heard little news about court or cultural affairs in London. Yet they are eager to welcome Ben Jonson, and to pay him their homage in the fields; and dance, entrancingly, in a circle about him as their piper plays. What did Ben Jonson mean to these shearers? What had he done—what was he doing—that had touched them most, and that so demanded their respect? How had his reputation been built, and how had it spread so far?

By 1618, it is tempting to suggest, Ben Jonson had already emerged as Britain's first literary celebrity; as a person whose name carried throughout the kingdom, in much the same way that the name of Byron or Dickens, in an age of speedier communication, would later resonate throughout Europe. Even Shakespeare's name, just two years after his death, might not have stirred the shearers of North Berwick into action; might not indeed ever have reached their ears. How Jonson had managed by this period of time to achieve such extraordinary fame, how he had already become such a living legend, is part of a larger puzzle which the following chapters of this book will try to resolve.

§§

Six years earlier, while staying at another great house in the south of England, Jonson had had cause to praise the generosity of his hosts, Lord and Lady Lisle—Robert and Barbara Sidney, the parents of Mary Wroth. At Penshurst, so Jonson gratefully wrote, he was always well cared for, food and drink were always freely offered, 'Thy tables hoard not up for the next day.'

> Nor, when I take my lodging, need I pray
> For fire or lights or livery: all is there,
> As if thou then wert mine, or I reigned here...
> ('To Penshurst', *The Forest*, 2.71–4)

The house itself treated him (Jonson playfully wrote) as if he were its very owner, or as if he were the King himself—James too was an occasional visitor to Penshurst—and *reigned here*. Throughout his journey to Scotland, often following in the footsteps of the King, Jonson had been treated with a similar generosity by several of his hosts. While he was visiting Welbeck, an episode occurred which oddly recalls the lines from the poem 'To Penshurst'. Sir William Cavendish and his future bride, Elizabeth Howard, were obliged to leave the Abbey for a few days, 'and resigned the whole house to my gossip, commanding his steward and all the rest of the officers to obey my gossip in all things, which authority he did as freely put into execution'. Gladly seizing the proffered role, Jonson ordered a buck to be killed, and the wine cellar to be thrown open, and 'On Sunday my gossip reigned wholly, and gave entertainment to all comers.' While Jonson was sitting grandly at dinner a further message arrived from the absent hosts, 'with a commission to lay all the doors open to Mr Jonson, and that My Lady resigned all power and authority to him to do what he pleased. The house was his. And withal to entreat him they might have as good cheer as he would make them when he came home.' Jonson clearly enjoyed such free gestures, and was in turn unstinting to others along the way. Departing from a house at Stanton where he and his companion had stayed overnight, he gave 'to the gentle-woman of the house a piece, her daughter half a piece, and to every servant in the house two shillings'. A 'piece' was a recently introduced gold coin (more formally known as King James's unite), now worth twenty-two shillings. These were generous disbursements from a man of limited means, who often found cause, even on this same journey—partly no doubt on account of his casual way with money—to complain of his own poverty.[30]

It is perhaps within the context of mock-regal play just noted that one of the journal's more startling entries is to be read: that at Welbeck Abbey 'my gossip made fat Harry Ogle his mistress'. Henry Ogle was a kinsman of William Cavendish, who would have been in his late fifties around the time of Jonson's visit. Was there a sexual encounter between the two men? Did Jonson, a known womanizer, also fancy (fat, ageing) male partners? The diarist's amused way of noting this incident certainly arouses this suspicion, and may well reflect some bantering double entendre that occurred at the time. Yet a more innocent reading is also possible. Cavendish's formal commission to Jonson to act in his absence as the master of Welbeck must of necessity have been directed in part to the servants, so they would know that their real master wished them to obey any orders, however surprising, issued by the household's boisterous if distinguished guest. A chain of command involving those actually familiar with the running of the place might also be required: thus to supervise the killing of the buck, Jonson names 'Mr George Markham his woodman'. For domestic management, the master of the house must often have deferred to the mistress; and Jonson might here have nominated Ogle, as the senior family member left in residence, to serve in this capacity; in short, 'made fat Harry Ogle his mistress'. But like much else relating to the social and sexual lives of our ancestors, such an interpretation rests largely on guesswork. For all we can tell (and for all it can possibly matter) fat Ben Jonson and fat Harry Ogle might also have had a more intimate encounter one night at Welbeck Abbey.

§§

Jonson's unknown companion, having served his presumptive function, departed from Edinburgh on 5 October, taking a boat from Leith to Burntisland and from there a ship back to England.[31] During the previous fortnight, he and Jonson had been shown the sights of Edinburgh and surrounding regions, touring the northern side of the Firth of Forth, visiting Sir George Bruce's coalmine at Culross and inspecting his salt-pans and 'a rare water-work', and proceeding to Dunfermline, where Jonson was gracefully received by the Lord

Chancellor and others, and the two men were made 'burgesses'. Jonson and his companion lodged in Leith with a Mr John Stuart, 'water-baillie and skipper'.[32] When his host and his wife were obliged temporarily to depart for London, John Stuart insisted that Jonson 'use his house as his house, and command his servants as his own', an invitation his guest accepted with characteristic promptitude, inviting guests to the house, where he 'kept them all day'.

Later in the same month the Edinburgh town council admitted Jonson as an honorary 'burges and gildbrother', and in October they entertained him with a formal banquet costing the substantial sum of £221 6s. 4d., Scottish currency.[33] Jonson seems to have been impressed by Edinburgh—more so than King James, who had been dismayed the previous summer by the city's squalor, which was to be picturesquely recorded by the disaffected Sir Anthony Weldon, a notoriously unreliable witness who had accompanied King James on that occasion.[34] 'In a poem he calleth Edinburgh "The heart of Scotland, Britain's other eye",' noted Drummond contentedly, when Jonson visited him at Hawthornden around Christmas (*Informations*, 318). An *eye* is a bright place, an intellectual centre. By 19 January Jonson had returned from Hawthornden to Edinburgh, and left the city by the 25th of that month, stopping briefly in Leith, then turning for home.

The return journey in those winter months cannot have been so pleasant as the journey north, but Jonson evidently once more took his time, lingering with more friends and acquaintances along the way. On 10 May 1619 he wrote to Drummond from London to report that he had got back safely, and had received 'a most Catholic welcome', and that his accounts of the journey were 'not unacceptable to His Majesty', who 'professed (I thank God) some joy to see me, and is pleased to hear the purpose of my book'.[35] It has been conjectured that the Scottish journey signalled Jonson's disenchantment with the court and with King James, and his wish in particular to absent himself from London during the trial and execution of Sir Walter Ralegh, yet the affectionate interest which James displayed in Jonson's Scottish journey, and his intended 'book', scarcely seems to support such a conclusion.[36]

§§

Jonson was followed to Scotland by another, more eccentric, foot traveller, John Taylor the so-called Water Poet. Taylor was a former naval seaman who had served under Essex at Cadiz, and retired from the service with a gammy leg. He became a waterman on the Thames, and when trade fell away, turned to writing doggerel verses for various occasions: births, deaths, and marriages. He was a great favourite at court, and Jonson told Drummond in despair that King James regarded him as the greatest poet in the kingdom (*Informations*, 288–9). Taylor found a further source of income in undertaking a number of improbable expeditions on the wager principle: sailing on one occasion in a boat made of brown paper from London to Queensborough in Kent. (After three miles, the bottom fell out, but he somehow completed the journey.) Shortly after Ben Jonson's departure for Scotland, John Taylor set out after him, travelling however by a westerly route. He reached Edinburgh a week or so after Jonson's arrival, pushed on as far as Braemar, and was back in London by October. Taylor's wager was that he could walk to Scotland and back without taking any money with him, and without asking anyone for food, drink, or lodging. His tactic was to stare very intently at people he encountered along the way, until in embarrassment they would ask the servant with whom he travelled what the problem was, and he would tell them the nature of the bet. Though Taylor was sometimes obliged to sleep in haystacks, the strategy usually worked. Seven hundred and fifty of his backers, however, refused to pay up, some of them insisting (in the manner of Will Kemp's speculators) that he had not precisely fulfilled the terms of his contract. Taylor wrote a sharp satirical poem entitled *A Kiksey Winsey, or a Leery Come-Twang*, urging them to pay; and commemorated the journey itself in a rollicking pamphlet entitled *The Pennyless Pilgrimage*. Jonson told Drummond that 'Taylor was sent along here to scorn him' (*Informations*, 486): 'sent', presumably, by the court. The two poets however had a friendly meeting in Leith, where, as Taylor records, Jonson presented him with 'a piece of gold of two and twenty shillings to drink his health in England. And withal, willed me to remember his kind commendations to all his friends.'[37]

§§

Jonson's most important meeting during his Scottish journey was with William Drummond, a bachelor thirteen years his junior. Drummond had originally trained in the law, studying in Bourges and Paris after graduating from the 'Tounis College' (Edinburgh University) in 1605. He was a genuinely learned and cultivated man who had travelled in Europe, was something of a linguist, had read Du Bartas and Rabelais along with Tasso and

Sannazzaro in a French translation, and had sent home accounts of pictures he had seen in the Paris galleries. Drummond had been called to the Scottish bar, but after the death of his father in 1610 he retired, aged 24, to Hawthornden Castle where he lived alone with his fine collection of English, Greek, Latin, and Italian books, writing verses, mainly amorous and melancholy, and studying *imprese* and anagrams. He busied himself inventing things, often seemingly foreign to his gentle nature—box-pistols, pikes, battering rams—or of dubious usefulness to his present circumstances: telescopes and burning glasses, devices for converting salt water into fresh, and for measuring distances at sea. He took an intense interest in poets south, as well as north, of the border, owning copies of works by Sidney, Lyly, and Shakespeare, and of Michael Drayton, with whom he maintained a friendly correspondence. He had bought a copy of the quarto text of Jonson's *Volpone*, and had claimed mysteriously in 1612 to have read Jonson's epigrams (of which there is no known text earlier than the Folio of 1616).[38]

Hawthornden Castle, perched romantically on the steeply wooded banks of the River Esk seven miles south of Edinburgh, is today appropriately maintained as an international retreat for writers. The remains of a great sycamore tree beneath which Drummond and Jonson are said to have had their first meeting are still visible in the Castle grounds. Expectation would have been high on both sides at this meeting. Drummond would have been eager to talk with the famous writer whose works he had bought and read. Jonson, a great bibliophile, would have been drawn to Hawthornden almost as much by Drummond's books as by the man himself. They had many friends and interests in common, and to judge by their subsequent correspondence appear to have established a warm friendship. That there were also sharp differences of taste and temperament between the two men is apparent from the private notes which Drummond made throughout the visit, probably without Jonson's knowledge, and without any thought of publication. These notes, the *Informations to William Drummond of Hawthornden*, were finally published in a heavily excised and reordered state almost a century after the walk to Scotland in a folio edition of Drummond's writings prepared by Bishop John Sage and Thomas Ruddiman and published in Edinburgh in 1711. Meanwhile the original manuscript of the *Informations* vanished, having perhaps been borrowed by Sir John Clerk of Penicuik shortly after this edition was prepared, and subsequently perishing in a fire at Penicuik House in 1899.

In the early 1830s, however, the antiquarian scholar David Laing stumbled across a seemingly reliable transcript of the *Informations* in the Advocates' Library in Edinburgh—twelve cramped manuscript pages, written in an ungainly but generally legible hand—evidently made around 1700–2 by the Edinburgh physician and scholar Sir Robert Sibbald. Though the authenticity of this document was at one time questioned, fuller analysis confirms its genuineness as a careful (if not always fully comprehending) work of transcription, likely to bear a close resemblance to the lost original.[39] This vivid and extended version of the *Informations to William Drummond*, three times the length of the 1711 redaction, is an extraordinary and at times unique source of contemporary gossip, information, and opinion. Laing's discovery quickly excited the attention of his friend Sir Walter Scott, who in *Kenilworth* (1831) made use of a previously unknown anecdote concerning the death of Robert Dudley, Earl of Leicester, who 'gave a bottle of liquor to his lady which he willed her to use in any faintness; which she, after his return from court, not knowing it was poison, gave him; and so he died' (*Informations*, 271–3).[40]

That these two very different versions of the *Informations* also present quite acute problems of interpretation has not always however been recognized, least of all by their earliest readers. They have therefore become over the years a source not merely of information but misinformation, encouraging a number of tenacious myths about Ben Jonson's character.

Drummond's jottings were evidently intended simply as a private record, to remind him in future years of the views and opinions of his celebrated guest. Drummond was a methodical man, who kept zealous lists of books he had bought and read, and 'Memorials' recording the precise dates on which he had caught a cold or fallen downstairs. His notes on Jonson's visit are inspired by the same spirit of method, but are frequently abrupt, elliptical, and syntactically ambiguous: the absent verbs, the sparse punctuation, the floating pronouns, the precarious chain of transmission creating textual difficulties not always recognized by the unwary reader. There is a further problem in understanding the tone of these highly laconic notes. Jonson's reported opinions often sound like a series of curt and contemptuous judgements, hurled *ex cathedra*.

> That Donne, for not keeping of accent, deserved hanging.
> That Shakespeare wanted art.

That Sharpham, Day, Dekker, were all rogues, and that Minsheu was one.
That Abraham Fraunce in his English hexameters was a fool.
That next himself only Fletcher and Chapman could make a masque.

(*Informations*, 34–8)

Jonson's seeming contempt for Shakespeare in particular was to scandalize eighteenth- and nineteenth-century readers, forming the flimsy basis for an elaborate fiction concerning Jonson's character, which was supposedly marked by malevolence, jealousy, and ingratitude towards his former friend and greatest contemporary.[41] Yet perhaps the sharpness here may be, partly at least, that of Drummond himself, scornfully or amusedly noting in the privacy of his room some of the evening's highlights. What Drummond does not record is the larger conversational context that has prompted such utterances. Earlier editors invented the title *Conversations with William Drummond of Hawthornden*, yet these notes are not of 'conversations', as they chronicle (for the most part) Jonson's opinions alone.[42] To understand the point of many of Jonson's reported literary judgements it is necessary to remember the (never explicitly stated) tastes and opinions of Drummond himself, which might at times have provoked them.

The differences between Jonson and Drummond were partly temperamental, and partly explicable in terms of nationality and location. To Drummond, Jonson was too little interested in Scottish literary achievement, while Jonson for his part evidently considered his host out of touch with the latest literary fashion in London. Drummond's verses 'smelled too much of the schools, and were not after the fancy of the time' (76–7), and he hankered after the wrong poetic models. Drummond was a devoted admirer of the writings of Petrarch, and was indeed known as the Scottish Petrarch.[43] He dryly notes that Jonson 'cursed Petrarch for redacting verses to sonnets, which he said were like that tyrant's bed, where some who were too short were racked, others too long cut short' (42–4). Drummond regarded Sir Philip Sidney as the greatest of British poets, followed by Sir William Alexander and Samuel Daniel. Though Jonson held a high opinion of Sidney's writings, he spoke bluntly during his visit about the shortcomings of Sidney's writings, adding casually that 'Sir P. Sidney was no pleasant man in countenance, his face being spoiled with pimples' (12–13, 490–1, 173–4). He reported frankly that Sir William Alexander 'was not half kind unto him, and neglected him', and that Daniel, who was 'at jealousies with him', was 'a good honest man ... but no poet' (118–19, 110, 16).[44] Drummond greatly admired the learned George Buchanan, sometime tutor to the young James VI and I. Jonson told Drummond that he had informed the King somewhat boldly that 'Mr G. Buchanan, had corrupted his ear when young, and learned him to sing verses when he should have read them' (442–3).[45]

These are clearly the remarks of an energetic controversialist, but not necessarily one driven by jealousy and malice. The comment by Jonson 'That Shakespeare wanted art' is scarcely his final verdict on the nature of Shakespeare's genius, which is more spaciously declared in Jonson's poem 'To the Memory of the Author, My Beloved, Mr William Shakespeare, and What He Hath Left Us', prefixed to the 1623 First Folio, in which the quality of Shakespeare's *art* is singled out for specific praise. What Drummond chooses to record is a particular argumentative moment within a debate whose larger context is unknown. The notion of Jonson's supposed malignity towards his great rival was crushingly attacked by Jonson's nineteenth-century editor William Gifford, who unhappily invented at the same time a counter-mythology of even greater absurdity, proposing that William Drummond had elaborately lured Jonson to Scotland in order to ply him with drink, provoke him to rash utterance, and treacherously reveal to the world what he had said in the privacy of Hawthornden.[46] This legend of the 'treacherous host' prompted another nineteenth-century editor, Ezekiel Sanford, to devise a counter-counter narrative in which Ben Jonson is sent to Hawthornden by King James as an official spy to keep an eye on Drummond and test his political loyalties.[47]

Only when Jonson had departed from Hawthornden did Drummond attempt to record a considered assessment of his personal qualities in a formal 'character' sketch of a kind that often concludes biographical writings in this period.[48] The sketch tells us something not only about Jonson but also about the solitary William Drummond, who in his later years (as his best modern commentator has remarked) was to grow increasingly 'irascible, querulous, and self-righteous'.[49]

He is a great lover and praiser of himself, a contemner and scorner of others, given rather to lose a friend than a jest, jealous of every word and action of those about him (especially after drink, which is one of the elements in which he liveth), a dissembler of ill parts which reign in him, a bragger of some good that he wanteth, thinketh nothing well but what either he himself or some of his friends and countrymen hath said or done. He is passionately kind and angry, careless either to gain or keep, vindicative, but, if he be well answered, at himself. (554–60)

It is worth noticing what Drummond reluctantly concedes in this largely disapproving portrait of his opinionated, self-absorbed, hard-drinking, and evidently disconcerting guest. It is also worth noticing that the (seemingly) most severe word that Drummond uses to describe Jonson's temperament, 'vindicative', is used here in its more positive Latin sense, 'eager for judgement'.[50]

Before offering this final portrait, Drummond transcribes two poems which Jonson had sent him after departing from Hawthornden, in gratitude for Drummond's hospitality. The poems are accompanied by an affectionate dedication testifying to the warmth of friendship that existed between the two men.

To the honouring respect\
Born\
To the friendship contracted with\
Mr William Drummond,\
And perpetuating the same by all offices of lover hereafter,\
I, Benjamin Jonson,\
Whom he hath honoured with the leave to be called his,\
Have with mine own hand, to satisfy his request\
Written this imperfect song\
'On a lover's dust, made sand for an hour-glass' . . .

The second poem is introduced like this:

Yet that love when it is at full may admit heaping,\
Receive another; and this, a picture of myself.

This 'picture of myself'—'My Picture Left in Scotland' (as Jonson was later to call the poem, when he included it, with minor variations, in *The Underwood*, 9)—offers a vivid glimpse of Jonson in 1619, its seemingly gloomy portrait of the mountainous, forsaken, middle-aged poet deftly balanced by nimble variations of metre. Whether the doomed romance which the poem describes was real or imaginary it is impossible now to say, but the theme of lost love was certain to appeal to Drummond himself, being close to his personal situation and poetic taste.[51]

> I doubt that Love is rather deaf than blind,
> For else it could not be
> That she
> Whom I adore so much should so slight me,
> And cast my suit behind;
> I'm sure my language to her is as sweet,
> And all my closes meet
> In numbers of as subtle feet,
> As makes the youngest he
> That sits in shadows of Apollo's tree.
>
> Oh, but my conscious fears,
> That fly my thoughts between,
> Prompt me that she hath seen
> My hundred of grey hairs,
> Told six-and-forty years
> Read so much waste, as she cannot embrace
> My mountain belly, and my rocky face;
> And all these through her eyes have stopped her ears.
>
> (535–52)

On the final pages of *Informations* these verses stand in eloquent tension with Drummond's sharply adjudicative prose, offering contrasting and complementary 'pictures' of the troublesome poet affectionately departing from Scotland.

3

Debatable Land 1542–1572

DESPITE his seeming boastfulness about the achievements of his country-men, Jonson was of course—as Drummond well knew—not strictly a Sasse-nach but a homecoming Scot, whose ancestral territories lay in the western borders, about fifty miles to the south and west of Hawthornden, not far from Gretna Green. One powerful motive for Jonson's journey to Scotland must have been the wish to revisit his family's homeland, and it is probable that at some stage of the journey he veered accordingly towards Dumfries. 'His grandfather came from Carlisle,' Drummond noted in his account of Jonson's 'own life, education, birth, actions',

and he thought from Annandale to it; he served King Henry VIII, and was a gentleman. His father lost all his estate under Queen Mary; having been cast in prison and forfeited, at last turned minister. So he was a minister's son. He himself was posthumous born, a month after his father's decease...

(*Informations*, 176–81)

Jonson's sense of the precise movements of his father's family seems a touch unsure ('and he thought from Annandale to it'), but never having known his father he had not been able to verify such details at first hand. But his surrogate father, William Camden, could have told him much about Annan-dale, whose region and inhabitants he had described in *Britannia*:

In this territory, the Jonstons are men of greatest name: a kindred ever bred to war; between whom and the Maxwells there hath been professed an open enmity over long, even to deadly feud and bloodshed...[1]

The Johnstones or Johnstouns or Jonstons (as Camden has it)—the name is spelt in at least thirteen different ways in Scotland in this period, but always with a 't'—had lived in Annandale since the twelfth century, and had intermarried with Norman invaders at an early stage.[2] They were notorious not merely for their endless feuds against the Maxwells—whose faces they slashed with their dirks, to bestow what was known locally as the 'Lockerbie lick'—but as chief marauders and guardians of the Scottish borders.

Annandale lies within a relatively inaccessible reach of country near the Solway Firth. During the time of Robert the Bruce a part of this region—eight miles long and four miles wide, between the Esk, the Sark, and the Leven—became known as the Debatable Land, and served as a refuge for outlaws. Its inhabitants were a wild lot. Camden quotes the testimony of John Leslie, Bishop of Ross, on the men of Annandale and neighbouring Nithsdale patrolling the bank of the Solway Firth, spearing salmon from horseback, and conducting raids into English territories by night 'through desert by-ways and many winding cranks'.

When they have laid hold of a booty back again they return home likewise by night, through blind ways only, and fetching many a compass about. The more skilful any leader or guide is to pass through these wild deserts, crooked turnings, and sheep down-falls in the thickest mists and deepest darkness, he is held in greater reputation as one of excelling wit.

Jonson's ancestors were, in short, border thieves, equipped with a genial patter suitable to their trade:

But say they be taken: so fair spoken they are and eloquent, so many sugared words they have at will sweetly to plead for them, that they are able to move the judges and adversaries both, be they never so austere and severe, if not to mercy, yet to admiration and some commiseration withal.[3]

But the Johnstones were not only brigands and cattle rustlers. The leading members of the clan were aristocrats who held significant power in this embattled region, for many years a zone of warfare, pillage, and destruction.[4] Into this part of the borders the English made frequent raids, burning and looting towns and villages, while Scottish bands gathered their strength here for reciprocal forays down into England. The Johnstones controlled many of the comings and goings in this area, where skirmishes of considerable ferocity continued throughout several reigns. In his *Annals* of Elizabeth's reign,

William Camden records a wild English raid into the Scottish borders as late as 1570, two or three years before Jonson's birth, in which 300 villages were burnt and 50 castles razed to the ground, and Henry, Lord Scroope, 'wasted far and wide all over Annandale, the territories of Johnston, and others'.[5]

It was probably an earlier engagement with the English during the reign of Henry VIII, however—the Battle of Solway Moss in 1542—that was the cause of Ben Jonson's grandfather removing from Annandale to Carlisle.[6] The Battle of Solway Moss was the culmination of growing animosity between England and Scotland following Henry's break with Rome in 1533. Threatened with isolation within Europe, Henry had watched with concern while Scotland strengthened its allegiances with other Catholic powers. James V's marriage with Mary of Guise in 1538 had confirmed Scotland's 'auld alliance' with France, while James's skilful treaty with the Pope soon after-wards secured a regular annual payment to Scotland of £10,000 from the Vatican, ostensibly to establish a College of Justice in Scotland but actually to ensure Scotland's continuing loyalties to the Church of Rome. England's northern borders now looked especially vulnerable to possible Catholic invasion. Late in 1542 Henry marshalled English troops at Newcastle, Ber-wick, and Carlisle to prepare for a crushing move against the Scots. When the Duke of Norfolk crossed briefly with English troops into Scotland, 18,000 Scots in return moved into England near Gretna and began to burn houses along the Esk. On 24 November, on the marshy ground of Solway Moss, just one mile into England, the Scots were surprised by 3,000 English troops, and fled in panic. It was a shameful defeat. Few were killed on the field of battle—a mere twenty Scots and seven Englishmen—but numerous Scots were drowned as they fled from the scene, their bodies being hauled out of the Esk in the nets of fishermen in the days to come. The English troops rounded up 1,200 prisoners, including some of distinguished rank—2 earls, 5 lords, 500 lairds and gentlemen—along with 3,000 horses and large quantities of weapons. Learning of the scale of this defeat and his army's refusal to follow his nominated leader, Oliver Sinclair, James V took to his bed, and within three weeks was dead.

Henry's greatest triumph lay in his manner of dealing with the prisoners taken at Solway Moss. Separating the twenty most distinguished prisoners from the others, he ordered that they be brought immediately to London, speaking neither to each other nor anyone else on the way. They entered Westminster, each wearing a red St Andrew's cross, and after brief detention at the Tower of London were released on parole and placed in the custody of various nobles and high-ranking gentlemen. Over the three days of Christmas Henry entertained them generously at Hampton Court. On New Year's Eve they were banqueted by the Lord Mayor of London, and on New Year's Day they were permitted to return to Scotland. Before they left London, all twenty of the prisoners signed a declaration agreeing that Henry should have custody of James's daughter Mary, the future Queen of Scots, born a week before James's death, and that Mary should eventually marry Prince Edward. Ten of the prisoners secretly signed another document declaring that if the sickly Mary should die, Henry ought immediately to become the King of Scotland.

The other Scottish prisoners were taken to the English garrisons in the north. It is likely that Ben Jonson's grandfather was amongst this group. Writing from Carlisle on 29 November 1542, Sir Thomas Wharton, Deputy-Warden of the West Marches, includes a 'Maister Johnston' in his list of 'Noble men and gentlemen of Scotland taken prisoners upon Eske and thereabouts, by the King's Highness's subjects on Friday, the xxiiij day of November'.[7] Various Johnstones must have shifted across the border at various times, and it cannot be proved beyond doubt that this 'Maister Johnston' was the playwright's grandfather. None the less, the conjunction of evidence here—a move from Annandale direct to Carlisle, an acceptance of service under Henry VIII at a time when the English king was actively wooing the more distinguished of his defeated adversaries—strongly favours the identification.

Scotland was officially a Catholic country until 1560. In shifting from Scotland to England and accepting service under Henry, Jonson's grand-father would have swapped not merely his national allegiances but, almost certainly, his religious allegiances as well. During the latter half of the sixteenth century countless men and women throughout Scotland and Eng-land changed their faith in this manner, under duress or of their own free will, moving from Catholicism to Protestantism or the other way about, while many more wavered or equivocated in their beliefs. Jonson's grandfather was in this sense typical of his age, and his story may seem an ordinary one. Yet it strikingly illustrates the dilemmas and necessities of the times, and, in particular, of the region in which he lived. Those who lived in the Debatable Land had particular reason to know the value of adaptability. For this area of the borders was 'debatable' not merely in relation to legal title—who owned this territory was never clear—but in its national and religious loyalties as well. Its inhabitants were well known for taking pay from either side, fighting for the Scots, spying for the English, committing themselves finally to neither cause. The Johnstones were not, as a clan, a notably steadfast lot. Faced with a massive loss of Scottish leaders after the Battle of Solway Moss, James V sent letters a day or two before his death to 'Master Maxwell and the Lord of Johnston to be head of that country' of the borders. A contemporary observer expressed amazement that, even in such extreme circumstances, James should now have trusted such turncoats. 'Those the King makes rulers of his borders he has kept in prison seven or eight years,' wrote Sir George Douglas on 16 December 1542. He has intended 'divers times to have smitten off their heads'; he has 'taken their goods and slain their friends. That he should make them his principal captains shows in what necessity he stands.'[8]

Jonson's grandfather and father seem to have stuck loyally to their new faith after the move to England, but his father was to find himself caught between contending forces of another sort when the reformist reign of Edward VI (1547–53) was succeeded by the bloody regime of Mary.[9] From February 1555 until her death in November 1558 Mary vigorously enforced a return to the religion of Rome, reviving medieval statutes to enable church and secular authorities to deal with cases of supposed heresy. Those who refused to recant were often imprisoned or burnt at the stake, and their land and goods, if judged of sufficient value, forfeited to the crown. Two hundred and seventy-three Protestants, including the Oxford martyrs, Bishops Ridley, Latimer, and Cranmer, were burnt for their beliefs during Mary's reign. It was during this time of persecution that Jonson's father suffered imprisonment and 'lost all his estate'—a phrase which suggests that his life until then had been relatively prosperous. He managed at least to escape with his life, but is likely to have remained in prison until November 1558, when, with the accession of Elizabeth, religious persecution took quite a different turn. It was probably at this point that Jonson's father journeyed south to London, and 'at last turned minister' in the Church of England.

In its southward progress, the family name shifted to the commoner English spelling 'Johnson'. When he came to adult life, Ben was to favour the spelling 'Jonson', the version of his name that appears in his published work from 1604 onwards, and in all surviving examples of his autograph. That he felt a continuing affinity with his Scottish forebears, however, is evident from his remark to Drummond of Hawthornden that 'His arms were three spindles or rhombi; his own word about them, *percontabor* or *perscrutator'* (*Informations*, 466–7). These have been shown to be the arms of the Johnstones of Annandale. The motto that Jonson himself added—*percontabor* means 'I shall enquire', and *perscrutator*, 'an enquirer'—stresses his empirical, questing nature, his constant appetite (like that of the Host in *The New Inn*) to scrutinize human character, 'and make odd discoveries'.[10]

The abrupt revolution in the fortunes of Jonson's father strikingly prefigures the equally abrupt revolutions that were to occur within Jonson's own career, as he shifted on more than one occasion between Whitehall and a state prison, between the houses of wealthy patrons and conditions of dismal poverty. His spiritual shuttling between the English and Roman religions can be seen likewise, in the longer perspective of family history, to have its precedent in the movements of his grandfather between country and country, faith and faith. Throughout his long career Jonson was to retain many of the natural instincts of the border dweller: the capacity above all, in his moral and professional life, to shift ground while professing to have remained forever in the same spot. Constancy and change, as twin imperatives, were to exercise a powerful hold upon his personal life, as they were on his creative imagination.

4

Influences 1572–1588

NEITHER the place nor the date of Jonson's birth is known with complete certainty. Thomas Fuller in his *History of the Worthies of England* (1662) assumed that Jonson was born in Westminster, but confessed to having no evidence to support this belief (for 'I cannot with all my industrious inquiry find him in his cradle'). The city of Westminster at this time contained only two parishes, St Margaret's and St Martin-in-the-Fields, neither of whose registers shows any record of Jonson's birth. It seems likely in fact that Jonson was born not in Westminster, but somewhere in or near the City of London.[1] The year of Jonson's birth has been disputed, but the evidence now strongly suggests that he was born in 1572, on a day and month that he himself names with characteristic precision in a poem written towards the end of his life, honouring his friend Sir Kenelm Digby:[2]

> Witness his action done at Scandaroon,
> Upon my birthday, the eleventh of June,
> When the apostle Barnaby the bright
> Unto our year doth give the longest light...
> (*The Underwood*, 78.13–16)

Digby had achieved a famous naval victory over the French and Venetian fleet near Scandaroon in Turkey on 11 June 1628. Jonson's announcement that 11 June was also his own birthday seems unambiguous, but it too has been, surprisingly, the focus of scholarly dispute.

To modern minds, it may not seem to matter much on which day Ben Jonson happened to have been born. In Elizabethan England, the settling of such a detail was, however, a serious business, for the particular day, month, hour, and minute of each person's birth—facts sometimes meticulously recorded in family bibles and memorials—were commonly reckoned to possess a vital significance.[3] From the particular conjunction of stars that reigned at this crucial moment, so it was still widely believed, each individual's character was shaped, and the course of their lives determined. Astrology commanded respect not just amongst the credulous and under-educated, but across the entire spectrum of society. The Queen herself and members of the court circle kept a prudent eye on the heavens; the Earl of Leicester consulted the celebrated astrologer John Dee in order to find a propitious day for Elizabeth's own coronation.[4] Learned men and women, including many of Jonson's closest friends and associates, believed passionately and literally in the influence of the stars. Jonson's own schoolmaster, William Camden, attributed various natural and human disasters (even Elizabeth's infatuation with Leicester) to astral influences.[5] Jonson himself could scarcely escape the spell of this powerful intellectual system. He was fascinated by astrology, though deeply sceptical of its claims. John Dee and his fellow-practitioners Simon Forman and Edward Kelly he evidently regarded as charlatans, yet he studied their art with close attention. 'He can set horoscopes, but trusts not in them,' noted Drummond of Jonson in 1619 (*Informations*, 234).

Astrology rested on the fundamental belief that the stars and planets inhabited a realm of the heavens beyond all change and decay, from which they exerted influence on the mutable regions below. This central supposition about the unchanging nature of the heavens was increasingly challenged throughout Jonson's lifetime by the new astronomical discoveries of Galileo, of which Jonson was sharply aware. In the very year of Jonson's birth a new star was observed in the heavens, a source and omen of doubts to come. Another new star, observed by Kepler in September 1604 and shown by Galileo in 1605 to lie in the supposedly unchanging region of the heavens beyond the moon, is wryly alluded to in Jonson's *Volpone* (1606), as attracting the excited attention of Sir Politic Would-be (who finds it 'strange! | And full of omen!', 2.1.37–8). Galileo's powerful new telescope, constructed in 1609, led to the crucial detection of sunspots—observed and discussed in England also by Thomas Harriot—a further evidence of heavenly mutability and decay.

By the end of the seventeenth century the entire system of astrology would be largely discredited; but in Jonson's day the issue was more finely poised.

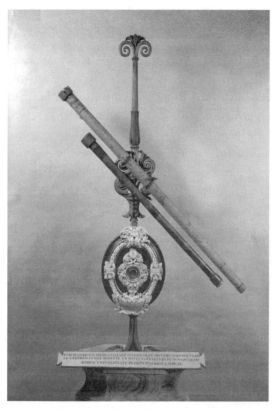

Fig. 8. Seeing the future: Galileo's telescope. 'But here's my jewel: my perspective,' says the Master of the New Exchange, London's grand new shopping mall in the Strand, in Jonson's recently discovered entertainment, *Britain's Burse*, written to celebrate the opening of this building in April 1609. 'I will read you with this glass the distinction of any man's clothes ten, nay twenty mile off, the colour of his horse, cut or long tail, the form of his beard, the lines of his face ... But I am promised a glass shortly from a great master in the catoptrics, that I shall stand with o'th' top of Paul's, when the new spire is built, and set fire on a ship twenty leagues at sea in what line I will by parabolical fiction.' Jonson is characteristically alert to the very latest scientific developments. In 1609 the English astronomer Thomas Harriot had begun to experiment with optic lenses acquired from Holland, and in July of that year was to point a primitive telescope, with startling results, at the moon. In Venice in June of the same year—two months after Jonson's entertainment— Galileo Galilei, realizing the revolutionary potential of this instrument, worked at high speed from mathematical principles alone to produce a version of his own (pictured above) with sixtyfold magnification, which he demonstrated from the Tower of St Mark's to an astonished Doge, pointing it, with sensational results, at his home town of Padua, fifty kilometres away, then out to sea, where hitherto invisible ships immediately became apparent. Harriot's and Galileo's astronomical observations were shortly to confirm Copernican theory, ushering in a new conception of the universe. Jonson was fractionally ahead of their discoveries, having already sceptically glimpsed the commercial potential of this thrilling new toy.

Jonson's own sympathies lay firmly with the doubters. His comedies repeat-edly ridicule those who place trust in the astrological arts, such as Dame Purecraft in *Bartholomew Fair*, who has her nativity-water cast 'by the cunning men in Cow Lane' to help her find a husband (1.2.36–8), or the tobacconist Abel Drugger in *The Alchemist*, who consults with Subtle over his horoscope and the identification of his fortunate days (1.3). Jonson himself, as he reported to Drummond, had cozened a lady by impersonating 'an old astrologer in the suburbs': 'and it was himself disguised in a long gown and a white beard at the light of a dim-burning candle, up in a little cabinet reached unto by a ladder' (*Informations*, 234–8). Drummond would have enjoyed this story, for he shared Jonson's general scepticism about the claims of astrology; yet he evidently did not dismiss the science entirely, as he owned a number of books and manuscripts on astrological subjects.[6] In this ambivalence he was probably typical of his age.

Sir Kenelm Digby, the subject of Jonson's 'birthday' poem, was a close friend of Jonson's during the latter stages of his life and acted after Jonson's death as his literary executor. The two men had much in common, including intermittent attachments to the Church of Rome and to Gresham College. An eager experimental scientist and early member of the Royal Society, Digby was also an avid astrologer. His (still extant) personal horoscope, drawn up in his own hand (Fig. 9), reveals the precise disposition of the stars at the moment of his birth on 11 July 1603.[7] It has been argued that Jonson's reference in the Digby poem is actually to Digby's birthday and not to his own, and that the text should read, as some inferior versions do, 'upon *his* birthday, the eleventh of June': but the horoscope shows clearly that July, not June, was the month of Digby's birth. By a freakish chance, however, Digby was eventually to die on 11 June 1665, prompting an enthusiastic elegist to marvel, somewhat inaccurately, over the symmetries of his life: his birth, death, and famous naval victory at Scandaroon all seemingly occurring on the same day.[8] This was precisely the kind of calendrical patterning—found also in the coincidental birth and death dates of Robert Burton, another firm believer in astrology, and of Shakespeare, who died on St George's Day, the day on which he was (putatively) born—which seemed to establish beyond all doubt the existence of astral powers and cosmic design. Jonson's poem more light-heartedly celebrates the happy accident that interweaves his own fortunes—'my birthday'—with those of Digby: 'Witness his action done at Scandaroon.' It is a human, not a stellar, influence that draws the men

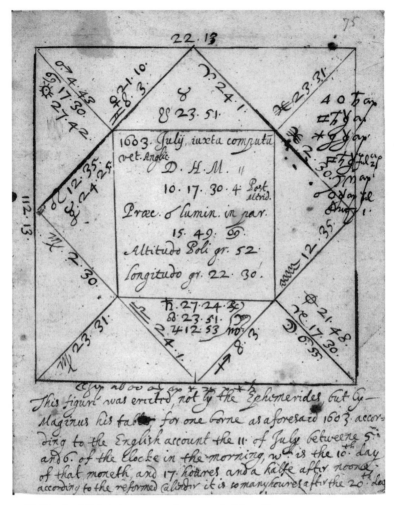

Fig. 9. Sir Kenelm Digby's horoscope, drawn up by himself.

together—Kenelm's beloved wife Venetia—and their shared devotion to poetry. The poem also celebrates the felicitously interwoven fortunes of the two poets whom Digby most admired, Edmund Spenser and Ben Jonson himself: for the day of Jonson's birth, 11 June, was a day that Spenser had famously celebrated in his *Epithalamion*, 'Barnaby the bright': the longest day in the old Julian calendar.[9]

Jonson's birthday fell at a period of the year which attracted a variety of popular beliefs and customs. St Barnabas Day marked the beginning of the summer solstice, and was 'taken for the whole time, when the days appear not for fourteen days together either to lengthen or shorten'. Midsummer Day itself was celebrated towards the end of this two-week period, on St John's Eve (23 June).[10] During the 'sun-sted' or solstice, witches and dragons were thought to be at their most active, mischievously poisoning wells and rivers. Bonfires were lit and brooms strategically placed outside houses to keep such creatures away, while fernseed carried on the person was reckoned to give additional protection. Up until about 1570 such fires were kindled in London itself at midsummer, but this custom was now in decline.[11] The period was by tradition a good time for lovers. Young women seeking husbands sowed hempseed or plucked a rose at midnight, which was thought to make eligible partners promptly materialize. Jonson would probably have regarded such traditions, to judge from the evidence of his comedies, with the same amused scepticism with which he regarded astrology. The teasing, shadowy world that Shakespeare invokes in *A Midsummer Night's Dream*, with its intricate layering of natural and faery events, is not, on the whole, Jonson's comic territory. In *The Alchemist* it is a credulous clerk—fired by the belief that 'a rare star' reigned at his birth (1.2.123–4)—who longs to see the Queen of the Fairies: who turns out to be a prostitute dressed in a sheet, aided by a couple of fellow-tricksters. For Jonson, as for many of his contemporaries, fairies—like witches and dragons and bonfires and horoscopes and other forms of systematic magic—were on the way out, as his near-contemporary at Westminster and lifelong friend, Richard Corbett, memorably observed.

> Witness those rings and roundelays
>   Of theirs, which yet remain,
> Were footed in Queen Mary's days
>   On many a grassy plain;
> But since of late Elizabeth,
>   And later, James, came in,
> They never danced on any heath
>   As when the time hath been.[12]

But the fairies had not quite vanished from the England into which Jonson was born, or from Jonson's mature imagination. Mab the Fairy Queen and her 'bevy of fairies' were indeed to make their appearance in the entertainment that he wrote for Anne of Denmark and her son Henry Frederick on Midsummer Day 1603 'as they first came into the Kingdom', when 'an artificial ring' was 'cut in the path' at Althorp to emphasize the fairy presence (*The Entertainment at Althorp*, title page; 27–8). 'Artificial' is the operative word here, as the seemingly supernatural sign is revealed as a product of human artifice. Jonson's device is a conscious rhetorical hyperbole, amused, sophisticated, half-ironical, signalling his belief not in the supernatural world but in the power of the new Stuart dynasty, which might (who knows?) call up the impossible fairies at that entrancing midsummer moment.

For the powers that primarily interested Jonson were not mythological or extraterrestrial in nature, but political and social. The influences that shaped his universe came not from the stars or the creatures of the forest but from particular men and women whose conduct and learning he admired. 'Good men are the stars, the planets of the ages wherein they live, and illustrate the times,' Jonson wrote in *Discoveries* (789–90). It was as a star that he was to figure Shakespeare, elevated in the heavens, 'with rage | Or influence' chiding or cheering the drooping stage through the formidable example of his work ('To the Memory of my Beloved, the Author, Mr William Shakespeare', 76–7). It is a star that he likewise figured Prince Arthur (alias Prince Henry), displaying his 'flame | And influence' in *Prince Henry's Barriers* (73–4). A similar trope imagined the brilliant Lucy Harington, Countess of Bedford, outshining and outdoing the planet Venus: 'I meant the day-star should not brighter rise, | Nor lend like influence from his lucent seat' (*Epigrams*, 76.7–8). The influences here are all decisively human, and humanistic in character. Astrology, like fairy lore, may have lost its literal credibility, but its potency lingers in Jonson's metaphorical language. Though Jonson's religious commitments were deep, the decisive influences on his own character came in a similar fashion from human beings, living and dead. 'His life was of humanity the sphere,' he wrote of the young Henry Morison, who had died at 21 (*The Underwood*, 70.52). Jonson's poem to the memory of Morison and to his friend Lucius Cary imagines the two men as stars, but stars of 'humanity': a word, central to Jonson's vocabulary, suggestive both of classical studies, *literaria humaniorem*, and social intercourse; what he calls in another poem the 'well-made choice of friends and books' (*Epigrams*, 86.2). To trace the formation of Jonson's own character, it is to the influence of these friends and books, the example of the living and the dead, that we must now turn.

§§

Jonson was born, as Drummond records, 'a month after his father's decease'. The unlucky minister of religion who had lost his estate under Mary would have not left much for his widow and infant son to inherit, for the annual income of a minister of religion at this time was extremely modest, and the young boy was 'brought up poorly' (*Informations*, 180–1). While he was still a 'little child' in 'his long coats', however, his mother married again, this time to a bricklayer, and the family moved to Hartshorn Lane, near Charing Cross.[13] The bricklaying stepfather has been plausibly identified as Robert Brett, a man of comfortable means who lived in the precise area mentioned by Fuller. Brett contributed personally to the cost of building at St Martin's, and had risen to become Master of the Tylers' and Bricklayers' Company by the time of his death on 29 August 1609.[14] No record of Brett's will or marriage has been found, and disappointingly little is known about Jonson's mother, apart from one anecdote that Drummond records, testifying to her remarkable courage at the time of her son's imprisonment in 1605.[15] A recent scholar wonders whether she may be the Rebecca Brett who was buried at St Martin's on 9 September 1609, just a few days after Robert Brett's own death: an attractive guess.[16] Brett had other sons, presumably by Jonson's mother, who eventually inherited his business: John Brett, who was baptized on 1 January 1581/2 and buried on 3 December 1618, and Robert Brett, who was baptized on 22 March 1583/4, married Mariam Poulter on 28 January 1609, and died on 26 September 1618. Five other Bretts listed in the baptismal register of St Martin-in-the-Fields in the 1580s and 1590s (three of whom died in infancy) could have been part of this same family.[17]

From his earliest years, Jonson would thus have felt the influence of two fathers, one living and one dead. The dead father's chief legacy would have been spiritual rather than material, for the widow of this 'grave minister' (as Anthony à Wood called him) would no doubt have ensured that their son was piously brought up.[18] Such a household always kept a Bible or two at hand: a copy of the Vulgate, and perhaps of the Geneva Bible—the so-called 'Breeches Bible' (from its translation of Genesis 3: 7, where Adam and Eve make themselves not aprons but breeches of fig-leaves), prepared by English exiles in Switzerland during the

Marian exile, and first published in 1560. As the eldest child, separated by more than ten years in age from his stepsiblings John and Robert, Ben enjoyed special status and responsibilities within the family. Nothing is known of his feelings towards the stepfather who was now the family's chief provider. By the time he reached late adolescence, however, it is clear that Jonson had come to detest the bricklaying business which he seemed destined to inherit. To have younger stepbrothers ready to carry on their father's trade 'which he could not endure' was undoubtedly a relief to him (*Informations*, 181–3).

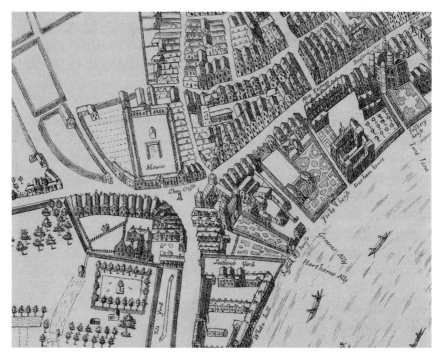

Fig. 10. Hartshorn Lane—marked here as 'Hartshorne Ally', next to Scotland Yard—two decades after Jonson's death: from William Faithorne's 'Exact delineation of the Cities of London and Westminster and the Suburbs', 1658. Jonson lived here with his family during his childhood years. While Hartshorn Lane itself remained a sordid alleyway, the adjacent sites between the Strand and the river formed a highly desirable residential area, lined with palaces that had formerly belonged to the Church and were now largely owned by members of the aristocracy. Robert Cecil's New Exchange, whose opening Jonson helped celebrate with his *Entertainment at Britain's Burse*, is centrally visible on the Strand.

Hartshorn (or Christopher) Lane, the family's new place of residence, was a small lane running from the Strand through to the Thames. It was not a salubrious place to live.[19] The 'great sewer' that ran down the centre of the lane was liable to overflow in bad weather, threatening both the health of the inhabitants and the foundations of the adjacent houses. This large open drain brought effluent of all kinds from St Martin's Lane down into the Thames. Later in life Jonson was to memorialize the sights and (more particularly) smells of another great sewer, Fleet Ditch, in his mock-heroic poem 'On the Famous Voyage'. The poem may well be touched by memories of childhood adventures outside his house in Hartshorn Lane, where, as at Holborn, the air was often 'as hot, as at the muster | Of all your night-tubs, when the carts do cluster, | Who shall discharge first his merd-urinous load' (*Epigrams*, 133.63–5). The lane gave direct access to the river, and carts constantly trundled back and forth to Pinfold's Wharf. A century later it was reported that houses in Hartshorn Lane 'do not fetch very high rents because of the noise generated by carting so none but the very poor will live there'. In 1720 John Strype described it in similar terms, as 'a place much clogged and pestered with carts repairing to the wharfs; and therefore not well inhabited'.[20] Brett did what he could to improve this unpromising scene: a lease of 1586 mentions 'the little garden lately made over the sewer or ditch by Robert Brett'.[21] In the 1630s a new piped sewer and pumping station was to be constructed in Hartshorn Lane, but the area evidently remained quite sordid.[22]

Many of the residents of Hartshorn Lane were small tradesmen, and the parish of St Martin's was home to many families connected with the building trade: carpenters, stonemasons, bricklayers, wood-mongers, and the like, often employed by the Queen's Works. There was work to do in the neighbourhood, for the Strand was becoming a fashionable place to live, and a number of grand new houses were being erected; some thirty years later, Jonson was to capture some of the growing attraction of the new 'west end' in his comedy *Epicene* (1609).[23] But it was still a rough district around Charing Cross, infested by many of the city's thieves, tricksters, prostitutes, dedicated drinkers, and petty criminals, and notorious for its 'stirrings'.[24] The cross after which the place took its name now stood in a state of advanced decay, aptly symbolizing the general condition of the area as a whole. Running northward from the west end of the Strand around the bottom of St Martin's Lane lay a network of courts and lanes known as the Bermudas; to the east end of the Strand near the church of St Clement Danes were the Straits, a similar maze of alleys and courtyards. In the early 1760s the houses in Hartshorn Lane would be pulled down to make way for the erection of Northumberland House. In a further more extensive redevelopment in 1829, this whole area of the city was swept away to allow for the construction of Trafalgar Square, whose generously radiating spaces were ideally suited for large public gatherings of national rejoicing and social protest. In Jonson's time its intricate character encouraged more deviant kinds of public and private behaviour. This is the area haunted by those shady operators Engine and Everill in *The Devil Is an Ass*, and passionately denounced by the high-minded Justice Overdo in *Bartholomew Fair*: 'Look into any angle o' the town—the Straits, or the Bermudas—where the quarrelling lesson is read, and how do they entertain the time, but with bottle-ale and tobacco?' (2.6.60–2). It is the home of extortionists, whose 'very trade | Is borrowing; that but stopped, they do invade | All as their prize, turn pirates here at land, | Have their Bermudas, and their Straits i' the Strand' (*The Underwood*, 13.79–82).

Jonson's formal education began, so Fuller reports, 'in a private school in St Martin's church', the small elementary school maintained by the church of St Martin-in-the-Fields, not far from Hartshorn Lane. Here children were taught to read and write in English, and to master basic grammatical skills. The routines of such schools were tedious and demanding: 'no man loves a prison worse', one veteran of the system was to recall many years later. Slow learners and high-spirited pupils alike received regular floggings, a practice that Jonson was later to condemn as 'deformed, and servile' (*Discoveries*, 1204).[25] Yet he evidently flourished in this unpromising atmosphere, and at the age of 7 or thereabouts was ready for advancement to the place that was to shape his future character and career: Westminster School. Many years later Drummond noted Jonson's remark that he had been 'put to school by a friend (his master, Camden)' (*Informations*, 181–2). In one reading of this characteristically ambiguous jotting, the 'friend' might be William Camden himself, who was at this time second Master at Westminster. 'Friend' is a word that Jonson always used with measured care, and warmly invoked in relation to Camden, whom he later celebrated in a famous phrase: 'Alumnus olim, aeternum amicus': 'a pupil once, a friend for ever'. But the 'friend' who is mentioned in Drummond's note may well have been a third party, a teacher or churchwarden at St Martin's School, perhaps, who recognized the young boy's outstanding abilities, and helped to negotiate his entry to Westminster.[26] Whatever the case, William Camden and Westminster School were soon to prove the greatest formative influences of Jonson's early life.

§§

The Royal College of St Peter in Westminster—to give the school its grandly formal name—stood in a different, and altogether more agreeable, quarter of the city, on the edge of the countryside.[27] A short walk in almost any direction would take a boy at once into the fields. To the north of the school lay St James's Park, and beyond the Park were fields leading to the rural villages of Hampstead and Highgate. To the west of the school stretched the road to Chelsea, and to the south, beyond the subterranean brook that flooded after heavy rain, were the marshes of Tothill (or Tuttle) Fields, a large open area which since at least the time of Henry III had been used for tournaments and fighting and the settlement of wagers, and for the annual Tothill Fair. Archers and train bands exercised here, and for those in search of quieter pleasures there was an artificial maze to wander in. In the remoter parts of the Fields conjurors reportedly practised their diabolical and forbidden arts: Gossip Tattle in *The Staple of News* is said to know 'who conjured in Tuttle Fields, and how many, when they never came there' (Intermean after Act 3, 28–9).

If the school gave easy access to such rural scenes and practices, it stood also at the heart of Westminster, and indeed (politically) of the nation: alongside the Abbey, and a few hundred yards from the Palace of Westminster, which until the reign of Henry VIII had served as a royal residence, and was now the seat of law and government. Boys at Westminster could watch the great lawyers and politicians of the day bustling past the school with their shoals of clerks, petitioners, and litigants, and had merely to cross the precinct in order to hear these orators in action. Less desirable characters gathered in the vicinity of the Abbey, which offered sanctuary to criminals and vagrants. Sightseers thronged to this area, and were free to enter the school itself. These visitors, popularly known as 'plump walkers', could watch the boys at their lessons, question them on points of learning, or challenge them to make verses on a given theme or debate a particular topic.[28]

The impact of Westminster School on the young Jonson was profound and long-lasting. It has been suggested that the school gave Jonson 'his first introduction to the intricate and often apparently meaningless divisions of the Elizabethan hierarchy';[29] but Westminster was notably non-hierarchical in composition, and would have offered Jonson a new and distinctive view of the complex structures of contemporary society, and his possible place within them. The school had been refounded by Queen Elizabeth in 1560 with new statutes providing forty Queen's Scholarships designed to attract talented children from poorer families, such as Jonson's own, who had been at the school for a year. No boy could be elected a Queen's Scholar if he had more than £10 per annum as his inheritance. While this financial bar was not always strictly applied, the very existence of such an enlightened policy made the school distinctive. 'The insistence on an ostensibly competitive entry to scholarship, rather than one in which Dean and Prebendaries nominated boys,' writes a recent historian, 'made Westminster unique among the great schools until the mid-nineteenth century.'[30] Queen's Scholars were educated free of charge; they resided in a dormitory within the school precincts, and took all their meals together with the Dean, Prebendaries, and college officers. Several boys from humble backgrounds who were admitted to Westminster around this time as Queen's Scholars became notable writers in later life: Thomas Randolph and William Cartwright, for example, both considerably younger than Jonson, but both to be drawn eventually into the select circle of his friends; and (in another generation) Abraham Cowley, who was to acknowledge his intellectual debts 'to the example and learning of Ben'.[31]

Jonson himself, being privately supported, was enrolled at Westminster however not as a Queen's Scholar but as an oppidan or 'townsboy', who attended the school daily from 6 a.m. to 6 p.m. He may have lodged near the school, but more probably resided at home, trudging to school early each morning from Hartshorn Lane along the muddy Strand (where, in *The Devil is in Ass*, 1.1.72–3, lawyers on horseback 'come dabbled from Westminster Hall') and home again to his family at the end of each day.

Westminster School attracted boys not merely from a wide range of social classes, but, like other great public schools of the day, from all parts of England: in 1592, shortly after Jonson's departure from Westminster, the sixty-four candidates admitted to the school came from no fewer than seventeen different counties.[32] William Camden's unrivalled acquaintance with families throughout the length and breadth of the country would no doubt have helped to extend the geographical diversity of the school, and his robustly independent approach to the question of genealogy may likewise have strengthened its relatively democratic temper. In Camden's opinion, families were to be valued for their accomplishments, not for their antiquity. 'There are some peradventure who apprehend it disdainfully and offensively', he wrote in the preface to *Britannia* in 1610, 'that I have not remembered this or that family, when it was not my purpose to mention any but such as were more notable, nor all of them truly (for their names would fill whole volumes) but such as happened in my way according to the method I proposed to myself.' Camden's social philosophy was deeply congenial to Jonson, according comfortably with his own social origins and aspirations, and becoming in time central to his own mature vision of the nature of social merit.[33]

So far from merely replicating the hierarchical divisions of Elizabethan society, Westminster School set the sons of squires, lawyers, clergy, tradespeople, artisans, and aristocrats on a relatively equal social footing, its gradations depending less upon birth and wealth than upon intellectual merit. In such a community, a quick-witted boy from a humble family might soon achieve distinction through single-minded ambition and application. The school thus offered Jonson unique opportunities for social advancement. Many of the friendships that he formed at Westminster with future churchmen, scholars, lawyers, diplomats, and politicians and with young aristocrats were of lasting benefit to him in later life. Amongst his near contemporaries at Westminster were the future antiquary Robert Cotton, from whose generous friendship and superlative library Jonson was later to profit; and Dudley Carleton, destined to become the most brilliant diplomat in Europe, and (as it happened) an acute observer of the court performances of Jonson's masques and entertainments. Several of Jonson's school companions were to make their names as poets, including William Alabaster, later a don in Cambridge and author of Latin tragedies and verses. Alabaster was to cause a stir by converting to Catholicism in 1597, just a few months before Jonson's own conversion to Rome. Hugh Holland was another friend of Jonson's at Westminster who was later to convert to Catholicism. Holland subsequently wrote a life of Camden, who ranked Holland and Jonson with the 'most pregnant wits of these our times, whom succeeding ages may justly admire'.[34] He and Jonson were eventually to write verses to the memory of William Shakespeare that would stand at the head of the First Folio in 1623. Other future writers entered Westminster shortly after Jonson himself had left the school: Richard Corbett (the fareweller of fairies), Henry King, George Herbert, William Strode, Giles Fletcher, and Brian Duppa. Corbett, King, and Duppa were to become close friends of Jonson in his middle years, and Duppa was eventually to edit the collection of memorial verses, *Jonsonus Virbius*, published in 1638 after Jonson's death.

If Westminster School offered opportunities for friendship, it was also a highly competitive place. A pupil's survival and advancement depended upon his ability to perform confidently before an audience of students, teachers, and the occasional 'plump walker'. Students from all forms of the school were taught together in the one room in the Cellarer's building in Dean's Yard: here both junior and senior students watched each other in action, and critically assessed each other's performances. The system encouraged intellectual quickness, and an element of histrionic display. These qualities were much in evidence during the 'wrangling' competitions with other church schools, where the boys disputed 'in verse, contending about the principles of grammar, or the perfect tense of supines', and during the annual three-day ritual of oral examining known as the Election: the gruelling process by which younger boys were selected for admission into the school, some as Scholars or 'minor candidates', and promising senior boys picked out as 'major candidates' to proceed to Christ Church, Oxford, or Trinity College, Cambridge. Latin was the regular language of class instruction. Any boy who spoke English, or said more than three words wrong in a rule, or made three mistakes in an exercise immediately became class dunce or *custos*. All questions in class were directed first to the unfortunate *custos*, before being put to other boys, one of whom would sooner or later fall into some similar error, and be forced to take on the dunce's role. The mockery of dullards and slow-witted characters in Jonson's comedies—of Mattheo in *Every Man In His Humour* for his mispronounced Latin, for example—recalls the atmosphere of teasing and rivalry in the Westminster classroom.

Many years later, advising an unknown lord (perhaps William Cavendish, Earl of Newcastle) about the education of his sons, Jonson warmly commended the advantages of a schooling of this kind. Education at home had many drawbacks, offering the children overmuch protection. 'For which cause I wish them sent to the best school, and a public; which I think the best,' wrote Jonson; 'To breed them at home is to breed them in a shade; where in a school they have the light and heat of the sun.' A school will give the boys two vital things which they would lack at home: the possibility of forming friendships, 'some to last till their age', and a sense of proper competition:

Therefore I like no private breeding. I would send them where their industry should be daily increased by praise, and that kindled by emulation. It is a good thing to inflame the mind, and though ambition itself be a vice, it is often the cause of great virtue. Give me that wit whom praise excites, glory puts on, or disgrace grieves: he is to be nourished with ambition, pricked forward with honour, checked with reprehension, and never to be suspected of sloth. (*Discoveries*, 1163–201)

Jonson seems here to be gratefully remembering the kind of stimulus, based on 'emulation', which his own schooldays had provided.

The daily routines at Westminster, like the curriculum itself, followed the model of Eton, for which detailed accounts survive. A document in the hand of Archbishop Laud, a Prebendary of the Abbey from 1620 to 1628, describes the routines at Westminster School at a slightly later period of the school's history; they would not have changed much since Jonson's time.[35] The day began early:

about a quarter of an hour after five in the morning we were called up by one of the monitors of the chamber with a *surgite* ['get up!'], and after Latin prayers we went into the cloister to wash, and thence in order two by two to the school, where we were to be by six of the clock at the furtherest.

A couple of boys known as the *monitores immundorii* ('the filth inspectors') presided over the washing ritual. The oppidans or day boys arrived at the school, the boys dressed in their monastic garb for lessons, and other monitors checked attendance. The Usher led the boys in prayer at 6 o'clock, then lessons commenced. At 8 there was a pause for 'beaver'—a brief snack—'and recollection of ourselves and preparation for future exercises', and dinner was taken at 11 a.m. The afternoon classes resumed at noon, and continued until supper at 6 p.m., when the oppidans returned to their lodgings. During mealtimes the boys listened to readings from the Old and New Testaments. Prayers were said in Latin six times a day. At 8 p.m. the boys in theory went to bed, 'pouring out prayers' (as the Eton prescription has it), but preparation was necessary for the following day's study, and they often worked in relays through the night, one boy waking the next and passing on what he had learnt. Even as a day boy, Jonson would have needed to prepare carefully for the next day's classes, and his own later habits of nocturnal working may well have been formed at this time.[36] The regime was recognized as arduous, and during the day an exhausted boy might seek permission to 'dor' in class, dozing briefly with his head on his hands. Lessons continued throughout the week, forty-six weeks a year: not even Sundays were free, and holidays were held to a minimum. In a later period, under the headmastership (1638–95) of the notorious Richard Busby—who boasted of having flogged sixteen future bishops of the Church of England as well as the future poets Prior and Dryden, and the budding philosopher John Locke—Westminster was renowned for the severity of its discipline. In Jonson's day,

Fig. 11. Westminster Scholar by Rudolph Ackermann, 1816.

under the headmastership of Edward Grant and Camden, his Second Master (who succeeded Grant as Headmaster in 1593), it would have been a more benign place, though discipline was still strictly maintained, and beatings still occurred.

In the lower division of the school the boys were trained essentially in the principles of grammar, while in the upper division they concentrated primarily on the rules of rhetoric. They began in the first form by studying the Latin exercises prepared by Juan Luis Vives, the great Spanish humanist, and the *Distichs* of the third-century BC writer Dionysius Cato, a schoolbook widely used in Renaissance Europe to teach principles of syntax and proverbial morality; sixteenth-century editions of the work often incorporated the *scholia* or annotations of Erasmus. They also read the *Dialogues* and *Confabulationes Pueriles* of the Swiss teacher Corderius, which helped them to develop spoken skills in Latin. In the second and third forms they began to read the comedies of Terence along with Erasmus' *Colloquies*, Aesop's *Fables* (in Latin, not Greek), and eventually some Sallust and a selection of Cicero's letters. In the afternoons the Master would read them the *Apothegms* of Erasmus. In the fourth form their principal texts were Ovid's *Tristia*, Cicero's *De Officiis*, along with more Terence and Sallust, and readings from Ovid's *Fasti* in the afternoons. At this stage, too, they made a start on their Greek grammar—a year earlier than at Eton and other schools, in order to allow time for the study of Hebrew in the top form—cutting their teeth on Lucian's *Dialogues*, a work for which Jonson retained a strong affection.[37] In the fifth form they studied the Latin historian Justin, together with Ovid's *Metamorphoses* and Cicero's discourse on friendship, *De Amicitia*. Their study of Greek continued with Plutarch and Isocrates, and the afternoons were diversified with readings from Horace, Lucan, or Seneca's tragedies. In the sixth and seventh forms they read Caesar, Livy, Virgil, Demosthenes, and Homer in the mornings and certain other authors in the afternoons, including Martial. Hebrew grammar was taught in the seventh form, and the Psalms were studied in both Greek and Hebrew. In addition to this formidable programme of reading, there was some provision also for music in the upper school.

Laud's notes give a sense of how lessons were conducted in the sixth and seventh forms.

Between 6 and 8 a.m. we repeat our grammar parts (out of Lily for Latin, out of Camden for the Greek), 14 or 15 being selected and called out to stand in a semi-circle before the master and other scholars, and there repeated 4 or 5 leaves in either, the master appointing who should begin, and who should go on with such and such rules.

'Lily' was the famous Latin grammar of William Lily, first printed in 1527, that had long been a standard textbook in Tudor schools; 'Camden' was William Camden's equally celebrated adaptation of the elementary Greek grammar prepared in 1575 by the school's Headmaster, Edward Grant. The afternoons began as follows:

Betwixt 1 to 3, that lesson, which, out of some author appointed for that day, had been by the master expounded unto them (out of Cicero, Virgil, Homer, Euripides, Isocrates, Livy, Sallust etc.) was to be exactly gone through, by construing and other grammatical ways, examining all the rhetorical figures and translating it out of verse into prose, or out of prose into verse; out of Greek into Latin, or out of Latin into Greek. Then they were enjoined to commit that to memory against the next morning.

The training in memory was an essential part of the educational system; Fridays and Saturdays were 'repetition days', when the boys were required, as a test of memory, to repeat what they had learnt throughout the week. Jonson later claimed (as we have seen) that he was able to remember all of his own writings well into middle age, and to 'repeat whole books that I have read, and poems of some selected friends, which I have liked to charge my memory with' (*Discoveries*, 346–65). During his visit to Scotland in his late forties, Jonson recited many of his own poems, as well as poems by his friends (*Informations*, 62–70, 80–90, etc.). The basic training at Westminster School must certainly have helped him to develop these remarkable gifts.

Laud's notes continue:

Betwixt 4 and 5 they repeated a leaf or two out of some books of rhetorical figures, or choice proverbs and sentences collected by the master for that use. After that they were practised in translating some *dictamina* out of Latin or Greek, and sometimes turning Latin and Greek verse into English verse. Then a theme was given to them whereon to make prose and verses, Latin and Greek, against the next morning.

Dictamina were sayings or precepts. Years later, Jonson playfully remembered (and domesticated) the word in his poem 'A Celebration of Charis', when the adored but tantalizing Charis—laying down the law like some classical authority—proffers her account of the ideal lover: 'Her Man Described by Her Own

Dictamen' (*The Underwood*, 2.9). Jonson's light-hearted use of the Latinate term—so characteristic of his poetry as a whole, as it switches easily between native and classical modes—comes from a flexibility acquired at an early age at Westminster School, where exercises in translation provided a foundation for original composition. Noting Jonson's 'opinion of verses' in 1618–19, William Drummond observed 'that he wrote all his first in prose, for so his master Camden had learned him' (*Informations*, 293). This technique, developed primarily in relation to classical translation, was to serve later generations of Westminster poets with equal profit, as did the school's more basic philosophy of learning through emulation. Like Jonson, George Herbert, Henry King, Abraham Cowley, and John Dryden all became accustomed at Westminster to think and write independently through developing an intimate familiarity with the best classical authors, much of whose work they came to know by heart. This method was warmly advocated by Jonson himself in later life:

For the mind and memory are more sharply exercised in comprehending another man's things, than our own; and such as accustom themselves and are familiar with the best authors, shall ever and anon find somewhat of them in themselves, and in their expression of their minds, even when they feel it not; be able to utter something like theirs, which hath an authority above their own. (*Discoveries*, 1237–41)

The authors who were read and emulated were not merely those from the classical past. For William Camden maintained a lively interest in English poetry, and it is reasonable to suppose that he encouraged his better pupils, such as Jonson, to read not merely classical but also vernacular verse. Pupils at Westminster were expected to try their hand in English at various verse forms, including the epigram (at which Jonson came in time to excel). In his *Remains Concerning Britain* (1605), Camden was to discuss the achievements of earlier English writers of epigrams and epitaphs, and to review more generally the work of English poets: of Chaucer, for example, 'our English Homer', from whom he quotes a long passage from *The Nun's Priest's Tale*, and of Sir Philip Sidney, whom he had known personally at Oxford: 'Will you have all in all for prose and verse?', he wrote; 'take the miracle of our age, Sir Philip Sidney.'[38] Jonson had a good knowledge of earlier English poets, including John Skelton, whose style he imitated deftly on more than one occasion, and of Chaucer, Gower, Lydgate, and Spenser, whom he introduces as characters ('the Poets') in his masque *The Golden Age Restored* in 1616. The 'god-like Sidney' (*The Forest*, 12.91) was to become a particular guiding light for Jonson, one of his 'great masters of wit and language' (*Discoveries*, 651–2). It is likely that Jonson's acquaintance with these authors began during his schooldays under Camden, a man absorbed as much by the achievements of modern Britain as by those of classical antiquity.

In a revealing passage in the *Discoveries*, Jonson speaks of the desirability of a graduated education, which introduces appropriate texts to young children according to their age and intellectual capacity:

And as it is fit to read the best authors to youth first, so let them be of the openest and clearest. As Livy before Sallust, Sidney before Donne. And beware of letting them taste Gower or Chaucer at first, lest falling too much in love with antiquity, and not apprehending the weight, they grow rough and barren in language only.... Spenser, in affecting the ancients, writ no language; yet I would have him read for his matter, but as Virgil read Ennius. (*Discoveries*, 1274–8, 1281–3)

What is striking about Jonson's educational programme as proposed here in the mid- to late 1620s is the easy pairing of English and classical authors, and the unhesitating modernity of his examples. Donne was still living at the time this passage was written, yet he is firmly included in Jonson's curriculum: as an author to be read at a slightly later stage of the child's progress (to be sure), but that is because he is hard, not because he is a contemporary. Antiquated writers, and those such as Spenser who affected antiquity, he regards indeed with caution, as providing poor models for those learning to write in their own language. It is tempting to think that Jonson is here remembering the eclecticism of Camden's own educational philosophy, and Camden's keen interest in English writing, modern as well as ancient. The academic study of English literature is usually reckoned not to have been developed until almost 200 years after Jonson's period at Westminster School: first, in the Scottish universities, and a good deal later than that, in universities south of the border. Yet for Jonson the study of contemporary and historical English poetry is naturally included within his programme for young pupils. If we ask why Jonson, an outstanding classical scholar, did not elect (as many of his contemporaries did) to write verses himself primarily in Latin or in Greek, choosing instead to excel in vernacular poetry, the answer may lie—partly, at least—in the powerful influence of William Camden.[39]

Boys in the upper school often established a close relationship with their teachers and other senior figures living within the Westminster precinct. Lancelot Andrewes, for example, during his time as Dean of Westminster

(1601–5), 'in the evenings would send for the elder boys to the Deanery, and teach them Greek and Hebrew from eight to eleven o'clock'.[40] While Jonson was still a pupil at Westminster, Elizabeth's former Chancellor, Sir John Fortescue, was living within the school in the Prior's House (later Ashburnham House). Fortescue, who had supervised Elizabeth's own studies, was a considerable scholar; Camden described him as 'an excellent man and a good Grecian'.[41] It is possible that Camden would have introduced Fortescue at some stage to such a promising pupil as Ben Jonson. Camden's own social origins were humble (his father had been a painter), but through his scholarship he had achieved a position of some social significance. He had a wide range of influential acquaintances both at home and abroad, and was able in turn, in the years to come, to introduce Jonson, the poor bricklayer's stepson, to people of power and distinction. It was perhaps through Camden's mediation, for example, that Jonson first became personally acquainted with members of the Sidney family, with his future patron, William Herbert, third Earl of Pembroke, and with scholars such as Sir Henry Savile (Provost of Eton, Warden of Merton College, editor of St Chrysostom, translator of Tacitus) and the great Dutch classicist and poet Daniel Heinsius.[42] When Jonson in 1616 saluted Camden as that 'most reverend head, to whom I owe | All that I am in arts, all that I know | (How nothing's that?)' (*Epigrams*, 14.1–3), he acknowledged the deep intellectual debts that he had incurred at Westminster School. But Camden was the making of Jonson in a social sense, as well. If Jonson was born under a lucky star, the name of that star was William Camden.

§§

Jonson became acquainted with one further art at Westminster that was to be of immense, if unforeseen, importance to him in the years to come. This was the art of the theatre. The school was famous for its annual productions of the Latin play, a regular event at Westminster since the headmastership of Alexander Nowell (1543–55).[43] The play was performed in the College Hall, and on at least two documented occasions (in 1564 and 1565) had been watched by Queen Elizabeth herself, who, as patroness of Westminster School, took a close interest in the school's activities. Surviving records of payment for early performances at the school show that these plays were quite elaborately staged. Costumes were hired from the Office of the Revels and transported by river to Westminster. Thunder barrels were brought in, along with men to operate them. A stage was erected in the hall, and scenery built: a couple of houses of wood and canvas for one play; the city, towers, and temple of Jerusalem painted on canvas for another. Musicians were hired, and properties devised: crowns and beards and ivy wreaths for small boys aspiring to the dignity of age, vizards and whips and flaxen hair for those impersonating the furies. Rushes were strewed on the floor, perfumes scattered, and men employed 'to watch the glass windows when the play was'.[44]

The Latin play was designed as a part of the boys' general classical education, and to help them in particular to speak confidently in Latin. They were issued with ink and paper, and told to write out their parts, and get them by heart. Nowell had introduced the comedies of Terence to the Westminster curriculum 'for the better learning the pure Roman style',[45] and Terence's plays, along with those of Plautus, were particular favourites also for performance—as they continue to be at the school to this day, where the tradition of the Latin play is maintained. Jonson's interest in Terence evidently continued into later life, for he acquired a fifteenth-century manuscript of Terence that is now in the library of St John's College, Oxford,[46] and refers repeatedly to Terence's comedies throughout his own work. The first prologue to *Epicene* (for example) alludes familiarly to the opening lines of the prologue to Terence's *Andria*, with its famous insistence that drama, before all else, must please the people:

> Truth says, of old the art of making plays
> > Was to content the people, and their praise
> > Was to the poet money, wine, and bays.
> But in this age a sect of writers are
> > That only for particular likings care,
> > And will taste nothing that is popular.
> With such we mingle neither brains nor breasts...
> > (*Epicene*, first prologue, 1–7)

> *Poeta quom primum animum ad scribendum adpulit,*
> *id sibi negoti credidit solum dari,*
> *populo ut placerent quas fecisset fabulas.*
> > (*Andria*, prologue, 1–3)

['When the playwright first steered his thoughts towards authorship, he supposed his sole business was to see that his plays pleased the people.'][47]

Terence's prologue soon proves tetchier than its agreeable opening might suggest, as he goes on—in a manner anticipating Jonson's own mature embattled style—to berate obtuse critics who have misunderstood the point of his adaptation of Menander, and to instruct his audiences to judge the matter for themselves. Jonson alludes to this same prologue again in the Induction to his late comedy *The Magnetic Lady*, this time with explicit reference to Westminster School.

Damplay You have heard, boy, the ancient poets had it in their purpose, still to please this people?
Probee Aye, their chief aim was—
Damplay Populo ut placerent (if he understands so much).
Boy Quas fescissent fabulas. I understand that, sin' I learned Terence i' the third form at Westminster. Go on, sir. (29–34)

There is something paradoxical about this learned swapping of tags from Terence to support the proposition that drama should appeal to the general public. Jonson's populism was always constrained, and it is not surprising that in the epilogue written for a court performance of *The Magnetic Lady* he roundly declares that it is not the people's approval that he ultimately seeks, but that of the monarch: 'To which voice he stands, | And prefers that, 'fore all the people's hands.'[48]

As the stage came under increasing attack from puritan critics during Elizabethan times, Westminster's policy of encouraging theatrical performance did not meet with universal approval, but the Latin play continued at the school notwithstanding.[49] In *The Staple of News* (1626) Jonson allows Gossip Censure to voice her disapproval of such libertarian practices:

They make all their scholars playboys! Is't not a fine sight, to see all our children made interluders? Do we pay our money for this? We send them to learn their grammar, and their Terence, and they learn their play-books? (42–9)

'Do we pay our money for this?' Gossip Censure's words almost suggest the anxiety of a Westminster parent, who in her muddled complaints fails to realize that 'Terence' and 'play-books' may be synonymous. For Jonson, on the other hand, education and the theatre—as his Westminster training had taught him—were necessarily and intimately involved. Plays must be designed to please the people, yes, but they must also be designed to instruct. After the success of his greatest comedy, *Volpone*, Jonson would address the

Universities of Oxford and Cambridge at some length on this matter, marking his distance from the generality of writers for the English stage.

It was to Oxford or Cambridge that a clever Westminster School boy would expect to proceed as he approached the age of 18. As his schooldays drew to an end, Jonson's ambitions would naturally have turned in this direction. But problems, and other callings, lay ahead.

5

Conflicts 1588–1592

CONFLICT was an idea that came easily to Jonson, and coloured his vision of the world. Life itself was a battleground upon which Catholic and Protestant forces struggled for supremacy, and the powers of good and evil, like opposing battalions, were pitted against each other in never-ending warfare. In an epigram addressed to William Herbert, Earl of Pembroke, in 1616 Jonson spoke of

> this strife
> Of vice and virtue, wherein all great life
> Almost, is exercis'd; and scarce one knows
> To which yet of the sides himself he owes.
> (*Epigrams*, 102.5–8)

This sharply divided moral universe resembles that of Calvin, with whose work Jonson appears to have been familiar.[1] It is a universe that is both rigid and unstable, whose opposing forces, though locked in perpetual combat, are uncertain in their allegiances, switching sides as occasion offers.

> They follow virtue for reward today,
> Tomorrow vice, if she give better pay:
> And are so good and bad just at a price,
> As nothing else discerns the virtue or vice. (9–12)

The role of the poet, as Jonson in his maturity came to perceive it, was akin to that of a brilliant general, spotting the enemy's troops, knowing the strengths of his own, and bringing the one into confrontation with the other. The poet, he wrote in *Discoveries*, must have an 'exact knowledge of all virtues, and their contraries; with an ability to render the one loved, the other hated, by his proper embattling them' (744–5). *Embattling* is a word that nicely captures Jonson's view of the creative, as of the spiritual, life. The sharply antithetical structure of court masque and antimasque which Jonson came in time to perfect, sometimes expressed through 'barriers' or solemn court tournaments in which opposing parties warred against each other in mock encounters, was in many ways congenial to his temperament.

Jonson's early life was itself notably conflicted. A naturally pugnacious man, he was caught up repeatedly in physical combat, both at home and abroad. He faced mental conflict as well, most obviously during these years in the choice of a profession. Jonson is often regarded as a determined and single-minded character, who, knowing his own destiny from the outset, methodically established and pursued a career as a writer. But throughout these early and restless years there can have been very few certainties in Jonson's life. Family expectation and need pulled him in one direction, personal ambition in another. Would he follow in the footsteps of his stepfather Robert Brett, the master-bricklayer, or aspire to a life of scholarship and creativity, like that of his mentor William Camden? Jonson for a time sought to resolve this question by following neither pathway, but recruiting instead for military service, merging his personal conflict within the wider framework of national and religious combat. Fighting would become a habitual response which was to govern much of Jonson's behaviour, for better or for worse, throughout his later life.

§§

The earliest biographical narratives offer very different accounts of Jonson's departure from Westminster School and his activities in the years that followed. William Drummond records that Jonson was 'taken from' the school before completing his education, 'and put to another craft (I think was to be a wright or bricklayer), which he could not endure' (*Informations*, 182–3). This was probably in 1587, while Jonson was 15 years of age. Other less reliable evidence suggests that he might have lingered on at the school a year or two longer.[2] Jonson's familiarity with Hebrew, from which he draws his examples in his *English Grammar*, is sometimes thought to support this view, for it was only in the uppermost form at Westminster that this language was taught. His knowledge of Hebrew need not have been acquired at Westminster, however, for private instruction in this language was readily available in London at this time, and Jonson in any case was quite capable of studying by himself. Much of his impressive learning was acquired through private application, outside the confines of an institution. Though he was fully aware of the perils of self-tuition—'he that was only taught by himself had a fool to his master', he noted tersely in *Discoveries* (16)—there was always a touch of the autodidact about him. He told William Drummond with evident pleasure that he had honorary degrees from both Oxford and Cambridge, though he had never completed a course of study at either university: 'He was a Master of Arts in both the universities, by their favour, not his study' (*Informations*, 191).

It is possible nevertheless that Jonson briefly studied at Cambridge. Thomas Fuller in his *History of the Worthies of England* (1662) records that Jonson 'was statutably admitted into St John's College in Cambridge' after leaving Westminster School, but for want of funds was soon obliged to abandon his studies and return home. Jonson's name does not appear in the records of either St John's College or Cambridge University, however, and as Fuller himself was not even born until twenty years after the events he purports here to describe, his testimony has usually been regarded with suspicion. But Fuller had a prodigious memory and an intimate knowledge of the University, whose history he had written. His own father had been a Fellow of St John's at the very time that Jonson is said to have been a student in the College, and if he was not the actual source of Fuller's information he would at least have been able to corroborate or deny the story. The possibility of Jonson's association with St John's is strengthened by a request made to him early in 1615 by the then President of the College, Robert Lane, that he 'pen a ditty' to celebrate the visit of King James to the College in March of that year. James was to visit most of the Cambridge colleges on this occasion; that Jonson should have been invited to write on behalf of a single college, rather than the University as a whole, strongly suggests the existence of a particular link with St John's.[3]

It would have been understandable for William Camden to have directed Jonson, one of his most gifted pupils, to this place. Cambridge was the leading centre of humanist scholarship and Protestant debate in Tudor England; and within Cambridge, St John's had long been regarded as the most intellectually distinguished of the University's various halls and colleges.

Thomas Nashe, a student at St John's in the years immediately preceding the period of Jonson's probable residence, was to hail his college as 'that most famous and fortunate nurse of all learning . . . an university within itself, shining so far about all other houses, halls, and hospitals whatsoever, that no college in the town was able to compare with the tithe of her students'.[4] Nashe was looking back on the great days of St John's earlier in the century, when men such as Sir John Cheke and Roger Ascham—outstanding Greek scholars both, and strong advocates also of vernacular learning, tutors in turn to the future Elizabeth I—were associated with the College. By the 1580s, in Nashe's eyes at least, the intellectual atmosphere had changed: the College was now dominated by the puritan faction, and was more narrowly dedicated to training future priests for the ministry. The puritan element strengthened its hold on the College in 1586 with the appointment of a new Master: William Whitaker, Regius Professor of Divinity, pre-eminent Anglican divine, and 'one of the greatest men the College has ever had'.[5] A brilliant Greek scholar and skilful biblical exegete, Whitaker was known for his strong opposition both to Catholicism and Lutheranism, and for his sympathetic interest in Calvinist doctrine. Strongly supported by Archbishop Whitgift and Lord Burghley, who had engineered his appointment to the mastership, Whitaker was to rise to further places of distinction within the Church of England, and to bring the College itself to new intellectual heights.

If Jonson indeed attended St John's, as seems entirely possible, he would have entered the College as a sizar, one of the poorer students who made his way by doing menial tasks (sweeping rooms, fetching water, waiting on table) in return for his keep, subsisting largely on food left over from the College meals, and following as best he could the demanding routines of undergraduate life. The names of sizars were not regularly entered in the College register, and it is not surprising therefore (since the University records for this period are also missing) that no trace of Jonson's short period of residence remains.[6] All students of St John's shared rooms with a Fellow of the College and other students, and usually slept more than one to a bed. They rose at 4 a.m. or earlier, worked long hours, attended regular prayers and lectures, and faced fines or flogging for deviations from the College's strict regime. For an eager student, however, the potential rewards of such a life were considerable. Whitaker's example was clearly inspirational. His formidable learning, writes a historian of St John's, spread itself over the whole society, where by his example, instruction and encouragement he raised such an emulation amongst his fellows as to make others learned as well as himself; to that degree, that the society in his time was looked upon as somewhat more than a private college. He himself, who was no boaster, used to style it an university...[7]

It was at St John's that the still-evolving doctrines of the Church of England were tried and tested. Jonson's interest in Calvinist theology, in which Whitaker was especially skilled, might well have been awakened during this period.

Even the briefest of stays in such a place at such a time would have intensified the general appetite for learning that Camden had instilled in Jonson at Westminster School, encouraging him to see himself, in however attenuated a sense, as a 'university man'. Throughout his later life Jonson would continue to value and cultivate his friendships with scholars at Cambridge and Oxford. In the epistle prefixed to the quarto edition of *Volpone* in 1607 he was to address the two universities with robust frankness, as though speaking gratefully at last to his intellectual equals. By 1615 he had probably acquired his honorary degrees from both universities. In the 1620s he was to become so closely identified with a group of academic friends at Christ Church, Oxford, that even the curmudgeonly Anthony à Wood, long entrenched as a Fellow of Merton, would freely claim him as an Oxford writer, 'for at Cambridge his stay was but short, and whether he took a degree in that University, I cannot learn of any'. Such was the ultimate veneration for Jonson's learning that in his old age he would be hailed, somewhat extravagantly, as being in himself 'Our third, and richest university'.[8]

§§

Whatever academic ambitions Jonson may have entertained as a young man at Cambridge quickly came into collision with hard reality. For 'want of further maintenance', Fuller reports, Jonson returned to London after a few weeks in order to work with his stepfather, helping 'in the building of the new structure of Lincoln's Inn'.[9] Searching through the Black Books of Lincoln's Inn, the American scholar Mark Eccles discovered that in 1588 the large sum of £298 7s. 11d. was paid for the building of a brick wall 'at the upper end of the Backside toward Holburne', along with a gate towards Fickett's Field (a piece of ground about ten acres in extent, now known as Lincoln's Inn

New Square), and another gate in the brick wall towards the pump. While the records fail to name the workmen employed on these tasks, they show that payments for the minor repairs were made to 'Thomas Brett, "le Bricklayer" '. Eccles concluded that this was the project upon which Jonson and his stepfather were engaged. This supposition is not without its problems. Since Eccles conducted this research, it has been shown (for one thing) that Jonson's stepfather was not Thomas Brett, but almost certainly Robert Brett. Payments were in fact made to Robert (not Thomas) Brett for minor repairs to walls near Holborn in 1590 and 1591. It is possible that Jonson was engaged with his stepfather on this task, but his return from Cambridge and the start of his apprenticeship as a bricklayer must have commenced well before this date.[10]

If Fuller's story of Jonson's brief period at Cambridge is accepted as true, it remains unclear why Jonson should have abandoned his studies and returned to London when he did. Nashe had supported himself as a sizar at St John's over many years, and there is no obvious reason why Jonson, when short of personal funds, could not have done the same. The most likely explanation is that Brett faced a temporary crisis in his business, and that pressure was applied on Jonson to help the family out. Antony à Wood, writing a century after the event, placed the blame for Jonson's return on 'his silly mother'. John Taylor the Water Poet, in an elegy written at Jonson's death, accused his ignorant stepfather, who despised education, and 'therefore did command his stepson Ben, | From learned studies to come home again'.

> Then was he forced to leave the academ',
> And lay by learning (that unvalued gem);
> Behold a metamorphosis most strange:
> His books were turned to bricks, a sudden change...[11]

Whatever the explanation for Jonson's sudden return, Taylor's conceit has a certain poetic truth: for books and bricks were indeed to become contrasting symbols in Jonson's life, and learning and labouring the two opposed professions to which he was variously called and driven.

Fuller pictures Jonson with a trowel in one hand and a book in the other, torn between an occupation he despised and a vocation he longed to pursue. Taunts about his early career as a bricklayer were to follow him throughout most of his professional life. Whenever his writing faltered, his critics were wont to remark unkindly that he should now return to his former work.

Jonson is the 'wittiest fellow of a bricklayer in England', one character ironically remarks in the second part of *The Return From Parnassus*, a play presented by Cambridge students in 1601; 'He were better betake himself to his old trade of bricklaying,' responds his companion; 'a bold whoreson, as confident now in making of a book, as he was in times past in laying of a brick.' 'Put off thy buskins, Sophocles the Great,' jeered Sir John Davies a few years later, 'And mortar tread with thy disarmed shanks.' 'The masque on Twelfth Night is not commended of any,' grumbled Sir Nathanael Brent after the performance of Jonson's *Pleasure Reconciled to Virtue* in 1618; 'the poet is grown so dull that . . . divers think fit he should return to his old trade of bricklaying again.' After the failure of *The Magnetic Lady*, Alexander Gil offered similarly caustic advice in 1633: 'But to advise thee, Ben, in this strict age, | A brickhill's fitter for thee than a stage.'[12]

It is curious then to find that Jonson in fact persevered in the bricklaying trade throughout a remarkably long period of his life. The quarterage book of the Tylers' and Bricklayers' Company shows that he must have been a freeman (or fully qualified member) of the Company by 29 June 1596, when he paid his quarterly dues for a period going back to Michaelmas 1595 and probably to Michaelmas 1594. After 1602 Jonson evidently stopped paying his dues, yet on 1 May 1611 he resumed his membership with a payment of 11s. 4d., retrospectively covering the previous eight years. An entry in the Company's records for the payment of 10s. 8d. 'for wine and sugar for Benjamin Jonson' around this time suggests that his colleagues may have celebrated his return in appropriate style.[13] It might be suspected that Jonson's continued membership of the guild was a hedge against unemployment, and that he returned to bricklaying during periods of financial need, when work in the theatre or at court was slack. Yet Jonson's obvious strong dislike for such work renders such an explanation intrinsically improbable, and would scarcely account for his resumption of guild membership in 1611, when he was in high demand as a dramatist and a writer of court masques and private entertainments. There were, however, other benefits for Jonson in keeping up his guild membership. To begin with, the London livery companies, as David Kathman has recently shown in illuminating detail, were intricately involved in activities of the City's professional theatrical companies, and in particular with its apprenticeship system. Apprentice players were often bound to masters who were freemen of a particular company, such as the Grocers or Drapers or Goldsmiths, even though, as apprentices, they

89

were trained exclusively for the stage, and gained no special knowledge of the trade which their company was designed to support. On 1 May 1612, a year after resuming his membership of the Tylers' and Bricklayers' Company, Jonson himself was able to bind John Catlin, son of John Catlin, deceased, a Birmingham bricklayer, as his apprentice for a term of eight years.[14] A talented apprentice, if rented to a theatrical company, might prove a profitable source of income. In Jonson's *Christmas His Masque* (performed in 1616) Venus confesses she has been tempted to rent out her 'playboy' son Cupid in this manner to the King's Men on a weekly basis.

Guild membership also served, more significantly, as an avenue to citizenship and therefore to social advancement. As late as 1618 Jonson was welcomed to the City of Edinburgh not as a celebrated writer but as 'inglisman burges and gildbrother in communi forma'. 'Burges', the Scottish term for a citizen or freeman, implies that Jonson had served his apprenticeship to full term, and 'gildbrother' that he was still closely associated with the Tylers' and Bricklayers' Company at this advanced stage of his career. Such qualifications eased his ready acceptance by the civic community in Edinburgh. In 1628, his guild membership made possible his appointment as Chronologer to the City of London.[15]

Guild membership in early modern England conferred other benefits and obligation, designed to foster a system of close community and support. As a member of the Tylers' and Bricklayers' Company, Jonson would have been required to attend all Company meetings at Bricklayers' Hall in Aldgate Street, as well as the funerals of other Company members and the annual Lord Mayors' processions to Westminster, fines being exacted for non-attendance at these events. The Company offered practical help moreover to individual members who were in personal difficulty through sickness, debt, imprisonment, or other circumstances: a system of friendly aid from which Jonson might well have benefited on more than one occasion. Though he must have maintained close and regular contact with the Company throughout a significant period of his writing life, Jonson evidently chose not to refer publicly to this continuing association with a trade which had all too frequently exposed him to ridicule. Yet there is no reason to suppose that the association was at odds with Jonson's development as a writer. On the contrary: in at least one respect, through the obligation imposed on all guild members to attend the annual Lord Mayors' shows, it may well have stimulated his powers of invention, and ultimately helped his advancement in a surprisingly different social quarter.[16]

The Lord Mayors' shows took place each year on 29 October (St Simon and St Jude's Day) to celebrate the inauguration of the new Lord Mayor. The mayoral party progressed along the Thames by barge to Westminster, accompanied by the barges of various London companies, adorned with banners and streamers, with trumpets sounding and small bands playing. After taking the oath at Westminster, the Lord Mayor returned downstream with his fleet to Baynard's Castle, while a land procession made its way from St Paul's Churchyard to the Guildhall. Here the assembled company took dinner, afterwards returning to St Paul's for divine service. The day was enlivened by dramatic exchanges and encounters which took place at strategic locations along the route. These dramatic pageants were devised and pre-sented by various London companies, who competed eagerly to outdo each other's inventions. Their actors were usually children, though from time to time professionals such as Richard Burbage and John Lowin are known to have taken part. In the early years of Elizabeth's reign, the drama of the Lord Mayors' shows was relatively static, consisting largely of set speeches recited along the way. Towards the end of the century and throughout James's reign, the drama grew more sophisticated, as companies began to call upon the services of professional dramatists such as George Peele, Thomas Dekker, Anthony Munday, Thomas Middleton, John Webster, and Thomas Heywood. In October 1604 Jonson himself was to be recruited by the Haberdashers' Company to devise the Lord Mayor's show for that year, and was paid the sum of £12 'for his device, and speech for the children'. That year's celebrations involved 'a fair pageant, chariot and a lion, two galleys, fire works, banners, streamers, and all other things', including mer-maids, a man 'that went on stilts to make room', and a company of ninety or a hundred bachelors attending on the Lord Mayor, suitably attired in furs and crimson satin hoods.[17] As a member of the Tylers' and Bricklayers' Guild, Jonson would by that time have been a seasoned observer of these annual shows, and have had an intimate knowledge of their conventions. Though the records of the Company show that a further sum of £1 10s. was paid 'for printing the books of the device', no copy of Jonson's work for the Company survives, and Jonson himself did not bother to include this piece, or indeed any of his civic entertainments, amongst the works he wished to preserve for posterity. Instead, he chose publicly to disparage such occasions, and the hacks who wrote repeatedly for them. Antonio Balladino, 'Pageant Poet to the City of Milan' in *The Case Is Altered*, is a thinly disguised portrait of Anthony Munday, a prolific deviser of Lord Mayors' shows. In Jonson's 'The Famous Voyage' the smells encountered by the courageous voyagers along Fleet Ditch, the sewer-like tributary of the Thames, rival those of 'the Lord Mayor's foist': the word 'foist' meaning a barge, but also a fart—Jonson's evident evaluation of the occasion (*Epigrams*, 133.120).

Despite such open scorn for the pageantry of the City, Jonson must have derived some at least of his skills as a writer of court masques from an intimate knowledge, gained through long association with the London guilds, of the drama associated with the Lord Mayor's show. Significantly, the Lord Mayor's show and the court masque both achieved their finest form during the first half of the seventeenth century, when writers such as Jonson were invited to write both for the livery companies and for the reigning monarch. These two forms of entertainment differed from each other in some obvious ways. The Lord Mayor's show was a public event, a civic parade in full grandeur through the streets of London and along the river to the delight of the citizenry, while the masque was an exclusive occasion, to which access was strictly controlled: an enactment of 'more removed mysteries' devised for a monarch who disliked, and chose whenever possible to avoid, the public gaze. Yet as David M. Bergeron has shown, these forms also had many scenic and thematic features in common. Both presented large-scale allegorical pageants depicting triumphs of civic or national harmony and prosperity. Both employed spectacular and at times identical mechanical devices: clouds that dissolved as a figure of sun-like importance approached, globes that rotated on their axes and opened in sections to disgorge their human contents. Both came in time to develop similar structural features, the mayoral shows mimicking (for example) the bipartite division of court masque and antimasque. At those times when the King himself was obliged to progress through the streets of the city, the formal distinction between civic and courtly pageantry was hard to draw. In 1604, the very year that he was employed by the Haberdashers' Company to devise the Lord Mayor's show, Jonson was also to write *Part of the King's Entertainment* to celebrate James's progress through the streets to Westminster to open his first parliament. At the height of his career Jonson continued to write entertainments for the livery companies which were staged at costly banquets attended also by the King.

Yet such long-term benefits of an association with the Tylers' and Bricklayers' Company lay still in the future. For a young man with literary ambitions, the day-to-day labouring with his stepfather must have seemed dull and arduous. The working hours were long, and Jonson can have had little energy left at the end of the day for serious study or reflection. Between the months of March and September, Elizabethan labourers were required by statute to be at work at or before five o'clock in the morning, and not to depart until seven or eight in the evening, occasional breaks being provided for eating, drinking, and sleep.[18] At some point during his early labours with Robert Brett, Jonson decided to escape. He may have felt an exasperation similar to that he was to express, some three decades later, in 'An Epistle to a Friend, to Persuade Him to the Wars', a poem that eloquently asserts the superiority of a life of vigorous action over one of drudgery or moral inertia.

> Wake, friend, from forth thy lethargy: the drum
> Beats brave and loud in Europe, and bids come
> All that dare rouse, or are not loath to quit
> Their vicious ease, and be o'erwhelmed with it.
> It is a call to keep the spirits alive
> That gasp for action, and would yet revive
> Man's buried honour in his sleepy life,
> Quick'ning dead nature to her noblest strife.
> (*The Underwood*, 15.1–8)

If the pathways to scholarship seemed no longer open to Jonson, military service might at least provide an honourable alternative to the life of a navvy. The drum that he now heard beating brave and loud in Europe was that of the English expeditionary forces, mustering for further campaigns in the Low Countries. Its sound was enticing.

§§

Since the mid-1560s the seventeen provinces of the Burgundian or Habsburg Netherlands—the so-called Low Countries, occupying most of the area of present-day Holland, Belgium, and Luxembourg—had been in open revolt against the rule of Philip II of Spain.[19] The provinces in the south were soon subdued, but those in the north would continue to fight for another eighty years for their independence, which was ultimately achieved with the Peace of

Westphalia in 1648. The Dutch communities grouped together under the hopeful title of the United Provinces were in fact quite diverse in language, religion, and social background, and the Dutch army contained significant Catholic as well as Protestant elements. Yet the Revolt of the Netherlands may fairly be represented as a struggle between the forces of northern Protestantism and the might of Catholic Spain, and as such was of deep and growing concern to England in the years leading to the Armada. Elizabeth's attitude to the conflict was cautious but calculating. While the brilliant Spanish Governor Alexander Farnese, Duke of Parma, swept to successive victories, she continued to resist any attempt to draw England into direct confrontation with Spain. In the autumn of 1585, however, as the Dutch situation worsened, Elizabeth finally agreed to give qualified assistance to their cause. Firmly declining the suggestion that she assume sovereignty of the United Provinces, she undertook through the Treaty of Nonsuch to send an army of 5,000 foot and 1,000 horse into the Low Countries on the understanding that England receive full financial compensation for this help when the war came to an end. In the meanwhile she held as security the key strategic towns of Flushing and Brill, and the Castle of Rammekins.

In September 1585 the English forces departed for the Low Countries under the command of the Queen's favourite, Robert Dudley, Earl of Leicester, who soon incurred Elizabeth's displeasure by accepting the office of Governor General of the United Provinces, thereby compromising the very distance she herself had been at pains to preserve. Leicester returned home in 1587 after suffering a number of disastrous military losses, and died the following year—in sinister circumstances, if the story that Jonson reported to Drummond many years later is to be credited.[20] Even as a young man, Jonson would have heard something of these campaigns, in which Leicester's nephews, Sir Philip and Sir Robert Sidney—the former, a figure of growing importance in his creative and intellectual life; the latter, a future friend and patron—had served with distinction. Sir Philip's heroic death at Zutphen in 1585 had quickly become the stuff of legend. 'Who falls for love of God shall rise a star,' Jonson was to write in *Underwood* 15, many years later: a maxim certainly borne out by Sidney's rapid posthumous fame.[21] To the young Ben Jonson, a glorious death in the Low Countries may well have seemed more attractive than a lifetime of laying bricks.

Though the date of Jonson's enlistment is unknown, it is likely that he recruited for service early in 1591, when special efforts were being made to increase the English presence in the Netherlands. In the spring of that year Maurice of Nassau, commander of the army of the States-General, began his first campaign to drive the Spanish from the inland provinces of the north. With the help of English forces and brilliant tactical advice from the English general Sir Francis Vere, who had served with distinction under Leicester, Maurice secured Zutphen in May, Deventer in June, and Nijmegen in October. In his later *Commentaries*, Vere was to describe with evident pleasure some of his more cunning ploys during these campaigns, such as his plan at Zutphen, where he disguised some of his younger soldiers as countrywomen bound for market, with weapons concealed in their baskets as they waited by the river—seemingly for the ferry, but actually to storm the gateway of the town's fort.[22] Vere was accompanied by his younger brother Sir Horace, who served as a lieutenant in his company of foot. Sir Horace was later to serve with distinction under Essex at Cadiz, before entering into service with the Dutch, and scoring a series of notable victories against Spanish forces. Jonson was to celebrate his deeds in his *Epigrams*, as one

> whose fame was won
> In th'eye of Europe, where thy deeds were done,
> When on thy trumpet she did sound a blast,
> Whose relish to eternity shall last.
>
> (*Epigrams*, 91.5–8)

Both Vere brothers were wounded in the summer of 1592 during the success-ful siege of Steenwyck, but assisted Maurice in its capture, and in the recovery of Coevorden that autumn. Jonson may have been involved in some or all of these campaigns.

Many years later Jonson recounted to Drummond with obvious relish his proudest achievement during this period of campaigning, his defeat, in single combat, of a champion from the opposing army: 'In his service in the Low Countries he had, in the face of both the camps, killed an enemy and taken *opima spolia* from him' (*Informations*, 184–5). *Opima spolia* are the arms or spoils traditionally seized by the victor from his defeated opponent; the Latin phrase hints at the antiquity of the custom.[23] In earliest times, one-to-one fighting of this kind was undertaken by opposing kings or leaders as a way of avoiding wider bloodshed amongst their men. In Jonson's day the custom was still vividly remembered on the English stage, though less often practised on the battlefield.[24] The few known instances of such one-to-one encounters

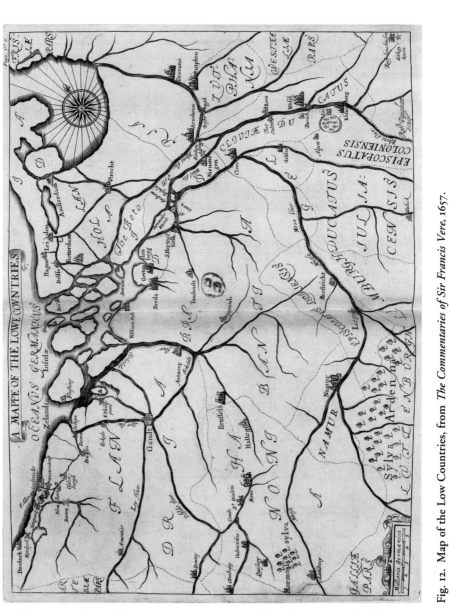

Fig. 12. Map of the Low Countries, from *The Commentaries of Sir Francis Vere*, 1657.

in this period involved opposing generals, rather than rival foot-soldiers. One such episode occurred in 1591, during the very period that Jonson was serving in the Netherlands, when Robert Devereux, Earl of Essex, the English general at the siege of Rouen, challenged Villars, the head of the beleaguered French garrison, to a similar single combat. After an elaborate exchange of letters, Villars refused the challenge.[25] That Jonson should have been selected from the ranks to fight 'in the face of both the camps' as his army's champion suggests that he had already distinguished himself in earlier campaigns through particular feats of strength and courage. His victory on this occasion would have earned him a measure of local fame, and brought him to the notice of his superior officers.

Jonson probably returned to England with the first contingent of home-coming troops in the autumn of 1592. Though his period in the Netherlands had been brief, his military experiences were to leave a trace on his subsequent writings. They might well have given him, as Julie Sanders has argued, a vivid practical introduction to the republican ideals (stemming largely from Venice) for which the Dutch troops were contending in their struggle against Spain.[26] And they affected his work in other more incidental ways. In the characters of Captain Tucca in *Poetaster*, of Bobadilla, the impoverished, quick-tongued braggart of *Every Man In His Humour*, and of Captain Hungry, the shifty mendicant of *Epigrams*, 107, Jonson ridiculed bogus veterans of the European wars, who posed as heroes of battlefields they had never seen. Bobadilla's plan to defeat the enemy in a mere 200 days with the help of nineteen chosen swordsmen in a series of single combats looks almost like an amused, parodic memory of Jonson's own heroic performance in the Netherlands. Jonson's ridicule of Captain Tucca appears to have caused offence however to other, more honest, veterans of these campaigns, whose understanding he felt obliged to beg in the Apologetic Dialogue of *Poetaster*.

> Strength of my country, whilst I bring to view
>   Such as are mis-called captains, and wrong you
> And your high names, I do desire that thence
>   Be nor put on you, nor you take offence.
> I swear by your true friend, my muse, I love
>   Your great profession; which I once did prove,
> And did not shame it with my actions, then . . .
>   ('To the Reader', [131–40])

Many years later, in a more distant memory of his campaigning experiences, Jonson has Merecraft in *The Devil Is an Ass* contrast the fashionable pleasures of London with the dreariness of day-to-day life in the Low Countries. In the taverns of London, Merecraft proudly declares, one may dine on 'Pheasant and godwit', while in the Low Countries the diet is 'cheese, salt-butter, and a pickled herring'. In London one dresses in 'Scarlet, gold lace, and cut-works', while folk over there go drably in 'worn cloth and fustian'. Here, there are sexual luxuries, 'lechery | In velvet', while the pleasures in Holland are mean and limited: for a penny, 'a leap o' your host's daughter, | In garrison'; for twopence, the wife of the camp provisioner (3.3.24–33). While Jonson's satire here is characteristically complex—the excitements of London are more pernicious, as well as more intense, than those of Holland—the unrelieved torpor of campaigning life in the Low Countries is sharply registered. Jonson was evidently unimpressed by 'the gross Dutch' (as he calls them elsewhere, *Epigrams*, 107.5), and would no doubt have shared the grumpy opinion of a somewhat later English traveller who characterized Holland as 'the great bog of Europe', 'a green cheese in pickle', and 'the buttock of the world'.[27] London, for all its vices, was a place of richer pleasures, and, for a young man at the outset of his career, richer possibilities.

Yet Jonson's period of military service in the 1590s had scarcely resolved the problems from which he had hoped to escape. If he had established a measure of independence through his time in the Low Countries and proved beyond doubt his courage as a fighter, he had still not yet managed to find his vocation. The way ahead was still unclear. The conflict in his mind continued.

6

Entering the Theatre 1594–1597

ON his return from the Low Countries, Jonson 'betook himself to his wonted studies', as he told William Drummond of Hawthornden many years later (*Informations*, 184). Jonson was not a man of independent means, however, as Drummond was, and despite the gentlemanly ring of this phrase he could not have maintained himself long in a life of private scholarship. What money he brought back from the Low Countries would soon have run out. That he returned, even briefly, to bricklaying seems unlikely, given his obvious loathing for his stepfather's trade. Perhaps he found temporary work as a private tutor, as he did in later years, but no evidence of such employment survives.

With the rapid expansion of theatrical activity in London of the 1590s, however, another and potentially more rewarding line of work was now opening up, whose attractions Jonson is likely to have viewed with sharply divided feelings of excitement and distrust. Though destined to become one of the supreme practitioners of the English theatre, Jonson would also prove to be its most scornful and outspoken critic. The theatre of his day, he would write despairingly in a few years' time, was a place in which 'nothing but ribaldry, profanation, blasphemy, all licence of offence to God and man, is practised' (*Volpone*, Epistle, 28–9). These words were addressed to the Universities of Oxford and Cambridge, whose qualities evidently seemed to Jonson altogether more enticing than those of the metropolitan theatre with which he was by then embroiled. At a later and even more disenchanted moment of his career Jonson would speak with deeper bitterness of 'the loathèd stage', as a place he wished to quit for ever ('Ode to Himself',

1629)—and would then decide, with an ambivalence that marked his entire career, to return once again to its embrace.

Yet at some moment in the early 1590s Jonson suppressed whatever misgivings he might have felt, and resolved to try his luck on the London stage. The timing and circumstances of this, the most significant decision of his life, are quite unknown. It is possible that he was driven not by any great ambition to excel in this new profession, but by an altogether simpler fact that was to dog so much of his career: the pressing need for money.

§§

Jonson's ambivalent feelings about the theatre were to some extent mirrored within the community at large. The playhouses that had sprung up in and around London during his own lifetime testified to the great and growing popularity of the theatre amongst all sectors of the population, but also served as a focus for civic and religious disapproval. The earliest venues for the professional players in London since the 1560s and 1570s had been the inn-yards and indoor halls at places such as the Bel Savage on Ludgate Hill, the Bell Inn and the Cross-Keys in Gracechurch Street, and the Bull Inn in Bishopsgate Street, where the much-loved Richard Tarlton had played, and the rousingly patriotic drama of *The Famous Victories of Henry V* had been staged.[1] The performances in these places attracted large and potentially disorderly crowds of onlookers, and were viewed with increasing concern by preachers and city authorities alike. After a series of ineffective attempts at regulation, the Common Council of the City of London in December 1574 under the direction of the Lord Mayor, Sir John Hawes, drew up a detailed order designed to curb theatrical activity in the city, forcing the players to seek other venues beyond the reach of the Council. During Jonson's early schooldays in the late 1570s, new amphitheatres designed for theatrical and related activities began to appear just outside the northern limits of the city. The first of these new structures, the Theatre—a large timber playhouse, with a circular performance area, and multiple galleries—was built in 1576 in the grounds of a former Benedictine priory at Shoreditch by James Burbage, a player and joiner, whose son Richard was in time to gain fame as Shakespeare's—and Ben Jonson's own—leading actor, and one of the great theatrical performers of his generation. The following year a second public amphitheatre, the Curtain, was built nearby, apparently serving for a time as a kind of auxiliary playhouse (or 'easer') to the Theatre, with which it was financially linked.[2]

The location of these two playhouses was critical both to their survival, and to the reputation they soon attracted. The Theatre and the Curtain were situated in the Liberty of Halliwell or Holywell, in the Middlesex parish of St Leonard's, Shoreditch, just outside the Bishopsgate entrance to the City of London, and lay therefore also just outside the jurisdiction of the City Council. This was open land, not far from Finsbury Fields, and close to the route of the old Roman road to the north.[3] There were many taverns here to serve the needs of travellers and other thirsty characters, and the area had become notorious for its bands of unruly vagrants, and its occasional scuffles and commotions. Bobadilla in *Every Man In His Humour* was to name Shoreditch as one of the 'divers skirts i'the town' in which he had been accosted by groups of strolling swordsmen, 'some three, four, five, six of them together, as I have walked alone' (4.7.434–6 (F)). Iniquity in Jonson's *The Devil Is an Ass* promises to lead young Pug on a wild drinking spree to this same notorious area as they 'survey the suburbs' of London (1.1.59–62). During the summer of 1584 a casual assault on an apprentice who had been lying on the grass outside the Theatre led to an escalating series of fights, prompting the Lord Mayor and his aldermen finally to petition the Privy Council 'for the suppression and pulling down' of the Theatre and the Curtain. The order was obtained, but evidently not carried out, and the two playhouses continued to stand, and to vex the authorities, for years to come.[4]

According to John Aubrey, whose testimony on such matters is not always to be trusted, it was in this troubled area on the outskirts of the city that Jonson began his dramatic career. After his return from the Low Countries (so Aubrey believed) Jonson 'acted and wrote, but both ill, at the Green Curtain, a kind of nursery or obscure playhouse somewhere in the suburbs (I think towards Shoreditch, or Clerkenwell)'.[5] There is no other surviving evidence however to support Aubrey's somewhat hesitant statement, though later in the decade Jonson would certainly be associated with the Curtain playhouse, where *Every Man In His Humour* was to be performed by the Lord Chamberlain's Men in the autumn of 1598.[6] It is likely that Aubrey (or his informant, J. Greenhill) was muddled in his recollection of the precise sequence of events in Jonson's early life, for other evidence suggests that Jonson's theatrical career began in an entirely different quarter of London, on the notorious Bankside.

On 14 November 1594, Jonson was married to Anne Lewis in the church of St Magnus the Martyr. Little is known about Anne, whom Jonson would later curtly describe to Drummond as 'a shrew yet honest' (*Informations*, 192), though she will enter the story more fully at a later stage.[7] The event must have changed Jonson's life in many ways, intensifying in particular his financial anxieties and the need to find continuing employment. The location of the church of St Magnus the Martyr gives a clue into the likely place and nature of Jonson's earliest theatrical work. One of the oldest churches in London—later destroyed in the Great Fire and rebuilt by Wren—St Magnus the Martyr lay at the bottom of Fish Street Hill, by the foot of London Bridge, and was close to the parish of St Mary Overies (now St Saviour's), across the river in Southwark. This was theatrical territory, the home of many players employed at the nearby playhouses along the Bankside: the Rose, Newington Butts, and Paris Garden. As Mark Eccles has persuasively argued, the Jonsons' choice of this church for their marriage suggests that Ben was working at one or other of these theatres at this period.[8] This idea gains further support from a taunting exchange in Thomas Dekker's *Satiromastix* (1601), in which Horace—a character obviously modelled on Jonson himself—admits to having once played the part of Zulziman (an unknown character in some now-lost tragedy) at Paris Garden on the Bankside (4.1.150–3).

The Bankside district extended along the Surrey side of the Thames from St Saviour's Church and Winchester House to the present site of Blackfriars Bridge. As one of the liberties of the City, it was not subjected to regular civic control, and thus, like Shoreditch, offered convenient sanctuary for players and other dubious types. Nominally under the jurisdiction of the justices of Surrey, the Bankside was in fact controlled by the Bishop of Winchester, who in the twelfth century had been granted one of the three manors that made up the borough. This was London's red-light district, home to the many prostitutes familiarly known as 'the Bishop's geese'—'Bred on the Bank in time of popery, | When Venus there maintained the mystery', as Jonson wryly put it in a later poem (*The Underwood*, 43.142–4). It was also the main area in London for bull- and bear-baiting. Paris (or Parish) Garden, where Jonson is said to have played the part of Zulziman, was the principal venue for these popular sports, though the site was now used also for theatrical entertainments. A huge wooden amphitheatre open to the sky and capable of accommodating at least 1,000 spectators, Paris Garden had been the scene of a spectacular accident in 1583, when the seating collapsed and many were killed and injured. The preacher John Field—father of Jonson's future protégé the actor and dramatist Nathan Field—viewed the incident, which occurred on the sabbath, as a direct sign of God's just anger.[9] In 'The Famous Voyage' Jonson was to describe the stench that wafted from 'Bears' College' (as he ironically called the place), and from the barge that crossed the Thames daily with rotting meat to feed its learned inhabitants (*Epigrams*, 133.117–18).[10] The bears were supervised by an officer known as the Keeper of the Royal Game (a position held for some years by the actor Edward Alleyn, after his retirement from the stage) and were occasionally transported to Whitehall to take part in royal entertainments. The manor of Paris Garden had been bought in 1589 by the theatrical entrepreneur Francis Langley, who erected the Swan playhouse here around 1595. Jonson may have played the part of Zulziman either at the Swan or at Paris Garden itself, but in either case it would have been within smelling distance of the bears, just a few steps away from the city's brothels.

Jonson would have been employed as a 'hired man', or jobbing actor, in receipt of a weekly wage. He probably picked up further work at other Bankside theatres, such as Philip Henslowe's Rose, or its southerly neighbour, Newington Butts. Dekker's gibes in *Satiromastix* suggest that Jonson worked not only in the metropolis, however, but also in the provinces. 'Thou hast forgot how thou amblest (in leather pilch) by a play-wagon, in the highway' (4.1.161–5), says Tucca to Horace, alias Jonson, tauntingly recalling his earlier days as 'a poor journeyman player' taking 'service among the mimics' in a travelling company. Despite the obvious mockery here, there was nothing inherently disreputable in this kind of work. All of the major theatrical companies travelled regularly, especially, though not only, at times when plague forced the closure of the London playhouses, as it had done, for example, in the years 1592 and 1593.[11] The frontispiece to Jonson's 1616 folio edition of his *Works* (Fig. 13) remembers the ancestry of this tradition, depicting Thespis, the semi-legendary inventor of tragedy, travelling with his cart through an Attic landscape.[12] Yet touring through the country towns would scarcely have been a glamorous business, as Jonson's own reference in *Poetaster* to walking 'with thy pumps full of gravel . . . after a blind jade and a hamper', in order to 'stalk upon boards, and barrel heads, to an old cracked trumpet' (3.4.137–9) vividly suggests.

Fredson Bowers has plausibly suggested that the troupe with which Jonson was travelling was Pembroke's Company, who were on the road in 1595–6.[13]

Fig. 13. Thespis and his cart: William Hole's engraved title page (detail) for Jonson's 1616 Folio *Works*.

This company, originally created some twenty years earlier by Henry Herbert, second Earl of Pembroke, had enjoyed mixed fortunes over the years, but was undergoing a brief revival in the early 1590s, owing perhaps to the influence of Henry Herbert's third wife Mary Sidney (mother of William Herbert, the third Earl and Jonson's future patron). It has been suspected that both Shakespeare and Jonson may have worked for Pembroke's Men in the early 1590s. Though Jonson was certainly a member of the company at a somewhat later stage, the evidence connecting him with it in this very early period now seems frail.[14] Pembroke's Men evidently flourished during 1591, to judge from their popularity at court at that time, but failed to survive the extended period during which the London playhouses were closed because of plague in 1593. The company broke up in August of that year, but the patent survived, and some members of the company continued to travel. Jonson may well have gone with this latter group two or three years later.

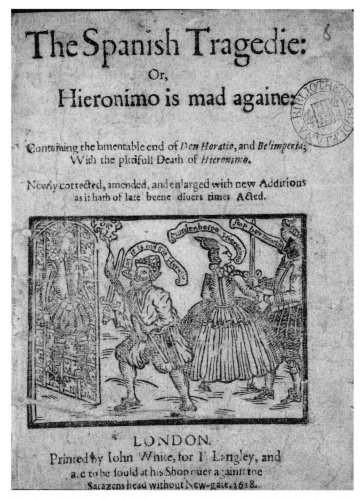

Fig. 14. *The Spanish Tragedy: Or, Hieronimo is Mad Again*: detail from 1615 title page.

On the road, Jonson seems to have played the celebrated role of the royal marshal Hieronimo, crazed by the murder of his son and his thwarted search for justice, in Kyd's *The Spanish Tragedy*. 'I ha' seen thy shoulders lapped in a player's old cast cloak, like a sly knave as thou art,' says Captain Tucca to Horace in *Satiromastix*, 'and when thou ran'st mad for the death of Horatio, thou borrowed'st a gown of Roscius the stager' (1.2.434–8). *The Spanish Tragedy* enjoyed immense popularity in this period. Henslowe's *Diary* reveals that between 1592 and 1597 it was performed twenty-nine times under his auspices alone. It was regularly performed at a variety of London theatres after that date, and was still in repertory through to the 1640s. With its thrilling blank verse measure and sensational dramatic set-pieces—the brooding ghost of Andrea and his companion Revenge, entering ominously from beneath the stage; the young Horatio stabbed and hanged during his love encounter with Bel-Imperia in the garden bower; his father Hieronimo running distractedly in his nightshirt, and biting his tongue out at the final catastrophe—*The Spanish Tragedy* would have been an obvious piece for a touring company to have taken to the provinces in the 1590s. The language of Kyd's play seems to have worked in Jonson's head like an old tune that he could never quite expel. Humorous and parodic echoes of *The Spanish Tragedy* are to be found throughout his own subsequent work from his first surviving play, *The Case Is Altered* (1597), through to *The Staple of News* in 1625: an unsurprising residue of allusions from a one-time actor with a powerful memory who had once learnt much of the play by heart.

Aubrey reports that Jonson 'was never a good actor, but an excellent instructor'.[15] The opinion this time sounds convincing. Jonson evidently stopped acting as soon as he began to enjoy some success as a writer—unlike Shakespeare, who continued to act for the Chamberlain's Men well after the point at which he had established himself as the company's principal writer. Had Jonson been in any way remarkable as an actor he might similarly have wished to continue performing. Jonson was on good terms with leading players of the day such as Alleyn and Burbage, and with such younger actors as Salomon Pavy, Dick Robinson, and Nathan Field, whom he seems to have trained and encouraged. He was evidently a daunting spectator of his own plays in performance. Dekker's Sir Vaughan in *Satiromastix* forbids Horace (alias Jonson) to 'sit in a gallery, when your comedies and interludes have entered their actions, and there make vile and bad faces at every line ... to make players afraid to take your part' (5.2.340–5). Jonson was later humorously to depict himself in similar fashion, nervously glimpsed by the characters of his own plays. '[H]e do' not hear me, I hope,' says the garrulous Carlo Buffone in *Every Man Out of His Humour* (Grex before Act 1, 308), glancing about apprehensively for the author of the play. 'I am looking lest the poet hear me,' says the equally talkative Stage-Keeper in the Induction to *Bartholomew Fair* (6). Gossip Mirth in the Induction to *The Staple of News* describes having seen the play's author in the tiring house 'rolling himself up and down like a tun' in sweaty agitation as he issues last-minute directions to the actors (50–1). In the playhouse as in print, Jonson clearly wished to maintain strict control over the interpretation of his own work, and was well aware of the effect this dominance created. Not until the arrival of Bernard Shaw would another London dramatist maintain so severe an eye on the conduct of his players.

It is clear none the less that Jonson's initial engagement with the theatre was as an actor, and that he only gradually and incidentally picked up additional work as a writer. His early commissions were essentially backroom jobs, patching up old plays, and working collaboratively with other members of the troupe to produce new plays at high speed. The pressures of the repertory system were intense, and the appetite for new plays was insatiable. Andrew Gurr points to the schedule of Henslowe's Admiral's Men, who in the mid-1590s were performing six different plays each week at the Rose. In 1594–5 the company 'staged seventeen new plays, at a rate of roughly one a fortnight. In 1595–6 they produced seven new plays in fifteen weeks. In 1596–7 it was five in eleven weeks.'[16] Rehearsal times were short, and the players were skilled at improvisation, and creative adaptation of the texts they received for performance. Dramatic authorship was an unglamorous, largely anonymous, and often collective affair. Audiences would often have been drawn to the theatre to see a star performer in action, such as the great Edward Alleyn, rather than to view the work of a particular author, of whose identity they would in most cases have been unaware. Significantly, there was still no agreed term to describe a dramatic author; the words *dramatist* and *playwright*, according to the *Oxford English Dictionary*, not entering the language until after the Restoration. Yet as it happens, the latter term was used—and possibly invented—by Jonson himself, many decades earlier. Three epigrams published in the folio edition of his *Works* in 1616 are addressed to a disreputable character named *Playwright*, who knocks up plays (it is implied) in much the same manner that a wheelwright assembles a wheel, taking bits and pieces that come readily to hand.[17] The disparaging coinage shows all too clearly what Jonson thought of the trade to which he himself had been drawn.

Jonson in time would do much to transform the status of the dramatic author in early modern England, boldly asserting his moral dignity, critical authority, and quasi-legal rights of textual ownership. Above all, he would make the dramatic author a *visible* figure—nominally visible on the title pages of his works, imaginatively visible through the language of his own dramatic creations ('I am looking, lest the poet hear me'), and literally visible, it would seem, on at least one occasion—the Apologetical Dialogue to *Poetaster*—as an actual stage presence. *Poet* was the term Jonson chose to describe his own professional role, both in and out of the theatre, but he would use the term discriminatingly, only of those whose work and actions met his own exacting standards. In the Epistle to *Volpone* he would set out in ringing terms the priest-like offices and function of the poet, as one who is

able to inform young men to all good disciplines, inflame grown men to all great virtues, keep old men in their best and supreme state, or, as they decline to childhood, recover them to their first strength; that comes forth the interpreter and arbiter of nature, a teacher of things divine no less than human, a master in manners; and can alone, or with a few, effect the business of mankind . . . (18–22)

At the outset of Jonson's career, however, these high-minded ideals may not have formed the sole or even the dominant motives that drew him towards dramatic writing. He was also driven by the need for money: a commodity which, as a recently married man, he could scarcely afford to ignore.

The life of all theatrical companies in the 1590s was highly precarious. The wages of a hired man varied considerably from season to season, from company to company, and indeed at times within a single company. Jonson probably earned between five and ten shillings a week while playing in London, and less than that while touring. Through his writing he would have gained a vital supplementation to his income. For delivering a complete new play an author was likely to receive anywhere between £5 and £10, and additional sums could be earned for the writing of prologues and epilogues, or of new scenes to enliven old plays. Though the work was demanding, such earnings over a year could be considerable. After studying the pay of professional playwrights in this period, G. E. Bentley was led to conclude that they 'made more money than other literary men of their time, and more than they could have made as schoolmasters or curates—professions which might have been open to many of them'.[18] Jonson himself took a rather different view of the matter, reporting to Drummond in 1619 that 'of all his plays he never gained two hundred pounds', and wishing 'he might have been a rich lawyer, physician, or merchant', since poetry had beggared him (*Informations*, 446, 493–4). Yet this was still considerably better than bricklaying, or the life of a hired man.

§§

By 1597 Jonson was certainly working for Pembroke's Men, as is clear from troubles that were to erupt in July of that year after the company's staging of Jonson's and Nashe's satirical comedy *The Isle of Dogs*. *The Isle of Dogs* was probably not the first of Jonson's works, however, to have been performed by Pembroke's Men. Though the dates cannot now be established with complete certainty, it is likely that the company presented *The Case Is Altered*, Jonson's earliest surviving single-authored play, in May or June of this same year.[19] *The Case Is Altered* survives despite Jonson's own wishes, for he made no known attempt in later years to claim it as his own. The title page of the 1609 quarto edition confidently names Jonson as sole author of the play, yet the edition was evidently not authorized by Jonson, and the play was not to be included in the folio edition of his *Works* in 1616. Jonson's characteristic touch is evident throughout the piece, both in small turns of phrase and action, and in larger devices and preoccupations that would come in time to dominate his comic writing.[20]

'The case is altered' is a phrase traditionally associated with the great jurist Edmund Plowden, a staunch Catholic who one day (according to legend) was defending a client accused of hearing Mass, when he learnt that the celebrant was in fact a layman, who had dressed as a priest and embarked on this ritual in an attempt to ensnare suspected Catholics; at which discovery Plowden is said triumphantly to have declared, '*The case is altered*: no priest, no mass.' It is a story that nicely resonates with Jonson's own later experiences as a recusant, and also with a characteristic habit of progression within his own comedies, when a new set of circumstances, or alternative identity of a seemingly familiar character, is suddenly produced, *altering the case*, and forcing the action to swerve abruptly off in a new and hitherto unforeseen direction.[21] This early comedy shows Jonson experimenting with this narrative method, pushing it at times—especially in the flurrying revelations of the play's concluding scenes, when 'the case is altered!' is the repeated, astonished cry—to a point of near-hilarity.

The Case Is Altered is modelled on two of Plautus' comedies which Jonson probably first encountered at Westminster School: *Captivi* (*The Captives*) and *Aulularia* (*The Pot of Gold*). Both of these plays involve the final discovery of long-lost and supposedly dead characters; by bringing their plots together, Jonson intensified the element of surprise. Count Ferneze in *The Case Is*

Altered, like his prototype Hegio in *The Captives*, has been separated from his two sons. Camillo, the elder son, vanished when a child during the capture of Vicenza some twenty years earlier, and is presumed dead. Camillo is in fact alive, having been discovered and brought up, under the name of Gasper, by the French leader, Chamont, and is now serving with the French army. In the course of new campaigns between the French and the Italians, the Count's second son, Paulo, is captured by the French, while Gasper (Camillo) and his companion Chamont—son of the lord who originally found and adopted the lost infant—are seized by the Italians. The Count arranges to recover Paulo by exchanging him for Chamont, but his plan is foiled when Gasper and Chamont agree to swap identities, Gasper posing as Chamont, and Chamont as Gasper. Infuriated to discover he has the wrong man, the Count threatens to kill Gasper, but in a curious moment of super-sensory insight—unlike anything in Jonson's mature drama, though curiously like an episode in his later life, when he had a premonitory vision of his own recently dead son (*Informations*, 198–206, see below, 179–80)—the Count draws back, sensing the need to spare his victim. In a series of rapid fifth-act revelations, Gasper is shown to be the Count's long-lost son Camillo, and the second son, Paulo, is also restored to his father.

The play's subsidiary plot, taken from *The Pot of Gold*, presents a similar mix of concealments, aliases, and last-minute discoveries, as the seemingly impoverished Jaques de Prie is shown to be Melun, the former steward of Lord Chamont, who absconded many years earlier with Chamont's fortune and his daughter Isabel; and Jaques's apparent daughter, Rachel, proves to be none other than Isabel herself. The scenes in which Jaques gloats privately over his ill-gotten wealth owe something perhaps to *The Jew of Malta* as well as to Plautus, and show Jonson exploring a device that he would bring to perfection in his later comedies: the idea of a 'centre attractive'—an object of desire that serves to draw characters magnetically to some central location (a house, a fairground) and, generally, in due course, to their downfall.[22] The dream of fabulous wealth furnishes the magnetism in many of Jonson's plays: 'the great herd, the multitude, that in all other things are divided, in this alone conspire, and agree: to love money,' as he wrote later in *Discoveries* (1033–4). Jaques in *The Case Is Altered* is plagued by constant visitors who, he believes, come to his house in quest of his gold, drawn—as he supposes, in a superlative flight of paranoid fantasy—by its very smell. He therefore buries his gold in dung in a desperate attempt to divert them. But gold is not in fact the 'centre attractive' in this comedy, for these visitors are drawn to Jaques's house not by his money (of the very existence of which they are largely ignorant), but by the beauty of his apparent daughter, whom they all wish to marry. The 'centre attractive' of the play turns out to be love, not money, and for Jaques, as he recognizes this benign turn of events, *the case is altered*. Though it is possible to see in this early comedy the potential ingredients for a future, darker, comedy such as *Volpone*, *The Case Is Altered* is still in some obvious ways an apprentice piece, lacking full tonal and structural cohesion, shifting uneasily as it does from satiric to romantic mode. Is it love indeed, as the play's ending seems to assert, that makes the world go around, or is it perhaps, as the comedy has elsewhere suggested, the love of money? On this basic question, for all its busy plotting, the play has not quite reached an answer.

§§

Jonson's next dramatic venture, *The Isle of Dogs*, written in collaboration with Thomas Nashe and performed by Pembroke's Men at 'one of the playhouses on the Bankside' (almost certainly Francis Langley's Swan theatre) in July 1597, was an altogether bolder affair than *The Case Is Altered*, bringing Jonson into immediate collision with the authorities for the first, but by no means the last, time in his dramatic career. Spurred on, perhaps, by his older collaborator's 'spirit quick as powder, sharp as steel'—as he described Nashe in an elegy on his death, a few years later—Jonson moved decisively now into the dangerous world of Elizabethan political satire.[23] As no text of *The Isle of Dogs* survives, it is impossible to know precisely how and why the play was regarded as offensive, but the official response was swift and severe. Shortly after performances began, an informer's complaint about the piece found its way to Elizabeth's chief interrogator, Richard Topcliffe, who in a letter of 10 August refers to the unnamed bearer as 'the first man that discovered to me that seditious play called *The Isle of Dogs*'.[24] Topcliffe evidently referred the complaint to the Privy Council, who in turn instructed him to investigate the matter. Forewarned of trouble, the two authors and members of the company must swiftly have destroyed whatever copies of the play remained in their possession. Nashe fled at once to the safety of Great Yarmouth in Norfolk. In his absence, his lodgings in London were raided and papers seized, but the play, like its co-author, had vanished without trace.

Fig. 15. Francis Langley's Swan theatre (built 1596) in Southwark, on the south bank of the Thames, where *The Isle of Dogs* was performed in the summer of 1597; home of Pembroke's Men. Drawing by Arendt van Buchell (Arnoldius Buchelius) from a sketch by Johannes de Witt, made around 1596–7. 'Of all the theatres', wrote de Witt in Latin, 'the largest and most magnificent is that one of which the sign is called in the vernacular the Swan theatre; for it accommodates in its seats three thousand persons, and is built on a mass of flint stones, and supported by wooden columns, painted in such excellent imitation of marble that it is able to deceive even the most cunning. Since its form resembles that of a Roman work, I have made a sketch of it above.'

In late July or early August, however, Jonson and two fellow-players from Pembroke's company, Robert Shaa and Gabriel Spencer, were arrested and committed to Marshalsea Prison. The rest of the company prudently took to the road, moving with speed towards Bristol, where they were encamped a few days later.

On 15 August 1597 the three players were examined by the Privy Council court, meeting at Greenwich. The case was heard by the Lord Treasurer, William Cecil, Lord Burghley; the Secretary, Sir Robert Cecil; the Lord Chamberlain, George, second Lord Hunsdon; the Controller of the Household, Sir William Knollys; the Chancellor of the Exchequer, Sir Walter Mildmay; and Lord North.[25] The three men were accused of indulging in 'lewd and mutinous behaviour' by performing a play 'containing very seditious and scandalous matter'. One of the three was described as 'not only an actor, but a maker of part of the said play'. While this accusation is clearly levelled at Jonson, it is conceivable that Shaa and Spencer had made their own passing contributions to the piece, through improvised dialogue or other means. Two years later Nashe coolly dismissed *The Isle of Dogs* as 'the infortunate imperfect embryon of my idle hours'. 'An imperfect emryon I may well call it,' he continued, 'for I having begun but the induction and first act of it, the other four acts, without my consent, or the least guess of my drift or scope, by the players were supplied, which bred both their trouble and mine to it.'[26] While Nashe implies that it was the players who were collectively and substantially responsible for whatever had caused offence in *The Isle of Dogs*, his disclaimer is clearly tactical, and not to be taken at face value. In 1599, as Nashe wrote these words, he was still in grave trouble with the authorities and 'sequestered' in Norfolk, away 'from the wonted means of my maintenance' and the officers of the law; the nonchalant tone is largely assumed. Though the troubles the play had occasioned in London were by this time well and truly over, Nashe was evidently still unwilling to return to the metropolis. In June of that year all of Nashe's writings were formally burnt in the famous 'bishops' bonfire' in London, when the bishops further decreed 'that no satires of epigrams be printed hereafter'. Francis Meres in 1598 teasingly refers to Nashe's continuing exile in Norfolk, and similar taunts are to be found in the Cambridge play *The Second Part of the Return From Parnassus* in 1601, the year of Nashe's death.[27]

It fell immediately to Richard Topcliffe and his team to determine who had been responsible for the offending play, and to what degree. Topcliffe was ordered to examine all three prisoners more closely to discover 'what is become of the rest of their fellows that either had their parts in the devising of that seditious matter, or that were actors or players in the same, what copies they have given forth of the said play and to whom, and such other points as you shall think meet to be demanded of them'.[28] Now in his mid-sixties, Topcliffe was a notoriously brutal interrogator, skilled in the arts of torture, which he routinely applied when examining Catholic and other political prisoners. His henchmen were similarly disposed. Giles Fletcher, Remembrancer of the City of London, had been employed by the Privy Council in the early 1590s to examine recusants, and would have been equally at home with these techniques. Roger Wilbraham, who was later to examine the Earl of Essex's followers after their abortive uprising in 1601, had matching skills. The two Middlesex magistrates who aptly completed the squad, Thomas Fowler and Richard Skevington, had been authorized the previous year to use instruments of torture when examining 'Egyptians and wanderers'.[29]

Whatever treatment the three players received during their time in Marshalsea, however, evidently failed to break their spirits, or to elicit the information the Privy Council was after. Jonson was proud of his own defiance. 'In the time of his close imprisonment under Queen Elizabeth', he told Drummond many years later, 'his judges could get nothing of him to all their demands but "ay" and "no". They placed two damned villains to catch advantage of him, with him, but he was advertised by his keeper. Of the spies he hath an epigram' (*Informations*, 194–7). It is tempting to wonder if the 'two damned villains' about whom the prison officer gave timely warning were the same two spies whom Jonson in a poem written some years later promises a friend will *not* be present at the supper party which he is preparing for him:

> And we will have no Poley or Parrot by,
> Nor shall our cups make any guilty men,
> But, at our parting, we will be as when
> We innocently met.
> ('Inviting a Friend to Supper', *Epigrams*, 101.36–9)

Robert Poley (or Pooley) was a notorious agent who had been present, as Jonson would have known, at the fatal stabbing of Christopher Marlowe at Deptford in 1593; 'Parrot'—possibly the minor poet Henry Parrot—was another informer. Both had worked for Elizabeth's spymaster-general Sir Francis Walsingham. In the epigram to which he refers in his remarks to Drummond, Jonson contemptuously notes the inevitable fate of such men, to be ultimately discarded by the very system that has employed them:

Spies, you are lights in state, but of base stuff,
Who, when you've burnt yourselves down to the snuff,
Stink, and are thrown away. End fair enough.

('On Spies', *Epigrams*, 59)

Jonson's encounter with the spies must have sharpened his natural caution and instinctive awareness of the dangers of unguarded talk: a topic to which he returns repeatedly in his later writings. 'How much better is it to be silent, or at least to speak sparingly!' he wrote in his commonplace book, *Discoveries*, in the 1620s. For there is 'a wall or parapet of teeth set in our mouth to restrain the petulancy of our words; that the rashness of talking should not only be retarded by the guard and watch of our heart, but be fenced in and defended by certain strengths placed in the mouth itself, and within the lips' (*Discoveries*, 237–41). These are the stoical arts—'the plain and passive fortitude' of Lepidus, 'To suffer, and be silent'—that Jonson was to depict in developed form just a few years after his imprisonment at Marshalsea, in his tragedy of *Sejanus* (4.294–5).

A warrant for the release of Jonson, Spencer, and Shaa was signed at the court at Richmond on 2 October 1597. Topcliffe and his men had evidently failed to extract the evidence they needed to force a prosecution, and the three players were free to depart on 8 October. But *The Isle of Dogs* affair had already precipitated a larger crisis for the London theatre companies. For on 28 July, in an astonishingly severe and wide-ranging edict evidently prompted by the play's performance, the Privy Council had decreed that 'no plays shall be used within London or about the City, or in any public place during this time of summer' and that 'those playhouses that are erected and built only for such purposes shall be plucked down—namely the Curtain and the Theatre near to Shoreditch, or any other within that County'. London's theatre proprietors were ordered 'to pluck down quite the stages, galleries, and rooms that are made for people to stand in, and so to deface the same as they may not be employed again to such use'. In justification of this swingeing command, the Privy Council's letter spoke merely of the 'great disorders' caused 'by lewd matters that are handled on the stages, and by resort and confluence of bad people'. Though no play or company is specifically named in the order, a note by Henslowe in his diary in August 1597 makes it clear that the 'restraint is by the means of playing *The Isle of Dogs*'—a fact confirmed by surviving letters from Topcliffe to Sir Robert Cecil, and from the Council to magistrates in Surrey.[30] Had these orders been carried out, the most fertile period in the history of the English theatre—the great age of *Hamlet* and *King Lear* and *Macbeth* and *The Tempest*, of *Sejanus* and *Volpone* and *The Alchemist*, of *The Changeling* and *The Revenger's Tragedy*—might simply never have occurred. Yet happily, things went otherwise.

Remarkably, the playhouse proprietors appear simply to have ignored the Privy Council's most radical instruction. So far as we can tell, no attempt was made to demolish or deface the Theatre, the Curtain, or any of the London playhouses during the summer of 1597.[31] After the release of the three actors from Marshalsea on 8 October, the restraint on playing was treated with similar disregard, for on 11 October Henslowe's men began to perform again at the Rose, though the closure order was still officially in place. Once Jonson, Shaa, and Spencer had walked free, it must have been clear that the larger case against the London companies and their playhouses had also collapsed, and that performances could resume with impunity. Henslowe, a shrewd businessman, seems to have remained undaunted throughout the entire *Isle of Dogs* affair, confidently signing up new players to work at the Rose theatre for the Lord Admiral's Men even during the most seemingly threatening stage of proceedings: Richard Jones on 6 August, William Borne (or Bird) on 10 August. Perhaps (as Glynne Wickham has argued) Henslowe was aware that, for all its apparently wide-ranging language, the edict was really aimed against Pembroke's Men—who indeed never recovered from this period of closure—and Francis Langley's Swan theatre.[32]

The questions nevertheless remain: why had *The Isle of Dogs* ignited such powerful feelings in the first place? and whatever can the play have been about? The title of the lost work may give a possible clue to its general nature. The Isle of Dogs is a narrow strip of land on the north bank of the Thames downriver from the City, which nowadays forms part of the London Docklands area in the Borough of Tower Hamlets. The name may derive from the (now disputed) fact that Henry VIII once kennelled his hounds on this marshy peninsula, which lay just across the Thames from the royal palace at Greenwich. In Jonson's day the area had become a refuge for debtors and petty criminals. Its immediate proximity to the Queen's palace must have presented rich opportunities for ironic reflection. It may be significant that in Jonson's later co-authored comedy *Eastward Ho!* the play's most daring satirical scene is also set, in what looks like a deliberately provocative allusion to the earlier play, on this same stretch of land, which the bedraggled knight Sir Petronel Flash, clambering ashore after suffering shipwreck in the Thames, at first imagines is the coast of France. It is here, on 'the coast of Dogs', facing the royal palace, that the play's most controversial exchanges about James and his Scottish favourites take place. In 1606, the year following the performance of *Eastward Ho!*, the dramatist John Day antagonized the authorities with a play that worked the same vein of anti-court satire, which was cheekily entitled, in further deliberate recall of Nashe's and Jonson's original work, *The Isle of Gulls*. Through a process of what might be called satirical topography, the Isle of Dogs had by this date acquired a suggestive power of its own, the very hint of its name alerting an expectant audience to anticipate what was to come.

As William Empson ingeniously demonstrated many years ago, the word 'dog' in Elizabethan times invoked an intriguing range of meanings. Through their fawning and hand-licking ways, dogs are often associated in Elizabethan satire with the behaviour of courtiers. Through another conjunction of ideas, however, they are linked with the Cynical philosophers, and with the writing of satire, traditionally seen as an aggressive or 'snarling' form. Nashe himself neatly encapsulates this double interpretation in *Summer's Last Will and Testament*: 'Cynics they are, for they will snarl and bite,' says Will Summers, of dogs; 'Right courtiers to flatter and to fawn.' Moll Cutpurse in Dekker and Middleton's play *The Roaring Girl* more precisely locates these tendencies as she speaks of one who 'hath been brought up in the Isle of Dogs, and can both fawn like a spaniel, and bite like a mastiff, as he finds occasion' (5.1.111–13).[33] One might guess that in Nashe's and Jonson's imagination 'the Isle of Dogs' was an ironic mirror of the idealized world of Elizabeth's court, and a place that attracted the delighted attention of satirists: a kind of royal kennels, a natural home to sharp-fanged writers.

But Nashe's and Jonson's satire must have gone considerably further than this. 'Seditious' and 'slanderous' are words that recur in the court records and correspondence relating to *The Isle of Dogs*; taken together, they strongly suggest that the play made libellous reference to recognizable individuals in high places: quite possibly, to members of the Privy Council, and conceivably (as Charles Nicholl has suggested) to the Queen herself.[34] Countering similar accusations of libel later in his career, Jonson would always strenuously—if at times disingenuously—insist that his satire was general in nature, and not particular; that he attacked the vice, and not the person. But this work of his earliest years may not have been defendable in quite this way. Eight years later, in a letter written to Robert Cecil from another prison where he had been confined for his part in writing another play, *Eastward Ho!*, which had also given grave offence to those in authority, Jonson appeared to confess that *The Isle of Dogs* had indeed satirized the behaviour of particular individuals. Cecil had been one of the privy counsellors who had investigated *The Isle of Dogs*, and must therefore have known the nature of the original charges. In appealing to him for help in this second crisis, Jonson attempts to assure Cecil that the present play is not like its predecessor.

I protest to your honour, and call God to testimony—since my first error, which yet is punished in me more with my shame than it was with my bondage—I have so attempered my style that I have given no cause to any man of grief; and if to any ill, by touching at any general vice, it hath always been with a regard, and sparing of particular persons. I may be otherwise reported, but if all that be accused should be presently guilty, there are few men would stand in the state of innocence. (Letter 3)

Which 'particular persons' did *The Isle of Dogs* offend? Did the play allude in some way, as one scholar has suspected, to the King of Poland, whose Ambassador had called on Elizabeth on 23 July 1597, just a few days before the troubles over the play erupted? Or did it glance, as others have wondered, at the late Lord Chamberlain, Henry Brooke, eighth Lord Cobham, who had died in March 1597, just a few months before the staging of *The Isle of Dogs*, and who was soon to attract further satirical attention—so a series of elaborate puns on brooks and cobs in these works appears to suggest—in *Nashe's Lenten Stuff*, Jonson's *Every Man In His Humour*, and Shakespeare's *1 Henry IV* and *The Merry Wives of Windsor*?[35] In the absence of firmer evidence, almost anything is possible, but if these were the only provocations it is hard to see quite why the play should have caused such acute agitation in government circles.

Neither England's relations with Poland nor the lingering sensitivities of the Cobham family were in themselves matters of the highest political concern in England during the summer of 1597. Of far greater moment were the growing danger of a new assault upon England from a revived Spanish armada, and the potential instability at home caused by the mounting rivalry between Robert Devereux, second Earl of Essex, and the Cecils, father and son: William Burghley, the ageing Lord Treasurer, whose role as Elizabeth's chief counsellor Essex fiercely coveted, and Sir Robert Cecil, the

Secretary, who Burghley just as ardently hoped would inherit this position himself. These two anxieties, foreign and domestic, were intimately linked. Impatient for military exploit, Essex tried to impress upon Elizabeth the need for immediate action against Spain. The Cecils counselled caution, believing the dangers of a Spanish attack to be less pressing than troubles in Ireland. Essex was appointed to the post of Master of Ordnance on 19 March 1597, and by May of that year was busy preparing for an assault upon Spain. In early June he received his commission from Elizabeth to undertake this expedition. He planned to make a pre-emptive strike on the armada gathered at Ferrol, to seize Spanish treasure ships, and establish a permanent garrison in the Azores at the island of Terceira. His ambitions created considerable anxiety at court. Elizabeth herself had second thoughts about the expedition, asking Essex sharply how, if he gained Terceira, he would manage to prevent its immediate recapture by the Spanish.[36]

In July 1597, the month in which *The Isle of Dogs* was presented at the Swan theatre, Essex had set off regardless with a fleet of twenty ships on what would prove to be an ultimately disastrous expedition to the Azores and the beginning of his own steep fall from power. His fleet had run into unseasonable storms and been forced back into harbour at Falmouth, where it was waiting until it could resume its journey. This was the highly volatile moment at which Nashe's and Jonson's play was presented at the Swan. It is impossible to be sure that these were the events to which the play, with misplaced facetiousness, managed somehow to refer, but a casual allusion to the Islands voyage, or to the imagined threat from Spain, or to current manoeuvrings for power by Essex and the Cecils, might easily have ignited the fuse.

If this is indeed the context of the now-lost play, its title would have had a particular resonance. From earliest times, both the Canaries and the Azores had been widely known as the home of fierce native dogs. Pliny the Elder in the first century AD noted 'the multitude of dogs of a huge size' on Gran Canaria—whose very name, deriving ultimately (via French and Spanish variants) from Latin *canaria insula*, 'the isle of dogs', testifies to this reputation.[37] This Isle of Dogs was one of the so-called Fortunate Isles, which by the time of Arnobius in *c.* AD 300 were collectively known as the Canaries.[38] By the sixteenth century, when both the Canaries and the Azores were important staging posts for the Spanish fleets on their way to the Indies, these ferocious mastiffs had been trained to guard this otherwise vulnerable territory, and the treasure ships that took harbour there.[39]

Such a context would encompass, rather than replace, the customary assumption that *The Isle of Dogs* contained some slighting reference to the Cobham family. Essex had a particular dislike for Sir Henry Brooke, eighth Lord Cobham, who was brother-in-law to Essex's chief rival at court, Robert Cecil. Essex had done his best to ensure—unsuccessfully, in the event—that Cobham would not be appointed to the vacant office of Warden of the Cinque Ports, preferring his own candidate, Robert Sidney. Caustic remarks about Cobham might well have formed one ingredient in the play's satirical mix. In the absence of a text we simply cannot tell.

The one surviving textual trace of the play, however, does hint at its possible association with Essex and his followers. A manuscript in the possession of the Duke of Northumberland at Alnwick Castle contains a number of minor works by Francis Bacon, who served as Essex's adviser in the 1590s. A surviving outer sheet of the manuscript (Fig. 16) lists a number of writings which the manuscript once contained, and includes the entry: 'Isle of dogs frmn^t | by Thomas Nashe inferior plaiers'.[40] While the 'fragment' itself has long disappeared, the inscription appears to suggest that the piece had once been of interest to Essex and his circle. F. J. Burgoyne, who edited the Alnwick manuscript more than a century ago, wondered if Jonson might have been associated with Bacon's scriptorium or literary workshop at some stage during the 1590s.[41] The evidence for such an association is both weaker and stronger than Burgoyne supposed. Weaker, because the testimony of Archbishop Tenison that he cites from later in the century, that 'Mr Benjamin Jonson (the learned and judicious poet)' was one of those who had helped with the translation of Bacon's *Essays* into Latin, refers to work that Jonson might have undertaken several decades later, in the 1620s, not to any activities of the scriptorium during the 1590s.[42] Stronger, because the conjecture can be supported by a number of contextual considerations.

Following the example and encouragement of his stepfather the Earl of Leicester, Essex was at pains during the 1590s to bring together a lively and learned group of scholarly advisers to guide him on academic and political affairs.[43] As Essex destroyed many of his papers before giving himself up after his failed uprising in 1601, the composition of his secretariat is known only in part. The young, restless, academically precocious Ben Jonson certainly fits the general profile, however, of those whom Essex sought to attract, and was in turn a warm admirer of the 'noble and high' Earl, as he called him many years

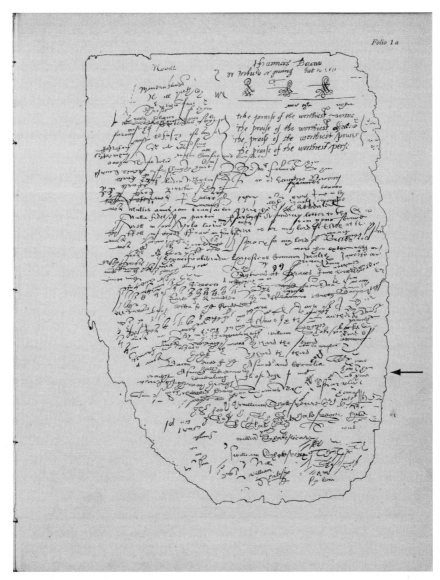

Fig. 16. 'Ile of dogs frmn'| by Thomas Nashe inferior plaiers': this jotting (centrally, towards the bottom) on the cover sheet of a manuscript held at Alnwick Castle (MS fo. 1) is the sole surviving textual trace of Jonson and Nashe's notorious play *The Isle of Dogs*, which brought all theatrical activity in London in 1597 to a temporary—and almost to a permanent—halt. Neither the 'fragment' nor the text as a whole exists today.

later (*Discoveries*, 653). Jonson was also to maintain undiminished admiration for the 'learned and able' Francis Bacon, even after his fall, praising him as one

who hath filled up all numbers, and performed that in our tongue which may be compared or preferred either to insolent Greece or haughty Rome. In short, within his view, and about his times, were all the wits born that could honour a language or help study. Now things daily fall: wits grow downward and eloquence grows backward, so that he may be named and stand as the mark and ἀχμή of our language. (*Discoveries*, 656–62)

Jonson is clearly referring here not simply to Bacon as an individual but also to the remarkable intellectual group that was gathered around him during an earlier historical period—'within his view, and about his times, were all the wits born that could honour a language or help study'—and that had now dispersed. This sounds very much like a nostalgic personal recollection of the Bacon/Essex circle of the late 1590s. Jonson was well acquainted with a number of members of this group, whose qualities he had subsequently praised in his *Epigrams* and *The Forest*.[44] Jonson's *Epigram* 95 (for example) praises Sir Henry Savile, the learned Warden of Merton College, Oxford, for his translation of Tacitus' *Histories* and *Agricola*, written under Essex's patronage in the early 1590s. Tacitus' reading of history in terms of its underlying causes had been of considerable tactical importance to the Essex circle during this period.[45] Jonson told William Drummond that the address to the reader prefixed to Savile's translation of Tacitus' *Histories* and signed 'A.B.' had in fact been written by Essex himself, and that 'The last part of the book the gentleman durst not translate for the evil it contains of the Jews'— fragments of information that suggests an unusually intimate knowledge of the intellectual operations of the Essex circle (*Informations*, 285–7).

To summarize these speculations: it is tempting to conclude that *The Isle of Dogs* was a political satire concerned with the recent debate about the Spanish threat and the Azores expedition; that the piece was generally friendly to Essex, and tactlessly critical of the Cecils, father and son—both of whom were members of the Privy Council court that tried the case. The fortunes of Jonson and Robert Cecil were to be entangled in a variety of ways, through patronage and legal investigation, in the years to come. Their first confrontation at Greenwich cannot have been easy, but Cecil must at least have recognized in Jonson an unusual talent that might ultimately be channelled to other ends.

7

Saved by the Book 1597–1598

FEW plays from the early modern period had such a sensational reception as *The Isle of Dogs*, but many were to share its ultimate fate: to vanish virtually without trace. The number of plays from this period that have perished far exceeds those that have managed to survive. Over 3,000 plays were probably written and performed in London between 1560 and 1642, yet only about 500 of these are known to exist today.[1] The causes of loss are various. Fear of legal reprisal no doubt prompted the sudden disappearance of one or two dramatic manuscripts as well as *The Isle of Dogs*, but the regular working conditions of the theatre accounted for most of the losses. Plays were technically the property of the theatrical company for which they had been written. Publication of a new (or newish) play was sometimes thought to boost theatrical attendances, and was becoming a popular stratagem around the time that Jonson started work as a dramatist. During the 1590s most of Shakespeare's plays, for example, were systematically published by the Lord Chamberlain's Men about two years after their first performance, seemingly to increase playhouse revenue.[2] Like modern paperbacks, quarto editions were inexpensive and easily portable. In Jonson's *Every Man In His Humour*, the would-be fashionable young man about town, Matheo, goes visiting with a copy of *The Spanish Tragedy* in his pocket, and needs little encouragement to read 'a number of fine speeches' from the play. Yet many plays failed to make it into print, either because their publishable value was thought to be negligible, or because publication seemed in conflict with their box office potential. Busy theatre companies, uncertain how to judge this issue, might simply set the manuscripts aside, with predictable consequences. In the 1630s Thomas Heywood grumbled that his own plays, 'by shifting and changing of companies, have been negligently lost; others of them are still retained in the hands of some actors, who think it against their peculiar profit to have them come in print'.[3]

Jonson was well aware of the vulnerability of such manuscripts, and also of the new opportunities offered to writers through the rapid expansion of the book trade during the last decade of Elizabeth's reign. In his determination to seek early publication for so many of his plays and other writings, Jonson differed from most of his theatrical and literary contemporaries. As a consequence, a smaller proportion of Jonson's plays, and of his total writing oeuvre, is 'lost' than is the case with many other authors of the period. Yet the number of Jonson's works that do not survive is considerably larger than is often supposed.[4] Of the numerous plays that he wrote, in particular, at the outset of his career, most are known only by name, or through some general reference. Jonson was a discriminating writer, who did not attempt to preserve everything he wrote. Moreover, he viewed the book trade, as he viewed the theatre itself, with distinct ambivalence. Though he chose eventually to publish many of his poems and masques in the folio edition of his *Works* in 1616, he continued—like many of his aristocratic and gentlemanly contemporaries—to circulate his poems in manuscript amongst chosen friends. He spoke with distaste in his *Epigrams* about the 'vile arts' of his own bookseller, who sought to promote the very book in which, ironically, these poems of sharp detraction were distributed to a wider readership; and deplored the illiterate customers who ignorantly fingered its pages: 'termers or some clerk-like serving man | Who scarce can spell the hard names; whose knight less can' (*Epigrams*, 3.9–10). At this moment of exceptional literary achievement in England, somewhere between half and two-thirds of the population were probably unable to read or write.[5] And of those who were able to read, so Jonson indignantly insisted, few read with proper understanding. In the quarto edition of *Catiline*, published in 1611 after failing in the theatre, Jonson was to address 'The Reader in Ordinary' with heavy disdain.

The muses forbid that I should restrain your meddling whom I see already busy with the title and tricking over the leaves: it is your own. I departed with my right when I let it first abroad. And now, so secure an interpreter I am of my chance that neither praise nor dispraise from you can affect me.

A second and more tersely admiring dedication is addressed 'To the Reader Extraordinary': 'You I would understand to be the better man, though places in court go otherwise. To you I submit myself and work. Farewell.'

While grumbling about the ignorance and impercipience of most of his readers, Jonson was also quick to recognize the benefits of publishing his plays, and happy to ignore the strict legal rights of the companies for which the plays had specifically been written. Publication gave a seeming permanence to works that might otherwise be regarded as ephemeral, and that were not always, as a genre, highly esteemed at this time.[6] It committed works that had been casually dismissed in the playhouse—such as *Sejanus* and *Catiline,* for which he had held the highest hopes—to the more considered verdict of discriminating readers. It redeemed the accidentals of theatrical performance and reception. '*The New Inn,* or, *The Light Heart: A Comedy*', reads the title page of the 1631 octavo edition of Jonson's *The New Inn,* a late comedy that had fared unhappily in the playhouse:

As it was never acted, but most negligently played by some, the King's Servants, and more squeamishly beheld by others, the King's subjects, 1629. Now at last set at liberty to the readers, His Majesty's servants and subjects, to be judged. 1631. By the author, B. Jonson.

The notion that a play, through publication, was *at last set at liberty* from the confinement of the theatre may seem surprising, coming from a dramatist who manipulated so superlatively the physical and psychological resources of the playhouse, yet the statement eloquently conveys the depth of hostility Jonson felt at times to 'the loathèd stage', and the confidence he placed in the power of the printed word.

Publication also served to highlight the (otherwise, up until then, fairly subdued) role of the dramatic author, and nurture what one scholar has aptly termed 'the bibliographical ego'.[7] It was through strategic publication of his works that Jonson was eventually to make his career as a writer, step by careful step. 'Ego' is the operative word here, for in publishing his plays Jonson was at pains to highlight his own achievement rather than any collective effort. He made no apparent effort to publish plays that he had written with others, apart from *Sejanus*, a play in which he confessed that 'a second pen had good share' of the writing while carefully removing the work of his collaborator and substituting what he called 'weaker (and no doubt less pleasing)' passages of his own ('To the Readers', 31–5). *Eastward Ho!*, which Jonson had written jointly with George Chapman and John

Marston, was published in quarto apparently without Jonson's authorization, and was not reprinted in his 1616 Folio. Jonson's persistent wish to highlight his own individual literary achievements, rather than those of his collaborators, affects in particular our knowledge of the work he undertook at the very outset of his career. For Jonson made no apparent effort to publish or otherwise preserve the plays he wrote in these early years in association with other writers from Philip Henslowe's stable: writers for whom (as his later contemptuous comments to William Drummond made clear) he entertained a generally low opinion.[8]

Throughout this early phase of his career Jonson was nevertheless obliged to work, however grudgingly and with whatever tensions, as part of a theatrical collective. Collaboration was an essential feature of early modern dramatic authorship, speeding the rate of production as competing companies battled to meet the huge demand for new plays. The commercial value of Jonson's writing talents was quickly spotted. An exchange of payments recorded on 28 July 1597 has been thought to imply that Henslowe was seeking to attract him away from Pembroke's company to become a sharer in the Admiral's Men.[9] This was the very day on which the Privy Council order for the demolition of London playhouses was issued, and Jonson would soon have had other pressing matters to worry about. The absence of further recorded payments suggests that, for whatever reasons, Henslowe's move came to nothing. Over the next two years, however, Henslowe employed Jonson regularly as one of his writers, recording payments to him for a number of plays about which little or nothing is otherwise known. On 3 December 1597 he noted a loan to Jonson of twenty shillings 'upon a book which he was to write for us before Christmas next after the date hereof which he showed the plot unto the company'.[10] On 18 August the following year Henslowe lent the Lord Admiral's Men the sum of £6 to pay Jonson and two other members of his team, Henry Porter and Henry Chettle, 'for a book called *Hot Anger Soon Cold*'. This play, presumably a comedy, was almost certainly completed, but no record of its performance survives.[11] Anger was a topic of some interest to Jonson, whose surviving comedies often involve virtuosic displays of wrath, and characters such as Humphrey Wasp in *Bartholomew Fair*, who seem in a constant state of ire or agitation. The late Peter Barnes (the English comic dramatist, a big admirer of Jonson's work) once acutely remarked that Jonson's characters, like those of Dostoevsky, seemed 'perpetually angry, or perpetually drunk; in the sense that they continuously reveal themselves'.[12] Jonson himself was perceived by William Drummond as a man 'passionately kind and angry' (*Informations*, 559). Anger was a topic also of interest to Porter, best known to posterity as the author of *The Pleasant History of the Two Angry Women of Abingdon*, performed at the Rose theatre at a slightly later date by the Admiral's Men. The third partner in this composition, Henry Chettle, was an industrious collaborator who is known to have worked on forty-nine plays for Henslowe between 1598 and 1603. He and Porter had just finished working together on a play called *Black Bateman*, part two. Jonson, a relative newcomer to such tasks, may have been brought in as 'coadjutor' (a relatively junior role) to help with *Hot Anger*.[13]

Jonson evidently wrote other plays in these early years whose very titles are today unknown. In September 1598 Francis Meres was to include both Porter and Chettle in a list of English writers 'the best for comedy amongst us'. Jonson's name does not appear in Meres's list of comic writers, but he is mentioned as being amongst 'our best for tragedy'.[14] Nothing whatever is known about the tragedies that Jonson must have written by this date, not even their themes or titles. By August 1599, however, Jonson was evidently at work with Thomas Dekker on another tragedy whose text has vanished, though its theme and title are this time known. *The Lamentable Tragedy of Page of Plymouth* was a domestic tragedy based on the real-life story—already familiar through ballads usually attributed to Thomas Deloney—of Ulalia Page and George Strangwidge, who were both hanged in March 1591 in Barnstaple, Devon, for conspiring to murder Ulalia's husband. *Page of Plymouth* was probably performed by the Lord Admiral's Men in September 1599.[15] Jonson and Dekker were soon to collaborate again, together with Henry Chettle and one 'other gentleman' (possibly John Marston), on another now-lost work for the Lord Admiral's Men, *Robert II, King of Scots*, that may have been staged by early October, though no record of its performance survives.[16] Robert II, son of Robert the Bruce and King of Scotland from 1371 to 1390, known as 'the Steward', is commonly regarded as the founder of the Stuart dynasty; his reign was marked by internal and cross-border feuding that might have held particular interest for Jonson in relation to his own family's history in the debatable lands around Annandale.

§§

Yet whatever merit these early works might have had, none (in Jonson's eyes) evidently deserved publication, or prompted subsequent nostalgic comment.

Jonson himself marked the real beginning of his dramatic career with the comedy he was to place in its revised format at the very head of his *Works* in 1616, and dedicate affectionately to his old mentor, William Camden. *Every Man In His Humour* was performed by the Lord Chamberlain's Men at the Curtain theatre in late September 1598. The date of this performance is known from a letter from Tobie Matthew to Dudley Carleton on 20 September, telling how a gentleman lost 300 crowns 'at a new play called *Every Man's Humour*'.[17] Why Jonson had chosen to offer this play to the Lord Chamberlain's Men rather than to Henslowe's company, the Lord Admiral's Men, remains unclear. It is possible he was attracted by the recent successes of the Chamberlain's Men and the work in particular of its leading writer, William Shakespeare; who, according to a story of dubious authenticity recounted for the first time in 1709 by Shakespeare's first editor, Nicholas Rowe, was instrumental in having the play performed, through 'a remarkable piece of humanity and good nature'.

Mr Jonson, who was at that time altogether unknown to the world, had offered one of his plays to the players in order to have it acted, and the persons into whose hands it was put, after having turned it carelessly and superciliously over, were just upon returning it to him with an ill-natured answer, that it would be of no service to their company, when Shakespeare luckily cast his eye upon it, and found something so well in it as to engage him first to read it through, and afterwards to recommend Mr Jonson and his writings to the public. After this they were professed friends, though I don't know whether the other ever made him an equal return of gentleness and sincerity.

It is not merely the late emergence of this story that arouses suspicion, but the manner in which the events are then elaborated in order to accommodate a tenacious eighteenth-century view of the imagined characters of Shakespeare and Jonson: the one, gracious, gentle, generous, gifted; the other, surly, grudging, envious, and ungrateful.[18] What is certain however is that Shakespeare acted in *Every Man In His Humour,* his name significantly heading the list that appears in Jonson's 1616 Folio of 'principal comedians' who originally presented the play in 1598, being bracketed alongside that of the company's leading player, Richard Burbage. The play thus brought together in creative conjunction for the first time Shakespeare and Jonson, the two great dramatic geniuses of the English theatre: the one, in his vigorous prime, the other, at the very outset of his career. The encounter was to have a notable impact on the work of both men.

Despite its nominal location in Florence, the earliest surviving version of *Every Man In His Humour* (that of the quarto of 1601) clearly takes as its theme the foibles and fashions of late Elizabethan London. In Jonson's revision of the comedy, published in the folio edition of his *Works* in 1616, this sense of social immediacy is intensified, the play's setting being shifted to the more recognizable neighbourhoods of London, its characters renamed and domesticated, the play as a whole offering, as Jonson's prologue challengingly declares, 'deeds and language such as men do use, | And persons such as Comedy would choose | When she would show an image of the times...' (21–3). Yet the striking novelty of Jonson's comedy, its power thrillingly to present 'an image of the times', was already clearly evident in the original version of the play. It signalled to Shakespeare and to the Lord Chamberlain's Men that a new dramatist had arrived, and that a new kind of dramatic writing—urban in setting, contemporary in reference—was now beginning to emerge.[19]

The world of *Every Man In His Humour*, like that of the London it mirrored, is one of high social mobility and finely calibrated social gradations: of dress, language, income, habitation, and leisurely pursuit. Stephano, the naive young man from the country, and Matheo, his urban counterpart, both aspire—as so many did in the last years of Elizabeth's reign and the early years of her successor's—to be seen as *gentlemen*, a status whose acquisition (they imagine) rests on the possession of a cloak, the fineness of a stocking, the ingenuity of an oath, the taking of tobacco, the quality of a weapon. Literacy itself—the ability to read, and to possess a book—is viewed as a social marker. For Stephano, hawking and hunting are important avenues to gentlemanly standing; he has bought himself 'a hawk and bells and all' and lacks 'nothing but a book to keep it by' (1.1.31–2). Like the books that Matheo has purchased—Marlowe's *Hero and Leander*, from which he has filched some verses to pass off as his own, and his treasured *Spanish Tragedy*, from which he liberally recites—the book that Stephano craves is hardly an item of humanistic learning, but rather a bluffer's appurtenance, an aid to social advancement.

Social climbing was a practice that Jonson, the bricklayer's stepson, now making his own way up through the ranks, would continue to ridicule throughout his writing career. It was the great phenomenon of his age, in which even those at the highest levels of power in England, such as William Cecil, Lord Burghley (targeted perhaps for this very tendency in this very play), were deeply implicated.[20] Musco, the clever servant of the comedy, contrives his own advancement by dropping a few rungs on the social ladder, disguising himself in 'the habit of one of your poor *desperviews*, your decayed, ruinous, worm-eaten gentleman of the round, such as have vowed to sit on the skirts of the city (let your provost and his half-dozen of halberdiers do what they can), and have translated begging out of the old hackney pace to a fine, easy amble . . .' (3.2.7–11). A *desperview* was a beggar, of whom there were plenty on the streets of London in the late 1590s. Many were vagrants or 'masterless men', a group now growing in such numbers that they were officially regarded as a threat to the social order. Just a few months before the performance of Jonson's play, the Parliament of 1597–8 had passed two Acts proposing measures to deal with 'maimed, idle, and disorderly soldiers and sailors returning from the wars'.[21] It is a delicious irony that Musco, posing as such a masterless man, should be rebuked by his actual master, Lorenzo, who, failing to recognize him, urges him to return to the wars, or seek the 'service of some virtuous gentleman' (2.2.65–7).

It is from these same continental wars, of which Jonson himself had had intimate knowledge earlier in the decade, that the play's great comic creation, Bobadilla, has also returned, now fantasizing freely about the campaigns he has undergone, and victories won. Bobadilla's very name identifies him incongruously with the Spanish rather than the Dutch forces whom the English troops had been sent to assist: a Don Francisco de Bobadilla had been commander of the Spanish military forces on board the Armada of 1588.[22] Bobadilla's grandest scheme, of overcoming the enemy through a series of individual duels rather than 'holding wars generally' (4.2.45–67), may seem like a comic memory of Jonson's own victorious single combat in the Low Countries just a few years earlier.[23] Jonson would certainly have encountered such boastful, indigent, yarn-spinning, fraudulent veterans as Bobadilla on the streets of London; in Captain Hungry of *Epigrams*, 107, he satirizes much the same type or humour.

The word *humour* was a legacy of Galenic medical theory, which held that a person's character was determined by the proportion in which the bodily humours—choler, blood, phlegm, and black bile—happened to be mixed. Choler made you angry; blood made you sanguine or cheerful, phlegm made you stolid, black bile made you melancholic. By the 1590s 'humour' was commonly used in a further extended sense to mean simply a whim, a fancy, a caprice, or a mere affectation: as Stephano and Matheo in this comedy each choose to adopt a melancholy pose, which they regard as a suitably modish and 'gentleman-like' humour. While Jonson viewed such abuses of the term with a mixture of exasperation and ironic delight, he continued throughout his dramatic career to populate his comic world with characters whose dominant or obsessive qualities—anger, jealousy, cowardice, extravagance, garrulity—were (in this special sense of the term) recognizably *humorous*. Jonson had used the word 'humours' repeatedly throughout *The Case Is Altered* the previous year to describe his characters' traits and foibles. His liking for humours comedy would have been further encouraged by the example of George Chapman's *The Blind Beggar of Alexandria* (1596) and *A Humorous Day's Mirth* (1597), and also perhaps, as several small verbal touches suggest, by a dramatic character who had proved a great favourite in the repertoire of the Lord Chamberlain's Men during the preceding months: Shakespeare's Falstaff: that 'trunk of humours', as Hal sardonically calls him (*1 Henry IV*, 2.4.495), and his faithful band of 'irregular humorists'.[24]

If Shakespeare's example could influence Jonson, however, the reverse was also true, for Shakespeare's experience of performing in Jonson's comedy was to affect his own subsequent practice. Though it is not known which role Shakespeare played in *Every Man In His Humour*, one character in particular was to remain indelibly in his mind: Thorello, the obsessively jealous merchant, whose broodings over the imagined infidelities of his wife Bianca Shakespeare was to recall in his own tragedy of *Othello* just a few years later. 'Bane to my fortunes: what meant I to marry?' asks Thorello in Jonson's play, in a meditation which Othello was soon to retrace, beginning with a similar question, 'Why did I marry?' (*Every Man In His Humour*, 3.3.15–25; *Othello*, 3.3.245–56). 'Sweetheart, will you come in to breakfast?', Bianca asks her anxious husband, placing her hand solicitously on his forehead as he complains of an aching forehead (1.4.181–212). 'I pray thee, good sweetheart, come in', begs Desdemona of Othello, starting to bind his brow with her handkerchief when he similarly speaks of 'a pain upon my forehead, here' (3.3.277–93, at 287).[25]

One further echo of Jonson's comedy in a later Shakespearian play has a curiously ironic relevance to events that were soon to erupt within the arena of Jonson's own life. In *Every Man In His Humour*, Thorello, the anxious merchant, rebukes his brother-in-law Prospero for the troubles he has brought to their house in the course of the day. Prospero protests to Thorello and Bianca that their troubles are all imaginary, and that no mischance has actually occurred:

Prospero No harm done, brother, I warrant you. Since there is no harm done,
anger costs a man nothing, and a tall man is never his own man till he be
angry...
Bianca Ay, but what harm might have come out of it!
Prospero Might? So might the good warm clothes your husband wears be
poisoned, for anything he knows, or the wholesome wine he drunk even now
at the table. (4.3.7–8, 13–16)

'No harm done': Shakespeare remarkably gives these precise words to another
character named Prospero in a play written towards the close of his career, as
he reassures his daughter that no mischance has arisen that day from his
contrivances:

> *Prospero*   Be collected:
> No more amazement: tell your piteous heart
> There's no harm done.
> *Miranda*   O, woe the day!
> *Prospero* No harm.
> (*The Tempest*, 1.2.13–15)

No harm done is a phrase that succinctly describes the comic action of *Every Man
In His Humour*, a play in which domestic calamity of one kind or another is
constantly imagined, but never actually occurs. In the scene outside Cob's house
at the opening of the fifth act Jonson brings this pattern of apprehension and
relief to a brilliantly cascading climax, as one character after another is drawn to
Cob's house, expecting to find at this location the clinching evidence of their
worst fears. All of these fears prove in turn to be misplaced, products merely of
an overheated imagination. The pattern recurs in the final scene of the play, as
Doctor Clement flourishes his long sword over the terrified Musco, who kneels
before him; announcing, first, that he must cut off Musco's legs, then suddenly
bidding him stand. 'How dost thou now?', he asks. 'Dost thou feel thyself well?
Hast thou no harm?' (5.3.87–103).

§§

No harm done: while Jonson's comedy was still playing to amused audiences
at the Curtain theatre, presenting a charmed world in which no real hurts
were inflicted, a more serious drama was soon to commence in the world just
beyond the theatre. On 22 September 1598 a quarrel broke out between

Jonson and Gabriel Spencer, one of the two actors with whom Jonson had been imprisoned at Marshalsea the previous year during *The Isle of Dogs* affair. Spencer had left Pembroke's Men after his release from Marshalsea, and was now a leading member of Henslowe's company, the Lord Admiral's Men, who were playing at the Rose theatre. It is possible that his quarrel with Jonson turned, as one scholar has suggested, on questions of professional loyalty: on Jonson's abandonment of the Admiral's Men, his sale of *Every Man In His Humour* to the rival company of the Lord Chamberlain's Men, and his failure to have completed the play for which Henslowe had commissioned him on 3 December 1597.[26] Yet the precise circumstances of the disagreement, which might equally have arisen out of some personal difference, are in fact unknown. Some twenty years after the event, William Drummond laconically noted Jonson's version of the affair:

since his coming to England, being appealed to the fields, he had killed his adversary, which had hurt him in the arm, and whose sword was ten inches longer than his; for the which he was imprisoned, and almost at the gallows. (*Informations*, 186–90)

The 'fields' to which Jonson was summoned by Spencer for this fight were at Hoxton, a semi-rural area to the north of London which served as a quiet recreational spot for those in search of cakes and ale, as an exercising area for the military train bands, and as a suitably remote location for would-be duellists. (Hoxton was to feature in the revised folio version of *Every Man In His Humour* as Stephen's place of residence, from whence 'it's but crossing over the fields' to arrive at Moorgate, neighbouring the city: 1.3.71.) Though strictly illegal at the time, duelling was a common activity in the 1590s, and swordplay a modish practice, as is evident again from Jonson's comedy, in which Bobadilla solemnly demonstrates to Matheo some essential moves and passes with the aid of his bedstaff. Challenges were difficult to refuse, as Bobadilla's experience in the play again bears out. Earlier in 1598 Sir Melchior Leven, a Dutchman, was reported to have 'refused to fight Sir Charles Blount in Paris on the ground that the King hath forbidden duels, whereat all do mock him'.[27] The Italian fencing-master Vincentio Saviolo, then resident in London, devoted a chapter of his celebrated treatise on swordsmanship to a careful consideration of 'How gentlemen ought to accept of any quarrel, in such manner that they may combat lawfully'.[28]

Gabriel Spencer was buried at St Leonard's, Shoreditch, on 23 September 1598, the day following the fatal encounter. Philip Henslowe reported the incident in sombre terms a few days later to his son-in-law Edward Alleyn, then absent in Sussex with his wife Joan:

assure you that I do not forget now to let you understand news, that I will tell you some, but it is for me hard and heavy. Since you were with me I have lost one of my company which hurteth me greatly, that is Gabriel, for he is slain in Hoxton Fields by the hands of Benjamin Jonson, bricklayer. Therefore I would fain have a little of your counsel, if I could.[29]

The theatre was a volatile profession in late Elizabethan England, and fatal quarrels between players and dramatists were not unknown. John Heminges, a member of Shakespeare's own company, had married in 1588 Rebecca Knell, the 16-year-old widow of William Knell, a member of the Queen's Men who had been killed by his fellow-actor John Towne at Thame in Oxfordshire while the company had been on tour the previous year. On 6 June 1599 a 'John Day of Southwark, yeoman'—probably the dramatist John Day, scornfully characterized by Jonson as a rogue (*Informations*, 36)—was to assault another member of Henslowe's team, Henry Porter, who died the following day of his wounds. Porter and Jonson had worked together with Chettle two years earlier on *Hot Anger Soon Cold*.[30] On 3 December 1596 Gabriel Spencer himself had been involved in a similar fatal affray while at the house in Shoreditch of a barber named Richard Easte, where 'divers insulting and reproachful words' were exchanged between Spencer and another man present, James Feake. Feake picked up a copper candlestick and made to throw it at Spencer. Spencer instantly struck Feake with his unsheathed rapier, then drove the rapier, still in its sheath, through Feake's right eye to the brain, from which agonizing injury Feake eventually died three days later.[31] Like Jonson himself, Spencer was clearly a powerful and quarrelsome man, with a reputation for violence.

In October 1598 Ben Jonson, 'yeoman', was formally arraigned at the Justice Hall in the Old Bailey for the manslaughter of Gabriel Spencer. The indictment—translated from the abbreviated legal Latin of the courtroom record—reveals that Jonson

with a certain sword of iron and steel called a rapier [*gladio de ferro et calibe vocat' a Rapiour*], of the price of three shillings, which he then and there had in his right hand and held drawn, feloniously and wilfully struck and beat the said Gabriel, then and there with the aforesaid sword giving to the same Gabriel Spencer, in and upon the same Gabriel's right side, a mortal wound, to the depth of six inches and the breadth of one inch, of which mortal wound the same Gabriel Spencer then and there died instantly in the aforesaid fields at Shoreditch in the aforesaid County of Middlesex. And thus the aforesaid jurors say upon their oath that the aforesaid Benjamin Jonson feloniously and wilfully slew and killed the aforesaid Gabriel Spencer at Shoreditch aforesaid in the aforesaid County of Middlesex in the aforesaid fields...[32]

When this account is compared with that given by Jonson to William Drummond many years later, two seeming oddities emerge. The first concerns the nature of the weapon with which Jonson slew Gabriel Spencer. Jonson's claim that Spencer's sword 'was ten inches long than his' suggests that he himself might have been armed with a short sword, and Spencer with a rapier. The rapier was a long, pointed, two-edged sword, sometimes as much as a yard and a quarter in length, commonly used for thrusting rather than cutting, with a complex hilt to protect the hand. It had been a relatively unknown weapon in England until the 1570s, when it gained rapid popularity as a more practical instrument for individual fighting than the short sword, which up until then was regarded as the English national weapon.[33] The indictment record however reveals that Jonson's weapon was actually not a short sword, but a rapier (or *Rapiour*). Nothing is said about its length, which may not have been of direct concern to the court. Rapiers certainly came in differing sizes, and it is conceivable Jonson's weapon was significantly shorter than Spencer's, though nothing in the court record confirms that part of his story. Was Jonson exaggerating as he recounted this incident to Drummond?

The second disparity between the two accounts concerns the way in which the combat started. Jonson's remark to Drummond implies that he himself was not the challenger, having been simply 'appealed to the fields' by Spencer. In the courtroom, however, Jonson makes no reference to this fact, as the endorsement of the indictment makes clear: *Cogn' Indictament pewtit librum legit ut Cl'icus sign' cum lra T Et del' iuxta formam statut' &c.*, 'He confesses the indictment, asks for the book, reads like a clerk, is marked with the letter T, and is delivered according to the form of the statute, &c.' Yet as Jonson certainly knew, duelling was an illegal activity, no matter who issued the initial challenge. Hence he simply entered a plea of guilty to the charge of manslaughter before asking for 'the book' and reading 'like a clerk'. By this latter request, Jonson was seeking benefit of clergy, a technical loophole which originally allowed ordained clergy to claim that they were outside the jurisdiction of the secular courts, permitting them to be tried instead under canon law. Over time this benefit was extended to anyone who could read the so-called 'neck-verse' or test of literacy. This was Psalm 51 (numbered Psalm 50 in the Vulgate and Septuagint), beginning appropriately *Miserere mei, Deus, secundum misericordiam tuam*, 'Have mercy upon me, O God, according to thy loving kindness' (in the Geneva translation), a passage that might easily be committed to memory even by the illiterate. An Elizabethan statute of 1575 changed the basic nature of this exemption, allowing benefit of clergy to be pleaded after conviction but before sentencing; offenders would thus have their cases heard by secular rather than by ecclesiastical courts. The plea of benefit of clergy did not cancel the conviction, but might change the nature of the sentence for first-time offenders from hanging to branding, and perhaps a year's conviction. By successfully reading this verse, Jonson escaped the gallows. His ability to read had saved him from an almost certain death. His goods however were confiscated, and, like all such offenders, he was branded with a hot iron in the fleshy part of the thumb of the right hand probably with the letter M (for manslayer) (T, for thief, mentioned in the court record, looks like a clerical error). Such a brand, immediately visible when the right hand was lifted up again in a courtroom, ensured that the benefit could be claimed only once.[34]

Jonson found himself, in the idiom of the day, 'saved by the book': an appropriate form of salvation for one who placed such trust in the printed word. From time to time both he and his detractors were to allude, with various degrees of playfulness, to this perilous episode in his life. 'First, the title of his play is *Cynthia's Revels*, as any man that hath hope to be saved by his book can witness', says one of the mischievous children in the Induction to that comedy a couple of years later, as he explains its subject matter to the audience (40–2). The title and location of the dramatic scene were at times displayed on stage in Elizabethan times, for literate members of the audience to read; Jonson humorously encourages a secondary understanding of the boy's words *saved by the book* for those with knowledge of his recent circumstances. Humour of a less friendly kind is to be found in Dekker's *Satiromastix*, performed just a few months later, in 1601: 'thou ... read'st as legibly as some that have been saved by the neck-verse', says Asinius Bubo to Horace, alias Jonson; 'read, *lege*, save thyself and read', says Tucca to Horace later in the play. 'Art not famous enough yet, my mad Horastratus, for killing a player ...?' he asks, then adding a further suggestive detail: 'Thou art the true arraigned poet, and should have been hanged, but for one of these part-takers, these charitable copper-laced Christians, that fetched thee out of purgatory—players, I mean—theatrians (pouch-mouth), stage-walkers...' (1.2.139–42; 4.1.169–70; 4.2.84–5; 4.3.252–57). Tucca's somewhat contorted gibe suggests that the Lord Chamberlain's Men themselves ('part-takers', 'players', 'theatrians', 'stage-walkers') had saved Jonson from execution, perhaps by testifying to the nature of the quarrel or to his personal character. Jonson's own plea of benefit of clergy, rather than any intervention by the players, is likely to have been the determining factor in saving him from the gallows, though their testimony might well have helped to secure his imme-diate release from custody.

Jonson himself in later plays continued to refer glancingly to this legal device in a manner that might well have awakened memories amongst knowing members of the audience of his own narrow escape from the gallows years earlier. One of the running jokes in *Bartholomew Fair* (1614) is that Cokes's irascible tutor, Humphrey Wasp, is actually himself illiterate, and is consequently unable to make head or tail of the wedding licence with which he has been entrusted. He tetchily dismisses any attempt to have the docu-ment either shown to him or explained. 'That's well—nay, never open or read it to me; it's labour in vain, you know', he exclaims. 'I am no clerk, I scorn to be saved by my book: i'faith, I'll hang first. Fold it up o' your word and gi' it me' (1.4.4–6). As late as 1625 Jonson seems fleetingly to recall his earlier brush with the law when he has Mistress Tattle—one of the garrulous, empty-headed commentators watching his own comedy, *The Staple of News*—speak admiringly of the play's author as a man who (astonishingly) knows how to read and write: 'He is an errant learned man that made it', she says, 'and can write, they say, and I am foully deceived but he can read too' (Intermean 1, 33–4). The latter phrase, 'he can read too', seems deliberately pointed. It is remarkable that Jonson himself should have chosen to refer, however obliquely, to this humiliating incident so many years after the event. Yet the escape from hanging was clearly a defining moment in his life, and one that remained in the public memory as well as in Jonson's own. Three or four years after Jonson's death, his former patron William Cavendish, Earl of Newcastle, was to give a further admiring twist to this familiar motif in verses addressed 'To Ben Jonson's Ghost'. 'Is any infidel?', he writes, referring to those who might entertain doubt about Jonson's supreme power as a writer. 'Let him but look | And read. He may be saved by thy book.'[35] The *book* which secures salvation is now, in Cavendish's lines, no longer the Bible, but the writings of Jonson himself that had recently been published in the Second Folio of 1640–1.

§§

While Jonson was awaiting trial in Newgate prison and 'almost at the gallows', an event occurred that was to change the course and character of his life. 'Then took he his religion by trust of a priest who visited him in prison,' William Drummond reported years later, with characteristic terseness; 'Thereafter he was twelve years a papist' (*Informations*, 189–90). Though Drummond does not record the name of the priest whose arguments for conversion to the Church of Rome Jonson took 'by trust', it has been plausibly suggested that the priest was a certain Father Thomas Wright, a sturdily independent Yorkshireman who in his youth had studied at William Allen's Catholic seminary at Douai—a favoured training ground for priests wishing to join the English Mission—and subsequently at the English College in Rome, where he had been admitted, not without difficulty, to the Jesuit Order, and ordained in 1586.[36] Wright later taught as Professor of Hebrew in Milan, and in a variety of other institutions throughout Europe, including the seminary in Valladolid recently established by the influential Jesuit Father Robert Persons. Persons seems to have taken a particular liking to Wright, and to have shielded him from the worst of the troubles that were shortly to follow. For in 1594 the Jesuits moved to expel Wright from their Order, on the grounds that he had expressed 'extravagant opinions', the nature of which can be gathered from an unpublished Latin tract of that time 'by one Wright, a priest as it seems, of the College of Douai'.[37] The arguments set out in this brief essay, however repugnant they may have been to the Jesuits, provide an important clue as to why Jonson could at least have listened to Wright with attention while in prison in 1598, and have made at that moment what might otherwise seem to have been, in strictly prudential terms, a reckless decision.

Wright's tract addresses a central and recurrent dilemma for English Catholics: whether their ultimate loyalty lay with their monarch, or with the Pope in Rome, who had supported a Spanish invasion of England as a means of restoring the true religion. The Pope's view on this matter had been firmly accepted by the Jesuit Order. Wright was above all a loyal Englishman, however, despite his years of service in Jesuit seminaries abroad. His tract, entitled *An licitum sit catholicis in Anglia arma sumere, et aliis modis, reginam et regnum defendere contra Hispanos* ('Whether Catholics in England may use arms and other means in defence of the Queen and the kingdom against the Spanish'), displays a fierce mistrust of the Spanish character and of Spanish motives for conquest, and vigorously contests the authority of the Pope to offer instruction on what (so Wright argues) was a purely secular question of political allegiance. While the Spanish 'pretend religion', Wright maintains, it was a mere 'lust of ruling' that actually drove their imperial expansion. Spain's recent hostilities against the Dutch were primarily motivated not by a wish to extend the Catholic faith, but rather to impose new and unlawful taxes and penalties upon the Dutch people, who, with the aid of Protestant allies such as England, had legitimately resisted their incursions. Spain's present designs upon England, Wright goes on, were to be similarly understood. It was in the clear interests of all good Catholics in England to support Elizabeth in her present resistance to a possible Spanish invasion. Such strenuously loyalist arguments, while hardly in themselves grounds for a conversion, might at least have won the general assent of Jonson, as a veteran of recent campaigns in the Low Countries and no obvious lover either of Spain or of the Spanish.

Wright narrowly survived the attempt to expel him from the Society, but prudently chose to leave the Jesuits of his own volition. In June 1595 he returned openly to England as a secular priest, and put himself at the mercy of Anthony Bacon, confidential secretary to the Earl of Essex. Wright evidently knew that Essex had recently afforded protection to two Catholic laymen, and that he was cautiously interested in gaining Catholic support for his personal cause. From his recent contacts in Spain, Wright had a further valuable card to play. He could offer fresh news about the political intentions of the King of Spain, who—so he dutifully informed Essex—was planning to arrive in England with an army the following spring. When Essex passed this information on to the Privy Council it was scornfully dismissed by Burghley as idle gossip, but subsequently found to be true. Wright's value as a loyalist informer, and as a handy pawn in Essex's strategic play with Burghley and Cecil, was at once established. For a time Wright enjoyed the favour and protection of Essex and of Francis and Anthony Bacon, mixing freely with members of Essex's circle, including Lord Mountjoy and the earls of Rutland and Southampton. If Jonson also had close contact with this circle in the late 1590s (as argued more fully in the previous chapter), then it is entirely possible he and Father Wright could have met at some stage before their crucial encounter in Newgate in 1598.

As the struggle for political ascendancy between Essex and the Cecils intensified, however, Wright's personal situation grew less secure. Wary of Wright's outspokenness and his potential usefulness to Essex, Burghley insisted that he be kept under restraint in the house of the Dean of Westminster, Dr Gabriel Goodman. Here Wright remained throughout 1596 and 1597, despite repeated efforts by the Bacons to secure his release, and an offer by Essex himself to send him again to Europe to work as a spy. From Goodman's house, as Wright complained in a letter to Essex, he was dispatched to 'two most close and unwholesome prisons', the Gatehouse and Bridewell—the latter, a favourite place of detention for troublesome religious prisoners—and 'spoiled of all my books and writings, not only Catholic but also Protestant, debarred of all company and humane conversation'.[38] At the time of his meeting with Jonson in 1598, Wright was still technically a prisoner, but evidently enjoyed a limited freedom to visit other prisoners held in neighbouring London gaols. His meeting with Jonson was nevertheless a high-risk affair, for under an Elizabethan statute of 1581, any attempt to convert an English subject to the Roman Catholic faith was a treasonable offence, which carried the appropriate penalty.[39]

Wright was widely suspected of having converted others already to Rome, and in particular a poet and divine with whom Jonson was well acquainted, Dr William Alabaster. Alabaster was a brilliant scholar who had been with Jonson at Westminster School, and subsequently moved to Cambridge, where he was soon to be elected a Fellow of Trinity College, and be drawn into the powerful orbit of the Earl of Essex. In 1596 Alabaster had joined Essex as a chaplain on the Cadiz expedition, and later that year had accepted from him a wealthy living in Cornwall. In 1597, while visiting Dean Goodman at Westminster, Alabaster had his first encounters with Father Thomas Wright. At the beginning of his period of detention Wright had been instructed to talk regularly with Anglican divines who, it was hoped, might persuade him to adopt their faith. In the course of his conversations with Alabaster, however, the tables were turned, for it was Alabaster, not Wright, who was persuaded of the error of his ways. The news of Alabaster's conversion was discovered when letters from Wright were intercepted by the authorities. Writing to Essex, however, Wright strenuously denied that he had ever converted Alabaster, while Alabaster himself attributed his change of faith merely to his having read an inspirational book by William Rainolds.[40] Whatever the final truth of the matter, Wright must obviously have possessed impressive powers of persuasion, which Jonson—who is likely to have known of Alabaster's recent experiences—might well have respected.

One further accomplishment of Father Wright's evidently caught Jonson's particular attention. Wright had recently completed a treatise on the human emotions entitled *The Passions of the Mind in General*, which he was shortly to present in person to the Bishop of London, the official censor, arguing that it contained nothing contrary to the interests of the state or of established religion, and seeking permission for the book to appear under official government auspices. A pirated edition of *The Passions of the Mind* was to be published in 1601, and a second, authorized, edition three years later, bearing a tributary sonnet 'To the Author' by Ben Jonson. Five editions of the book were to be published over the next twenty-five years. At some stage before its first publication—quite possibly, in Newgate prison, while awaiting trial—Jonson had studied this work of moral psychology with unusual care. Wright's work, when closely read (so Jonson's sonnet declares), would show the discerning reader 'Each subtlest passion, with her source and spring'. Jonson's own ways of conceptualizing human character (as one critic has noted) were remarkably close to those set out in Wright's treatise.[41] In a patriotic essay prefixed to the treatise, moreover, Wright had contrasted the fox-like cunning of the Italian and the Spanish people with the simplicity of the English character. It is a contrast that Jonson, who had never visited Italy, might well have remembered when he came a few years later to write his greatest comedy, *Volpone*, with its duplicitous Venetian confidence men, and gullible English visitors.[42]

But even granted such intellectual sympathies and mutual respect, the larger question remains. Why should Ben Jonson, at such a troubled moment of his life, have chosen to renounce the religion of his country in favour of the religion of Rome, especially at a time when recusancy ('refusing' or abstaining from the Anglican communion) attracted such official suspicion and crippling penalties? The question might more easily be answered if a work of Jonson's called *Motives* had survived, though the genre to which this now-lost essay seemingly belongs—of writings purporting to explain why their authors have changed their faith—is notoriously unreliable, as well as notoriously subject to loss.[43]

Jonson's conversion has sometimes been explained as an impulsive and irrational act, characteristic of a man of 'ungovernably strong and violent passions' and 'strong aggressive and libidinous drives', who, having recently killed a colleague in illegal combat and himself fearing immediate death by execution, converted to Rome on account of 'an equally strong disposition toward dependence and submission'.[44] Yet it is rash to conclude that Jonson would have taken a decision of this magnitude without strenuous analysis and debate. Rational argumentation, as well as sheer impulsiveness, is likely to have guided his behaviour at this significant moment in his life. Thomas Wright's teachings alone would have urged him to pause, argue, and reflect. In *The Passions of the Mind in General* Wright had conceded that the passions must be reckoned a force for good in spiritual life, and not just for evil, and that any attempt to suppress or extinguish them, in the manner of the Stoics, was radically mistaken. But the passions (as Wright went on to argue) needed also to be controlled, or they would trouble the soul as political agitators trouble the state, and 'rebel against Reason, their lord and king, or oppose themselves one against another'.[45] In decisions of great spiritual consequence one must therefore be prompted by reason rather than by passion alone. Jonson was evidently impressed by this line of thinking. In a poem written not long after his meeting with Thomas Wright, he was to stress the role of 'wakeful reason, our affections' king', lamenting the fact that 'our affections do rebel' ('Epode', *The Forest*, 11.13, 21). 'For passions are spiritual rebels, and raise sedition against the understanding', he wrote again later in *Discoveries*, 22–3. Even the garrulous Lady Would-be in *Volpone* appears to have digested this basic maxim: 'as we find our passions rebel, | Encounter 'em with reason', she urges the unfortunate Volpone (3.4.101–2). Jonson not only placed a high valuation on reason, but also took a keen interest in questions of theological doctrine, as later episodes in his life—his debates with the Dean of St Paul's and the Archbishop of Canterbury's Chaplain in 1606, his attendance at an extended disputation in Paris in 1612 on the nature of the real presence—strongly suggest.[46] What then were the possible theological arguments that might have persuaded him to convert to Catholicism in 1598?

One argument in particular in favour of conversion is likely to have impressed itself upon Jonson as he awaited trial for manslaughter in his cell at Newgate: namely, the promise of absolution offered by the Catholic Church through its Sacrament of Penance. Absolution, it is true, was also available to members of the Anglican Church, though its efficacy in the eyes of some seemed less assured, being vested not in a sacrament but in the (possibly fallible) declaration of an individual minister. Priests of the Church of Rome could offer a seemingly more potent form of absolution that appeared to come, through the due stages of apostolic succession, directly from God himself.[47] Wright's writing and example may moreover have assured Jonson that loyalty to the Catholic Church was not incompatible with loyalty to an English Queen. Whatever the final reasons behind his conversion may have been, Jonson maintained his faith resolutely for a dozen years, through one of the most trying periods for members of the Catholic Church in England.

The religion of England had swung back and forth over the past three reigns, and the pendulum was not yet stable. Religious conversion and re-conversion were common occurrences in late Elizabethan England.[48] Many who conformed outwardly with the official religion of the country felt a continuing attraction to the older beliefs and rituals which were still quietly practised, especially in more remote areas of the kingdom. It was ironical that the son of an Anglican clergyman who had lost his entire estate during the reign of Bloody Mary should now adopt the religion that his father had stoutly resisted—and by so doing, find himself equally at odds with the authorities of the day. 'That conversion will always be suspected that apparently concurs with interest,' Dr Johnson was later to remark, as he reflected in *The Lives of the English Poets* on John Dryden's adoption of Catholicism.[49] Ben Jonson's adoption of Catholicism eighty years earlier certainly did not concur with interest: in terms of his personal safety and advancement it was a decidedly risky move, as he was shortly to discover. Yet it was a move that may not have been made entirely without political forethought. By 1598, Elizabeth's age and weariness were in evidence, and her days as England's monarch were clearly numbered. While she refused to display any interest or preference in questions concerning the succession, that topic had become one of urgent and widespread speculation both in England and in neighbouring countries: nowhere with more intensity than in Catholic circles, where the prospects of establishing on the English throne a successor sympathetic to the Catholic cause were being keenly assessed.[50] Many Catholics looked hopefully to the Earl of Essex, whose Catholic sympathies and connections were to come under particular scrutiny at his eventual trial in 1601. In 1598, Thomas Wright and William Alabaster were amongst the hopeful (if at times dubious) onlookers. Ben Jonson probably shared their qualified optimism. A convicted felon, branded on the thumb, stripped of what limited goods and money he possessed, hardly in high favour amongst his theatrical colleagues (one of whose members he had recently slain), he had not much else to be hopeful about at this particular moment in his career. But he had at least been saved from the gallows. He had found a new religion, and a new circle of allied friends and acquaintances. And he had written a comedy which—in his own estimation, at least—could mark the true starting point of his career.

8

Global Satire 1598–1601

THE death of Gabriel Spencer seems to have brought Jonson's rapidly accelerating dramatic career to an abrupt, if temporary, halt. In the month of Jonson's release from Newgate, Philip Henslowe wrote laconically in his diary, 'Lent unto Robert Shaa and Juby the 23 October 1598 to lend unto Mr Chapman on his play book and two acts of a tragedy of Benjamin's plot the sum of £3.' The subject of this 'tragedy of Benjamin's plot' is entirely unknown, as is Henslowe's reason for paying George Chapman, rather than Jonson himself, to complete it. Perhaps Henslowe was not much inclined to put further work in the way of a man who had just killed a leading member of his company, or perhaps he assumed that Jonson, following his trial for manslaughter, would not be around to complete the play himself.[1] Whatever the case, no further record of Jonson's employment in the theatre is found for nearly a year after his discharge from prison. Two of his (now-lost) co-authored plays, *Page of Plymouth* and *Robert II, King of the Scots*, were performed in the late summer of the following year, but his next major dramatic work, *Every Man Out of His Humour*, was not to be staged until the final weeks of 1599.

Meanwhile, another form of writing seems to have taken Jonson's attention: for it is at this point of his life—newly released from prison, newly converted to Catholicism—that he began to write the first poems that have survived into modern times. These would not have been, in any literal sense, his first poetic efforts. As a schoolboy, Jonson would have been required to compose verses in both Latin and English as part of the normal system of learning at Westminster School. He probably continued to write occasional poems throughout the 1590s. None of these pieces, however, was published or otherwise preserved before 1599. His earliest surviving poems differ in some obvious ways from those of his maturity. In his *Epigrams* and in *The Forest*, both published in the 1616 Folio, Jonson attempted, through the careful selection of his addressees, to re-create imaginatively a significant part of that larger society in which he lived. His early poems show no such scope or intention. They are more private verses, often addressed to figures who are in some sense or another marginalized: living out of fashion, out of favour, outside the established Church, outside of the metropolis. They are the work of a writer who is still himself living at the very edges of his society, conscious of his vulnerability and his own status as a partial outsider. It is significant that even the most accomplished of Jonson's early poems, the 'Epistle to Elizabeth, Countess of Rutland' (presented to the Countess on New Year's Day, 1600, and later published as *The Forest*, 12), should begin with a long and intricate sentence, winding over nineteen lines, elaborating his prime disqualification for place or presence at court: his total lack of the commodity which draws all others to this location: 'almighty gold'. 'I, that have none to send you, send you verse.' Confidence and insecurity here are curiously mixed. Jonson was quite literally without resources at this moment: later in the same month, he was to be prosecuted for debt in Westminster Hall, and incarcerated at Marshalsea prison, where he had previously spent time after the *Isle of Dogs* affair.[2] But he was not without ambition. The challenge is that of one who has nothing but his genius to declare: of the gifted pretender, standing sceptically, critically, at the threshold, scorning the court, but waiting none the less his chance to get in.

Jonson's earliest datable poem is addressed to a staunch fellow-Catholic with whom he probably became acquainted soon after his release from Newgate in the autumn of 1598: Thomas Palmer, former Principal of Gloucester Hall and Fellow of St John's College, Oxford, now living 'in old and decrepit age' in Exeter.[3] Some time that year Palmer had begun to compile a manuscript book of botanical emblems entitled *The Sprite of Trees and Herbs,* which he intended to present to Elizabeth's Lord Treasurer, William Burghley. Burghley however had died in August of 1598 while the book was still in preparation, and *The Sprite of Trees and Herbs* was presented instead to Burghley's son, Robert Cecil, on 1 January 1599. Jonson may perhaps have thought it prudent at this moment to restore good relations with Cecil, who had been one of his interrogators during *The Isle of Dogs* episode a year or so earlier. But his tributary poem, placed at the head of Palmer's manuscript collection, shows a deeper interest also in the condition and cultural codes of Catholic life, with which he was now becoming closely acquainted. Emblems were sometimes used in this period by Catholics in order to convey truths which for one reason or another could not be openly spoken. Jonson was to maintain a lively interest in this art throughout his later life. In 1619 William Drummond wrote to Jonson detailing at some length the coded and ambiguous emblems that Mary Queen of Scots had devised during her long period of imprisonment in Scotland and England to convey rallying messages to the Duke of Norfolk and other supporters.[4] It was through the work of Thomas Palmer, the first major emblematist in England, that Jonson first became sharply aware of the strategic uses of emblematic art, and perhaps, in a more general sense, of the veiled and indirect forms of utterance associated with the day-to-day pressures of Catholic life.[5]

Jonson chose always to present himself as a forthright man, and in modern times has been praised as an exponent of 'the plain style'. T. S. Eliot went so far as to characterize Jonson's poetry as being 'of the surface'—while adding at once that such poetry 'cannot be understood without study'.[6] Jonson is often indeed a lucid and direct writer, though he was also at times obliged—never more pressingly than in his early years as a Catholic—to adopt another form of writing, that proceeded by hints, obliquities, gaps, suppressions, and poised ambiguities. His poem of praise to Thomas Palmer is an early example of this style, speaking darkly as it does of the 'travails' the learned Catholic had suffered seemingly on account of his faith, then climaxing curiously in a rapturous run of asterisks, as—'giddy with amazement' at the qualities of Palmer's work—the poet falls 'down | In a deep trance; ***** | *****' and has no more to say. For reasons never explained—the inadequacy of the poet? the nature of the emblems? the private allegiances of their maker?—the central subject of this poem remains finally unutterable, issuing merely in a set of typographical markers.[7]

Similarly guarded in style, similarly indicative of his own shifting allegiances in these difficult early years, is Jonson's Ode to James Fitzgerald, fifteenth Earl of Desmond, written shortly before Fitzgerald's release from the Tower of London in October 1600. James Fitzgerald's father, Gerald fitz James Fitzgerald, 'the rebel Earl' (c.1533–1583), had been a notoriously troublesome figure in Ireland who, like his son, had suffered lengthy periods of incarceration in Dublin Castle and the Tower of London after feuding bitterly over many years with his traditional family rival Thomas Butler, tenth Earl of Ormond. Proclaimed a traitor by Elizabeth in 1574 and subjected to attainder in 1582, Fitzgerald was finally captured and beheaded by Ormond's men, acting on English instructions, on the borders of Kerry and Cork in 1583. Though his personal religious beliefs remained unclear, Gerald Fitzgerald had been commonly regarded in Rome and Spain and by Jesuits and recusants in England as a potential leader of the Catholic cause in Ireland. His son James Fitzgerald (c.1570–1601), to whom Jonson's Ode is addressed, had been imprisoned initially as a surety for his father's good behaviour, but was also seen as a possible flashpoint for Catholic revolt. He was finally released from the Tower at the initiative of the Earl of Essex, acting in his capacity as Lord Lieutenant of Ireland, and restored to the family title, granted a pension of £500 p.a., and dispatched to Munster in the hope that he would help pacify the region. His mission was a complete failure. Arriving to an enthusiastic welcome in Kilmallock, county Limerick, he immediately alienated the predominantly Catholic population by attending services of the Protestant Church of Ireland, thus surrendering whatever power he might otherwise have had as a negotiator between the local Geraldines and the opposing forces of fitz Thomas and of Hugh O'Neill, Earl of Tyrone. In March 1601 Desmond returned, a disappointed man, to England, and eight months later, at the age of 31, was dead.

Jonson's Ode must have been written some time between Essex's initial proposal in October 1599 that Fitzgerald be released from the Tower, and the Queen's agreement to that request on 1 October 1600: an event which the poem, in its cautious, admonitory fashion, hopefully foresees:

> But to yourself, most loyal lord,
>   (Whose heart in that bright sphere flames clearest,
> Though many gems be in your bosom stored,
>   Unknown which is dearest)
>   If I auspiciously divine,
> As my hope tells, that our fair Phoebe's shine
>   Shall light those places
>   With lustrous graces,
> Where darkness with her gloomy-sceptred hand
>   Doth now command;
> Oh, then, my best-best loved, let me importune,
>   That you will stand
> As far from all revolt, as you are now from fortune.
>   (*The Underwood*, 25.53–65)

Jonson could scarcely have addressed Fitzgerald in such intimate terms (as 'my best-best loved') had not the two men already developed a close personal relationship, nor could he have spoken so confidently of the Queen's ('fair Phoebe's') intentions without a reliable source of information from the highest levels at court. These circumstances point yet again to the probability of Jonson's continuing contact with the circle surrounding the Earl of Essex, which included at this time many expectant Catholic followers, such as Sir Christopher Blount, Sir John Davies, Sir Charles Danvers, John Littleton, Sir William Parker, Charles and Josceline Percy, and priests such as Father Thomas Wright, who had come under Essex's protection.[8] Jonson might have become acquainted with Fitzgerald through Father Wright, a regular prison visitor, or through Sir John Salusbury, a Catholic follower of Essex living in Denbighshire, Wales, with whom Jonson seems to have developed a close relationship at this time, and amongst whose papers the poet's autograph copy of the Desmond Ode is to be found.

If the Desmond Ode suggests Jonson's continuing closeness at this time to the Essex circle, it also more clearly reveals a growing caution on Jonson's part about Essex's own political ambitions, and his chances of ultimate success. The poem's plea to Fitzgerald 'That you will stand | As far from all revolt, as you are now from fortune' points to Essex's current difficulties and the possibility of further troubles to come. Throughout 1599 tension between Essex and Elizabeth had mounted over the Irish campaign and Essex's repeated failure to crush the Earl of Tyrone's forces. Exhausted by illness and exasperated by his Queen's insistent dispatches from England, Essex finally left Ireland in late September intent on a personal confrontation with Elizabeth. On the morning of 28 September he burst impetuously into the Queen's private chamber at Nonsuch Palace to remonstrate with Elizabeth as she was still dressing, but after prolonged discussions throughout the day found himself a prisoner at York House. So applicable to Essex himself is the poem's timely warning to stand 'far from all revolt' that one scholar has even wondered whether the Ode in its earliest state was not addressed to Essex rather than to Desmond.[9] While this is not a necessary or likely conclusion, it is characteristic of Jonson's carefully ambiguous style at this time that so many of the poem's references—to honour, misfortune, endurance, noblesse, detention—might apply with equal aptness to Essex as to Desmond. Essex, himself a master of Delphic utterance, would have known in how many ways a poem such as this might be read.[10]

Jonson's considerable powers as a poet show in flashes in these early poems, but were not to develop fully until the first decade of James's reign. By 1616, more securely established in his career as court poet and returned to the bosom of the Anglican Church, Jonson would choose, significantly, to exclude such poems as the Desmond Ode and the verses to Palmer and other Catholic acquaintances from his major poetic collections, *Epigrams* and *The Forest*. Though the Desmond Ode was clearly in circulation in manuscript during the early years of the new century—its lines are parodied by Thomas Dekker in the second scene of *Satiromastix* in 1601—the poem did not find its way into print until after Jonson's death, appearing as the twenty-fifth poem of *The Underwood* in the 1641 Folio, where it is tactfully described as a poem 'Writ in Queen Elizabeth's Time, Since Lost, and Recovered'. More than once throughout his long career Jonson found it convenient to 'lose' certain of his own texts in this way, either through an act of deliberate destruction or by a prudent setting-aside. Not everything that he wished to say as a poet could be said directly, and even his more oblique and guarded utterances were not always suitable for widespread distribution. As a writer ambitious for advancement, he picked his way forward with special care.

§§

The comparatively slow emergence of Jonson's poetic powers is particularly evident when contrasted with the prodigious early achievement of John Donne. Donne and Jonson were exact contemporaries, both born in 1572. By the early years of the new century they were already close friends. It is likely they met at some stage during the 1590s through the intellectual networks associated with the Earl of Essex, or through the Catholic community in London, with whom Donne, who had now abandoned the religion of his birth, still retained significant links, and with whom Jonson, whose recent conversion had taken him in a contrary direction, was becoming increasingly acquainted. Jonson evidently read Donne's startling new poems with full attention as they emerged through the 1590s. 'He esteemeth John Donne the first poet in the world in some things,' noted William Drummond of Jonson in 1618–19,

His verses of the lost chain he hath by heart; and that passage of 'The Calm', that dust and feathers do not stir, all was so quiet. Affirmeth Donne to have written all his best pieces ere he was twenty-five year old. (*Informations*, 80–3)

None of Jonson's own poems written before (or even during) his twenty-fifth year has survived, but it was in this period of early manhood, in Jonson's view, that Donne had produced his most remarkable work. Donne's elegy 'The Bracelet' ('the lost chain', as Drummond calls it here) was probably written around 1593, when Donne was about 21. 'The Calm', with its companion piece 'The Storm', was written in 1597, as Donne—who turned 25 in that year—travelled with forces under the joint command of the Earl of Essex, Lord Howard of Effingham, and Sir Walter Ralegh on their impetuous expedition to the Azores.[11] These poems of Donne's from the 1590s Jonson had committed to memory and was able to recite admiringly in Scotland more than twenty years later. His strong residual admiration for Donne— 'Whose every work of thy most early wit | Came forth example, and remains so yet' (*Epigrams*, 23.3–4)—is always evident, even as he grumbles from time to time to Drummond about the obscurity or excesses or metrical irregularity of his friend's verses.[12]

One group of Donne's verse writings in particular evidently made a deep impression on Jonson during the 1590s. These were Donne's *Satires*: 'Rare poems', as Jonson later called them, when presenting a manuscript collection of these verses to Lucy, Countess of Bedford—Donne's (and his own) patroness—in an act of friendly intercession (*Epigrams*, 94.6). There were other verse satirists whose work might well have engaged Jonson's attention to a greater or lesser degree during the last years of Elizabeth's reign: Joseph Hall, John Marston, William Rankins, John Weever, Everard Guilpin, to name just a few. Yet none of these writers could match John Donne in wit, verve, and colloquial directness, in the astonishing simulation of a voice that could be by turns sardonic, exasperated, amused, passionately argumentative:

> Kind pity chokes my spleen; brave scorn forbids
> Those tears to issue which swell my eyelids,
> I must not laugh, nor weep sins, and be wise,
> Can railing then cure these worn maladies?
> Is not our mistress fair religion
> As worthy of our soul's devotion,
> As virtue was to the first blinded age?
> (Satire 3, 1–7)[13]

Jonson must at some stage have wondered whether this style of writing, so often casually described in modern times as 'dramatic', could not in a literal sense be transferred to the stage. Might not the satirical targets that Donne had so deftly attacked—the tedious companion, the foppish traveller, the spruce courtier, the absurd rituals of court attendance, the colossal expenditures on fashionable dress—be vividly paraded and wittily exposed within the theatre? Might not comedy itself be seen as a legitimate outgrowth of ancient satire? The *comical satires* that Jonson was soon to produce—the term itself was his own—are recognizably Donneian both in tone and subject matter. Whole scenes in the third act of Jonson's *Poetaster* (1601) involving the tenacious bore Crispinus, for example, are virtually lifted from Donne's first and fourth *Satires*, which are themselves modelled on a well-known Satire (1.9) of the Roman poet Horace. Many small touches in *Every Man Out of His Humour*—Jonson's next theatrical venture, performed by the Lord Chamberlain's Men late in 1599—have a similar Donne-like bravura: the comically recurring scenes involving the impoverished legal student Fungoso (for example) ardently following the fashion 'afar off, like a spy', yet never quite catching its latest extravagant turns.

The stance of the satirist, railing at the excesses of fashionable society and the venality of a court which he simultaneously hoped to enter, might well have been congenial to Jonson at this particular moment in this career, though it is risky, as ever, to assume too exact a correspondence between Jonson's personal disposition and the forthright views expressed by the satirical spokesmen of his plays. There were in any case other, more strictly professional, reasons why Jonson in the late 1590s might have wished to initiate this new species of comic writing, which cast its fierce beam on the foibles and follies of contemporary society, and stood at such obvious variance with the vein of gentle romantic comedy that Lyly and Shakespeare had made so popular throughout the decade. Jonson's satirical comedy challenged the basic terms and territory upon which comedy in England, up until this moment, had been played out.[14] The ringside conversations that occur between Mitis and Cordatus as they observe the action of *Every Man Out of His Humour* stress the novelty of the enterprise, and also, paradoxically, its thoroughly traditional nature. They assert and defend the dramatist's 'liberty' (his *licentia* or 'free power') to plunder various elements from wherever he wishes: from old English drama, from the festive traditions of Inns of Court revelry, from the ancient comedy of Aristophanes, and from what is boldly said to be the true origin of all comic action, ancient satire: for 'that which we call *comoedia*', remarks Cordatus, 'was at first nothing but a simple and continued satire, sung by one only person' (Induction, 246–8). Authentic comedy, in short—so Jonson's own advocates insist from the sidelines—has its origins not in romance but in ancient satire. What the audience is now watching is the real thing. Jonson's persistent strategy from this point forward in his career would be to depict his kind of comedy—through choruses and prologues and epilogues and other meta-theatrical devices—as normative, and the conventions of Shakespearian comedy as risibly deviant; contrary both to common sense and to the most ancient traditions of the theatre.

Jonson's comical satire threw down a remarkable challenge not just to his theatrical rivals, however, but also—with far greater bravery—to civil and ecclesiastical authority as well. For satire was a form of writing that Elizabeth's official censors of published works, the bishops of Canterbury and London, had chosen just a few months earlier to declare illegal. In a severe and apparently far-reaching edict of 1 June 1599, Bishops Whitgift and Bancroft, troubled by the subversive and unsettling nature of many recent publications in London, had firmly decreed 'that no satires or epigrams be printed hereafter', and ordered the immediate destruction of satirical writings by Thomas Nashe, John Marston, Joseph Hall, and others. For Jonson flagrantly to have prepared for performance just a few months later a drama announcing itself to be a 'comical satire' was an act of some audacity—especially when it is remembered that he had been imprisoned just a couple of years earlier for collaborating with Nashe in the composition of a satirical drama that had caused supreme offence, and that he had only recently been released once more from a prison where he had been held on another grave charge that might equally have cost him his life. The late Elizabethan move to comical satire is sometimes explained as an ingenious manoeuvre by writers to circumvent the 1599 ban, which had spoken of printed satire, but said nothing about performance. Yet Jonson's initiation of the genre was a more confrontational act than such an explanation suggests. It directly challenged the letter as well as the spirit of the ban. Within a few months of the play's first performance, a quarto edition of *Every Man Out of His Humour* would be published by William Holme with the defiant words *comical satire* provocatively displayed across its title page.[15]

Yet the new play was designed first and foremost not for publication but for performance: to exploit the resources of a brand new theatrical venue on the Bankside that was already exciting the playgoers of London, and proving a superlative arena for the work of Jonson's greatest theatrical rival.

§§

During the final weeks of 1598, the members of Shakespeare's company, the Lord Chamberlain's Men, had been facing a serious professional crisis. The lease of their usual home in Shoreditch, the Theatre, the oldest playhouse in London, had expired at the end of the previous year. Throughout 1598 they had been forced to perform in other venues, such as the nearby Curtain theatre—where *Every Man In His Humour* itself had been performed—as they waited for their new indoor playhouse in Blackfriars, in which James Burbage had heavily invested, to be completed. But problems had arisen with the Blackfriars site. Influential residents in the neighbourhood had objected to the noise and disruption they imagined the new playhouse would cause, and work on the building had come to a halt. Meanwhile the landlord of the Theatre, Giles Allen, was threatening to dismantle their former playhouse, and to appropriate the materials from which the building had originally been constructed by James Burbage in 1576. In the last days of December 1598, with Giles Allen away in Essex, members of the company took the law into their own hands, and began to demolish the Theatre themselves. Carefully numbering the individual timbers, they carted them across the city to storage on the north bank of the Thames.

Early in 1599, under the supervision of master-carpenter Peter Street, work began on the erection of a new playhouse for the Chamberlain's Men on a newly acquired site on the south bank of the Thames. The timbers from the old playhouse were ferried across the river and used in the construction of an amphitheatre that was circular in appearance but probably in fact polyangular (as the bending of timber was not an Elizabethan skill), having perhaps as many as twenty-four sides. The new playhouse had a diameter of about 100 feet, thatched galleries, exterior staircases, two narrow entry doors, and a large rectangular thrust stage, and may have accommodated as many as 3,000 spectators.[16] It was known as the Globe. The name had reference not only to the shape of the building, but to the familiar belief that the world itself might be regarded as a theatre, and the theatre in turn regarded as a microcosm of the world. 'I have considered our whole life is like a play,' Jonson was later to write in his commonplace book, *Discoveries* (784–5), 'wherein every man, forgetful of himself, is in travail with another.' Jonson was drawing here on the best-known medieval authority for this ancient belief, John of Salisbury's *Policratus*, the probable source also of the famous tag thought to have served as the motto of the Globe playhouse, *Totus mundus agit histrionem* ('the whole world plays the actor') which may have been displayed, perhaps on a standard, at the theatre, along with 'a figure of Hercules supporting the Globe'. Jaques' well-known speech 'All the world's a stage', in *As You Like It* (2.7.140), has often been seen as a self-conscious reference to this motto of the new playhouse where Shakespeare's comedy is thought to have been performed, not long after the staging of *Every Man Out of His Humour*.[17]

In his first work for the Globe theatre, Jonson chose to exploit the full physical resources of this new venue through a novel style of dramatic construction, presenting the action of *Every Man Out of His Humour* through

Fig. 17. The first Globe theatre, as depicted by Amsterdam engraver Claes Jansz Visscher in his *View of London* in 1616. As Visscher's drawing reveals, the Globe was polyangular, rather than strictly circular, in structure.

sixteen successive scenes which establish (as one critic has put it) a series of 'long swelling movements' in 'a rhythm that would be obvious to an audience or reader right from the beginning' of the play. In the play's central act, six successive scenes are set in St Paul's Walk, the central aisle of the largest building in London, which served at the time as a popular social meeting place. Jonson skilfully exploits the spatial axes of the new Globe theatre to depict this vast cathedral, which (it is subtly implied) serves as a microcosm of the city as a whole.[18] Like Shakespeare in *As You Like It*, Jonson seems also to have played self-consciously on the name of the new theatre. *Every Man Out of His Humour* satirizes the follies and misdemeanours of what is called repeatedly, in an apparently deliberate gesture of universal inclusiveness, *the world*. 'The world' is variously characterized—by Asper, the play's 'free spirit', bent on 'controlling the world's abuses', and by his alter ego Macilente and the snarling cynic Carlo Buffone—as 'impious', 'reeling', 'iron': as deeply corrupted by sin and folly (Induction, 2–4, 2.1.376, 2.2.165). 'The world' is all that the Globe theatre contains, symbolizes, and presents, including the very audience itself—the 'thronged round' of play-goers (Induction, 49)—who, in this circular auditorium, surround and observe the action of the play.

These expressions of what might be termed, in a double sense, *global satire*—satire designed for performance at the Globe theatre; satire that denounces, without exception, all quadrants and sectors of society—do not pass unchallenged in Jonson's play. Though Asper's fearless character may seem at moments to match Jonson's own—Asper is 'one whom no servile hope of gain or frosty apprehension of danger can make to be a parasite either to time, place, or opinion'[19]—he is also depicted as a raving, wide-eyed, moralizing fanatic, with little understanding of the world he so radically condemns. 'Unless your breath had power | To melt the world and mould it again', as the moderating figure of Cordatus coolly reminds him (Induction, 46–7), the world will remain very much as it is.

Yet this swingeing, universalizing style of satire was to draw the amused attention of Jonson's contemporaries, and to be associated closely with Jonson's own attitude to the society in which he lived. Thomas Dekker in 1601 responded ironically to Jonson's new mode of writing when he dedicated his own comedy *Satiromastix*, also performed at the Globe theatre, 'To the World'. Through the character of Jaques in *As You Like It*, Shakespeare

Fig. 18. Paul's Walk, the middle aisle of St Paul's Cathedral, was a fashionable meeting place in Jonson's day, and the setting for a central scene in *Every Man Out of his Humour* (3.1), performed at the Globe theatre in 1599. John Earle in his *Microcosmography* (1628) was punningly to describe it as 'the land's epitome, or as you may call it, the lesser Isle of Great Britain. It is more than this, the whole world's map, which you may here discern in its perfectest motion, jostling and turning... The noise in it is like that of bees, a strange humming or buzz, mixed of walking, tongues, and feet: it is a kind of still roar or loud whisper. It is the great Exchange of all discourse, and no business whatsoever but is here stirring and afoot.' This engraving of the Walk by Wenceslas Hollar is from William Dugdale's *The History of St Paul's Cathedral*, 1658.

appears also to glance humorously at the more extreme rhetoric of moral denunciation that Jonson's comical satire had brought into fashion.

> *Jaques*   Give me leave
> To speak my mind, and I will through and through
> Cleanse the foul body of th'infected world…
>   (*As You Like It*, 2.7.58–60)

Jaques' lavish denunciation of 'th'infected world' seems to mock Asper's similar impatience with 'the impious world', and his extravagant language of moral reform:

> *Asper*   Tax me freely.
> Let envious critics with the broadest eyes
> Look through and through me. I pursue no favour.
>   (*Every Man Out of His Humour*, Induction, 59–61)

Tax and *taxing* are favoured words also of Jaques (2.7.71, 2.7.85–7), whose *through and through* cleansing of the world's illnesses mirrors the very idiom of Asper. Duke Senior's response casts a passing rebuke not only at Jaques but also (it would seem) at the new genre of comical satire, from which Shakespeare quite deliberately marks his distance:[20]

> Most mischievous foul sin in chiding sin,
> For thou thyself hast been a libertine,
> As sensual as the brutish sting itself,
> And all th'embossed sores and headed evils
> That thou with licence of free foot hast caught
> Wouldst thou disgorge into the general world.
>   (*As You Like It*, 2.7.64–9)

In the small and intensely competitive arena of late Elizabethan theatre Jonson and Shakespeare were clearly observing each other's practice with a sharp eye, as these exchanges testify. Jonson peppers his play with sly and not always respectful references to the work of his great rival. ' "Reason long since is fled to animals", you know,' remarks the foppish character Clove with due solemnity to his equally foolish companion, Orange, in *Every Man Out of His Humour* (3.1.150–1), comically echoing Antony's words in *Julius Caesar*, played at the Globe theatre just a few months earlier: 'O judgement, thou are fled to brutish beasts, | And men have lost their reason' (3.2.106–7). 'Et tu

Brute,' murmurs Carlo Buffone bathetically near the end of *Every Man Out* to Macilente, who moves in with his companions to seal up Carlo's lips with hot wax: recalling Caesar's famous words as he succumbs to the last of the assassins' knives (*Julius Caesar*, 3.1.77). 'Beg a plaudit for God's sake', says Macilente pleadingly to the audience at the end of the play, 'But, if you, out of the bounty of your good liking, will bestow it, why, you may, in time, make lean Macilente as fat as Sir John Falstaff.' Not all of these passing quips need be seen as unfriendly; the last indeed frankly acknowledges the great popular success of Shakespeare's *Henry IV*. Since the early eighteenth century, however, they have often been taken as evidence of a supposed quarrel between Shakespeare and Jonson that erupted around this time, and continued (in some Victorian elaborations of this narrative) more or less unabated until Shakespeare's eventual retirement from the stage a decade or so later.[21]

One passage in particular in *Every Man Out of His Humour* has often been read as a hostile gibe by Jonson at Shakespeare's social ambitions. In the third act of the play the character Sogliardo, a man 'so enamoured of the name of gentleman that he will have it though he buys it', reports on the coat of arms he has just purchased for himself for the sum of £30. In designing the arms the herald has depicted a boar without a head, rampant, along with 'a hog's cheek and puddings in a pewter field'. Invited to admire the design, the pompous knight Puntarvolo ironically remarks, 'Let the word be *Not without mustard*. Your crest is very rare sir' (3.1.193). The phrase which Puntarvolo suggests might adorn Sogliardo's new insignia, 'Not without mustard', is the punch-line in a well-known anecdote that is related in Thomas Nashe's novel *Pierce Penniless*. A 'mad ruffian' is caught one day in a storm that threatens to destroy the ship on which he is travelling. When his companions drop to their knees and swear to amend their ways if delivered from this impending disaster, he follows suit, assuring the Almighty that he will never again eat haberdine (or salt cod) if he is safely delivered from the tempest. When the weather clears, he adds a small rider: '"Not without mustard, good Lord, not without mustard"—as though it had been the greatest torment in the world to have eaten haberdine without mustard.'[22] Puntarvolo's recitation of this phrase in *Every Man Out of His Humour* is the feeblest of witticisms, triggered merely by the word *without*. The upstart Sogliardo, being 'without brain, wit, anything, indeed, ramping to gentility', has been aptly represented by the herald in the shape of a boar without a head: hence his motto, Puntarvolo facetiously adds, might appropriately be 'Not without mustard'.

The remark nevertheless has commonly been seen as a satirical reference by Jonson to the Shakespeare family's acquisition in 1596 from Sir William Dethick, Garter King of Arms, of a patent for a coat of arms bearing the motto NON SANZ DROICT: *not without right*. The motto was evidently intended to assert beyond all question the family's right to bear arms, though surviving drafts reveal that the clerk originally wrote, with unfortunate ambiguity, 'non, sanz droit', then 'Non, Sanz Droit' before hitting on the more confidently capitalized and unpunctuated version of the phrase. There is in fact no evidence, however, that Shakespeare or any member of his family ever used this motto, which does not appear on the Stratford monument or on the gravestone of Shakespeare's daughter Susannah.[23] If Puntarvolo's line was intended as a joke at Shakespeare's expense, it was a joke that would hardly have meant much to an audience at the Globe. Nor is it at all clear that the line was actually aimed at Shakespeare. The *not without...* formula of the motto is entirely commonplace, being regularly found in courtly and heraldic contexts. In Jonson's next play, *Cynthia's Revels*, the semi-allegorical figure of Eucolos (known for 'duly respecting others') is formally described in a similar phrase—'not without respect, but yet without difficulty'—as he is ushered into the presence of the queenly Cynthia, who adopts similar periphrases in her own regal pronouncements ('Not without wonder, nor without delight...', etc., 5.4.34, 5.3.1, 5.4.34). *Non sine sole* ('Not without glory') is the motto inscribed on the famous Rainbow portrait of Elizabeth I in 1600 (see Plate 6). 'Not without mustard' is an amused echo of such familiar courtly phrases, which need not have any further and more specific satirical intent.

The last years of Elizabeth's reign and the early years of James's succession saw an astonishing increase in the granting of arms to claimants such as John and William Shakespeare, anxious for social advancement. Between 1560 and 1589 the College of Arms issued 2,320 new grants of arms, and 1,760 further grants were made between 1590 and 1639. Such figures in part reflect abuses within the College itself, as unscrupulous heralds found ways to accommodate the new appetite for arms, and to secure for themselves a steady source of additional revenue. It was precisely the existence of such flagrant malpractices within the College of Arms that led to the appointment in October 1597 of Jonson's former mentor, William Camden—a man lacking formal training in heraldry, but renowned for his learning and integrity—as Clarenceux Herald of Arms. Working under the watchful eye of the Cecils, father and son, Camden strove to fulfil his formidably difficult brief: to curb irregularities within a famously quarrelsome and ill-disciplined institution, to bring the College more firmly under royal authority, and to transform the basic role of the College in response to the profound and rapid changes that were then reshaping English society. In the first of these missions he gained dubious help from his cantankerous colleague Ralph Brooke, York Herald of Arms, who in the early years of the new century began methodically to investigate the recent activities of his fellow-herald Sir William Dethick, whom he accused of granting armigerous status to twenty-three undeserving recipients. High in Brooke's list of 'mean persons' who had improperly been granted arms by Dethick was 'Shakespeare the player', whose coat of arms in any case, Dethick alleged, too closely resembled that of Lord Mauley. Dethick—an even more violent and foul-tempered man than his adversary—responded vigorously, and with Camden's support and assistance successfully defended the granting of arms to Shakespeare, and the design in question.[24]

Camden, who was to suffer a lifetime's slow torture from Brooke (a dogged and pedantic critic of Camden's own great work, *Britannia*), must have

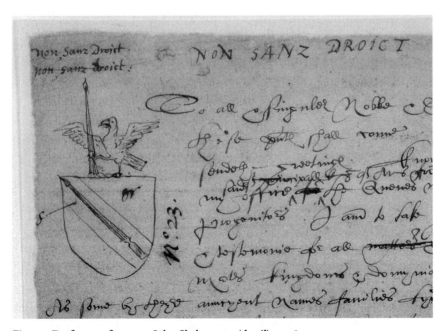

Fig. 19. Draft coat of arms to John Shakespeare (detail), 1596.

observed the exchanges between Dethick and Brooke with sharply divided feelings.[25] So too would Jonson himself, who, like Camden, was acutely aware of abuses in the current granting of arms, yet conscious also of the need to reform the dubious system of inherited honours attaching to the old nobility which the College of Arms had long sustained. Throughout his plays and poems Jonson continued to satirize undeserving recipients of arms, like Sogliardo in *Every Man Out of His Humour*, and Mongrel Esquire of *Epigrams*, 48, who purchases himself a coat of arms to brandish proudly in combat, only to fling it away at the first taste of battle in order to speed his departure from the field:

> His bought arms Mong not liked; for his first day
> Of bearing them in field, he threw 'em away;
> And hath no honour lost, our duellists say.

Equally undeserving in Jonson's eyes, however, were those complacent members of the aristocracy who failed to uphold the traditions for which their ancestors had originally received their arms and titles. Such are the 'tempestuous grandlings' in 'A Speech According to Horace', who indolently devolve their military and political obligations to those of lower standing:

> Let poor nobility be virtuous; we,
>   Descended in a rope of titles, be
> From Guy, or Bevis, Arthur, or from whom
>   The herald will. Our blood is now become
> Past any need of virtue. Let them care
>   That in the cradle of their gentry are,
> To serve the state by counsels and by arms;
>   We neither love the troubles nor the harms.
>   (*The Underwood*, 44.79–86)

It has sometimes been assumed that Jonson's own social situation would have placed him beyond any hope of acquiring arms in his own right. Jonson, writes one recent critic,

as the stepson of a bricklayer and, from October 1598, a branded and convicted felon was well aware that he had no chance whatsoever of being granted armigerous status. Even his schoolmaster and friend William Camden, Clarencieux King of Arms from 1594, could not fix this for him. Jonson decided, instead, to develop for all it was worth his 'rare' status, as a creative genius who was also an exceptional scholar.[26]

Plausible though this assumption might seem—how indeed, one might ask, could a man with such crippling social disabilities as Jonson ever hope to acquire arms?—it does not correspond with the known facts. For, astonishingly, Jonson did somehow manage to acquire armigerous status during the early years of the new century. When he and his wife Anne were brought before the London Consistory Courts to answer charges of recusancy in January 1606, the indictment records of the Court clearly declare his status to be that of 'Armiger', one entitled to bear heraldic arms.[27] Precisely how and when Jonson was granted this status is unknown, but it is reasonable to suppose that Camden, who had been in office as Clarenceux Herald at Arms since 1597 (not 1594), might have offered his assistance. Talking with William Drummond in Scotland about heraldry many years later, Jonson described his own arms in a little detail, as we have already seen (Ch. 3 above).[28] Jonson also told William Drummond that he possessed a personal *impresa*: 'a compass with one foot in centre, the other broken; the word, *deest quod duceret orbem*' (*Informations*, 457–8): 'that which might draw the circle (*or that which might guide the world*) is missing': a powerful visual and verbal reminder of the necessary imperfections of a fallen world.[29]

For a bricklayer to have acquired a coat of arms was not altogether unknown in this period: William Middleton, for example—father of the dramatist Thomas Middleton, and a reasonably well-to-do member of the Tylers' and Bricklayers' Company—had been granted a coat of arms as early as 1568. But the potential incongruity of such honours was clearly evident to contemporary observers. In a cancelled passage in *The Arte of English Poesie* of 1589—which survives uniquely in Jonson's personal copy of the book, now in the Grenville collection at the British Library—George Puttenham remarked on the inappropriateness of a bricklayer taking for his personal *impresa* the device of Attila the Hun with its martial motto, *ferro et flamma*, 'with sword and fire'.[30] The uncertainties of armigerous status and complexity of heraldic language were a topic of comic mirth for Jonson—'some harrot of arms; he shall give us a gudgeon', declares Juniper in *The Case Is Altered*, 4.7.150–1—as they were for Shakespeare in *Merry Wives of Windsor*, where Slender proudly boasts of his uncle, Justice Shallow, 'who writes himself Armigero in any bill, warrant, quittance, or obligation—Armigero' (1.1.7–8). Such jokes are indicative of deeper uncertainties of the day that impinged directly on the personal lives and social ambitions of both dramatists.

It is hard therefore to maintain the picture of Jonson as plebeian underdog, barking at Shakespeare, the pretender to gentility. Both Shakespeare and Jonson in their different ways had legitimate aspirations to social advancement; both were, in Jonson's resonant phrase, 'in the cradle of their gentry'; both used their creative talents to move ambitiously upwards through society. Jonson is unlikely to have satirized Shakespeare for acquiring a grant of arms which Camden would soon be required to defend, especially at a time when Jonson himself was preparing to bid for arms.[31] Jonson's own social ascent was to prove even more spectacular than Shakespeare's, starting as it did from a position of such seemingly impossible disadvantage, moving so swiftly to the highest levels of acceptance, recovering so acrobatically from seemingly fatal falls.

§§

As the old century gave way to the new, Ben Jonson—the bricklayer's stepson, the Catholic convert, the branded and convicted felon, the vexatious writer of forbidden satire—began, against all odds, to prepare his approaches to the privileged world of Elizabeth's court. Jonson made his first and not wholly successful signal for royal attention in the concluding scene of *Every Man Out of His Humour*, in which the envious satirist Macilente, observing the figure of the Queen (played by a boy actor) passing over the stage, instantly falls to the ground, 'dumb and astonished'. Miraculously purged of his humour by the mere sight of the impersonated monarch, Macilente declares himself now ready to praise the virtues of the late Elizabethan state. 'Why, here's a change!' he adds, in some surprise at his own volte face. The moment might be seen as a hinge not just in the movement of the play— clumsily anticipating the subtler transformations of Jonson's Jacobean court masques—but also in Jonson's own career, as his creative attention swings abruptly from satirical denunciation to courtly panegyric. The scene was not well received in early performances of the play at the Globe, however, when, as Jonson later frankly confessed, 'many seemed not to relish it', though it was played without objection at court in the Christmas season of 1599, where the Queen herself, rather than an actor, served as the object of adoration. Some point of decorum had evidently been breached in the original version of the scene, which Jonson revised for subsequent publication of the play in quarto in 1600, and once more for its publication in his First Folio in 1616.[32]

In his next play, *The Fountain of Self-Love, or, Cynthia's Revels*, performed 'by the then Children of Queen Elizabeth's Chapel' at Blackfriars theatre some time between 2 September 1600 and May 1601, and (probably) on 6 January 1601 at court, Jonson made his second and even bolder approach to the ageing, childless, and increasingly wilful Queen, with whose personal vanities and eccentricities he was already familiar. 'Queen Elizabeth never saw herself after she became old in a true glass,' Jonson reported nearly twenty years later to William Drummond of Hawthornden:

they painted her, and sometimes would vermilion her nose. She had always, about Christmas evens, set dice that threw sixes or five (and she knew not they were other) to make her win and esteem herself fortunate. That she had a *membrana* on her which made her uncapable of man, though for her delight she tried many. (*Informations*, 261–5)[33]

In *Cynthia's Revels* Jonson chose to figure Queen Elizabeth in a more flattering mythological guise as the virgin huntress Cynthia (or Diana), seeking her attention through one of his most beguiling lyrics:

> Queen and huntress, chaste and fair,
> Now the sun is laid to sleep,
> Seated in thy silver chair,
> State in wonted manner keep;
>   Hesperus entreats thy light,
>   Goddess excellently bright.
>
> Earth, let not thy envious shade
> Dare itself to interpose!
> Cynthia's shining orb was made,
> Heaven to clear, when day did close.
>   Bless us then with wishèd sight,
>   Goddess excellently bright.
>
> Lay thy bow of pearl apart,
> And thy crystal-shining quiver;
> Give unto the flying hart
> Space to breathe, how short soever;
>   Thou, that makest a day of night,
>   Goddess excellently bright!

Gracious though the lyric is, its allegorical fiction was flimsily transparent, barely concealing its bold political subtext. In classical mythology, 'the flying hart' for whom the lyric pleads 'Space to breathe, how short soever' was of course the hunter Actaeon, who had glimpsed Cynthia/Diana and her nymphs bathing naked in a fountain near the valley Gargaphia, and as a punishment for this offence had been changed by Cynthia into a stag and torn to pieces by his own hounds. When the play was performed at court in January 1601, the figure of 'Actaeon' could denote only one person: Elizabeth's former favourite Robert Devereux, Earl of Essex, who, just fifteen months earlier, had angrily burst into the Queen's presence at Nonsuch Palace while she was still only partially dressed and in the company of her maids of honour, and since then had been languishing in a state of grave disfavour. Until late August 1600 Essex had been held in detention at York House. He had been formally interrogated by his fellow privy counsellors, and reprimanded for his conduct in Ireland. His former follower and ally Francis Bacon had spoken damagingly against him. His health had deteriorated sharply. In October 1600, in a crucial indication of royal disfavour, Elizabeth denied renewal of his lucrative lease on sweet wines. During the final months of the year Essex had been negotiating desperately with James VI in Scotland, whom he hoped would still succeed Elizabeth on the English throne, and with Charles, Lord Mountjoy, in Ireland; and also in all likelihood with prominent political figures in France.

During January 1601, the very month in which *Cynthia's Revels* is thought to have been performed at court, Essex was beginning to prepare the disastrous coup which was shortly to lead to his rapid downfall.[34] On Tuesday 3 February a group of his most loyal supporters met at Drury House to discuss the possibility of taking a direct delegation to the Queen, and of requesting the arrest and prosecution of Essex's personal enemies on charges of treason and corruption. Rumours in London began nevertheless once more to intensify that Essex entertained more radical designs: that he was in league with Spain, that he was plotting against the Queen's very life, that he intended to seize the crown for himself. On Saturday 7 February Essex received a summons to report immediately to the Lord Treasurer's house to face further questioning. Fearing a plot on his life, he remained behind at Essex House, coolly playing a game of tennis while a group of his followers that included Lord Monteagle, Sir William Constable, Sir Christopher

Blount, Sir Charles Percy, Henry Cuffe, Edward Bushell, and Ellis Jones went off to the Globe theatre, where the Lord Chamberlain's Men, on instructions from Essex's steward, Sir Gelly Meyrick, were performing a play about Richard II—almost certainly, Shakespeare's *Richard II*—whose central theme of royal deposition was suspiciously pertinent to the political situation of the day. The following day, having received further demands to report for questioning, Essex decided to march at once into the City with his followers and seek protection from the Lord Mayor and Aldermen who would be assembling that morning for divine service. He led into the City a group of about 300 men who wore swords but were otherwise peaceably equipped, and arrived around midday at the house of the sheriff of London, Sir Thomas Smythe, whom he believed was sympathetic to his cause. But neither Smythe nor the City offered Essex support, and the gates were firmly closed against his men. Making his way with difficulty back to Essex House, Essex was arrested and taken off later that night to the Tower of London.

On 19 February Essex, along with his friend and supporter the Earl of Southampton, was formally tried for treason at Westminster Hall. Essex was accused of favouring toleration for English Catholics, of being a secret Catholic, and of plotting with England's enemy Spain to seize the crown for himself; and once more faced hostile interrogation from his former ally Francis Bacon. Denying that he had ever intended to cause personal injury to the Queen or to seize the crown, Essex finally confessed under pressure to other charges brought against him, freely incriminating at the same time a number of his most faithful followers. On 25 February 1601, now in a calmer and more dignified state of mind, Essex was summarily executed in the courtyard of the Tower of London.

If played at court (as seems highly probable) on the very eve of these catastrophic events, *Cynthia's Revels* would have looked quite plainly like an appeal to Elizabeth to relax her punitive attitude towards her former favourite. 'Hesperus entreats thy light, | Goddess excellently bright': in classical legend, Hesperus (son of Japetus, brother of Atlas) is said to have ascended Mount Atlas in order to make observations of the stars, but never returned. His name was later given to the planet Venus, when it appears as the evening star. The name Hesperus had already been connected with the Earl of Essex, whom Edmund Spenser had hailed in similar terms (as Jonson would have remembered) as 'Radiant Hesper' in his wedding poem, 'Prothalamion', in 1596.[35] In January 1601 'Hesperus' was still an apt, though distinctly optimistic, designation for Essex, figured here as a star who might still shine in the heavens more fully illuminated by that even more radiant body Cynthia, the moon.

Whether this elaborate fiction was devised by Jonson entirely on his own initiative or (like the performance of *Richard II* that was soon to follow) at the prompting of Essex's followers it is impossible now to say. Either way, the evidence suggests that Jonson was still in close contact and sympathy with Essex and his circle on the eve of the rebellion, and that, like many Catholics at the time, he still retained some dwindling hope of Essex's eventual ascendancy. As a bid for royal leniency towards Essex, however, *Cynthia's Revels* was unfortunately timed, and doomed inevitably to failure. The court performance of the play seems, unsurprisingly, not to have gone down well.[36] As a bid by Jonson himself for personal recognition at court the play was equally unsuccessful. The ambitions of the scholar Criticus in the play ('A creature of a most perfect and divine temper', 2.3.93) to ingratiate himself in court favour might well have appeared to some observers to be uncomfortably close to those of Jonson himself. Criticus is not necessarily or wholly a portrait of Jonson himself: the name happens to be one which he later gave to an interlocutor, modelled on his friend John Donne, in his now-lost commentary on Horace's *Ars Poetica* (*Informations*, 58–60), and the character is in any case quite obviously idealized. Yet this sober-suited 'candle-waster' who 'smells all lamp-oil with studying by candlelight' (3.2.9) sufficiently resembled Jonson himself to attract the mirth and ridicule of his fellow-dramatists in the satirical skirmishes that were shortly to follow, and to dampen his own immediate chances of a favourable reception at court.

§§

Jonson's *Poetaster: or, The Arraignment* was performed at Blackfriars by the Children of Queen Elizabeth's Chapel in the winter of 1601.[37] Set in the Rome of Augustus Caesar, *Poetaster* is marked by the curious blend of high idealization and satirical gloom that had by now become a characteristic feature of Jonson's writing. Its idealistic vision (not unrelated, perhaps, to Jonson's current hopes for a personal welcome at court) focuses on the role of the poet as counsellor and companion to the monarch. In a climactic scene in the play (5.2), Augustus Caesar rises to his feet to acknowledge the entry of Virgil, whom he seats beside him in a more elevated chair, inviting the poet to read aloud from his latest work, the *Aeneid*. Virgil chooses significantly, in a play much concerned with envy and detraction, to read to Augustus a passage from Book 4 of the *Aeneid* describing the progress of *fama*, or false report. The scene eloquently conveys Jonson's view of the ideal relationship of poet and monarch, of tutor and governor: a matter he was to ponder deeply in the years to come. By the late 1620s, drawing on his experience as poet to the Stuart court and on the writings of the Spanish humanist Juan Luis Vives, Jonson could describe the relationship as follows:

Learning needs rest: sovereignty gives it. Sovereignty needs counsel: learning affords it. There is such a consociation of offices between the prince and whom his favour breeds, that they may help to sustain his power, as he their knowledge. (*Discoveries*, 47–50)

A *consociation of offices*—an intimate, symbiotic, and mutually beneficial relationship that might be achieved between poet and monarch—was a matter about which Jonson had some personal, though not always positive, knowledge at this advanced point of his career. In 1601 Jonson had no such experience. He was still in his late twenties, still strongly tainted by his criminal record, by his new-found religion, and by his own ungainly attempts to attract royal favour. To have entertained any thoughts, however indirectly, about a possible role for himself as court poet and adviser under the ageing and wayward Elizabeth seems little short of remarkable, but is testimony to the strength of his ambitions at this early moment of his career.

Yet *Poetaster* not only idealizes the high calling of the supreme poet such as Virgil or Horace; it also exposes and excoriates the would-be poet, the *poetaster*—the *OED* credits Jonson with the first usage of the word, in *Cynthia's Revels* (2.4.15), to denote 'a petty or paltry poet; a writer of poor or trashy verse; a rimester'—as a positive menace to society. In this regard the play can be seen as a kind of Elizabethan forerunner of Pope's *Dunciad*.[38] Demetrius and Crispinus, two struggling pretenders to poetry—thinly disguised caricatures of Jonson's real-life rivals Thomas Dekker and John Marston—are formally arraigned before a court presided over by Augustus Caesar and Virgil and found guilty of maliciously going 'about to deprave and calumniate the person and writings of Quintus Horatius Flaccus here present: poet and priest to the muses' (an idealized portrait of Jonson himself) and of 'taxing him falsely of self-love, arrogancy, impudence, railing, filching by translation, etc.' (5.3.190–1, 194–5). Crispinus is forcibly given an emetic to purge him of his pretensions, and vomits up a number of neologisms found in Marston's works: 'glibbery', 'lubrical', 'snotteries', 'turgidous', 'prorumpted'.

In early performances, the play was evidently known by the title Jonson ultimately chose to use, more prudently, in quarto and folio publications of the play as a less prominent sub-title: *The Arraignment.* 'What's here? *Th'Arraignment?*' says the figure of Envy in the opening moments of the play, reading from a title board probably displayed above the Blackfriars tiring house, and musing aloud on the possible significance of this title. To audiences in 1601, as Tom Cain has persuasively argued, this title is bound inevitably to have suggested one famous recent event: the trial of Essex in February of that year.[39] Essex, like Horace in Jonson's play, had been the object of envy and calumny throughout much of his career. In the months leading to the February rising, his actions and intentions had been widely disparaged through 'libels' and forged writings generally attributed to his enemies Sir Walter Ralegh and Henry Brooke, eighth Lord Cobham. In both the poetic and political spheres (so Jonson's play implies), *fama* or false report has worked as a malign and destructive force. In both spheres—the play might be thought also, more daringly, to hint—the libels have been without foundation: Essex, like Horace, being innocent of the allegations brought against him. The two poetasters who are arraigned in Jonson's play are deservedly punished for their defamatory activities, and Horace's name is ultimately vindicated. Similar disparagements however brought Essex to his untimely death, and have remained unpunished.

Some such innuendo, whether wholly intended or partly imagined, was evidently detected by the authorities after early performances, landing Jonson and the players in immediate trouble. Jonson's later dedication of the folio text of *Poetaster* to his friend Richard Martin of the Middle Temple gratefully acknowledges Martin's role as 'a noble and timely undertaker' on the play's behalf 'to the greatest Justice of this kingdom'. Martin, a high-spirited barrister who regularly played the Prince d'Amour or Lord of Misrule in the Middle Temple's Christmas revels, had recently been elected MP for Barnstaple in Devon, and was soon to attract attention in the House through his courageously outspoken attacks on monopolists, and other abuses of power and privilege. In time he would join the circle of wits and poets that included Jonson, Fulke Greville, Francis Beaumont, John Donne, John Hoskyns, and others that would gather regularly at the Mermaid tavern in Bread Street. The 'greatest Justice of this kingdom' with whom Richard

Martin argued on behalf of Jonson's play was none other than Sir John Popham, the formidably severe judge who had recently presided over Essex's trial. The exchanges between these two adroit and tough-minded lawyers concerning the play's rights to be staged would certainly have been vigorous. Popham—'a huge, heavy, ugly, man', according to Aubrey, with a dubious past of his own, but possessed of exceptional stamina and technical mastery of the law—could hardly have failed to observe that certain episodes in Jonson's play glanced at Popham's own recent role in Essex's trial. The interrogation of the actor Histrio in Act 4 scene 4 of *Poetaster* by the unsavoury magistrate Lupus seems (for example) to recall Popham's own questioning of the actor Augustine Phillips about the performance by the Lord Chamberlain's Men at the Globe on 7 February 1601 of Shakespeare's *Richard II*, at the request of Essex's followers.[40] Both Martin and Popham however were members of the Middle Temple, which in 1601 harboured other former supporters of Essex, Catholic sympathizers, and personal friends of Jonson, and maintained its own lively traditions of free-speaking theatrical performance. In the event, the spirit of tolerance prevailed and Jonson's play was allowed to proceed, though its author had once again sailed perilously close to the wind.

Whether the play represented any kind of victory for Jonson, psychologically or otherwise, is another question. To identify oneself so publicly with a figure accused of 'self-love, arrogancy, impudence, railing, filching by translation' and smelling like a goat is a risky tactic, even if those accusations are shown finally to be largely based on malice. *Poetaster* was soon to receive its humorous comeuppance. While still completing the play Jonson must have been uneasily aware that Dekker was already at work on his skittish counter-attack *Satiromastix*, which was performed (first privately, by the boys of Paul's Company, then publicly at the Globe by the Lord Chamberlain's Men) not long after the first presentation of *Poetaster*. *Satiromastix* teasingly exposes many of Jonson's more obvious authorial pretensions: his ostentatious behaviour in the playhouse—making vile faces in the gallery while his plays are acted, venturing triumphantly onto the stage when they are concluded—his lofty denials of personal animosity, his boasted intimacy with the monarch.

Composed though it is with obvious speed and knockabout glee, *Satiromastix* is one of the genuinely amusing texts in the often rather barren and baffling theatrical exchanges of these years that Dekker himself termed the *poetomachia*, or Poets' War—otherwise known in more recent times as the Stage Quarrel or War of the Theatres.[41] A prolific yet perpetually impoverished writer, Dekker had worked prodigiously for Henslowe since early in 1598, composing (as part or sole author) over forty plays during the next four years, including two in partnership with Jonson during 1599, *Page of Plymouth* and *Robert II, King of the Scots*. For all his industry, Dekker had been twice imprisoned for debt, in 1598 and 1599. Jonson had mocked him in *Poetaster* in the character of Demetrius Fannius, a 'dresser of plays' (3.4.261), and was to quarrel with him sharply a few years later when the two men collaborated on an entertainment designed to welcome James on his progress in 1604 to Westminster. Many years later Jonson would characterize Dekker to Drummond brusquely as a rogue (*Informations*, 36). Whether Jonson's targeting of Dekker in *Poetaster* had been prompted by a specific incident it is impossible now to say; their mutual antagonism may simply have arisen from the more general tensions of collaborative work. Clearly regarding Dekker as a mere hack, Jonson had been embarrassingly obliged to occupy the same stables, and even at times to work in harness with him.

Jonson's volatile relationship with John Marston may have developed in a similar way. Another member of Henslowe's team, Marston was almost certainly the 'Mr Maxton' who worked alongside Jonson, Dekker, and Chettle in the composition of *Robert II* in 1599.[42] Later he would collaborate again with Jonson and with George Chapman in the disastrous venture of *Eastward Ho!* Jonson fought constantly with Marston, both through his writings and face to face, and blamed him for starting the Poets' War. 'He had many quarrels with Marston', Drummond later noted of Jonson; 'beat him, and took his pistol from him; wrote his *Poetaster* on him. The beginning of them were that Marston represented him in the stage' (*Informations*, 216–18). Jonson's beating of Marston is perhaps remembered in *Epigrams*, 68, 'On Playwright', where, in a wonderful comic imagining, the writer is presented as a kind of unthinking automaton, a clockwork toy that goes on writing even when forcibly hit:

> Playwright, convict of public wrongs to men,
>   Takes private beatings, and begins again.
> Two kinds of valour he doth show at once:
>   Active in's brain, and passive in his bones.

Just how and why and in what spirit Marston 'represented' Jonson on stage is still a matter of dispute. The character of the learned Chrisoganus in

Histriomastix (1599 or earlier) was perhaps intended as a representation of Jonson, as was the character of Brabant Senior in *Jack Drum's Entertainment* (1600), though to modern eyes these portraits seem on the whole more flattering than hostile.[43] Jonson retaliated by satirizing Marston in the characters of Clove and Orange in *Every Man Out of His Humour* and of Hedon in *Cynthia's Revels*, and again more openly in the character of Crispinus in *Poetaster*. These attacks do not seem to have caused any long-term damage or resentment on Marston's part. By 1603 he felt able to write commendatory verses on the publication of *Sejanus*; by the following year he could describe Jonson in the dedication to *The Malcontent* as *poetae elegantissimo, gravissimo* ('the most discriminating and weighty poet') and sign himself *amico suo, candido et cordato* ('his frank and sincere friend'); a year later the two men were working together once more, on *Eastward Ho!* The resilience that Jonson humorously depicts in 'To Playwright' may well have been part of Marston's character; it was certainly a necessary quality in the essentially collaborative world of the early modern theatre.

A similar robustness characterized the behaviour of the theatrical companies themselves, which, for all their rivalries, were bound by common interests and networks of fellowship.[44] The so-called War of the Theatres grew out of genuine conflicts intrinsic in the competitive theatrical system of the day, which also however necessarily demanded a certain pragmatism and readiness to compromise. Such qualities are not conspicuously evident, however, in the Apologetical Dialogue which Jonson wrote as a pendant to *Poetaster*, which 'was only once spoken upon the stage' before being 'restrained . . . by authority', but subsequently published in the quarto and folio editions of the play. This dramatized epilogue presents the character of The Author—possibly played on stage by Jonson himself—reflecting in his study on 'sundry impotent libels then cast out (and some yet remaining) against me, and this play', and recalling 'that Virgil, Horace, and the rest | Of those great master spirits did not want | Detractors then, or practisers against them'. While professing supreme indifference to the tactics of his adversaries, Jonson tacitly concedes, through this lengthy and exasperated harangue, that the poetasters have now got through his armour. He has not yet found his rightful place in the glittering world of the court, and not yet shaken loose from his mediocre rivals. His satirical ambitions have been derided not only by Dekker and Marston, but by the minor versifiers John Weever and Nicholas Breton, and even perhaps—if a passing quip in the anonymous

Cambridge comedy *The Return from Parnassus* is to be credited—by Shakespeare himself, who is said to have given Jonson, in return for the emetic administered to Crispinus in *Poetaster*, 'a purge that made him beray his credit'.[45] This phase of his life is over: the *world* has defeated him, and comical satire is a game he will no longer play. And 'since the Comic Muse | Hath proved so ominous to me', he now 'will try | If Tragedy have a more kind aspect'.

A new chapter of Jonson's life was about to begin.

9

The Wolf's Black Jaw
1601–1603

'LEAVE me,' says the character of The Author to his visitors in the closing moments of the Apologetical Dialogue to *Poetaster*,

> There's something come into my thought
> That must be sung, high and aloof,
> Safe from the wolf's black jaw and the dull ass's hoof. (225–6)

The prospect of retreating entirely from society, of living somewhere wholly remote—'Safe from the wolf's black jaw and the dull ass's hoof'—appealed strongly to Jonson at intervals throughout his career, though never more powerfully than in the closing years of Elizabeth's reign.[1] A kick from the dull ass had been one thing—Dekker and Marston had done their worst—but a bite from the wolf's black jaw was quite another. The 'wolf' in Jonson's imagining was the Elizabethan state itself, its 'black jaw' ready to crush at any time the deviant and the dissenter. Jonson had felt its power already in Marshalsea and Newgate prisons, and knew all too well how his co-religionists had at times been treated by Elizabeth's officers. Years later at Hawthornden he would talk with William Drummond about the Catholic poet and martyr Robert Southwell, tortured by the Queen's executioner Richard Topcliffe in the Tower in 1592 and ultimately dispatched by Sir Edward Coke with the calm instruction 'that he should be carried to Newgate from whence he came, and from thence to be drawn to Tyburn upon an hurdle, and then to be hanged and cut down alive, his bowels to be burned before his face, his head to be stricken off, his body to be quartered and disposed at Her Majesty's pleasure'. Southwell was a poet whose talents Jonson greatly admired, yet he had no wish to follow his ultimate fate. But now that Essex was dead, how could Jonson, the leading Catholic poet of the next generation, ever find protection? How, even more perplexingly, could he hope to find advancement?

Jonson's literary efforts had failed so far to impress the aged and increasingly vacillating Queen, and he would make no further attempt to celebrate her reign. Elizabeth's power was fading fast, though by refusing for so long to name her successor, she had kept the country in a state of extended agitation and suspense. 'There are twelve competitors that gape for the death of that good old Princess, the now Queen, the eldest prince in years and reign throughout Europe or our known world,' wrote Thomas Wilson in 1600.[2] For English Catholics the situation was especially perilous. Of the twelve contenders for the English throne, their best hopes lay with James VI of Scotland, whose sympathies towards Catholic beliefs and practices were well known. Yet with the death of Essex—James's chief ally and advocate—those hopes (again) had been severely shaken. Sensing a political opening, Robert Cecil had begun secretly after Essex's death to correspond with James himself, warning him nevertheless (through his chief negotiator, Henry Howard, Earl of Northampton) of rising Catholic numbers and expectations in England, with which he needed to deal warily.[3]

Jonson's decision to live quietly at this moment, away from the pressures of public life, was understandable. So too was the interest he now began to take in the writings of the ancient Stoics and their Renaissance commentators. If the society in which you live becomes intolerable, so the Stoic writers advised, you can always withdraw from public life, cultivating in private, as best you can, your own capacities and resources. If you cannot attain or keep those things you crave and love, then you must learn to value them in another way, moderating your passion for acquisition and affection. If fortune rebuffs you, you must ride above it, regarding with equal wariness your good luck and your bad. 'Ill fortune never crushed that man whom good fortune deceived not,' Jonson was later to write at the beginning of his commonplace book, *Discoveries*, drawing freely on the writings of the Roman philosopher Seneca.

I therefore have counselled my friends never to trust to her fairer side (though she seemed to make peace with them) but to place all things she gave them so as she might ask them again without their trouble: she might take them from them, not pull them; to keep always a distance between her and themselves.[4]

Distance was a quality that Jonson seems particularly to have valued also at this earlier moment of his career: distance not merely from the vagaries of fortune, but from the court, from his friends, and from the turmoil of domestic life.

The portrait of himself that Jonson presents in the Apologetical Dialogue is that of a man living in monkish seclusion, spending 'half my nights and all my days | Here in a cell, to get a dark, pale face, | To come forth worth the ivy, or the bays' (220–2). No hint is given of the possible comfort or companionship afforded by his marriage and family life. His wife Anne is absent from the scene, as she is almost invariably from Jonson's writing. But how accurate a picture do these lines give of Jonson's life around this time; how solitary a life was he actually living? Jonson's verses on the death of a six-month-old daughter, Mary ('On my First Daughter', *Epigrams*, 22), give a rather different sense of his domestic circumstances, offering a rare glimpse of Anne Jonson, and of the couple's shared grief and affection.

> Here lies, to each her parents' ruth,
> Mary, the daughter of their youth;
> Yet all heaven's gifts being heaven's due,
> It makes the father less to rue.
> At six months' end she parted hence
> With safety of her innocence;
> Whose soul heaven's Queen (whose name she bears),
> In comfort of her mother's tears,
> Hath placed amongst her virgin train;
> Where, while that severed doth remain,
> This grave partakes the fleshly birth;
> Which cover lightly, gentle earth.

Tom Cain has plausibly suggested that this 'first daughter' may be the 'Maria Johnson' whose baptism on 8 February 1601 is recorded in the parish register of St Martin-in-the-Fields.[5] If this identification is accepted, then Mary's death 'At six months' end' would have occurred around August of that year, at the outset of the satirical warfare in which her father was then engaged, adding to the stresses of what had already been for Jonson an especially difficult year.

The infant Mary would have had two elder brothers. Joseph, 'the sone of Beniamyne Johnson', had been baptized at St Giles without Cripplegate—the next parish to Shoreditch, where Jonson was then working for the Lord Chamberlain's Men—on 9 December 1599. Nothing more is known about Joseph, and in this period of high infant mortality it is possible that he too failed to survive into adult life. The eldest child of the family, born probably in 1596, had been given the father's name of Benjamin. He died of the plague in 1603; perhaps in August or September of that year, when the mortality rates in London were at their height.[6] Jonson was away from home at the time, staying at Sir Robert Cotton's estate Conington in Huntingtonshire, in the company of William Camden. Years later Jonson told William Drummond that he had had a premonition of the boy's death, seeing one night 'in a vision his eldest son, then a child and at London, appear unto him with the mark of a bloody cross on his forehead, as if it had been cutted with a sword; at which, amazed, he prayed unto God...'. In earlier times, the mark of a red cross had been regarded as a talisman against the plague, but by Jonson's day its symbolism had changed: a large red cross 'fourteen inches in length and the like in breadth' was commonly painted or nailed on the doors of houses visited by the plague, to discourage entry and signify that the inhabitants were either dead or dying.[7] In Jonson's distracted vision this familiar symbol has become an actual wound on the boy's forehead, 'bloody', 'as if it had been cutted with a sword'. In the morning, distressed by the dream, Jonson went to the room where Camden was sleeping. Camden assured him the vision was a figment of his imagination, 'at which he should not be disjected', but in the meanwhile 'comes there letters from his wife of the death of that boy in the plague. He appeared to him, he said, of a manly shape, and of that growth that he thinks he shall be at the Resurrection' (*Informations*, 198–206).

Jonson's vision of his own doomed child could well have been triggered (it would be tempting these days to suggest) by guilt or anxiety at having left his family in the dangerously infested city while he travelled alone to the relative safety of the countryside. In Jonson's own time, however, dreams and visions were interpreted in terms of other, more mysterious causes that lay beyond the realm of individual behaviour or rational explanation. Izaak Walton tells a curiously similar story of a 'dreadful vision' experienced by John Donne while he was travelling in France in 1612, when Donne saw his wife, whom he had left behind in England, passing twice through his room, 'with her hair hanging about her shoulders, and a dead child in her arms'. Though assured by his friends that what he had seen was 'some melancholy dream', Donne was so shaken by the vision that he sent a servant back to England to enquire after his wife's condition. After twelve days the servant returned to report that he had found Anne Donne 'very sad and sick in her bed', having been delivered of a dead child on 'the same day, and about the very hour that Mr Donne affirmed he saw her pass by him in his chamber'. 'This is a relation that will beget some wonder,' adds Walton thoughtfully, 'and it well may; for most of our world are at present possessed with an opinion that visions and miracles are ceased.' Yet souls may at times vibrate in sympathy, Walton goes on, as two lutes, 'both strung and tuned to an equal pitch', may do when one is touched. Though Jonson does not offer such an explanation for his own unsettling experience, the story he told to Drummond—along with other tales of the bizarre and the uncanny elsewhere in the *Informations*—reveals a dimension of his character that is not always evident in his own (typically more rational and more sceptical) creative work: a fascination with the coincidental, the inexplicable, the supernatural.[8]

Jonson's mind must have turned often during the previous months to the loss of children, for on 22 June 1602 Philip Henslowe had commissioned him to write two works in which this theme would have been vividly present: a play about Richard III (*Richard Crookback*: now lost, with no surviving record of its performance) which is likely to have included some treatment of Richard's murderous dealings with the young princes in the Tower, and several additional scenes for Kyd's highly popular *Spanish Tragedy*, in which he had once played the starring role of Hieronimo, the royal marshal who runs mad after the murder of his son Horatio.[9] Jonson addresses the theme of parental loss in a more direct and measured way in his poem on the death of his first son (*Epigrams*, 45). The poem draws upon biblical as well as stoical wisdom, figuring the boy, like all loved possessions, as merely lent by heaven; as a debt that—like some strict Old Testament bargain—must now be punctually repaid. His thoughts may well have been prompted by the opening verses of Deuteronomy 15:

1. At the end of every seven years thou shalt make a release.
2. And this is the manner of the release: Every creditor that lendeth aught unto his neighbour shall release it; he shall not exact it of his neighbour, or of his brother; because it is called the Lord's release.[10]

Yet this austere philosophy is countered by subtle movements of mood and metre, as the poem shifts back and forth between calm acceptance and small resurgences of feeling: the last two syllables in each of its first two lines—'and joy', 'loved boy'—gently resisting what appears at first to be a definitive statement of dismissal in the first four feet of the pentameter.

> Farewell, thou child of my right hand, and joy;
>   My sin was too much hope of thee, loved boy.
> Seven years thou wert lent to me, and I thee pay,
>   Exacted by thy fate, on the just day.
> Oh, could I lose all father now! For why
>   Will man lament the state he should envy?
> To have so soon 'scaped world's and flesh's rage,
>   And, if no other misery, yet age?
> Rest in soft peace, and, asked, say here doth lie
>   Ben Jonson his best piece of poetry;
> For whose sake, henceforth, all his vows be such,
>   As what he loves may never like too much.

In early modern England, the names of children who had died in their youth or infancy were often bestowed on subsequent children of the same family. A few years later the Jonsons would have another Benjamin, whose baptism ('Beniamin Johnson sonne to Beniamin') is registered at St Anne's, Blackfriars, on 20 February 1608. The life of this boy, too, may have been brief, for the burial of 'Benjamin Johnson sonne to Benjamin' is recorded at the same church on 18 November 1611. This was probably the same child, though the entry could conceivably refer to another 'Beniamen Johnson fil. Ben' whose baptism was registered at St Martin-in-the-Fields nineteen months earlier, on 6 April 1610—following some days after the baptism of 'Elis. daughter of Ben Johnson', recorded at St Mary Matfellon on 25 March 1610. Anne Jonson can hardly have been the mother of all of these children, but Ben Jonson might well have fathered them all, as well as other children, legitimate and illegitimate, whose births have not been traced.[11] 'In his youth given to venery,' noted Drummond laconically in his account of Jonson's early life (*Informations*, 219). The relative commonness and flexible spelling of the poet's surname in London at this time makes certainty in these matters difficult. It seems likely nevertheless that a boy named 'Bedford Johnson' whose baptismal record at St Martin-in-the-Fields on 1 February 1616 has recently been discovered by Tom Cain, is indeed Ben Jonson's son. The identity of the mother is again unknown, though 'Bedford' may be a tribute to Lucy, Countess of Bedford, who was possibly offering Jonson assistance at that time.[12] On 4 March 1638 the baptism is recorded at St Martin's church of 'Beniamin f[ilius] Bedfordi & Elizab: Johnson': yet another Ben Jonson, who may well have been (as Cain very plausibly conjectures) the grandson of the poet, who himself had died just seven months earlier.

Despite his professed love of constancy and of dwelling securely and contentedly 'at home', Jonson seems not then to have been a notably faithful husband. He spent a good deal of his time moreover away from home, in the houses of friends and patrons. 'Ben Jonson the poet now lives upon one Townshend and scorns the world,' wrote John Manningham, a law student at the Middle Temple, in his diary in February 1603, reporting gossip from his (and Jonson's) friend Thomas Overbury. 'He married a wife who was a shrew yet honest,' Drummond later recorded Jonson as saying; 'Five years he had not bedded with her, but remained with my Lord Aubigny' (*Informations*, 192–3).[13] While marital unhappiness could well have been the principal cause for these absences from home, other factors may also have played their part. Sir Robert Townshend, youngest son of the naval commander Sir Roger Townshend of Raynham (died 1590; a big landholder in Norfolk, Middlesex, and Essex), was a wealthy member of Parliament and generous patron to a number of writers at this time, including John Fletcher, who was later to describe him as 'the perfect gentleman'.[14] Jonson's period of residence with Townshend seems to have followed a period of serious illness which he suffered late in 1602 or early in 1603. In a letter addressed to Sir Robert Cotton, once thought to have been written towards the end of his life but now convincingly reassigned to this earlier period—requesting topographical information about the Campania region of Italy which he would turn to use in his tragedy *Sejanus*—Jonson speaks of himself as 'infirm', and 'as a man but faintly returning to his despaired health'.[15] It is possible Jonson had been touched by an early wave of the plague that was soon to devastate London, and to bring on the death of his own son. Whatever the nature of this illness, it seems to have taken him perilously close to death. His stay with Townshend would have allowed him a period of convalescence in a residence no doubt more spacious and tranquil than the Jonsons' family home in Blackfriars. Under Townshend's protection he could progress in relative peace with his next work, the tragedy of *Sejanus His Fall*, which required intensive study of the story's various classical sources. Jonson probably completed the acting version of the play by the late spring of 1603.[16] In 1605 he was to present a copy of the quarto edition of *Sejanus* to Townshend with a grateful inscription: 'The testimony of my affection and observance to my noble friend, Sir Robert Townshend, which I desire may remain with him, and last beyond marble.'[17]

Jonson's other and crucially significant patron with whom he resided during these years was King James's cousin Esmé Stuart, seventh Seigneur d'Aubigny, to whom the 1605 quarto edition of *Sejanus* is dedicated 'in just confession of the bond your benefits have, and ever shall hold upon me'. Jonson expressed his further thanks to Aubigny in a poem that was published eventually amongst his *Epigrams* in 1616, though probably written a dozen or so years earlier.

> Is there a hope that man would thankful be
>   If I should fail in gratitude to thee,
> To whom I am so bound, loved Aubigny?
>   No; I do therefore call posterity
> Into the debt, and reckon on her head
>   How full of want, how swallowed up, how dead
> I and this muse had been if thou hadst not
>   Lent timely succours, and new life begot:
> So all reward or name that grows to me
>   By her attempt, shall still be owing thee.
> And than this same I know no abler way
>   To thank my benefits: which is, to pay.
>
> (*Epigrams*, 127)

'How full of want, how swallowed up, how dead | I and this muse had been...': these lines are generally read as conventional hyperbole, but the newly redated letter to Cotton suggests another way in which they might be understood. Jonson could still have been suffering from the lingering effects of his debilitating illness when the two men first met in the late spring or early summer of 1603. His reference here to the 'new life' which Aubigny brought him may signify, quite literally, a physical as well as a creative and material renewal which this period of residence afforded him after a dangerous and seemingly depressive period in his life.

Fig. 20. Aubigny-sur-Nère (Haut-Berry, France) in 1589, home town of Jonson's patron Esmé Stuart, Seigneur d'Aubigny.

These were not however the sole 'benefits' which the residence with Esmé Stuart, Seigneur d'Aubigny, would have conferred. Aubigny may well have assisted Jonson financially, conceivably with an annual pension of £100, as Charles Stanhope (a far from reliable witness) repeatedly asserts in marginal scribbling on his personal copy of Jonson's 1640 Folio.[18] More vital still was the access to court favour that his friendship made possible, and the ready protection that Aubigny, as a fellow-Catholic much beloved of the King, could give to Jonson and to his wife during a period in which they risked incurring severe penalties for their refusal to accept Anglican communion.

Esmé Stuart had grown up at Château de la Verrerie in Aubigny-sur-Nère, a charming—and still to this day emphatically Scottish—small city in Haut Berry, in the Loire region of France. The Stuarts of Aubigny were a Catholic branch of the Scottish royal family who were resident in France from 1422 to 1672, having been granted the Seigneurie of Aubigny in 1423 by the French King as a reward for their help against the English. They commanded two military companies, the Scots Men-at-Arms and the Scots Guards, and were vigorously involved in all of the major French wars of the period.[19] Educated at home by his mother and subsequently at the University of Bourges, Esmé had entered the service of Henri IV in 1600 before travelling to Scotland to join his elder brother Ludovick, Duke of Lennox. It is possible Jonson met the two brothers in 1602, when they were briefly in London. In 1603, following Elizabeth's death, Esmé was amongst the large Scottish entourage that accompanied James on his progress south from Edinburgh to London, where he was naturalized as an Englishman on 24 May 1603. He took up residence in Blackfriars, living (it is thought) in the great house formerly belonging to Lord Cobham near Playhouse Yard next to the Blackfriars theatre (later Apothecaries' Hall) that with Cobham's conviction in 1603 had been forfeited to the crown, and had now passed formally to Ludovick.[20] It would have been a convenient location for Jonson, with ready access both to the Blackfriars theatre and to his own family home.

Esmé Stuart's house in Blackfriars would also have provided, even more importantly, a haven within which Jonson could continue to observe his religious beliefs and practices, safe from the wolf's black jaw. To lodge in the house of a noble Catholic family was a familiar stratagem for recusants who wished to hear a private Mass and to escape the interrogations of the Consistory Court. Robert Southwell himself had found sanctuary in this fashion with Lord Vaux and later at the Countess of Arundel and Surrey's house in the Strand.[21] The Blackfriars house was doubly secure on account of the special hold which Esmé Stuart had on James's affections. The origins of their unusual friendship—which would prove decisive to the development of Jonson's career—lay in the extraordinary attachment that James had developed in Scotland three decades earlier, while still in his early adolescence, to Esmé's father, also known as Esmé Stuart, c.1542–1583, sixth Seigneur d'Aubigny. This older Esmé Stuart, an impoverished, adventurous, unscrupulous, and strikingly handsome man, red-bearded and smoothly spoken, had been dispatched to Scotland by Vatican authorities in 1579 ostensibly to witness James's state entry into Edinburgh. Unknown to James, however, Esmé's real mission (as one Jesuit confided in secret correspondence) was 'to settle the affairs of Scotland' in the interests of Rome.[22] Esmé arrived in Edinburgh bedecked in jewels and the latest French fashions. The 13-year-old James, too long confined in Stirling Castle with the austere George Buchanan, was entirely bedazzled. To the consternation of his political advisers and the senior ministers of the Kirk, he began to devolve titles, honours, assets, and political responsibilities on his French cousin. Outwardly renouncing his Catholic beliefs and declaring himself a convert to Presbyterianism, the older Esmé remained closely in touch with the Guises in France and the Spanish Ambassador in Paris, who in 1582 sent two Jesuits secretly to Scotland with letters of credence from Philip II of Spain and from the Pope, instructing Esmé to raise an army, invade England, secure the release of Queen Mary, and thus help to restore the Catholic faith in both England and Scotland. This bold conspiracy was thwarted by the sudden capture of James himself by the Earl of Gowrie, who held James prisoner at Ruthven Castle and forced him to order Esmé Stuart's immediate departure from Scotland. By the time of his arrival in Paris in May 1581, Esmé was gravely ill, and within a few days was dead; Jesuit observers were convinced that he had been poisoned in London on his journey home. On his deathbed he requested that his body be buried at Aubigny and his heart be dispatched, as a token of his love, to James in Edinburgh, to whom he commended the care of his children: Ludovick, the young Esmé (Jonson's future patron), and their three sisters, Harriet, Mary, and Gabriela.

Devastated by these events, James issued a proclamation declaring that Esmé senior had died in the Presbyterian faith, and threatening the death penalty to anyone rash enough to deny this assertion. He ordered Esmé's eldest son Ludovick to be fetched at once from France to assume the title of Duke of Lennox, and arranged suitable marriages for the two eldest daughters.[23] When young Esmé arrived in England in 1603, James treated him with special love and fondness. He created him a Gentleman of the Bedchamber, thus placing him in the powerful innermost group of royal advisers within a structure established by Esmé senior on the French model in 1580, which Ludovick now controlled.[24] During the following years James showered young Esmé with gifts and favours, granting him concealed crown lands worth £1,000 a year, and arranging in 1609 his marriage to the wealthy Katherine Clifton, daughter and heir to Sir Gervase Clifton, sealing the match with the substantial sum of £18,000. Jonson was to praise her virtues in *The Forest*, 13.

Esmé continued to move periodically back and forth between England and France, managing the family estates at Aubigny and visiting his formidable mother, Katherine de Balsac, who lived on at Château de la Verrerie into the 1630s. Jonson would at times have had the spacious house in Blackfriars mainly to himself. Soon he was to write a comedy about a quick-witted man leading a double life in a large and partly neglected house 'here, in the Friars', whose indulgent master was sometimes out of town. (Is it merely a coincidence that Aubigny, like Lovewit in *The Alchemist*, appears to have had estates in Kent, and an interest in the cultivation of hops?[25]) Through Esmé's appointment as Gentleman of the Bedchamber, Jonson would have enjoyed access to powerful Scottish courtiers such as the poet Sir William

Fowler, uncle of William Drummond of Hawthornden and former intimate associate of Esmé Stuart senior. Fowler now served as secretary to Queen Anne, and was closely involved in arrangements for masquing at court; his acquaintance would have been valuable to Jonson at the outset of his career as masque-writer to the Stuart court. He would also have enjoyed, more crucially still, a means of access to the King himself and his Queen, a passionate lover of dancing and of the new form of courtly celebration that Jonson and his collaborator Inigo Jones were about to bring into being.

§§

In 1616 Jonson was to dedicate the folio edition of *Sejanus His Fall* to Aubigny, recalling as he did so that the tragedy 'in your lordship's sight suffered no less violence from our people here than the subject of it did from the people of Rome'. Jonson's learned tragedy, forcefully rejected by the London audiences who came to see it, suffered an identical fate (so Jonson implies) to that of its subject Sejanus, one-time favourite of the emperor Tiberius, whose body, after his fall from grace, was torn limb from limb by the Roman mob. If this first disastrous performance of *Sejanus* was indeed witnessed by Aubigny when it was 'first acted in the year 1603 by the King's Majesty's Servants' (as the Folio title page was to declare), it must have been after Aubigny's arrival in London in early May of that year and before the theatres were closed down for an extended period later that month on account of the plague. There was in fact a week in the middle of May, as the play's most recent editor has shown, when Aubigny (like his brother, a keen theatregoer) could have seen *Sejanus* performed at the Globe theatre by Shakespeare's company, the Lord Chamberlain's Men (soon to become known as the King's Men).[26] With Shakespeare himself in the cast, possibly playing the part of the emperor Tiberius, this would have been the hottest ticket in town. Given the unusual sensitivity that existed at this time concerning the writing of history, and the reputation Jonson himself had gained as writer capable of dealing in political innuendo, the play is likely also to have been awaited with particular alertness and expectation.

The ban which Bishops Whitgift and Bancroft had imposed upon the writing of satire and epigrams on 1 June 1599 had been accompanied by a further prohibition on the writing of history, an activity viewed at that time with special unease. The writings of the Roman historian Tacitus, with their searching analyses of corruption and double-dealing at the imperial court—a major source for Jonson in the writing of *Sejanus*—had been a particular focus of suspicion.[27] Tacitus was read with great attention in Europe during the final years of the century, following the publication of the great edition of his work by the Belgian scholar Justus Lipsius. In England, the Earl of Essex and a group of Oxford scholars closely connected with his cause had shown particular interest in his work. They included Henry Cuffe, Regius Professor of Greek, soon to become Essex's secretary, and Henry Savile, Warden of Merton College, who in 1591 had published the first English translation of Tacitus, the four books of his *History* and the *Agricola* along with an original section of his own, *The End of Nero and the Beginning of Galba*, and the scholar Richard Greneway, whose English translation of Tacitus' *Annales* and *Germanica*, published in 1598, had been dedicated significantly to Essex. Jonson was familiar with the work of all these men and that of Tacitus himself, whom he would recommend years later to William Drummond as revealing 'the secrets of the council and senate'. Greneway's translation Jonson condemned as 'ignorantly done in English', though this did not prevent his borrowing from it during his composition of *Sejanus*. The translation undertaken by 'most weighty Savile', on the other hand, Jonson warmly praised, along with Savile's own discerning qualities as a historian; in him 'the soul of Tacitus' still lived (*Epigrams*, 95). Essex himself, he told William Drummond, had approved Savile's undertaking, and had written the prefatory address to the translation that was signed 'A.B.' (*Informations*, 10, 104–5, 285–7, 481–2).[28]

The principal fear about Tacitean historiography lay in its capacity to compare past and present times, and to reflect adversely, through the subtle use of historical parallelism, on current political rulers, policies, and systems of government. The case that had most troubled the Elizabethan authorities, prompting the bishops' prohibition on the writing of history in June 1599, was that of the historian and civil lawyer John Hayward, whose account of *The First Part of the Life and Reign of Henry IV*, detailing the events leading to the downfall of Richard II and the rise of Henry Bolingbroke, had been published in London in February 1599 with a Latin preface flatteringly dedicated to the Earl of Essex. Sensitive to the possible force of a parallel between herself and Richard II and fearful of Essex's Bolingbroke-like ambitions, Elizabeth instructed Francis Bacon to examine Hayward's text more closely for evidence of possible sedition. Having read Hayward's work with care, Bacon reported that he had found evidence of felony, for Hayward had appropriated entire sentences from Tacitus' work and translated them into English, but not of sedition. In June, however, a second 'corrected' edition of Hayward's book with a new 'epistle apologetical' was seized and burned while in the press, and Hayward, along with his publisher John Wolfe, was repeatedly interrogated by crown officials. Hayward's history of Henry IV was cited against Essex during his Star Chamber hearing in June 1600 and cited once more at Essex's trial following the failed rising of February 1601.

Investigating the case against Hayward on behalf of the crown, the Attorney-General Sir Edward Coke—no friend to the Essex faction—noted that Hayward 'selecteth a story two hundred year old, and publisheth it this last year; intending the application of it to this time'.[29] *Application* was a practice that Jonson viewed with unwavering contempt. In *Poetaster*, with Hayward's case no doubt vividly in his mind, he has the poet Virgil vigorously denounce this habit:

> 'Tis not the wholesome sharp morality
> Or modest anger of a satiric spirit
> That hurts or wounds the body of a state,
> But the sinister application
> Of the malicious, ignorant, and base
> Interpreter, who will distort and strain
> The general scope and purpose of an author
> To his particular and private spleen. (5.3.117–24)

In *Sejanus* Jonson mounts an altogether more ingenious attack on the practice of application. He shows the Roman historian Cremutius Cordus accused by the imperial authorities of 'comparing men | And times': of indulging the very practice of 'parallel' history that had landed John Hayward in trouble with the authorities in London in 1599. Cordus' offence is to have written admiringly of Cassius and Marcus Junius Brutus, the assassins of Julius Caesar. By having 'a Brutus brought in parallel— | A parricide, an enemy of his country', Cordus is said to have implied that Tiberius himself, the present Caesar, deserves to suffer the same fate as his predecessor (3.390 ff.). Cordus' writings, like those of John Hayward, are taken off to be burnt: an act of folly deplored by Arruntius:

Oh, how ridiculous
Appears the Senate's brainless diligence,
Who think they can, with present power, extinguish
The memory of all succeeding times! (3.471–4)

Jonson's tactics here are audacious. In a scene ridiculing the 'brainless diligence' of those who find contemporary allusions within historical narratives—whom he likens, in his quarto address 'To the Readers', to 'common torturers', 'whose noses are ever like swine spoiling and rooting up the muses' gardens' (20–2)—he brazenly plants an unmistakable contemporary allusion of his own: to the recent activities of Elizabeth's bishops in publicly burning what they judged to be seditious, immoral, and libellous books, such as Hayward's history of the reign of Henry IV.[30]

'Of all styles he loved most to be named honest', Jonson was later reported as saying (*Informations*, 507), yet at moments such as these he is clearly also playing the fox, protesting the innocence of his own rewriting of Roman history, while boldly inserting a less-than-innocent critique of contemporary English authorities. His double bluff did not however escape the eye of his 'mortal enemy' Henry Howard, Earl of Northampton, on whose initiative he 'was called before the Council for his *Sejanus*, and accused both of popery and treason by him' (*Informations*, 251–2). Howard was an able but shrewdly opportunistic politician, flexible in his political and religious loyalties as in his sexual preferences. Second son of the poet Henry Howard, Earl of Surrey, and brother of Thomas Howard, Duke of Norfolk (executed in 1572 for his ambitions to marry Mary, Queen of Scots, and restore England to Catholicism), Howard had learnt from an early age how to play both ends of the field. After his brother's death he had acted as one of the principal agents for Mary, Queen of Scots, yet had taken care simultaneously to cultivate favour with Elizabeth and Burghley. Gaining a position of trust with Essex during the 1590s, he came eventually to regard Essex's activities with suspicion, took no part in the rising of 1601, and shifted his allegiance to the Cecil faction. Later he would shift his allegiances once more, deserting Cecil for the King's new favourite, Robert Carr. He had assumed a key role in negotiations with the future James I, who on his succession to the English throne treated him with particular favour. (In satirical literature of the day he would be dubbed 'His Majesty's earwig'.) Though widely suspected of retaining loyalty to the Catholic faith in which he had been raised, Howard conformed outwardly to the established religion, zealously pursuing trouble-some Catholics and serving on several commissions to expel Jesuits and seminary priests from the country.[31]

Howard's cleverness was not to be denied. He was a learned humanist scholar, a former Cambridge don fluent in Greek, Latin, French, Italian, and Spanish, well read in the works of Tacitus, Machiavelli, and Bodin, and skilled in the arts of political and theological argumentation. Jonson is bound nevertheless to have regarded him with suspicion. His writings were florid, and laced with flattery towards the King and those by whom he stood to benefit, while his personal lifestyle was dandified and extravagant. His atti-tude to the Catholic community must have seemed at times duplicitous. The two men's relationship deteriorated beyond repair after a scuffle broke out, for reasons unknown, between Jonson and one of Howard's attendants on St George's Day 1605, as Howard was being solemnly inducted into the Order of the Garter at Windsor Castle (*Informations*, 250–1). Howard's move to bring Jonson before the Privy Council to answer charges relating to *Sejanus* might have been made later that same year, possibly (as Cain has conjectured) as late as November, during the Council's investigations into the Gunpowder Plot.[32] By that time, the quarto edition of *Sejanus* was already in print, and the interrogation could have focused on the published text. Yet the elaborate annotation Jonson furnishes for that edition, vouching for the play's histor-ical accuracy, together with his free admission that the text 'in all numbers, is not the same as that which was acted on the public stage', seems to imply that troubles had already overtaken the play after its first performance.[33] It is entirely possible that the original acting text of the play contained even more daring and inflammatory material than is evident in the surviving quarto and folio texts.

Given these uncertainties, it is not easy therefore to know precisely what the fuss was about when Jonson was summoned before the Privy Council, and how exactly the charges of 'popery and treason' were sustained. Though Jonson's tragedy concerns the downfall of a court favourite, there can have been little correspondence in Jonson's mind between the deserved fate of the corrupt Sejanus and the sudden fall from grace of the 'noble and high' Essex (*Discoveries*, 653)—or of recently favoured, now demoted, members of the court of whom Jonson had a lesser opinion, such as Ralegh or Cobham.[34] Nor do the surviving printed texts suggest how this narrative of Sejanus' fall might have been thought to reflect seditiously or popishly on recent or current royal authority. Jonson's play might have provoked contemporary observers not through any set of one-to-one correspondences, but in a more diffused and insidious manner: through its portrayal of the operations of a deeply corrupt Roman imperial court, which—so it is hinted, but never directly stated—closely resembled the operations of their own system of governance.

'You're rarely met in court,' says Silius admiringly to Sabinus in the opening moments of the play, as the two men meet, and measure their distance from the centre of power; 'indeed this place is not our sphere.' 'No, Silius, we are no good enginers', the other replies,

> We want the fine arts, and their thriving use
> Should make us graced or favoured of the times.
> We have no shift of faces, no cleft tongues,
> No soft and glutinous bodies that can stick
> Like snails on painted walls, or on our breasts
> Creep up, to fall from that proud height to which
> We did by slavery, not service, climb. (1.2–11)

Silius' one decisive act later in the play will be to denounce in the Senate the fickleness of 'doubtful princes' (3.303), before taking his own life. Sabinus and his companions Arruntius and Lepidus will stand literally as well as morally to one side of the play's central action, watching, waiting, warning, lamenting, but never intervening. Their stance of stoical detachment, of careful distance from the vagaries of fortune and the centres of power, resembles that which Jonson had chosen himself to adopt and to describe in the Apologetical Dialogue to *Poetaster*. Against the Machiavellian skills of political manipulation and advancement that Jonson had studied with care when composing *Sejanus*, he posits the contrasting skills of political survival, learnt not merely from books but from personal experience, both as a Catholic and as a writer whose work had already on several occasions aroused the suspicions of those in authority.[35] 'What are thy arts—good patriot, teach them me,' says Arruntius to Lepidus late in the play. 'Arts, Arruntius?', Lepidus replies,

> None but the plain and passive fortitude
> To suffer and be silent; never stretch
> These arms against the torrent; live at home,
> With my own thoughts, and innocence about me,
> Not tempting the wolf's jaws: these are my arts. (4.290, 293–8)

The society that Jonson depicts in *Sejanus* closely resembles that of Catholic communities in London during the last years of Elizabeth's reign and the early years of James's succession: a society intimidated by the constant threat of surveillance, forced often, like the members of Agrippina's household, to maintain silence or communicate in whispers, equivocations, or code ('They all lock themselves a'late, | Or talk in character', 3.333–4), a society in which, as Silius puts it,

> your state
> Is waited on by envies, as by eyes;
> And every second guest your tables take
> Is a fee'd spy, t'observe who goes, who comes,
> What conference you have, with whom, where, when,
> What the discourse is, what the looks, the thoughts
> Of every person there, they do extract
> And make into a substance. (2.442–9)

In such a society, restraint, passivity, fortitude, and withdrawal seem the only available qualities and strategies to embrace. Those, like Sejanus, who trust to fortune, trying to ascend the political heights, will sooner or later, like snails with their soft and glutinous bodies, come unstuck, as the play sententiously insists:

> Forbear, you things
> That stand upon the pinnacles of state,
> To boast your slippery height. When you do fall,
> You pash yourselves in pieces, ne'er to rise,
> And he that lends you pity is not wise. (5.875–9)

Yet those who distance themselves entirely from political action, who merely watch and wait—as the play gloomily concludes—may not themselves fare much better. No place was wholly safe from the wolf's black jaw. The deep pessimism that *Sejanus* reflects is one that Jonson himself must have felt for a time during the final years of Elizabeth's reign, as he contemplated his prospects for survival, and for his future as a writer.

By the time the composition of *Sejanus* was completed and the play was ready for performance, however, a new monarch (as fate would have it) was already on the throne. The political climate of Britain was beginning dramatically to change, and so too were Jonson's prospects of advancement. New opportunities lay ahead, but with these lay also new political dangers.

10

Scots, Plots, and Panegyrics
1603–1605

ELIZABETH lapsed into her final illness towards the end of March 1603, with the question of the succession still unresolved. James VI of Scotland had powerful claims to the English throne, being Henry VII's eldest lineal representative and most obvious heir. But James was formally excluded from the succession under the terms of Henry VIII's will (which had later been endorsed by Act of Parliament), and was further disqualified by his status as an alien, born outside 'the realm of England'. Public discussion of the succession had been banned as treasonable. A clear pronouncement by the Queen was needed to break the deadlock, but her only comments on the matter up to this time had been teasing and ambiguous. On the day before her death, however, as her young cousin Sir Robert Carey was later to report, she appeared at last to signal her choice.

On Wednesday, the twenty-third of March, she grew speechless. That afternoon, by signs, she called for her Council, and by putting her hand to her head, when the King of Scots was named to succeed her, they all knew he was the man she desired should reign after her.

By the early hours of the following morning the Queen was dead. Carey resolved to convey the news to James in Scotland by the speediest possible means. Pre-empting the official dispatches, barely waiting to hear of the Privy Council's endorsement of James's succession, he set off at once on his famous non-stop ride to Edinburgh, bearing a blue sapphire ring that the King had entrusted to Carey's sister Lady Scrope, with instructions that it be returned at once as a signal that Elizabeth had died. Early on 24 March Lady Scrope had thrown the ring from a window of Richmond Palace to her brother, waiting on horseback below. After less than three days' hard riding Carey arrived at Holyrood Palace in an exhausted state. 'I was quickly let in, and carried up to the King's chamber. I kneeled by him, and saluted him by his title of England, Scotland, France, and Ireland. He gave me his hand to kiss, and bade me welcome.' Looking at the ring, James said, 'It is enough: I know by this you are a true messenger.'[1]

Carey's hectic ride to Scotland was not entirely disinterested. Hours after his arrival at Holyrood, he begged James to reward him with appointment as a Gentleman of the Royal Bedchamber—a promise the King at once granted, but was later to deny, deciding instead to reserve these coveted places in his innermost cabinet for his fellow-countrymen. Carey's scramble to ingratiate himself with James was deplored by many at the English court, who began nevertheless also to position themselves for favour from the new King. In early April, as James and his Scottish contingent began to progress in stages southward from Edinburgh, many of his new English subjects flocked towards the border to meet them. Robert Cecil and Henry Howard, the chief engineers of his succession, were amongst the throng. Howard rode on to join the Scottish entourage in Newcastle, while Cecil, delayed with Privy Council business in London, finally met his new King in York on 18 April. 'Though you are but a little man,' declared James, looking at his diminutive English negotiator, 'we will shortly load your shoulders with business.' Cecil was soon to become James's most trusted adviser, 'thrice-honoured' by him (in Ben Jonson's own phrase) as Baron Cecil of Essendon in May 1603, Viscount Cranborne a year later, and first Earl of Salisbury in 1605. Having already succeeded his late father as Secretary of State and Master of the Court of Wards, Cecil was to become Lord Treasurer in 1608, thus holding simultaneously, in an unprecedented monopoly, the three most powerful offices of state. Henry Howard and his nephew Thomas were also to enjoy great favour from James, both soon being admitted to the Privy Council and elevated to their respective earldoms of Northampton and Suffolk. Together, these three men were to form the powerful 'trinity of knaves' that was to dominate political life in England during the first decade of Stuart rule. Each man was to be of crucial significance to Jonson, who was now also beginning to consider his future position at the newly forming English court.[2]

Jonson had made no effort to join the chorus of poets lamenting the death of the old Queen. 'His muse another path desires to tread,' his former collaborator Henry Chettle pointedly remarked.[3] Jonson had become increasingly disenchanted with Elizabeth, and had now in any case another Queen to celebrate: Anne of Denmark, whose passionate love of dancing and court spectacle was to govern his fortunes over the next decade and a half. In early June, Anne began her own journey south from Edinburgh to London, accompanied by her 9-year-old son Prince Henry Frederick, newly created Duke of Cornwall (with whom, after a period of enforced separation, she had now been reunited), and a cavalcade of attendants. Jonson was invited to devise a three-day entertainment to greet the Queen and Prince at Althorp, Sir Robert Spencer's estate in Northamptonshire, during the midsummer period (25–7 June) 'as they came first into the kingdom'. The event attracted a large throng of the nobility, eager to catch a glimpse of the new royal family as they entered England. The 13-year-old Anne Clifford, taken off by her aunt to witness the entertainment, commented with awe on 'the infinite number of lords and ladies' who had crowded into the estate.[4] Sir Robert Spencer was absent from Althorp at the time of the visit, and his aunt Alice, dowager Countess of Derby—widow of the theatrical patron Ferdinando Strange and now married to Sir Thomas Egerton, Lord Keeper of the Great Seal of England—may have acted as hostess in his place. It was perhaps from this formidable lady, as Leeds Barroll has conjectured, that Jonson received his commission to prepare this entertainment. This was a turning point in Jonson's fortunes, allowing him to display his artistic talents to the new Queen at the earliest possible moment as she entered the kingdom.[5]

James himself had planned to make his formal entry into the City of London appropriately on St James's Day, 25 July. By the time he had reached the capital on 7 May, however, the plague that was eventually to cause the death of Jonson's own son had already reached alarming proportions, and the King prudently decided to postpone all public celebrations until it had receded. The royal coronation was held with minimum ceremony on the scheduled date, but the triumphal entry into the City did not finally take place until 15 March of the following year. Jonson was commissioned to prepare speeches for three of the eight pageants sponsored by the City's livery companies and by Italian and Dutch merchants living in London, designed for performance at arches erected at strategic points throughout the City of London. The dramatist Thomas Middleton and the headmaster of the

Merchant Taylors' School, Richard Mulcaster, were invited to contribute single speeches, and Jonson's old rival Thomas Dekker to prepare another three speeches, as well as the overall narrative of the event, published later that year as *The Magnificent Entertainment Given to King James, Queen Anne his Wife, and Henry Frederick the Prince, upon the Day of His Majesty's Triumphant Passage from the Tower through his Honourable City and Chamber of London.* Dekker's grudging allusions in this account to Jonson's role suggest, unsurprisingly, that the collaboration had not been an easy one; the antagonism between the two writers, sharpened by fresh competitiveness on this occasion, was to continue for many years.

Hundreds of carpenters and craftsmen working under the direction of Stephen Harrison, a joiner and architect appointed to oversee the operation, constructed the ornate arches, forty to seventy feet tall, through which the King passed ceremoniously in his five-hour journey through the City, pausing as he did so at each station to hear the verses of praise and welcome read. 'Never came man more longed for, more desired, | And being come, more reverenced, loved, admired,' declared Jonson's Genius Urbis—the Genius of the City, impersonated by the actor Edward Alleyn—at the arch at Fenchurch Street. At Temple Bar and the Strand, Jonson's verses welcomed the monarch again. Four days later, as James progressed towards Westminster to open his first parliament, Jonson saluted the King once more, as 'the glory of our western world', in a *Panegyre* modelled on classical panegyrics by Claudian and Pliny, offering as he did so certain tips about kingly conduct he had taken diplomatically from James's own treatise on regal governance written for Prince Henry, *Basilikon Doron.* Moving with speed to anticipate the publication of Dekker's account of the royal entry, Jonson strengthened his claims for royal favour with a small and carefully presented quarto of his own, containing each of his three early works of greeting to James and his family: *The King's Entertainment, A Panegyre,* and *The Entertainment at Althorp.*[6]

Jonson's welcome to the new monarch and his consort reflected the optimism felt amongst certain sections of the Catholic community in London, who cautiously expected under James the advent of a more tolerant regime. It reflected too Jonson's hopes for personal advancement at a rejuvenated court at which his own literary abilities would be more fully recognized. In *The King's Entertainment,* anticipating an analogy that would become a common feature of poetic panegyric in the following century, he likened James to the emperor Caesar Augustus, under whose benign and

Fig. 21. Londinium from Stephen Harrison's *Arches of Triumph*, 1604.

peaceful rule in Rome poets and poetry had flourished.[7] Jonson had hopefully invoked the same Augustan analogy in *Poetaster* three years earlier, but in *Sejanus* had given a darker view of the likely relationship between writers and rulers. With James's accession, kings and poets were again—in Jonson's verses, at least—happily reunited. Their association was succinctly expressed through a favourite classical tag of Jonson's, *Solus rex et poeta non quotannis nascitur*, with which he concluded his *Panegyre*. New consuls and proconsuls are created annually, said the Roman poet and rhetorician Publius Annius Florus, 'only kings and poets are not born every year'.[8] James himself was not merely a king but also a poet, about whose early efforts in verse Jonson, in later conversation with William Drummond, would incidentally express some scorn (*Informations*, 442–3). In the early raptures of James's reign, however, he was prepared to overlook these shortcomings.

> How, best of kings, dost thou a sceptre bear!
> How, best of poets, dost thou laurel wear!
> But two things rare the Fates had in their store,
> And gave thee both, to show they could no more.
> (*Epigrams*, 4.1–4)

James not only combined in his own person these 'two things rare', but had Jonson as an aspiring court poet eager and ready to guide and advise him.

The advent of the Stuart dynasty therefore marked for Jonson a potential new beginning both for the nation and for himself. In *The King's Entertainment* he invoked the figure of Janus Quadrifrons, who looks in multiple directions: forwards, to prosperous times to come under James, and backwards to what had been, as he boldly declared, the altogether less happy regime of his predecessor, Elizabeth.

> No more shall rich men, for their little good,
> Suspect to be made guilty, or vile spies
> Enjoy the lust of their so murdering eyes;
> Men shall put off their iron minds and hearts,
> The time forget his old malicious arts
> With this new minute, and no print remain
> Of what was thought the former age's stain. (497–503)

Nowhere is Jonson's contempt for the political atmosphere of late Elizabethan England, his profound hope for better things to come, more vividly expressed than in these outspoken lines. In a series of short poems written early in James's reign, Jonson further celebrated his new monarch's peaceful policies, his wish to unite the kingdoms of Scotland and England, his exemplary rule, and his preservation both from plotters and from plague.[9]

Jonson was clearly working hard to ensure his acceptance by the new regime, but remained nevertheless a wary observer of the new court, acutely conscious of his own marginal and irregular status. On Twelfth Night 1604, in an episode which seemed almost to symbolize that dubious standing, he and his friend Sir John Roe had been forcibly ejected by the Lord Chamberlain, Thomas Howard, first Earl of Suffolk (nephew of Jonson's 'mortal enemy', Henry Howard), during the performance of a masque at Hampton Court. The masque was probably *The Vision of the Twelve Goddesses*, by Samuel Daniel, a rival of Jonson's for court favour; Jonson and Roe may perhaps have voiced their opinions of the work—Anne's first commissioned masque since her arrival in the capital—in somewhat too boisterous a fashion.[10] In a verse epistle addressed to Jonson immediately after the event, Roe conveyed his disdain not just for the masque but for the 'riot and excess' of the court itself, whose members 'Contemn learning, and all your studies flout'.

> If the Queen masque or King a-hunting go,
> Though all the court follow, let them. We know
> Like them in goodness that court will ne'er be,
> For that were virtue, and not flattery.
> Forget we were thrust out; it is but thus,
> God threatens kings, kings lords, as lords do us.[11]

Roe was a close and beloved friend of Jonson's, and shared many of his personal characteristics: courage, wit, generosity, impetuosity, and financial recklessness. Two years after this event Roe was to die of the plague (so Jonson reported to Drummond) in his very arms: an astonishing testimony to the intimacy of their relationship, given the justly feared virulence of the disease. In his short lifetime Roe had seen service in Ireland and the Low Countries, travelled in Russia, fought a couple of duels, and squandered a considerable fortune. He was 'an infinite spender', Jonson declared, who 'used to say, when he had no more to spend he could die' (*Informations*, 139–40). Many of Roe's closest friends and associates were Catholic, and it is likely he shared their religious loyalties and allegiances. In Lent 1605, according to a report by one of Cecil's spies, Roe was at the Horns tavern in Carter Lane, London, in the company of a number of the Gunpowder conspirators, including Robert Catesby, Francis Tresham, and Thomas Winter. Though he may have been privy to the conspirators' plans, he was away in the Low Countries in October and November of that year, and was spared any involvement in the repercussions that followed.[12]

Jonson and Roe were thus at once insiders and outsiders at James's court, scorning many of its habits and fashions, 'thrust out' at moments for their temerity, yet—in Jonson's case, at least—ready also to be lured in. Jonson's ambitions for employment at court might have seemed misplaced, even in some ways outrageous. He was a difficult, quarrelsome, vain, pedantically learned, hard-drinking member of the wrong faith, tainted with a criminal record; a satirist of court manners accused in the past of sedition; a man with known enemies in the inner circle of James's advisers. But even those enemies must have recognized his immense talents, and the great strategic value his recruitment would bring to the newly established Stuart court, which looked to celebrate its own glories and blazon the policies of James before the assembled ambassadors of Europe. Jonson's Catholicism was not in itself an insuperable barrier to employment at court. During James's reign as during Elizabeth's, talented artists were often viewed with tolerance, whatever and despite their beliefs. William Byrd, a Catholic, directed the music of the Chapel Royal under Elizabeth, and attended James's coronation although he and his family were under investigation at the time for so-called Popish practices, and he himself had been formally excommunicated since 1598.[13] Anne of Denmark, whose patronage was crucial to Jonson's acceptance at court, was widely thought to have converted to Catholicism. James's own religious position was marked by a mixture of ambivalence and calculation. A central element of his strategy of government was his toleration of loyal Catholics and crypto-Catholics. The latter group included, ironically, Jonson's 'mortal enemy' Northampton—a patron, as it happened, of certain talented Catholics such as Byrd, but a zealous persecutor (as Jonson was soon to learn to his cost) of others who did not wholly meet his own standards and definitions of loyalty.[14]

Jonson had influential friends amongst the group of ladies attending Queen Anne, which included a number of former political allies of the Earl of Essex. The Queen's particular favourite and most powerful member of the circle, Lucy, Countess of Bedford, would warmly have endorsed (and may

Vandyke's original Drawing, from which the Print by Van. Voerst was taken, in the Book of Vandyke's Heads. Given me by the Duke of Devonshire.

Burlington

Fig. 22. Inigo Jones by Van Dyck.

even have proposed) his employment at court.[15] Jonson and she were already well acquainted, his affectionate verses inscribed in a gift-copy to her of *Cynthia's Revels* ('Go, little book, go little fable . . .') testifying to the intimacy of their friendship from as early as 1601. Whatever the source of their prompting, Jonson's commissions were not long in coming. A few months after his expulsion from Daniel's masque at Hampton Court, he was invited to prepare a May Day entertainment welcoming the King and Queen at Sir William Cornwallis's house at Highgate. Not long afterwards he received the coveted commission to write for the court's Christmas season of 1604–5. On 6 January 1605 those at Whitehall would see Jonson's first masque composed in collaboration with Inigo Jones, *The Masque of Blackness*, followed by revivals at court of two of his successful early comedies, *Every Man Out of His Humour* on 8 January and *Every Man In His Humour* at Candlemas, 2 February.

§§

Inigo Jones and Ben Jonson had probably not known each other long when they started to work together on *The Masque of Blackness* in December 1604. Jones had been travelling extensively over the past several years, and had only recently got back to London. Most of his time had been spent in Italy, where he had become adept in the language, and had studied with excitement the work of Palladio and Vitruvius. At the Medici court in Florence he may have witnessed the spectacular productions of Bernardo Buontalenti, which he certainly knew through printed accounts. Jonson had never been to Italy, but his classical learning was superior to Jones's. Years later he would mockingly note Jones's use of 'mistook names out Vitruvius', whose *De Architectura* Jones had probably read in an Italian translation rather than in the original Latin with which Jonson was familiar. Even less kindly—even less reasonably, given his own family background—Jonson was to taunt Jones, the son of a Welsh clothworker, on his humble origins: 'you that first began | From thirty pound in pipkins, to the man | You are' (*An Expostulation with Inigo Jones*, 8, 1–3). 'Pipkins' are pots and pans: Jonson is referring to a common commercial practice of the day known as 'commodity', whereby goods were bought on credit from a money-lender, and resold cheaply for ready cash. Inigo Jones, so Jonson's innuendo suggests, must have started life on borrowed money, and worked his way up from there. In another late work of Jonson's that caused particular offence to Jones, *A Tale of a Tub*, he glances satirically at the trade in which Jones is thought to have been employed as a young man: In-and-In Medley is a joiner.[16] But at the start of James's reign, in this era of astonishing social mobility, both Jonson the bricklayer and Jones the joiner, each highly sensitive about his social origins, each in his early thirties and full of artistic energy, found themselves working in surprising partnership for the new royal dynasty.

The temperamental differences between Jonson and Jones were in time to provoke quarrels of legendary dimensions, which might to some degree be ascribed to tensions within the evolving form of the masque itself. Court masques were generally designed for performance on one night only, and were mounted at a huge financial cost; expenditure on *The Masque of Blackness* alone was rumoured to have run well over budget to a total sum of nearly £3,000. After the performance the elaborate scenery was dismantled, and at times borne away by members of the audience as souvenirs of the occasion—abandoned, as Jonson colourfully put it, to 'the rage of the people'.[17] However magnificent in nature, the visual splendours of the court masque might therefore seem 'but momentary and merely taking' in relation to the text itself, which (in Jonson's determined vision) was 'impressing and lasting', designed for the edification of 'posterity' and as an enduring monument to the Stuart dynasty. The difference between Inigo Jones's work and his own might therefore be represented analogically (Jonson believed) as that between body and soul: the former, doomed in time to be 'utterly forgotten', the latter to be preserved eternally. This analogy was not merely highly provocative; it failed also to convey the high valuation that Jonson actually placed on the visual symbolism that lay at the heart of the court masque. Though he mocked at times those who were dazzled merely by outward appearances—'the Curious', he called them in a later masque, *Time Vindicated*: 'the Eye'd, the Ear'd, and the Nos'd'—he knew, as Jones did, how much the success of the court masque depended on an act of informed observation. He was deeply interested in the significance of emblems and *imprese*, and in the work of the major Renaissance commentators on iconography, such as Andrea Alciati, Cesare Ripa, and Vicenzo Cartari. 'Whoever loves not picture is injurious to truth, and all the wisdom of poetry,' he later declared in *Discoveries*, 1083. As recent scholarship has shown, Jonson's and Jones's artistic and philosophical positions were in general more closely aligned and compatible than the traditional view of their partnership once suggested.[18] Their collaboration was to flourish for more than two decades. Enriched by the work of musicians such as Alfonso Ferrabosco—who joined Jones and Jonson on *The Masque of Blackness* in 1604—and choreographers such as Thomas Giles, their combined genius would produce some of the most intricate and superlative artistic creations of the English Renaissance.

Fig. 23. Inigo Jones, A Daughter of the Niger, from *The Masque of Blackness*.

The Masque of Blackness, to judge from the startled comments of diplomatic observers of the occasion, caused something of a sensation when first presented at Whitehall at Twelfth Night 1605. Even at their first entry into the Banqueting House the arriving guests would have noticed certain changes in the traditional arrangements for such occasions. A single stage had been constructed at one end of the hall, forty feet square and four feet high and running on wheels: the action was to be concentrated in this one location, not dispersed around the hall, as was customary. Jones's scenic landscape—of small woods with scenes of hunting, changing then to an artificial sea with billowing waves, flowing (as it seemed) on to the shore—could be observed in true perspective from only one, central, point in the hall, at which, with symbolic aptness, the King was seated. More striking still was the masque's central device which Queen Anne herself had dictated: her entry, along with the eleven other ladies of the court—including Lucy, Countess of Bedford, and Katherine, Countess of Suffolk (wife of the Lord Chamberlain, Thomas Howard, who had ejected Roe and Jonson from Daniel's masque at Hampton Court a year earlier)—seated on a scallop shell, 'all painted like blackamoors, face and neck bare', dazzlingly bejewelled and 'strangely attired'. The shell was borne into the hall on a mobile wave, 'stuck with a chevron of lights', and escorted by six huge sea monsters. The blackened ladies in due course alighted, and danced with gentlemen of the court, though 'Their apparel was rich, but too light and courtesan-like for such great ones', as Sir Dudley Carleton disapprovingly reported, and blackness 'became them nothing so well as their red and white'.[19] *The Masque of Beauty*, Jonson's intended sequel to *The Masque of Blackness*, was to present these graceful blackamoors (their numbers now expanded to sixteen) miraculously transformed back to their natural colours, seated on a slowly rotating Throne of Beauty, accompanied by 'a multitude of Cupids' pelting each other with golden apples, drawn across the stage on a floating island. This sequel was not to be performed, however, until 10 January 1608, and then without Jones's involvement. In the intervening years, Anne was to be much preoccupied with the birth and death of her two daughters, the Princesses Sophia and Mary, while Jonson himself would be engaged on other masquing commissions, loyally celebrating the political ideals and aspirations of the Stuart monarchy.[20]

§§

Whatever optimism he may have felt about the new regime, Jonson continued to view the Jacobean court with a certain wariness. In addition to its habitual shortcomings, the place was now overrun by Scotsmen, revelling in their newly acquired authority. In his journey south to London in 1603 James had been accompanied by several hundred of his fellow-countrymen, many of whom he proceeded to honour and place in positions of political trust. Some were made members of his powerful inner cabinet, as Gentlemen of the Bedchamber, and many more were dubbed as knights. As

James quickly discovered, knighthoods provided a welcome source of revenue for the crown. In the first four months of his reign he created no fewer than 906 new knights, and by the end of 1604 the figure had risen to 1,161. This was three times the total pre-existing number of knights in England.[21] The newly created knights quickly became the object of resentment and satire. Many were Scottish, and their presence at court could be seen as oppressive. The future bishop Godfrey Goodman, a household chaplain of Queen Anne's in the early years of the reign, grumbled at the number of Scottish 'hang-bys' (or hangers-on) at court, and the unpleasantness of their company: 'They were nasty for want of clean linen.'[22] Jonson himself had Scottish blood in his veins, and had celebrated the symbolic union of Scotland and England in the first of his pageants for *The King's Entertainment* early in 1604; both his livelihood and (as he was soon to discover) his very life depended on a Scottish monarch and his Scottish advisers. To make fun of James's unworthy knights, as Jonson was to do repeatedly during the early years of his monarch's reign, was one thing. But to mock the Scots, as common prudence should have warned him, was quite another.[23]

Early in 1605, however, Jonson rashly embarked on a piece of collaborative writing with George Chapman and John Marston that made incidental and seemingly light-hearted fun of James and his Scottish knights. The jointly authored comedy *Eastward Ho!* was presented at Blackfriars theatre by the Children of the Queen's Revels—a boys' company, known for their daringly satirical work—in late July or August of that year. The play was a quickly penned response to *Westward Ho!*, a comedy by Thomas Dekker and John Webster that had been performed in London just a few months earlier. The titles of both plays recall the familiar cries of the Thames watermen—Dekker and Webster would later retaliate with a further work entitled *Northward Ho!*—but carry also a further symbolic suggestiveness. To travel towards the east, so many of the characters in *Eastward Ho!* fondly imagine, is to encounter immense riches, and gather a prodigious fortune. Sir Petronel Flash turns hopefully to the City of London, on the eastward side of the metropolis—the area later known as the East End, now growing indeed in wealth and substance[24]—to recoup the large sums he has just paid to obtain his knighthood, and marries Gertrude, the flighty daughter of Touchstone, a wealthy goldsmith: who, to Sir Petronel's dismay, cuts her off abruptly from her expected fortune. Sir Petronel persuades his penniless bride that he has a rich castle somewhere in the east of England, to which Gertrude now hopefully journeys, while Petronel himself embarks on an eastward journey of his own that will take him downriver and, as he imagines, across the seas to Virginia, where fabulous fortunes are surely to be made. His ship breaks up in a storm, and the bedraggled Petronel comes ashore, as he thinks, on the coast of France, though in fact—as he is informed by a passing gentleman—at the Isle of Dogs, opposite the royal palace of Greenwich. This is the notorious region invoked by Jonson's and Nashe's earlier comedy of 1597. The very mention of the Isle of Dogs might well have alerted an expectant audience to some risky business to come. They were not to be disappointed. The Isle of Dogs is another destination that lies to the east of London, 'Where radiant beams of lusty Sol appear' (1.1.127)—home of the rising sun, the new monarch, James, a place where (so Touchstone's apprentice Quicksilver firmly believes) fortunes of a greater kind are now to be made. The passing gentleman—a Scotsman, as his accent has already revealed—turns out to be none other than King James himself, who murmurs to his companion as he leaves, 'I ken the man weel; he's one of my thirty-pound knights' (4.1.140).

At the time of the play's performance, the real King James was away on his summer progress to Oxford, accompanied by many of his courtiers, including Thomas Howard, Earl of Suffolk—the Lord Chamberlain who had ejected Jonson and Roe forcibly from the Banqueting House eighteen months earlier, whose permission should have been obtained before the comedy was performed. Staging unlicensed and often risqué plays at this time of the year had become a common stratagem amongst the companies, and this breach of protocol, rather than the subsequent publication of the play, was in all likelihood the rationale (if not the primary trigger) for the actions followed.[25] Years later, Jonson gave this account of these events to William Drummond:

He was delated by Sir James Murray to the King for writing something against the Scots in a play, *Eastward Ho!*, and voluntarily imprisoned himself with Chapman and Marston, who had written it amongst them. The report was that they should then had their ears cut and noses. (*Informations*, 207–10)

Nothing in the surviving 1605 quarto text of *Eastward Ho!*, whose printing had probably begun but not been concluded by the time the authors were imprisoned, quite accounts for the severity of the treatment that was threatened on this occasion. The brief mimicry of James's own voice (if this was indeed what was attempted at this moment) along with other passing

Fig. 24. George Chapman, who was imprisoned with Jonson for their comedy *Eastward Ho!,* jointly authored with John Marston. Jonson told William Drummond that Chapman was 'loved of him' (*Informations,* 126). By the 1630s, however, Chapman's 'Invective' suggests that the two men's relationship had cooled. This engraving, attributed to William Hole, appeared as a frontispiece to Chapman's translation of *The Whole Works of Homer* in 1616.

jokes in the play about the behaviour of the Scots may be disrespectful, but scarcely seem to warrant a punishment involving physical mutilation: a standard punishment for sedition.

Yet as in the case of *Sejanus,* the printed text does not fully reveal the nature of the play as originally presented. As close textual analysis reveals, a number

208

of deletions were made from the text of *Eastward Ho!* during the process of printing. Some of these deletions are indicated merely by generous spaces left in an otherwise crowded page; their nature can only be guessed at. Others can be identified from the survival of a rare complete copy of the first issue of the original quarto, which contains two passages deleted from later printings.[26] Both occur in the third act of the play as the sea-captain Seagull is describing the settlement at Virginia: a pleasant place, he says, where one can live freely, 'without sergeants, or courtiers, or lawyers, or intelligencers' (i.e. spies). Then he goes on, in words the printer saw fit to remove:

only a few industrious Scots, perhaps, who indeed are dispersed over the face of the whole earth. But as for them, there are no greater friends to Englishmen and England, when they are out on't, in the world than they are. And for my part, I would a hundred thousand of 'em were there; for we are all one countrymen now, ye know; and we should find ten times more comfort of them there than we do here. (3.3.30–5)

The second deleted passage followed immediately: 'You may be an alderman there and never be a scavenger; you may be a noble man and never be a slave' (3.3.36–8). A further passage that was allowed to remain in the quarto text is likely to have given particular offence to Sir James Murray, the Scottish courtier who brought the impeachment against the three authors, and to his brother Sir John Murray. These two men were the sons of Sir Charles Murray of Cockpool in Annandale—the very region of Scotland, ironically, from which Jonson's own family hailed. Sir James Murray was one of James's new knights, who had been dubbed by the King at Hampton Court on 5 August 1603. Sir John Murray, later to be ennobled as Earl of Annandale, was a powerful favourite of James's, and a man with whom (had the authors pondered the matter) it was especially unwise to meddle.[27] In the second act of *Eastward Ho!* the conversation of the play turns to the difficulties of life at court, where (so one character remarks) it seems necessary to please not only 'an imperious lord', but 'every trencher-bearer, every groom that by indulgence and intelligence crept into his favour, and by panderism into his chamber. He rules the roost; and when my honourable lord says, "it shall be thus", my worshipful rascal, the groom of his close-stool, says, "it shall not be thus", claps the door after him, and who dares enter?' (2.2.61–9). The Groom of the Stool was the officer who had special responsibility for the

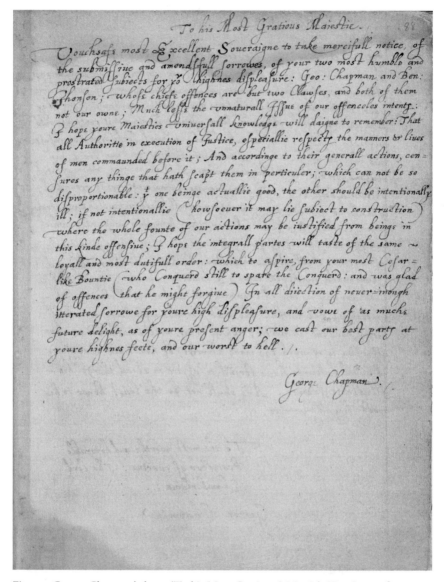

Fig. 25. George Chapman's letter 'To his Most Gratious Maiestie', King James, from prison, where he and Ben Jonson had been imprisoned following the unauthorized performance of their comedy (jointly authored with John Marston) *Eastward Ho!* (Not in Chapman's hand.) 'Vouchsafe most Excellent Soueraigne to take mercifull notice, of the submissiue and amendsfull sorrowes, of your two most humble and prostrated subiects for your highnes displeasure: Geo: Chapman and Ben: Ihonson; whose chiefe offences are but two Clawses, and both of them not our owne...'

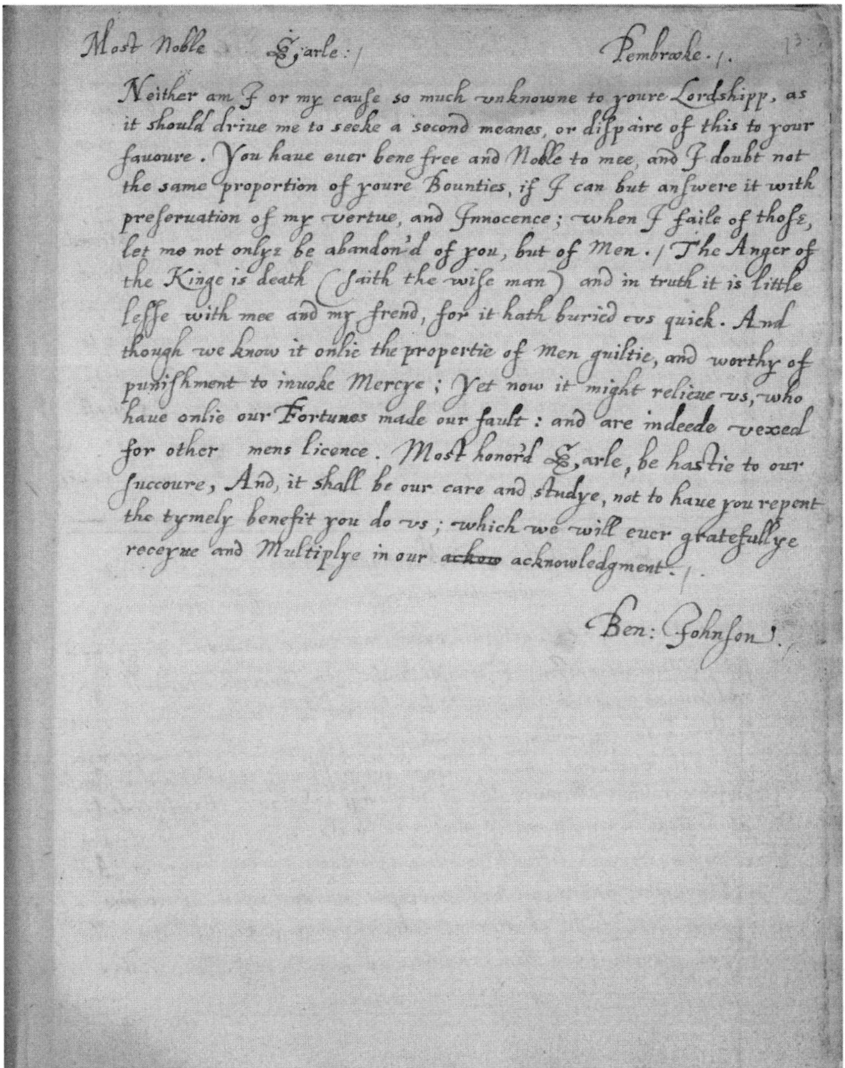

Fig. 26. Jonson's letter from prison to William Herbert, Earl of Pembroke, appealing for his help after *Eastward Ho!* (Not in Jonson's hand.) 'Neither am I or my Cause so much vnknowne to your Lordshipp, as it should driue me to seeke a second meanes, or dispaire of this to your fauoure. You haue euer bene free and Noble to mee, and I doubt not the same proportion of youre Bounties, if I can but answere it with preseruation of my vertue, and Innocence; when I faile of those, let me not onlye be abandon'd of you, but of Men.'

King's most intimate functions. The present holder of this position happened to be none other than Sir John Murray.

Some sense of the gravity of the events that followed was revealed in 1901, when the London bookseller Bertram Dobell came upon a seventeenth-century manuscript book containing, amongst other items, a group of ten letters written from prison by Ben Jonson and George Chapman. The letters appealed to some of the highest figures in the land for help in the two men's present troubles, which had evidently been occasioned by their authorship of some unnamed play. Dobell identified the letters, not without difficulty, as referring to the episode concerning *Eastward Ho!* that Jonson had reported to William Drummond in 1618–19.[28] Though this identification has been cautiously accepted by subsequent scholars, the letters remain puzzling in a number of ways. While Chapman speaks in this correspondence of two offending clauses in the play for which, he insists, neither he nor Jonson was responsible, no mention is anywhere made of the third author of *Eastward Ho!*, John Marston.[29] Perhaps Marston by this time had eluded the authorities, or was being held, without Chapman's and Jonson's certain knowledge, in another prison, and their silence was designed to protect him. Jonson's later claim to Drummond that he had 'voluntarily imprisoned himself with Chapman and Marston' seems in any case doubly strange: for not only was Jonson (on the evidence of these letters) *not* imprisoned with Marston; he appears moreover not to have 'voluntarily imprisoned' himself at all. On the contrary, he repeatedly complains throughout the correspondence that he has been forcibly committed to jail without fair hearing or examination, on the strength of mere 'rumour'. Perhaps Jonson, years after the event, had decided to improve the story of his clash with the authorities, or perhaps Drummond had misreported an anecdote that might in any case not have emerged with perfect clarity as Jonson, fortified with his host's late-night liquor, reminisced about past adventures.

Whatever the case, the letters, in their number, persistency, and urgency of tone, testify eloquently to the seriousness of the situation in which Jonson and Chapman now found themselves. Seven of the letters are written by Jonson, and are addressed to Robert Cecil, recently created Earl of Salisbury; to Philip Herbert, Earl of Montgomery, and his brother William Herbert, Earl of Pembroke; to the Lord Chamberlain, Thomas Howard, Earl of Suffolk; to Esmé Stuart, Lord Aubigny; and to an unnamed lady, who is perhaps Lucy, Countess of Bedford. Of the three letters by Chapman, two are directed to Suffolk, and one to King James. These multiple petitions, probably written between 30 August and 4 September 1605, were ultimately effective, and the authors were released some time thereafter: certainly before 9 October, when (as we shall shortly see) Jonson is known to have been at liberty, and already beginning to dabble with other kinds of mischief. Chapman's correspondence with Suffolk strongly suggests that Aubigny had made a personal intervention to James on the authors' behalf. An otherwise unexplained large financial payment made by Salisbury to Sir John Murray late in 1605 may also have smoothed the ruffled Scottish feathers, and eased the two authors' final exit from prison.[30] Jonson celebrated their release with characteristic gusto, though his report of the occasion to Drummond, with its vivid cameo of his formidable mother, underscores the gravity of the situation from which the men had narrowly escaped.

After their delivery he banqueted all his friends: there was Camden, Selden, and others. At the midst of the feast his old mother drank to him, and show him a paper which she had, if the sentence had taken execution, to have mixed in the prison among his drink, which was full of lusty strong poison. And that she was no churl, she told she minded first to have drunk of it herself. (*Informations*, 210–15)[31]

§§

The question persists: why should Jonson, at this early stage of his association with James—while evidently admiring of his King's policies, and eager himself for professional advancement—have chosen to satirize the powerful Scottish courtiers and, by implication, the monarch himself upon whose favours he was so dependent? His willingness to subscribe to a piece of high-spirited anti-Scots satire in 1605 cannot simply be explained as a whimsical or reckless act. It also reflects the deeper political currents that were beginning to move opinion in London in the early years of James's reign, and the concerns that Jonson himself, for all the rhetorical confidence that had shaped his welcome to the new dynasty, may also privately have felt.

Antagonism to the Scottish presence in London was widespread at this time, especially, but by no means solely, amongst Catholic communities. The Scots had been a rare sight in the English capital prior to 1603; now they were everywhere, speaking to each other in a language which, in the south of the country, was barely understood. 'The King teacheth him Latin every morning', remarked Thomas Howard to Sir John Harington in 1606, of

Robert Carr; 'and I think someone should teach him English too, for, as he is a Scottish lad, he hath much need of better language.'[32] The gibe took an additional sting from the fact that all of the royal favourites were, like Carr, Scottish lads, and that despite James's efforts to balance the Privy Council with equal numbers of Scots and English, his inner circle of Bedchamber advisers, in the earliest period of his reign, were Scottish to a man. To make matters worse, their often extravagant debts were being paid off from the national exchequer.[33] The preference given to the Scots riled not only all English contenders for courtly office, but members of the Catholic community in London as well.

In mid-July 1605, some days before the first performances in London of *Eastward Ho!*, a young soldier from Yorkshire named Guy Fawkes travelled to Madrid in the hope of soliciting Spanish support for a political coup in England. The principal grievance that moved English Catholics and 'the English Peers apart from the Catholics', so Fawkes informed the Spanish councillors, was James's habit of appointing Scots to all positions of power and trust.

He has granted many of the highest offices to Scots. To the Earl of Mar he has handed the governance both of his son, the prince of Wales, and of that province as well. He made Lord Home, a Scot, the governor of the town of Berwick which is at the frontier of Scotland. Near his person everyone in his Chamber are Scots, wherever there is an English official he has placed another Scotsman. He has made a Scot named Thomas Erskine the Captain of his Guard and this captain has dismissed 100 Englishmen who were outside of the muster, but he has not appointed others. The chancellor of the Duchy of Lancaster is a Scot. He has given bishoprics to two Scotsmen. He has allowed the Scots, his favourites, to represent whomever they wish to their own profit. He has granted knighthood to them, receiving from some 300 ducats, from others 600 and in that fashion they become rich with the money of Englishmen.

These were not merely matters of religion, Fawkes stressed. The differences went deeper than that, and were basically ethnic in nature.

There is a natural hostility between the English and the Scots. There has always been one, and at present it keeps increasing through these grievances, so that even were there but one religion in England, nevertheless it will not be possible to reconcile these two nations, such as they are, for very long.[34]

Anti-Scottish feeling of this kind was not confined to the Catholic community. It had been building more generally in England throughout the previous year, erupting at times in surprising quarters. On 24 June 1604 the Earl of Southampton, Lord Danvers, and Sir Henry Neville, all former Essex conspirators, were arrested and interrogated. According to the Venetian Ambassador, Southampton had 'been rumoured by his enemies to be plotting to slay several Scots much about the person of the king', with James's chief adviser, Sir George Hume, as his first intended victim. Though the three men were released after questioning the following day, the incident says much about the general nervousness of the times, and the growing hostility towards James and his countrymen shown not only by Catholics but also by other members of the community.[35]

Many Catholics, however, felt deep disappointment that the toleration they had expected from James had seemingly come to nothing. The priests William Watson and Francis Clarke had journeyed to Edinburgh in 1602 to ask James if he would relax the laws against Catholics after his accession. Advised secretly by Cecil of the dangers of such a move, but anticipating the possible need for Catholic support to secure the succession, James had given the priests an encouraging but non-committal answer. In the early months of his reign, fines for recusancy were substantially remitted, and Catholics seemed at first to enjoy a greater freedom than hitherto. Yet this honeymoon was short-lived. Safely established on the English throne, James famously remarked (or was rumoured to have remarked), 'Na, na, gud faith, we's not need the Papists now.' In a sudden reversal of his initial policies, tougher penalties against Catholics followed. Moves by Catholics to unnerve or unseat the new King had been made in England even before his coronation. The very day on which Queen Anne and her son Henry, having barely entered the kingdom, had been enjoying the spectacle of Jonson's *Entertainment at Althorp*—25 June 1603, Midsummer Day—was initially chosen by one group of Catholic conspirators (led by Sir Griffin Markham, a country squire, and the two disgruntled priests, Father Watson and Father Clarke) as the ideal moment to kidnap King James at Windsor Castle, carry him off to the Tower, and forcibly demand toleration for Catholics, along with the removal of those privy counsellors who were known to be unsympathetic to the Catholic cause. Though this absurd adventure, known to history as the 'Bye' Plot, came in the end to nothing, rumours of a possible coup against James about this time were rife, and may even have reached the ears of the royal party and their hosts at Althorp. The more serious 'Main' Plot, involving an alleged move by Lord Cobham, his brother George Brooke, Sir Walter Ralegh, and Lord Grey of Wilton 'to destroy the king and all his cubs' and place his cousin Arbella Stuart on the throne, though likewise aborted, had given further cause for vigilance and alarm. In February 1604, using the foiled Bye Plot as his pretext, James issued a proclamation abruptly ordering all Jesuit and seminary priests to leave the country by 19 March, a move that further angered the Catholic community.[36]

Growing discontent with James's handling of the Catholic question led soon to an even more extreme measure: the formation of a plan early in 1604 by a group of five Catholic desperadoes to blow up the House of Lords the following year on the occasion of the state opening of Parliament, thus destroying King James, Prince Henry, the now detested Robert Cecil (seen as a particular enemy of Catholic interests), along with other leading ministers. The inspiration for this coup came from Robert Catesby, a Northamptonshire gentleman who had been associated with the failed Bye Plot. As core confidants, Catesby recruited his cousin Thomas Winter, a Yorkshireman named John Wright and his brother-in-law Thomas Percy, and the malcontent soldier Guy Fawkes (conveniently, an expert on explosives), now back from his unsuccessful mission to Spain. Between the hatching of the so-called Gunpowder Plot and its final discovery in November 1605, a further eight conspirators were enlisted, including Francis Tresham, another veteran of the Bye Plot. Anti-Scots feeling played a powerful part in this new conspiracy. After its exposure, a list of Scots targeted for death was allegedly found in the rooms of some of the plotters. Guy Fawkes himself, in response to a question from James himself on 5 November, was to comment sharply that his hopes for the Scots through this conspiracy had been 'to have blown them back into Scotland'.[37]

Seen in this larger context of political alarm and disquiet, the detention and questioning of the authors of *Eastward Ho!* during the late summer of 1605 was not altogether surprising. What wider contacts and associations (their interrogators might well have asked) did the authors have with other anti-Scottish, anti-Stuart movements during this long summer? What were those gibes about James and his countrymen actually intended to achieve? Such questions are no easier to answer now than they were in 1605. It would be surprising, however, if Jonson at least, through his wide network of Catholic acquaintances and his informants at court, did not have some knowledge prior to the writing of *Eastward Ho!* of current murmurings and

Fig. 27. The Gunpowder conspirators.

manoeuvrings within the Catholic community. Even in the early summer he may well have had some inkling of the existence of the Gunpowder Plot. By the time of his release from prison in the autumn, he must certainly have had a clearer idea of what was afoot, for on or about 9 October, less than a month before the intended coup, he attended a supper party at William Patrick's hostelry in the Strand, the Irish Boy, together with a number of the leading conspirators: Robert Catesby (who lodged at this address), Francis Tresham, Thomas Winter and his brother-in-law John Ashfield, Sir Josceline Percy (a brother of Henry Percy, Earl of Northumberland, and former follower of Essex), Lord Mordaunt, and one other guest 'unknown to William Patrick or any of his house'.[38]

Jonson's precise role in relation to the Gunpowder Plot remains obscure. Was he an accomplice or adviser to the conspirators, a neutral observer at their discussions, or (as some have conjectured) an agent planted by Sir Robert Cecil to flush out the conspiracy?[39] None of these options is especially creditable to Jonson, and none can be definitively excluded. The last, however, may seem to be the least likely. After the exposure of the Plot, Jonson persevered in the Catholic faith, despite all difficulties, for another five years, remaining on close and friendly terms with his co-religionists. None of his contemporaries ever hinted at the possibility of his having acted disloyally. Espionage was a practice for which he continued to express particular contempt, and to associate with the bad old days of the late Queen and her detested spymaster Francis Walsingham. Jonson was in any case wary of Cecil, knowing of his enmity to Essex in years past, and to Catholics in England at the present time.[40] The two men's relationship had never been easy. Cecil had been one of Jonson's interrogators during *The Isle of Dogs* affair in 1597, as Jonson had recalled with some embarrassment when appealing to Cecil in autumn 1605 for help once more following his imprisonment in relation to *Eastward Ho!*, describing the earlier episode as 'my first error, which yet is punished in me more with my shame than it was with my bondage' (Letter 3). Years after Cecil's death in 1612, in the privacy of Hawthornden, Jonson was to express his scorn for Cecil, who 'never cared for any man longer nor he could make use of him' (*Informations*, 274). Publishing in his 1616 Folio two poems of dutiful praise that he had addressed to Cecil during his lifetime (*Epigrams*, 63 and 64), Jonson carefully followed them with a new poem, 'To my Muse' (*Epigrams*, 65), that begins exasperatedly: 'Away, and leave me, thou thing most abhorred, | That hast betrayed me to a worthless lord' (*Epigrams*, 63, 64, 65). The clear implication as these poems are read in sequence is that the 'worthless lord' is none other than Cecil himself.

According to one persistent tradition, the Gunpowder Plot was a conspiracy fabricated—or at the very least, manipulated—by Cecil himself in order to discredit and eliminate troublesome members of the Catholic community. But while Cecil may have had some general fear of a possible Catholic strike, he is unlikely either to have manufactured or have had any knowledge of the Plot prior to 26 October 1605.[41] That evening the Catholic peer William Parker, Lord Monteagle, disturbed him at supper at Whitehall in order to show him an anonymous letter that had been delivered to him earlier that night at his house at Hoxton, warning him that Parliament was likely to 'receive a terrible blow' on 5 November, and that he should therefore make some excuse to avoid attendance at Westminster on that day. Monteagle was a former follower of Essex, and had himself been associated in recent years with the extremist Catholic faction; his wife was the sister of the conspirator

Francis Tresham, the probable author of the anonymous letter. Since James's accession, Monteagle had declared himself a loyal adherent to the new regime. Like Jonson himself, however, he still inhabited (metaphorically speaking) the border country, the debatable land that lay between conformity and dissent, and—again, like Jonson—was well positioned to hear rumours and warnings circulating from both directions. Following his exposure of the Plot, he was to receive from the government a reward of lands worth £200 a year and an annual pension of £500 for his crucial role in averting a national catastrophe. Jonson was in due course to direct a congratulatory epigram to Monteagle, hailing him as 'saver of my country', and protesting that this reward was not enough.

> Lo, what my country should have done (have raised
>   An obelisk or column to thy name,
> Or, if she would but modestly have praised
>   Thy fact, in brass or marble writ the same)
> I, that am glad of thy great chance, here do!
>   And, proud my work shall outlast common deeds,
> Durst think it great, and worthy wonder, too . . .
>   (*Epigrams*, 60.1–7)

James happened to be out of town on the day the letter of warning was delivered, hunting near Royston. Cecil chose not to disturb him with the rumour until after his return on 1 November. On learning of the alarm, James ordered that a search be made of the Parliament building by a number of counsellors, headed by Suffolk as Lord Chamberlain. Patrolling the parliamentary cellars on 4 November, the team came upon a tall man, apparently a servant, guarding a suspiciously huge quantity of firewood in a part of the building rented by Thomas Percy. Towards midnight on the same date, the King ordered a second and more thorough search to be conducted, which led to the discovery of thirty-six barrels of gunpowder stacked behind the firewood, ready to blow the entire building sky-high.

The tall man was at once arrested, and in the early hours of the following morning was brought into the royal bedchamber for questioning by James and members of the Privy Council. He gave his name as John Johnson, son of Thomas Johnson and his wife Edith Jackson; he was a Catholic, he said, from Netherdale in Yorkshire, and 36 years of age. He freely confessed that he had intended to blow up Parliament, but stoically refused to say much else, or to incriminate others. James was both tantalized and impressed. 'We all thought we had found some new Mutius Scaevola born in England,' he later remarked, recalling the legendary Roman who had been captured while attempting to assassinate Lars Porsena, and had held his hand over burning coals to show his fortitude under questioning.[42] Pondering the situation, James decided to send for a priest and a torturer, whose combined ministrations might encourage the suspect to speak. Cecil was put in charge of the investigation, along with the Attorney-General, Sir Edward Coke, and six other privy counsellors serving as his fellow-commissioners: Sir John Popham (the formidable Lord Chief Justice who had conducted the investigation into *Poetaster*) and the earls of Nottingham, Suffolk, Northampton, Devonshire, and Mar. 'John Johnson'—whose true identity, as Guido Faux (or Guy Fawkes), was soon to be revealed—was taken off to the Tower of London. 'The gentler tortures are to be first used unto him', James instructed, '*et sic per gradus ad ima tenditur* ["and so by degrees proceeding to the worst"]; and so God speed your good work.'[43] Meanwhile a suitably compliant Catholic priest had to be found in order to persuade the suspect that it was his moral duty now to disclose to his interrogators further details concerning the Plot, and in particular the names of his fellow-conspirators. To help with this task, the services of Ben Jonson were now enlisted.

On 7 November, Jonson received a warrant from the Privy Council instructing him to 'let a certain priest know (that offered to do good service to the state) that he should securely come and go to their Lordships, which they promised in the said warrant upon their honours'.[44] The next day Jonson wrote at length to Cecil, confessing that, for all his efforts, he had been unable to trace the priest in question, but was continuing to work zealously on his behalf.

My most honourable Lord,
May it please Your Lordship to understand there hath been no want in me, either of labour or sincerity in the discharge of this business, to the satisfaction of Your Lordship and the state. And whereas, yesterday, upon the first mention of it, I took the most ready course (to my present thought) by the Venetian Ambassador's chaplain, who not only apprehended it well, but was of mind with me, that no man of conscience or any indifferent love to his country would deny to do it; and withal engaged himself to find out one, absolute in all numbers, for the purpose, which he willed me (before a gentleman of good credit, who is my testimony) to signify to Your Lordship in his name. It falls out since that that party will not be found (for so

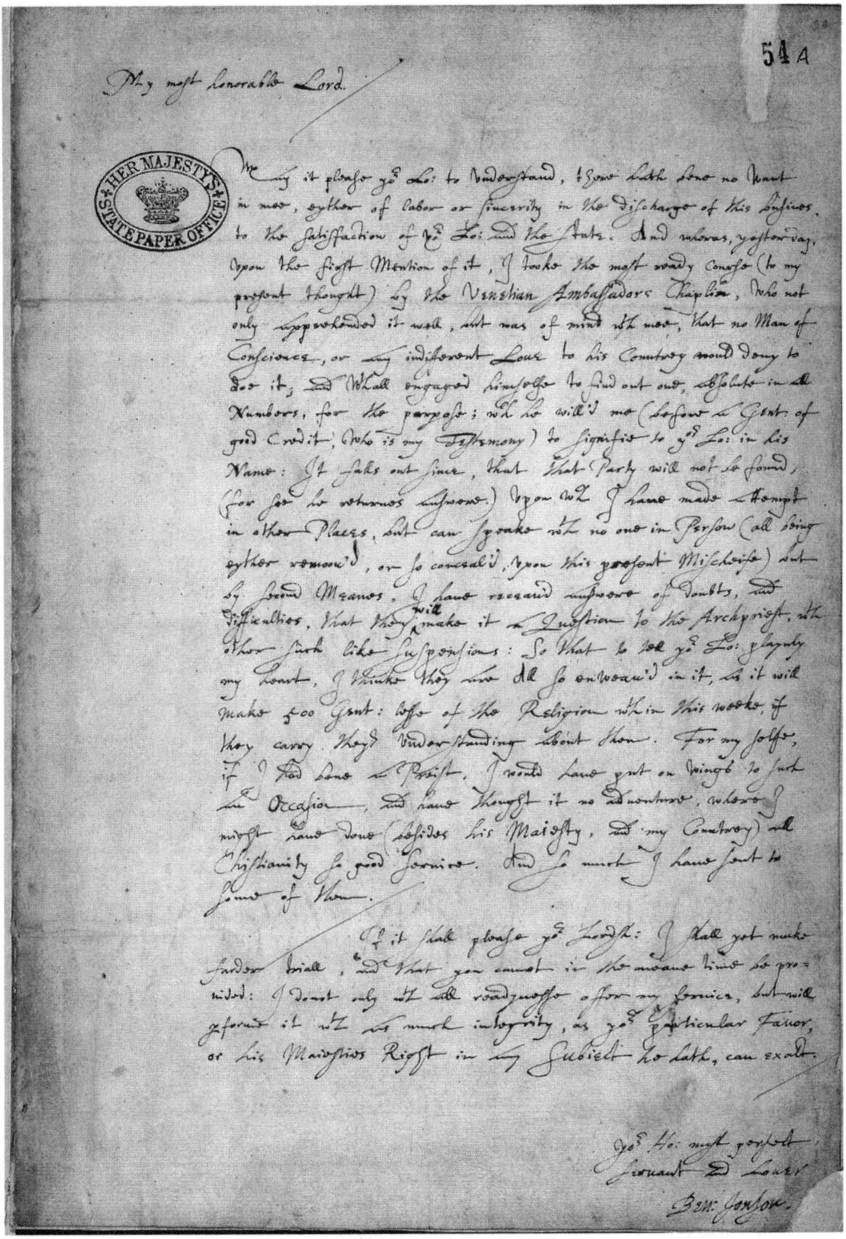

Fig. 28. Jonson's letter to Robert Cecil, 7 November 1605, holograph in *CSPD, James I,*
November 1605.

he returns answer). Upon which I have made attempt in other places, but can speak with no one in person—all being either removed or so concealed upon this present mischief—but by second means, I have received answer of doubts and difficulties, that they will make it a question to the Archpriest, with other such like suspensions; so that to tell Your Lordship plainly my heart, I think they are all so inweaved in it, as it will make five hundred gentlemen less of the religion within this week, if they carry their understanding about them. For myself, if I had been a priest, I would have put on wings to such an occasion, and have thought it no adventure, where I might have done—besides His Majesty, and my country—all Christianity so good service. And so much I have sent to some of them.

If it shall please Your Lordship, I shall yet make farther trial, an that you cannot in the meantime be provided. I do not only with all readiness offer my service, but will perform it with as much integrity as your particular favour, or His Majesty's right in any subject he hath, can exact.

Your Honour's most perfect
servant and lover,
Ben Jonson[45]

In its eager protestations of loyalty and frank recognition that the Plot had been damaging to the Catholic cause, Jonson's letter typifies the general nervousness felt amongst the Catholic community in the immediate wake of the Gunpowder Plot. The Venetian Ambassador, Nicolò Molin, whose chaplain Jonson had been consulting, was well aware of the dangers to which his fellow-countrymen in London and Catholics in general were now exposed, as his coded messages back to Venice and his chaplain's immediate readiness to cooperate with Cecil's enquiries make clear. On 22 November Molin was to assure James of the continuing affection of the Doge and Senate of Venice and their relief at his preservation. The Catholic Archpriest, George Blackwell—also mentioned in Jonson's letter—acted with similar promptness after the discovery of the Plot, publicly condemning the conspiracy, ordering the secular priests over whom he had authority to behave in a peaceable manner, and appealing to the Pope to reinforce these calming instructions.[46]

If, as the evidence tends to suggest, Jonson had not been acting hitherto as an agent of Cecil's but rather as a confidant of the conspirators, the discovery of the Plot radically changed the situation. Not just Jonson's career at court but his very survival hung on his readiness now to collaborate with the commission of enquiry. And if, as Tom Cain has suggested, Jonson's appearance before the Privy Council at this time was not merely to assist the commission but to answer charges of 'popery and treason' in relation to *Sejanus*, it is conceivable that a deal of some kind was struck at this moment: the charges being dropped in exchange for Jonson's readiness to pursue enquiries on behalf of the commission amongst the Catholic community.[47] In these conflicting circumstances, pragmatic considerations must finally have won out.

The unnamed priest that Jonson was asked to bring before the Privy Council may well have been his old friend the former Jesuit Father Thomas Wright, who did indeed come before the commission—possibly as a result of Jonson's further and more diligent searches—a few days later, with a warrant 'sub-signed with twelve Privy Councillors' hands'. Wright arrived too late, however, to fulfil his intended role, to persuade Guy Fawkes 'that he was bound in conscience to utter what he could of that conspiracy', for Fawkes's Roman resolution had by now broken, and on 7, 8, and 9 November he had already made his confessions.[48] It has recently been suggested, however, that Wright may not have been the primary candidate that the Privy Council sought, but a substitute brought in when the priest in question was not to be found. The wanted priest may have been Father Thomas Strange, a close associate of the Jesuit superior, Henry Garnet. Educated at Oxford and Gray's Inn, Strange had become a lay Jesuit in Rome, had worked for the Catholic cause in Dunkirk, and recently completed a huge Latin 'compendium of all the sciences', dedicated to his 'most dear friend', the conspirator Robert Catesby. Jonson and he were well acquainted; just a few years earlier, Strange had presented Jonson with his personal copy of the Tridentine Vulgate Bible. He was also well known to the authorities, and had recently offered assistance to the government (as the words of Jonson's warrant from the Privy Council might suggest) in return for some unstated favour. In a report to Cecil on 5 November, Lord Chief Justice Popham had named Father Strange as a person of interest, and on 7 November the priest had actually been arrested north of Warwick, though this news was slow to reach London. Father Strange was to be kept for years in solitary confinement in the Tower of London, where he was repeatedly interrogated and tortured, left hanging by his wrists for periods of six hours at a time, and becoming as a consequence a total cripple. He was never convicted, but was eventually ransomed and exiled to Belgium, where he spent the remainder of his life.[49]

Jonson was fortunate to have escaped such a fate, and the even more severe penalties that were soon to be executed on the Catholic companions with whom he had been at supper at the Irish Boy on 9 October.

II

Following the Plot 1605–1607

SINCE James's accession Jonson had acted by turns as an apologist for the new King and as a satirist of his manners and countrymen; as a celebrator of the magnificence of the Jacobean court and scourge of its dubious values; as a confidant of the Gunpowder conspirators and as a go-between for their chief inquisitor, Robert Cecil; as a Catholic hare who might seem at times to be running with the Protestant hounds. Barely extricated from his various scrapes over *Sejanus, Eastward Ho!*, and the Gunpowder conspiracy, Jonson now found himself, in another revolution of fortune, returned to temporary favour at court. He received a commission to prepare a masque in celebration of the forthcoming marriage of a young couple from opposed dynasties: Robert Devereux, third Earl of Essex—son of the recently executed second Earl and his wife Frances (daughter of Elizabeth's spymaster Sir Francis Walsingham and widow of Sir Philip Sidney)—and Frances Howard, daughter of the present Lord Chamberlain, Thomas Howard, Earl of Suffolk, and his wife Katherine Knyvett. This was not a love match, nor was there any immediate prospect of its physical consummation; the groom was not yet 15 years of age, and his bride was a mere four months older. Immediately after the wedding, the young Earl was to be sent off on a three-year period of continental travel, after which the couple would be permitted to begin (so it was hopefully supposed) a normal life of marital cohabitation. The marriage was designed by James to fortify an alliance between the potentially feuding families of Devereux, Howard, and Cecil. He hoped to ease hostility between the young Earl of Essex and Robert Cecil (whom Essex regarded as the agent of his father's downfall) and to strengthen ties between Cecil and the Howard faction, who together made up the central power group within his Privy Council.

The Howards

Thomas Howard 1473–1554
2nd Earl of Surrey, 3rd Duke of Norfolk.
m. (i) Anne, d. of Edward IV,
m. (ii) Elizabeth née Stafford
Attained 1547, but escapes execution

Henry Howard 1516/17–1547
Earl of Surrey, the poet
Attained and executed for treason
[Jonson commends in Discoveries, 647–8]

Henry Howard 1540–1614
1st Earl of Northampton
[Jonson's 'mortal enemy': Informations, 250–2]

Thomas Howard 1538–72
4th Duke of Norfolk
Conspires to marry Queen of Scots
Attained and executed

m. (i) Mary née Fitzalan 1539–57   m. (ii) Margaret née Dudley 1540–64   m. (iii) Elizabeth née Leybourne d. 1567

Philip Howard 1557–95
13th Earl of Arundel
Imprisoned and attainted
for Catholic associations

m. Anne née Dacre 1557–1630

Thomas Howard 1561–1626
restored in blood 1584
1st Earl of Suffolk
Lord Chamberlain
[Escorts Jonson from masque, 1604,
Informations, 113; appealed to
from prison, 1605: Letter 2; addressed,
Epigrams, 67]

Margaret Howard c. 1560–91
marries Robert Sackville c. 1560/61–1609
2nd Earl of Dorset

Richard Sackville 1589–1624
3rd Earl of Dorset

Edward Sackville 1590–1652
4th Earl of Dorset
[addressed, Und. 13]

Thomas Howard 1585–1646
14th Earl of Arundel, 4th Earl of
Surrey, 1st Earl of Norfolk
Art collector, politician
[dances in Hymenaei, Haddington,
tilts in Prince Henry's Barriers]

m. (i) Mary Dacre 1563–78
m. (ii) Katherine Knyvet c. 1564–1636
Countess of Suffolk [who dances in Blackness,
figures in Mary-lord, ?1618: Informations, 308]

Frances Howard 1590–1632
m. (i) Robert Devereux,
3rd Earl of Essex
[marriage celebrated in Hymenaei]

m. (ii) Robert Carr, Earl of Somerset
[marriage celebrated in A Challenge at Tilt
and The Irish Masque; Carr addressed
in verses 'To the most noble. . .']

Catharine Howard, d.1673
m. William Cecil 1591–1668
Viscount Cranbourne
[she dances in Queens; she
and Frances refuse to dance
in Love Restored]

Elizabeth Howard 1586–1658
m. (i) Sir William Knollys
c. 1545–1632
m. (ii) Edward 4th
Lord Vaux 1588–1661
[she dances in
Blackness, Hymenaei]

Henry Howard
d. 1616
[tilts in
Challenge at Tilt]

A simplified genealogy, indicating Jonsonian connections. Thomas and Katherine Howard had at least seven sons and four daughters.

To all of these principal figures—Robert Cecil, Thomas and Henry Howard, and James himself—Jonson now had powerful, if complex, bonds of obligation. Coming as it did at the end of a turbulent year, the commission offered him a chance to repay in some measure his debts to Salisbury and Suffolk, to placate his 'mortal enemy' Northampton (great-uncle to the bride, and principal match-maker for the occasion), to affirm his loyalty to the present regime, and to consolidate his position as principal poet at the Stuart court.[1] Jonson called the masque *Hymenaei*, and deftly associated the marriage of Robert Devereux and Frances Howard with a larger political event that was currently exercising the King, the proposed Union of England and Scotland. Having successfully united the crowns of England and Scotland, James was now looking for a closer association of the two nations which might ultimately involve a common parliament, legal system, religion, language, and name (in the new formulation, neither 'England' nor 'Scotland' but 'Britain'). In his first address to the English Parliament in 1604 James had described the proposed Union of Scotland and England through a series of analogies, culminating—happily for Jonson's purposes—in a comparison with the sacrament of marriage. Has God 'not made us all in one island', James asked, 'compassed with one sea and of itself by nature indivisible?'

And now in the end and fullness of time He hath united the right and title of both kingdoms in my person, alike lineally descended of both the Crowns, whereby it is now become like a little world within itself, being intrenched and fortified round about with a natural and yet admirable strong pond or ditch. What God hath conjoined let no man separate. I am the husband and all the whole isle is my lawful wife; I am the head and it is my body; I am the shepherd and it is my flock.[2]

In *Hymenaei*, presented in the old Banqueting House at Whitehall on 5 and 6 January 1606, Jonson drew ingeniously on these analogies, to which Inigo Jones, with virtuosic skill, gave literal embodiment. Before a Roman altar (modelled perhaps on an antique altar which Jonson had seen at his friend Robert Cotton's estate at Conington), Hymen, god of marriage, blessed the young couple, while the figure of Reason paid tribute to the political wisdom of the King in bringing the Scots and English together, and in negotiating at long last a peace with Spain: 'Long may his Union find increase | As he, to ours, hath deigned his peace' (381–2). A microcosm or globe, 'filled with countries, and those gilded, where the sea was expressed heightened with silver waves', rotated magically (it seemed) of its own accord, 'for no axle was seen to support it', though as the news-writer John Pory reported, it was actually turned by Jonson himself, half-concealed behind the altar. The male masquers, representing the four humours and four affections, leapt from the globe, fought amongst themselves, and were pacified by the figure of Reason. Brilliantly attired, their shoes of 'azure and gold, set with rubies and diamonds', the ladies of the court descended spectacularly from above, 'not after the stale downright perpendicular fashion, like a bucket into a well', Pory explained, 'but came gently sloping down' and danced their measures. On the second night, in a formal tournament reminiscent of those beloved by the bridegroom's father, the second Earl of Essex, the forces of Truth and Opinion engaged in mock-battle over the relative virtues of celibacy and marriage.[3]

Hymenaei was an elegant and erudite exercise in wishful symbolism, but the various types of *union* which the masque so elaborately celebrated proved in real life to be altogether harder to achieve. Robert Devereux and Frances Howard were never to consummate their marriage, which was eventually to terminate (as we shall see) in scandal and divorce. Nor was the political union between England and Scotland, a subject already of sharp contention and debate, to be fulfilled within the lifetime of any of the spectators of Jonson's masque. Not until 1707, and then in significantly modified form, was this goal at last to be achieved. As for the hoped-for relationship between the 'trinity of knaves': that was to be held in place, partly at least, through a less official kind of union, as Robert Cecil and Katherine Howard, Countess of Suffolk, continued (so popular gossip had it) to conduct their clandestine liaison, with the tacit collusion of the Countess's husband Thomas Howard, Earl of Suffolk. Between the large aspirations of the court masque and the political reality lay a considerable gulf, which seemed, in this instance at least, to be barely bridgeable.[4]

§§

Despite the vision of peace and unity promoted through Jonson's masque, the fear of Catholic unrest in England was still a vivid reality. 'Every day something new about the Plot comes to light, and produces great wrath and suspicion,' the Venetian Ambassador Nicolò Molin had reported in late December; 'everyone is armed and ready for any event.' Just four days after the performance of *Hymenaei*, two more Gunpowder conspirators, Robert Winter and Stephen

Littleton, were finally rounded up and brought to justice. On the very same day Ben and Anne Jonson were summoned to appear at the London Consistory Court to face charges of recusancy.[5] The discovery of the Gunpowder Plot, so Jonson had informed Robert Cecil confidently in his letter of 8 November, would 'make five hundred gentlemen less of the religion within this week, if they carry their understanding about them', yet neither he nor Anne had chosen to vary their religious habits or allegiances. Penalties for recusancy had increased in the weeks following the Plot's discovery. All persons of a status to retain servants were now fined £10 per month if they absented themselves from church. Recusants were forbidden to travel more than five miles from their homes, to practise at the bar, to act as attorneys or physicians, to hold property accruing to them from marriage, to execute trusts connected with wills, or to act as guardians to minors. Tougher legislation was soon to follow, giving the King the right to seize recusant land, and imposing an Oath of Allegiance on convicted recusants and those who had not received communion at least twice within the period of a year.[6]

The Jonsons were instructed to return to the Court in late April to answer the charges levelled against them. The prosecution had alleged that while the couple 'refuse not to come to divine service' in the Parish of St Anne's, Blackfriars, they had 'absented themselves from the communion, being often-times admonished, which hath continued as far as we can learn ever since the King came in'. Jonson now responded that he and his wife did 'go ordinarily to church and to his own parish church and so hath done this half year'; and that his wife, 'for anything he knoweth, hath gone to church and used always to receive the communion, and is appointed to receive the communion tomorrow'. These words clearly imply that at this stage the couple were living apart, yet they might also have been designed, through their very imprecision, to protect Anne, about whom Ben insists he knows nothing incriminating. As for himself, he still harboured (so he said) theological doubts, and 'hath refused to receive the communion until he shall be resolved either by the minister of the parish or some other in the scruple he maketh therein'. Jonson was no doubt playing strategically for time at this moment, knowing the Protestant passion for what was called 'persuasion through conference': the duty imposed on clergy by the sixty-sixth canon of 1604 to engage in disputation with wayward Catholics.[7] John Overall, Dean of St Paul's, Regius Professor of Divinity at Cambridge, and a formidable theological disputant, was assigned to the case, along with the Archbishop of

Canterbury's chaplain, Zacharius Pasfield, and other leading clerics. Their subsequent debates, like most 'persuasions' of this nature, clearly failed to convince the errant believer, but must have been robust occasions. (Had the requirement been imposed just a few years later, Jonson might actually have been asked, in an even more spectacular encounter, to dispute with Overall's successor as Dean of St Paul's, his friend John Donne.) In a further and altogether more serious charge,[8] Jonson was said to be 'by fame a seducer of youth to the popish religion'; the words *by fame* implying however that this allegation was based on rumour rather than evidence. Jonson strenuously denied 'both the fact and the fame thereof or ever going about to seduce or persuade any to the popish religion'. Further hearings of these same charges were held in May and June. The Jonsons were fined a total of thirteen shillings for persistently abstaining from communion, before proceedings were 'stayed at seal', that is, halted without a final decision being taken. James had found it prudent to exercise some leniency in the application of the recusancy laws at this time; convicted recusants were often released after petition, or acquitted if there was good evidence of church attendance, as there appears to have been in the Jonsons' case.[9] It has been conjectured that some influential person might also have intervened on Jonson's behalf; conceivably this might again have been his Catholic patron Esmé Stuart, Seigneur d'Aubigny.[10]

§§

Jonson's comic masterpiece *Volpone: or, The Fox* was performed by the King's Men at the Globe theatre in mid-March 1606. Jonson had written the play with uncharacteristic speed, as he reveals in its Prologue, responding triumphantly to critics such as Thomas Dekker who in the past had derided him for his tortoise-like slowness in composition. Such critics

> ... when his plays come forth, think they can flout them,
>   With saying, 'He was a year about them'.
> To these there needs no lie but this his creature,
>   Which was, two months since, no feature;
> And though he dares give them five lives to mend it,
>   'Tis known, five weeks fully penned it:
> From his own hand, without a coadjutor,
>   Novice, journeyman, or tutor. (11-18)[11]

If 'two months since' the play had 'no feature', then Jonson cannot have started work on *Volpone* before mid-January 1606. If 'five weeks fully penned it', he must then have delivered the completed text to the King's Men by the end of February to allow sufficient time for the play's immediate rehearsal and performance in the middle of March. The play therefore must have been written from start to finish in the interval between the Jonsons' first appearance in the Consistory Court on 9 and 10 January and their second appearance on 20 April, during a period of continuing national vigilance and anxiety in the aftermath of the Gunpowder Plot.

Given this genesis, it is not surprising that *Volpone* should be so much concerned with *plots* and *plotters*, words whose recurrence throughout the play might have given a small *frisson* to early audiences in their passing recall of recent events and alarms in England. 'I told you, sir, it was a plot', declares the English traveller to Venice, Sir Politic Would-be, triumphantly to his companion Peregrine, at the opening of the play's fourth act. Absorbed by his own 'dearest plots' and 'projects', Sir Pol finds conspiracies and 'tricks of state' wherever he looks, but fails to perceive the central plot on which the action of the comedy turns: the conspiracy between the Venetian *magnifico* Volpone and his servant Mosca to fleece the legacy-hunters of their wealth and bring Celia, the wife of the merchant Corvino, to Volpone's bed. In Pol's amusing mix of officiousness and imperceptiveness Jonson may perhaps be glancing at recent government busy-bodying in England over the Gunpowder Plot. Other small touches throughout the play may likewise have awakened memories of the recent conspiracy: the lawyer Voltore's daring courtroom suggestion (for example) that the genuineness of Volpone's seeming frailty be tested by the immediate application of goads, burning irons, the *strappado*, and the rack: instruments of torture similar to those by which Guy Fawkes and his fellow-conspirators had themselves been recently tested in London (4.6.31ff.). Mosca's ironic suggestion that Voltore's statue should be erected in St Mark's for his 'worthy service to the state' by his 'discovery' of a seeming 'plot' between Bonario and Celia (5.667, 60, 44) might equally have seemed to an alert audience like an ironic reference to the fulsome thanks that had recently been offered in London to Lord Monteagle for his part in uncovering the Gunpowder conspiracy.[12]

Celia and Bonario, as it happens, are entirely innocent of this alleged plot, which has been contrived by Mosca himself. At the conclusion of the play Mosca is denounced by the first Avocatore as 'the chiefest minister, if not plotter, | In all these lewd impostures'. *Plotter* was a very new word in 1606:

the *OED*'s first example of its usage as a synonym for 'conspirator' is from that very year, where it is used in relation to those involved in the recent 'Jesuits' treason', the Gunpowder Plot. Coincidentally, the word *plotter* had also just entered the language in another, dramaturgical, sense, to describe a writer who devises the action or 'plot' of a play: thus Francis Meres in 1598 could describe Anthony Munday to be 'our best plotter' in the realm of comedy. By 1606 the supreme plotter in the English theatre was not Munday but Jonson himself—the first known user, incidentally, of the word *plot*, in the sense of 'The plan or scheme of any literary creation, as a play, poem, or work of prose fiction' (whose first occurrence the *OED*, *sb*.6, belatedly dates to 1649), and of *counter-plot*, a word first found in *Volpone* ('I'll try your salt-head, | What proof it is against a counter-plot,' says Peregrine of Sir Politic Would-be, 4.3.25).[13] In both of its lexical senses, the word 'plotter' suggests a capacity for secrecy, complexity, narrative manipulation, and surprise: qualities with which Jonson now had some acquaintance, both in art and in life, and which he was to demonstrate in abundance in the extraordinary final movement of *Volpone*.[14]

At the end of *Volpone*, after many surprising turns, the play's two principal plotters are severely punished: Mosca is condemned to a whipping and perpetual confinement to the galleys, while Volpone is 'to lie in prison, cramped with irons', till he is 'sick and lame indeed' (5.12.123–4). Celia is formally separated from her husband and sent home to her father with her dowry trebled, and she and Bonario go their separate ways. Jonson is reaching here for a new kind of drama that pushes at the very frontier of comedy, scorning the happy resolutions that had characterized much English comedy (including his own) up until that time, with their final betrothals, reunions, and rewards. Coleridge was dismayed by Jonson's failure to have united Celia and Bonario in marriage at the ending of the play, which Yeats was nevertheless to admire for its pathos and 'cold implacability'.[15] Others have felt that in the final movement of the play Jonson is turning, so to speak, against himself and his own best powers, suppressing the very energies from which the action of the comedy has sprung.[16] Certainly the ending of *Volpone* differs markedly from that of *Every Man In His Humour*, where the feats of the clever servant Musco are finally admired and forgiven by Doctor Clement; and the endings of later comedies such as *Epicene*, where Truewit in the play's closing moments cheerfully applauds both his own plots and the counter-plotting of his companion Dauphine ('Well, Dauphine, you have lurched your friends of the better half of the garland, by concealing this part of the plot!'), and *The Alchemist*, where Face's mischievous contrivances are viewed with amused tolerance by his returning master, who is 'A little indulgent to that servant's wit'. In each of these cases the 'art' and 'wit' that are admired seem to belong not merely to the characters within the play but also in some sense to the dramatist himself. At the end of *Volpone*, however, that collusive bond between the author and his own busily plotting characters, though not wholly broken (as Volpone's final epilogue attests), has been severely weakened. Even within the canon of Jonson's own drama this is an unusual ending, which Jonson was to defend at length in his Epistle addressed to the Universities of Oxford and Cambridge and prefixed to the 1607 quarto edition of the play, after it had been performed with evident success in those two cities.[17]

It is tempting to ask whether contemporary political events in England could in any way have affected Jonson's attitude to comedy at this particular moment. His Epistle to the two Universities is at pains to assert the authority and status of the poet, almost (as one critic has plausibly suggested) as if to challenge and counter the legal authority to which so many of Jonson's Catholic friends had recently been subjected.[18] The role of the comic poet, the Epistle insists, is 'to imitate justice, and instruct to life': the dramatist in some way assuming, within the sphere of comedy, an adjudicative role that mirrors and, in moral terms, excels that of civic administrators. Poetry herself, Jonson vows in a passage of surprising violence at the end of the Epistle, will punish through her agents 'the vile and slothful', and

out of just rage incite her servants (who are *genus irritabile*) to spout ink in their faces, that shall eat farther into their marrow, into their fames; and not Cinnamus the barber with his art shall be able to take out the brands, but they shall live, and be read, till the wretches die, as things worst deserving of themselves in chief, and then of all mankind.

Recently branded himself with a hot iron for causing the death of Gabriel Spencer, Jonson now vows, as a servant of Poetry, to brand her enemies in the face with corrosive ink, occasioning their disgrace and ultimately their death. The poacher has here turned gamekeeper with a vengeance. The sentences fizz with righteous anger as Jonson, a friend and ally of many of the Gunpowder conspirators, now threatens literary malefactors with equal punishment in the name of the poetic law.

Volpone is a play which has traditionally invited both biographical and autobiographical interpretation, though such *ad hominem* readings, for all their attraction, have often proved curiously difficult to sustain.[19] Wary of the hostile methods of 'invading interpreters', wounded by recent readings of *Sejanus* and *Eastward Ho!*, Jonson takes particular pains in *Volpone* to cover his tracks, deflecting or otherwise complicating what might otherwise be seen as local or personal allusions. By setting the play in Venice, a city-state whose political system was entirely different from that of Britain, he minimized the risks of any direct 'application' to the local scene.[20] Where personal allusion is suspected— that Sir Politic Would-be might be (for example) a caricature of Jonson's friend Sir Henry Wotton, then British Ambassador in Venice—the suspicion is confused by further possibilities: that Sir Politic may be modelled rather on the eccentric adventurer, diplomat, and spy Sir Anthony Sherley, or even, more daringly, on Jonson's own patron and bugbear Robert Cecil, Earl of Salisbury.[21] The more such possibilities accumulate, the more difficult it becomes to read the play in terms of particular identifications and precise historical allusions.

It has recently been suggested, however, that Robert Cecil might be 'shadowed' in *Volpone* not just in the character of Sir Politic Would-be but in an altogether more pervasive way.[22] For Cecil (it is argued) was sometimes referred to by contemporaries as a 'fox', as Volpone is, and he resembled Volpone in certain other respects, being (for example) an upstart nobleman, lacking an ancient lineage. Cecil was moreover a short and ill-formed man, and audiences at the Globe might have thought him mocked in the figure of Nano, Volpone's dwarf. He was widely disliked, as is clear from the range and vigour of scurrilous libels published at his death in 1612. Many Catholics believed that he had fabricated the conspiracy he was now busily investigating. For a variety of reasons therefore it might have seemed an opportune moment to have satirized Cecil on the London stage. But there would also have been grave dangers in so doing, as the dramatist John Day discovered when he mocked Cecil too openly as the hunchback Dametas in his play *The Isle of Gulls* that same year: an act that led to the imprisonment of the leading players of the company that presented the comedy, and the abrupt withdrawal of its royal patronage. For Jonson to have satirized Cecil openly through the agency of the King's Men at the Globe theatre would have been even more hazardous, given Jonson's present position: so recently extricated from danger (as he had been) over *Eastward Ho!* and the Gunpowder Plot, so dependent (as he was) on Cecil for future commissions for both royal and civic occasions. Whatever the tensions and pressures inherent in this complex relationship of unequal but mutual dependency, this would have been an acutely perilous moment for Jonson to have attempted any sustained ridicule of Cecil on the public stage. Any transparent satire of Cecil, of the kind represented by (say) Gay's *Beggar's Opera* or Pope's *Epistle to Augustus* or Byron's *Vision of Judgement*—satires whose principal targets (Sir Robert Walpole, George II, Robert Southey, respectively) are fairly evident to readers and playgoers—would hardly have been thinkable. If Jonson does indeed satirize Robert Cecil in *Volpone* (and some doubt must hang over this very proposition) he does so in an altogether more covert way, through a fleeting, subliminal, and finally incoherent pattern of possibly suggestive reference, in a process that might more accurately be described not as satire but crypto-satire, a form so vaporous as to remain at all times firmly deniable. It is as hard for modern scholars to establish beyond any doubt that Jonson ridicules Robert Cecil in *Volpone* as it might have been for government officials in 1606. If the case is accepted, however, these glimpses of his presence in the play might be taken, like hisses of escaping steam, as evidence of the intense pressure under which Jonson felt himself to be working in the months following the discovery of the Gunpowder Plot.

Jonson's other writings at this time were more discreet, as he strove to establish his credentials as a loyal subject of the King. On 22 March, while *Volpone* was probably still playing at the Globe, the rumour spread through London that James had been stabbed with a poisoned knife while hunting near Woking. Coming as it did a mere six days before the scheduled trial of Father Garnet for his alleged involvement in the conspiracy, the rumour sparked widespread alarm: the court was locked and its guard doubled, and Tower Bridge was drawn up. The report soon proved to be no more than a 'happy false rumour', as Jonson called it in a poem of congratulation he quickly dispatched to the King, stressing his loyal concern, as one of James's 'jealous subjects', for His Majesty's present and future safety: 'For we, that have our eyes still in our ears, | Look not upon thy dangers, but our fears' (*Epigrams*, 51.9–10). Over the coming years, Jonson the jealous subject would continue to coexist with Jonson the stubborn recusant and Jonson the court satirist, just as Jonson the public entertainer would continue to live alongside Jonson the unforgiving critic of the public stage. While proclaiming his steadfastness and unity of purpose, Jonson, like his own creation, Volpone, moved with the agility of a player from one role to the next.

12

Employment 1607–1610

IN his Epistle to the two Universities prefixed to the quarto edition of *Volpone* in 1607 Jonson spoke contemptuously of the London stage as a place where 'nothing but the garbage of the time is uttered, and that with such impropriety of phrase, such plenty of solecisms, such dearth of sense, so bold prolepses, so racked metaphors, with brothelry able to violate the ear of a pagan and blasphemy to turn the blood of a Christian to water' (67–70). The heat of Jonson's attack is perhaps surprising. He sounds more like a puritan opponent of the stage at this moment than one of its most superlative practitioners, fresh from a recent triumph at the Globe. It was an odd time furthermore to utter a complaint of this kind about the London theatres, which over the previous three or four years had seen the first performances of *Macbeth, Troilus and Cressida, All's Well That Ends Well, Antony and Cleopatra, Othello, King Lear, Measure for Measure,* and *Timon of Athens,* of Middleton's *The Changeling* and *Michaelmas Term,* and of Marston's *The Fawn* and *The Malcontent*—to name just a few highlights from a moment in theatrical history that, in its range and brilliance, remains unsurpassed to the present day.[1]

Jonson must no doubt have been genuinely shocked by certain aspects of the London theatre of his time. In his old age he was shocked even by certain aspects of his own earlier dramatic writing. Visiting him in Westminster in the 1630s, his Christ Church friend George Morley, now Bishop of Winchester, reported that Jonson was 'much afflicted that he had profaned the scripture in his plays, and lamented it with horror'.[2] It is entirely possible, as Barbara Mowat has persuasively argued, that Jonson took pains in later redactions of his plays to remove or modify oaths uttered by characters in his early drama not out of fear of legal reprisal stemming from the 1606 Act to Restrain the Abuses of Players (as has traditionally been thought) but from an awareness of a rapidly changing public sensitivity, which he may well himself have shared, to questions of profanity.[3] In the Epistle to *Volpone* Jonson was moreover addressing his friends in the Universities of Oxford and Cambridge, thanking them for their reception of his play, and covertly signalling, perhaps, his preference for a life of scholarship over that of a writer for the London theatre. Later in his career, as we shall see, he would be honoured by both the universities, and welcomed into the worlds of Christ Church, Oxford, and Gresham College, London. He relished the company of scholars in London such as Thomas Farnaby, 'the chief grammarian, rhetorician, poet, Latinist, and Grecian of his time' (according to Anthony à Wood), and members of the intellectual circle of Sir Walter Ralegh, to whose ambitious undertaking *The History of the World* he was recruited as a contributor. He enjoyed close links with the group associated with the Society of Antiquaries, which included his friends William Camden, Robert Cotton, and John Selden.[4]

Even at the height of his dramatic career, the theatre remained for Jonson simply one of several arenas in which he had chosen to work, and a place he continued to regard with a certain wariness and distrust. His employment as principal masque-writer at the Stuart court was more lucrative than writing for the stage: 'Of all his plays he never gained two hundred pounds,' he grumbled to William Drummond, *Informations*, 446, while £40 was the usual payment for a masque. It was also an occupation that satisfied Jonson's deepest instincts concerning the proper role and function of the poet, as guide and counsellor to the monarch.[5] Moreover, it conferred a kind of celebrity which went beyond that of the theatre, bringing him to the notice of aristocratic and diplomatic observers and at times, through their reports, to national and international attention. From these contacts at court, further commissions for private employment might sometimes follow. Jonson maintained strong links of quite another kind with the City of London, renewing his membership of the Tylers' and Bricklayers' Company in 1611, and receiving further commissions for professional work from other livery companies.[6]

Through these various networks and affiliations, Jonson achieved a position of social prominence that was unusual, if not unique, for a writer in early modern England, and that differed significantly from that of his greatest rival.

Shakespeare was a well-known and highly regarded figure at Whitehall, where the King's Men were regularly summoned to perform and where many of his plays made their first appearance. Yet he was first and foremost a man of the theatre, his energies being largely consumed not just by the writing of plays but by the multifarious tasks of company management. Throughout most of his career his loyalties lay with a single company, the Lord Chamberlain's Men (later known as the King's Men), the premier troupe of the day. Jonson was less constant in his preferences, though, as David Bevington has recently shown, not quite as promiscuous as G. E. Bentley in a classic study forty years ago once influentially suggested.[7] For Jonson favoured two companies above all others. The first went under various names at various times as it experienced some reorganization over the years, being known at first as the Chapel Royal or the Children of Queen Elizabeth's Chapel, then, under the sponsorship of Queen Anne after 1603, as the Children of Blackfriars (where the company played from 1604 to 1608) and next as the Children of Whitefriars (their home from 1609 to 1613). Around 1614–15 this troupe appears to have merged with the Lady Elizabeth's Men for whom Jonson wrote *Bartholomew Fair*. The second company with which Jonson was closely associated over a considerable period of time was the Lord Chamberlain's (or King's) Men, which presented the two comedies which marked the significant starting point of his dramatic career, *Every Man In His Humour* and *Every Man Out of His Humour*, and performed the majority of his plays in the years that followed.

Yet even when this element of continuity in Jonson's theatrical work is acknowledged, it is clear that his professional life was by no means centred exclusively on the playhouse. He moved watchfully between different centres of power: the playhouse, the printing house, the academy, the city, and the court.[8] The present chapter offers a glimpse of the variety of Jonson's writing life at the height of his career, looking in turn at the work he undertook for a London company, then for an aristocratic patron, then for the public theatre, and lastly for the court.

§§

On 16 July 1607 the members of the Merchant Taylors' Company gathered at their guild-hall in London for a banquet to celebrate the regular election of their Master and Wardens, and the induction of Prince Henry to their company.[9] The King himself, who had recently been admitted to membership of the rival Clothworkers' Company, had also consented to be present, and the members of the Merchant Taylors' Company, who, like the Clothworkers, were manoeuvring for royal favour, had felt some nervousness in preparing for this occasion. To celebrate James's entry to the City four years earlier they had called on one of the schoolmasters at Merchant Taylors' School to write a speech that was then recited by one of the scholars, but this amateurish effort had evidently not gone down well. It was agreed that for the present occasion more professional assistance should be sought. The Master of the Company, Sir John Swinnerton, was therefore 'entreated to confer with Master Benjamin Jonson the poet about a speech to be made to welcome His Majesty, and for music and other inventions which may give liking and delight to His Majesty, by reason that the Company doubt that their schoolmaster and scholars be not acquainted with such kind of entertainments'.[10] For his services Jonson would be paid a fee of £20, out of a total expenditure for the company that evening of £1,061 5s. 1d.

The provisions for the banquet were of Rabelaisian proportions. Swans, godwit, shovellers, partridges, owls, cuckoos, ringdoves, pullets, ducklings, teal, peacocks, rabbits, leverets, and a great turkey were prepared for the table, along with 1,300 eggs, three great lobsters and 200 prawns, salmon, salt fish, plaice, sole, dory, carp, and tenches, sirloins and ribs of beef, mutton and lambs' dowsets, neats' tongues and sweet breads, and to conclude the evening, figs, dates, prunes, currants, almonds, strawberries, gooseberries, cherries, pears, apples, damsons, oranges, and quinces. Twenty-eight barrels of beer were provided to slake the diners' thirst, together with more than 440 gallons of wine. The 13-year-old Prince Henry banqueted in the body of the hall, while his father, never comfortable in crowded company, dined in a separate room that had been constructed in the gallery above, with a hole specially cut in the wall to allow him to watch the proceedings below. Before retiring to this separate chamber, however, he progressed with the Master through the hall, which had been richly decorated with flowers, and sat at the upper end in a chair of state to view the entertainment that Jonson had devised. Then 'a very proper child, well spoken, being clothed like an angel of gladness with a taper of frankincense burning in his hand, delivered a short speech containing eighteen verses, devised by Master Ben Jonson the poet, which pleased His Majesty marvellously well'.[11] A ship suspended in the rafters of the hall—a symbol of the company—had been lowered to the level of the spectators. The three musicians who were aboard, dressed as mariners

(John Allen, Thomas Lupo, John Richards), then sang three songs written by Jonson and set by the court musician John Cooper. For nearly 400 years these songs were regarded as lost, but two have now turned up among the Salisbury papers at Hatfield House and been confidently identified by Gabriel Heaton and James Knowles as belonging to this sequence.[12] In the first song, the sailors gaze out into the hall, professing amazement at the stellar company they see, and the King seated before them.

> *Captain*   Jolly mate, look forth and see
> What lights those be;
> The air doth glow as if the stars
> Were all at wars.
>
> *Mate*   I know not what they are.
> In all my hours at seas
> I have not seen such lights as these.
>
> *Captain*   Is not the one that fixèd star
> That guides us out at sea so far,
> The glory of the North?
>
> *Mate*   It is! And those the fires that shine
> About our tacklings, and divine
> Clear calms and safety, when we're forth.
>
> *All three*   Double, oh, double then our joys, and say
> Their wish'd sight ne'er brought a happier day.
>
> *Captain*   Nothing could more welcome be
> To us than he,
> Who doth our course abroad direct,
> At home protect.

James is reported to have enjoyed the songs, especially the (still lost) farewell song, which he 'caused...to be sung three times over', before retiring upstairs to his private chamber, where musicians from the Chapel Royal choir continued to play for him. The musical provision for the evening was almost as rich as the banquet itself, with a dozen lutenists, six wind-instrumentalists playing cornets and 'loud music', as well as the City musicians and the King's and Prince's drummers and trumpeters. The organist and composer John Bull 'in a citizen's gown, cap, and hood, played most excellent melody upon a small pair of organs placed for that purpose only', giving rise to a later rumour—erroneous in all particulars—that the national anthem ('God save the king'), with words written by Ben Jonson, was played and sung for the first time on that occasion.[13] There were understandable complaints that the words of the singers were at times inaudible. But the King and the Prince must nevertheless have been well pleased by the evening's entertainment. The Company had agreed, after some debate, that a small gift to them both would not go amiss, and James was accordingly presented before he departed with a purse containing £100 in 20 shilling pieces, and Henry with another purse of £50 in 20 shilling pieces.

The survival of part of this entertainment amongst the Salisbury papers is not altogether surprising. Robert Cecil, as the King's principal Secretary, and Thomas Howard, Earl of Suffolk, as Lord Chamberlain, had been closely involved in the preliminary negotiations for the evening.[14] There was a further political dimension to the event with which both men would have been concerned, and of which Jonson, who had fought in the Protestant cause in the Low Countries years earlier, would have been sharply aware. James was attempting to bring the long-drawn-out struggle between the United Provinces and Spain to a final conclusion; and while wishing to signal England's general support for the Dutch cause, was reluctant to commit his country to further costly expenditures on their behalf. Members of the Dutch diplomatic mission were included in the guest list for the Merchant Taylors' banquet, as a tactful sign of continuing English goodwill—but at no expense to the royal coffers.

§§

Ten months later, Cecil chose to employ Jonson himself for an entertainment of a very different kind at Salisbury House celebrating his own appointment on 6 May 1608 as Lord Treasurer.[15] The entertainment itself has vanished, though the poem which Jonson presented to Cecil on this occasion has not. It begins:

> Not glad, like those that have new hopes or suits
>   With thy new place, bring I these early fruits
> Of love, and what the golden age did hold
>   A treasure, art: condemned in the age of gold ...
>   (*Epigrams*, 64.1–4)

The 'early fruits | Of love' mentioned in these somewhat unpropitious opening lines may be either the poem that Jonson now is writing, or the entertainment that he has prepared, or more probably both. They represent 'A treasure, art', a gift that Jonson now offers to his difficult and demanding patron, with whom he maintains (so he struggles to suggest) a relationship untainted by financial consideration. Later he would have occasion to complain more openly about Cecil's lack of respect for those whom he employed ('Salisbury never cared for any man longer nor he could make use of him', *Informations*, 274) and his lack of generosity as a patron. The tensions between the two men were considerable, which may in itself explain why Jonson later chose to exclude this work and *Britain's Burse* from his 1616 Folio.[16] *The Entertainment at Salisbury House* seems to have been designed to celebrate Cecil's intellectual achievements (set in his library, it focused partly on his collection of books and maps) along with his attainment of the high office of Lord Treasurer formerly held by his father William Cecil, Lord Burghley, and his energetic building programme in the area of Westminster.[17] A conjuror, a juggler, and a 'flying boy' were somehow involved, together with figures representing Fancy and Confusion; while a single surviving sketch by Inigo Jones, who was also associated with this event, shows rocks and a classical archway.[18]

Nearly a year later Cecil employed Jonson and Jones once more for another entertainment designed to celebrate this time the opening of the New Exchange, Cecil's grand new shopping mall. This ambitious commercial development was located on the site of Durham House (the former palace of the bishops of Durham) in the Strand—the principal thoroughfare joining the cities of London and Westminster, now fast becoming a fashionable place of residence for the wealthy. It was designed to rival Sir Thomas Gresham's famous Royal Exchange, and to draw custom away from the City of London to the West End, a prospect that was already causing anxiety amongst London shopkeepers. Inigo Jones had been commissioned to prepare initial plans for the building (see Fig. 29a), and although his designs were (in Lawrence Stone's words) 'far in advance of anything which had yet been built in England', they failed to appeal to Cecil's conservative taste.[19] An alternative design by Robert Smythson (Fig. 29b) was approved, and the building itself—involving a covered neoclassical arcade more than 200 feet long and an internal corridor, with shops on the ground and first floors, and cellars beneath—was constructed at some speed, opening on 11 April 1609 with a festive event attended by King

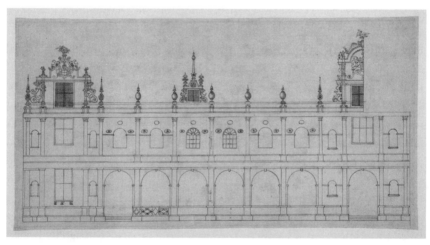

Fig. 29a and 29b. Inigo Jones's design for Robert Cecil's shopping arcade in the Strand, the New Exchange (above), was finally rejected in favour of that by Robert Smythson (below), erected in 1609.

James, Queen Anne, Prince Henry and Prince Charles, and Princess Elizabeth, accompanied by members of the court and the London diplomatic community. In a gesture embracing Cecil's mercantile hopes and James's plans for a united kingdom, the new building was named Britain's Burse.

Jonson and Jones prepared *The Entertainment at Britain's Burse* under the direction of Cecil's somewhat officious private secretary Thomas Wilson, who relayed instructions from his employer with a precision that may at times have rankled with these two notoriously independent spirits.[20] Until recently, no text of the entertainment was thought to have survived, but in 1996 James Knowles discovered, excitingly, amongst the papers of Sir Edward Conway—later Viscount Conway and Secretary of State to James I and Charles I—in the Public Record Office (now the National Archives) a transcript which seems more or less faithfully to reflect the final acting version of the piece.[21] The entertainment is presented by three actors: Nathan Field (as the Key Keeper, or Porter of the Burse), William Ostler (as the Master), and Giles Cary (as the Shop Boy). All of these actors would shortly appear also in Jonson's *Epicene*. The exotic contents of the shopping exchange are on display as the entertainment begins, and the Boy, in a bold piece of patter, begins to tout them to the distinguished company.

Shop Boy What do you lack? What is't you buy? Very fine China stuffs of all kinds and qualities? China chains, China bracelets, China scarves, China fans, China girdles, China knives, China boxes, China cabinets, caskets, umbrellas, sundials, hourglasses, looking-glasses, burning-glasses, concave glasses, triangular glasses, convex glasses, crystal globes, waxen pictures, ostrich eggs, birds of paradise, musk-cats, Indian mice, Indian rats, China dogs, and China cats? Flowers of silk, mosaic fishes? Waxen fruit and porcelain dishes? Very fine cages for birds, billiard balls, purses, pipes, rattles, basins, ewers, cups, cans, voiders, toothpicks, targets, falchions, beards of all ages, vizards, spectacles? See, what you lack? (50–9)

The entertainment vividly suggests the new range of Eastern luxury goods now available to shoppers in Jacobean London, shifting back and forth from the realm of the possible (porcelain 'tralucent as amber and subtler than crystal') to that of delicate fantasy: combs devised to prevent the hair from turning grey;

carpets wrought of *paraquitos'* feathers; umbrellas made of the wing of the Indian butterfly; ventolas of flying fishes' fins; hangings of the island of Cochin, which, being but a natural cobweb of that country, last longer than your gilded leather; paper made of the barks of trees and ink to carry dry in your pocket; and thousand such subtleties which you will think to have cheap now at the next return of the Hollanders' fleet from the Indies. (116–22)

The entertainment concluded with a shower of gifts to the assembled guests, modest items (rings with poesies) for some, and offerings of some magnificence for the royal party: a silver plaque worth 4,000 crowns depicting the Annunciation for Queen Anne; a rich caparison, 'the whole furniture for a horse, and for a proud horse indeed', for Prince Henry. *The Entertainment at Britain's Burse* offers an intriguing glimpse into the culture of consumerism in London in 1609, into the determined efforts of Robert Cecil to aggrandize his own commercial estate and political position, and (not least) into Jonson's creative range and versatility.

§§

A touch of irony as well as of fantasy may well be evident in the spiel that Jonson gives to the Shop Boy in *Britain's Burse*, as he runs through the goods available for sale in the New Exchange. For in promoting Cecil's new commercial endeavour in this entertainment Jonson can barely suppress the sense of satirical amusement that he elsewhere directs against those who, in this age of lavish expenditure, are so taken by that new and exciting phenomenon: shopping. 'What do you lack?' is a cry that will next be heard in *Bartholomew Fair* (2.2.24–5), as Lantern Leatherhead offers the tawdry wares of Smithfield to those who pass by: 'What do you lack? What is't you buy? What do you lack? Rattles, drums, halberds, horses, babies o'the best? Fiddles o'the finest?' What these customers *lack* (Jonson seems to imply) is common sense, and the power to resist the acquisitive urge. In *Epicene*, performed just a few months after *Britain's Burse*, he revisits the fashionable area of the New Exchange he had recently helped to celebrate, and inspects some of its customers more closely. The desperately sociable Sir Amorous La Foole has acquired a lodging in the Strand where he can shout his invitations at people passing by in carriages, or 'watch when ladies are gone to china houses, or the Exchange, that he may meet 'em by chance and give 'em presents, some two or three hundred pounds' worth of toys, to be laughed at' (1.3.26–9). And in his next great comedy, *The Alchemist*, the tricksters Subtle and Face attempt to persuade Dame Pliant, the rich young widow from the country, that by marrying the supposed Spanish count they have enticed to the house (who is in fact the suspicious Londoner Surly, though

they don't yet know that) she will have all the pleasures of the rapidly expanding
metropolis at her disposal, including, above all, shopping:

Face   ... her pages, ushers,
   Footmen and coaches—
Subtle   Her six mares—
Face   Nay, eight!
Subtle To hurry her through London to th'Exchange,
   Bedlam, the China-houses—
Face   Yes, and have
   The citizens gape at her and praise her tires!
   And my lord's goose-turd bands, that rides with her! (4.4.45–50)

Like *Epicene* and other comedies of Jonson's maturity, *The Alchemist* is
startlingly up to the moment in its setting and its allusions, playing directly to
the current pretensions and anxieties of its audiences. The principal anxiety of
the year in which the play was first performed was the plague, which had
descended upon London in 1610 with unusual severity, forcing the closure of
the playhouses from mid-July to late November (along with other places of
public resort), and prompting an exodus from the city.[22] During this period
of closure the members of the King's Men were themselves obliged to leave
town, and in September presented *The Alchemist* in Oxford. It is likely that
the comedy had already been performed in London shortly before the closing
of the theatres in July. In congregating at such a moment in such a risky
venue as the playhouse, the original audiences may well have felt some of the
nervousness experienced by Lovewit, the master of the house in Blackfriars in
which the play is set, on his return to London at the end of the play after a
period of voluntary exile at his hop-yards in Kent, when his butler Jeremy,
alias Face, inventively suggests that the house has been visited by the
plague ('Breathe less, and farther off', says Lovewit in alarm, 5.2.15). When
the weekly deaths in London exceeded forty, the theatres were obliged to
close, in accordance with a restraint order of 1608. This tally included deaths
in the out-parishes that had not previously been taken into account in the
earlier figure for theatre closure, of thirty deaths per week.[23] Such calculations
are vital to the three conspirators in *The Alchemist* if they are to know
how long Lovewit is likely to remain out of town, and what time they
have at their disposal. 'Oh, fear not him,' says Face early in the play;
'While there dies one a week | O' the plague, he's safe from thinking toward

London' (1.1.182–3). Lovewit's return at the end of the fourth act catches the trio by surprise.

Subtle   You said he would not come
  While there died one a week within the liberties.
Face No, 'twas within the walls.
Subtle   Was't so? Cry you mercy,
  I thought the liberties. What shall we do now, Face? (4.7.115–19)

The liberties are the areas of London outside the city walls, encompassing a large geographical area. On this misjudgement, the dénouement of the play depends.[24]

Though it is not known for certain at which of the two venues of the King's Men, Blackfriars or the Globe, the play was first presented, *The Alchemist* is likely to have been performed at Blackfriars, in the same district that the play is set.[25] Through these conjunctions of time and place, Jonson creates a suggestive parallel between the activities of the three rogues who have taken over Lovewit's empty house in Blackfriars during this time of plague and the activities of the King's Men themselves, operating in another house in Blackfriars (or is it perhaps the same house?): the theatre.

The fraudulent operation that Subtle, Face, and Doll set up in Lovewit's house centres on a practice that had flourished in England (as elsewhere in Europe) for many centuries, and that was still seriously regarded by many in Jonson's day. Though the researches of the Royal Society would help in due course to undermine the premises of alchemy, a belief in its feasibility lingered on; no less a scientist than Sir Isaac Newton would in due course secretly conduct his alchemical investigations.[26] Just eight years after the staging of Jonson's comedy, Francis Bacon—who disapproved of the practices of alchemists, but shared many of their larger aspirations—was to give his approval for a patent to be granted to Sir Giles Mompesson (the original of Massinger's Sir Giles Overreach in *A New Way to Pay Old Debts*) to make gold and silver lace with copper in a new 'alchymistical' way.[27] The quest of the alchemists was to discover, through successive processes of refinement, the elixir that would turn base metals to gold, while simultaneously restoring the possessor's health and beauty, and, in the full-blown version of the dream, conferring eternal life. The bogus laboratory that Subtle and Face install in the house resembles the more serious laboratory that the learned Dr John Dee had set up in his house at Mortlake for alchemical experimentation in 1571.

Dee, a formidable scholar in many reputable (as well as some less reputable) branches of learning, had died in 1609, the year before the performance of Jonson's comedy. Though his diaries had not yet been published, Jonson was evidently familiar with his activities, and seems to have modelled the character of Subtle in part upon him. Jonson had a sceptical fascination with the arts that had so entranced John Dee, and owned a copy of *Liber sacer*, also known as the *Sworn Book of Honorius* (one of the key texts for ritual magic in pre-Reformation England) that had previously been in Dee's possession.[28]

Jonson's Subtle professes not merely to be as an alchemist, however, but to possess exceptional powers of perception and knowledge. He is a magus or cunning-man, who can answer questions on any topic and teach 'Anything whatever'; 'His art knows all' (3.4.42; 4.4.66).[29] He counsels the young tobacconist, Drugger, on the precise layout of his shop (being evidently knowledgeable in some early form of *feng shui*), and on his lucky and unlucky days which he knows by reading his horoscope. He pretends to further knowledge of Drugger's character and fortune through metoscopy, or study of his face. He offers to teach Dapper the rules for gambling, and Kastril the grammar, logic, mathematics, and rhetoric of quarrelling, as well as of fencing. He can advise Dame Pliant on fashion, the art she has come to London to learn, tell her fortune through the art of palmistry, and guide her as to the wisdom of remarriage. He is 'a rare physician' who is treating a deranged lady (Doll, as it happens) for her mental troubles. He can inform a sailor's wife whether her husband is at present away with the pirates in the Mediterranean, and a waiting maid if she will ever have precedence of her mistress. He is an expert on hair-loss, as was another real-life contemporary and possible model for the character of Subtle, Simon Forman, who was likewise skilled in 'astrology, geomancy, medicine, divination by facial moles, alchemy, and conjuring' and much in demand from a credulous public, conducting (it is said) 8,000 consultations between March 1596 and 1603 on a wide range of problems.[30] Not long after the performance of *The Alchemist*, Forman was to be consulted by Frances Howard, at the outset of an episode that would impinge in other ways on Jonson's life, about the best way to attract the attentions of an unnamed lord, who was soon to become her husband.[31]

Jonson brilliantly combines the central premiss and promise of alchemy, that of transmutation, with a major preoccupation of the day, social mobility. Those who call to see the wise man at his house in Blackfriars all wish in some way to be transformed, as the metals themselves are said to be transformed by the alchemical processes. None can express their dreams on this matter more eloquently than Sir Epicure Mammon.

> We will be brave, Puff, now we ha' the med'cine.
> My meat shall all come in in Indian shells,
> Dishes of agate, set in gold and studded
> With emeralds, sapphires, hyacinths, and rubies.
> The tongues of carp, dormice, and camels' heels
> Boiled i' the spirit of Sol and dissolved pearl
> (Apicius' diet 'gainst the epilepsy),
> And I will eat these broths with spoons of amber,
> Headed with diamond and carbuncle.
> My foot-boy shall eat pheasants, calvered salmons,
> Knots, godwits, lampreys. I myself will have
> The beards of barbells served instead of salads,
> Oiled mushrooms, and swelling unctuous paps
> Of a fat pregnant sow, newly cut off,
> Dressed with an exquisite and poignant sauce,
> For which I'll say unto my cook, 'There's gold,
> Go forth and be a knight.' (2.2.71–87)

Social change (in Jonson's ironical perception) is driven entirely by gold: even Mammon's cook—once Subtle has perfected the elixir—can now go out to buy himself a knighthood. At the conclusion of the play, his dreams shattered, Mammon 'will go mount a turnip-cart and preach | The end o' the world within these two months' (5.5.81–2). Most of the characters at the end of Jonson's comedy remain what they have always been, base metals, wholly themselves, wholly untransmutable. Yet some changes have occurred. Through the quickness of his wits, Jeremy the butler, alias Captain Face, has improved his standing with his master, Lovewit, who, thanks to Face's skills, has acquired a young rich widow for his wife. Dame Pliant herself—though not married precisely to a Spanish count—has entered happily into marriage and the metropolis, to the satisfaction of her brother Kastril.

And the author himself, along with the King's Men who have presented this comedy—so Jonson suggests, in an epilogue that is spoken by Jeremy or Face or perhaps by the actor playing those roles ('Speak for thyself, knave,' says Lovewit, with a delicious ambiguity)—have not done badly, either. 'Gentleman', says 'Face',

> My part a little fell in this last scene,
> Yet 'twas decorum. And though I am clean
> Got off from Subtle, Surly, Mammon, Doll,
> Hot Ananias, Dapper, Drugger, all
> With whom I traded, yet I put myself
> On you, that are my country, and this pelf,
> Which I have got, if you do quit me, rests
> To feast you often, and invite new guests. (5.5.157–65)

'Pelf' is a word that means booty, but also rubbish, nicely conveying Jonson's own dual valuation of the commodity for which everyone in the play has ultimately been scrambling. Gold may be fine to possess, though it is also, in the last estimate, trash. The *pelf* of these final lines is at once the loot Face or Jeremy has acquired through his illicit activities in Lovewit's house, and the booty of the box office, the money that the company itself has acquired from trusting playgoers who have likewise come to their home in Blackfriars to witness this performance of the comedy. They are genially invited to return to the theatre again, this time with their friends, to be relieved of their money once more.

The sense of ironic complicity here between the players and the rogues whose actions they depict makes for a kind of comedy that differs markedly from Jonson's earlier great comic masterpiece *Volpone*. *The Alchemist* is a play more tolerant, more delightedly collusive, more willing to embrace the spirit of mischief that drives the action of its intricately constructed plot. Jonson appears more ready now to accept the energies of the theatre about which he had expressed such stern misgivings just three years earlier. Perhaps it was true, as he had said with such force in the Epistle to *Volpone*, that the theatre does utter 'nothing but the garbage of the time', but on occasions such garbage may actually turn out to be gold.

§§

Part of Jonson's livelihood was earned at yet another venue, the court, where despite the crown's financial problems, money flowed in greater abundance. On 2 February 1609, just two months prior to the presentation of *Britain's Burse* at the New Exchange, Jonson's *The Masque of Queens* was performed at the Banqueting House at Whitehall. Though the masque was intended to cost no more than £1,000, total expenditures on the evening finally exceeded three times that sum, much of the additional cost being attributable to the elegant costumes created by Inigo Jones, and part to the ingenious machinery which Jones deployed on this occasion, a combination of *scena ductilis* (or sliding flats) and *machina versatilis* (or revolving scenery).[32] Jonson was encouraged by Queen Anne to perfect for this occasion a new structural device towards which his more recent masques of *Haddington* and *Hymenaei* had been tending: 'a foil or false masque' to precede her entry, or what Jonson himself was to call, in the first known use of the term, an *antimasque* (*Queens*, 9–10). The variant forms of this word—'ante-masque' (i.e. an entry preceding the principal masque) and 'antic-masque' (a grotesque or fanciful show)—capture some, though not all, of the term's essential meaning, which also signifies an entertainment that is directly antithetical to the style and values displayed in the main masque, and that will as a consequence be suddenly and spectacularly expelled at the entry of the principal dancers.

The Masque of Queens opens with an antimasque entry of 'twelve women in the habits of hags, or witches, sustaining the persons of Ignorance, Suspicion, Credulity, etc., the opposites of Good Fame' (11–12). The witches, played by male actors, are 'all differently attired: some with rats on their heads, some on their shoulders, others with ointment pots at their girdles; all with spindles, timbrels, rattles, or other venefical instruments, making a confused noise with strange gestures' (21–3), and speaking their several charms. Here is the recitation of the third witch:

> The owl is abroad, the bat and the toad,
>   And so is the cat-a-mountain;
> The ant and the mole sit both in a hole,
>   And frog peeps out o' the fountain;
> The dogs they do bay, and the timbrels play,
>   The spindle is now a-turning;
> The moon it is red, and the stars are fled,
> But all the sky is a-burning:
> The ditch is made, and our nails the spade,
> With pictures full, of wax and of wool;
> Their livers I stick with needles quick;
> There lacks but the blood, to make up the flood.
>   Quickly, Dame, then bring your part in,
>   Spur, spur, upon little Martin,
>   Merrily, merrily, make him sail,

A worm in his mouth and a thorn in's tail,
Fire above and fire below,
With a whip i' your hand to make him go. (58–75)

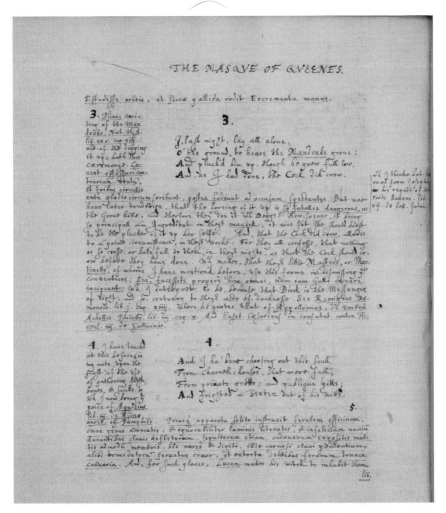

Fig. 30. Presentation copy of *The Masque of Queens* in Jonson's own hand, prepared for Prince Henry (BL Royal 18 A xlv, fo. 7ᵛ).

The hags perform their 'magical dance, full of preposterous change and gesticulation, but most applying to their property: who at their meetings, do all things contrary to the custom of men, dancing back to back and hip to hip, their hands joined, and making their circles backward to the left hand, with strange fantastic motions of their heads and bodies' (313–17). With a blast of loud music the hags abruptly vanish, and the main masque begins, the sliding flats being drawn aside to reveal 'a glorious and magnificent building, figuring the House of Fame', a throne 'erected in the form of a pyramid and circled with all store of light' on which are seated twelve ladies of the court, headed by Queen Anne ('Bel-Anna, royal Queen of the Ocean'). Representing twelve formidable female figures from history and legend— 'Penthesilia, the brave Amazon', 'Swift-foot Camilla, queen of Volscia', 'The virtuous Palmyrene, Zenobia', and others (406–8, 358ff.)—the ladies process in triumphal chariots drawn across the stage by eagles, lions, and griffins, the defeated hags chained abjectly to their wheels.

On closer inspection, the seemingly simple bipartite structure of *The Masque of Queens* presents more ambiguities than might immediately be apparent. What looks at first like an unreserved celebration of queenly power (it has been argued) is in fact mediated through the male figure of Heroic Virtue, and is in quiet tension with the masculinist realities of the Stuart court, headed by King James.[33] The force of the antimasque, moreover—built upon popular belief, fuelled by James himself, in the literal existence and malign power of witches—may not be entirely extinguished at the end of the masque, where the witches are still in full view as potent, though now servile creatures, trudging at the wheels of the ladies' triumphal chariots. James had for many years been a fervent believer in the existence of witches and sorcerers, whom he regarded as people of loose morals who had become 'detestable slaves of the Devil', as he put it in his *Demonology*, published first in Edinburgh in 1597 and reissued in 1603 after his arrival in London.[34] Through the potions and poisons and waxen figures furnished them by the Devil, witches (he believed) could raise storms, and cause madness, impotency, sexual frenzy, or death. Witches moreover had directed their powers against him personally, throwing cats into the sea tied to the severed limbs of corpses in order to raise storms while he was sailing to Denmark to collect his bride, and seeking through chants and waxen images to bring about his death. James's *Demonology* is a profoundly misogynist work, whose basic assumptions are in obvious tension with the feistily

Plate 1. William Drummond of Hawthornden. Anonymous painting on wood, 1623.

Plate 2. During their first visit to Scotland in 1842 Queen Victoria and Prince Albert were taken by the Duchess of Buccleuch to Hawthornden Castle on the River Esk, where Jonson had stayed with William Drummond over the winter of 1618–19. Painting by Sir William Allen, oil on canvas, 1844.

Plate 3. William Camden, scholar and antiquary, by Marcus Gheeraerts the younger, 1622. Jonson's teacher at Westminster School and lifelong friend is depicted here in old age, a year before his death.

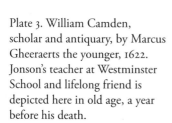

Plate 4. Robert Devereux, 2nd Earl of Essex, after Marcus Gheeraerts the younger, c.1596, the year of the Cadiz expedition. Jonson may have been drawn into Essex's circle about this time.

ANNO DNI. 1591.
ÆTATIS SVÆ 18.
ANTES ALIADO
QVELO QVE

This was for youth, Strength, Mirth, and wit that Time
Most count their golden Age; but t'was not thine.
Thine was thy later yeares, so much refind
From youths Drosse, Mirth, & wit; as thy pure mind
Thought (like the Angels) nothing but the Praise
Of thy Creator, in those last, best Dayes.
Witnes this Booke, (thy Embleme) which begins
With Love; but endes, with Sighes, & Teares for sins.
Will: Marshall sculpsit.   IZ: WA:

Plate 5. John Donne by William Marshall. This engraving is based on a now-lost portrait made in 1591, when Donne was not yet 20. Jonson believed that Donne, 'the first poet in the world in some things', had 'written all his best pieces ere he was twenty-five years old': *Informations*, 80–3.

NON SINE SOLE
IRIS.

Plate 6. Elizabeth I as Iris: the Rainbow portrait, *c.*1600. Attributed to Marcus Gheeraerts (d. 1635); oil on canvas. The motto, *non sine sole*, means literally 'not without the sun' (on which the radiance of the rainbow depends), and by extension, 'not without glory'.

Plate 7. Jonson's 'mortal enemy', Henry Howard, later Earl of Northampton. Painted in 1594 by an unknown follower of the London-based Flemish artist Hieronymus Custodis.

Plate 8. King James VI and I, by John de Critz the younger.

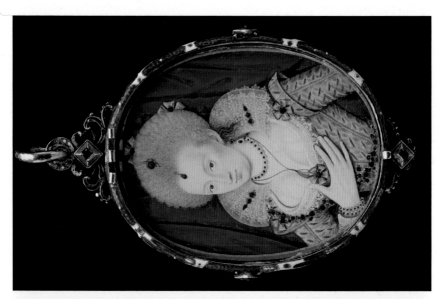

Plate 9 (right). Queen Anne of Denmark. Studio of Nicholas Hilliard, vellum on playing card, c.1610. Plate 10 (left). 'Lucy, you brightness of our sphere, who are | Life of the muses' day, their morning-star!' (*Epigrams*, 94.1–2). Jonson's friend and patroness Lucy Harington, Countess of Bedford, in masquing costume; attributed to John de Critz the elder.

Plate 11. Jonson's patron William Herbert, 3rd Earl of Pembroke, hailed in the dedications to both *Catiline* and *Epigrams* as 'the great example of honour and virtue'. Studio of Daniel Mytens.

Plate 12. King James VI and I in procession to Parliament. From the *Album Amicorum* (or *Book of Friends*) of Michael van Meer, a Dutchman who lived most of his life in Hamburg but visited London in 1614–15, when James's relations with his Parliament were particularly fraught (see Chapter 16).

Plate 13. Henry Frederick, Prince of Wales, on horseback, escorted ominously by the figure of Time, *c.*1610, a couple of years before his early death. Portrait by Robert Peake.

Plate 14. Penshurst Place, Kent, home to the Sidney family since 1552.

Plate 15. William and Robert Sidney, sons of Lord and Lady Lisle, c.1610, artist unkown (English School). Jonson acted as tutor to William Sidney at Penshurst in 1611: see Chapter 14.

Plate 16. Lady Mary Wroth and her mother, Barbara Gamage, Lady Lisle, by Marcus Gheeraerts the younger.

Plate 17. Sir Walter Ralegh and his eldest son Walter, Jonson's troublesome charge on their continental travels in 1612–13 (see Chapter 14). Artist unknown.

Plate 18. Sir Thomas Overbury by Sylvester Harding after Marcus Gheeraerts the younger.

Plate 19. Jonson's patron Robert Cecil, 1st Earl of Salisbury, by John de Critz. 'Salisbury never cared for any man longer nor he could make use of him,' said Jonson to William Drummond after Cecil's death (*Informations*, 274).

Plate 20. George Villiers, 1st Duke of Buckingham, favoured courtier of James VI and I and later of his son Charles I. Attributed to William Larkin.

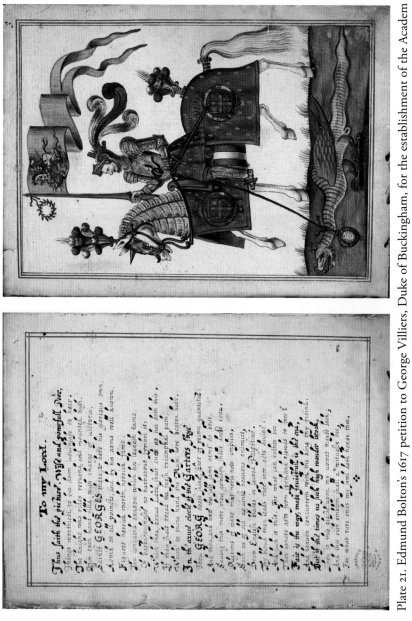

Plate 21. Edmund Bolton's 1617 petition to George Villiers, Duke of Buckingham, for the establishment of the Academ Roial (BL Harley 6103, 2ᵛ, 3). Ben Jonson was named as a foundation member of this new body (see Chapter 17).

Plate 22. Jonson's learned friend John Selden, by an unknown artist. 'He was very tall, I guess about six foot,' wrote John Aubrey of Selden, 'sharp oval face; head not very big; long nose inclining to one side; full popping eye (grey).'

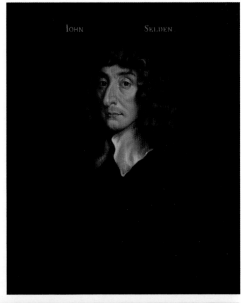

Plate 23. Venetia Digby on her death-bed, by Van Dyck. ''Twere time that I died too, now she is dead,' wrote Jonson, 'Who was my muse, and life of all I said' (*The Underwood*, 84.ix.1–2).

Plate 24. Sir Kenelm Digby, by Van Dyck. Jonson's friend and literary executor.

feminist display presented, under Queen Anne's watchful eye, in the main masque of *The Masque of Queens*. Women, so James suggests in the *Demonology*, are twenty times more likely to become servants of the Devil than men, 'for as that sex is frailer than man is, so it is easier to be entrapped in these gross snares of the Devil, as was over-well proved to be true by the serpent's deceiving of Eva at the beginning, which makes him the homelier with that sex' ever since.[35]

Jonson cites *Demonology* respectfully near the beginning of the lengthy and erudite notes he provided, supposedly at Prince Henry's request, for the 1609 quarto edition of the masque. In view of this citation and his massive marshalling of learned authorities on the subject of witchcraft it is tempting to conclude that Jonson shared the King's general beliefs about witches, and perhaps about women in general. Yet Jonson in fact makes little use of James's treatise in the masque, drawing some of his details about the alleged behaviour of witches instead (though he is discreetly silent about his sources) from the very work that James's *Demonology* set out specifically to refute: Reginald Scott's *The Discovery of Witchcraft*, published in 1584.[36] Scott's *Discovery* is a sceptical and humane investigation of the phenomenon of witchcraft and of the factors leading to the persecution of poor and elderly women throughout Europe at this time. With remarkable courage, Scott maintained that there were no witches in England in his day and that those who had been executed for witchcraft were in fact innocent. With equal boldness he attacked other contemporary forms of credulity and superstition, including astrology, alchemy, and conjuring. Refusing to accept the account of the fall offered in Genesis, he was in no danger of sharing the view later entertained by James of the intrinsic weaknesses of the female sex.

Scott was in short precisely the kind of author who, in his hard-headed attitude towards popular beliefs and superstitions, was likely to appeal strongly to Jonson. There is in fact a fragment of new evidence that Jonson had studied Scott's writings with care. In 1619 Drummond noted that Jonson 'scorned that simplicity of Cardan about the pebble-stones of Dover, which he thought had that virtue, kept between one's teeth, as to save him from being sick' (*Informations*, 427–9). In his sceptical discussion of the supposedly magical power of certain stones in *The Discovery of Witchcraft* Scott had recorded the opinion of the celebrated Italian physician Gironimo Cardano 'that stones do good', even if the seals inscribed upon them—totemic insignia such as lions and serpents, thought to have special power—have little force. And he goes to recount an anecdote that has a distinctly Jonsonian air:

An excellent philosopher, whom (for reverence unto his fame and learning) I will forbear to name, was overtaken by his hostess at Dover, who merrily told him that if he could retain and keep in his mouth certain pebbles lying at the sea-shore he should not perbreak [vomit] until he came to Calais, how rough and tempestuous so ever the seas were. Which when he tried, and being not forced by sickness to vomit, nor to lose his stones, as by vomiting he must needs do, he thought his hostess had discovered unto him an excellent secret, nothing doubting of her amphibological speech; and therefore thought it a worthy note to be recorded among miraculous and medicinable stones, and inserted it accordingly into his book among other experiments collected with great industry, learning, travel, and judgement. All these toys help a subtle cozener to gain credit with the multitude.

Scott's anecdote forms part of a larger attack upon popular (and scholarly) credulity. 'Hereunto' (he continued) 'belong all manner of charms, periapts, amulets, characters, and such other superstitions, both popish and profane: whereby, if that were true which either papists, conjurors, or witches undertake to do, we might daily see the very miracles wrought indeed which Pharaoh's magicians seem to perform.'[37]

Jonson's learned notes to *The Masque of Queens*, while seeming to support a belief in the literal existence of witches, may in short be largely lapwing activity, to distract attention from Jonson's own doubts on this very subject. He cites classical authorities (as the masque's latest editor has noted) with more enthusiasm than contemporary authors, and the witches themselves are named (as Martin Butler observes) to designate 'an intellectual or moral flaw rather than supernatural evil: Ignorance, Suspicion, Credulity, Falsehood, Murmur, Malice, Impudence, Slander, Execration, Bitterness, Rage, and Mischief'.[38] There is little evidence of Jonson's personal attachment to James's beliefs about witches. James's attitude towards witches was in fact to change as time went by, and in *The Devil Is an Ass* (as we shall see, 347–8) Jonson was able to pay a quiet compliment to his King's new-found scepticism on this subject. But for Jonson in 1609 to have expressed misgivings about such matters would not have been prudent or decorous. The court masque was not a vehicle in any simple sense for Jonson's own views, but needed to reflect opinion (however divided) of those who commissioned his work. His own 'voice', despite his protestations to the contrary, was not singular or constant. Each employer, each location offered different opportunities and constraints. Like Jeremy the butler or Captain Face, Jonson himself needed swiftly to adapt to changing circumstance.

13

Communities 1607–1612

JONSON was now in close touch with an unusual range of communities: religious, scholarly, theatrical, poetic, legal, parliamentary, civic, aristocratic. *Community* is a word that appears to imply social cohesion. Raymond Williams speaks of it as a 'warmly persuasive' term. 'Unlike all other terms of social organization (*state, nation, society*, etc.)', he writes, 'it seems never to be used unfavourably, and never to be given any positive opposing or distinguishing term.'[1] In the seventeenth century, moreover, the notion of community was highly prized: 'Levellers, clubmen and Cavalier poets all evoked the word community, associating it with patriotism and even civilization itself,' writes Conal Condren.[2] Yet it was a term that often barely concealed the tensions and fissures that actually existed within and between loosely defined sectors of society. The so-called English Catholic community, for example, to which Jonson now belonged, was in fact (as we shall shortly see) a deeply fractured group, whose members held a wide range of often sharply opposed views on social, political, and ecclesiastical issues. Where precisely Jonson situated himself within this community, how he reconciled his religious loyalties with his loyalties to the state, were pressing questions that faced him in the years following the collapse of the Gunpowder Plot.

In a poem written early in his Catholic years, Jonson had hopefully depicted divine love as a unifying, socializing force, that

> ... bears no brands nor darts
> To murther different hearts

> But in a calm and god-like unity
> Preserves community.
>
> ('Epode', *The Forest*, 11.51–4)

In a period marked by bloody, fractious, and seemingly endless wars of religion, the notion that divine love 'Preserves community' was a bold stroke. It was equally bold of Jonson to have reprinted this poem with its central proposition unchanged in 1616, some years after converting back to the Anglican faith, as if the word 'community' applied with equal appropriateness to either religion, or signified some larger, more capacious concept within which the warring factions of the Christian Church might somehow sit peaceably, side by side.

§§

To which community—and to which *part* of that community—did Jonson's loyalties in the early years of James's reign ultimately belong? In the immediate wake of the Gunpowder Plot, the government saw fit to introduce, along with harsher penalties on recusancy, a new Oath of Allegiance, which put such questions immediately to the test. The Oath of Allegiance was ostensibly designed 'for the better trial of how His Majesty's subjects stand affected in point of their loyalty and obedience', but also, as Catholics themselves quickly recognized, to deepen existing rifts between discordant elements within the Catholic community.[3] Approved by the House of Commons on 27 May 1606 through an 'Act for the Better Discovery and Repressing of Popish Recusants', the Oath required assent to the proposition

that our Sovereign Lord King James is lawful and rightful King of this realm and of all other His Majesty's dominions and countries; and that the Pope neither of himself, nor by any authority of the Church or See of Rome, or by any other means with any other, hath any power or authority to depose the King, or to dispose of any of His Majesty's kingdoms or dominions, or to authorize any foreign prince to invade or annoy him or his countries or to discharge any of his subjects of their allegiance and obedience to His Majesty, or to give licence or leave to any of them to bear arms, raise tumult, or to offer any violence or hurt to His Majesty's royal person, state, or government, or to any of His Majesty's subjects within His Majesty's dominions.

Through its successive clauses the Oath increased in rhetorical intensity, requiring those who took it to declare, without equivocation or evasion, that they did from their hearts 'abhor, detest, and abjure, as impious and heretical, this damnable doctrine and position, that princes which be ex-communicated or deprived by the Pope may be deposed or murthered by their subjects, or any other whatsoever'.

The Oath caused immediate confusion within the already divided Catholic community in England, just as its devisers, Robert Cecil and Archbishop Bancroft, had hoped it would. Since Elizabeth's accession, the precise lines of religious authority for Catholics resident in England had been shifting and uncertain. Deep divisions had existed for years between the Jesuits, who adhered closely to papal instructions from Rome, and the secular priests, who worked outside any closed order, and often adopted a more independent position. When the secular priest Father George Blackwell was appointed Archpriest of the Catholic Church in England in 1598, the terms of his appointment—intended to placate the contending parties, but having pre-cisely the reverse effect—obliged him to consult with the Superior of the Jesuits and others of that order over any matter of importance. The require-ment outraged many of the secular priests, thirty-one of whom, subsequently known as the Appellants, protested vigorously to Pope Clement VIII in Rome. In a series of briefs and bulls over the next few years, punctuated by further protestations from the Appellants, Pope Clement attempted to mod-erate the situation, finally instructing Blackwell in 1602 to communicate no business whatever to the Provincial of the Jesuits or any members of his Order, lest such consultations merely provoke further quarrels and animosity between the two groups.

The introduction of the Oath of Allegiance threw the already perplexed Blackwell and the Catholic community as a whole into greater turmoil. Blackwell reminded his clergy that it was the Pope's wish that they should behave peaceably in all civil matters, and advised them therefore to accept the Oath. But the new Pope, Paul V, at once contradicted this advice, roundly condemning the Oath, and suggesting that those who refused to take it might be regarded as martyrs, reminding English Catholics 'of the singular virtue, valour, and fortitude which in these last times doth no less shine in your martyrs than it did in the first beginning of the church'. The Pope's interven-tion drew a stinging riposte from King James, who in a tract entitled *Triplici nodo, triplex cuneus* scornfully rejected the notion that those who refused to take the Oath could legitimately be regarded as martyrs. The controversy concerning the Oath continued for several years, prompting bitter exchanges between Rome and London, and between different sectors of the Catholic community within England.

Jonson would have been acutely aware of this controversy, which bore directly on his own situation in the years leading up to his own re-conversion to the Church of England in 1610. He might well have explored the central issues with John Overall, Dean of St Paul's, and with the Archbishop of Canterbury's chaplain, Zacharius Pasfield, during the consultations the Consistory Court had instructed him to undertake at this time. He must also have discussed these questions with his friend John Donne, whose learned treatise of 1610, *Pseudo-Martyr*, was a major contribution to this debate. *Pseudo-Martyr* was Donne's first significant publication, and of crucial importance to Donne's eventual preferment by James to the deanship of St Paul's. The subject of martyrdom was a sensitive one for Donne, and he refers famously in the opening of *Pseudo-Martyr* to the sufferings of his own family, to which Thomas More (whose credentials for martyrdom James had at one point queried in *Triplici nodo*) had belonged. Yet Donne comes down firmly in this treatise in support of James's views, declaring that those who refuse to take the Oath of Allegiance cannot legitimately be described as 'martyrs'. 'There may be an inordinate and corrupt affectation of martyrdom,' he writes, a pseudo-martyrdom, which needs to be resisted. A good Catholic, Donne concludes, may take the Oath without in any way compromising his religion. Though Donne and Jonson had switched their religion in opposite ways— Donne from Catholicism to Anglicanism, Jonson, the other way about—they may have had broadly similar views on the significance and legitimacy of the Oath, and it is almost certain that Jonson would have willingly subscribed to the Oath. The position it staked out, pledging ultimate loyalty to the monarch of England rather than to the Pope of Rome, was broadly similar to that adopted by Father Thomas Wright in the 1590s, which Jonson evidently had found congenial.[4] Jonson, like Donne, had no special wish to be a martyr. He did not identify with the extreme Catholic position in these matters, and had no particular fondness for papal authority or for continental powers such as Spain. And like Donne, he had a career to build, which would have been seriously jeopardized had he decided to refuse the Oath. He was a moderate and a loyalist, ready to declare his allegiance to James and to attend Anglican services for the sake of 'community'. Yet he was sufficiently independent still to refuse the next step, the act of communion itself, insisting on his own honest 'scruple' and his continuing adherence to the beliefs and protocols of the Church of Rome.

It is intriguing to observe how wider questions of social conformity—the manner in which an individual chooses to resist or succumb to the behavioural norms of the community in which he lives—continue to preoccupy Jonson at this time, and inform his next major work for the theatre: *Epicene, Or, The Silent Woman*, performed late in 1609 or early in 1610 at the small indoor theatre of Whitefriars, a former Carmelite priory, by the company soon to be known as the Children of Her Majesty's Revels.

§§

Epicene is a comedy about a man who lives (so far as he can achieve this impossible dream) entirely outside society, having a pathological hatred of noise and of other people. Morose is a solitary and a misanthrope: a man without a community. He has taken up residence off the Strand, in a street 'so narrow at both ends that it will receive no coaches nor carts nor any of these common noises', devising within his house 'a room with double walls and treble ceilings, the windows shut and caulked; and there he lives by candlelight', 'a huge turban of nightcaps on his head, buckled over his ears' (1.1.133–4, 146–8, 115). Morose's style of life is deliciously riddled with contradiction. Hating noise, he has come to live in one of the busiest and most fashionable areas of the town, in the newly developing area of the West End.[5] Loathing conversation, he has a garrulous barber in attendance, and talks himself with inordinate prolixity. Craving solitude, he is hoping now to marry a silent wife, in order to beget an heir and disinherit his nephew Sir Dauphine Eugenie. Dauphine, with his high-spirited companions Clerimont and Truewit, and the obligingly cooperative Collegiate Ladies, have resolved in return to torment and defeat him. Morose's bride, Mistress Epicene— surreptitiously schooled in this role by Dauphine—is revealed to be, moments after marriage, not silent at all, but a prodigious talker; and more startlingly, in the closing moments of the play, not a woman at all, but a boy dressed as a woman. The play concludes not with the rewards and fulfilments traditionally expected at the end of a comedy, but with divorce, frustration, and the scornful dismissal of its central character: 'Now you may go in and rest, be as private as you will, sir,' says Dauphine to Morose; 'I'll not trouble you till you trouble me with your funeral, which I care not how soon it come' (5.4.174–6).

In modern times Morose has been regarded not as a realistic character but as a monstrous caricature, part of 'a fantastic comic conceit, an extravagant exaggeration of human folly, to which all of the more realistically conceived characters and incidents have reference'.[6] Nearer to Jonson's day, John Dryden saw Morose in another light, being 'assured from divers persons' (in the words of his spokesman Neander in *An Essay of Dramatic Poesy*) 'that Ben Jonson was actually acquainted with such a man, one altogether as ridiculous as he is here represented'.[7] Given Jonson's sensitivity to the possibility of 'applied' readings of his work at this time, it is unlikely that Morose would have been modelled directly on a single person in quite the manner that Dryden here suggests. Stung by the accusation that the play contained an unflattering allusion to the King's cousin Lady Arbella Stuart, Jonson had indeed insisted that *Epicene* was not a play about real-life people at all—'For he knows, poet never credit gained | By writing truths, but things like truths well feigned' (second prologue, 9–10).[8] Yet however 'feigned' or exaggerated a dramatic character ultimately proves to be, it may often be inspired by everyday experience. It is tempting to wonder whether Jonson, in developing the character of Morose, might not have recalled the familiar condition of Catholic priests in England at this time, who were often obliged to live in a manner not unlike that of Morose, hidden away from the world within the houses of their protectors: in window-less priest-holes, padded and protected to exclude noise and to prevent their possible detection. George Blackwell himself had lodged for seven or eight years in the house of a Mrs Meany in Westminster in this way, remaining in constant fear of discovery and arrest, being rescued on one occasion by the Catholic Countess of Arundel and Surrey, who (as already noted, p. 184 above) had sheltered the Catholic fugitive Robert Southwell in earlier times in the same fashion in her house in the Strand—the very area of London in which Morose himself has chosen to live. Here Blackwell was

... forced for his own and the gentlewoman's security he lived with to hide himself in a secret place of the house when search was made after [him] by the heretics [i.e. Protestant vigilantes]; and being in great danger of being taken or famished by reason that all the Catholics of the house were carried away to prison, and heretic watchmen put into the house to keep it and hinder any from helping him.[9]

It is striking that Morose should be spoken of repeatedly in the play as a 'martyr', who believes that Dauphine and his company 'are authors of all ridiculous acts and monuments are told of him' (1.2.9–10). *Acts and Monuments* was the formal title of John Foxe's huge work popularly known as *The Book of Martyrs*; Morose is casting himself in the martyr's role. 'Take courage', says Truewit to Morose tauntingly later in the play as the uninvited revellers begin to enter his house, 'put on a martyr's resolution. Mock down all their attempting with patience. 'Tis but a day, and I would suffer heroically' (3.7.9–10). In 1609 these repeated references to martyrdom might well have reminded audiences of the highly contested issues surrounding the Oath of Allegiance: whether those who refused to take the Oath should properly be regarded as 'martyrs', or whether such a self-isolating act was to be seen as merely wilful, as a form of pseudo-martyrdom. *Epicene* is a highly topical play (as critics have often noted) in its frequent references to local happenings, fashions, and events. Less often noted is the play's engagement with more perplexing issues such as these that were currently touching Jonson in his life as a Catholic.[10]

In a curious turn of events during the eighteenth century, the character of Morose was to be confused with that of Ben Jonson himself, who came to be regarded as the real-life model upon whom the character of this noise-hating misanthrope was based. In *Epicene*, so it was imagined, Jonson was really writing about himself. In 1750 the London bookseller and Drury Lane prompter W. R. Chetwood declared of Jonson: 'Whether he first appeared upon the stage as a poet, or an actor, is uncertain, for he was both; the chief part, we are told, he performed in his latter capacity, was the character of Morose (a picture, it is said, which he drew from himself) in his own play, *The Silent Woman*.'[11] Chetwood's vague belief that Jonson was to be identified in these ways with Morose is unconfirmed by any surviving evidence, but formed part of the larger eighteenth-century imagining of the sharply contrasting characters of Jonson and Shakespeare (the one gloomy, the other gentle) already noted. Elements of these stereotypes survive into modern times, being found most notably in the notorious Freudian analysis of 'Morose Ben Jonson' by the American critic Edmund Wilson.[12]

Yet it is difficult to imagine Jonson at this stage of his life as harbouring misanthropic or unsociable tendencies, or to elide his notably gregarious personality in any way with that of his own dramatic character, Morose. For what *Epicene* finally celebrates and affirms (with whatever harshness) are the pleasures of sociable living, of 'company' and communality, with which Jonson himself at this time was coming increasingly to identify. During the final years of Elizabeth's reign he had chosen indeed to withdraw for a time from the world of the court and the theatre, casting himself, in the Apologetical Dialogue to *Poetaster*, as a fugitive from society, who cultivated as best he could the stoical virtues of fortitude, self-sufficiency, and detachment. With the advent of the Stuarts, however, Jonson had re-emerged as a more public and socially responsive figure. His masquing commissions at court had opened up a wider range of friendships and acquaintances than he had hitherto enjoyed, with parliamentarians, diplomats, members of the judiciary, and of the court circle. Questions of governance, statecraft, and social organization were increasingly capturing his interest. He was reading with attention the works of Bodin, Machiavelli, Contarini, and the Italian civic humanists, alongside the classical texts on which those writers drew.[13] 'Commonwealth', 'common good', 'public good', 'state', 'nation' are terms that appear with increasing frequency in his works at this time, together (significantly) with the word *patriot* in its newly emerging sense, as one who loves his country, of which Jonson is the first known user.[14] Patriotism—the duty owed by loyal citizens to the imagined community of 'Britannia' (that hopeful amalgam of England, Scotland, and Wales that James was attempting to fashion and promote)—was fast becoming a central and defining issue in the years following the Gunpowder Plot. By 1610, however, the word 'patriot' had acquired an additional sense, to describe someone who championed the interest of the country against those of the King. And it was with such patriots, through the social circles in which he was now beginning to mix, that Jonson was now beginning to come into frequent contact.

§§

One of the new and rapidly spreading social pleasures in Jacobean London was the advent of *clubs*: small associations of friends and like-minded companions who met regularly at designated taverns and eating-houses for drinking, dining, and animated conversation. John Aubrey, who surveyed the growth of this phenomenon with interest, believed that the term *club* derived from the hefty weapon that members of these groups had been known occasionally to carry for protection while walking the town together.[15] Jonson was a leading member of one of the most celebrated of early seventeenth-century London clubs, which some time before 1611 began to meet (according to the testimony of one of its company, the prodigious foot traveller Thomas Coryate) on the 'first Friday of every month at the sign of the Mermaid in Bread Street in London'. The members of this club, whom Coryate saluted from his travels in India as 'The Worshipful Fraternity of Sirenaical Gentlemen' ('Sirenaical', from the French word for 'mermaid', *sirène*), were fondly, if not always accurately, remembered in later times as a company of poets, as in Keats's 'Lines on the Mermaid Tavern':

> Souls of poets dead and gone,
> What Elysium have ye known,
> Happy field or mossy cavern,
> Choicer than the Mermaid Tavern?
> Have ye tippled drink more fine
> Than mine host's Canary wine? . . .

Donne and Jonson were certainly members of the Mermaid group, as was Jonson's old friend from Westminster School the Catholic Welsh poet Hugh Holland, and the dramatist Francis Beaumont, as his well-known lines to Jonson from the country suggest:

> What things have we seen
> Done at the Mermaid? Heard words that have been
> So nimble, and so full of subtle flame
> As if that everyone from whom they came
> Had meant to put his whole wit in a jest
> And had resolved to live a fool the rest
> Of his dull life . . .

But the Mermaid Club was not primarily or uniquely a poetical company. Keats may well have been misled in this regard by William Gifford, who in his recent edition of Jonson's works, published just two years before Keats wrote his lines on the Mermaid tavern, had confidently recruited other poets to membership of the Club, including the man he claimed to have been the Club's initiator, Sir Walter Ralegh, who had in fact been confined to the Tower of London since 1603 and was scarcely able therefore to participate in its activities; along with Shakespeare, whom Gifford imagined conversing with Jonson 'in the full flow and confidence of friendship' in those 'lively and interesting "wit-combats"' that Thomas Fuller had spoken of a century and a half earlier. Fuller's testimony was itself in fact belated and dubious; he was an 8-year-old boy living in Northamptonshire when Shakespeare died in Stratford in 1616, and had no first-hand knowledge of these legendary encounters, which he nowhere associates (in any case) with the Mermaid tavern. Shakespeare may well have drunk from time to time in the Mermaid and the nearby Mitre taverns before his retirement to Stratford, and quite possibly on occasions with Jonson, but there is no real evidence to associate him with the Club (which continued to meet well after his departure) or to support the notion of the two men's supposed wit-combats.[16]

Other Syrenaics were associated principally with the law, with Parliament, or with activities at court. The Club's importance to Jonson was political as much as literary. There was the barrister and wit Richard Martin, courageous parliamentary critic of monopolies, who had come to Jonson's defence just a few years earlier in the troubles over *Poetaster*. There was the learned lawyer (later judge) and parliamentarian John Hoskyns, whose outspoken remarks in Parliament against the Scots and royal expenditures were eventually to see him dispatched to the Tower of London. Jonson was to transcribe extended passages from Hoskyns's rhetorical treatise *Directions for Speech and Style* into his commonplace book, *Discoveries*. When Hoskyns asked to be adopted as a 'son of Ben', Jonson is said to have replied that such a relationship was impossible, for Hoskyns, from whom he had learned so much, was already his father: ''twas he that polished me.'[17] There was Donne's close friend with whom he shared chambers at Lincoln's Inn, Christopher Brooke. A minor poet associated with the pastoral revival of 1613–16, Brooke had also written a dramatic work, *The Ghost of Richard III*, about which Jonson wrote some appreciative verses. Brooke too was a fierce defender of parliamentary rights and privileges. Along with Martin and Hoskyns and other Syrenaics—such as William Hakewill and Sir Robert Phelips, two Cornish MPs who aggressively criticized royal imposts and demands during James's early parliaments—he gave the Club its spirited, oppositional air, exposing Jonson to a freely critical assessment of the policies of the Stuart court. Jonson's masquing colleague and collaborator Inigo Jones was another member of the Club, as was Sir Henry Goodere, a former follower of Essex, now courtier, landowner, and close friend of Donne and Jonson. Jonson had visited Goodere's estate at Polesworth in Warwickshire for 'a few days' sport', observing his friend hawking, and inspecting his library (*Epigrams*, 85, 86).

The Mermaid Club helped both to sharpen Jonson's political instincts, and to deepen his love of sociability. The Mermaid and Mitre taverns are mentioned familiarly throughout his writings. It is 'At Bread Street's Mermaid having dined, and merry' that the two adventurers in Jonson's 'Famous Voyage' 'Proposed to go to Holborn in a wherry' (*Epigrams*, 133.37–8), travelling bravely in their small vessel up the 'merd-urinous' passage of the Fleet Ditch. The quality of the Mermaid's wine, nostalgically recalled by Beaumont from the country where he makes do with an inferior vintage ('O, we have water mixed with claret lees, | Drink apt to bring in dryer heresies | Than beer') is remembered also by Jonson in his poem 'Inviting a Friend to Supper':

> But that which most doth take my muse and me
> Is a pure cup of rich Canary wine,
>   Which is the Mermaid's now, but shall be mine;
> Of which had Horace or Anacreon tasted,
>   Their lives, as do their lines, till now had lasted.
>   (*Epigrams*, 101.27–32)

§§

In the Epistle prefixed to the 1607 quarto text of *Volpone* Jonson had sketched 'the offices and function of a poet', and the poet's responsibilities to the larger society in which he lived. Stimulated perhaps by contact with his parliamentary friends at the Mermaid, Jonson began increasingly to recognize that such a society is not simply given; it must also in some sense be created; and that the poet's role in its creation might be as potent as the statesman's. A decade or so later, developing a hint from Sidney's *Apology*, Jonson was to elaborate this perception in his commonplace book, *Discoveries*.[18]

I could never think the study of wisdom confined only to the philosopher, or of piety to the divine, or of state to the politic. But that he which can feign a commonwealth (which is the poet) can govern it with counsels, strengthen it with laws, correct it with judgements, inform it with religion and morals is all these. We do not require in him mere elocution, or an excellent faculty in verse, but the exact knowledge of all virtues, and their contraries; with ability to render the one loved, the other hated, by his proper embattling them. (*Discoveries*, 729–45)

The poems that Jonson began to assemble towards the end of the first decade of James's reign as his first book of *Epigrams* were designed to present, in a more ambitious and coherent manner than those he had written after his conversion to Catholicism in 1598, a collective portrait of the larger community in which he lived: a feigned 'commonwealth', headed by the King himself, along with its statesmen, scholars, soldiers, legislators, diplomats, poets, actors, musicians, and ladies of the court, saluted by their distinguished names, as in a roll of honour: 'Camden, most reverend head, to whom I owe | All that I am in arts, all that I owe'; 'Lucy, you brightness of our sphere, who are | Life of the muses' day, their morning star!'; 'Jephson, thou man of men, to whose loved name | All gentry yet owe part of their best flame!' (*Epigrams*, 14, 94, 116). The personal characteristics of these exemplary figures are seldom detailed; instead, the reader is invited to look in some way through or beyond the poems to these subjects as they exist, unvaryingly, within the society they are said to adorn. Here for example is how Jonson addresses his patron William Herbert, third Earl of Pembroke (*Epigrams*, 102):

I do but name thee, Pembroke, and I find
    It is an epigram on all mankind,
Against the bad, but of, and to the good:
    Both which are asked to have thee understood.
Nor could the age have missed thee, in this strife
    Of vice and virtue, wherein all great life,
Almost, is exercised; and scarce one knows
    To which, yet, of the sides himself he owes.
They follow virtue for reward today,
    Tomorrow vice, if she give better pay:
And are so good and bad at just a price,
    As nothing else discerns the virtue or vice.
But thou, whose noblesse keeps one stature still,
    And one true posture, though besieged with ill
Of what ambition, faction, pride can raise,
    Whose life ev'n they that envy it must praise;
That art so reverenced, as thy coming in
    But in the view doth interrupt their sin:
Thou must draw more, and they that hope to see
    The commonwealth still safe, must study thee.

Once Pembroke has been *named*, so it is implied, the epigram in his praise has virtually been written. Jonson curiously deflects any further accounting of his exemplary qualities, which will nevertheless, if closely studied by the reader, keep the 'commonwealth still safe'. This modest final turn, implying that the subject of the poem has already more fully acquitted themselves than the poet would ever be capable of doing, is characteristic of the collection. Thus an epigram to John Donne similarly concludes:

> All which I meant to praise, and yet I would,
> But leave, because I cannot as I should.
> (*Epigrams*, 23.5–10)

Within these poems, as Stanley Fish has remarked, everything important seemingly 'happens off stage'. The society of the *Epigrams* is never fully described or revealed. Instead, so Fish suggests, it is merely hinted at, gestured towards, as an admirable network of like-minded members who (it is assumed) would recognize and respect each other's values. It is what Fish calls, in a suggestive phrase, *a community of the same*.[19]

More closely observed, however, this community is not as homogeneous as it might at first seem. For one thing, Jonson's *Epigrams*, like his court masques— created out of the poet's 'exact knowledge of all virtues, and their contraries'— present a sharply polarized world, its exemplary figures constantly 'embattled' against their moral anti-types: the deliberately unnamed, generic figures, enemies of the true commonwealth, 'My Lord Ignorant', 'Something that Walks Somewhere', 'Court-Worm', 'Sir Cod the Perfumed', 'Sir Voluptuous Beast', 'Don Surly', 'Person Guilty', 'Cheverel the Lawyer', 'Old Colt', 'Sir Luckless Woo-All', 'Groom Idiot', 'Court-Parrot', etc. (*Epigrams*, 10, 11, 15, 19, 25, 28, 30, 37, 39, 46, 58, 71, etc.). Pembroke himself is poised heroically within 'the strife | Of vice and virtue, wherein all great life, | Almost, is exercised', defined (one might say) by his stance in relation to his assumed opposites. The 'feigned' community of the *Epigrams* is moreover in subtle tension with the actual community in which the poet lives, being organized, as a poem early in the sequence forewarns us, according to more egalitarian principles than generally determine precedence in Jacobean Britain:

> May none whose scattered names honour my book
> For strict degrees of rank or title look;
> 'Tis 'gainst the manners of an epigram;
> And I a poet here, no herald am.
> ('To All to Whom I Write', *Epigrams*, 9)

Its praiseworthy members are not identical with those currently in power at Whitehall. Notably absent from the collection are several of James's current favourites, including Jonson's 'mortal enemy' Henry Howard, Earl of Northampton; the amiable Scotsman Lord Hay, whose extravagant outlay, as Master of the Robes, on James's personal attire had run up massive household debts; Robert Carr, Earl of Somerset, another Scot, whose scandalous marriage to Frances Howard Jonson would soon be obliged to commemorate; and Philip Herbert, Earl of Montgomery, who (in Clarendon's words) had 'pretended to no other qualification than to understand horses and dogs very well', and had thereby won his way to James's heart.

Philip's elder brother William Herbert, Earl of Pembroke, nevertheless plays a dominant role in the *Epigrams*, as 'the great example of honour and virtue' to whom Jonson dedicates the collection. Pembroke was the most remarkable patron of his age, and a man whose political ideals were considerably closer to Jonson's own. He stood however at some remove from the inner circle at court. Wealthy, generous, and cultivated, he had supported the work of many writers, including Shakespeare and Jonson himself, to whom he gave £20 each new year to purchase books (*Informations*, 239–40). 'You have ever been free and noble to me,' Jonson had written to Pembroke from prison in 1605, appealing for his assistance after the *Eastward Ho!* affair (Letter 7), and implying a friendship already of some duration. Clarendon was to describe Pembroke as 'the most universally loved and esteemed of any man of that age'; as

A man very well bred, and of excellent parts, and a graceful speaker upon any subject, having a good proportion of learning, and a ready wit to apply it, and enlarge upon it; of a pleasant and facetious humour, and a disposition affable, generous, and magnificent.

Yet despite such qualities, Clarendon added, Pembroke was 'rather regarded and esteemed by King James, than loved and feared'.[20] He had opposed the alliance with Spain, which James had supported, and was one of the counsellors who proposed the calling of a Parliament in 1615. Though he remained on good terms with Robert Cecil, Pembroke was deeply disliked by Henry Howard, and by James's current favourite, Robert Carr, whose fall he hastened by successfully promoting George Villiers as an alternative candidate. Despite these difficulties, by 23 December 1615 Pembroke had gained the coveted post of Lord Chamberlain, which amongst its various duties carried responsibility for censorship. Jonson's dedication to the *Epigrams*, published in the First Folio of 1616, may have been smuggled into the text at the last moment while the volume was in production, both as a tribute to Pembroke and as a protection to Jonson himself: for the publication of epigrams, along with satires and histories, had been specifically forbidden by the Bishops' Ban of 1599, which was still technically in force at this time.[21] These short poems of praise and dispraise, presenting Jonson's ideal 'commonwealth', were in some sense therefore still illicit, carrying 'danger in the sound' (Dedication, 5). They not only ignored certain figures who were currently in power, but, as Martin Butler has observed, daringly championed others 'whose relationship with the centre was conflicted, or who, when the *Epigrams* were collected (probably in 1612), stood only at the edges of power'.[22]

Some of these figures celebrated in the *Epigrams* were former members of the Essex circle, while others had been connected in some fashion with the Gunpowder conspirators. Sir Henry Savile, Warden of Merton College, Oxford, and later Provost of Eton College, whom Jonson addresses in *Epigrams*, 95 (for example), had been closely associated with Essex throughout the final decade of the Earl's life, and briefly imprisoned after Essex's failed coup of 1601, when his study at Eton was raided, and papers relating to Essex and his circle removed. After Essex's downfall, Savile had acted as protector to his son, the young Robert Devereux—the future third Earl, whose marriage with Frances Howard Jonson was to celebrate in *Hymenaei*—who came to live with him in the Warden's lodgings at Merton.[23] Jonson is at pains in the *Epigrams* to stress Savile's present political loyalty and probable fame in the years to come. His past activities are nowhere explicitly mentioned, but their shadow crosses the page.

> For who can master those great parts like thee,
> That liv'st from hope, from fear, from faction free;
> That hast thy breast so clear of present crimes
> Thou need'st not shrink at voice of after-times,
> Whose knowledge claimeth at the helm to stand,
> But wisely thrusts not forth a forward hand,
> No more than Sallust in the Roman state!
> As, then, his cause, his glory emulate.
>
> (*Epigrams*, 95.17–24)

When Jonson wrote these lines, perhaps around 1611, Savile was no longer a politically suspect figure, but had opted for a life of quiet scholarship;

he 'wisely thrusts not forth a forward hand'. Jonson compares him with the Roman historian Sallust, who withdrew from public life following charges of political misdemeanour, and devoted himself to writing the history of Rome for the years immediately following the abdication of Sulla. Sallust's *Bellum Catilinae* ('The War with Catiline')—a major source for Jonson's own tragedy on this subject in 1611—traces the course of the conspiracy of the Roman patrician Catiline, sometimes seen as a prototype of Essex's rebellion.[24]

Savile's friend and fellow-Mertonian Sir Henry Neville, whom Jonson addresses in *Epigrams*, 109, was another former follower of Essex. Arrested at Dover while attempting to flee the country after the abortive rising of February 1601, Neville had been imprisoned in the Tower, fined the sum of £10,000, and stripped of his diplomatic posting as English Ambassador in France. Though released at James's accession and in due course politically rehabilitated, Neville had nevertheless failed in his attempted mediations to secure the 'great contract' between James and the Commons in 1610, and was again briefly imprisoned after the dismissal of the Addled Parliament of 1614. Though widely seen as a worthy successor to Robert Cecil as Secretary of State in 1612, Neville had failed also to secure that post. Jonson presents him none the less as one who 'serves nor fame nor titles', a figure of admirable if unfashionable 'virtue' (*Epigrams*, 109.2–3), and a deserving member of his ideal commonwealth.[25] William Parker, Lord Monteagle, recently returned to royal favour and praised by Jonson in *Epigrams*, 60, for his role in the discovery of the Gunpowder Plot, had been another follower of Essex, for which he had been fined £4,000 and dispatched to the Tower in 1601. Sir John Roe, a close acquaintance (as we have seen, 199–200) of the Gunpowder conspirators, is the recipient of three affectionate epigrams (27, 32, and 33), and his younger brother William (on whose behalf Jonson had appeared as a witness in a Chancery suit of 5 May 1610) is addressed twice (70, 128), as is their cousin Thomas of the Middle Temple, the future English Ambassador to Mughal India and Constantinople, a warm admirer of Jonson's writings (98, 99).[26]

Jonson's poetic community is thus made up of former dissidents as well as present stalwarts of the state, pretenders to greatness and 'caterpillars of the commonwealth' as well as those deserving of esteem. It is a community tenuously held together, criss-crossed with fault-lines and fractures; characterized not by its sameness, but by its multiplicity and difference, reflecting tensions of which Jonson in his own life was now growing increasingly aware.

14

Travels 1611–1613

IN a suggestive short tale entitled 'Proofs of Holy Writ' Rudyard Kipling imagines Shakespeare and Jonson working together on a translation of chapter 60 of the Book of Isaiah for King James's new Bible, due to go to press in 1610. They look first at the sonorous opening of the Vulgate text— 'Surge, illuminare, Jerusalem, quia venit lumen tuum, et Gloria Domini super te orta est. Quia ecce tenebrae operient terram et caligo populous'— and next, with general disapproval, at the efforts of earlier translators, surreptitiously appropriating however the odd phrase as they go. Their work moves ahead in excited spurts, punctuated by doubts, hesitations, and further wrestlings with the subtleties of the text. Gradually the majestic rhythms of the Authorized Version begin to emerge: 'Arise, shine; for thy light is come, and the glory of the Lord is risen upon thee. For, behold, the darkness shall cover the earth, and gross darkness the people: but the Lord shall arise upon thee, and his glory shall be seen upon thee. And the Gentiles shall come to thy light, and kings to the brightness of thy rising...'[1]

Though it is natural to suppose that James would have engaged these two supreme writers of the age, each at the height of his powers, on a project to which he attached such high importance, there is no evidence that either Shakespeare or Jonson was ever so employed. Throughout the period during which King James's Bible was in preparation, Jonson's status as a Catholic would moreover have made his participation in such an undertaking improbable. The question of translation was itself a matter of contention at this time between Catholics and Protestants, who differed on the wisdom of making the sacred text widely accessible to the laity. The preface to the Authorized

Version speaks sharply of the attitude of 'Popish persons' towards translated scripture, and the address of 'The Translators to the Readers' continues to berate Catholics for their views on this question.[2]

Jonson may nevertheless have been safely back in the Anglican fold by the time the King James Bible was actually published in 1611. The precise date of his re-conversion is unknown; Drummond merely records that, having accepted Catholicism in 1598, Jonson thereafter 'was twelve years a papist' (*Informations*, 189–90). Jonson's change of religion is likely to have been prompted by a momentous event that had occurred on 14 May 1610, when the French king Henri IV—who had himself notoriously moved back and forth between the two religions—was stabbed to death in his carriage by a Catholic fanatic named François Ravaillac while caught in a tangle of traffic in the streets of Paris. Henri IV had been greatly admired by English visitors to France, including Jonson's friend Sir Thomas Overbury, who had met with him privately in Paris the previous year. Overbury had wondered, ominously, what might occur within France and more widely throughout Europe should Henri ever meet with a sudden death.

Sure it is that the peace of France, and somewhat that of Christendom itself, is secured by this Prince's life: for all titles and discontents, all factions of religion there suppress themselves till his death; but what will ensue after; what the rest of the House of Bourbon will enterprise upon the King's children, what the House of Guise upon the House of Bourbon; what the League, what the Protestants, what the Kings of Spain and England, if they see a breach made by civil dissension, I choose rather to expect than conjecture, because God hath so many ways to turn aside from human foresight, as he gave us a testimony upon the death of our late Queen.[3]

Two weeks after the assassination, Ravaillac was taken to the scaffold at the Place de Grève, scalded with burning sulphur, molten lead, boiling oil, and resin, his arms and legs then being attached to horses which were driven away in opposite directions, ripping his limbs from his body. This bloody climax to the French wars of religion caused terror on both sides of the Channel. After two decades of relative calm in France, civil conflict—so it seemed— was about to break out once more, fulfilling the darkest fears of Overbury and other English observers. Arriving in Paris within a month of the assassination, the English Ambassador Sir Thomas Edmondes wrote in alarm to James, believing France to be on the very brink of civil war.[4] Though Ravaillac had insisted under extreme torture that he had acted entirely alone in murdering

Fig. 31a. Henri IV of France assassinated by François Ravaillac.

the King, rumours of a wider Catholic conspiracy persisted. Twenty-three previous plots to murder Henri were already known to the authorities. Alarmed by the possible ramifications of this event, James issued a proclamation on 2 June 1610 forbidding English Catholics access to his court or to that of Queen Anne or Prince Henry, and further tightened the requirements surrounding the Oath of Allegiance, insisting that Catholics renounce the sovereignty of the Pope and pledge their loyalty to the King of England. For many English Catholics, the severity of these measures effectively spelt the end of a professional career, forcing them either to leave the Church of Rome or to leave the country. Camden's successor as Headmaster at Westminster School, Richard Ireland, a convert to Catholicism, chose the latter course, surrendering his position and fleeing to France to avoid exposure.[5]

Camden himself, a staunch Protestant since his Oxford days, was meanwhile recruited by Matthew Sutcliffe to serve, along with John Hayward, as a historical adviser at James's newly established Chelsea College at Thameshot,

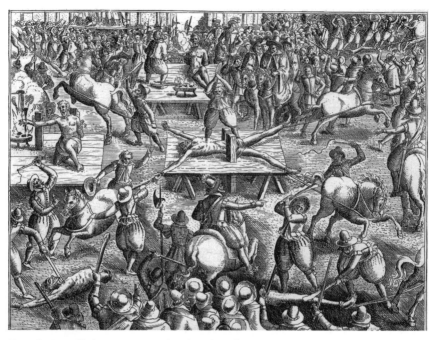

Fig. 31b. Ravaillac's execution in the Place de Grève, Paris.

a kind of anti-Catholic think-tank or (in the words of Thomas Fuller) 'spiritual garrison, with a magazine of all books for that purpose, where learned divines should study and write in maintenance of all controversies against the papists'.[6] If Jonson talked with Camden at this time about the spiritual dilemma that faced him, one can imagine the advice he would have received. At some unknown moment probably in mid-1610 he decided to return to the Church of England, and marked the event with characteristic gusto. 'After he was reconciled with the church and left off to be a recusant,' notes William Drummond, 'at his first communion, in token of true reconciliation, he drank out all the full cup of wine' (*Informations*, 241–2). In the Catholic Church at this time the cup was not offered to lay communicants; Jonson's gesture enthusiastically celebrated one significant difference between the two faiths.[7] Though Jonson had now returned formally to the Church of England, he would maintain later in life close friendships with Catholics such as Kenelm Digby and Richard Weston, and an interest in Catholic beliefs and practices. In 1619 Drummond would describe him as being 'For any religion, as being versed in both' (*Informations*, 561).

§§

On hearing the news of Henri IV's assassination in Paris in May 1610, King James's eldest son Prince Henry Frederick is said to have taken to his bed for several days, repeating the words, 'My second father is dead.'[8] The French King had been one of the two contemporary figures (the other was Maurice of Nassau) whom the young Prince most idolized; theirs were the only portraits adorning his gallery at St James's Palace. He had more in common with both these men than with his actual father, James, for he cared little about hunting and scholarship, or his father's wish to promote the cause of European peace. He was zealous instead in the practice of martial and physical arts, in his passion for horsemanship, and in his unremitting opposition to Catholicism. 'None of his pleasures savour the least of a child,' wrote Antoine le Fèvre de la Boderie, the French Ambassador, of the 12-year-old Henry in 1606, 'He studies two hours a day, and employs the rest of his time in tossing the pike, or leaping, or shooting with the bow, or vaulting, or some other exercise of that kind . . .'[9] Since March 1609 Prince Henry had been following intently the escalating sequence of events in the tiny German duchies of Clèves and Juliers between the Ruhr and the lower reaches of the Rhine, where the death of the existing ruler, Duke Jean-Guillaume, had prompted a crisis of succession that threatened to provide a flashpoint for a major war in Europe between Protestant and Catholic powers. In May 1610—the very month of his death, as conspiracy theorists were not slow to note—Henri IV had been massing troops in alliance with the United Provinces and the Union of German Protestant Princes in preparation for an assault against the Habsburg powers, who were in turn readying themselves to take over the small German states. Prince Henry was eagerly hoping to fight alongside his hero and to involve England in the fray when the news of the French king's assassination arrived.[10]

The death of Henri IV horribly disfigured what should have been a triumphant year for Prince Henry, which had begun with the performance of Jonson's masque of *Prince Henry's Barriers* on 6 January, and was to proceed via further celebratory events—a water pageant on 31 May at Chelsea with a fleet of City boats and barges, the performance of Daniel's masque, *Tethys' Festival*, in early June—to his investiture on 4 June as Prince of Wales and Earl of Chester, and the recruitment of his household in November.

Though the Privy Council, concerned by the financial problems currently besetting the royal family, had urged postponement of Henry's investiture for two years, the Prince was impatient to achieve his new status at the earliest possible moment, and a special tax had been approved for the purpose in February 1609. By the end of 1610 the 16-year-old was said to have recruited nearly 500 members to his newly established household.[11] The new year was to open with a further celebration by Jonson and Inigo Jones in the Prince's honour, the masque of *Oberon* (1 January 1611).

Jonson had been acquainted with the young Prince since his arrival with Queen Anne in England in 1603, recognizing his appetite for military leadership in his words of welcome at Althorp:

> Oh, shoot up fast in spirit, as in years;
> That when upon her head proud Europe wears
> Her stateliest tire, you may appear thereon
> The richest gem, without a paragon.
> Shine bright and fixèd as the Arctic star,
> And when slow time hath made you fit for war,
> Look over the strict ocean, and think where
> You may but lead us forth, that grow up here
> Against a day when our officious swords
> Shall speak our action better than our words. (284–93)

By the end of 1609, however, as Jonson began to compose *Prince Henry's Barriers*, it was less easy for him to endorse the politics of a young prince determined to root out recusancy at home and combat Catholic power abroad through a programme of military force. Jonson was in all likelihood still himself a Catholic at this time, and his own religious sympathies would have been in obvious tension with those of the Prince he was supposed to celebrate, whose military ideals were in turn directly opposed to his father's policies of peace. *Prince Henry's Barriers* had necessarily therefore to be an exercise in compromise. The strains are at times detectable in the verse: as when, in rehearsing to Henry the exploits of his royal predecessors, Jonson wavers as to the precise lesson to be learnt, as if striving to please simultaneously father and son:

> These, worthiest prince, are set you near to read,
> That civil arts the martial must precede;
> That laws and trade bring honours in and gain,

And arms defensive a safe peace maintain.
But when your fate shall call you forth t'assure
Your virtue more, though not to make secure,
View here what great examples she hath placed . . . (etc.) (204–10)

Preparations for the June investiture were left in the hands of Robert Cecil, who was eager to establish himself in the young Prince's favour. Samuel Daniel was invited to prepare the masque to celebrate this occasion, perhaps (as Roy Strong has suggested) because the Prince's mother perceived some lack of complete harmony between Jonson and her son. Whether or not *Tethys' Festival* was perceived as a success, the commission for the 1610/1611 Christmas season returned to Jonson.[12]

Henry chose to appear in the Christmas masque in the guise of the fairy prince, Oberon, whom Spenser had associated in *The Faerie Queene* with the Protestant champion, Henry VIII. The masque was characterized by some of Jones's most brilliant technical effects: beginning with a scene of rocks that opened, through a series of sliding flats, to reveal 'the frontispiece of a bright and glorious palace, whose gates and walls were transparent', which in turn opened once more to disclose a 'nation of fays . . . some with instruments, some bearing lights, others singing; and within, afar off in perspective, the knights masquers sitting in their several sieges; at the further end of all, Oberon in a chariot, which to a loud triumphant music began to move forward, drawn by two white bears, and on either side guarded by three sylvans, with one going in front.' The two white bears were probably actors dressed in bear-skins, though two scholars have recently suggested that they may have been polar bears that had been captured as cubs near the Arctic circle in May 1609 and retained by Philip Henslowe for use in theatrical events and entertainments.[13] Jonson tactfully chooses on this occasion to say less about the conflicting aims of war and peace, and strikes a happier balance of admiration for the young Prince and homage to his father.

Melt earth to sea, sea flow to air,
  And air fly into fire,
Whilst we, in tunes, to Arthur's chair
  Bear Oberon's desire;
  Than which there nothing can be higher,
Save James, to whom it flies;
But he the wonder is of tongues, of ears, of eyes.

Who hath not heard, who hath not seen,
   Who hath not sung his name?
The soul that hath not, hath not been,
   But is the very same
   With buried sloth, and knows not Fame,
Which doth him best comprise.
For he the wonder is of tongues, of ears, of eyes. (216–30)

Fig. 32. Inigo Jones's final costume design for Prince Henry as Oberon, the fairy prince, in Jonson's *The Masque of Oberon*, 1611.

Fig. 33. Oberon's palace: Inigo Jones's final design for *The Masque of Oberon*, 1611, involving a series of sliding flats, unfolding successively to reveal an ever-deepening set of perspectives.

Despite the need for financial restraint at this time, *Oberon* was a costly masque whose total budget ran well in excess of £1,000, though as Henry was not in control of the budget for this occasion, his largest ambitions—such as having the masquers perform on horseback—were not fulfilled. The failure a year earlier of the so-called Great Contract between James and his Parliament, designed to ensure the continuity of funding for royal expenditures—a complex and controversial negotiation, which Robert Cecil had tried assiduously to broker—resulted in an altogether more austere budget for the masque that followed a year later (6 January 1612), *Love Restored*, of around £280. By the time of Cecil's death in May 1612 the crown was half a million pounds in debt, and running an annual deficit of £160,000.[14] In a poem addressed about this time to Sir Robert Wroth, Jonson speaks caustically of 'the short bravery of the night': 'the jewels, stuffs, the pains, the wit | There wasted, some not paid for yet!', commending Wroth's good fortune in living at some distance from the city and the court (*The Forest*, 3.9–12). Later in life Jonson would deplore at greater length the extravagance of masquing at court:

Have I not seen the pomp of a whole kingdom, and what a foreign king could bring hither also to make himself gazed and wondered at, laid forth as it were to the show, and vanish all away in a day? And shall that which could not fill the expectation of few hours, entertain and take up our whole lives, when even it appeared as superfluous to the possessors, as to me that was a spectator? The bravery was shown, it was not possessed; while it boasted itself, it perished. It is vile and a poor thing to place our happiness on these desires. Say we wanted them all: famine ends famine. (*Discoveries*, 1001–8)

Yet whatever private feelings Jonson may have had about the extravagance of these occasions, he found himself nevertheless obliged in *Love Restored* to enter a plea on the King's behalf for a more liberal masquing budget. The character of Plutus in *Love Restored* echoes the actual complaints of many of James's critics and advisers, but is presented as a grudging, Malvolio-like figure, whose puritanical objections to court extravagance are not to be taken seriously.

I tell thee, I will have no more masquing; I will not buy a false and fleeting delight so dear. The merry madness of one hour shall not cost me the repentance of an age.... Let 'em embrace more frugal pastimes.... Away! I will no more of these superfluous excesses.

Jonson's readiness to support the royal cause is obviously pragmatic: his own financial state, as well as the King's pleasures, depended upon the steady flow of available masquing revenue. The case is put with skill and humour. But the tensions within his own position are nevertheless evident, and might well have been a topic of spirited conversation between Jonson and his parliamentary friends when they met at the Mermaid tavern.

§§

Jonson's most profound political fears and imaginings could at times be more freely expressed in his works for the public stage than in his court masques, constricted as the latter were by the need to present a view of events not too greatly at variance with that of his royal patrons. *Catiline His Conspiracy* was probably the first stage work that Jonson wrote after his return to the Anglican Church.[15] Though the play may appear at first to be a painstaking exercise in ancient history, it can be seen too as a work responsive to current events in Europe that is also curiously predictive of troubles to come in England in the years immediately following Jonson's death. *Catiline* was performed some time before 29 August 1611 by the King's Men either at the Globe or Blackfriars (it is not known which). It is a learned piece for which Jonson entertained the highest hopes, but its first performance proved a disaster, the audience growing restive during Cicero's long speeches in the fourth act, finally making it impossible for the players to proceed. Jonson's response was to publish the work immediately in a quarto edition with a dedication to William Herbert, Earl of Pembroke, lamenting the darkness that now covered the age, and confidently predicting a better verdict from posterity. This prediction was partly, but only partly, fulfilled: the fortunes of the play were to revive remarkably later in the century, only to decline sharply in the centuries that followed. The title page of the second quarto of *Catiline* published in 1635 (two years before Jonson's death) spoke of the tragedy being 'now acted by His Majesty's Servants with great applause'. *Catiline* was read with close attention during the closure of the theatres, and performed with frequent success at the Restoration, Charles himself contributing £500 for one production in 1667 (so Samuel Pepys notes) to help with the purchase of sixteen scarlet robes to be worn by members of the company. 'This play is still in vogue on the stage, and always presented with success,' wrote the theatre historian Gerard Langbaine in 1691.[16] According to G. E. Bentley's researches, *Catiline* emerges, astonishingly, as the most frequently cited play of all of Jonson's and Shakespeare's dramatic works throughout the seventeenth century. 'There can be little doubt', Bentley writes, having surveyed the evidence, 'that not *Hamlet, Lear, Othello,* or *Macbeth,* but *Catiline* was the premier English tragedy in the minds of seventeenth-century writers.'[17] Why should *Catiline* have enjoyed this surprising surge to popular favour during the later part of the seventeenth century? And why, to pose a more basic question, should Jonson have been moved to dramatize the story of Catiline's conspiracy in 1610–11?

In a study of the tragedy more than forty years ago Barbara De Luna attempted to show that *Catiline* offered an elaborate 'parallelograph' to the events of the Gunpowder Plot, with which Jonson had been personally entangled some six years earlier. In De Luna's somewhat over-determined reading of the tragedy and its supposed background, Jonson's motives for constructing this elaborate set of parallels at this particular moment of his life are never fully explained, the exercise being viewed simply as 'a kind of private joke, between the dramatist and "the initiate few"'.[18] That *Catiline* should at times awaken memories of the Gunpowder Plot as well as of the several other plots that England (and Scotland) had experienced since the final decade of the previous century is not surprising, but exact one-to-one allusion of the kind De Luna seeks to establish here, lending itself to schematic 'application', is not characteristic of Jonson's methods at this stage of his career; whatever tactics he may have adopted in his apprentice years, his habits of political reference by now were more wary, oblique, and intermittent, as already noted in relation to *Volpone*. That Jonson, so soon after his return to the Anglican Church, should have sought to develop such a detailed parallel between the Catilinarian and Gunpowder conspiracies, either as a 'private joke' or in renunciation of a chapter of his life about which he now felt acute remorse, seems moreover basically implausible. A more relevant context for an understanding of *Catiline* may be the period of terror in which the play was actually written during the months following the assassination of Henri IV in Paris: a period known to the French as *la grande peur*, when (as we have seen) the prospect of civil war erupting on either side of the Channel kept both nations in a state of constant vigilance and alarm.

Through his multiple connections with the Catholic community and sources of foreign intelligence at court, Jonson was well positioned to observe these current fears, and to imagine what might occur in England, a country at present so sharply divided over issues of religion, which might one day, like the body of Ravaillac, be torn brutally apart. More than one writer for the early modern London stage had depicted the horrors of civil war: Shakespeare in his *Henry VI* plays; Thomas Lodge, in *The Wounds of Civil War*; George Chapman, in *Caesar and Pompey* (to go no further with this list). The basic theme of Jonson's tragedy was not novel, though his experience of civil unrest over the previous decade—through his contacts with the Essex group and the Gunpowder conspirators—was intimate, and his awareness of the particular anxieties of 1610–11 acute. Jonson's consciousness of the present relevance of the story of Catiline may help to explain the particular value he attached to the play, his confidence in believing that 'posterity' would come in time to appreciate its significance, and the actual trajectory of the play's reputation during the course of the seventeenth century, as so many of the tragedy's major issues—the legitimacy of rebellion, the duties of the citizen, the protection of the commonwealth—became burning topics of the day.

For all its air of learned antiquarianism, *Catiline His Conspiracy* is thus an oddly prophetic play, drawing on the past in order to read the political future. In developing a vision of civil war Jonson recalls the great archetype of such internecine conflict against which, in early modern England, present troubles were often measured: the long series of domestic Roman struggles beginning with those between Lucius Cornelius Sulla, Roman general and leader of the *optimates* party, and his rival Gaius Marius, leader of the *populares*, extending from 88 to 82 BC (the so-called First Roman Civil War), continuing with the conflict between Pompey and Julius Caesar between 49 and 45 BC (the Second Civil War, culminating in Caesar's defeat of Pompey at the battle of Pharsalus in 48 BC), and concluding with the Third Civil War (44 to 30 BC) between Mark Antony and Caesar's heir, Octavian, and Antony's final defeat at the Battle of Actium. The conspiracy of Lucius Sergius Catilina occurred between the First and the Second Civil Wars in 62 BC, marking a critical moment within this series of internal conflicts as the late republic shifted inexorably towards imperial rule.

In historical terms, as Jonson well knew, each phase of these civil troubles had built upon what had gone before. Many saw Catiline as Sulla's natural successor or reincarnation, who, disappointed in his quest for consular office, prepared for his political coup—the assassination of Cicero, the murder of numerous senators, the firing of the city, the seizing of power—by recruiting veterans from Sulla's army to assist his cause. Jonson re-creates this sense of cumulative and successive disturbance by introducing Sulla at the outset of the play in the form of a ghost, who bequeaths to Catiline all of the various evils with which he himself has been traditionally associated.

> What all the several ills that visit earth,
> Brought forth by night with a sinister birth,
> Plagues, famine, fire could not reach unto,
> The sword, nor surfeits, let thy fury do.
> Make all past, present, future ill thine own,
> And conquer all example in thy one. (1.49–54)

Catiline's conspirators in turn excitedly recall 'the days of Sulla's sway, when the free sword took leave | To act all that it would!'

Catiline	And was familiar

With entrails as our augurs!

Cethegus	Sons killed fathers,

Brothers their brothers.

Catiline	And had price and praise.

All hate had licence given it, all rage reins.

Cethegus Slaughter bestrid the streets and stretched himself
To seem more huge, whilst to his stainèd thighs
The gore he drew flowed up and carried down
Whole heaps of limbs and bodies through his arch.
No age was spared, no sex.

Catiline	Nay, no degree.

(*Catiline*, 1.229–39)

Through passages such as these Jonson builds up a powerful sense of cyclical history, of the past impinging constantly upon the present, which in turn may presage the future. The horrors here described might be thought to recall the recent massacres of the French wars of religion as well as those of ancient Rome, and to hint at similar slaughter now feared both in France and England. It was the seemingly predictive force of *Catiline* that must in large measure have made the play so compelling to later readers and playgoers, and made this (today, so neglected) work much talked of in the years following Jonson's death.

§§

Jonson's dedication of *Catiline* in 1611 to William Herbert, Earl of Pembroke ('the first of this race that ever I dedicated to any person'), marked his growing attachment at this time, both personally and politically, to the interrelated families of Herberts and Sidneys. At some stage during the summer of 1611 Jonson appears to have abandoned London for a period of several months and to have taken up residence with Pembroke's uncle Robert Sidney and his wife Barbara, née Gamage (Lord and Lady Lisle), at Penshurst Place, near Tonbridge in Kent. The friendship between Robert Sidney and Ben Jonson probably began soon after Sidney's appointment in 1603 as Queen Anne's Lord Chamberlain, when masquing business is likely to have brought them together. Sidney was a highly cultivated man, devoted not merely to affairs of state but to the writing of poetry, to musical performance, and the discerning collection of books. Jonson was on affectionate terms with the Sidneys' equally talented daughter, Mary, Lady Wroth—whom we have already met, coming out to greet Jonson on the first stage of his long walk to Scotland—and had addressed two admiring poems to her (*Epigrams*, 103, 105), along with another to her younger sister Philip, named after her famous uncle (*Epigrams*, 114).[19] Later in life, Lady Mary was to embark on an affair with her cousin, Jonson's patron William Herbert, Earl of Pembroke, further complicating the already close relationship between the two families and leading to the birth of two illegitimate children.

The first indication of Jonson's presence at Penshurst in 1611 comes in a letter from Lord Lisle to his wife on 21 July of that year which contains an aside about their son William (Mary's younger brother): 'I am glad to hear of Will Sydney's care to follow his book,' writes the boy's father; 'If he list, he may do himself much good with Mr Johnson and he cannot any way please me better.' For many years, the 'Mr Johnson' mentioned here was thought to an Oxford graduate named Robert Johnson, one of the King's Chaplains.[20] As Michael Brennan and Noel Kinnamon have recently shown, however, there is no other evidence linking Robert Johnson in any way with the Sidney family, and every reason to suppose that Lord Lisle is referring here rather to Ben Jonson—who seems to have been staying at Penshurst in 1611, and was almost certainly present in November of that year for the twenty-first birthday celebrations of William Sidney, for which he wrote a somewhat stern congratulatory ode (*The Forest*, 14).[21] William was a moody and troublesome boy, and his father's letters show concern for his 'melancholy' and lack of serious application.[22] Along with his younger brother Robert, William had matriculated from Christ Church, Oxford, in 1607, but it is not known how much time either of the boys had then spent at the University. A Mr Bird had been hired as William's tutor at Penshurst, but had insulted Lady Lisle when she tried to advise him on her son's education, and had also evidently quarrelled with William himself, who had then stabbed him with a knife. On 15 January 1609 William had been granted a licence to travel in the company of Pembroke's (and Jonson's) friend the poet Benjamin Rudyerd, but this journey was evidently not undertaken. A few months before Jonson's arrival at Penshurst, William had been knighted (8 January 1611), and in May there were reports of his taking up a position in the Low Countries as Lieutenant-Governor to his father, but this plan likewise failed to materialize. It must have been around this time that Jonson was recruited as a tutor to

The Sidneys and Herberts

Sir William Sidney 1482–1554 m. Anne Pagenham, d. 1543

Sir Henry Sidney 1529–86   m. Mary Dudley 1531–86 ['Sir P. Sidney's mother, Leicester's sister, after she had the little pox never show herself in court thereafter but masked': *Informations*, 269–70]

Ambrosia Sidney *c*.1564–75

Thomas Sidney 1569–95 m. Margaret Dakins 1571–1633

Sir Robert Sidney 1563–1626 Lord Lisle 1st Earl of Leicester ['To Penshurst', *For.* 2]

m. (i) Barbara Gamage d. 1621 ['Thy lady's noble, fruitful, chaste withal': *The Forest*, 2.90]   m. (ii) Sarah Smythe

Sir Philip Sidney 1542–86 [amongst the 'great masters of wit and language', *Discoveries*, 651–2]
m. Frances Walsingham 1567–1632

Mary Sidney 1561–1621 [completes Philip's translation of the Psalms: *Informations*, 152–3]
m. Henry Herbert *c*.1538–1601 2nd Earl of Pembroke

Philip Herbert 1584–1650 1st Earl of Montgomery 4th Earl of Pembroke [addressed, Letter 7]

Sir William Sidney 1590–1612 [whom Jonson tutors; birthday ode, *The Forest*, 14]

Philip Sidney 1594–1620 [*Epigr.* 114] m. John Hobart d. 1647 2nd baronet

Robert Sidney [resembled Sir Philip Sidney, 'no pleasant man in countenance', *Informations*, 173–5]

and seven siblings

Elizabeth Sidney 1585–1612 ['nothing inferior to her father . . . in poesy', *Informations*, 259; addressed, *Epigr.* 79, *Forest*, 12; *May Lord.*]

William Herbert 1580–1630 3rd Earl of Pembroke [Jonson's patron; dedicatee of *Catiline*, *Epigrams*; addressed, *Epigr.* 102, Letter 8; gifts to Jonson, *Informations*, 239–40]

m. Mary Talbot 1580–1650

m. Roger Manners 1576–1612 5th Earl of Rutland [who 'accused her that she kept a table to poets', *Informations*, 278]

Mary Sidney *c*.1587–*c*.1653 ['fair crown of your fair sex', *Epigr.* 103; 105; *Und.* 28; dedicatee of *The Alchemist*; dances in several of Jonson's masques]

m. Sir Robert Wroth 1576–1614 ['unworthily married on a jealous husband', *Informations*, 275–6; addressed, *The Forest*, 3]

James 1614–16; William and Catherine b. *c*.1623 fathered by William Herbert, Earl of Pembroke replace the wounded Mr Bird, who had now been dismissed from his position, and to direct William in his studies. Jonson had several clear qualifications for this post. He was a genuinely learned scholar who was also physically tough, and clearly sympathetic to the family—a quality that is apparent in his birthday ode to William:

> 'Twill be exacted of your name, whose son
>   Whose nephew, whose grandchild you are;
>   And men
>   Will, then,
>   Say you have followed far,
> When well begun;
>   Which must be now;
>   They teach you how.
>   And he that stays
>   To live until tomorrow hath lost two days.
> So may you live in honour as in name,
>   If with this truth you be inspired;
>   So may
>   This day
>   Be more and long desired:
> And with the flame
>   Of love be bright,
>   As with the light
>   Of bonfires. Then
>   The birthday shines when logs not burn, but men.
>   (*The Forest*, 14.41–60)

The note of urgency in these lines—'he that stays | To live until tomorrow hath lost two days', etc.—was sadly all too apt, for on 3 December 1612 William was to die of smallpox at Baynard's Castle, the Earl of Pembroke's London residence.

It was probably during the late summer of 1611 that Jonson wrote 'To Penshurst', a poem that—for all its classical memories—reveals an intimate knowledge both of the estate and of the family that it celebrates.[23] Most of the features of the grounds mentioned here may still be traced four centuries later.

> Thou hast thy walks for health, as well as sport:
>   Thy Mount, to which the dryads do resort,
> Where Pan and Bacchus their high feasts have made

Beneath the broad beech, and the chestnut shade;
That taller tree, which of a nut was set
　　At his great birth, where all the muses met.
There, in the writhèd bark, are cut the names
　　Of many a sylvan, taken with his flames;
And thence the ruddy satyrs oft provoke
　　The lighter fauns to reach thy lady's oak.
Thy copse, too, named of Gamage, thou hast there,
　　That never fails to serve thee seasoned deer,
When thou wouldst feast, or exercise thy friends.
　　The lower land, that to the river bends,
Thy sheep, thy bullocks, kine and calves do feed:
　　The middle grounds thy mares and horses breed.
Each bank doth yield thee conies; and the tops
　　Fertile of wood, Ashour and Sidney's copse,
To crown thy open table, doth provide
　　The purpled pheasant with the speckled side:
The painted partridge lies in every field
　　And for thy mess is willing to be killed.
　　　　　　　　　　　　　(*The Forest*, 2.9–30)

'That taller tree' is the oak, still standing today at Penshurst, grown from an acorn said to have been planted on the day of Sir Philip Sidney's birth, 30 November 1554. As Jonson would have known, Suetonius reports that a poplar had been planted in similar fashion on the day of Virgil's birth.[24] Towering over the neighbouring trees, the oak now suggests the pre-eminence of the great departed figure it commemorates, but also symbolizes the entire Sidney dynasty, the family's burgeoning tree, part of the larger *forest* which Jonson was carefully imagining in the collection of poems he was putting together at this time. Another tree, 'thy lady's oak', along with the copse 'named of Gamage', are identified with Lady Lisle herself, who according to tradition was taken in labour under an oak tree in the grounds of Penshurst, which thereafter was known as 'My Lady's Oak'; and who is also said to have fed deer in the copse that bore her name.[25] The 'tops' of the trees are 'fertile' not just in their production of deer and pheasant, but in their apparent identity with the Sidney family itself.

Jonson was intimately familiar however not just with the topography of the estate, but also with the precarious financial state of its owners, and with other anxieties they were experiencing at this time.[26]

Now, Penshurst, they that will proportion thee
  With other edifices, when they see
Those proud, ambitious heaps, and nothing else,
  May say, their lords have built, but thy lord dwells. (99–102)

Despite that firm last statement on which the poem concludes—'thy lord dwells'— Lord Lisle was frequently absent from Penshurst during these years, his duties at court taking him away from the estate for extended periods of time. His affectionate letters to his wife reveal the extent to which he was missing her company and that of their children, and the day-to-day pleasures of the estate. More worryingly still, he was under severe financial pressure. 'For I was never in that case in my life as I am now,' he writes on one occasion,

For besides mine interest, debts I owe 2,000 *l.* in London, for most part of which I either am or shall presently be sued. The household debts and many of them to poor and clamoursome persons come to a thousand pound: a sum that I think you did not imagine. I protest I should not have looked for but that I see it: but in them is contained the debts about Penshurst also . . . I have not money to pay the interest [that] grows due, nor to buy necessary clothes for this winter, nor to pay for men's meat or horse meat.[27]

Despite these constraints, and the rival demands of at least four other properties he was attempting to maintain in addition to Penshurst, Sidney was not exercising much financial caution, but freely indulging in the purchase of clothes, of fabrics, and of books. His anxieties were magnified by the more ostentatious lifestyle of some of his fellow-courtiers, and their lavish building programmes, such as that of the Earl of Dorset at nearby Knole, or of Robert Cecil, Earl of Salisbury, within the City of Westminster and in his country property at Theobalds, a house which displayed many of the ostentatious architectural features dismissively noted in the opening lines of the poem, as features that Penshurst is said to lack—black and white marble, polished pillars, a roof of gold, a fenestrated lantern 'whereof tales are told'.[28] Jonson nowhere openly refers to the Sidneys' current financial difficulties. His poem, on the other hand, tactfully implies that in the 'ancient pile' of Penshurst, with its more modest and proportionate dimensions, the Sidneys maintain a style of life that is at once more generous and more egalitarian than that to be found in the 'proud, ambitious heaps' of other, wealthier, families. The 'liberal board' of Penshurst flows

With all that hospitality doth know!
Where comes no guest but is allowed to eat,
  Without his fear, and of thy lord's own meat:
Where the same beer and bread, and self-same wine
  That is His Lordship's, shall be also mine;
And I not fain to sit (as some this day
  At great men's tables) and yet dine away. (59–66)

Both in classical and early modern times, it was a common habit to serve different food to the more and less distinguished guests. Classical satirists such as Juvenal and Martial had wryly commented on this custom ('Why do I dine without you, although, Ponticus, I am dining with you?', asks Martial) and Jonson's lines could well have been taken as a simple recall of their well-known sallies.[29] But a later remark of Jonson's to William Drummond of Hawthornden particularizes the allusion:

Being at the end of my Lord Salisbury's table with Inigo Jones, and demanded by my lord why he was not glad, 'My lord', said he, 'You promised I should dine with you, but I do not', for he had none of his meat. He esteemed only that his meat which was of his own dish. (*Informations*, 243–6)

Together with the lines from 'To Penshurst', the anecdote nicely encapsulates Jonson's contrasting feelings about these two great dynasties and the style of life each represented. Robert Cecil may well have been a wealthier and more politically powerful man than Robert Sidney, but Jonson leaves it in no doubt as to which of these patrons, in human and social terms, is to be preferred.

§§

It is tempting to wonder whether Jonson's now-lost pastoral play *The May-lord* could have been performed that summer at Penshurst Place.[30] Little is known about this work apart from Drummond's tantalizingly brief note:

He hath a pastoral entitled *The May-lord*. His own name is Alken; Ethra, the Countess of Bedford's; Mogibell, Overbury; the old Countess of Suffolk, an enchantress; other names are given to Somerset's lady, Pembroke, the Countess of Rutland, Lady Wroth. In the first story, Alken cometh in mending his broken pipe. Contrary to all other pastoral, he bringeth the clowns making mirth and foolish sports. (*Informations*, 307–12)

This account leaves it unclear as to whether *The May-lord* was a fully dramatized work that had actually been performed, perhaps in the grounds or interior of a great house such as Penshurst, or a text more akin to Spenser's *The Shepherd's Calendar*, intended essentially for reading. If it was indeed written for performance, then the real-life figures mentioned here might be assumed to have played the roles with which they are associated: Lucy, Countess of Bedford playing the part of Ethra (Greek εφρα, 'bright'), and so on. If on the other hand the work was not designed for performance, these figures might simply have been in some way 'shadowed' or 'personated' in their fictional counterparts. They need not have been collectively present, or even aware of the work's existence, or for that matter even alive, at the time that the pastoral was composed. These alternative readings allow for very different conclusions as to the likely date of the work and its possible character.

The May-lord was traditionally the young man who was elected to preside over the festivities of May Day. His reign—like that of his consort, the May-lady or Queen of the May—was of strictly limited duration, like that of the chambermaid Pru in the sports that are organized in Jonson's later comedy *The New Inn*. If the pastoral was indeed performed at Penshurst on 1 May 1611 it is possible that William Sidney or his brother Robert might have been chosen for this role. The title of the work seems consciously to recall that of Sir Philip Sidney's entertainment *The Lady of May* that had been performed at Wanstead Abbey in Essex (the estate of Sidney's uncle the Earl of Leicester) during a visit by Queen Elizabeth in May 1578 or 1579. And several of those who are named in relation to *The May-lord* of course have strong Sidneyan connections: there is Sir Philip Sidney's daughter Elizabeth, Countess of Rutland, and Robert Sidney's daughter Mary, Lady Wroth, and her cousin and future lover William Herbert, Earl of Pembroke.

But could all of those named in connection with *The May-lord* possibly have been at Penshurst in the summer of 1611, and is it likely they could have been persuaded to act together in a work of this kind? It was quite uncommon in this period for aristocrats to indulge in amateur theatricals of this kind which involved speaking roles; Jonson's masque of *The Gypsies Metamorphosed* was to be something of an innovation in this regard. Furthermore, the supposed participants in this drama formed a very unlikely mix. It is hard to imagine the formidable Katherine Howard ('the old Countess of Suffolk', wife of the Lord Treasurer and mother to Frances Howard) equably assuming the role of 'an enchantress' (or witch), and of Sir Thomas Overbury acting alongside the Countess's daughter Frances Howard ('Somerset's lady'), who—as we shall see in the following chapter—was soon to be responsible for his death.

It is even harder to think of Overbury acting in the company of Elizabeth Manners, Countess of Rutland, to whom he had recently made unwelcome advances, or indeed of Jonson himself, with whom as a consequence he had now fallen out. Jonson was an admirer of the Countess, whom he reckoned 'nothing inferior to her father in poetry' (*Informations*, 159–60), though he was aware that her marriage to Roger Manners, fifth Earl of Rutland, had its problems. In a verse epistle written as early as 1600 he had praised the Countess's verses with their 'high and noble matter', and spoken affectionately of her husband ('your brave friend and mine'), who was travelling abroad, wishing them both the birth of a son within the coming year. But that last wish could not be fulfilled, for the simple reason that Manners, as Jonson later came to realize, was impotent—a fact that may partly have prompted his constant travelling.[31] When he came to publish the poem as *The Forest*, 12, Jonson therefore deleted its last eight lines, concluding tactfully 'Who, wheresoe'er he be ... *The rest is lost.*' Though the marriage was fragile, the Countess remained loyal to her absent husband, as Overbury discovered when—soliciting Jonson as his accomplice—he made a disastrous bid for her favour. This is how Drummond was later to report Jonson's account of the resulting fiasco:

Sir Th. Overbury was in love with her, and caused Ben to read his *Wife* to her, which he, with an excellent grace, did, and praised the author. That the morn thereafter he discorded with Overbury, who would have him to intend a suit that was unlawful. The lines my lady kept in remembrance, 'He comes too near, who comes to be denied.' (*Informations*, 159–64)

The means of courtship that Overbury had proposed to Jonson—that he should read to the Countess from Overbury's own poem *The Wife*—was curious, to say the least, for the work itself ironically advocates chastity: 'in part to blame is she | Which hath without consent been only tried; | He comes too near, that comes to be denied.' The Countess took the poem's advice quite literally, and rejected the suit. 'Overbury was first his friend, then turned his mortal enemy,' reported Jonson (*Informations*, 127), mortified perhaps by his own discreditable role as go-between in the courtship of a lady he seems greatly to have admired.[32]

In view of these circumstances it seems unlikely that *The May-lord* was performed at Penshurst during the summer of 1611, or indeed that it was performed at all. *The May-lord* is more likely to have been a work designed for private study that Jonson began to write in 1618, soon after the Countess of Suffolk's corrupt financial practices had been brought to the attention of James, who had ordered her to leave the court and London and retire to Audley End. By this time too her daughter's responsibility for Overbury's murder had been legally proven, and the name 'Mogibell' (Greek μογοσ, 'suffering') might appropriately have been used of Overbury, in a fuller knowledge of how he had met his end.

§§

Jonson's stay at Penshurst probably concluded soon after William Sidney had celebrated his majority in November 1611, when he would have returned to London to prepare for the presentation at court of *Love Restored* in the Christmas season.[33] During his time at Penshurst he had also begun to put together a second poetic collection, *The Forest*, which he would eventually publish, along with his *Epigrams*, in the folio edition of his *Works* in 1616. This was a smaller, carefully organized, sequence of poems, fifteen in number, some reflecting his recent time at Penshurst or addressing members of the Sidney family. Standing near the head of the collection are the two companion poems addressed 'To Penshurst' and to Lady Mary's husband Sir Robert Wroth, appraising his peaceful life at Durrants, one of his estates in the parish of Enfield, just outside London, 'Free from proud porches or the gilded roofs, | 'Mongst lowing herds and solid hoofs.' Towards the end of *The Forest* are two poems directed admiringly to Elizabeth, Countess of Rutland, and Katherine, Lady Aubigny, the wife of Jonson's patron Esmé Stuart. In the body of the collection are some lighter pieces, including the familiar lyric 'Drink to me only with thine eyes', and two short translations from Catullus ('Come, my Celia' and 'Kiss me sweet') that had last been heard in a more sinister context, sung by Volpone in Jonson's comedy to the hapless wife of the merchant Corvino, as part of his attempted seduction; and a poetic exercise ('That Women Are But Men's Shadows') teasingly assigned to Jonson by Mary Herbert, Countess of Pembroke, to resolve a playful argument with her husband. Two linked poems, 'Praeludium' and 'Epode' (*The Forest*, 10 and 11), written around 1601, interestingly testify to Jonson's early associations with Sir John Salusbury and the Essex circle.[34]

At the opening and conclusion of the collection Jonson places two poems of a seemingly more personal character. 'Why I write not of Love' (*The Forest*, 1) bemoans the poet's inability to write amorous verses, as 'Love is fled, and I grow old'. Jonson was still in his early thirties at this time, and would go on to write a number of love poems that would appear eventually in his later collection *The Underwood*. The present lament is in part witty hyperbole, in part a hint as to the character of *The Forest*, which—unlike the usual run of fashionably amorous songs and sonnets—moves frequently into a graver mode, as in the poem which concludes the collection, 'To Heaven':

> Good and great God, can I not think of thee,
> > But it must straight my melancholy be?
> Is it interpreted in me disease
> > That, laden with my sins, I seek for ease?
> Oh, be thou witness, that the reins dost know
> > And hearts of all, if I be sad for show,
> And judge me after: if I dare pretend
> > To aught but grace, or aim at other end.
> > > (*The Forest*, 15.1–8)

The pose of melancholy was often affected in Jonson's day by would-be gallants wishing to add an air of mystery to their character, as Jonson himself had humorously noted in his early comedies: Stephano in *Every Man In His Humour* is 'mightily given to melancholy', which Mattheo agrees is 'your only best humour' (Q, 3.4.64–5). Religious melancholy was a more serious matter, classified by commentators as an actual disease, issuing (according to Robert Burton) from the Devil himself and his 'instruments or factors, politicians, priests, impostors, heretics, blind guides', working through 'simplicity, fear, blind zeal, ignorance, solitariness, curiosity, pride, vain-glory, presumption', and giving rise to the dreaded state of specious piety.[35] Jonson struggles in this poem to resist that interpretation of his present gloom: he is not (he insists) 'sad for show' but from a consciousness of his actual spiritual condition.

> I know my state, both full of shame and scorn,
> > Conceived in sin and unto labour born,

Standing with fear, and must with horror fall,
　　And destined unto judgement after all.
I feel my griefs too, and there scarce is ground
　　Upon my flesh t'inflict another wound.
Yet dare I not complain or wish for death
　　With holy Paul, lest it be thought the breath
Of discontent; or that these prayers be
　　For weariness of life, not love of thee. (17–26)

The 'scorn' of which Jonson speaks is not that of the satirist, speaking disdainfully of the world's follies, but that of the sinner, whose qualities deservedly attract the condemnation of others ('Scorn', *OED*, 3†a). 'To Heaven', first published in the 1616 Folio and strongly coloured by Calvinist theology, was probably written some time after Jonson's return to Protestantism. Concluding a collection which celebrates the pleasures of feasting, hospitality, and social life, it acts as a reminder of a more devout, rigorous, and introspective element in Jonson's character: of his acute consciousness (in the casual, pregnant phrase of which he was master) that he was 'destined unto judgement after all'.

§§

Early in 1612 Jonson elected to travel abroad for more than a year in the company of a pupil every bit as demanding and troublesome as Will Sidney.[36] His new charge was the 19-year-old Wat Ralegh, son of the distinguished scholar, poet, and traveller Sir Walter Ralegh, who was still immured in the Tower of London. The young Ralegh, who was eventually to be killed at San Tomas during his father's expedition to Guiana in 1618, was notoriously wild; his Oxford tutor, Daniel Featley, reported him to have been addicted to 'strange company and violent exercises'. Aubrey described him as 'a handsome lusty stout fellow, very bold, and apt to affront. Spake Latin very fluently; and was a notable disputant and courser, and would never be out of countenance nor baffled; fight lustily'; and given to practical jokes. On one occasion during a session of 'coursing' (or formal disputation) at Oxford, Wat had 'put a turd in the box, and besmeared it about his antagonist's face'. On another, when dining in distinguished company with his father, he promised to behave 'mighty mannerly' but forgot himself halfway through the meal.

Sir Walter being strangely surprised and put out of his countenance at so great a table, gives his son a damned blow over the face. His son, as rude as he was, would not strike his father, but strikes over the face the gentleman that sat next to him, and said, 'Box about: 'twill come to my father anon.' 'Tis now a common-used proverb.[37]

Aubrey was to include Jonson among Wat's father's 'intimate acquaintance and friends', but the relationship of the two men was not without friction.[38] Jonson was to speak disgruntledly of Ralegh to Drummond, adding that 'the best wits of England were employed for the making of his *History*. Ben himself had written a piece to him of the Punic War, which he altered and set in his book' (*Informations*, 148–52).[39] Never an easy collaborator, Jonson may well have resented the manner in which Ralegh had appropriated and altered his work without acknowledgement in his *History of the World*, a project that was in preparation in William Stansby's printing house at the same time as Jonson's own folio edition of his *Works*. Jonson and Ralegh must have been intermittently in touch since work on the *History* had begun in 1607, and it is likely that Ralegh knew that Jonson had been acting recently as a tutor to a difficult pupil at Penshurst.

During the early years of James's reign the idea of the Grand Tour, as an essential part of a young man's education, was still strongly associated with the political interests of two powerful families, the Cecils and the Howards. After his wedding to Frances Howard in 1607, the young Robert Devereux (for example) was packed straight off to Paris, where he met with Henri IV. When Robert Cecil's son William Cecil, Lord Cranborne, married Frances Howard's sister Catherine the following year, he too was dispatched to Paris; and when Henry, Lord Clifford, married William's sister Lady Frances in July 1610 he too was sent off at once on his continental travels, beginning with a period in Paris during which he was attached to M. de Pluvenal's Academy, a fashionable place of study for young members of the French nobility.[40] Such programmes of travel were designed not only to bestow a cultural polish on the young English aristocrats, but to strengthen political bonds between the British and French courts, and to consolidate the personal influence of James's 'Trinity of Knaves'. Yet there were other reasons too why Englishmen, young and old, might choose to travel at this time. For committed Catholics and those with Catholic sympathies, the years immediately following the assassination of Henri IV might well seem a good time for leaving

England, with its zealous anti-Catholic legislation, and travelling abroad. Though no longer now formally a member of the Catholic Church, Jonson, like many of his former co-religionists, may have felt some relief at leaving England at such a moment, and curiosity to observe the more open display of Catholic beliefs and practices in continental Europe.[41]

A further and simpler motive for dispatching young men on the Grand Tour might be that their despairing parents had no idea what else to do with them. This could well have been the prime reason that Wat Ralegh was sent off to France in the company of Ben Jonson in 1612. There was no particular political advantage to be gained from the son's travels, and at this stage of his life Wat Ralegh must have seemed virtually beyond the reach of further education. Whatever the explanation, this combination of high-spirited pupil and hard-drinking tutor did not prove a success. Jonson reported the outcome to William Drummond.

Sir W. Ralegh sent him governor with his son, anno 1613, to France. This youth, being knavishly inclined, among other pastimes (as the setting of the favours of damsels on a cod-piece), caused him to be drunken and dead drunk, so that he knew not where he was; thereafter laid him on a car which he made to be drawn by pioneers [= workmen] through the streets, at every corner showing his governor stretched out, and telling them that was a more lively image of the crucifix than any they had; at which sport Ralegh's mother delighted much, saying, his father young was so inclined; though the father abhorred it. (*Informations*, 226–33)

The chaotic behaviour of Humphrey Wasp, the irascible and incompetent 'governor' of young Bartholomew Cokes in *Bartholomew Fair*, the first comedy Jonson was to write after returning to England in 1613, clearly reflects certain of Jonson's own experiences with his young charge on this eventful tour. A few years earlier, Sir Walter Ralegh had written a Polonius-like book of advice for his errant son which included a chapter entitled 'What inconveniences happen to such as delight in wine', which his son's governor might also have done well to have studied.[42] 'Favours of damsels' were love-tokens such as gloves, scarves, or ribbons, given by young ladies to the men they fancied, who customarily displayed them in a more discreet part of their attire. But Wat Ralegh's pranks with codpieces were as nothing compared with his principal feat, of displaying Ben Jonson's drunken body to the citizens of Paris as 'a more lively image of the crucifix than any they had'. This was an act which might well have landed the two travellers in quite serious trouble: for what Ralegh is here openly mocking is one of the more solemn rituals of the Catholic Church, the Feast of Corpus Christi, which—like other Protestant visitors—he must have watched with amusement and curiosity on the streets of Paris. Jonson's fellow-Syrenaic Thomas Coryate had observed this ceremony with some astonishment when visiting Paris in 1608, and discussed its significance at length with the great English Protestant scholar Isaac Casaubon, who was then resident in Paris. In his account of his visit to the city, Coryate describes 'rich cupboards of plate' being carried by priests through the streets of Paris near the Cathedral of Notre Dame, along with tables on which were 'costly goblets, and what not tending to pomp, that is called by the name of plate'. 'Upon the midst of their tables stood their golden crucifixes, with divers other gorgeous images', and elaborate rockeries, with water spouting out of jets.

Wherefore the foresaid sacred company, perambulating about some of the principal streets of Paris, especially Our Lady Street, were entertained with most divine honours. For whereas the bishop carried the sacrament, even his consecrated wafer cake, betwixt the images of two golden angels, whensoever he passed by any company, all the spectators prostrated themselves most humbly upon their knees, and elevated their hands with all possible reverence and religious behaviour, attributing as much divine adoration to the little wafer cake, which they call the sacrament of the altar, as they could do to Jesus Christ himself.

The procession in the morning lasted for two hours, and continued for a further two hours in the afternoon, attended this time by Queen Marguerite herself, who was carried along beside it on the backs of porters. This was not a ceremony (Coryate noted) which spectators, however sceptical, could afford to ignore.

If any godly protestant that hateth this superstition should happen to be amongst them when they kneel, and forbear to worship the sacrament as they do, perhaps he may be presently stabbed or otherwise most shamefully abused, if there should be notice taken of him.[43]

In so flagrantly parodying the Corpus Christi ceremony, Ralegh (and Jonson, his unconscious collaborator) may have been lucky to have escaped without assault or abuse from devout Parisians.

The Feast of Corpus Christi dramatically highlighted one essential difference between the Catholic and Protestant faiths: the belief in the Roman Church that Christ himself was literally, rather than just symbolically, present in the wine and wafer of the mass. The doctrine of the real presence stood at the centre of theological disputation at this time. While he and his young charge were in Paris, Jonson was invited to act formally as witness to one such debate on this subject, between two celebrated English-born controversialists of the opposing faiths: Daniel Featley, Wat Ralegh's former Oxford tutor, now household chaplain to the British Ambassador to Paris, Sir Thomas Edmondes, and Cardinal Richelieu's protégé and theological adviser Richard Smith. The company (including Jonson, the English writer Henry Constable, and others) met at noon on 4 September 1612 at the house of an Englishman, Mr Knevet, who had organized the occasion. Smith came attended by his cousin Mr Rainer, while Featley was accompanied by the English news-writer John Pory, who was resident at this time in Paris, serving as an agent or correspondent for George, Lord Carew.[44] Pory seems to have been charged with recording the main points of the debate, and Jonson with vouching for the accuracy of his account. The debate went on for nearly seven hours, with Smith defending and Featley disputing; another day's argumentation had been planned, with the roles reversed, but—due to Protestant trickery, so the Catholic supporters bitterly claimed—this never came about. Pory's and Jonson's joint testimony—published at a critical moment in 1630 when Smith, now Vicar Apostolic for England (with the title of Bishop of Chalcedon), was exerting considerable influence in the country—gives some sense of the highly technical and disputatious nature of the occasion:

In this relation we have omitted of set purpose all D. Smith's by-discourses, together with his proofs of the main, because they were against the third law [the agreement about the procedures for the debate]. And Mr Featley at this time took no notice of them in particular, but promised in general to answer them all, when it came to his course to answer. Now he was bound by the law only to oppose, and D. Smith only to give his answers, which are here truly set down, most of them out of his own writing, as we depose, who were present at this disputation.

I must willingly subscribe to the truth of that which D. Smith did voluntarily present to our eyes and ears; and for the rest, which is Mr Featley's, none of the adverse party can take any just exception to it.

J. P.

I profess that all things in this narration delivered and quoted out of D. Smith's autography are true out of my examination. And of the rest, I remember the most, or all; neither can I suspect any part.

B. J.[45]

Jonson's other recorded meeting in Paris was with Cardinal Jacques-Davy Duperron, son of a Huguenot refugee and one of France's leading intellectuals. A formidable scholar, preacher, wit, and controversialist, Duperron had been raised as Calvinist but converted to Catholicism as a young man, and had scored a famous triumph in converting Henri IV to the Catholic faith in 1593. He too had been involved in a notable debate concerning the real presence just a few years earlier with the French Calvinist leader Duplessis-Mornay.[46] He had strong literary tastes, and had delivered the funeral *éloge* at the death of Ronsard. His free translations of Books 1 and 4 of the *Aeneid* had aroused the curiosity of James I, to whom Duperron, at the King's request, dispatched a specially printed copy in 1612. When Jonson met with Duperron in Paris, however, he informed him with characteristic bluntness that his translations of the *Aeneid* 'were naught' (*Informations*, 50–1). As Jonson's French at this time was far from perfect, he was scarcely qualified to make such a judgement.[47] Possibly however the remark was not driven purely by literary considerations. As Jonson was aware, Duperron was in particular disfavour in England at that moment for his 'disrespectful carriage' towards King James, whose claims to represent the true Catholic Church by maintaining all truths considered necessary by the first Christians Duperron had recently refuted. John Pory had actually been sent to Paris early in 1612 to convey a formal response to Duperron prepared on the King's behalf by Bishop Lancelot Andrewes and the learned Protestant scholar Isaac Casaubon. Jonson may well have thought that a little personal rudeness on his part would help to drive home this message—or at least convey quiet gratification when reported in due course to James in London.[48]

Before long, Jonson and his protégé would take to the road once more. On 21 February/3 March 1613 the Paris business agent Jean Beaulieu wrote a letter of introduction, which Jonson evidently delivered in person, to William Trumbull, the British Resident in Brussels: a close friend and colleague of Thomas Edmondes, his opposite number in Paris.

... This gentleman Master Ben Jonson (who I am sure, cannot but be well known unto you by his reputation), having spent some twelve months' travel in this country, in Master Ralegh's company, who was committed to his charge by Sir Walter his father, hath now taken a resolution to pass by Sedan [to the north-east of Paris, in the Ardennes] into your parts... [it] will be sufficient to declare his virtuous inclination ... besides the testimony of his extraordinary and rare parts of knowledge and understanding, which make his conversation to be honoured and beloved in all companies; specially for the commendation he hath, not to abuse the power of his gifts, as commonly other overflowing wits use to do…This only particular I must require on his behalf…that…you do charge him, by the authority of your place, with the best cup of claret that Brussels shall afford, to remember the healths of his friends here…

A week later Beaulieu wrote again confidentially to Trumbull:

…At Master Jonsons entreaty I did accompany him with a letter of recommendation unto you, which I suppose he was desirous to have to prevent the rumour of some ill cross-business wherein he hath been interested here. What is good in him I was content to relate. And indeed he hath many worthy parts in him; for the rest you shall soon make a discovery thereof.[49]

The nature of this rumoured 'ill cross-business' is wholly unknown. Trumbull however, a man with puritan sympathies, was a particularly sharp observer of possible Catholic mischief, which over the years he had reported back methodically to Cecil in London. It is possible that Beaulieu might have harboured misgivings of Jonson's lingering Catholic affiliations which he was passing on to Trumbull for what it might be worth.[50]

If Trumbull was not already acquainted personally with Jonson at this time he was certainly well aware of his work, having received detailed notes from a London correspondent on the performance of *Oberon* at Whitehall two years earlier; this letter provides a valuable guide as to how the masque was actually performed.[51] He may also have been on good terms with Wat Ralegh's father—or have performed some particular favour on this occasion for Wat and his governor, for which he was soon to be rewarded by Sir Walter. The only known presentation copy of any of Ralegh's works is a first edition of *The History of the World* inscribed 'Ex dono Authoris, for Mr W Trumbull', which Trumbull received the year after the two men's visit to Brussels. Over the next few years Trumbull was to show a close interest in Ralegh's wavering political fortunes, and after his execution in 1618 he copied Ralegh's last verses, 'Even such is time', carefully in his own hand into the presentation copy of *The History of the World*.[52] Trumbull was a great lover and collector of books, and, despite the coded warnings he had received from Beaulieu about Jonson's character, may possibly have enjoyed this visit in March 1613 from two figures so intimately connected with the literary world of London.

From Brussels, Jonson and Ralegh moved on to Antwerp, where they arrived in early April.[53] They then journeyed north to Leiden, where (as David McPherson has shown) Jonson met with the formidable Dutch scholar Daniel Heinsius.[54] Heinsius was a scholar Jonson greatly admired, and with whom he had much in common. Over the previous two or three years Heinsius had edited the works of Horace and Aristotle's *Poetics*, written a treatise on tragedy based on the *Poetics*, *De Constitutione Tragoediae* (which Jonson was to follow extensively in his *Discoveries*), together with another on satire appended to the edition of Horace. He was one of the great European Protestant scholars that King James was currently attempting to lure to England as a polemicist for the reformed faith. Another such scholar, Isaac Casaubon, whom James had enticed from Paris back to London in 1610, was also begging Heinsius to come and work in England. At such a moment, Heinsius and Jonson would have had much to discuss.[55] It was through Heinsius' kindness that Jonson was able to achieve a considerable coup on behalf of his friend Thomas Farnaby, the London scholar and schoolmaster who was at that time working on his edition of the works of Martial. As Farnaby was uneasily aware, Heinsius' distinguished colleague in Leiden, Peter Scriverius, was also at that time working on his great edition of Martial. Through Heinsius' mediation, Scriverius allowed Jonson to transcribe his existing annotations and pass them on to Farnaby. This was no small favour: Farnaby's edition was published (with due acknowledgement to Jonson and the two Dutch scholars for their aid) in 1615; Scriverius' edition was not to appear for another four years. The meeting in Leiden between Jonson and Heinsius must certainly have been amiable, and may have been for Jonson one of the enduring memories of his continental tour.

The rest of Jonson's and Ralegh's itinerary in Europe is not clearly known, though a marginal scribbling by (the not always wholly reliable) Charles Stanhope in his personal copy of Jonson's 1640 Folio suggests the couple may have journeyed south: 'I kneaw Ben Jhonson at Lyons hee trauelld wth yoonge Walt Wrawleigh'.[56] If they did indeed venture in this direction they might well have called on Esmé Stuart's mother at the Château de la Verrerie at Aubigny-sur-Nère, though the archives at the Chateau and at Bourges today bear no trace of their visit.

By the end of June the pair were certainly back in London, as Jonson testifies in a later poem, 'An Execration upon Vulcan', written in 1623 to lament the loss of many of his own books and manuscripts in a house fire.

Jonson compares his own personal catastrophe with another larger conflagration that he witnessed in London with his own eyes on his return from his continental travels: the burning of the Globe theatre on 29 June 1613 during a performance of Shakespeare's *Henry VIII*, when a canon misfired into the thatched roof of the theatre. This (writes Jonson) was the 'cruel stratagem' of Vulcan himself,

> Against the Globe, the glory of the Bank.
> Which though it were the fort of the whole parish,
> Flanked with a ditch and forced out of a marish,
> I saw with two poor chambers taken in
> And razed, ere thought could urge, 'This might have been!'
>   (*The Underwood*, 43.132–9)

While Jonson had been travelling abroad, two events had occurred that had significantly altered the existing structures of political power at Whitehall, and made possible the emergence of new leaders, factions, and alliances. In May 1612 the increasingly unpopular and embattled Robert Cecil, Earl of Salisbury, had died after a painful and disabling illness, his death finally closing a long period of Cecilian political domination in England. Six months later, a more widely mourned death had followed: that of the young Prince Henry Frederick, carried off by typhoid while poised (so it seemed) at the very brink of a brilliant martial career. The political machinery of the country had been brought quite suddenly to a standstill, where it would for a time remain. The grief-stricken King was in no mood to take any significant policy decisions. The princely household, so recently brought together, was now no more. At Henry's funeral in Westminster Abbey on 7 December 1612, the white rods of office belonging to its members were formally broken, and tossed into his burial vault. The Prince's Great Standard, 'being a lion crowned, standing on a chapeau', was carried in the funeral procession, bearing a motto that had been suggested to the Prince by Jonson himself: *fax gloria mentis honestae*, 'fame is the incitement to honest minds'—or, as Milton would later rework the phrase, 'Fame is the spur that the clear spirit doth raise, | (That last infirmity of noble mind)' (*Lycidas*, 70–1).[57] This was a sentiment which, in all its complexity, Jonson would have cause to ponder in the years ahead.

15

Fame 1613–1616

SIR Walter Ralegh's *History of the World*, planned for the edification of the author's royal protector Prince Henry, was cut short when—in an 'unspeakable and never enough lamented loss'—'it pleased God to take that glorious Prince out of the world'.[1] The *History* was published by the London printer and bookseller William Stansby none the less in its unfinished state in an imposing folio edition in 1614. The frontispiece to the volume was engraved by Renald Elstracke from a design by Ralegh himself, probably devised in consultation with Ben Jonson, whose verses on 'The Mind of the Frontispiece to a Book' offer a commentary on its significance (Fig. 35).[2] In Elstracke's engraving (Fig. 34) the figure of History is shown bearing the world aloft, and trampling underfoot the decrepit figures of Death and Oblivion. Above the pediment stand two flamboyant winged figures holding curly trumpets to their lips, representing Good and Bad Fame. *Fama Bona,* dressed all in white and radiating light, rests her right hand controllingly on the circumference of the world. *Fama Mala,* spotty both in face and garment, mimics her stance, placing her left hand equally assertively on the opposing rim of the globe. Though the large all-seeing eye of *Providentia* watches over all, the fortunes of the world (so the design implies) are basically governed by these two figures of Good and Bad Repute. The word *fama* in Latin contains a range of meanings on a descending gradient from fame, honour, renown, report—in the generally positive senses of those terms—through to rumour, news, gossip (the fallible circulatory systems of the day), and thence, in a plummeting decline, to the more negative senses of the term: slander, blame, reproach, disgrace, dishonour.

Fig. 34. Good and Bad Fame: Ralegh's *History of the World* title page, 1614.

Throughout his career Jonson showed much interest in this complex and
unstable notion. In *Poetaster* (as we have seen) he allows the character of
Virgil to read to Augustus the great passage on this topic from the fourth
book of the *Aeneid*: recalling, at the very moment of his honouring by the
emperor, the operation of *fama* in its more malign and damaging form:

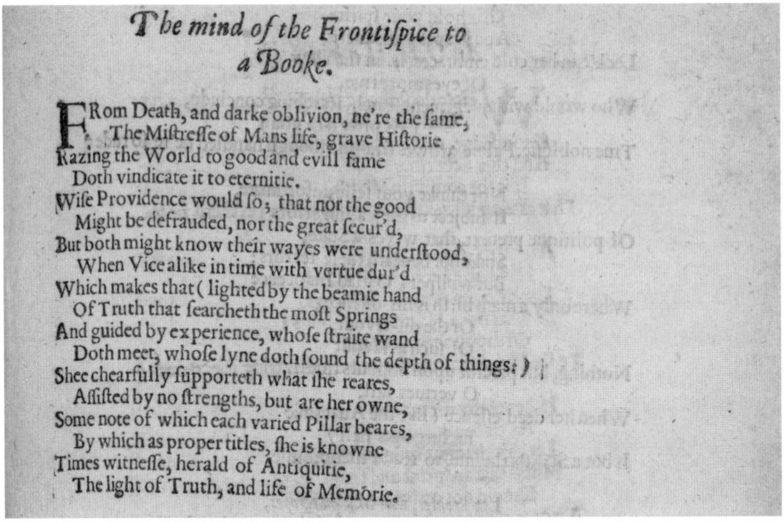

The mind of the Frontispice to a Booke.

FRom Death, and darke oblivion, ne're the fame,
    The Miftreffe of Mans life, grave Hiftorie
Razing the World to good and evill fame
    Doth vindicate it to eternitie.
Wife Providence would fo; that nor the good
    Might be defrauded, nor the great fecur'd,
But both might know their wayes were underftood,
    When Vice alike in time with vertue dur'd.
Which makes that (lighted by the beamie hand
    Of Truth that fearcheth the moft Springs
And guided by experience, whofe ftraite wand
    Doth meet, whofe lyne doth found the depth of things;)
Shee chearfully fupporteth what fhe reares,
    Affifted by no ftrengths, but are her owne,
Some note of which each varied Pillar beares,
    By which as proper titles, fhe is knowne
Times witneffe, herald of Antiquitie,
    The light of Truth, and life of Memórie.

Fig. 35. 'The Mind of the Frontispiece to a Book': Jonson's verses on Ralegh's frontispiece, *The Underwood*, 24, from Jonson's 1641 Folio.

> Fame, a fleet evil, than which is swifter none;
> That moving grows, and flying gathers strength;
> Little at first and fearful, but at length
> She dares attempt the skies, and stalking proud
> With feet on ground, her head doth pierce a cloud!

In *The Staple of News,* with a satirical eye on early developments in the field of journalism, Jonson presents an Office for the manufacture and dissemination of news. ''Tis the House of Fame, sir,' explains its Registrar as visitors enter his Office,

> Where both the curious and the negligent,
> The scrupulous and careless, wild and staid,
> The idle and laborious: all do meet
> To taste the *cornucopiae* of her rumours
> Which she, the mother of sport, pleaseth to scatter
> Among the vulgar. Baits, sir, for the people!
> And they will bite like fishes. (3.2.115–22)

In Jonson's late masque of *Chloridia* the figure of Fame is revealed standing precariously, trumpet in hand, on top of a globe (Fig. 36), surrounded by four

306

persons representing Poesy, History, Architecture, and Sculpture, 'who together with the nymphs, floods, and fountains make a full choir; at which Fame begins to mount, and moving her wings, flieth singing up to heaven'. This was evidently a tricky manoeuvre, which Inigo Jones carried off with the help of an invisible wire and the newly introduced fly gallery. Jonson later scornfully dismissed this virtuosic act ('The ascent of Lady Fame, which none could spy') as a mere attempt on Jones's part to hoist his own fame up to the heavens:

> O shows! Shows! Mighty shows!
> The eloquence of masques! What need of prose,
> Or verse, or sense, t'express immortal you?[3]

On his return from Europe in the summer of 1613 Jonson had particular cause to consider these various and contrary aspects of Fame. He encountered at once a simmering political scandal involving the King's favourite, Robert Carr, and a member of the country's most powerful political family, Frances Devereux, née Howard, Countess of Essex. Rumour about their relationship (as in Virgil's lines) was bowling along, and gathering strength on the way. The pair would in due course be disgraced, and dispatched to the Tower of London. Jonson himself was to be awkwardly, if in large measure unwittingly, caught up in this notorious scandal, being commissioned to celebrate the fortunes of the couple just as their actions were about to be legally exposed and condemned. Yet the years between his return from Europe and his departure on foot for Scotland were to be characterized for Jonson by fame of a more positive variety, as with the passing of Shakespeare and the publication of the first folio edition of his own collected works he began to emerge more clearly as the dominant literary figure of the day.

Though Jonson valued the fame that these years would bring, it was a quality he continued none the less to regard with mistrust. Good Fame, he knew, could easily convert to Bad, as the changing fortunes of Ralegh himself had shown. In October 1618, having returned empty-handed from his futile expedition to Guiana and gravely displeased King James, Ralegh was to be convicted of high treason, and executed at Westminster. Talking with William Drummond at Hawthornden a mere two months after this event, Jonson was to comment sharply on the fate of his old acquaintance: 'That Sir W. Ralegh esteemed more of fame than conscience' (*Informations*, 148). Conscience, as Jonson repeatedly maintained, was the force that must always

Fig. 36. Fame standing on a globe in *Chloridia* (1631): Inigo Jones's final design.

guide one's actions; fame was incidental, adventitious, unpredictable, having the power not merely to elevate but also suddenly to destroy.[4]

§§

Jonson returned to England in the summer of 1613 to find his former friend Sir Thomas Overbury incarcerated in the Tower of London, and Robert and Frances Devereux, the young couple whose marriage he had helped to celebrate seven years earlier in *Hymenaei*, now in open contention over the validity of their union.[5] Too young in 1606 (it was thought) to be thrown directly into married life, the pair had gone their separate ways straight after their marriage, Robert departing on his continental travels, while Frances returned to the care of her mother, the powerful Countess of Suffolk—not herself a model of virtue, if contemporary gossip was to be trusted. Frances had performed at court in *The Masque of Queens* in 1609, and in 1612 she and her young sister Catherine had appeared in *Love Restored*, causing something of a stir by refusing the young courtiers who asked them to dance.[6] Perhaps the two sisters regarded the young men as beneath their station; but by this date, as evidence that was to emerge at later trials would confirm, Frances had a new attraction in her life, the King's favourite, Robert Carr, and little time to spare either for inferior members of the court or for her husband, to whom she had given a cool reception when he returned from his travels in 1609 and proved incapable (so she alleged) of consummating the marriage. Some time before September 1611 she had consulted with her confidante Anne Turner and the conjuror Simon Forman about spells that might make an unnamed lord—thought to be Carr himself fall in love with her.

Handsome, agile, attractive, though speaking with a brogue that English observers found incomprehensible, Robert Carr was pre-eminent amongst the favoured Scottish courtiers who had accompanied James south to England in 1603. Taken into the royal household at Holyrood as a boy after the early death of his father, he had risen steadily in royal favour. At an Accession Day Tilt in 1607 he had broken a leg, and James had taken him into personal care, growing increasingly fond of him during the period of convalescence. By December of that year Carr had been awarded an annual grant of £600 and a knighthood, and admitted as a Gentleman of the Bedchamber. James continued over the next few years to grant Carr exceptional favours and privileges of access. An amiable and relatively undemanding companion to

Fig. 37. Frances Howard by Simon van de Passe.

the King, Carr did not concern himself much, in these early years, in affairs of state. By 1610, however, the nature of his position at court had perceptibly changed, as—under the close direction of his friend Sir Thomas Overbury, now employed as his private secretary—he began to busy himself more energetically with matters of government and royal policy, drafting the King's correspondence and arranging new political alliances. In March 1611 Carr was created Viscount Rochester; in May of that year, he was admitted as Knight of the Garter, and a year later was appointed to membership of the Privy Council. As Carr's power grew, so too did that of Overbury, who in turn became (as Francis Bacon put it) Carr's 'oracle of direction', controlling and dictating the political advice that Carr now freely offered the King.[7]

Jonson would have viewed Overbury's new ascendency with interest, but also perhaps with apprehension. The two men had quarrelled after

Overbury's bungled courtship of the Countess of Rutland, but still had many friends in common—John Donne, John Hoskyns, Richard Martin, Sir Thomas Roe, Benjamin Rudyerd—as well as many political beliefs and aspirations. To judge from certain of his reported remarks ('He said Robert Cecil followed the Earl of Essex's death not with a good mind'), Overbury had been sympathetic to Essex's cause, and evidently retained some support for former members of Essex's circle.[8] He was now attempting to broker alliances with men whom Jonson himself liked and admired: Henry Wriothesley, Earl of Southampton; William Herbert, Earl of Pembroke; Sir Henry Neville; Sir Ralph Winwood. Yet the game that Overbury was playing—managing the King's favourite, who he hoped in turn could manage the King—carried very high risks. Queen Anne had already taken strongly against Overbury, while James was growing increasingly suspicious of his manoeuvrings, and resentful of his close relationship with Carr.

Frances Devereux's infatuation with Robert Carr presented another and equally complex danger for Overbury, threatening not just his personal relationship with Carr, but his basic political hopes and ambitions. For if Frances were to be formally separated from the young Earl of Essex and married to the royal favourite, Robert Carr, this would bring the Howard family into a new and powerful alignment with the King, endangering the Pembroke/Southampton interests that Overbury was currently attempting to promote. While tolerant of Carr's flirtation with Frances Devereux, Overbury therefore urged his friend to abandon any thoughts of marrying her. In doing so, he antagonized not only the couple themselves but also the King, who was ready to indulge his favourite's ambitions and eager to remove Overbury from the political scene. In April 1613, probably at Carr's and Northampton's prompting, James offered Overbury an ambassadorial post in France, the Low Countries, or Muscovy. Overbury refused point-blank, pleading at first linguistic incompetence and then ill health. Angry at this intransigence, James dispatched him on a charge of contempt to the Tower of London, where, in an increasingly sickly state, he would spend the few remaining months of his life.

In the following month Frances sued for divorce from her husband, alleging his incapacity to consummate the marriage. The case was tried by a commission headed by George Abbot, Archbishop of Canterbury, assisted by three other bishops and six civilian lawyers and judges. The two most powerful members of the Howard clan, Frances's great uncle Henry, Earl of

Northampton, and her father Thomas, Earl of Suffolk, sensing their political opportunity, worked busily to support her suit. Impotence was one of the few available grounds for annulment in early modern England; it was the plea to which Jonson's Morose had resorted despairingly towards the end of *Epicene*, in the hope of finally ridding himself of his boisterous bride ('I am no man, ladies', he declares, 'Utterly unabled in nature, by reason of frigidity, to perform the duties or any the least office of a husband,' 5.4.35–7).[9] The use of this same plea in the Essex divorce case may or may not have been equally born of desperation. Evidence was given that Robert Devereux was impotent only with his wife, but capable of sexual relations with other women, prompting the charge (ultimately dropped from the proceedings) that Frances had exercised *malificium* or witchcraft on her husband. A jury of four ladies and two midwives inspected the bride, declaring her to be capable of sexual relations but still a virgin. A series of servants and other household witnesses testified to the couple's failure to consummate their marriage. Devereux himself, perhaps under pressure from his advisers (Pembroke and Southampton), was prepared to accept these assertions.[10] George Abbot, no friend to the Howard family, was cautious about the evidence, but when his commission failed to reach agreement on the case, James appointed two more commissioners, the bishops of Winchester and Rochester, who could be relied upon to achieve the desired result; and on 25 September 1613 the Essex marriage was formally annulled.

Ten days before the nullity was granted, Overbury died in the Tower of London after a painful illness. He had been suffering from nausea, vomiting, and permanent thirst, and had an ulcerous infection on his back. His gangrenous body was buried the same day. Nearly two years later, allegations would emerge that Overbury had been murdered in the Tower by poisons administered by his keeper, Richard Weston, at the instigation of Frances Devereux, working in collusion with her friend Anne Turner and with Carr himself. In 1613 the divorce proceedings and Overbury's mysterious death had prompted much gossip and speculation, but no talk of murder had as yet been heard, and the fortunes of Carr and his intended bride and the triumphant Howard faction appeared to be running high.[11] In October Carr was appointed to the Scottish Privy Council, and in December he was made Lord Treasurer of Scotland. On 4 November he was created Earl of Somerset and Baron Brancepeth, and was escorted to the throne in the installation ceremony by two senior members of the Howard family, the earls of Nottingham and Northampton, with their political rivals Pembroke and Southampton carrying his cap and hood, signalling a political compromise that had now tacitly been agreed.

On 26 December, in a lavish culmination to the year's disconcerting events, Robert Carr and Frances Devereux were married in the Chapel Royal: the very place where Frances had been married to Robert Devereux seven years earlier, with the same celebrant, Dr James Montague, Bishop of Bath and Wells and Dean of the Chapel Royal, officiating on each occasion. As the news-writer John Chamberlain noted in his reports of these events, the costs of the wedding itself, the attendant celebrations, and the King's extravagant gifts to the couple were largely met by the crown, despite the acute financial difficulties which James faced at this moment.[12] Ben Jonson, who had been invited to write *Hymenaei* in honour of Frances's first marriage in 1606, was called upon again to celebrate her new marriage to the King's favourite, and provided two masques, *A Challenge at Tilt*—the first part of which was presented on 27 December, the second on 1 January 1614—and *The Irish Masque*, performed on 29 December. In a week of almost non-stop festivity, Thomas Campion's *Somerset Masque* was presented at the Banqueting House on the evening of the wedding itself, while on Twelfth Night *The Masque of Flowers* was performed by members of Gray's Inn, largely financed by Francis Bacon, who was eager to repay political favours. On 31 December the Lord Mayor of London presented at the Merchant Taylors' Hall in Threadneedle Street an elaborate tribute from the City, Thomas Middleton's *The Masque of Cupids*. Middleton's masque was preceded by a torchlight procession through Cheapside 'accompanied by the father and mother of the bride, and all the lords and ladies about the court', the men 'well mounted and richly arrayed, making a goodly show; the women, all in coaches'.[13] Donne, Chapman, Jonson (see Fig. 38), and others offered congratulatory poems to the happy pair.

The apparently buoyant celebrations of the 1613 Christmas season were undermined nevertheless by a sense of misgiving, which at times found expression in the masques themselves. In Campion's masque 'Great Honour's herald, Fame' was accompanied by

> Deformed Error, that enchanting fiend,
> And wing-tongued Rumour, his infernal friend,
> With Curiosity and Credulity

Both sorceresses: all in hate agree
Our purpose to divert . . .

These allegorical figures were allowed, somewhat unsettlingly, to make an actual appearance in Campion's antimasque:

. . . Error first in a skin coat scaled like a serpent and an antique habit painted with snakes, a hair of curled snakes, and a deformed vizard. With him Rumour in a skin coat full of winged tongues, and over it an antique robe; on his head, a cap like a tongue, with a large pair of wings to it. Curiosity in a skin coat full of eyes, and an antique habit over it, a fantastic cap full of eyes. Credulity in the like habit painted with ears, and an antique cap full of ears.

Though ritually expelled from the proceedings during the course of the masque ('Vanish, vanish, hence confusion,' chants the figure of Harmony, accompanied by nine musicians), Error, Rumour, Curiosity, and Credulity would continue to dog the Somersets in real life over the coming months.

Jonson more prudently made no reference within his masques to the gossip surrounding this scandalous marriage. Like Pembroke, Southampton, and other former supporters of the Essex faction, he instead accepted the political situation that (with whatever force, crudity, and precariousness) had now been achieved. Invoking the myth of Eros and Anteros, *A Challenge at Tilt* playfully presents a contest as to which of two figures of Cupid (one allied with the bride, the other with the groom) was the true god of Love: a question resolved on the second day of the masque's performance through a tournament in the tiltyard at Whitehall watched by the King and Queen and the ambassadors of Spain and the Archduke and their ladies. Both Cupids, it was revealed, turned out to be true representatives of Love, their amorous opposition making its force more passionate and enduring. In a similar spirit, so the masque implied, the ritual combat between the tilters actually signalled a new political concord; 'a general reconcilement', as one witness put it, 'made between my lord of Howard and my lords of Pembroke, Southampton, etc. in this conjuncture'. As a sign of this new merger of interests, the bride's relatives in the tiltyard wore the groom's colours, while the groom's relative's wore the bride's.[14] Jonson's second offering on this occasion, *The Irish Masque at Court*, paid scant attention to the Somerset wedding, and may indeed have been designed originally as a quite separate celebration for the Christmas season: attempting as it does jocularly to deal with growing problems in James's programme of colonial rule in Ireland.[15]

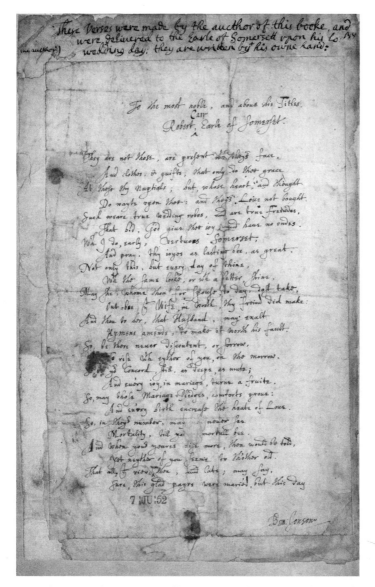

Fig. 38. Jonson's autograph manuscript of his poem 'To the Most Noble, and Above his Titles, Robert, Earl of Somerset' was delivered to Robert Carr on the day of his wedding to Frances Howard, 26 December 1613, and is today pasted into a copy of Jonson's Second Folio (1640–1) in the British Library (shelfmark C.28.m.11) that may once have belonged to Carr himself. Jonson chose not to include the poem amongst his *Epigrams* in the 1616 First Folio, nor to publish it elsewhere after the fuller story emerged of the poisoning of Sir Thomas Overbury in the Tower of London. Overbury is the 'friend' mentioned in line 12; the further reference is to his poem *The Wife*, 1614 (see Chapter 14, 292–3).

For all the wishful symbolism of the Somerset marriage masques, the new political alliance between the Pembroke/Southampton faction and the Carr and Howard group soon proved fragile and unworkable. The overwhelming problem of the day was how to deal with the King's massive and ever-mounting debts, a question which the so-called Addled Parliament met briefly and ineffectively to address in the spring of 1614.[16] The favoured solution of the Howard faction was increased revenue from 'projects' (patents or monopolies sold at profit to courtiers or other servants of the crown) and from a royal marriage alliance with Catholic Spain, strategies which the Pembroke faction strenuously opposed.[17] Despite Northampton's death in June 1614, the Howard faction managed nevertheless to retain its political supremacy throughout much of the year. Thomas Howard, Earl of Suffolk, was appointed Lord High Treasurer in July, and also inherited his uncle's posts of Lord Privy Seal and Warden of the Cinque Ports; while Carr himself, in a significant addition to his existing powers, was allowed to succeed Suffolk in the powerful position of Lord Chamberlain: a move especially galling to Pembroke, who had hankered after this office for himself.[18]

Yet from this point of high achievement, Carr's fortunes began quite suddenly to slide. During his August progress James had been introduced to a charming and strikingly athletic young man named George Villiers, to whom he had taken an immediate fancy. In the autumn Villiers was summoned to court, where his attractions were instantly registered. Bishop Goodman was to describe him as 'the handsomest-bodied man in England; his limbs so well compacted and his conversation so pleasing and of so sweet a disposition'.[19] Over the following months, in a deliberate bid to curtail Carr's influence, Pembroke and his close political ally George Abbot began quietly to promote Villiers's interests at court. Unsettled by these moves, Carr began unwisely to show his anger and irritation at the presence of the new rival. In November he deflected a move to appoint Villiers to the Bedchamber, securing instead the appointment of his own cousin and namesake, Robert Ker of Ancram. At Pembroke's prompting, the King then appointed Villiers as his personal cupbearer, to wait upon him at table every other month, and was soon seen to be taking obvious pleasure in his conversation and company.

The main testing ground however for the two court favourites would prove to be the masque prepared for the Christmas season: Ben Jonson's *Mercury Vindicated From the Alchemists at Court*, presented at the Banqueting House on 6 January 1615. The 'principal motive' for the masque, according to John

Chamberlain, was 'thought to be the gracing of young Villiers and to bring him on the stage', with his rival's cousin Robert Ker as a fellow-masquer.[20] Villiers was a dancer of exceptional skill and agility, capable of electrifying the sometimes leisurely dances of the court. Orazio Busino, chaplain to the Venetian Ambassador, was to describe Villiers's intervention at a potential disastrous moment in Jonson's later masque *Pleasure Reconciled to Virtue* (1618), when the King showed irritation with the languid progress of the dancers.

Last of all they danced the Spanish dance, one at a time, each with his lady, and being well nigh tired they began to lag, whereupon the King, who is naturally choleric, got impatient and shouted aloud: 'Why don't they dance? What did you make me come here for? Devil take you all, dance.' Upon this the Marquis of Buckingham, His Majesty's most favoured minion, immediately sprang forward, cutting a score of lofty and very minute capers, with so much grace and agility that he not only appeased the ire of his angry lord but moreover rendered himself the admiration and delight of everybody.

At this, the King kissed and embraced Villiers and patted his face 'with marks of extraordinary affection'.[21] In *Mercury Vindicated From the Alchemists at Court*, his debut performance at court, Villers must have taken equal pains to impress both the King and the assembled company with his virtuoso skills. James was evidently delighted with the masque, ordering a repeat performance two nights later.

Villiers's dancing would no doubt have been one element in the masque's success, but the theme itself is likely also to have amused and gratified the King. The 'vindication' of Mercury with which the masque is concerned is (in a now-obsolete sense of that word) his emancipation or deliverance, as well as the clearing of his name and the retribution carried out upon those who had oppressed him (*OED* †2, 3, †1.†b). In classical mythology Mercury had a mixed reputation. On the one hand, he was the god of thieves and pickpockets and similar ne'er-do-wells; yet he was also (as Jonson elsewhere noted) 'deorum hominumque interpres', the interpreter between gods and men, a semi-divine orator hailed as 'the president of language' and the 'sacred god of wit'.[22] Mercury had further qualities, as alert observers at Whitehall would have recalled: he was famously nimble on his feet, and had been appointed to serve as Jove's cupbearer. Lurking behind the classical figure it was therefore possible to glimpse the new favourite at court, George Villiers, whom the masque was also designed, in all senses of that term, to vindicate. At a further level of meaning Jonson plays with the fact that mercury was a central symbol and element in the process of alchemy, imagined by its practitioners to be 'the transformative substance without which the opus cannot be performed'; as such, it was subjected in the course of their experiments to much vigorous treatment.[23] 'I am their crude and their sublimate,' cries Jonson's Mercury in mock distress at this abuse,

their precipitate and their unctuous, their male and their female, sometimes their hermaphrodite: what they list to style me. It is I that am corroded and exalted and sublimed and reduced and fetched over and filtered and washed and wiped. What between their salts and their sulphurs, their oils and their tartars, their brines and their vinegars, you might take me out now a soused Mercury, now a powdered and pickled Mercury; never herring, oyster, or cucumber passed so many vexations. (39–47)

Jonson is here satirizing not only the claims, processes, and language of alchemy itself, but those courtiers who operate *like* alchemists, hoping 'to outwork the sun in virtue and contend to the great act of generation', and bring their own new 'men' into being (99–102). Jonson's masque wittily supports the King's right to make and unmake court officers as he sees fit, mocking those who assumed that this right was vested in themselves. In order to have registered these points with such stinging clarity, Jonson must have recognized that Somerset's days were already numbered, and that Villiers was the coming man: a realignment which his own masque, in its light-hearted and inventive way, no doubt helped to effect.

In the autumn of 1615 Somerset and his wife encountered an altogether more serious threat to their already-threatened position at court. For reasons unknown, Sir Ralph Winwood—a former Essex sympathizer, now recently appointed Secretary of State—had begun to take an interest in the circumstances of Sir Thomas Overbury's death in the Tower of London two years earlier.[24] In September Winwood informed King James that, having spoken at length with the Lieutenant of the Tower, Sir Gervase Elwes, he now had evidence that the Countess, with her future husband's connivance and the help of various accomplices, had been responsible for the murder of Overbury. At the Countess's instigation, so he believed, poisoned tarts and jellies had been passed to Overbury via his keeper, Richard Weston, along with poisoned enemas that had been administered by a hired apothecary's assistant, causing Overbury's agonizing death and the rapid putrefaction of his body. Alarmed by these reports, James instructed Lord Chief Justice Coke, assisted by Lord Ellesmere the Lord Chancellor and other commissioners, to investigate the matter. Somerset was placed under house arrest at Whitehall in October, and was soon obliged to surrender his seals and staff of office before being removed to the Tower. In early November the now-pregnant Countess was detained at Esmé Stuart's house in Blackfriars—a residence well known to Jonson, who had himself lodged here for several years and was now living nearby. This scandal was for Jonson, in every sense of the phrase, exceedingly close to home.

A series of sensational trials followed: of Overbury's keeper, Richard Weston, accused of colluding with the Countess to poison Overbury (hanged at Tyburn on 25 October); of the Countess's friend and confidante Anne Turner, accused of 'comforting, aiding, and assisting' Weston in these activities and of employing diabolical arts to achieve these ends (hanged at Tyburn on 14 November); of Sir Gervase Elwes, accused of conniving at these actions (executed outside the Tower of London on 20 November); of the apothecary James Franklin, accused of providing the poisons in question (hanged at Tyburn on 9 December); of Sir Thomas Monson, Master of Armoury at the Tower of London, on whose recommendation Richard Weston was appointed as Overbury's keeper (ultimately acquitted and released); and—at intervals, over a period from January to May 1616—of the Earl and Countess of Somerset themselves, indicted on charges of murder. The executions were spectacular public events, and the trials themselves likewise attracted huge public interest. Tickets were openly sold for admission to the hearings at Westminster Hall, where Inigo Jones and his assistants had erected a stage and several scaffolds to accommodate the crowds. At the hearing of her case on 12 January 1615 the Countess pleaded guilty to the murder of Overbury, but insisted that her husband was innocent. At the resumption of the trials in May, with Francis Bacon now prosecuting in place of Coke, the Countess expressed her sincere contrition, and the Earl maintained his plea of innocence. Both were finally convicted of murder and condemned to death, a sentence later commuted by royal pardon. The couple remained in tolerable comfort in the Tower of London until released in 1622, Somerset receiving a formal pardon in 1624.[25] But their fall from grace had been absolute. 'Stand whoso list upon the slipper top | Of court's estate,' Sir Thomas Wyatt had once famously written, translating a well-known chorus from Seneca's *Thyestes*, 'and let me here rejoice | And use

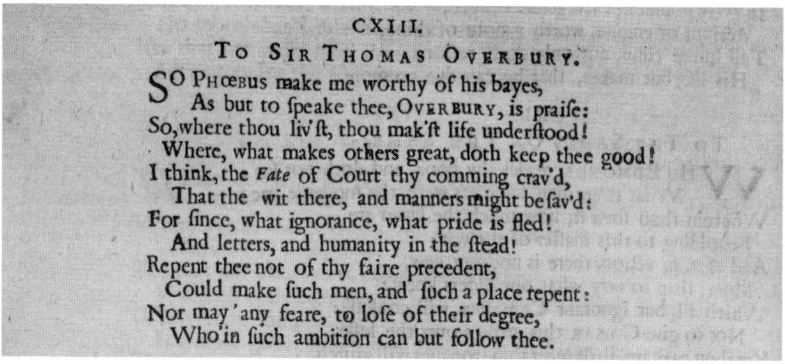

CXIII.

To Sir Thomas Overbury.

So Phœbus make me worthy of his bayes,
  As but to speake thee, Overbury, is praise:
So, where thou liv'st, thou mak'st life understood!
· Where, what makes others great, doth keep thee good!
I think, the *Fate* of Court thy comming crav'd,
  That the wit there, and manners might be sav'd:
For since, what ignorance, what pride is fled!
  And letters, and humanity in the stead!
Repent thee not of thy faire precedent,
  Could make such men, and such a place repent:
Nor may' any feare, to lose of their degree,
  Who in such ambition can but follow thee.

Fig. 39. 'To Sir Thomas Overbury', *Epigrams*, 113. Jonson told William Drummond that 'Overbury was first his friend, then turned his mortal enemy': *Informations*, 127. Yet despite his quarrel with Overbury, Jonson decided to include these admiring verses in his *Epigrams*, published in his 1616 Folio *Works*, after Overbury's agonizing death in the Tower of London.

me quiet without let or stop, | Unknown in court, that hath such brackish joys.' Some at James's court might have recalled these lines at the moment of the couple's downfall.

§§

The fall of Robert Carr signalled a political triumph for the party of William Herbert, Earl of Pembroke, who in November 1615 was at last appointed to the office that he had long coveted and that Somerset had now been obliged to renounce, that of Lord Chamberlain. Jonson's masque for the Christmas season, *The Golden Age Restored*—performed at the Banqueting House on 1 January 1616, while the Somersets were in custody, and their trials still proceeding—is a frank celebration of this extraordinary reversal of political fortune: of the reinstatement (even before the verdicts of the commission had been returned) of the country's judicial system, embodied in the figure of Astraea, goddess of Justice.[26]

> *Astraea* What change is here! I had not more
>   Desire to leave the earth before
>   Than I have now to stay;
>   My silver feet, like roots, are wreathed
>   Into the ground, my wings are sheathed,

And I cannot away.
Of all there seems a second birth;
It is become a heaven on earth,
    And Jove is present here;
I feel the godhead, nor will doubt
But he can fill the place throughout,
    Whose power is everywhere.

This, this, and only such as this,
The bright Astraea's region is,
    Where she would pray to live,
And in the midst of so much gold
Unbought with grace or fear unsold
    The law to mortals give. (176–93)

In a remarkably explicit reference to the passing of a corrupt regime at court under Somerset, the masque shows the figures of Avarice, Fraud, Slander, 'Corruption with the golden hands', Ambition, Pride, Scorn, Folly, Ignorance, and 'Smooth Treachery' (40–8) abruptly transformed into statues—a metamorphosis which (it is implied) has been achieved by James himself, figured here as Jove the Thunderer, who 'can endure no longer | Your great ones should your less invade, | Or that your weak, though bad, be made, | A prey unto the stronger' (7–10). In a possible hint at an impending change in his own position at court and a hoped-for rejuvenation of the arts under Pembroke, Jonson has Pallas Athena summon, along with Astraea and the Golden Age, a small band of distinguished English poets:

You far-famed spirits of this happy isle,
That for your sacred songs have gained the style
Of Phoebus' sons, whose notes the air aspire
Of th'old Egyptian or the Thracian lyre,
That Chaucer, Gower, Lydgate, Spenser hight,
Put on your better flames and larger light
To wait upon the age that shall your names new nourish,
Since virtue pressed shall grow, and buried arts shall flourish. (102–10)

These four poets are invited by Pallas to awaken certain 'semigods' who 'went away from earth' but may now be glimpsed in the present company, and are needed now as persons 'That justice dare defend, and will the age sustain' (119). The poets invoke these semi-divine figures, who are led out triumphantly by Somerset's old adversary and his wife's former husband Robert Devereux, Earl of Essex, to perform the first dance. The symbolism of the moment was unmistakable, and, for many in the audience, would have had a long resonance. The Essex faction, cheered and supported by the poets, was back in power; a new age was about to begin.

Chaucer, Gower, and Lydgate were poets whose work Jonson ranked highly and knew intimately; his *English Grammar* was to be illustrated by many quotations from their work. All three had been associated with the tradition of 'poetes laureat' that another of Jonson's favourite poets, John Skelton, had celebrated in his long discursive poem *The Garland of Laurel*, in which the Queen of Fame, Dame Pallas, and Skelton himself animatedly debate who should and should not be admitted to the House of Fame, a glittering edifice with turquoise and chrysolite floors, stairs of jasper and whalebone, walls pointed with diamonds, and palace gates adorned with the teeth of elephants. Edmund Spenser, the fourth of Jonson's 'far-famed spirits of this happy isle' in *The Golden Age Restored*, is a poet whom Jonson also admired despite a distaste for his antiquated language ('Spenser, in affecting the ancients, writ no language; yet I would have him read for his matter,' *Discoveries*, 1281–2); he is perhaps included here partly as a Protestant champion, who was admired by many in the political circle attending the present masque.[27] All four poets had been loosely associated with a laureate tradition that pre-dates the official creation in 1668 of the royal post of Poet Laureate, whose first incumbent was to be John Dryden. By the Christmas season of 1615/1616 Jonson is likely to have known that he himself was about to be drawn into this same tradition, and be awarded (on 1 February 1616, back-dated to 'the feast of the birth of our Lord God last past') a royal pension of 100 marks a year, 'in consideration of the good and acceptable service done and to be done' to James I. This honour encouraged Jonson to speak of himself boldly as the King's Poet, a position that appeared to balance that of the King's Architect, Inigo Jones, who had been appointed in October of the previous year as Surveyor of the King's Works. The duties of the King's Poet, Jonson humorously noted, were to serve as 'A kind of Christmas engine: one that is used, at least once a year, for a trifling instrument of wit or so' (*Neptune's Triumph*, 19–21).[28] Here was *fame* of a kind that was perhaps less slippery than Wyatt had once associated with court's estate, though it was also (as Jonson was well aware) open to mischance and the progressive adjustments of time.

§§

By 1616 Jonson's greatest contemporary had renounced not only the stage but also perhaps the metropolis as well, and been living quietly for several years— according to his first biographer, Nicholas Rowe, writing in 1709—'at his native Stratford', enjoying 'ease, retirement, and the conversation of his friends'.[29] The notion of Shakespeare's spending 'what remained to him of life in walking about a small, squalid country town with his hands in his pocket and an ear for no music now but the chink of the coin they might turn over there' has long puzzled and fascinated his readers, though apart from Rowe's statement there is little evidence to support the idea of his continuous residence in Stratford during these years.[30] Shakespeare certainly died how-ever in Stratford, and according to a local legend recorded many years later by the Reverend John Ward, vicar and physician in the parish from 1662, 'Shakespeare, Drayton, and Ben Jonson had a merry meeting, and it seems drank too hard, for Shakespeare died of a fever there contracted.' Though this late anecdote may well be apocryphal, it is possible that a meeting of some kind between these three men took place some time before Shakespeare's death on 23 April 1616. Jonson and Drayton had a stormy but sometimes amicable relationship. 'Drayton feared him, and he esteemed not of him,' Jonson told Drummond a couple of years later (*Informations*, 111), though subsequently he was to direct an admiring poem to Drayton, to show the world 'I can be a friend, and friend to thee'.[31] Drayton was from Warwick-shire, and often visited the village of Clifford Chambers near Stratford, where he had once been treated by the physician Dr Hall, husband of Shakespeare's daughter Susannah; Jonson might well have decided to accompany him on such an occasion. The wedding of Shakespeare's other daughter, Judith, to Thomas Quiney in February 1616 would have provided an appropriate opportunity for Jonson and Drayton to visit their old friend in Stratford and drink together, though their celebrations are unlikely in themselves to have been the cause of Shakespeare's 'fever' and subsequent death—some-times thought to have been caused by typhoid: a disease more likely to have been brought on by drinking water than wine (as Jonson might have noted with satisfaction).[32]

In what must seem to modern eyes an astonishing act of negligence or renunciation, Shakespeare appears during the final years of his life to have made no effort to bring his works together in collected form. His attitude to publication in general differed in certain ways from that of Jonson, who from his earliest professional years had methodically prepared quarto editions of his individual plays—including, defiantly, those which had not succeeded in the theatre and others over which he had no legal rights of ownership—confidently proclaiming his authorship on the title pages.[33] The contrast between the two authors is admittedly not as stark as once was imagined: Shakespeare and his theatrical company were by no means wholly indifferent or opposed to the publication of play-texts, but seem on the contrary (as Lukas Erne has persuasively argued) to have regarded the publication of his plays as conducive, rather than prejudicial, to their commercial success in the playhouse. While the company often left an interval of about two years between first performance of a play and its entry in the Stationers' Register, it seems to have found publication a useful means of reviving theatrical interest in plays that were no longer entirely new in performance. Of the first dozen or so plays that Shakespeare wrote for the Lord Chamberlain's Men, as Erne points out, 'not a single one that could legally have been printed remained unprinted by 1602'. Many of these carried the author's name, as Jonson's did.[34] Yet the evidence for Shakespeare's continuing interest in the publication of plays during the latter part of his career (post-1602) is less coherent and less compelling, and the notion that he might have begun to prepare a collected edition of his writings during his final years in Stratford remains entirely speculative, and based in part on dubious anecdote. If Jonson was the better known of the two writers by 1616 (as it seems reasonable to suppose) this was not only due to his more prominent position at court and to the diversity of his social contacts and literary ambitions, but also to his greater readiness to promote his own work, and exploit the massive and growing potential of the London book trade.

On 15 May 1612 Jonson's bookseller John Stepneth announced in the Stationers' Register his intention to publish 'A booke called, Ben Johnson his Epigrams'. No copy of this early printing of Jonson's *Epigrams* ('the ripest of my studies', as he was later to call them) is known however to exist, and it is likely the project came to nothing.[35] Meanwhile Jonson was beginning to prepare for a more ambitious collective publication of his writings by the printer William Stansby. By the beginning of 1615 Stansby seems to have had most of the material in hand for this collection, which was eventually published in folio format between 6 and 25 November 1616 as *The Works of Benjamin Jonson*. The long gestation period of the First Folio was due partly

Fig. 40. Jonson, *Works*, 1616 Folio, engraved title page by William Hole.

to the complexity of the task, partly to the volume of business that Stansby was currently handling and his difficulty in obtaining full rights to publish the material, and partly to Jonson's own last-minute tinkering with certain of the texts intended for inclusion.[36] Jonson's twentieth-century editors,

C. H. Herford and Percy and Evelyn Simpson, believed that Jonson took a close and continuous interest throughout this period in the preparation of this volume, calling into Stansby's printing house each morning to check its progress and supervise revisions. They consequently placed great weight on the Folio's textual authority, which they took whenever possible as copy-text for their own great Oxford edition of his collected writings (in eleven volumes, 1925–52), their own compositors mimicking the volume's typographical features—even certain of its typographical errors—with great fidelity.[37] Jonson himself affected a somewhat looser engagement with the 1616 Folio, implying that the selection and organization of its contents had been essentially a matter for the printer. 'When I wrote this poem, I had friendship with divers in your societies,' he says in his dedication of *Every Man Out of His Humour* to the Inns of Court; 'Now that the printer, by a doubled charge, thinks it worthy a longer life than commonly the air of such things doth promise, I am careful to put it a servant to their pleasures, who are the inheritors of the first favour borne it.' Recent scholarship suggests that Jonson was more closely involved with the production of the Folio than such a statement might imply. He is likely to have had a major say in the selection and arrangement of the contents of the volume and its physical appearance, even if he was not as minutely and continuously involved in its oversight as his Oxford editors once thought. Many of the corrections in the volume are probably the work of compositors rather than the author himself, whose personal engagement with the project may in any case have wavered towards the end.

The 1616 Folio comprises nine plays, thirteen court masques and four court entertainments, the *Panegyre* addressed to James on his entry to his first session of Parliament, and two substantial collections of poetry, the *Epigrams* and *The Forest*. Such a volume would in some respects have surprised Jonson's contemporaries. It was unusual, to begin with, for poets to publish collected editions of their work within their own lifetimes: the bulk of Sir Philip Sidney's writings, for example, were published only after his death, and the same would be true of John Donne's. It was even more unusual—to the point of oxymoron—for plays (then deemed a somewhat lowly form of writing) to be included within a folio volume bearing the imposing title *Works*. Jonson received some teasing on this point. A couple of later epigrams published in *Wit's Recreation* in 1640, though probably in circulation much earlier, give some flavour of the debate.

To Mr Ben Jonson demanding the reason why he called his plays 'works'
Pray tell me, Ben, where doth the mystery lurk,
What others call a play you call a work.

Thus answered by a friend in Mr Jonson's defence
The author's friend thus for the author says,
Ben's plays are works, when other's works are plays.[38]

Yet as the list of its contents just mentioned makes clear, Jonson's First Folio was by no means intended primarily or exclusively as a collection of plays, as Shakespeare's 1623 First Folio or Beaumont and Fletcher's 1647 Folio—for which it would be in other ways a powerful model—would later prove to be. The ornate frontispiece to the volume, engraved by William Hole (Fig. 40), might seem at first to promise otherwise.[39] On either side of the central panel proclaiming the title and authorship of the volume stand the figures of TRAGOEDIA and COMOEDIA, above two emblematic representations of the theatre. In the lower left panel is the wagon (PLAVSTRVM) in which Thespis, semi-legendary inventor of Tragedy, is said to have travelled through the Attic landscape, the vehicle serving as his primitive stage. At the lower right is depicted an ancient amphitheatre (VISORIUM) sunk beneath ground level; a Chorus with linked hands dance around an altar from which flames ascend; a sacrifice is being performed. Standing above the pediment are a SATYR with panpipes and a PASTOR or shepherd holding a pipe to his lips, representing Satire and Pastoral respectively. In a cartouche is a section of a Roman theatre (THEATRVM) resembling the Colosseum.

These images are not intended to indicate in any literal way the precise contents of the volume. Though the figure of Tragicomedy is dominant in the design (for instance), the Folio actually contains no example of tragicomedy, a form of writing that Jonson is not known ever to have attempted. Nor is there any pure example of Pastoral or of Satire—though pastoral elements can be found in certain of the poems and in masques in the Folio such as *Oberon* and entertainments such as *Althorp*, and satire is certainly mixed with comedy in works such as *Every Man Out of His Humour*. Nor are the images of theatres intended to imply that the contents of the Folio are predominantly dramatic in nature (as they are not). These symbolic images are better understood as representing in a more general way the scope and diversity of Jonson's authorial ambitions. In early modern times theatres were often thought of in much the same way as encyclopedias, as representing a

Fig. 41. The engraved title page by Renold Elstracke for the folio edition of King James's *Works*, published in the same year as Ben Jonson's First Folio.

gathering-together of human knowledge: as sites within which worldly thought and action might be contained and displayed.[40] In his dedication to Pembroke of the *Epigrams* Jonson refers to 'my theatre, where Cato, if he lived, might enter without scandal' (27–8). Jonson's 'theatre' here is clearly not in any literal sense a modern playhouse, but a carefully organized collection of poems which reveals and epitomizes the society in which he lives. The Folio as a whole serves as another, more capacious *theatrum*, containing and exhibiting the works that Jonson at this point of his career thought worthy of preservation. What the frontispiece displays however in a central image is only *half* a theatre: for in 1616, as Jonson perceives, he is only half-way through his literary career; with good fortune, more writings may still be to come.[41]

The tag from Horace's *Ars Poetica* (29) engraved around the pediment of the frontispiece—*singular quaeque locum teneant sortita decentem*—'Let each style keep the appropriate place allotted to it'—similarly refers not just to the various kinds of dramatic writing which Jonson himself had practised, but more generally to the different genres of literature in which he was by now a seasoned practitioner, and to the various social and intellectual domains to which he might now lay claim, or at least pay homage. The Folio sets out not just to accumulate Jonson's by-now numerous writings, but to display them also in their distinct and appropriate places, in order to signify the versatility and range of Jonson's literary achievement thus far, and his standing in the society of his time.

This purpose is even more clearly visible in the Catalogue that serves as the table of contents for the edition (Fig. 42), with its carefully organized columns of works and dedicatees. The latter list includes (at the head) 'the most learned and my honoured friend' William Camden, Jonson's former mentor to whom the revised text of *Every Man In His Humour* is dedicated; the quick-witted lawyer, politician, and fellow-member of the Mermaid Club Richard Martin, the 'noble and timely undertaker' who had come to Jonson's aid during the troubles over *Poetaster*; the King's cousin Esmé Stuart, Lord Aubigny, in whose house in Blackfriars Jonson had lived for five years, the generous patron who had helped him during the troubles over *Sejanus* and *Eastward Ho!*; Esmé's Scottish relative and friend Sir Francis Stuart (son of the Bonny Earl of Moray of border ballad fame), Gentleman of the Bedchamber, who had intervened to protect Jonson against charges of libel in *Epicene*; his old friend Mary, Lady Wroth, 'the lady most deserving her name

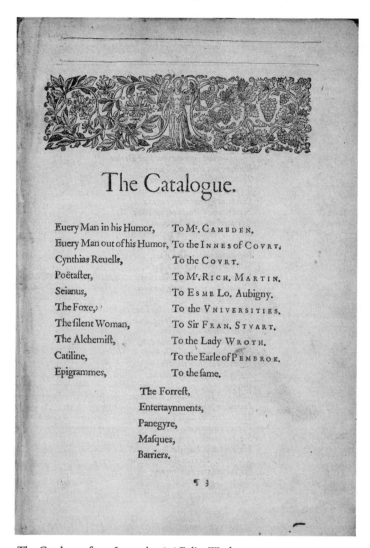

The Catalogue.

Euery Man in his Humor,	To Mr. CAMBDEN.
Euery Man out of his Humor,	To the INNES of COVRT.
Cynthias Reuells,	To the COVRT.
Poëtaſter,	To Mr. RICH. MARTIN.
Seianus,	To ESME Lo. Aubigny.
The Foxe,	To the VNIVERSITIES.
The ſilent Woman,	To Sir FRAN. STVART.
The Alchemiſt,	To the Lady WROTH.
Catiline,	To the Earle of PEMBROKE.
Epigrammes,	To the ſame.

The Forreſt,

Entertaynments,

Panegyre,

Maſques,

Barriers.

¶ 3

Fig. 42. The Catalogue from Jonson's 1616 Folio *Works*.

and blood', to whom *The Alchemist* is dedicated; and William Herbert, Earl of Pembroke, the recently appointed Lord Chamberlain, a significant figure within the Folio, as dedicatee of two of Jonson's most valued texts, *Catiline* and the *Epigrams*.[42] Along with the names of these distinguished individuals come those of institutions to which Jonson feels equally associated and indebted: the Inns of Court ('the noblest nurseries of humanity and liberty in the kingdom'), with which *Every Man Out of His Humour* is gratefully linked; the court ('the special fountain of manners'), remembered in the dedication of *Cynthia's Revels*; 'the most noble and equal sisters, the Universities of Oxford and Cambridge', thanked 'for their love and acceptance shown to his poem [*Volpone*] in the presentation'. From this list, it is curious to observe, the theatre and its representatives are conspicuously absent; and when Jonson speaks at all of the contemporary theatre in these preliminary statements—as he does in the epistle prefixed to *Volpone*—it is only with scorn, as a place of 'foul and unwashed bawdry', to be regarded with contempt. Jonson carefully positions both himself and his work at some distance from 'the loathèd stage', and in close proximity to other institutions and individuals he more deeply values. Fame for Jonson was not to be found within the narrow confines of the playhouse, but in the wider reaches of social, cultural, and intellectual life.

The scholar and jurist John Selden—'the law-book of the judges of England, the bravest man in all languages', as Jonson described him (*Informations*, 483–4)—contributed some admiring Latin verses to the 1616 Folio, praising Jonson as 'a man who patently deserves so many laurel wreaths', wondering what unpublished writings might still be on his desk, and eagerly looking forward to an eventual second collected edition of his writings. Selden's reference to laurel wreaths is perhaps significant in a year in which Jonson had been granted his royal pension, for Jonson about this time appears to have been asking Selden to explain to him the full traditions attached to the laureateship.[43] Many years later, in the second edition of his *Titles of Honor* (1631), Selden was duly to fulfil a 'promise to you, my beloved Ben Jonson' and describe in some detail the historical origins of the laureateship and its mode of operation. But by 1616 Ben Jonson, in Selden's opinion, had already acquired *notitia*, fame, through his collected writings. 'Venus was not so famous for her girdle,' Selden writes, 'or Apollo for his long hair, as you will be famous for your learned poetry, as a bright star by its ray surpasses the brightness of lesser stars.'[44] Here was fame as Jonson might have liked to know it: not 'with breath soon kindled, soon blown out', but captured in the words of a judicious friend, and enshrined in the seeming permanence of a printed book.[45]

16

Money 1614–1617

JONSON did not try to include in his 1616 Folio everything he had written up to that point of his career, but for various aesthetic and prudential reasons chose instead to exclude a number of texts. He omitted most of the poems he had written to Catholic friends and acquaintances soon after his conversion to the Roman Church in 1598. He omitted most of his apprentice work for the theatre, including plays written collaboratively and others that had brought him into trouble with the authorities. He rejected poems celebrating figures such as Ralegh and Somerset, whose reputation was now open to question, and he suppressed contextual information about the masques he had written for the two weddings of Frances Howard. He left out the civic entertainments he had written for the London livery companies, and certain entertainments commissioned by Robert Cecil, such as *Britain's Burse*.

More surprisingly, perhaps, Jonson also omitted a comedy he might well have included in the Folio had he so wished: *Bartholomew Fair*, performed two years earlier on 31 October 1614 at the recently opened Hope theatre on the Bankside and at Whitehall in the presence of the King the very next night, 1 November.[1] The reasons for this exclusion remain unclear, though it is possible Jonson felt that the play did not sit well with other material selected for the Folio. *Bartholomew Fair* marks a clear departure from Jonson's existing dramatic work and indeed from earlier comic writing in England. It is a huge piece, longer in running time than almost any other play of the early modern theatre. It has nearly forty speaking parts, presenting a challenge to Lady Elizabeth's Company that could only comfortably be met because of its recent merger with another company, the Children of the

Queen's Revels. The play is unusual too in structure. T. S. Eliot once remarked that Jonson's dramatic skill lay less in plotting than 'in doing without plot'; and while that is scarcely an accurate characterization of *Bartholomew Fair*, which is plotted with extraordinary intricacy and attention, the play may appear to lack the more sharply defined action of Jonson's earlier comedies—which in plays such as *Volpone* and *The Alchemist* is pithily stated in a preliminary verse 'argument'.[2] In *Bartholomew Fair* dramatic action, in the traditional sense of that term, is replaced by what might rather be called *activity*: urgent, random, uncoordinated, digressive. Busy, the name of the puritan elder at the centre of many of the play's disturbances, is a word that also captures a quality in the comedy itself. Leading his little party through the fair at Smithfield in the third act of the play, Busy urges them forward in a linear progression that neither he nor the comedy itself seems capable of achieving: 'So, walk on in the middle way, foreright; turn neither to the right hand nor to the left. Let not your eyes be drawn aside by vanity, nor your ear with noises.' Constantly rationalizing and equivocating, 'ever in seditious motion', Busy moves always at a tangent to the direction towards which he apparently sets his face. His peculiar mode of propulsion curiously resembles the devious structure of the comedy itself.

Nor is it entirely clear where *Bartholomew Fair* begins and ends. In the Induction, the Stage-Keeper apologizes for an apparently delayed start ('Gentlemen, have a little patience, they are e'en upon coming instantly') yet—though an unwary audience may not realize this fact—the play is already now under way. At the conclusion of the fifth act Bartholomew Cokes proposes to 'ha' the rest of the play at home' (5.6.95). He is referring of course to the puppet play about Hero and Leander that was rudely interrupted in the fairground by Zeal-of-the-Land Busy, which he now wants to see to the end; but there is a further curious sense that the larger drama we have been watching will now be continued in another place, and that the line between life and art cannot easily be drawn. Defying as it does both narrative convention and comedic expectation, *Bartholomew Fair* must have tantalized and amused its earliest audiences in much the same way that *Waiting for Godot* did its first audiences in the 1950s, or *Tristram Shandy* its early readers in the 1760s. Conscious of the experimental character of *Bartholomew Fair*, Jonson wrote a now-lost 'apology' for the play which he read to Drummond in 1618.[3] With the same awareness, he may simply have judged it inappropriate for inclusion within a preliminary gathering of his writings. Many years later, when preparing for the publication in 1631 of a Second Folio collection of his *Works*, he was to place *Bartholomew Fair* at the head of this new volume, according it the same symbolic position that he had given to *Every Man In His Humour* in the First Folio of 1616, and implying that this play also in some way marked the start of a new phase in his career.

Jonson might also have hesitated for another reason over the inclusion of *Bartholomew Fair* in the 1616 First Folio. The play glances at times quite sharply at (still unresolved) social and constitutional issues of the day, including the King's own policies, and could have been seen as bringing too strong a whiff of controversy to a volume designed more to consolidate Jonson's past achievements than to provoke present debate. The genesis of the play had been protracted. Jonson seems to have begun drafting it in 1613, and at that time to have given anxiety to his friend Hugh Holland by too openly satirizing Inigo Jones in the character of the puppeteer later called Lantern Leatherhead, but in early drafts known as 'Inigo Lantern'. In July 1613 John Donne, after consulting with his (and Jonson's) friend Sir Henry Goodere, persuaded Jonson to vary the text in order to calm Holland's fears and avoid any trouble with Inigo. 'There was nothing obnoxious but the very name,' Donne later reported to Goodere after a successful meeting with Jonson, 'and he hath changed that'.[4]

Jonson seems also to have consulted around this time with his scholarly friend John Selden about the precise meaning of the biblical text prohibiting cross-dressing which was regularly invoked by puritanical writers such as Philip Stubbes and William Prynne to justify their opposition to theatrical performance: 'The woman shall not wear that which pertaineth unto a man, neither shall a man put on a woman's garment,: for all that do so are abomination unto the Lord thy God' (Deuteronomy 22: 5).[5] Zeal-of-the-Land Busy is to cite this text righteously in *Bartholomew Fair* as he demolishes Lantern Leatherhead's puppet show in the fairground—'my main argument against you is that you are an abomination: for the male among you putteth on the apparel of the female, and the female of the male' (5.5.77–9)—only to retreat in astonishment as Leatherhead lifts the skirts of the puppets, revealing them to have no sex whatever. In a long and erudite letter to Jonson in 1616 Selden offered a historical interpretation of this well-known prohibition, tacitly endorsing his friend's satire of puritanical extremism. Selden was to reflect more generally in an intriguing passage in his *Table Talk* on the philosophical stance Jonson takes in the comedy.

Disputes in religion will never be ended, because there wants a measure by which the business should be decided. The puritan would be judged by the word of God: if he would speak clearly, he means himself, but that he is ashamed to say so; and he would have me believe him before a whole church, that have read the word of God as well as he. One says one thing, and another another; and there is, I say, no measure to end the controversy. 'Tis just as if two men were at bowls, and both judged by the eye: one says 'tis his cast, and the other says 'tis my cast; and having no measure, the difference is eternal. Ben Jonson satirically expressed the vain disputes of divines by Inigo Lanthorn disputing with a puppet in his *Bartholomew Fair*. It is so; it is not so; it is so; it is not so; crying thus one to another a quarter of an hour together.[6]

Jonson had had close experience of 'the vain disputes of divines' during his recent sojourn in Paris, when the words 'it is so', 'it is not so' (or their equivalents) must have tiresomely re-echoed throughout the seven-hour disputation he witnessed on the nature of the real presence. During Jonson's time at Hawthornden, Drummond noted he was 'For any religion, as being versed in both', *Informations*, 561). This position of sceptical detachment is one with which John Selden, closely in touch and in tune with Jonson during these years following his return to the Anglican Church, plainly found sympathetic.[7]

§§

Religious disputatiousness was not however the only problem troubling the kingdom while Jonson was drafting *Bartholomew Fair*. A graver crisis, that moved to flashpoint in the months preceding the first performance of the play, turned on a matter which Jonson had always found of absorbing interest: *money*—or in this case (to be more precise) the absence of money. The royal treasury was now in an alarmingly depleted state. Jonson had been well positioned to observe the astonishing expenditures by James and Anne since their arrival in London in 1603: the Queen being accompanied at that time, it was said, by 250 carriages and 5,000 horses. They had spent lavishly on court entertainment, on gifts to friends and courtiers, on jewellery, on personal attire, on household attendants and accoutrements. 'Neither now, nor at any subsequent time,' comments a historian of the period, 'is there the slightest indication that James had any sense of the value of money or of the meaning of the balance of debit and credit.'

He seems to have been incapable of understanding the fact that a considerable income and even the occasional presence of large amounts of coined money in the hands of the tellers of the exchequer were entirely compatible with a condition verging on bankruptcy. As long as there was money, or any other resources available to his hands, James was inclined to exercise that spirit of generosity which he had been compelled to suppress so long in Scotland.[8]

While negotiating the Great Contract in the Parliament of 1610, Robert Cecil had attempted to argue that, despite the traditional belief that the King should live off his own, Parliament owed it to James to provide substantial support towards his annual charges. In return, existing royal prerogatives which at present provided revenue—from feudal tenures, from impositions, and from the unpopular Court of Wards—would undergo significant reform. The constitutional implications of this proposal had alarmed many defenders of ancient parliamentary rights, including several of Jonson's closest friends and associates from the Mermaid circle.

In February 1614 the King summoned a new Parliament, hoping it would grant him his urgently needed financial support, as its 1610 predecessor had signally failed to do.[9] During the brief and fiercely argumentative session that followed, Bishop Richard Neile—who four years later would entertain Ben Jonson at Durham, on his northward journey to Edinburgh—attracted derision from the Commons by suggesting that impositions were an untouchable part of royal prerogative ('a *noli me tangere*'): a position he later defended, with tears in his eyes, before the Lords. Enraged by Neile's interference in the deliberations of the Commons, Jonson's friend Sir Thomas Roe entered an order to disable Neile 'either to be about the King or to be a bishop or to be amongst reasonable men, but to run away and bewail his estate in the woods amongst wild beasts'. Another of Jonson's close friends, the lawyer, satirist, and rhetorician John Hoskyns, spoke with equal vehemence against the influence of the Scots on royal policy, declaring that a wise prince would send these strangers home, as Canute had done with his Danish followers, lest a bloodbath like the Sicilian Vespers follow. Deeply angered by this language and realizing the hopelessness of his case, James dissolved Parliament abruptly on 7 June. It had passed no legislation, and therefore earned the sobriquet 'addled', being judged as useless as a putrefied egg. Hoskyns, along with three other malefactors, was summoned before the Privy Council, charged with having made seditious speeches, and dispatched to the Tower, where he would remain for another twelve months.[10] In mid-July 1614 William Trumbull reported that Brussels was 'filled with an expectation and rumour of an open rebellion in England ... upon the abrupt dissolving of the late unhappy parliament', and that the King was 'in some danger of a new powder plot'.[11]

To prepare, at such a volatile political moment, a comedy suitable for presentation not only to a public audience but to the King and his retinue at Whitehall cannot have been easy. Jonson must have felt considerable sympathy with the oppositional stance taken by Hoskyns, Roe, and their colleagues in the Commons, but it was scarcely appropriate to revive these issues in a comic entertainment at court. Though Jonson carefully avoids in *Bartholomew Fair* any direct or satirical reference to the recent feuding between King and Parliament, the play touches openly from time to time on contentious matters of the day: the problems of 'governance' in private and domestic life and, by implication, in the nation as a whole; the precariousness of authority at every level of society, from the King himself to the judge of the court of Pie-Powders in Smithfield Fair; the difficulties of judgement, in literature as in life. In the predicament of Grace Welborn, a ward of the crown unhappily bound to a foolish guardian, Justice Overdo, the play highlights the much-resented system of royal wardships which had been the subject of bitter debate over recent months. Overdo's tirade against 'that tawny weed, tobacco' in the second act of the play also touches on a sensitive topic of the day, recalling James's own declaration, in his *Counterblast to Tobacco* in 1604, that the drug was a social evil which the monarch, as 'physician of his politic body', was bound to exterminate from the commonwealth. This fine-sounding sentiment had recently been compromised by James's move to impose new duties on the importation of tobacco into the kingdom, in order to benefit the crown.[12]

Even more daringly, the comedy might be thought to reflect indirectly, through the follies of its central character, on the current predicament of the King. For Bartholomew Cokes, like James, has a dire problem with money. Delighting in the pleasures of the fairground, he seems eager, despite the protests of his irascible governor Humphrey Wasp, to buy up everything he sees.

Cokes [*To Leatherhead*] Those six horses, friend, I'll have—
Wasp How!

Cokes And the three Jews' trumps; and half a dozen o' birds, and that drum (I have one drum already) and your smiths—I like that device o' your smiths very well. And four halberds—and (le' me see) that fine painted great lady, and her three women for state, I'll have.

Wasp No, the shop; buy the whole shop, it will be best, the shop, the shop!

Leatherhead If his worship please.

Wasp Yes, and keep it during the Fair, bob-chin.

Cokes Peace, Numps. [*To Leatherhead*] Friend, do not meddle with him, an you be wise, and would show your head above board; he will sting through your wrought nightcap, believe me. A set of these violin I would buy, too, for a delicate young noise I have I' the country that are every one a size less than another, just like your fiddles. I would fain have a fine young masque at my marriage, now I think on't—but I do want such a number of things. (3.4.59–73)

Cokes is finally to leave the Fair having lost everything he possessed: 'myself, and my cloak and my hat, and my fine sword, and my sister, and Numps, and Mistress Grace (a gentlewoman that I should ha' married) and a cut-work handkercher she ga' me, and two purses today. And my bargain o' hobby-horses and gingerbread, which grieves me worst of all' (4.2.65–9).

Bartholomew Fair is (by and large) a tolerant play, which upholds the legitimacy of the theatre and the pleasures of holiday recreations against puritanical attack: an approach certain to be found congenial by James himself, who (as Jonson remarks in the prologue to the play) had been troubled since his accession to the throne by the 'rage' of puritans, and was himself soon to defend holiday custom in his royal *Book of Sports*.[13] Yet in an ironical counter-movement, the play also satirizes, in the character of Bartholomew Cokes, the naivety of play- and fair-goers, and their readiness to part so easily with their money, for such tawdry rewards. 'What petty things we wonder at, like children that esteem every trifle, and prefer a fairing before their fathers!', Jonson was later to observe in his commonplace book, *Discoveries*.

What difference is between us and them, but that we are dearer fools, coxcombs at a higher rate? They are pleased with cockleshells, whistles, hobby-horses, and such like; we with statues, marble pillars, pictures, gilded roofs, where underneath is lath and lime, perhaps loam. Yet we take pleasure in the lie, and are glad we can cozen ourselves. Nor is it only in our walls and ceilings, but all that we call happiness is mere painting and gilt, and all for money: what a thin membrane of honour that is! And how hath all true reputation fallen, since money began to have any! Yet the great herd, the multitude, that in all other things are divided, in this alone conspire and agree: to love money. They wish for it, they embrace it, they adore it, while yet it is possessed with greater stir and torment than it is gotten. (*Discoveries*, 1025–36)

The love of money, in this complex vision of the world, serves as one of the great human universals; as a central force that ironically draws together the otherwise disunited 'great herd, the multitude'.

§§

Throughout his career Jonson studied with intense interest the power invested in money: a commodity of which (as he was always keen to stress) he himself was habitually in short supply. In verses included by Robert Allot in *England's Parnassus* in 1600 (which may originally have formed part of a now-lost early play), Jonson considered the link between wealth and erotic success:

> Gold is a suitor never took repulse;
> It carries palm with it where'er it goes,
> Respect, and observation; it uncovers
> The knotty heads of the most surly grooms,
> Enforcing iron doors to yield it way,
> Were they as strong rammed-up as Etna gates...

In his Epistle to Elizabeth, Countess of Rutland, written around this same time, he saw gold as being also the vital commodity for entry into court, 'for which all virtue now is sold | And almost every vice' (*The Forest*, 12.2–3). In *Volpone* and *The Alchemist*, gold—or the mere rumour of gold—has an almost physical, olfactory power to draw the gullible to its supposed location, forming the 'centre attractive' around which the comedy proceeds. In *The Staple of News*, wealth is ironically personified in the figure of Pecunia, 'princess' or 'infanta of the mines', universally adored and worshipped for her powerful charms.

Jonson was writing in a period in which immense fortunes were being made and lost from land sales, from overseas ventures, and from lucrative projects of sometimes dubious legality, often run in conjunction with the crown. He was personally acquainted with some of the more spectacular beneficiaries, such as Thomas Sutton, the founder of Charterhouse, who had made a huge fortune from northern coalfields, money-lending, and the acquisition of land, having ridden south to London, it is said, with two horse-loads of money, which he soon converted into even greater wealth.[14] Aubrey was not alone in believing that Sutton, who kept hopeful beneficiaries in suspense by changing his will with bewildering frequency, furnished the 'hint' for Jonson's *Volpone*.

The latter end of his days he lived in Fleet Street at a woollen-draper's shop opposite to Fetter Lane, where he had so many great chests full of money that his chamber was ready to groan under it; and Mr Tyndale, who knew him and I think had money of him on mortgage during his law-suit . . . was afraid the room would fall.[15]

Jonson would also have been acquainted with the wealthy merchant and financier Lionel Cranfield, a member of the Mitre group and close friend of Jonson's own intimate associates Richard Martin, John Hoskyns, John Donne, and Inigo Jones.[16] A keenly intelligent and cultivated man, Cranfield had built his fortune first in the cloth trade, then through investment in land and financial advice to the crown, largely in partnership with his fellow-financier Sir Arthur Ingram, whom Menna Prestwich has judged 'perhaps the most unscrupulous tycoon of the age' and the probable model for Jonson's character Meercraft in *The Devil Is an Ass*.[17] Ingram had secured huge subsidies from the crown to back his development of works in alum, a project which, so far from helping the royal treasury, soon proved a financial disaster. Cranfield himself, a steadier hand, began meanwhile to gain the trust of the King, and would eventually be recruited to replace two of James's most inefficient officers, the absurdly extravagant Lord Hay, as Master of the Wardrobe (who on one occasion had ordered twenty suits for himself for a twenty-day mission to France, only to discover the fashion had changed, and the designs needed all to be changed), and Thomas Howard, Earl of Suffolk, who, busying himself with grandiose building schemes at Audley End, had proved a delinquent and self-serving Lord Treasurer.

Jonson was to become more closely acquainted with the activities of another immensely wealthy and soon-to-be notorious projector, Alderman William Cockayne.[18] Cockayne, who had endeared himself to James through a number of large and timely financial loans, was a leading member of the Eastland Company, a rival trading company to the Merchant Adventurers, who held a monopoly on the exportation of undyed and undressed cloth. In a bid to break this monopoly, Cockayne proposed an alternative project: a prohibition on the export of all undyed and undressed cloth in order to boost exportation of cloth that had been already locally dyed and dressed. This scheme would provide (so he argued) increased work for local dyers and dressers, enhanced prices for English cloth abroad, and greater revenue for the crown. Impressed by the scheme, James gave his consent to the disbanding of the existing Company of Merchant Adventurers, and the creation in 1614 of a new King's Company of Merchant Adventurers to take this proposal forward. Gradually, however, it became evident that Cockayne's arguments were badly flawed. The quality of English dyeing was poor, and the Baltic countries to which the cloth was principally sent resented this rebuff to their own (less costly and more efficient) local dyeing industries, and refused to purchase the cloth at all, thus triggering a major trading crisis within England and aggravating the already serious financial problems of the crown.

On 8 June 1616 Alderman Cockayne invited King James to a lavish banquet at his house in Broad Street to thank him for his sponsorship of the new Merchant Adventurers' Company, and commissioned Ben Jonson to prepare a suitable entertainment to mark the occasion. Throughout the year the Privy Council had been investigating complaints about the new company's practices and viability, and disturbances amongst merchants in Hamburg, its staple trading city in Europe. Many on the Council, deeply concerned by these reports, wished to see the Company immediately dissolved. James himself had continued to support the Company despite persistent warnings from his counsellors, but was clearly wavering and perplexed about its future. A large gesture from the Company, as Cockayne shrewdly perceived, was clearly needed at this moment to boost the King's confidence. Efforts were made, without success, to secure him a gift of £50,000.[19] In the end a lesser presentation from the Company was made to him that evening at Alderman Cockayne's house in the form of a gold basin which, as John Chamberlain reported to Dudley Carleton, had 'as many pieces in it as together made up the sum of £1,000, the Prince after the same manner with £500, so that the whole charge of that feast stood the new company in more than £3,100, the thanks remaining wholly with the Alderman who at parting was knighted with the city-sword'.[20] Jonson may well have felt some scepticism about this self-interested exchange of gifts and about the project itself, which had been promoted by Henry Howard and Robert Carr, and was likely therefore to have been warily regarded by Pembroke and his faction. In a year's time Cockayne's project had collapsed. The new Company was dissolved, and the old Merchant Adventurers' Company restored to its former status, but lasting damage had by then already been done to the English cloth trade.

No text survives of the entertainment which Jonson devised for the evening at Cockayne's house on 8 June 1616, but it is briefly described by a second news-writer, George Gerrard, in a further dispatch to Dudley Carleton the following week.

Hitherto of things done, yet I must add one more, which I had almost forgot. The King was invited by Alderman Cockayne and the New Company of Merchant Venturers to a dinner in London. They made a great feast, gave him a present of £1,000 in a basin and ewer of gold, which, because it wanted nigh £300 of that value in weight, they made it up with £20 pieces. To the Prince also a present. And for the King's better contentment, they presented dyers, weavers with their shuttles, and cloth dressers, speaking by way of interlude to grace themselves and their industry. After this was presented certain Hamburgians, with great bellied doublets, all drunk, which spake such language as Ben Jonson put into their mouths, only for merriment. But this, they say, is taken so ill that the Lord Ambassador here, Sir Noel Caron, hath been with the Lords to complain of it.[21]

Jonson's drunken Hamburgians were presumably intended as caricatures of German merchants or manufacturers who had been frustrated by Cockayne's venture, though as the intervention of Ambassador Sir Noel de Caron, Lord of Schoonewalle, implies, the Dutch must also have seen themselves slighted by the presentation.[22] There was particular reason on this occasion for members of the Company to feel resentment towards the Dutch, for a recent Dutch edict banning the import into the Netherlands of dyed and dressed cloth was severely damaging the Company's trade, and would eventually prove one of the main causes of the Company's downfall.[23] Yet it was not a good move to have offended Ambassador Caron, an exceptionally wealthy man who was a particular favourite of James, to whom he had already advanced several substantial loans. The following year, when, despite crippling debts, James resolved to make his royal progress back to Scotland attended by a stupendous retinue of court retainers, it was Caron who organized a £20,000 loan from the merchant strangers of London, contributing substantially himself to this sum. Combined with a further loan of £100,000 from the Corporation of London, Caron's generosity (from which he obtained no interest) made it possible for James to travel to Scotland in his preferred style. Jonson's robust entertainment at Alderman

Cockayne's house had evidently done no lasting damage to diplomatic relations between the Dutch and the English—or at least to personal relations between Caron and the King. But Jonson may have seen enough of projectors and profiteers by now to furnish him with materials for a new comedy; and enough of his King's extravagances to prompt him eventually to travel himself to Scotland in more frugal style, following the example of his fellow-Syrenaic Thomas Coryate in his peregrinations across Europe, which John Taylor the Water Poet would also later emulate in his significantly titled *Penniless Pilgrimage.*[24]

§§

'But what is a projector?' asks Fabian Fitzdottrel eagerly in *The Devil Is an Ass*—Jonson's next comedy, presented by the King's Men at Blackfriars theatre in mid-autumn 1616, a few months after the entertainment at Alderman Cockayne's house—when told that Merecraft—'the wit, the brain, the great projector | I told you of'—has arrived in town. Though still a sufficiently new phenomenon to invite such a question, *projectors* (and the projects they promoted) had been a topic of much interest in England for at least a decade, being seen by some as the principal means of restoring strength to the now-enfeebled royal coffers. Land reclamation projects of the kind which Merecraft commends as an investment to Fitzdottrel in *The Devil Is an Ass* (draining the fens, Fitzdottrel is assured, will undoubtedly earn him a dukedom) had been considered by Lord Treasurer Dorset in 1606, and rejected in 1613 by the committee set up under Sir Thomas Parry to look at new projects, but were well under way in England at the time of the play's performance. In the years 1613–16 projecting in England was at its zenith.[25] Money was plentiful everywhere except in the royal treasury, interest rates were low, and foreign trade was flourishing; proposals for new and lucrative ventures, such as those ironically floated in *The Devil Is an Ass*—for trading in raisins, bottle-ale, forks, dog-skins, cosmetics, toothpicks, etc.—were being regularly canvassed. The projectors promoting these (often dubiously viable) schemes were successfully amassing their private fortunes. Fabian Fitzdottrel, though hitherto more interested in conjurors and dealers in black magic, is keen to hear more about these new men. 'But what is a projector?', he asks; 'I would conceive.'

Engine   Why, one, sir, that projects
Ways to enrich men, or to make 'em great,
By suits, by marriages, by undertakings
According as he sees they humour it.
Fitzdottrel Can he not conjure at all?
Engine   I think he can, sir –
To tell you true—but you do know, of late
The State hath ta'en such note of 'em, and compelled 'em
To enter such great bonds, they dare not practice. (1.7.9–17)

Jonson's portrayal of projectors in *The Devil Is an Ass* landed him once more in trouble with the authorities; he was 'accused' (so he told William Drummond) over the play's references to 'the Duke of Drownland', and 'the King desired him to conceal it' (*Informations*, 319, 322–3). 'It' is likely to have been in this case not the general satire on the draining of the fens, which remained in the text prepared for publication in 1631, but a more specific reference to some identifiable individual. Somerset's cousin Robert Ker, and Archibald Campbell, the seventh Earl of Argyll, have been suggested as possible targets, but the reference might conceivably have been to some even more eminent figure of the day.[26]

Jonson's comedy concerns a young devil named Pug, who longs to spend some time on earth, and is finally granted a day's leave from hell to go off to London and cause mischief. He is outwitted at every turn by the citizens of that city, and returns finally to hell, chastened by his experiences. The play ironically inverts a familiar pattern of English religious drama. 'According to *comoedia vetus* in England,' as Jonson explained to William Drummond, 'the devil was brought in either with one Vice or other; the play done, the devil carried away the Vice. He brings in the devil so overcome with the wickedness of the age that thought himself an ass' (*Informations*, 319–22). *Comoedia vetus* ('old comedy') is the English morality drama, in which a character representing some form of human vice was carried off finally by the Devil to hell, there to suffer eternal torment: a tradition recalled in some fashion in a number of recent popular plays, including Marlowe's *Doctor Faustus*, and two comedies written (partly or wholly) by Jonson's old adversary Thomas Dekker: *The Merry Devil of Edmonton* (1608) and *If This be Not a Good Play, The Devil is In't* (1612). Yet as Jonson's Satan ruefully confesses to Pug in *The Devil Is an Ass*, such traditions are entirely irrelevant 'now', given the way 'vice stands in the present year... Six hundred and sixteen' (1.1.80–1), when evil need not come from hell, but thrives of its own accord spontaneously here in London. Raising the Devil, as Faustus once did with blasphemous daring, seems nowadays less bold an act than the feats of projectors, who raise money (or the spectre of money) with nonchalant ease.

> *Merecraft*   Sir, money's a whore, a bawd, a drudge,
> Fit to run out on errands: let her go.
> *Via pecunia!* When she's run and gone,
> And fled and dead, then will I fetch her again
> With aqua-vitae out of an old hogshead,
> While there are lees of wine, or dregs of beer,
> I'll never want her. Coin her out of cobwebs,
> Dust, but I'll have her! Raise wool upon eggshells,
> Sir, and make grass grow out o' marrow-bones,
> To make her come. (2.1.1–10)

In *The Devil Is an Ass* the power of money has defeated the power of the Devil, and become a central focus of devotion and belief. The worlds of finance and religion (the comedy reminds us) have much in common, as terms such as *credit* and *trust* suggest. At the outset of the play Satan warns Pug 'to keep us in credit' on his mission to London by performing with expert devilry, and to use his 'credit with the hangman' to secure a body to inhabit for the day. 'A devil, and could not keep a body entire | One day!', he remarks on his return; '*That, for our credit.*' (Pug: 'How is the name of Devil | Discredited in me!', 5.6.48–9, 3–4.) The word 'credit' at this time (Latin *credo*, to trust or believe) meant reputation, believability, a concept equally important for a would-be borrower of money and a devil conscious of growing popular scepticism concerning his very existence. Credit transactions (as Craig Muldrew has shown) were still a relatively new phenomenon in England, and had grown dramatically during the early years of James's reign on account of the shortage of coinage: a need that James's introduction in 1613 of farthing tokens was largely calculated to address.[27] The granting of credit had originally depended upon the lender's close personal acquaintance with the borrower and knowledge of his financial soundness, though more complex trading negotiations in the late sixteenth century had led to longer chains of credit, which involved the need to *believe* in the financial trustworthiness of a person one did not personally know.[28] And as with all matters of belief—belief (for example) in the existence of hell, or of the Devil, or of witchcraft, or demonic possession—there was always the chance that one's trust was misplaced. Behind the assurances of borrowers and financiers, as behind the beguiling talk of the projectors, there might well be—so Jonson's comedy suggests—nothing substantial at all, just the dust and dregs and cobwebs from which (as in Merecraft's words) a dream of wealth had been ingeniously fabricated.

The dangers of credit transactions are nicely played out in a small piece of trickery in *The Devil Is an Ass*. Fabian Fitzdottrel is advised by the projector Merecraft and his broker, Engine, to send 'Some little toy', 'A diamond ring of forty or fifty pound', to a Spanish lady who will coach his wife in the manners and deportment appropriate to her anticipated status as a duchess. What Fitzdottrel does not know is that the 'Spanish lady' is none other than Wittipol—the young man who is courting Fitzdottrel's wife—dressed in female garments borrowed from the actor Dick Robinson—who (in a nicely self-reflexive Jonsonian joke) was probably playing the part of Wittipol himself in the first performance of *The Devil Is an Ass*. Fitzdottrel admits he does not have ready money to buy such a ring, but Merecraft assures him he will secure credit for this transaction from his goldsmith, Gilthead. Gilthead duly arrives at the opening of the third act with his son Plutarchus, to whom he explains the situation.

> I am called for now in haste by Master Merecraft
> To trust Master Fitzdottrel, a good man—
> I've enquired him, eighteen hundred a year,
> His name is current—for a diamond ring
> Of forty, shall not be worth thirty; that's gained. (3.1.9–13)

Trust lies at the centre of this (by now, rapidly expanding, multiply fraudulent) transaction: Merecraft will assure Gilthead that Fitzdottrel is a man to whom credit may be advanced, Gilthead will sell Fitzdottrel the ring for more than it is worth, Merecraft will arrange for it then to be stolen back. Plutarchus nervously asks his father if he does not trust too much. 'Boy, boy,' replies Gilthead, *'We live by finding fools out to be trusted'* (3.1.16). Jonson sees with remarkable clarity the ease with which the emerging trading practices of his day are open to fraud and exploitation, how scams are contrived, fortunes made, and financial dreams dissolve. The modern financial world of collapsing investment schemes, absconding financiers, and plummeting global markets seems not very far away.

In the final act of the play Jonson turns with equal scepticism to credulity (or misplaced credit) of another and more traditional kind: the belief in diabolical possession. Fabian Fitdottrel, entranced by the charms of the 'Spanish lady', has unwittingly conveyed his entire estate to the very man who is courting his wife: Wittipol, who promises in turn to retain the estate for the wife's benefit. Merecraft and Everill, aghast at the miscarriage of their plot to defraud Fitzdottrel themselves, urge Fitzdottrel to pretend he was possessed by the Devil at the time he signed his feoffment, thereby invalidating the deal.

> *Merecraft* It is the easiest thing, sir, to be done.
> As plain as fizzling; roll but wi' your eyes,
> And foam at th' mouth. A little castle-soap
> Will do't, to rub your lips: and then a nutshell,
> With tow and touchwood in it to spit fire.
> Did you ne'er read, sir, little Darrel's tricks,
> With the boy o'Burton, and the seven in Lancashire,
> Sommers at Nottingham? All these do teach it.
> And we'll give out, sir, that your wife has bewitched you—
> *Everill* And practised with those two, as sorcerers. (5.3.1–10)

All of the cases of fraudulent diabolical possession instanced here by Merecraft had occurred during the last years of Elizabeth's reign, and involved the notorious puritan preacher and exorcist John Darrel. But in 1616 the question of diabolical possession and the power of witches was also of urgent and compelling interest to King James himself, who in his earlier years had been an ardent believer in demonology and a zealous hunter of witches, but had now grown increasingly sceptical about such matters.[29] During his summer progress in 1616 James had visited Leicester in order personally to interrogate a young boy named John Smith who had recently testified against fifteen women accused of witchcraft: a case to which Merecraft now refers.[30]

> Sir, be confident,
> 'Tis no hard thing t'outdo the devil in:
> A boy o' thirteen year old made him an ass
> But t'other day. (5.5.48–51)

John Smith had vividly described to the court the nature of these women's familiars—a horse, a dog, a polecat, a fish, a toad, a dog—whose noises, during apparent fits of diabolical possession, he imitated dramatically in the courtroom. In the course of his interrogations, James exposed the boy as a fraud, and after further examination five of the women accused of witchcraft were released. For others, the King's discovery came too late; one had already died in prison, and nine others had been executed earlier in the summer. In the final scene of *The Devil Is an Ass*—a passing compliment to James's detection of this deceit—Fabian Fitzdottrel fools the great judge Sir Paul Eitherside with his sham fits of demoniac possession, as John Smith had fooled Sir Humphrey Winch, the judge who had presided at the Leicester witch trials earlier that summer. 'A practice foul | For one so fair,' declares Sir Paul, suspecting Fitzdottrel's frantic behaviour to have been prompted by his wife's witchcraft. '*Hath this then credit with you?*' asks Wittipol. 'Do you believe in't?' echoes his friend Manly (5.8.53–5).

Human credulity (so Jonson's comedy suggests) takes many forms. A belief in the power of witches and the power of the Devil—those crucial elements in late medieval eschatology—may not differ greatly from a belief in the power of projectors and financiers, and the systems of future payment so central to the now emerging capitalist system of the modern world. Focusing precisely, as ever, on matters of immediate topical concern in England— 'Now, as vice stands this present year', in 'six hundred and sixteen'—Jonson looks with equal scepticism at the inherited systems of belief which his society is struggling at this moment to discard, and at those it is now beginning eagerly to embrace.

17

Scholarship 1619–1630

BY the late spring of 1619 Jonson had returned to London after ten months of journeying to Scotland and back. He may have felt unsettled on arrival in the metropolis, and have lodged initially with friends. 'The uncertainty where to direct letters hath made me this time past not to write,' wrote William Drummond from Edinburgh to Ben Jonson in London on 30 April 1619 (Letter (e), *CWBJ*). 'I am arrived safely,' Jonson replied on 10 May, and 'have somewhat in hand, which shall look upon you with the next' (this was a poem—now lost, perhaps never completed—in memory of Queen Anne, who had died two months earlier). By 1 July Drummond was still no wiser as to Jonson's whereabouts. 'The uncertainty of your abode was a cause of my silence this time past,' he wrote once more; 'I have adventured this packet upon hopes that a man so famous cannot be in any place either of the city or court where he shall not be found out' (Letter (f)). Before his departure for Scotland Jonson had been living in Blackfriars, where Coryate in his *Traveller for the English Wits* in 1616 had addressed him 'at his chamber'. By January 1620 he had moved to Cripplegate, as a passing reference to this location suggests in a bill from one of Prince Charles's grooms, dispatched 'to warn Master Ben Jonson the poet and the players at the Blackfriars to attend His Highness that night following at court'.[1] Later still he would shift to Westminster, spending his final years (as Aubrey records) 'in the house under which you pass as you go out of the churchyard into the old palace; where he died'.[2] Nothing is heard of Anne Jonson over these years; either she and Ben had finally separated by this time, or she was no longer living. The register of the church of St Giles, Cripplegate, records the marriage on 27 July 1623 of

'Beniamyne Johnson and Hester Hopkins'.[3] It is possible that this 'Benia-myne Johnson' was indeed the poet, as this was the very parish in which he was living at this time, though the absence of any subsequent reference to a wife (or later, a widow) suggests that Jonson's remarriage—if this is what the record indicates—cannot have lasted long. His last years were spent, if not entirely without female companionship, then at least in a non-married state. Despite periods of illness and financial difficulty, these last years of his life were not only surprisingly creative; they were a time in which he was able to devote himself in a more single-minded fashion than ever before to scholarly pursuits, and fulfil some at least of his large humanistic ambitions.

Jonson did not stay long in London after getting back from Scotland. On 17 July 1619 he was in Oxford to receive the degree of Master of Arts, and had probably by that time already begun a longer period of residence at Christ Church. Later in the century Anthony à Wood, compiling his biographical dictionary of distinguished Oxford alumni, was to list Ben Jonson amongst their number, and explain the reasons for this inclusion and for the College's wish to bring him to the University.

His own proper industry and addiction to books, especially to ancient poets and classical authors, made him a person of curious learning and judgement, and of singular excellence in the art of poetry. Which, with his accurate judgement and performance, known only to those few who are truly able to judge of his works, having gained from the most eminent scholars of his time (especially from the learned Selden) an increasing admiration, Dr Richard Corbett of Ch. Ch. and other poets of this University did in reverence to his parts invite him to Oxon, where continuing for some time in Ch. Ch. in writing and composing plays, he was, as a member thereof, actually created M. of A. in 1619; and therefore upon that account I put him among the Oxford writers...[4]

Earlier that same year Jonson had told Drummond that 'He was Master of Arts in both the universities, by their favour, not his study' (*Informations*, 191). His honorary degrees must therefore by that time have already been approved by statute (or in the parlance of the universities, *graced*) by both Oxford and Cambridge, though there is no surviving record in either univer-sity of these decisions. The ceremony in Oxford on 17 July was to induct Jonson formally into the degree, for which he was presented by his patron, the Earl of Pembroke, who was by then the University Chancellor.[5] When did Jonson first learn that he was to be honoured by the two universities? In what is sometimes seen as an autobiographical allusion by Jonson at the opening of the revised version of *Every Man In His Humour* in the 1616 Folio, the elder Knowell had spoken proudly of his son:

> He is a scholar, if a man may trust
> The liberal voice of fame in her report,
> Of good account in both our universities,
> Either of which hath favoured him with graces. (1.1.10–14)[6]

If these lines are taken as self-referring, then Jonson might well have been 'favoured...with graces' by both Oxford and Cambridge some time before the publication of his *Works* in 1616. Jonson was probably in Cambridge at the time of James's visit in March 1615 to witness the King's ceremonial welcome at St John's, for which he had been invited to 'pen a ditty'.[7] He may well have been a witness of (if not a participant in) the chaotic mass conferral that occurred during this visit, when 'Degrees were vilely prostituted to mean persons, such as apothecaries and barbers', and indeed to anyone, qualified or unqualified for this honour, who pressed forward hopefully clad in cap and gown.[8] In Jonson's *The Staple of News* Pennyboy Junior reveals that the clerk Thomas Barber 'Was made, or went out Master of Arts in a throng, | At the university' (1.5.126–7): a probable allusion to this event (or to an earlier occasion, for similar scenes had occurred during James's visit to Oxford in 1605). In 'An Epistle to a Friend, to Persuade Him to the Wars' Jonson speaks of 'flatterers, spies, | Informers, *masters both of arts and lies*, | Lewd slanderers, soft whisperers that let blood...' (*The Underwood*, 15.163–6), the sardonic phrase here italicized perhaps referring once more to the cheapening of university honours on these occasions.

By a curious chance, Jonson's principal friend and sponsor at Christ Church, the poet and future bishop Richard Corbett, had travelled across to Cambridge in 1615 to observe the events associated with the King's visit, and had composed a humorous versified account of the rival university's conferral ceremony.

> The King being gone from Trinity,
> They made a scramble for degree:
> Masters of all sorts, and all ages,
> Keepers, subsizars, lackeys, pages,
> Who all did throng to come aboard,
> With, 'pray make me *now*, good my Lord.'[9]

Corbett and his friends at Christ Church (together with the Earl of Pembroke, the University Chancellor) would have ensured that the Oxford ceremony honouring Ben Jonson four years later was of a more dignified and appropriate nature. Corbett, ten years younger than Jonson, had come to Christ Church from Westminster School, as had many scholars and Students at the College. The connection between the two institutions was close—Christ Church elected four King's Scholars from Westminster a year, who enjoyed the status of a Fellow from the moment of their arrival in Oxford—and helps to explain the College's promptness to honour this distinguished former member of the school.[10] Corbett (according to Anthony à Wood) was esteemed as 'one of the most celebrated wits in the University, as his poems, jests, romantic fancies and exploits, which he performed *extempore*, showed'.[11] 'His conversation was extreme pleasant,' John Aubrey noted; he was 'very facetious, and a good fellow', showing certain unusual qualities as a cleric.

After he was D. of Divinity he sang ballads at the cross at Abington on a market day. He and some of his comrades were at the tavern by the cross... [when] the ballad singer complained he had no custom, he could not put off his ballads. The jolly doctor puts off his gown, and puts on the ballad singer's leathern jacket, and being a handsome man and had a full rare voice he presently vended a great many, and had a great audience.[12]

Jonson must have admired Corbett's ready wit, and enjoyed his company. The two men had probably known each other for some years, having perhaps first met through their common friend Sir Francis Stuart, or some other members of the Mermaid Club.[13] Jonson had known and admired Corbett's father Vincent, a nurseryman of Whitton in the parish of Twickenham, who died on 29 April, about the time that Jonson got back to London from Scotland. Jonson mourned the loss of 'a friend and father' in affectionate lines that may have been written early during his stay at Christ Church.

> Dear Vincent Corbett, who so long
> Had wrestled with diseases strong
> That though they did possess each limb,
> Yet he broke them, ere they could him,
> With the just canon of his life,
> A life that knew nor noise, nor strife,
> But was, by sweet'ning so his will,

> All order and composure still;
>> His mind as pure and neatly kept,
>> As were his nurseries, and swept
> So of uncleanness or offence,
> That never came ill odour thence:
>> And add his actions unto these,
>> They were as specious as his trees.
>> *(The Underwood,* 12.7–20)[14]

Richard Corbett's career was just beginning to take off at the time of Jonson's visit to Oxford. In June 1620 he was to be elected Dean of Christ Church, and the following year James appointed him a royal Chaplain 'on account of the quaintness of his preaching and the brightness of his fancy'.[15] The first of these appointments Corbett seems to have owed to the influence of the now powerful royal favourite George Villiers, Marquis of Buckingham.[16] Later he would seek favour from William Laud, who had likewise been indebted to Buckingham for his initial rise to power and in 1630 was to become an energetic Chancellor of the University. Corbett had a closer accommodation to these figures and to members of the former Howard faction than Jonson might always have found comfortable: qualities probably offset, however, by Corbett's mischievous and companionable nature.

The Oxford to which Jonson came in 1619 was enjoying a period of remarkable growth after a century of relative inactivity.[17] New buildings had been appearing at Lincoln, Exeter, St John's, University College, and at nearby Merton, where under the wardenship of Jonson's friend Sir Henry Savile the imposing Fellows' quadrangle had recently been built. The handsome Jacobean structures of the newly endowed Wadham College had now been completed, as had the Arts End of the new Bodleian Library, and the old Schools had also undergone rebuilding; while at Christ Church itself the library in the old monastic refectory had also been recently remodelled and refitted. Christ Church's great hall, the largest hall in either Oxford or Cambridge, served as the centre of the University's theatrical life.

Since 1554 the College had been committed to presenting two comedies and two tragedies a year, one play in each pair in Latin and the other in Greek: all of these plays being presented in the College hall. The most ambitious performances were staged during the monarch's periodic visits to the University. It was here in Christ Church that in August 1605 James had been regaled (if at times somewhat wearied) by a series of Latin plays written by Oxford dons, with settings specially designed for the occasion by Inigo Jones. Many years later, for the visit of Charles, Henrietta Maria, the Elector Palatine, and Prince Rupert to Oxford in 1636, Jones was again in charge of the theatrical settings in the hall, which included 'very sumptuous' machinery for William Strode's comedy *The Floating Island* which gave 'the perfect resemblance of the billows of the sea rolling, and an artificial island, with churches and houses waving up and down and floating, as also rocks, trees, and hills'.[18]

Strode, a protégé of Corbett's and former Westminster scholar, was one of the promising younger poets at Christ Church at the time of Jonson's stay.[19] Other writers at Christ Church at this time included Thomas Goffe, author of *The Tragedy of Orestes*, a couple of tragedies on Turkish themes (*The Courageous Turk* and *The Raging Turk*), and a pastoral, *The Careless Shepherdess*, that was revived around 1638 at the Salisbury Court playhouse by Queen Henrietta's Men; and Barten Holyday, author of a comedy called *Technogamia, or The Marriage of Arts* that had been acted 'with no great applause' at the College in 1617 and may have been retouched by Jonson before being presented, with equal lack of success, to an impatient King James at Woodstock in 1621.[20] Pleasing the King on these occasions was not always easy. Robert Burton, the future chronicler of melancholy, who was also at Christ Church at this time, had not fared much better while seeking to entertain James with his now-lost pastoral *Alba* in 1605, when 'if the Chancellors of both Universities had not entreated His Majesty earnestly he would have gone before half the comedy had been ended'.[21] Burton's comedy *Philosophaster*, which satirized alchemists and other pretenders to learning, had been performed at Christ Church the year before Jonson's arrival, with Goffe taking the principal role. Burton was at pains to point out in his introduction to the printed text that he had begun to write this work in 1606, before Jonson himself had thought of tackling the same theme in *The Alchemist* in 1610. Jonson and Burton would have had many intellectual interests in common, and shared in particular a passion for books, of which Burton, soon to become Librarian of Christ Church, was already a prodigious collector. Antony à Wood reported that, despite Burton's serious scholarly interests, 'I have heard some of the ancients of Ch. Ch. often say that his company was very merry, facete, and juvenile, and no man in his time did surpass him for his ready and dextrous interlarding his common discourses among them with verses from the poets or sentences from classical authors'.[22]

Jonson would also have had contact at Christ Church with Brian Duppa, a respected scholar and devoted Royalist who would in time act as tutor to Prince Charles, the future Charles II. A lover and writer of poetry, Duppa was a central, animating figure in the group of Christ Church writers.[23] At the time of Jonson's visit to Oxford, Duppa had just been appointed junior proctor in the University. A few years after Jonson's stay at the College, he would win the patronage of Edward Sackville, fourth Earl of Dorset, a friend of the Duke of Buckingham; and through Buckingham's influence go on to become Dean of Christ Church in 1628. He was to be a moderate supporter of William Laud during Laud's time as Vice-Chancellor of the University, before becoming Vice-Chancellor himself in the early 1630s and securing a series of bishoprics, culminating in his appointment towards the end of his life as Bishop of Winchester in 1660. Duppa seems to have encouraged Jonson during his stay at Christ Church to complete an epic poem on which he was then engaged. Many years later Duppa's friend Sir Justinian Isham was to refer in passing to 'the epic poem to which Ben Jonson was encouraged by your Lordship. Though this hath already come to no maturity, yet such prizes have commonly the fate of great buildings, to be left imperfect with a footing. And when all is finished they are but high lanterns for light in respect of the true sunshine.'[24] This was probably the same 'epic poem, entitled *Heroologia*', that Jonson had mentioned to William Drummond earlier in the year, 'of the worthies of his country roused by fame', which Jonson planned to dedicate 'to his country'. 'It is all in couplets,' Drummond added, 'for he detesteth all other rhymes' (*Informations*, 1–3). 'Heroologia' means literally 'a history of heroes'. What Jonson—intrigued once again by the permutations of fame—was evidently contemplating at this moment was a kind of versified dictionary of national biography. Though his rhyming epic never saw the light of day, a similarly titled work, *Heroologia Anglica*, was to be published in 1620 by the London bookseller Henry Holland, containing brief lives (all written in Latin prose) of statesmen, scholars, churchmen, navigators, and other distinguished citizens from the time of Henry VIII to the early years of James I, illustrated by fine-quality engravings. Holland's work would be a model for later biographical dictionaries such as Thomas Birch's *Heads of Illustrious Persons of Great Britain* (1743), with its engravings by Jacobus Houbraken and George Vertue: a pantheon of national worthies including that by-now most celebrated of English writers, Ben Jonson himself.[25]

§§

Jonson had probably left Oxford by December 1619 and established himself in his new lodgings in Cripplegate, on the north side of the city between Moorgate and Aldersgate, and near to the Barbican: the very district in which Shakespeare had lodged for several years with the French family of Mountjoys.[26] The time Jonson had spent amongst the dons seems to have sharpened his appetite for scholarly work. Over the next few years the theatre was to have only an intermittent hold on his attention, as he occupied himself increasingly with a variety of learned tasks: with writings on statecraft, divinity, philology, history, poetics and rhetoric, and with the translation and presentation of classical and modern texts. The scholarly resources in London for such work were scarcely inferior to those on offer in Oxford or Cambridge, and the presence of a remarkable network of learned friends in London would have provided Jonson with constant stimulus and support. He himself had always been keen to maintain a substantial personal library, drawing on the generous annual gift of £20 from the Earl of Pembroke 'to buy books' (*Informations*, 239–40). The size of his collection would have varied considerably over the years, however, for he was prodigal with his money, ran periodically into debt, and was obliged on occasions to sell his books (probably his sole significant asset) in order to make ends meet: 'Sundry times he hath devoured his books,' he told Drummond, 'i.e. sold them all for necessity' (*Informations*, 253); 'all' (if literally taken) suggesting not merely an occasional selective cull but a total periodic clearance of the collection. Many of Jonson's books survive and are readily identifiable today by his characteristic signature, his marginal annotations, and his personal motto, *tanquam explorator* (see Fig. 43).[27]

The survival of multiple copies of certain titles from Jonson's library suggests that he at times acquired second copies of books that he had formerly owned, but had been forced to part with. Some of his books were sold on to friends such as John Selden, whose remarkable personal library, bequeathed after his death to the Bodleian Library in Oxford, contains a number of books whose title pages bear the autographs both of Selden and Jonson himself.[28] Selden and Jonson also borrowed books on occasions from each other's collections. In the preface to his *Titles of Honor*, published in 1614, Selden

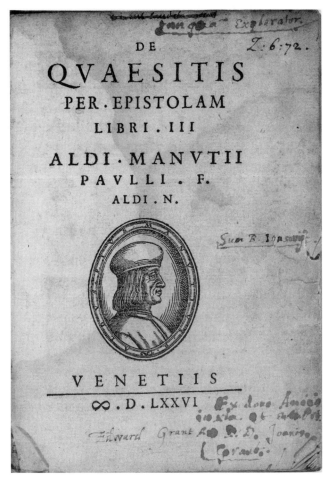

Fig. 43. Jonson's signature and personal motto, *tanquam explorator*, are inscribed on this copy of Aldo Manuzio the younger's *De Quaesitis per Epistolam Libri III*, Venice, 1576, three books of commentary on Roman antiquities that were once in Jonson's possession (and are now in Cambridge University Library). The book also bears the signature of an earlier owner, Edward Grant, who was Headmaster of Westminster School when Jonson was a student; and a Latin inscription declaring the book to have been the gift to Jonson 'of my close and erudite friend, the Reverend John Grant' (Edward Grant's son, who is perhaps glanced at in *The Magnetic Lady*: see 420 below). Jonson found the tag *tanquam explorator* in an epistle of Seneca (2.2), who had found it in turn in the writings of the Greek philosopher Epicurus. *Soleo enim et in aliena castra transpire, non tamquam transfuga, sed tamquam explorator*, writes Seneca: 'for I am wont to cross over even into the enemy's camp—not as a deserter, but as a scout.' The motto signals the spirit in which— so Jonson believed, as Seneca and Epicurus had believed before him—all reading should ideally be conducted, in a spirit of free but self-possessed enquiry; not forsaking one's own beliefs, but to explore the ideas of others.

had thanked Jonson for allowing him to consult his personal copy of the writings of the Greek scholiast Arsenius, paying warm tribute as he did so to Jonson's intellectual attainments: 'I went, for this purpose, to see it in the well-furnished library of my beloved friend, that singular poet Master Ben Jonson, whose special worth in literature, accurate judgement and performance, known only to that few which are truly able to know him, hath had from me, ever since I began to learn, an increasing admiration.'

Like many scholars in Jacobean London, both Selden and Jonson frequently drew on the greatest library of the day: that of their friend Sir Robert Cotton (Fig. 44). Cotton's extraordinary library was an academic meeting place that (as one commentator has said) 'probably did more to advance the cause of scholarship than the combined patronage of Oxford and Cambridge'.[29] It attracted readers and donors not only from around Britain but from continental Europe, such as the great French scholar Nicolas-Claude Fabri de Peiresc, who presented books to the collection.[30] It incorporated books and manuscripts that had been in the possession of the learned John Dee, whose stupendous library at Mortlake represented what Frances Yates once described as 'the whole Renaissance': items which Dee made accessible, in a similarly generous spirit, to readers from many parts of Britain and many countries. Cotton methodically acquired books and manuscripts too from the libraries of Prince Henry (which in turn included items from the collection of John, Lord Lumley); of Robert Cecil (with its fine collection of maps and political papers); of the disgraced Garter King of Arms, William Dethick; of Cotton's own patron Henry Howard, Earl of Northampton; and finally of Cotton's great mentor himself, William Camden.[31] Cotton's library was at first located in Blackfriars, where Jonson himself was then living. Late in 1602 or early 1603, while suffering from severe illness, Jonson wrote to Cotton begging the loan of a book that would give him precise topographical information about the Campania region, so he might trace more exactly the possible movements of the emperor Tiberius at the end of Act 3 of the tragedy of *Sejanus*, which he was then writing; adding, 'The book shall be returned this night without excuse'.[32] Many readers were less punctilious in returning Cotton's books and manuscripts; while several books 'Which noble Carew, Cotton, Selden lent' to Jonson himself, relating to the reign of Henry V which Jonson was attempting to chronicle, were destroyed in the fire that damaged his lodgings in 1623 (*The Underwood*, 43.100).[33] Later Cotton and his library moved to the Strand. In 1622 he acquired a large four-storey house

Æsculapius hic Librorum ærugo, Vetustas
Per quem nulla potest Britonum consumere chartas.

T. Cross sculpsit.

Fig. 44. Portrait of Robert Cotton engraved by Thomas Cross.

within the Palace of Westminster which he named Cotton House, where the library was methodically organized into collections named after the Roman emperors, whose busts adorned the house. Here, during the late 1620s, Jonson and Cotton once again became close neighbours; and though Jonson now found it increasingly difficult to get about, he could still have borrowed books from the library with the help of friends and servants. A visitor to Cotton House in 1692 reports having seen Ben Jonson's portrait on display there, along with a portrait of Cotton himself: an apt pairing of two of Camden's most learned pupils, and most avid bibliophiles.[34]

Antiquarian scholarship, as both Cotton and Selden had good cause to know, was not always seen as a harmless or disinterested pursuit in seventeenth-century England. During the last years of Elizabeth's reign, the small group known as the Society of Antiquaries (or 'Antiquaries' College'), whose members included William Camden, Robert Cotton, John Stow, and Henry Spelman, had met regularly at Derby House and sought to establish themselves as a kind of national academy under royal protection. Their petition to the Queen for a royal charter, however, had been unsuccessful, and to their disappointment they fared no better under James, who feared their enquiries might drift from ancient to modern times, and reflect on contemporary 'matters of state'.[35] In November 1629, driven by similar fears, Charles ordered the closure of Robert Cotton's library, which he perceived as a meeting place for dissidents and source of historical evidence potentially damaging to royal interests. Cotton had been one of the growing band of critics of the power wielded by the royal favourite George Villiers, Duke of Buckingham, who in retaliation had been urging Charles for some years to shut down this troublesome institution. Cotton himself was eventually allowed limited access to his own building under the supervision of a clerk of Council who held the keys, but died in 1631, still mourning the forced closure of his unrivalled library.[36]

At a time when the respective powers of the crown, Church, and Parliament were being sharply debated, any scholarly enquiry into the historical origins and consequent legitimacy of contested rights, privileges, and procedures could be seen as politically inspired, however neutrally intended. This was precisely the kind of intricate, learned work which John Selden—'the law-book of the judges of England, the bravest man in all languages', as Jonson called him (*Informations*, 483–4)—was pre-eminently equipped to undertake. Jonson had praised his skills in a verse epistle prefixed to Selden's *Titles of Honour* in 1614:

What fables have you vexed! What truth redeemed!
Antiquities searched! Opinions disesteemed!
Impostures branded, and authorities urged!
What blots and errors have you watched and purged
Records and authors of! How rectified
Times, manners, customs! Innovations spied!
Sought out the fountains, sources, creeks, paths, ways,
And noted the beginnings and decays!

(*The Underwood*, 14.39–46)

Fig. 45. Portrait of Ben Jonson by George Vertue.

Vexing, searching, purging, branding, rectifying, and (marvellous word) *disesteeming* in this supremely authoritative manner, Selden constituted a distinct threat to holders of supposedly time-honoured privilege.

The potentially dangerous nature of his seemingly remote academic enquiries is well illustrated in a project with which both Cotton and Jonson were involved (Cotton, as a partial contributor, Jonson as a subsequent supporter), *The History of Tithes*: Selden's account of the origin and legitimacy of ecclesiastical tithes, a subject of much dispute and litigation in the early years of the century.[37] These enforced taxes were regularly payable not merely to parish clergy, who depended upon this income for their livelihood, but also to laymen who had purchased tithing rights after the dissolution of the monasteries. Holders of such rights commonly asserted that ecclesiastical tithes were due not simply by law but by virtue of divine right. In examining the foundations of this claim, Selden concluded that the law provided a stronger basis for the levying of tithes than did any notion of divine right, which he regarded with due scepticism. Outraged at this implied limitation on their traditional rights, the bishops at court—with the sole exception of Lancelot Andrewes, Bishop of Winchester—responded (in Selden's own image) like angry hornets, swarming about King James and persuading him to take punitive action.

James at this time had never heard of John Selden, but (ever eager to parade his own knowledge) welcomed this opportunity to indulge in a bout of academic disputation. The *History of Tithes* had been clandestinely printed and published without licence in November 1618 by William Stansby (the publisher of Jonson's First Folio).[38] In mid-December Selden found himself summoned to Theobalds (James's residence in Hertfordshire, twelve miles from London) for a viva voce examination with the King. He went nervously to this interview, as he recalled in later life, accompanied by two friends, his colleague and chamber-mate Edward Heyward and Ben Jonson, *poetarum ille facile princeps* ('easily the foremost of poets').[39] Jonson was very familiar with Theobalds, having celebrated the formal transfer of the estate's ownership from Robert Cecil to Queen Anne in an entertainment for the King and Queen in 1607. Had he indeed been present on this occasion, he would have been able to introduce Selden to the King, and ease the inevitable tension of the meeting—which was evidently enjoyed by James at least, who in laboriously playful mood required Selden to write three palinodes (or penitential poems) on the significance of the number 666 in the Book of Revelations, on

Calvin's opinion of that Book, and on the proposition that Christ was born on 25 December. This cannot have been exactly the outcome the bishops were looking for, but firmer measures were in store for Selden, who was required by the King early in 1619 to appear before the Court of High Commission and the Privy Council and apologize in both places for what he had written.

Though Selden himself clearly remembers Jonson having been with him at Theobalds in mid-December 1618, his memory must have been at fault, for Jonson at this time was away in Scotland. A few days after his supposed appearance at Theobalds, he was actually staying with William Drummond at Hawthornden Castle near Edinburgh. Selden was recalling these events in 1653, many years after they occurred, and may have confused their sequence. For James did summon Selden on two subsequent occasions to answer questions about *The History of Tithes*, once to Whitehall and once again at Theobalds—on the latter occasion (described in a letter to Sir Edward Herbert of 3 February 1620 as having occurred 'recently') when he was treated 'as if actually on trial' for having circulated handwritten notes rebutting the formal refutations of the *History* that James had commissioned.[40] It must have been on this last occasion that Jonson accompanied John Selden to Theobalds, and stood by him during his difficult interrogation by the King.

The meeting at Theobalds (however conjecturally reconstructed) offers a suggestive glimpse into Jonson's own political position in the late Jacobean years. In the presence of the King whose policies he officially celebrates, Jonson asserts his friendship with a tough defender of constitutional rights. Fresh from his stay with the Oxford bishops (both present and future), he offers his support to a sceptical critic of episcopal power. Jonson's mediating position is governed in part by pragmatism, as he picks, characteristically, a middle pathway through the political controversies of the time. Yet it is rooted, too, in profound respect for the most prodigiously learned of the many remarkable scholars whom he had the good fortune to count amongst his friends.

§§

It was about this time Jonson and a number of these friends—poets, wits, lovers of learning, members of the so-called 'tribe of Ben'—began regularly to meet in the Apollo Room on the first floor of the Devil and St Dunstan tavern in Fleet Street, near Temple Bar, created in imitation of the Apollo Room once maintained (according to Plutarch) by Lucullus, a well-known gourmet as well as a great lover of books, where the most extravagant and delicious of dinners were served to his special friends.[41] A terracotta bust of Apollo, attributed to Edward Marshall, which stood in the room where Jonson and his companions met, is still preserved today in the building that has replaced the original tavern in Fleet Street (which was demolished towards the end of the eighteenth century). Jonson's verses of welcome, painted on a panel over the door at the entry to the room, can also still be seen today.

> Welcome, all who lead or follow
> To the oracle of Apollo:
> Here he speaks out of his pottle,
> Or the tripos, his tower bottle.
> All his answers are divine:
> Truth itself doth flow in wine.
> 'Hang up all the poor hop drinkers',
> Cries old Sim, the king of skinkers;
> He the half of life abuses
> That sits watering with the muses.
> Those dull girls no good can mean us;
> Wine, it is the milk of Venus
> And the poets' horse accounted.
> Ply it, and you all are mounted;
> 'Tis the true Phoebeian liquor,
> Cheers the brain, makes wit the quicker,
> Pays all debt, cures all diseases,
> And at once three senses pleases.
> Welcome, all who lead or follow,
> To the oracle of Apollo!

The 'old Sim' commemorated in these lines was Simon Wadlow, the inn-keeper and head tapster (or 'skinker') at the Devil and St Dunstan. Over the mantelpiece of the Apollo Room, engraved in marble, were the twenty-four Latin rules of the Club, the *Leges Convivales*, translated into English many years later by Alexander Brome, beginning as follows:

> Let none but guests or clubbers hither come,
> Let dunces, fools, sad, sordid men keep home;

Let learned, civil, merry men be invited,
And modest, too; nor the choice ladies slighted.
Let nothing in the treat offend the guests;
More for delight than cost prepare the feasts;
The cook and purveyor must our palates know;
And none contend who shall sit high or low...[42]

§§

The remarkable group of scholars and writers working in London during the latter years of James's reign, while often meeting together convivially in this way in taverns and private libraries, had no collective identity, recognition, or institutional base. The attempt by the Society of Antiquaries to establish themselves as a national academy (as we have just seen) had come to nothing. Earlier efforts to establish a learned academy under royal protection, such as that of Sir Humphrey Gilbert in Elizabeth's time, had similarly failed to gain momentum. The embryonic Academy Royal that was developing around Prince Henry, with its emphasis on the study of languages, mathematics, and horsemanship, terminated with the Prince's death in 1612. Yet the learned academies that now flourished in continental Europe, such as the Accademia Nazionale dei Lincei, established in Rome in 1603 by the 18-year-old Prince Cesi and boasting Galileo Galilei amongst its members, set an attractive model which scholars in England viewed with some envy.[43] In 1617 Jonson's friend Edmund Bolton set out the first of his several proposals for the establishment in England of a national academy that would enjoy the monarch's support and protection.[44] Bolton was an impoverished Catholic scholar who was on friendly terms with Cotton, Selden, Camden, and other leading antiquarians of the day, and had known and admired Jonson and his work for many years. Early in 1606 the two men had faced the Consistory Court together on charges of recusancy. The following year Bolton had contributed some Latin verses to the quarto edition of *Volpone*, praising Jonson as one who had studied Greek and Roman drama *tanquam explorator*, as an explorer, and had provided Britain with a learned drama of its own. In *Hypercritica*, a work unpublished in his lifetime, he candidly declared that he had 'never tasted English more to my liking, nor more smart, and put to the height of use in poetry, than in that vital, judicious, and most practicable language of Benjamin Jonson's poems'.[45] Bolton too was a minor poet who had contributed verses to *England's Helicon*, Camden's *Britannia*, and other volumes, and the author of more ambitious works such as *The Elements of Armories*, a study on heraldry published in 1610.

Bolton proposed that the new Academ Roial (as he called it) should receive an annual grant from the crown of £200 and have its headquarters at Windsor Castle. All of the Academy's members would be permitted to wear special ribbons and badges designed by Bolton himself, and to make appropriate adjustments to their coats of arms. There were to be three tiers of membership. At the highest level was a group of grandees known as the Tutelaries, comprising the Lord Chancellor, Knights of the Garter, and the Chancellors of the two Universities. Then came the Auxiliaries, who were selected members of the aristocracy. They were followed by the rank and file, the scholarly foot-soldiers known appropriately as the Essentials. Bolton's preliminary list of eighty-four scholars, poets, and artists nominated as Essentials included Robert Cotton, Henry Spelman, Inigo Jones, George Chapman, John Selden, Michael Drayton, Edward Coke, and Ben Jonson. The earliest version of this proposal was directed to King James through the mediation of the Duke of Buckingham, to whom Bolton was distantly related; the pages reproduced in Plate 21 capture the spirit of the entire venture. The primary function of the new Academy—the proposal grandly, if somewhat vaguely promised—was to be the promotion of ORDER, DECORUM, and DECENCIE (words emphatically inscribed in large upper-cased letters) and the suppression of Confusion and Deformitie. As Bolton's thoughts developed, he proposed more specific functions to the Academy: that it should control the licensing of all non-theological books in England, for example, keep a constant register of 'public facts', monitor the translation of all learned works, hold meetings every quarter and annually on St George's Day.

James was impressed by this grand proposal, and flattered by the role in which Bolton had cast him, as Britain's King Solomon, presiding over a house of wisdom like that which Bacon was also coincidentally imagining at this time. He pledged his support to the scheme, but died in 1625 before the new Academy could be created. With his death, the scheme itself collapsed, for Charles I, despite specific written instructions from his father, showed no interest in taking it forward. Four decades were to pass before the Royal Society was established under the protection of Charles II, and another three centuries would elapse before the creation of the real successor to Bolton's scheme, the British Academy.[46]

Election as an Essential to the Academ Roial was not the only honour that Jonson narrowly escaped around this time. Writing to Sir Martin Stuteville on 15 September 1621, the Reverend Joseph Mede declared that Jonson was about to be knighted, but that the proposal had run into trouble: 'for that his Majesty would have done it, had not been means made (himself not unwilling) to avoid it.'[47] Three weeks later Jonson was granted a patent for the reversion of the mastership of the Revels, in the event that Sir George Buck, the present Master, and Sir John Astley, who was next in line, should die before he did. In the event Astley outlived Jonson, thwarting him of the succession.[48] In a jocular exchange with Sir Dudley Carleton at The Hague the following month (17 November), John Chamberlain imagined Jonson's receiving a further honour. John Donne, he informed Carleton, had now been appointed as Dean of St Paul's: 'so as a pleasant companion said, that if Ben Jonson might be made Dean of Westminster, that place, Paul's, and Christ Church [home of Richard Corbett] should be furnished with three very pleasant poetical Deans.'[49] For all his scepticism about the role of bishops, Jonson might well have enjoyed mounting the pulpit, and delivering at least one robust sermon to an auditor more accustomed (so Jonson believed) to receiving flattery in church: 'He hath a mind to be a churchman,' he told Drummond, 'and so he might have favour to make one sermon to the King, he careth not what thereafter should befall him; for he would not flatter, though he saw death' (*Informations*, 254–6).[50]

§§

John Aubrey has left a vivid picture of Jonson's working habits.

He would many times exceed in drink (Canary was his beloved liquor), then he would tumble home to bed, and when he had thoroughly perspired, then to study. I have seen his studying chair, which was of straw, such as old women used, and as Aulus Gellius is drawn in.[51]

Late in 1623, perhaps after one such tumbling home to bed, Jonson suffered a domestic catastrophe: a fire in his lodgings, possibly caused by an overturned candle or spark from his chimney, destroyed a number of his books and papers. In 'An Execration upon Vulcan', his long poem comically but ruefully lamenting this event, Jonson lists some of his still unpublished writings lost in this conflagration.

But in my desk, what was there to accite
  So ravenous and vast an appetite?
I dare not say a body, but some parts
  There were of search and mastery in the arts:
All the old Venusine in poetry,
  And lighted by the Stagerite, could spy
Was there made English, with a Grammar too,
  To teach some that their nurses could not do,
The purity of language. And, among
  The rest, my journey into Scotland sung,
With all th'adventures; three books not afraid
  To speak the fate of the Sicilian maid
To our own ladies, and in story there
  Of our fifth Henry, eight of his nine year;
Wherein was oil, beside the succour, spent
  Which noble Carew, Cotton, Selden lent;
And twice twelve years' stored up humanity,
  With humble gleanings in divinity,
After the fathers, and those wiser guides
  Whom faction had not drawn to study sides.
How in these ruins, Vulcan, thou dost lurk,
  All soot and embers, odious as thy work!
                    (*The Underwood*, 43.85–106)

Fires of this sort were not uncommon in Jacobean London. A few years later, Jonson's 'Son, and contiguous neighbour' in Westminster, James Howell, was to write teasingly about another such blaze from which he had rescued Jonson in his lodgings, 'desiring you to look better hereafter to your charcoal fire and chimney, which I am glad to be the one that preserved from burning, this being the second time that Vulcan hath threatened you. It may be because you have spoken ill of his wife, and been too busy with his horns...'[52] It is impossible to know how trivial or serious an event the fire of 1623 actually was. Jonson's lamentation in the 'Execration' is obviously boosted by a certain comical overkill. His old friend and collaborator George Chapman (now on altogether less amicable terms with Jonson) was led to wonder somewhat unkindly how many of the works listed here as destroyed by fire had ever been written in the first place; but most appear to have been well advanced, and some were later to emerge in rewritten form.[53]

What is perhaps most striking about the list of lost writings, especially for those accustomed to thinking of Jonson primarily as a writer for the theatre, is that—apart from the 'parcels of a play, | Fitter to see the fire-light than the day' that Jonson mentions earlier in the poem (43–4)—nearly all of the works whose loss he mourns, with the possible exception of the versified account of his walk to Scotland, *A Discovery,* are serious works of scholarship. 'I dare not say a body, but some parts | There were of search and *mastery in the arts*': Chapman saw this last italicized phrase as a reference by Jonson to his recent honorary degree from Oxford, and it is indeed in the role of a distressed scholar, rather than as a frustrated playwright, that Jonson presents himself throughout the poem.[54] He deplores the loss of his commentary on the *Ars Poetica* of Horace (the 'old Venusine') in the light of the *Poetics* of Aristotle ('the Stagirite'), a work from which the *Ars Poetica* was commonly thought at this time to have derived. Jonson's commentary had been long in the making: he had referred to it many years earlier in the preface to the quarto edition of *Sejanus,* and during his time in Scotland had read it to William Drummond, who noted, 'It is all in dialogue ways; by Criticus he understandeth Dr Donne' (*Informations,* 324–5; cf. 58–61). Two different versions of Jonson's translation of Horace's work were to be published eventually after his death.[55] Though his *English Grammar* was destroyed in the 1623 fire, Jonson seems to have embarked almost immediately on a revised version, intended this time not merely for native speakers ('To teach some that their nurses could not do, | The purity of language'), but for 'strangers who are to live in communion and commerce with us' (Preface, 1–2). This work was still unfinished at the time of Jonson's death, and was published eventually in 1641 in the third volume of his Second Folio.[56]

Jonson also laments the loss of three books of his translation, undertaken at King James's request (and confidently announced in the Stationers' Register on 2 October 1623, just a few weeks before the fire), of John Barclay's hugely popular Latin novel *Argenis,* telling of 'the fate of the Sicilian maid'.[57] Jonson was probably personally acquainted with Barclay, who had died in Rome in 1621 a few days after the publication in Paris of *Argenis* (through the agency of Barclay's learned friend, Peiresc). The gifted son of a Catholic Scottish nobleman and his French wife, Barclay had grown up in France, and subsequently spent time at James's court, winning the King's favour and working for Robert Cecil. He had published in 1603 a Latin poem celebrating

James's coronation, and in 1605 a prose satire modelled on Petronius called the *Satyricon Euphormionis*, which he dedicated to James, whom he flatteringly portrays in the work under a fictitious name. *Argenis* is a political allegory, Royalist in tendency, which reflects in a thinly disguised fashion recent events in France (figured here as 'Sicily') and England ('Mauritania'), glancing at such scandals as the Overbury affair in England, and graphically depicting the turmoil in France under Henri III and Henri IV, where 'religion is banished and the laws neglected, the ways dangerous for travellers, houses and streets everywhere affected with rapine, fire, and fury; only the tents in the forlorn fields show glorious with bright armour'. Its subject matter would have been of particular interest to Jonson, but he could not bring himself to begin the translation all over again. The commission passed to Kingsmill Long, whose English translation of *Argenis* was published in 1625.[58]

§§

Through an odd coincidence, the destruction by fire of Jonson's own papers was swiftly followed by the publication of a monumental work which Jonson himself had helped in some measure to prepare: the dramatic oeuvre of his great friend and rival: *Mr William Shakespeare's Comedies, Histories, and Tragedies, Published According to the True Original Copies.*[59] Shakespeare's First Folio was edited by the two surviving members of the original company of the Lord Chamberlain's Men established in 1594: John Heminges and Henry Condell.[60] In preparing the volume for publication, these two would have been certain to have consulted with Ben Jonson, not just because he was the leading dramatist of the day and a former friend of Shakespeare's, but because he was also experienced (as they were not) in the ways of printers and booksellers; and was the author of another volume, published seven years earlier, that presented a powerful model for 1623 Shakespeare First Folio: the 1616 Folio of his own *Works*, published by William Stansby. Heminges and Condell had known Jonson for many years, having both acted in six of his plays: *Every Man In His Humour, Every Man Out of His Humour, Sejanus, Volpone, The Alchemist,* and *Catiline*. (Whether Heminges had ever acted in a play by Shakespeare is not known.) One critic has wondered whether Jonson, having been granted the opportunity to look over so many of Shakespeare's plays in manuscript while the Folio was in preparation at this time, and being free now at last of the competitive pressures that existed during Shakespeare's lifetime, might not have felt attracted by romance conventions which he professed to despise in earlier days, and tempted therefore to adopt them in certain of his own late comedies, such as *The New Inn* and *The Sad Shepherd*.[61]

Whatever the extent of his involvement, the stamp of Jonson's authority is clearly apparent in the 1623 Folio. At the outset of the volume, opposite the title page with its famous, if ungainly, portrait of Shakespeare, stand Jonson's verses 'To the Reader' (Fig. 46a), vouching for the fact that Martin Droeshout's engraving (Fig. 46c) was indeed 'for gentle Shakespeare cut', and (to the lasting confusion of those wishing to propose an alternative authorship) that the person depicted was indeed responsible for the works presented in this volume.

Did Jonson also help to draft the famous address 'To the Great Variety of Readers' that is signed by the two editors? Part of this address is indisputably the work of Heminges and Condell themselves, who report the miraculous fluency of the author whose working manuscripts they have inherited: 'His mind and hand went together, and what he thought he uttered with that easiness, that we have scarce received from him a blot in his papers.' Jonson was to regard this tribute with a certain reserve, as he later reported in his *Discoveries*.

I remember the players have often mentioned it as an honour to Shakespeare, that in his writing, whatsoever he penned, he never blotted out line. My answer hath been, 'Would he had blotted a thousand'. Which they thought a malevolent speech. I had not told posterity this but for their ignorance, who choose that circumstance to commend their friend by wherein most he faulted. And to justify mine own candour; for I loved the man, and do honour his memory (on this side idolatry) as much as any. He was, indeed, honest, and of an open and free nature; had an excellent fantasy, brave notions, and gentle expressions; wherein he flowed with that facility that sometime it was necessary he should be stopped. (*Discoveries*, 468–76)

Though Jonson and the players are in obvious tension here, other passages in the address 'To the Great Variety of Readers' are strongly suggestive of Jonson's own sentiments and phrasing. 'From the most able to him that

To the Reader.

This *Figure* that thou here feeſt put,
It was for gentle *Shakeſpeare* cut ;
Wherein the *Graver* had a ſtrife
With Nature to out-do the Life.
O, could he but have drawn his Wit
As well in Braſs, as he has hit
His Face ; the Print would then ſurpaſs
All that was ever writ in *Braſs*.
But ſince he cannot, Reader, look
Not on his Piĉture, but his *Book*.

B. I.

Fig. 46a. 'To the Reader' from Shakespeare's 1623 First Folio.

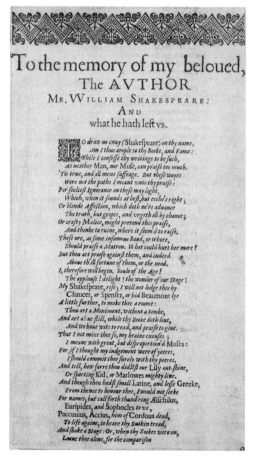

Fig. 46b. 'To the Memory of My Beloved, the Author, Master William Shakespeare, and
What He Hath Left Us.'

can but spell: there you are numbered. We had rather you were weighed,' the address begins tetchily,

Especially, when the fate of all books depends upon your capacities: and not of your heads alone, but of your purses. Well! It is now public, and you will stand for your privileges, we know: to read and censure. Do so, but buy it first. That doth best commend a book, the stationer says.

The opening statement resembles a comment in *Discoveries*, 365, 'Suffrages in parliament are numbered, not weighed.' The distinction between good and bad readers recalls Jonson's similar distinction in the quarto edition of *Catiline* between readers 'in ordinary' and readers 'extraordinary'. 'That doth best commend a book, the stationer says' echoes a similar gibe in Jonson's epigram to his own bookseller, John Stepneth, who 'Callst a book good or bad, as it doth sell' ('To My Bookseller', *Epigrams*, 3.2). 'From the most able to him that can but spell' is reminiscent of the same poem's mockery of the barely literate customers who come to inspect the books which the stationer has displayed for sale: 'some clerk-like serving-man | Who scarce can spell the hard names; whose knight less can' (9–10).[62] The sarcastic suggestion that readers 'Judge your six-penn'orth, your shilling's worth, your five shillings' worth at a time' resembles the terms proposed for the playgoers at the Hope theatre in the Induction to *Bartholomew Fair*, where 'It shall be lawful for any man to judge his six-penn'orth, his twelve penn'orth, so to his eighteen pence, two shillings, half a crown, to the value of his place—provided always his place get not above his wit,' the author having now 'departed with his right' (64–8). The notion of an author departing with his rights recurs frequently in Jonson's work, and crops up in this very address, when Shakespeare is said by his death to have 'departed from that right' to 'have set forth and overseen his own writings'.[63] 'And though you be a magistrate of wit, and sit on the stage at Blackfriars or the Cockpit to arraign plays daily, know these plays have had their trial already...' anticipates the famous opening of Jonson's 'Ode: To Himself', written after the failure of *The New Inn* in 1629:

> Come, leave the loathed stage,
> And the more loathsome age,
> Where pride and impudence, in faction knit,
> Usurp the chair of wit:
> Indicting and arraigning every day
> Something they call a play...[64]

The presence of so many small phrases characteristic of Jonson in this address strongly suggests that he may have had a hand in its composition.

Jonson's more significant contribution, however, both to the volume itself and to the course of Shakespeare's subsequent reputation, lay in the remarkable poem that follows this address in the preliminary pages of the Folio: 'To the Memory of My Beloved, The Author, Master William Shakespeare, And What He Hath Left Us' (Fig. 46c). Here Jonson sets out more spaciously the affection and admiration he felt for his great friend and rival, declaring Shakespeare's pre-eminence over all writers for the stage, both ancient and modern.

> For if I thought my judgement were of years
> I should commit thee surely with thy peers,
> And tell how far thou didst our Lyly outshine,
> Or sporting Kyd, or Marlowe's mighty line.
> And though thou hadst small Latin and less Greek,
> From thence to honour thee I would not seek
> For names, but call forth thundering Aeschylus,
> Euripides and Sophocles to us,
> Pacuvius, Accius, him of Cordova dead,
> To life again, to hear thy buskin tread
> And shake a stage; or, when thy socks were on
> Leave thee alone for the comparison
> Of all that insolent Greece or haughty Rome
> Sent forth, or since did from their ashes come.
> Triumph, my Britain, thou hast one to show
> To whom all scenes of Europe homage owe.
> He was not of an age, but for all time! (27–43)

'He was not of an age, but for all time!': this verdict may seem, four centuries on, like an uncontested truth, but in 1623 it was a bold prediction. No one had spoken in such terms of Shakespeare before, imagining so vividly his reputation in the years to come. Later readers of the Folio, while often drawing their own critical vocabulary from Jonson's poem, were at times discomfited by its one apparent glancing reservation: the suggestion that Shakespeare, for all his great powers, had 'small Latin and less Greek'. But Jonson was evidently familiar with a rhetorical strategy recommended by Quintilian to those seeking to praise a person of outstanding qualities: begin (said Quintilian) by describing any possible disadvantages your subject might

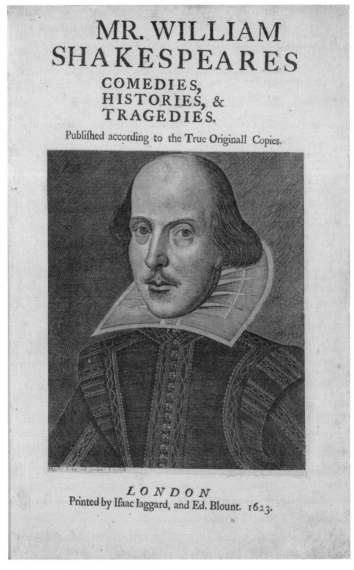

> # MR. WILLIAM
> # SHAKESPEARES
> ## COMEDIES,
> ## HISTORIES, &
> ## TRAGEDIES.
>
> Publiſhed according to the True Originall Copies.
>
> *LONDON*
> Printed by Iſaac Iaggard, and Ed. Blount. 1623.

Fig. 46c. Martin Droeshout portrait of Shakespeare, from 1623 First Folio.

be thought to have had (that he was a physically small man, for example), then go on to show how he overcame those disadvantages (that nevertheless he would fight with great courage).[65] Shakespeare, in Jonson's view, has not merely overcome his imagined deficiencies, but shown that the qualities he

375

supposedly lacked were never needed in the first place. Through his supreme genius he surpasses 'all that insolent Greece and haughty Rome | Sent forth, or since did from their ashes come'. He is the writer not just of England, but of the known world; the writer not merely of the present age, but for all time. Jonson's careful, considered, not-easily-won mode of praising gives this tribute its exceptional power. At such moments as these it is apparent that he is not just a considerable scholar, but also the first literary critic in England worthy of the name.

§§

On 20 October 1623 Ben Jonson was examined as a witness in a lawsuit in the Court of Chancery brought by Elizabeth, Lady Ralegh, widow of Sir Walter, about a disputed settlement of Sir Walter's estate following his attainder and execution. In the Chancery interrogatories and depositions, Jonson is described as '*Beniamin Johnson* of Gresham Colledge in London gent. aged 50 yeares & vpwards'.[66] Gresham College had been established in 1597 from an endowment deriving from the wealthy merchant and financier Sir Thomas Gresham (1518–79), founder of the Royal Exchange. Gresham College— located in Sir Thomas's former house in Bishopsgate on the northern edge of the city, and administered by the Corporation of London and the Mercers' Company—had been described by Sir George Buc in 1612 as 'the third university of England'.

This is a little university, or academy's epitome, as Rome, when it flourished, was *orbis epitome* in the conceit of Athenaeus and others, for in this College are by this worthy founder ordained seven several lectures of seven several arts and faculties, to be read publicly: to wit, a lecture of Divinity, a lecture of Civil Law, a lecture of Physic, a lecture of Rhetoric, a lecture of Astronomy, a lecture of Geometry, and a lecture of Music, by seven several renowned professors of these arts and learnings. And these lectures must be read only in the term times.[67]

C. J. Sisson, who discovered the court record in question, wondered whether Jonson might have taken refuge in the College after the fire in his lodgings, or alternatively have occupied rooms there by virtue of some office he held. He speculated that Jonson might have deputized for a time for the Gresham Professor of Rhetoric, Henry Croke, and that both the *Discoveries* and the revised version of Jonson's *English Grammar* might have had their origin in

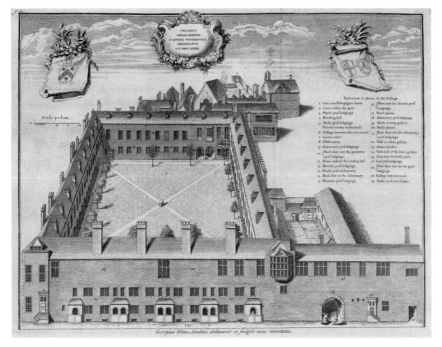

Fig. 47. Gresham College, London: engraving by George Vertue from John Ward's
Lives of the Professors of Gresham College, 1740.

lectures delivered at the College.[68] The ordinances and agreements of the
foundation required the Professor of Rhetoric to lecture twice each Saturday
during term time, first in Latin from 8 a.m. to 9 a.m. (for the benefit of
foreign students) and then in English from 2 p.m. to 3 p.m.[69] Was Jonson
then for a time an actual (or acting) professor at Gresham College?

The fact that Jonson enjoyed an association of any kind with the College is
in itself intriguing, yet it is unlikely that he actually held any formal office
there in the way that was once imagined, or that the texts in question were
originally delivered as Gresham lectures. There is no trace in the records at
the College of Jonson's attachment to the institution or of a period of absence
by Henry Croke that might have required the services of a deputy professor.[70]
Croke was the youngest professor ever to have been appointed at Gresham
College, having succeeded his cousin Charles Croke as Professor of Rhetoric
on 26 May 1619 at the age of 23, on the strength of a testimonial written by

Students (including Robert Burton) at Christ Church, Oxford, where he had recently studied. He continued in post until 13 April 1627, when he resigned to make way for his even younger brother-in-law (aged 19), Edward Wilkinson.[71] In the early years of his appointment he might well have felt in need of advice and support from a more seasoned scholar such as Jonson, who might in turn have been recommended to him through common friends at Christ Church. In that case Jonson's role at Gresham could well have been unofficial and advisory, but sufficiently recognized by the College to enable him to cite the connection at his court appearance, as a boost to his credentials. Though Sisson believed that Jonson's *Discoveries* bore the stylistic marks of oral delivery—the repeated use of the first-person singular pronoun, the promise to explore certain topics at a later stage—he failed to realize that such passages were usually taken over verbatim from the sources that Jonson happened to be following at the time.[72] Jonson's commonplace book seems rather to be a continuation of those meditations and transcriptions—the 'twice twelve years' stored up humanity'—whose loss he had lamented in 'An Execration upon Vulcan'. Sisson's theory could at best apply only to certain parts of the *Discoveries*, for other passages are datable to a period well beyond 1627, when Croke was no longer attached to Gresham College.[73]

Jonson's approach to learning was nevertheless much in the spirit of Gresham College, and of the institution which the College helped eventually to establish: the Royal Society.[74] This intellectual affinity is partly due to Jonson's continuing association with Francis Bacon, whose writings were strongly to inspire the agenda of the Royal Society. Jonson's intimate acquaintance with Bacon's writings is evident throughout *Discoveries*, as is his endorsement of Bacon's ambition to purge learning of its 'defects' or 'distempers', to sweep away the 'cobwebs' of the schoolmen.[75] Jonson was on close and friendly terms with Bacon during the late 1590s, as already noted, and around the time of his contact with Gresham College was probably translating Bacon's essays into Latin.[76] He had written verses in celebration of Bacon's sixtieth birthday on 22 January 1621, and may have been present at York House to read this poem at the lavish banquet held that night in Bacon's honour, when his fortunes stood at their height:

> Hail, happy genius of this ancient pile!
> How comes it all things so about thee smile?

> The fire, the wine, the men! And in the midst
> Thou stand'st as if some mystery thou didst!...
> (*The Underwood*, 51.1–4)

A mere three months later Bacon was to be impeached on charges of corruption. By June 1621, having been stripped of the office of Lord Chancellor, he would 'retire from the stage of civil action and betake myself to letters'.[77] Jonson remained loyal to Bacon after his dramatic fall from grace. 'My conceit of his person was never increased toward him by his place or honours,' he wrote in *Discoveries* (673–9),

But I have and do reverence him for the greatness that was only proper to himself, in that he seemed to me ever by his work one of the greatest men, and most worthy of admiration, that had been in many ages. In his adversity I ever prayed that God would give him strength; for greatness he could not want. Neither could I condole in a word or syllable for him, as knowing no accident could do harm to virtue, but rather help to make it manifest.[78]

Elsewhere in *Discoveries* Jonson offers a resonant tribute to Bacon's extraordinary powers as an orator:

Yet there happened in my time one noble speaker who was full of gravity in his speaking. His language (where he could spare, or pass by a jest) was nobly censorious. No man ever spake more neatly, more pressly, more weightily, or suffered less emptiness, less idleness, in what he uttered. No member of his speech but consisted of the own graces. His hearers could not cough or look aside from him without loss. He commanded where he spoke, and had his judges angry and pleased at his devotion. No man had their affections more in his power. The fear of every man that heard him was lest he should make an end. (637–44)

This homage to Bacon comes at the very head of Jonson's *scriptorum catalogus*, a list of the most eloquent scholars the nation has ever known: a list that includes such names as Sir Thomas More, Sir Thomas Wyatt, Sir Philip Sidney, the Earl of Essex, Sir Walter Ralegh, Sir Henry Savile, concluding with the present Lord Chancellor, Lord Egerton ('a grave and great orator, and best when he was provoked'), but looping finally and admiringly back to Bacon himself: 'But his learned and able (though unfortunate) successor is he who hath filled up all numbers, and performed that in our tongue which may be compared or preferred either to insolent Greece or haughty Rome' (645–62). It is a powerful tribute, echoing the very words that Jonson had used of Shakespeare ('Leave thee alone for the comparison | Of all that insolent Greece or haughty Rome | Sent forth, or since did from their ashes come') and exuding the same sense of national excitement.[79]

§§

Jonson had likened King James on his first arrival in England to the Roman emperor Augustus, and as James's reign continued that analogy seemed to become increasingly justified. Suetonius reports that Augustus, seeing the buildings of Rome to be so vulnerable to fire and flood, judged the city unworthy of its great role as capital of the Roman empire. He undertook a methodical programme of rebuilding in the city, and could finally boast, 'I found Rome built of bricks; I leave her clothed in marble.' These words were remembered many centuries later by Samuel Johnson when speaking in *The Lives of the English Poets* of the achievement of John Dryden: 'What was said of Rome adorned by Augustus, may be applied by an easy metaphor to English poetry embellished by Dryden—*lateritiam invenit, marmoream reliquit,* he found it brick, and left it marble.'[80] James himself in the latter years of his reign had a perception about London similar to Augustus' view of Rome, and in a series of proclamations from 1619 declared that all new buildings in London should henceforth be seen as ornaments to the city, and constructed not of timber but of brick or stone. Inigo Jones and Thomas Howard, Earl of Arundel, were given oversight of this ambitious programme.[81] It would be tempting again, by the further application of an easy metaphor, to see Ben Jonson and Inigo Jones—despite their notorious quarrels—as engaged throughout the 1620s in a parallel and complementary set of activities leading to the creation of a new 'Augustan' Britain. Jones, through his oversight of James's urban building programme and through his own inspired architectural work—the new Banqueting House, the reconstruction of Somerset House and of Covent Garden, the Queen's House at Greenwich, the Cockpit theatre—helped to transform London into what Jonson (echoing the words of William Camden) had called 'the proper seat of empire' (*The King's Entertainment,* 20–1). Jonson, through his scholarly labours in the same decade—his historical and philological writings, his attempt to memorialize the lives of English worthies, his help in preserving and presenting the plays of William Shakespeare, his efforts to purify and regularize the English language, his confidence that Britain could outstrip the cultural and intellectual achievements of insolent Greece and haughty Rome—paralleled the endeavours of his old rival and collaborator Jones. Together they were laying the foundations of a new Augustan world.

18

Growing Old 1619–1626

Scholarship and creativity for Jonson went hand in hand, and the contacts he enjoyed with learned friends at Christ Church and Gresham College after his return from Scotland served also to stimulate his original writing in at times unpredictable ways. If his engagement with the theatre diminished during these years, his ambition to remain James's principal masque-writer did not. 'Next himself only Fletcher and Chapman could make a masque,' he had told William Drummond with some satisfaction at Hawthornden.[1] Since Jones and he had first collaborated to present *The Masque of Blackness* in 1604–5, Jonson had prepared at least one masque for every subsequent Christmas season, with only three interruptions to this regular pattern. In 1606–7, owing to the influence of the Howard family, he had been passed over in favour of Thomas Campion, who was invited to compose a masque to celebrate the wedding of James's Scottish courtier Lord Hay and his bride Honora Denny. In 1612–13, when Jonson was away on his European travels, Campion, Chapman, and Beaumont had been recruited to provide the court's Christmas entertainments. And during Jonson's recent absence in Scotland over the winter of 1618–19, George Chapman had again been asked to take his place, and had presented *The Masque of the Twelve Months* as part of that season's festivity—as Jonson no doubt already knew, while he talked with Drummond that Christmas at Hawthornden.

For all his confidence in his powers of invention, however, Jonson must also have known that his position at court was not wholly secure. Queen Anne, a keen promoter of his work in earlier years, was no longer living. He himself had not merely missed a whole season at court, but had produced for the previous season a work that—though destined to inspire John Milton in due course to write his own masque of Comus—had been poorly received by its immediate audience. *Pleasure Reconciled to Virtue* had presented Prince Charles for the first time as a principal masquer, and allowed the figure of Hercules to rebuke Comus the belly-god for his 'drunken orgies' and addiction to swinish pleasure. Performed at the Banqueting House with unhappy timing on 6 January 1618 at the outset of a Privy Council campaign led by Lionel Cranfield designed to reduce conspicuous spending at court, the masque had been seen as part of the current austerity drive, and judged severely as a consequence: 'the invention proved dull,' declared John Chamberlain dismissively; 'not worth the relating, much less the copying out', agreed Nathaniel Brent. Presented again on Shrove Tuesday that year in revised format with the addition of a new action (*For the Honour of Wales*), the masque failed yet again to satisfy its spectators.[2] Finding himself again commissioned to prepare a masque for the 1619–20 season, Jonson was under particular pressure to deliver.

'One of our greatest poets—I know not how good a one—went to Edinburgh o'foot, and came back,' Jonson boldly announced in the new masque, *News From the New World Discovered in The Moon*, performed at court on 6 January and 29 February, as if humorously to remind its audiences why they had not heard from him of late.[3] A high-spirited and cleverly inventive work, *News From the New World* seems to have gone down well at court, and helped to ensure Jonson's continuing employment in subsequent Christmas seasons throughout the final years of James's reign.[4] *A Discovery* was the title of the versified account of the Scottish journey that Jonson was attempting to write at that time; and *discovery* in the larger sense of the term was a notion of constant interest to Jonson, as well as a popular word at the moment, whether used in relation to the reportage of news, voyages of exploration, philosophical debate, or scientific learning: all themes that converged within Jonson's new masque. The greatest scientific discovery of Jonson's age, destined to validate the theories of Copernicus and confound all previous cosmologies, was that of the telescope. A principal object of the discoverers' attentions had been the surface of the moon, the world from which—so Jonson's masque playfully suggests—some new information is now to be reported. While the masque skilfully satirizes the absurdities and extravagances of the just-emerging news industry, it also light-heartedly celebrates the most powerful new toy of the age, by which knowledge of far-off places can now be conveyed: 'Oh, by a trunk! I know it, a thing no bigger than a flute case,' exclaims the Printer. 'A neighbour of mine, a spectacle-maker, has drawn the moon through it at the bore of a whistle, and made it as great as a drumhead twenty times, and brought it within the length of this room to me I know not how often' (70–3).[5]

On 13 March 1610, as if in anticipation of the action of this masque, Sir Henry Wotton had written excitedly from Venice to Robert Cecil to convey 'unto his Majesty the strangest piece of news (as I may justly call it) that he hath ever yet received from any part of the world'. He enclosed with the letter a book that had just been published, entitled *Sidereus Nuncius* (*The Starry Messenger*), by Galileo Galilei:

who by the help of an optical instrument (which both enlargeth and approximateth the object) invented first in Flanders and bettered by himself hath discovered four new planets rolling about the sphere of Jupiter, besides many other unknown fixed stars; likewise, the true cause of the *via lactea*, so long searched; and lastly, that the moon is not spherical, but endued with many prominences, and, which is of all the strangest, illuminated with solar light by reflection from the body of the earth, as he seemeth to say. So as upon the whole subject he hath first overthrown all former astronomy—for we must have a new sphere to save the appearances—and next all astrology. For the virtue of these new planets must needs vary the judicial part, and why may there not yet be more?[6]

Galileo's principal discovery was that the moon, so far from being a perfect orb hanging in a zone beyond all change and decay, was (in his own account) 'uneven, rough, and full of cavities and prominences, being not unlike the face of the earth, relieved by chains of mountains and deep valleys'.[7] Ten years on, this discovery was still astounding news, de-centring earlier concepts of the structure of the universe, and prompting speculation by scholars—such as Jonson's Christ Church friend Robert Burton, in his soon-to-be-published *Anatomy of Melancholy*—about the possible existence of other habitable worlds.[8] The appearance in the heavens late in 1618 of a new comet had fuelled further conjecture about the possibility of change in regions previously deemed immutable. 'Say, shall the old philosophy be true? | Or doth he ride above the moon, think you?', wrote Richard Corbett, in a verse letter to the mathematician Thomas Aylesbury (a former Christ Church student): 'Is he a meteor fired by the sun, | Or a first body by creation?' Burton was similarly fascinated by the advent of the comet, and was busily exchanging ideas about its significance with yet another Christ Church scholar, Edmund Gunter, now Professor of Astronomy at Gresham College.[9] These recent activities and observations in the heavens are likely to have been a topic of lively conversation at Christ Church during Jonson's recent stay in Oxford, and might well have prompted his choice of topic for the Christmas masque.

In *News From the New World Discovered in The Moon*—conscious, as ever, of the magnifying power of rumour itself, which (as Virgil had remarked) gains vigour as it goes—Jonson wittily explores the excitements and questions raised by these new sightings and discoveries,

First Herald	Of a new world—
Second Herald	And new creatures in that world.
First Herald	In the orb of the moon—
Second Herald	Which is now found to be an earth inhabited!
First Herald	With navigable seas and rivers.
Second Herald	Variety of nations, polities, laws.
First Herald	With havens in't, castles, and port towns!
Second Herald	Inland cities, boroughs, hamlet, fairs, and markets!
First Herald	Hundreds, and wapentakes! Forests, parks, cony-ground, meadow-pasture, what not?
Second Herald	But differing from ours. (102–13)

Behind this light-hearted fantasy lay more serious philosophical questions. Did the imperfections now revealed in and beyond the moon imply that the world itself was in a state of advanced decay, as John Donne and others at the time feared? The 'new philosophy calls all in doubt', Donne had written in *The First Anniversary*,

> The element of fire is quite put out;
> The sun is lost, and th'earth, and no man's wit
> Can well direct him where to look for it.
> And freely men confess that this world's spent,
> When in the planets and the firmament
> They seek so many new; they see that this
> Is crumbled out again to his atomies.
> 'Tis all in pieces, all coherence gone...[10]

The shock of the new made the world quite suddenly look old. The doubts that had afflicted John Donne also privately worried Ben Jonson. 'No wonder if the world, growing old, begin to be infirm', he wrote in his *Discoveries* during the 1620s, for 'old age itself is a disease. It is long since the sick world began to dote and talk idly. Would she had but doted still; but her dotage is now broke forth into a madness, and become a mere frenzy' (215–18). But was it the world that was growing old, or was it merely the individuals within it? 'I cannot think Nature is so spent and decayed that she can bring forth nothing worth her former years', he wrote, in contrary mood, elsewhere in *Discoveries*, 'She is always the same, like herself: and when she collects her strength, is abler still. Men are decayed, and studies: she is not' (89–91).

Behind such seemingly general meditations it is difficult not to feel also the pressure of Jonson's personal anxieties, as he thought not just of the world growing old but of his own inevitable decline. While still a young man he had worried about the pains of growing old. Barely out of his twenties, bereaved of his 7-year-old son, he recalled that the boy at least would not grow old: having 'so soon 'scaped world's and flesh's rage, | And, if no other misery, yet age' (*Epigrams*, 45.7–8). While still in his thirties he had seen himself as already ancient: 'my numbers are so cold, | When love is fled, and I grow old' (*The Forest*, 1.11–12). By 1624, now in his early fifties, he felt himself to be 'as Anacreon old' (85 years of age, if Lucian's account of the Greek poet's life is to be trusted). In perhaps the same year he described himself in *The English Grammar* (1.6.25–6) as an *elementarius senex*, 'an old teacher of rudimentary knowledge'.[11] While there is no doubt a touch of gentle mockery in all these self-descriptions, Jonson seems also to be seriously pondering the problem of continuing creativity during the latter stages of life. 'If we look upon him while he was himself (for his last plays were but his dotages),' John Dryden was to write of Jonson in a distinctly two-edged compliment later in the century, 'I think him the most learned and judicious writer which any theatre ever had.'[12] '*While he was himself*' implies an abrupt cessation of Jonson's literary power and indeed of his fundamental character in the years following the publication of his First Folio. This view of the sharply declining trajectory of Jonson's career during the last twenty years of his life—of a lurch from 'himself' to another, less congenial, anti-self—was widely repeated in critical commentary until quite recent times. Yet despite Jonson's troubling health and acute financial difficulties during this last period of his life, it is possible also to see these final years as remarkably fertile and inventive: as a time in which Jonson found out new ways to be 'himself'.

§§

What the comet of 1618 was also imagined to portend—coming as it did (in Sir Henry Wotton's words) 'in a time of such motion in Bohemia, distraction of opinion in the Low Provinces, divisions in the court of France, and no firm estate yet of Italy'—was the occurrence of catastrophic events both at home and abroad.[13] The death of Queen Anne fulfilled the first of these fears, while the troubles in Bohemia, marking as they did the onset of the Thirty Years War, seemed ominously to answer the expectation of foreign disaster. As Jonson prepared his masque for the 1620–1 season, the crisis in Bohemia and the Palatinate was arousing intense debate in England.[14] Bohemia had long been a part of the Holy Roman Empire, but over recent times the largely Protestant population of the country had been growing increasingly restive with Catholic domination by the Austrian Habsburg dynasty. On 23 May 1618, in a spectacular gesture of rejection known to history as the Defenestration, members of the Council of Bohemia had actually thrown two senior Habsburg officials, along with a secretary, from an upper window of a castle in Prague. A year later, with equal boldness, they deposed the newly elected Habsburg King of Bohemia, Ferdinand of Styria, and offered the throne of the country instead to James's son-in-law Frederick, the Emperor of the Palatinate. Protestants in Bohemia and across Europe eagerly prayed that Frederick would accept this invitation, but as Frederick well knew, the risks of acceptance—and of thereby inflaming the wrath of the Habsburgs—were immense. Frederick's eventual acceptance of the throne and the couple's entry into Bohemia stirred great excitement in England as elsewhere, but their tenure of the new kingdom was to be short-lived. In November 1620 Frederick's forces were to suffer a crushing defeat at the Battle of White Mountain outside Prague, and after barely a year's occupancy of the kingdom, he and his 'Winter Queen', Elizabeth, were driven from the country. Unable to retreat to the Palatinate, which by now was overrun by Spanish troops who had arrived under the command of their general Ambrogio Spinola to assist the Austrian Habsburgs, Frederick and Elizabeth sought refuge instead in The Hague. James had no funds to wage a continental war and was eager to maintain his reputation as the peacemaker of Europe. He had reluctantly permitted 2,000 English volunteers to travel to Bohemia, but this force had been quickly overrun by a contingent of 25,000 troops sent in by the Emperor Maximilian II of Bavaria. He placed his chief hopes now on a political marriage between Prince Charles and the Infanta Maria, daughter of King Philip III of Spain, which might lead to the withdrawal of the Spanish forces in central Europe, and the eventual return of the Palatinate to Frederick. Aware that this strategy was viewed with considerable distrust and hostility at home, however, James began also to prepare an alternative plan: a possible military intervention in the Palatinate, or a 'diversionary war' in the Spanish Netherlands, to place further pressure on Spain for the restoration of the Palatinate. He therefore recalled Parliament in 1621, knowing the mood of many amidst the so-called puritan faction to initiate a full-scale intervention in Europe. A parliamentary vote of funds for military action would at least show James's Spanish friends that England meant business, and perhaps (so he trustfully thought) lead the way to an early negotiated resolution.

Jonson's new masque, *Pan's Anniversary, or, The Shepherds' Holiday*, was performed at court on 6 January 1621, just a few days before the new Parliament was due to sit.[15] The masque is a pastoral entertainment featuring a dancing contest between 'certain bold boys of Boeotia'—a juggler, a corn-cutter, a bellows-mender, a tinderbox man, a clock-keeper, a maker of mousetraps, a tailor given to prophecy, and a clerk—and a group of grave Arcadians, led by Arcas (alias Prince Charles), who dance their opponents into submission. The Boeotians—a people traditionally represented as dull and thick-witted, here obviously identified with the puritan advocates for European war—finally return to the scene abjectly wearing sheep's heads. Having triumphed over this rabble, the Arcadians offer a hymn of praise to 'Great Pan, the father of our peace and pleasure, | Who giv'st us all this leisure' (206–7): an evident tribute to King James and his policies of peace.

> Pan is our All; by him we breathe, we live,
> We move, we are. 'Tis he our lambs doth rear,
> Our flocks doth bless, and from the store doth give
> The warm and finer fleeces that we wear.
>   He keeps away all heats and colds,
>   Drives all diseases from our folds,
>   Makes everywhere the spring to dwell,
>   The ewes to feed, their udders swell;
>   But if he frown, the sheep, alas,
> The shepherds wither, and the grass. (151–61)

For Jonson to have celebrated James's capacities, and, in particular, his role as a peacemaker, so wholeheartedly at this awkward political moment might seem at first surprising. He had close friends and allies in the new Parliament—such as his own patron, the Earl of Pembroke, and Pembroke's political spokesman in the Commons, Sir Benjamin Rudyerd—who viewed James's peaceful policies with mistrust, and who favoured a more aggressive approach to the problems of central Europe. Many years earlier, Jonson himself had fought in the Protestant cause in the Low Countries against the forces of Catholic Spain. But the praise of peace that Jonson presents in *Pan's Anniversary* is likely to have reflected his own personal hopes and preferences in the 1620s, rather than any craven attempt to maintain royal favour. He had little fondness for faction, or for the notion of an apocalyptic struggle waged by Protestant militants against the papal Antichrist, being now, as Drummond had observed, 'For any religion, as being versed in both'. He was increasingly anxious about the fissures now developing between crown and Parliament at home and between contesting powers abroad. 'Pan is our all': the solution to present troubles (so the masque implies) rests only with the King, as the grand executor of peace.[16]

§§

As it turned out, the Parliament of 1621 did not concentrate solely on the problems of the Palatinate and of the prospective Spanish match, but turned its collective attention also to a domestic issue: the abuses surrounding the handling of patents and monopolies. By May, Francis Bacon had been forced out of the office of Lord Chancellor, and the King's favourite George Villiers, Marquis of Buckingham, had been subjected to hostile questioning regarding monopolies he had procured for his half-brother Sir Edward Villiers and his brother Kit Villiers. Though Buckingham was not himself a major monopolist, his growing power and intimacy with the King were attracting increasing suspicion, as was his perceived involvement with Spanish interests. By mid-year Buckingham had successfully deflected the personal charges brought against him, but was clearly feeling the wear and tear of parliamentary attack; the French Ambassador described him and his followers as being in the grip of *une grande mélancolie*.[17] Jonson's next masque, *The Gypsies Metamorphosed*, was probably commissioned around this time in an attempt to lift his spirits. The most lively and popular of all Jonson's masques, *The Gypsies*

Metamorphosed delighted the King and court and was performed at three separate locations in the course of the year: first, on 2 August at Burley on the Hill in the county of Rutland; then two days later, in slightly reworked format, at nearby Belvoir Castle; and then in late September or early October for a third time in a more fully revised version at Windsor. Burley on the Hill was an estate that Buckingham had acquired after his marriage in 1620 to Katherine Manners, daughter of Francis Manners, sixth Earl of Rutland, the owner of Belvoir Castle. Jonson had stayed with Francis Manners at Belvoir on his way to Scotland in 1618. In order to oversee arrangements for the masque's presentation at Burley and Belvoir, he now journeyed north once again into the area he knew well from his long walk to Scotland: the accounts reveal that he was paid £13 for the provision of a horse—the equivalent of a modern scriptwriter's rental car, to take him from site to site—as well as a fee of £100 for composition of the masque.[18]

Jonson's inspired device in this new masque was to present the Duke of Buckingham and leading members of the court as gypsies, living on the margins of the law, thriving through their charm and mischievous agility. Depicting Buckingham in such a role served to deflect the more serious questions that had recently been posed about his possibly illicit handling of monopolies, and to portray him instead as an endearing rogue—in the teasingly complex sense of that term once proposed by William Empson, where glamour, affability, and an allowable element of transgression all combine.[19] In a departure from courtly tradition, which permitted courtiers to enter the action of the masque by dancing, but not through song or speech, Jonson gave his aristocratic performers on this occasion lines to deliver. Thus Buckingham, as Captain of the Gypsies, was allowed not only to make his customary entry leading the dances, but also boldly to take the King's hand, and pronounce his fortune:

> *Captain* Could any doubt that saw this hand,
> Or who you are, or what command
>   You have upon the fate of things,
> Or would not say you were let down
> From heaven, on earth to be the crown
>   And top of all your neighbour kings?
> To see the ways of truth you take
> To balance business, and to make
>   All Christian differences cease,

Or till the quarrel and the cause
You can compose, to give them laws,
   As arbiter of war and peace.
For this, of all the world you shall
Be styled James the Just, and all
   Their states dispose, their sons, and daughters,
And for your fortune, you alone,
Among them all shall work your own
   By peace, and not by human slaughters.
This little from so short a view
I tell, and as a teller true
   Of fortunes, but their maker, sir, are you. (239–59)

While this speech was no doubt relished both by the King and by his favourite, it served also to simplify what was in fact at this moment a highly complex political situation. Relations between the King and Parliament throughout the year had been tense and at times explosive. By November the Commons was petitioning James 'speedily and effectually to take your sword into your hand', to undertake a war against Spain, and to ensure that 'our most noble Prince may be timely and happily married to one of our own religion'. When their successive petitions were ignored by the King, the Commons drew up a formal protestation affirming what they believed to be their traditional parliamentary rights and privileges. The protestation so angered James that he came in person to the Council chamber to announce the dissolution of the Parliament and tear the page containing the protestation from the Commons journal with his own hands.[20]

For all its wit, adroitness, and learning, *The Gypsies Metamorphosed*, like the masques that were shortly to follow, could barely conceal the political quarrels and fault-lines that were now becoming increasingly evident throughout the kingdom.[21] During these contentions Jonson was awkwardly placed. He is likely to have felt some sympathy with the arguments of his patriot friends in the Lords and Commons and—never a lover of Spain—to have had little trust in the likely success of current negotiations with Madrid; yet he also clearly shared James's wish to avoid if possible any military engagement in Europe. At the same time, as his 'Epistle to a Friend to Persuade Him to the Wars'—written around 1620 (see Ch. 5, 93 above)—makes plain, he keenly felt the attractions of recruiting for the

European wars, whose excitements offered a stark contrast to the emotional torpor of London.

> It is a call to keep the spirits alive
> That gasp for action, and would yet revive
> Man's buried honour in his sleepy life,
> Quickening dead nature to her noblest strife.
> (*The Underwood*, 15.5–8)

This scarcely amounted to a coherent political position, as Jonson must have been acutely aware. Peace (so one part of him declared) was the ultimate goal of the moment, yet war (so another internal voice maintained) was the most exhilarating option. At times he professed wholesale indifference to the burning political issues of the day, vowing a deeper attachment to matters of personal conduct and friendship. 'What is't to me whether the French design | Be or be not to get the Valtelline?' he wrote in 'An Epistle Answering to One that Asked to be Sealed of the Tribe of Ben' during the late summer or early autumn of 1623,[22]

> Or the States' ships sent forth belike to meet
>   Some hopes of Spain in their West Indian Fleet?
> Whether the dispensation yet be sent,
>   Or that the match from Spain was ever meant?
> I wish all well, and pray high heaven conspire
>   My prince's safety and my king's desire;
> But if for honour we must draw the sword,
>   And force back that which will not be restored,
> I have a body yet that spirit draws
>   To live, or fall a carcass in the cause.
> (*The Underwood*, 47.31–42)

Yet Jonson could hardly remain long detached from the questions which he here insists are none of his business. For the coming Christmas season he would be required to produce a masque celebrating Charles and Buckingham's expected return from Madrid in the company of the Prince's new bride-to-be, the Infanta Maria. By the autumn, however, it was clear that negotiations for the Spanish match had collapsed. On 5 October 1623 Charles and Buckingham arrived back in England without the Infanta, to scenes of huge national rejoicing. Jonson's new masque, *Neptune's Triumph for the Return of Albion*, designed for presentation on Twelfth Night 1624, had now

to celebrate a 'triumph' of a different kind from the one originally anticipated: the return of a Protestant hero, rather than the prospective husband of
a Catholic bride.[23] The role of a court poet, forced, as circumstances dictated,
to write in glorification of such contrary political outcomes, was not an easy
one to sustain. Nor was this the end of Jonson's problems with the new
masque, which threatened now to cause dire offence to the ambassadors of
the two countries that James was trying most earnestly to please: Spain and
France. Jonson had included 'many jests against the Spaniards' in the antimasque of *Neptune's Triumph* which now had to be removed.[24] Trouble then
broke out on the other political flank, as the French Ambassador—who,
according to diplomatic protocol, was expected not to come to the Twelfth
Night masque that year—announced his intention of attending the performance, and insisted he be given equal status to that of his Spanish counterpart.
James soon realized that it would be impossible to please both parties, and
that any performance of *Neptune's Triumph* would further expose the embarrassingly different foreign policies held by his son (who was attempting to
woo French interests) and himself. The masque was postponed to Shrovetide,
on the excuse that the King was indisposed, and then, the stalemate
continuing, abandoned altogether.[25]

Jonson must have found the entire experience acutely trying. 'Let me be
what I am,' he wrote in evident exasperation about this time in a poem that
expresses a further unease with the world of the court in which he had now
lived 'twenty year',

> Where I may handle silk as free and near
> As any mercer, or the whale-bone man
>   That quilts those bodies, I have leave to span;
> Have eaten with the beauties and the wits
>   And braveries at court, and felt their fits
> Of love and hate, and came so nigh to know
>   Whether their faces were their own or no ...
>   ('An Elegy', *The Underwood*, 42.29–36)

Jonson's prolonged closeness to the centres of political power, like his literal
closeness to the beauties and wits and braveries at court (handling their silks,
measuring their bodies, scrutinizing their faces as they ate and laughed) was
an experience that Jonson had begun to find not only thrilling but also
repugnant. He had no real wish to abandon his career as masque-writer at

court, yet he may have begun to think again around this time with renewed interest about a kind of work he had not undertaken for nearly a decade: writing for the stage.

§§

The Staple of News, Jonson's first work for the theatre since 1616, was performed at Blackfriars theatre in February 1626, and later the same month (probably at Shrovetide, 19–21 February) at the court of the newly crowned Charles I. James VI and I had died after a short illness on 27 March 1625, and in early May had been given a spectacular funeral, 'the greatest indeed that ever was known in England', reported John Chamberlain, 'there being blacks distributed for above 9,000 persons, the hearse likewise being the fairest and best fashioned that hath been seen, wherein Inigo Jones the Surveyor did his part'.[26] Further grand public events had been planned to usher in the new regime: a welcome to Charles's new French bride, Henrietta Maria; the royal marriage; the coronation of the new King and Queen, with a procession through the streets of London, in which five triumphal arches had been erected: one in Gracechurch Street by the Dutch community from the Dutch church at Austin Friars, who had recruited Jonson to help prepare their greeting to the royal couple. But a severe outbreak of the plague throughout the summer months had led to the postponement of these planned events. Charles was nevertheless crowned King of England in a somewhat curtailed ceremony at Westminster Abbey (Henrietta Maria being absent) on 2 February 1626, just a few days before the first performance of *The Staple of News* in London.[27] This event is referred to in the play itself, whose action is seen as occurring (in characteristically Jonsonian fashion) in the historical present, 'Now, at the coronation' (3.2.301). As the comedy opens, the young prodigal Pennyboy Junior 'draws forth his watch and sets it on the table', waiting for it to chime and usher in the moment of his majority. In a play so much concerned with questions of inheritance and patrimony, it is tempting to glimpse a veiled allusion, in the apparent death of Pennyboy Senior, to the recent death of James, and in the figure of Pennyboy Junior, 'the Golden Heir', to the problems of Charles's succession.[28]

However precisely such features are to be read—for Jonson at this stage of his career was skilled in the arts of denial and deflection—*The Staple of News* is a play that clearly exploits the powerful attractions of the *now* and the *new* in the London of 1626. The play itself is presented as a theatrical novelty: 'Mark but his ways,' says the Prologue of the author, 'What flight he makes, *how new*' (The Prologue for the Stage, 27–8). Jonson valued the presence of newness in his own work and that of others, and spoke scathingly of those whose tastes ran behind the times, who yearned after the theatrical models of an earlier generation.

He that will swear *Jeronimo* or *Andronicus* are the best plays yet shall pass unexcepted at here, as a man whose judgement shows it is constant and hath stood still these five and twenty or thirty years. Though it be an ignorance, it is a virtuous and staid ignorance; and next to truth, a confirmed error does well: such a one, the author knows where to find him. (*Bartholomew Fair*, Induction, 79–84)

Newness too was a quality valued in contemporary empirical enquiry, as the very titles of Bacon's works (*The New Organon*, *The New Atlantis*) testified.[29] Yet Jonson was wary about those who sought after newness for its own sake, like the antimasque characters Ears, Eyes, and Nose in *Time Vindicated To Himself and His Honours*: 'We only hunt for novelty, not truth' (214). 'Expectation of the vulgar is more drawn and held with newness than goodness,' Jonson wrote in *Discoveries*, 'we see it in fencers, in players, in poets, in preachers, in all where fame promiseth anything; so it be new, though never so naught and depraved, they run to it and are taken' (292–5).

For many years Jonson had satirized a particular aspect of this 'hunt for novelty': the insatiable English appetite for *news*.[30] 'Pray you, what news, sir, vents our climate?', Sir Politic Would-be had asked the traveller Peregrine in *Volpone* (2.1.18), in a greeting said to have been typical of Englishmen at this time whenever they met.[31] By 1620, however, the year of Jonson's *News From the New World Discovered in The Moon*, news was beginning to circulate in Britain in a rather different way, through the medium of print: initially in the form of small Dutch broadsheets written in English known as corantos, bearing reports, characteristically with a strong anti-Catholic bias, about current events in continental Europe. These in turn soon encouraged the production of similar publications by local syndicates in London.[32] In Jonson's *News From the New World* a character named 'The Factor' is said to dispatch printed news in weekly bulletins throughout the shires: a form of business that does not seem yet to have existed in England, though Jonson could imagine it happening any time soon.[33] In *The Staple of News*, building inventively once again on hints provided by contemporary practice, Jonson envisages an office or 'Staple' of news—ironically referred to as 'The House of Fame'—that operates rather in the manner of a modern news agency, with its correspondents (or 'emissaries') strategically located at key centres through-out the metropolis: the court, St Paul's, the Royal Exchange, Westminster Hall. From these vantage points they 'fetch in the commodity', dispatching to the Staple their various items of gossip, fantasy, and speculation, which are marketed then as 'news', being priced according to their relative rarity and interest. Ambrogio Spinola, so the emissaries report, has been appointed General of the Jesuits, who have presented him with a machine to hoist himself up into the moon 'And thence make all his discoveries!' The King of Spain has been chosen as Pope, and as Emperor too. A burning glass has been found in Galileo's study 'To fire any fleet that's out at sea'. An 'invisible eel' has been invented by 'one Corneliuson' 'To swim the haven at Dunkirk and sink all | The shipping there' (1.2.51; 3.2.36–43, 21–5, 52–5, 59–62).

The satire here is complex. While the play openly ridicules the fabrications and distortions of the emerging news industry, it also registers a certain fascination with some of the more exciting discoveries and inventions of the day. Burning glasses—large convex lenses that could be used to concen-trate the sun's rays and ignite fires in particular locations—had been used in naval warfare since classical antiquity, and had now, with the availability of superior lenses, become a subject of renewed scientific enquiry. Galileo is not known to have experimented with them, though he was certainly inter-ested in the potential usefulness of the telescope in naval warfare. But Jonson's friend William Drummond was experimenting with these devices at Hawthornden at precisely this time, and later in 1626 would apply for a three-year patent to manufacture 'A set of Burning Glasses of different kinds, by which, at whatever distance, whether on land or sea, any combustible stuffs, out of all reach of shot, may be set on fire'.[34] The 'Corneliuson' who is said to have invented 'the invisible eel' is the Dutch mechanical engineer Cornelis Drebbel, inventor of the perpetual motion machine at Eltham to which Jonson several times refers in his writings. Around 1620 Drebbel had constructed a rudimentary submarine propelled by oars within which he had travelled adventurously down the Thames from Westminster to Greenwich. Jonson is likely to have known Drebbel, who had been employed in the service of James and of the young Prince Henry early in James's reign, and often assisted with technical preparations for court entertainment. Jonson and Drebbel might also have met at Gresham College, as Drebbel was a friend of Henry Briggs, Gresham Professor of Geometry, who had in turn been closely acquainted with John Napier of Merchiston (the inventor of logarithms), another pioneer of submarine warfare and expert on burning glasses.[35]

Through his wide and unusual network of acquaintances, Jonson was in touch not only with scholars engaged in traditional fields of humanist enquiry but also with those working in the rapidly evolving areas of the new science. Though it has been suggested that Pennyboy Junior's plan in *The Staple of News* (4.4.82) to establish a 'Canter's College' may imply Jonson's disapproval of the educational programme provided by Gresham College, the seedbed of the Royal Society, the reverse seems more likely to have been the case. Gresham, with its broad sevenfold programme of study, seems rather to have served as a stimulus both to Jonson's scholarship and to his creative imagination. What he ridicules in *The Staple of News* is not Gresham College itself or the fields of study it promoted, but the reductive notion of a college devoted merely to the study of 'canting' (the specialized terms of art used by various social groups).[36]

Jonson viewed the new science with deep fascination, touched with occasional amusement and sardonic prophecy. Through alert observation of the latest discoveries and developments of his day, he could glimpse at moments aspects of the world in which we live today: see how the syndication of news, the fighting of wars, the conquest of space, the organization of finance might in time develop, and in time be corrupted. His mind was trained not only on the lessons of the past, but on the possible shape of the future. He was in this sense part of that new world that he also intermittently satirized.

§§

Yet as Jonson himself was acutely aware, there was another, less flattering, way of viewing his present state. By 1626 he might also be seen—as he allowed the Gossips in *The Staple of News* to report him—as a writer well past his prime: physically, mentally, and creatively spent. Towards the end of Jonson's comedy it is announced that the Staple of News has just blown up, and is now 'broke! Broke! Wretchedly broke!', 'all to pieces, quite dissolved!' (5.1.38–9). The author of the play, so the Gossips suggest, has perhaps suffered a similar fate, and also exploded: gone to pieces, failed his audiences,

Mirth	Bankruptly, indeed!
Censure	You say wittily, gossip, and therefore let a protest go out against him—
Mirth	A mournival of protests, or a gleek at least—
Expectation	In all our names—
Censure	For a decayed wit—
Expectation	Broken—
Tattle	Non-solvent—
Censure	And forever forfeit—
Mirth	To scorn of Mirth!
Censure	Censure!
Expectation	Expectation!
Tattle	Subsigned, Tattle. (Intermean 4.5; 60–71)

The suspicion that he might now be bankrupt (in more senses than one) returns with uneasy insistence in Jonson's work from this point on. "Tis true, I'm broke! Vows, oaths, and all I had | Of credit lost,' he writes in a poem probably composed about this time ('An Elegy', *The Underwood*, 38.1–2). 'I am now like an old bankrupt in wit, that am driven to pay debts on my friends' credits, and for want of satisfying letters, to subscribe bills of exchange,' he writes to his patron William Cavendish, Earl of Newcastle, in February 1631 (Letter 18.5–7). "Tis not alone the merchant, but the clown | Is bankrupt turned; the cassock, cloak, and gown | Are lost upon account!', he writes in his 'Epigram to our Great and Good King Charles on his Anniversary Day' in 1629, linking his personal state to that of the (by now, deeply indebted) nation at large; 'And none will know | How much to heaven for thee, great Charles, they owe!' (*The Underwood*, 64.19–22).[37]

But if Jonson's years were advancing and his physical resources diminishing, his creative talents were not yet totally exhausted.

19

Dying Late 1626–1637

An engraving of Jonson by Robert Vaughan made in or around 1627 shows a
scraggily bearded, heavily built figure, plainly dressed and crowned with
laurel, staring gloomily through an oval border whose inscription proclaims
him *doctissimi poetarum anglorum*, the most learned of English poets
(Fig. 48). The melancholy look may perhaps reflect the sharp decline in
Jonson's health that had occurred around the middle of the decade. Already a
heavy though decidedly athletic man at the time of his walk to Scotland, he
may by now have put on further weight; in 1626 Gossip Expectation in *The
Staple of News* described him as 'a huge overgrown play-maker' (Intermean,
4.6). In his 'Epistle on My Lady Covell', probably written about this time,
Jonson speaks glumly of himself as

> . . . a tardy, cold,
> Unprofitable chattel, fat and old,
> Laden with belly, and doth hardly approach
>   His friends, but to break chairs or crack a coach.
> His weight is twenty stone within two pound,
> And that's made up as doth the purse abound.
>   (*The Underwood*, 56.7–12)[1]

Some time in 1628 Jonson (as he later reported to his patron William
Cavendish) was 'strucken with the palsy', a phrase generally interpreted to
mean that he had suffered a paralytic stroke.[2] The onset of this illness 'made a
deep impression upon his body and his mind', according to Edward Hyde,
the future Earl of Clarendon, who had made Jonson's acquaintance in the

399

Fig. 48. Robert Vaughan's engraved portrait of Jonson, *c*.1627.

autumn of 1625 when he came as a young student to the Middle Temple, 'and stood at gaze, and irresolute what course of life to take'.[3]

A further dramatic occurrence in Jonson's life throws incidental light on his physical and mental state in 1628. On 23 August of that year the Duke of Buckingham, erstwhile favourite of James and close confidant of the present

King, was fatally stabbed while at Portsmouth by a professional soldier named John Felton. Felton had personal as well as political quirks and grudges which drove him to this act, which caused widespread rejoicing throughout much of the country. Buckingham's unpopularity had by this time achieved startling proportions. He had been closely identified with James's hated pro-Spanish policies, and accused of wielding too much power at court, of selling offices and honours, of obtaining titles for members of his family, of harbouring Catholic sympathies, of bungling recent military expeditions to Cadiz and Rhé, and of poisoning James on his deathbed. Many in England welcomed his assassination as a timely deed, and poems and ballads in praise of John Felton circulated throughout the country. It was suspected that one poem in particular, addressed 'To his Confined Friend, Mr Felton', might have been written by Jonson himself. Though it might seem prima facie unlikely that Jonson could have written in praise of a Protestant fanatic who had just assassinated his patron, he had never shown great fondness for Buckingham, and his friends John Selden and Robert Cotton had been outspoken critics of Buckingham's power and conduct. The verses in question, discovered in Cotton's house, urge the assassin, in the face of torture, to recall the power of stoical endurance. The tone of this advice is certainly characteristic of Jonson himself.[4]

> Enjoy thy bondage; make thy prison know
> Thou hast a liberty thou canst not owe
> To those base punishments; keep entire, since
> Nothing but guilt shackles the conscience.
> I dare not tempt thy valiant blood to weigh,
> Enfeebling it with pity, nor dare pray
> Thy act may mercy find, lest thy great story
> Lose somewhat of its miracle and glory.
> I wish thy merit laboured cruelty;
> Stout vengeance best befits thy memory,
> For I would have posterity to hear
> He that can bravely do, can bravely bear;
> Tortures may seem great in a coward's eye;
> 'Tis no great thing to suffer, less to die . . .

On 26 October Jonson was formally interrogated by the Attorney-General Sir Robert Heath about the verses, and asked whether he had ever seen them.

He answereth that he hath seen the like verses to these; and being asked where he saw them, he saith at Sir Robert Cotton's house at Westminster. Being further asked upon what occasion he saw them at that time, he saith that coming in to Sir Robert Cotton's house as he often doth, the paper of these verses lying there upon the table after dinner, this examinant was asked concerning those verses, as if himself had been the author thereof. Thereupon this examinant read them, and condemned them, and with deep protestations affirmed that they were not made by him, or had ever seen or heard them before, and the like protestations he now maketh upon his Christianity and hope of salvation.

Being asked about the authorship of the verses, Jonson responded that

he hath heard by common fame that one Mr Townley should make them, but he professeth truly that he cannot name any one singular person who hath so reported it. Being asked of what quality that Mr Townley is, he saith his name is Zouch Townley; he is a scholar and a divine by profession, and a preacher, but where he liveth or abideth he knoweth not, but he is a Student of Christ Church in Oxford.

Zouch Townley, who seems likely indeed to have been the author of these verses, was one of Jonson's Christ Church friends and Deputy Orator at Oxford; in 1623 he had delivered one of the two Latin orations given in the University on the death of William Camden. By the time of the interrogation, as Jonson must have been aware, Townley was fleeing to Holland, and unlikely to suffer as a result of Jonson's deliberately vague testimony. When he eventually returned to England, the two men's friendship continued apparently unabated.[5]

Some aspects of this episode remain mysterious: why the examination was ever initiated in the first place; why suspicion had fallen on Jonson; why Jonson, two nights after hearing Townley preach at St Margaret's Westminster, had arranged to have supper with him, and had presented him with 'a dagger with a white haft which this examinant ordinarily wore at his girdle' and to which Townley had evidently taken a liking.[6] What may reasonably be concluded is that Jonson (like Cotton, Selden, and Townley) was amongst the large group in England who saw Buckingham's death as constituting, in political terms, a relief rather than a disaster.

The incident also offers an intriguing glimpse into Jonson's customary routines at this time, 'coming in to Sir Robert Cotton's house as he often doth' from his house in Westminster to dine, inspect books, and exchange literary and political gossip—and perhaps on this occasion read with some

satisfaction the latest libellous verses circulating about Buckingham and his
assassin. Jonson's house near the Abbey belonged to the Dean and Chapter,
and 'stood between St Margaret's Church and Henry VII's Chapel and was
formerly known as the Talbot. It consisted of four rooms on the ground, first,
and second floors, with garrets over them. . . . One of the rooms on the first
floor is particularly described in a deed of sale of 1650 as being "over the
passage leading from the old Palace into the churchyard".'[7] It was sub-let to
an old lady with whom Jonson boarded at this time. That he could still walk
with ease the short distance from this house to Cotton's suggests that by this
stage of the year his stroke (if such it was) had not yet occurred. Later he
would find it more difficult to get about. In his 'Epistle Mendicant' written to
the Lord High Treasurer, Richard Weston, first Earl of Portland, in 1631 he
speaks of himself as wholly confined to his house and to his bed; likening
himself, in an extended metaphor, to a besieged city: surrounded, undermined, immobilized, starved of essential supplies, waiting for the end.

> Disease, the enemy, and his engineers,
> Want, with the rest of his concealed compeers,
> Have cast a trench about me, now, five years;
>
> And made those strong approaches, by faussebraies,
> Redoubts, half-moons, horn-works, and such close ways,
> The muse not peeps out one of hundred days;
>
> But lies blocked up, and straitened, narrowed in,
> Fixed to the bed and boards, unlike to win
> Health, or scarce breath, as she hath never been,
>
> Unless some saving honour of the crown
> Dare think it, to relieve, no less renown
> A bed-rid wit than a besiegèd town.
> (*The Underwood*, 71.5–15)

Yet Jonson was evidently still capable of leaving the house from time to time.
Writing early in 1631 to William Cavendish about the progress of a projected
second volume of his *Works* he complains about the delays of 'the lewd
printer', John Beale, adding with grim humour:

My printer and I shall afford subject enough for a tragicomedy, for with his delays and vexation I am almost become blind; and if heaven be so just in the metamorphosis to turn him into that creature he most assimilates, a dog with a bell, to lead me between Whitehall and my lodging, I may bid the world good night. (Letter 15.11–15.)

Troubled with poor vision, Jonson is still taking pains to read the proofs of his work with care, and is still able to walk, with whatever difficulty, through the streets of Westminster. If only Beale were his guide-dog rather than his printer, he murmurs, life might be a lot easier. On 3 May 1632 Jonson is recorded as having been amongst the group of esquires who walked in the funeral procession of Sir John Lemmon, former Lord Mayor of London, 'from Grocers' Hall to St Michael's Church in Crooked Lane', in company with a number of City dignitaries including the Town Clerk, the Auditor, the Beadle, and the Chamberlain.[8]

Financial necessity may have prompted his participation in this last event. On 2 September 1628 the City of London Court of Aldermen had appointed Jonson as Chronologer to the City in succession to the recently deceased dramatist Thomas Middleton. Jonson's duties would have been identical to those specified for Middleton: 'to collect and set down all memorable acts of this City and occurrences thereof' and be ready 'for such other employments as this Court shall have occasion to use him in', but not to print anything so written 'without the allowance and approbation of the Court'. In return Jonson was to receive 100 nobles (£33 6s. 8d.) a year.[9] When appointed to this post in September 1620, Middleton had been the first writer to receive an annual salary from the City of London for recording contemporary events in this way.[10] Coming in addition to Jonson's royal pension and annual benefactions from Pembroke and other patrons, along with payments for court masques and (on occasions) plays, this sum should have helped to provide Jonson with a modest but steady income. But whether on account of illness or indifference to the task in hand, Jonson failed to perform his required duties as City Chronologer, and on 10 November 1631 the Court was obliged to order 'that Master Chamberlain shall forbear to pay any more fee or wages unto Benjamin Jonson the City's Chronologer, until he shall have presented unto this Court some fruits of his labours in that his place'. Jonson noted this freeze on payment in a stinging postscript in a letter to Cavendish on 20 December (the unwelcome news having taken some time to reach him): 'Yesterday the barbarous Court of Aldermen have withdrawn their chanderly pension for verjuice and mustard, £33.6.8d' (Letter 17.40–1). Walking in Sir John Lemmon's funeral procession five months later must have been for Jonson a calculated act to show he was now more fully engaged with his civic duties.

During the last decade of his life Jonson was constantly troubled by a real or imagined shortage of money. Generous friends and patrons were often at hand, however, to help him. On 19 January 1629, not long after the advent of his palsy, the Dean and Chapter of Westminster Abbey granted Jonson £5 'in his sickness and want', probably at the initiative of the former Lord Keeper, Bishop John Williams, who had lost office after being markedly at odds with the policies of both Buckingham and Charles, and whom Jonson had praised in *The Underwood*, 61 for his moral and political integrity. In March of the same year Jonson thanked King Charles himself for a larger gift: 'A Hundred Pounds He Sent Me in My Sickness' (*The Underwood*, 62). In 1630, in response to a begging verse letter from Jonson—'The Humble Petition of Poor Ben, to the Best of Monarchs, Masters, Men, King Charles' (*The Underwood*, 76)—Charles converted Jonson's royal pension from 100 marks per year (£75) to £100, with the welcome addition of 'one Terse of Canary Spanish wyne yearly'. (A tierce was 42 gallons.[11]) On 3 November 1631 Queen Henrietta Maria made an *ex gratia* payment to Jonson of £40 'In consideration of pains taken by him in other service upon several occasions of masques and otherwise', the warrant being countersigned by the Queen's secretary Sir Robert Aytoun, a man who Jonson knew 'loved him dearly' (*Informations*, 120).[12] On 18 September 1634 the Court of Aldermen ordered the restoration of Jonson's pension as City Chronologer and the payment of 'all arrearages thereof', possibly at the prompting of another of Jonson's friends, Edward Sackville, Earl of Dorset (now Henrietta Maria's Lord Chamberlain), who had helped Jonson generously in the past.[13] Other friends and acquaintances lent Jonson money from time to time; some (including his protégé Nathan Field and the classical scholar Thomas Farnaby) being eventually obliged to take legal action in order to secure repayment.[14] Jonson at times settled his debts with other creditors by assigning them future portions of his royal pension.[15]

Why then should Jonson, with so many friends and benefactors to assist him, have found himself in such financial need during these years? Jonson's own grumbling explanation was that poverty was endemic to his calling: 'Of all his plays he never gained two hundred pounds,' he told Drummond, who also noted that 'He dissuaded me from poetry, for that she had beggared him, when he might have been a rich lawyer, physician, or merchant' (*Informations*, 446, 493–4). Yet Jonson's sources of income were more numerous and diverse than he was always ready to acknowledge, and in absolute terms he was not as impoverished as he professed to be.[16] Payment of the royal pension, it is true, was often tardy, as Jonson at times had occasion sharply and beseechingly to remind the officers of the Exchequer.

Father John Burges
Necessity urges
My woeful cry
To Sir Robert Pye:
And that he will venture
To send my debenture.
Tell him his Ben
Knew the time when
He loved the muses,
Though now he refuses
To take apprehension
Of a year's pension,
And more is behind:
Put him in mind
Christmas is near,
And neither good cheer,
Mirth, fooling, nor wit
Nor any least fit
Of gambol or sport
Will come at the court,
If there be no money;
No plover or cony
Will come to the table,
Or wine to enable
The muse or the poet,
The parish will know it.
Nor any quick warming-pan help him to bed:
If the 'chequer be empty, so will be his head.

(*The Underwood*, 57)

The main reason for Jonson's habitual poverty however was very simple: he enjoyed living generously. 'The use of things is all, and not the store,' says Pennyboy Canter in the final scene of *The Staple of News* (5.6.26), voicing a sentiment dear to Jonson's heart. Izaak Walton (reporting gossip from George Morley of Christ Church, Oxford, later Bishop of Winchester) gives a revealing glimpse of Jonson during his final years, sharing his pensions with 'a woman that governed him with whom he lived and died near the Abbey in Westminster; and that neither he nor she took much care for next week, and would be sure not to want wine, of which he usually took too much before he went to bed, if not oftener and sooner'.[17] James Howell, Jonson's next-door neighbour during his last years in Westminster, speaks of a 'solemn supper' given by Jonson in the 1630s in which 'there was good company, excellent cheer, choice wines, and jovial welcome', thanking him on another occasion 'for the last *regalo* you gave me at your *musaeum*, and for the good company'.[18] Jonson's complaints about poverty during this period of his life are in any case not always (perhaps) to be taken entirely literally: a certain exaggeration was perfectly in order in begging letters, so Erasmus had advised, to show 'how useless modesty is to a person in need' and how urgently relief was required.[19] Such letters called for art, wit, and at times a modicum of invention.

One of Jonson's most touching appeals for financial help was directed in 1631 to William Cavendish, Earl of Newcastle, Jonson's generous patron and benefactor during his last years (Letter 17). Another thoughtful friend, Sir Thomas Badger (so Jonson reports in this letter), had recently presented him with a pet fox, 'which creature, by handling, I endeavoured to make tame, as well for the abating of my disease as the delight I took in the speculation of his nature'. One morning that week Jonson had had a dream, in which a servant had come to his bedside, saying 'Master, master, the fox speaks.'

Whereat, methought, I started; and troubled, went down into the yard to witness the wonder. There I found my Reynard, in his tenement, the tub I had hired for him, cynically expressing his own lot, to be condemned to the house of a poet, where nothing was to be seen but the bare walls, and not anything heard but the noise of a saw, dividing billets all the week long, more to keep the family in exercise than to comfort any person there with fire, save the paralytic master; and went on in this way, as the fox seemed the better fabler of the two.

The fox then informs his master that the cellar is infested with moles. The royal mole-catcher is fetched, but says there is nothing he can do; only the King 'or some good man of a noble nature must help you'. 'This kind of mole is called a want, which will destroy you and your family, if you prevent not

the working of it in time; and therefore, God keep you and send you health.'
A 'want' is a species of mole, and *want* (so Jonson punningly continues) now
undermines the house in which he lives.

The interpretation both of the fable and dream is that I, waking, do find want the
worst and most working vermin in a house; and therefore my noble Lord and (next
the King) my best patron, I am necessitated to tell you. I am not so impudent to
borrow any sum of Your Lordship, for I have no faculty to pay; but my needs are
such, and so urging, as I do beg what your bounty can give me, in the name of good
letters, and the bond of an ever-grateful and acknowledging servant.

To your honour,
B. Jonson

Like the verses just quoted to John Burges, the letter to Cavendish is
dispatched expectantly in 'the week ushering Christmas'. Confessing one's
poverty, asking for aid, are not easy tasks, but in such witty and inventive
appeals Jonson during this late period of his life converted these hard
necessities to a minor art, avoiding self-pity and proving paradoxically
that—in terms at least of his rhetorical skills—he was less bereft than his
protestations might suggest.

§§

Jonson presents himself in this letter as living in deep solitude, where
'nothing was to be seen but the bare walls, and not anything heard but the
noise of a saw'. The house in which he lived at this time actually stood at a
central and busy location at the very heart of Westminster, near the Abbey,
the school, and the Great Hall: one of the four 'Cardinal Quarters' in *The
Staple of News* from which news is gathered, 'the field | Where mutual frauds
are fought, and no side yield', as he had once described it in a poem addressed
to Sir Anthony Benn, Recorder of London (*The Underwood*, 33.3–4). Friends
are likely to have called in regularly to see him, and he would not have been
starved of news and gossip. Nor was he forgotten by more distant benefactors
such as Cavendish himself, whose friendship he had enjoyed for many years:
'my best patron', as Jonson more than once called him.[20] Cavendish was by
now Earl of Newcastle upon Tyne and Lord Lieutenant of Derbyshire, and
one of the wealthiest men in the kingdom, with vast estates in the north of
England including his principal seats of Welbeck and Bolsover, where Jonson

had visited him on his way to Scotland. Being ambitious for court favour, he now spent time also in London, and around 1630 commissioned Robert Smythson to build him a town house in Clerkenwell. The relationship between patron and poet was based on mutual affection and regard. Cavendish was twenty years younger than Jonson, and a skilled fencer and horseman; Jonson had praised his skills in two epigrams later published as *The Underwood*, 53 and 59. He had inherited his father's great love of music, and throughout the 1630s employed at least five musicians and maintained a fine collection of musical instruments at Welbeck. He had a passion for architecture, and had taken extensive pains in the decoration of the Little Castle at Bolsover. He was an aspiring dramatist who modelled his practice in part on Jonson's own work: his comedy *Wit's Triumvirate, or The Philosopher*, written for performance before Charles and Henrietta Maria in the winter of 1635–6, has echoes of *The Alchemist*. 'No person since the time of Augustus better understood dramatic poetry,' wrote the theatrical historian Gerard Langbaine of Cavendish later in the century, 'nor more generously encouraged poets, so that we may truly call him our English Maecenas. He had a more particular kindness for that great master of dramatic poesy, the excellent Jonson, and 'twas from him that he attained to a perfect knowledge of what was to be accounted true humour in comedy.'[21]

During the 1630s William and his mathematically talented younger brother Charles encouraged the work of a distinguished group of experimental philosophers, including William's chaplain Robert Payne and his friend Thomas Hobbes, in the fields of optics, mathematics, and mechanics. Robert Payne was a graduate of Christ Church, Oxford, who, disappointed in his hopes to secure a Studentship at the College or to succeed Edmund Gunter as Professor of Astronomy at Gresham College in 1626, had come instead into Cavendish's employment, where he worked in close association with Hobbes. Both Payne and Hobbes were on intimate terms with Jonson. In a letter to Cavendish in 1633 Jonson spoke of Payne as his 'beloved friend', 'than whom Your Lordship could not have employed a more diligent and judicious man, or that hath treated me with more humanity' (Letter 19.3, 12–15). Jonson was in turn (as John Aubrey testifies) Hobbes's 'loving and familiar friend and acquaintance'. The intellectual interests of the three men were closely linked. Hobbes invited Jonson (along with his friend Robert Aytoun) 'to give their judgement on his style of his translation of Thucydides', published early in 1629, and it is possible that other areas of Hobbes's writing were influenced by conversations with Jonson and observation of his dramatic practice. Jonson's own thinking on questions of political organization is likely in turn to have been affected by contact with Hobbes—whom Jonson (so it has been suggested) may have represented in the character of Fitz-Ale, possibly played by Hobbes himself, in Jonson's *Entertainment at Welbeck* in 1633.[22]

Both Hobbes and Jonson were tenuously associated during the 1630s with another intellectual circle whose centre lay at the Oxfordshire village of Great Tew, home of Lucius Cary, Lord Falkland, 'a person of such prodigious parts of learning and knowledge' (as his friend Edward Hyde wrote after his death), 'of that inimitable sweetness and delight in conversation, of so flowing and obliging a humanity and goodness to mankind, and of that primitive simplicity and integrity of life, that if there were no other brand upon this odious and accursed civil war, than that single loss, it must be most infamous, and execrable to all posterity'. A dedicated Greek scholar who had studied closely the writings of the Greek historians and church fathers, Lucius Cary had 'contracted familiarity and friendship with the most polite and accurate men of [Oxford] university', who 'frequently resorted and dwelt with him, as in a college situated in a purer air; so that his house was a university bound in a lesser volume'.[23] Jonson is unlikely ever to have taken part in these famous gatherings, which occurred at Great Tew from 1634, when he was not in a fit state to move about the country. Hobbes too was away on the Continent from 1634 to 1636 but may have visited Great Tew after that date. Jonson and Cary are likely to have first met in London shortly after Cary's return from Ireland in 1629. It is possible Jonson had occasional contact in London with other members of the group, which included the theologians William Chillingworth, Henry Hammond, and George Morley, the Greek scholar John Hales, and the poets Sidney Godolphin, Edmund Waller, and Sir John Suckling. Jonson would certainly however have found congenial the central tenets of the Great Tew circle, especially as expressed through the writings of Chillingworth and Cary, who opposed war and violence, tolerated dissent, and (in line with the teachings of the Italian-born theologian Faustus Socinius) valued the application of reason in all questions of religion, looking for a middle path between the Roman and reformed faiths. Cary's mother, the formidable Lady Falkland, had recently converted to Catholicism and was herself a passionate converter of others, translating into English the writings of Cardinal Duperron, the outspoken advocate for Rome with whom Jonson had had his memorable encounter in Paris.[24] Hers was an influence Cary did his utmost to resist. Royalist in sympathy, pacific in temper, sceptical in discourse, wishing to distance themselves from the current 'brawls which were grown from religion', the Great Tew circle were in many respects a losing force in England of the 1630s, yet represented a position with which Jonson could broadly identify during the final years of his life. It is clear from Hyde's account that Jonson also received financial support from Cary at this time, being one of several 'whose fortunes required, and whose spirits made them superior to, ordinary obligations'.[25]

Jonson developed about this time another close and lasting friendship, with the scholar and adventurer Sir Kenelm Digby. Kenelm was the son of the mild-mannered conspirator Sir Everard Digby, executed in 1606 for his part in the Gunpowder Plot. Everard was said to have been in his day the handsomest man in all England. Kenelm himself was an equally striking figure: 'a man of very extraordinary person and presence', as Edward Hyde later recalled, 'which drew the eyes of all men upon him, which were more fixed by a wonderful graceful behaviour, a flowing courtesy and civility, and such a volubility of language that surprised and delighted.'[26] 'He was such a goodly handsome person,' John Aubrey similarly noted, 'gigantic and great voice, and had so graceful elocution and noble address etc. that had he been dropped out of the clouds in any part of the world he would have made himself respected.'[27] Kenelm Digby had been brought up as a devout Catholic, and despite a brief conversion to Protestantism in 1630 maintained a strong interest in the Roman faith to which he formally returned a few years later. As a young man he had studied for a time at Gloucester Hall, Oxford, with the noted mathematician and astrologer Thomas Allen, who at his death in 1632 bequeathed to Digby his extensive collection of scientific manuscripts. These Digby housed in a specially constructed wing of his house in Clerkenwell along with his own fine collection of manuscripts, and later donated to the Bodleian Library in Oxford. He had a wide range of scholarly interests, was an eager reader of English poetry, and admired in particular the work of Edmund Spenser, whose natural successor he believed Ben Jonson to be: 'when divine Spenser's sun was no sooner set,' he wrote, 'in Jonson a new one rose with as much glory and brightness as ever shone withal.'[28]

It is not known when Jonson and Digby first met, but their friendship seems to have flourished from 1629, when Digby returned to London after a couple of years of semi-authorized privateering in the Mediterranean, attacking and plundering ships from Spain and France, with whom England was now at war. Kenelm was at this time devotedly married to the celebrated beauty Venetia Stanley, with whom he had had a prolonged and tumultuous romance. Early in the couple's relationship, Kenelm's mother, who disapproved of the match, had dispatched him on the Grand Tour in the hope of ending the affair. In Paris, however, Digby had unwittingly caught the eye of the middle-aged Queen Mother, Marie de Médicis, whose unwelcome advances he attempted to avoid by fleeing the city, and then spreading a rumour that he had been killed in action. The news of his death reached Venetia in London, but his letters assuring her that he was still alive did not. In time she took up despairingly with other men, becoming the mistress first of Sir Edmund Wyld and then of Richard Sackville, third Earl of Dorset, with whom she had one or more children. Richard's younger brother Edward (Jonson's patron and friend) was said also to have been infatuated by her, and to have proposed marriage. After Digby's eventual return to London in 1623 he and Venetia met again, and in 1625, despite his mother's continuing disapproval, were secretly married.

Jonson's 'Epigram to My Muse, Lady Digby, on her Husband, Sir Kenelm Digby' (*The Underwood*, 78), probably written in the early 1630s, warmly praises Digby's personal qualities, and recalls his naval victories in the Mediterranean. It also suggests an easy intimacy in the couple's relationship both with each other, and with the ageing poet.

> Go, muse, in, and salute him. Say he be
>   Busy, or frown at first, when he sees thee
> He will clear up his forehead, think thou bring'st
>   Good omen to him in the note thou sing'st,
> For he doth love my verses, and will look
>   Upon them (next to Spenser's noble book)
> And praise them, too. Oh, what a fame 'twill be!
>   What reputation to my lines and me,
> When he shall read them at the Treasurer's board!
>   The knowing Weston, and that learnèd lord
> Allows them! Then what copies shall be had,
>   What transcripts begged! How cried up, and how glad,
> Wilt thou be, muse, when this shall them befall!
>   Being sent to one, they will be read of all. (19–32)

'Fame' is associated here not with the production of a printed book—a form of publication about which (as already noted in Chapter 7) Jonson entertained decidedly mixed feelings—but with the private circulation of his poems in manuscript amongst such discerning friends as the Digbys and Lord Treasurer Richard Weston, another influential patron of Jonson's during the last decade of his life.[29]

§§

Jonson's commitment to the theatre throughout these final years was intermittent, ambivalent, and marked by misadventure. None of the last three plays of Jonson's to be performed within his lifetime was accounted a success. *The New Inn*, performed by the King's Men at the Blackfriars theatre in late January or February 1629, was a resounding disaster. Jonson himself attributed its failure to the carelessness of the players and the malice of his critics: the comedy (so the title page of the 1631 octavo text of the play sternly declared) 'was never acted, but most negligently played, by some, the King's Servants, and more squeamishly beheld and censured by others, the King's subjects'. The critics themselves associated the failure of the play, performed soon after the onset of Jonson's palsy, with his 'decaying' health and 'declining wit'.[30] In the play's epilogue Jonson spoke openly of his illness, and with uncharacteristic misgiving foresaw the possible rejection of the piece: 'All that his faint and faltering tongue doth crave | Is that you not impute it to his brain. | That's yet unhurt, although set round with pain' (7–10). It is usually assumed that Jonson could not have been present at Blackfriars to witness this debacle, but at this time (as just noted) he was still capable of getting around the town, and his comments on the performance of individual actors and on the behaviour of the play's audience (and their 'confidence in rising between the acts, in oblique lines') may well be based on first-hand observation rather than report.

Despite its initial failure and nearly four centuries of neglect, *The New Inn* is a play with remarkable theatrical power, as Anne Barton compellingly argued a generation ago, and as John Caird's subsequent production of the play for the Royal Shakespeare Company soon confirmed.[31] Yet the play represents so startling a departure from the comic style of Jonson's early maturity that it is not altogether surprising that its original audience felt a sense of puzzlement and disorientation. The action of *The New Inn* takes place not in the city, the classic locus of Jonsonian comedy, but in a hostelry in the town of Barnet, eleven miles north of London on the Great North Road. The events are contrived not (in the usual Jonsonian fashion) by a group of scheming male tricksters but by a clear-sighted young woman, the chambermaid Prudence, who (in Jonson's words) 'is elected sovereign of the sports in the inn, governs all, commands, and so orders as the Lord Latimer is exceedingly taken with her, and takes her to his wife in conclusion'. Love is the force that—once more, uncharacteristically for Jonson—drives the play, and that forms a principal topic of disputation throughout its central acts, which are shaped by the traditions of Neoplatonism and medieval courtly debate. And the dénouement of the play, to compound its seemingly un-Jonsonian nature, draws on the time-honoured conventions of romance that, since his early venture into comedy in *The Case Is Altered*, Jonson had studiously avoided and seemingly scorned. Lord Beaumont reveals that he has just married a young woman at the inn named Laetitia, only to be told that his apparent wife is in fact a boy who has been dressed as a girl as part of the day's sports, and who is the son of Goodstock, the host at the inn. Trumping this announcement, an ancient Irish nurse, pulling the black patch from her eye, then reveals that she is Goodstock's long-lost wife who has been living undetected at the New Inn these past seven years, and that this apparent boy is their long-lost child: who (she insists) is not a boy but—as the doubly astonished Lord Beaumont now hears to his relief—a girl after all.

At the centre of the play are the speeches on the nature of valour delivered by Lovel—'a complete gentleman, a soldier, and a scholar' and 'a melancholy guest in the inn'—in the court of love pleadings organized by chambermaid Pru, queen of the day's sports. True valour, so Lovel maintains, is displayed not in the field of battle, but in the face of 'poverty, restraint, captivity, | Banishment, loss of children, long disease: | The least is death' (4.4.106–9). These were adversities of which Jonson himself had some acquaintance, either personally or through the experience of his closest friends. The character of Lovel, with his fondness for riding, fencing, 'letters, arms, | Fair mien, discourses, civil exercise' (1.3.44–52), has sometimes been seen as an admiring if glancing portrait of Jonson's patron William Cavendish. But Lovel's stress on the value of enduring hardship, avoiding aggression, and distancing oneself from the tumults of the time is also close to the emerging philosophy of Lucius Cary and other members of the Great Tew circle.

> A calm wise man may show as much true valour
> Amidst these popular provocations
> As can an able captain show security
> By his brave conduct through an enemy's country.
> A wise man never goes the people's way,
> But as the planets still move contrary
> To the world's motion, so doth he to opinion. (4.4.210–16)[32]

At such a moment early in 1629, on the eve of Charles's summoning of his last Parliament before the start of his eleven-year period of personal rule, such a reference to 'popular provocations' would have been seen to allude to the political agitations of the day. The exchanges between Lady Frampul and Prudence elsewhere in *The New Inn* (2.6.125–38, 249–5) concerning the legitimate extent of Pru's powers as queen of the day's sports appear to refer in similar fashion to the current constitutional crisis. 'Prince Power will never want her parasites,' says Lady Frampul in the tones of a discontented parliamentarian, as she complains about Prue's use of her newly conferred sovereign authority; 'Nor Murmur her pretences,' Prudence responds with regal dignity, putting the protester in her place (2.6.138–9). In a number of poems addressed to the King later in the same year Jonson condemns popular opinion in the same dismissive fashion. 'What can the poet wish his king may do, | But that he cure the people's evil too?', he writes in an epigram thanking Charles 'for a Hundred Pounds He Sent Me in My Sickness' (*The Underwood*, 62.13–14); the 'people's evil' probably referring to the outcry that followed Charles's proroguing of the Parliament amidst scenes of disorder in March of 1629. Such discontent is seen as an illness akin to scrofula (the 'king's evil'), and he wishes despairingly that Charles might cure it. 'O times! O manners! Surfeit bred of ease, | The truly epidemical disease!' he writes in Ciceronian fashion in another epigram addressed to the King on his anniversary day (27 March 1629), noting, again dismissively, the popular 'murmur' against Charles's political conduct (*The Underwood*, 64.17–18).

'Come, leave the loathèd stage,' Jonson wrote in a famous 'Ode: To Himself' after the failure of *The New Inn*,

Leave things so prostitute,
  And take the Alcaic lute,
Or thine own Horace, or Anacreon's lyre;
    Warm thee by Pindar's fire:
And though thy nerves be shrunk and blood be cold
    Ere years have made thee old,
  Strike that disdainful heat
  Throughout, to their defeat:
As curious fools, and envious of thy strain,
May, blushing, swear no palsy's in his brain.

  But when they hear thee sing
  The glories of thy king,
His zeal to God, and his just awe o'er men,
    They may, blood-shaken, then
Feel such a flesh-quake to possess their powers,
    As they shall cry: 'Like ours
  In sound of peace or wars
  No harp e'er hit the stars
In tuning forth the acts of his sweet reign,
And raising Charles's chariot 'bove his wain.' (41–60)

The vigorous commitment of these concluding stanzas is remarkable: Jonson is vowing not merely to quit the stage, but to devote his remaining energies to celebrating Charles and 'the acts of his sweet reign'. It has been suggested that Jonson's writing during the final period of his life was strongly coloured by nostalgia for the age of Elizabeth, and a general habit of retrospection.[33] But whatever fondness the late plays may show for earlier social customs and practices in England, it is worth recalling that Jonson was never entirely at ease with the political climate of Elizabeth's reign. His Caroline writings are more sharply attuned to contemporary events, and more strongly committed to the ideology of Charles's court than such a reading would suggest. Jonson was never as close temperamentally to Charles as he had been to his father, yet he remained substantially loyal to Charles's often unpopular policies throughout the 1630s and admiring of (and dependent on) his often unpopular counsellors, such as Richard Weston, whose power to 'stint the strife | Of murmuring subjects' he praises in a late poem (*The Underwood*, 77. 18–19).[34]

It was not with the King that Jonson's quarrel ultimately lay, but with the profession in which he had long reigned supreme: the loathèd stage.

Yet Jonson's departure from the stage proved only temporary. On 20 September 1632 the news-writer John Pory—with whom Jonson had spent time in Paris nearly twenty years earlier—informed Sir Thomas Puckering that 'Ben Jonson (who, I thought, had been dead) hath written a play against next term called *The Magnetic Lady*'.[35] Jonson's comedy *The Magnetic Lady: Or, Humours Reconciled* was licensed on 12 October, and performed not long afterwards by the King's Men at Blackfriars. Alexander Gil the younger, whose father Jonson had satirized in his masque *Time Vindicated to Himself and to his Honours* in 1623, attended an early performance along with two other former victims of Jonson's satire, Inigo Jones and Nathaniel Butter, in what seems to have been an orchestrated attempt to disrupt the play, which Gil scoffingly dismissed in doggerel verses as the product of Jonson's 'bedridden wit': a verdict that provoked sharp replies from Jonson himself and his friend Zouch Townley.[36] The final Chorus of *The Magnetic Lady* is said to have been 'changed into an epilogue to the King', but there is no record of a court performance. Later in the century *The Magnetic Lady* was 'generally esteemed an excellent play', yet despite some appreciative appraisals in recent times its performance record through to modern times has remained exceedingly sparse.[37]

Why did Jonson return to the loathèd stage in 1632, having seemingly bidden it a definitive farewell just three years earlier? There is no very obvious answer to this question, but a guess or two might be hazarded. It is possible that Jonson came to feel some unease at having broken off his long career in the theatre in 1629 in such an impetuous and dismissive way. *The Magnetic Lady* might be seen as his attempt to review and round off that career in a more harmonious fashion, and depart more peaceably from a profession in which he had worked for nearly forty years. In the Induction to the play the Boy who serves as the author's apologist sketches the progress thus far of his dramatic career.

Boy The author, beginning his studies of this kind with *Every Man In His Humour* and after, *Every Man Out of His Humour*, and since, continuing in all his plays, especially those of the comic thread whereof *The New Inn* was the last, some recent humours still, or manners of men, that went along with the times, finding himself now near the close or shutting up of his circle, hath fancied to himself in idea this magnetic mistress. A lady, a brave, bountiful housekeeper and a virtuous widow, who, having a young niece ripe for a man and marriageable, he makes that his centre attractive to draw thither a diversity of guests, all persons of different humours to make up his perimeter. And this he hath called *Humours Reconciled*.

Probee A bold undertaking! And far greater than the reconciliation of both churches, the quarrel between humours having been much the ancienter and, in my poor opinion, the root of all schism and faction, both in church and commonwealth. (75–89)

The Boy's mention here of 'the comic thread' recalls Jonson's adeptness in constructing Terentian plots of high narrative complexity, and the skill required in observing their development; for 'a good play', the Boy goes on, 'is like a skein of silk which, if you take by the right end, you may wind off at pleasure on the bottom or card of your discourse in a tale or so, how you will. But if you light on the wrong end, you will pull all into a knot or elf-lock, which nothing but the shears or a candle will undo or separate' (Induction, 105–9).[38] But the figure also hints at a continuity and consistency within Jonson's own comic writing, from the play he liked to see as marking the start of his dramatic career, *Every Man in His Humour*, through to the present moment.

What Jonson is spinning here is not merely another humours comedy but a narrative about his own creative life, whose thread (as he knows) is shortly to be cut. It is a simplifying narrative, which suppresses the elements of experimentation and also of failure within his dramatic work, suggesting a smooth progression from the start of his theatrical career to its conclusion. Like the figure of the compass which returns in a double capacity throughout the play—as a draughtsman's instrument that draws the perfect circle, and the mariner's instrument that points unerringly to the north—it suggests a degree of stability and cohesion within Jonson's work and life that he had never wholly achieved.[39] Jonson is performing the 'shutting up of his circle' in a seemingly placid manner, as if his angry rupture with the stage following the failure of *The New Inn* had never taken place.

'Where's one o' your masters, sirrah, the poet?', asks the hostile critic, Damplay in the Induction to *The Magnetic Lady*. 'Sir, he is not here,' answers the Boy, 'But I have dominion of the shop for this time under him, and can show you all the variety the stage will afford for the present.' Jonson probably did not get to see his own play in performance at Blackfriars on this occasion, though his presence is strongly felt throughout *The Magnetic Lady*, perhaps the most self-referential of all his writings.[40] The conversations between the

Boy, Damplay, and Probee that take place between the acts serve to direct the audience's responses not just to the play they are currently watching, but to Jonson's work as a whole. The author's past practice and opinions are constantly recalled throughout the play: 'Oh, he told us that in a prologue long since,' Damplay remarks casually at one point, after hearing some advice from the Boy (2 Chorus, 23). Even Jonson's style of dress at one point attracts a comment: 'his clothes shall never be the best thing about him, though; he will have somewhat beside, either of human letters or severe honesty, shall speak him a man though he went naked' (1 Chorus, 42–4). The characters within the play prove also to be familiar with Jonson's writings: the foppish courtier Sir Diaphanous Silk has read Lovel's speeches on valour from *The New Inn*, and assumes that Captain Ironside will know the play too. In an even bolder moment of theatrical self-consciousness, Master Compass remarks at one point that the rhyming speech he has just uttered was written by none other than the author of this play: 'Ben Jonson made it' (1.2.33–4).

The Magnetic Lady thus serves in part as a biographical fable, reminding its audiences of Jonson's own prolonged engagement with the theatre, and concluding, like the principal action of the play itself, in a spirit of reconciliation. The author who had impulsively left the loathèd stage just three years ago has now returned with a new offering. The fable is something of a romance, like the main action itself of *The Magnetic Lady*, in which Mistress Placentia, the presumptive heiress of the comedy, and her waiting-woman Pleasance turn out to have been exchanged as infants in their cradles, while Sir Moth Interest, the dislikeable usurer who controls his niece's fortunes, tumbles to the bottom of a well, from which he ultimately emerges contrite and 'A little wet'. Only through the agency of such conventions, it seems, can the humours—those fundamental differences of human character and temperament that had long formed the staple of Jonson's comedy, and are now (in Probee's view) the root cause of the 'schism and faction, both in church and commonwealth' that trouble England in the 1630s—ever be reconciled. Only through such conventions, likewise, can the enmity between Jonson and his audiences—represented here by the stubborn Damplay ('I care not for marking the play: I'll damn it, talk, and do that I come for,' 3 Chorus, 19–20)—ever be suspended.

Despite such touches of romance and retrospection and Jonson's seeming seclusion at the time of its composition, *The Magnetic Lady* is a play that is remarkably attuned to the contemporary world of London in 1632. Jonson is alert, as ever, to the new science: in his references to magnetism, the central metaphor of the play, he shows familiarity with current magnetic theory, including the writings of two scholars who had died just a few years previously (Lady Lodestone is teased for imagining they are still alive): the physician Mark Ridley—who had collaborated with Henry Briggs of Gresham College, brother of Jonson's friend Richard Briggs—and William Barlow, former chaplain and tutor to Prince Henry.[41] His allusions to other fields of knowledge in the play—mathematics, military strategy, law, politics, finance, medicine, and diplomacy—are similarly knowledgeable and up to date.[42] He is sharply aware of current theological controversy. Some malapropistic references by Dame Polish in the first act of the play to Arminianism—the liberal doctrines of the Dutch theologian Jacobus Arminius, disliked by Calvinists at this time and often associated with the high church preferences of Archbishop Laud and his followers—seem to have touched a nerve with ecclesiastical authorities, causing the play to be the subject of prolonged investigation from November 1632 to October 1633. Jonson's satire appears to be directed (it has recently been suggested) at Laudian practices at the London church of St Bartholomew-by-the-Exchange, whose rector, Dr John Grant, was the son of Jonson's former headmaster at Westminster School, Edward Grant. Such references reveal Jonson's ability to map out his late drama, as in the days of his early maturity, 'with a microscopic particularity'.[43] However this rich and long neglected play is finally to be judged, *The Magnetic Lady* is hardly the work of a dramatist out of touch with the society in which he lived. Bedridden though he may have been, his curiosity about the world beyond his house in Westminster was undiminished, as was his capacity to gather in the news.

A Tale of a Tub, the last of Jonson's plays to have been performed in his lifetime (by Queen Henrietta's Men at the Cockpit theatre, Drury Lane: licensed 7 May 1633), shows an equally remarkable acquaintance with Laudian practices within a particular but representative London parish, St Pancras, and the proclivities of its vicar, John Elborow; and with the tensions and nuances of local government within the (similarly representative) community of Finsbury to the north of London.[44] How did the largely house-bound Jonson manage to acquire such precise local knowledge at this late stage of his life? Partly perhaps through gossip with friends and acquaintances calling at his house, but also possibly through the impetus of his work as City Chronologer, despite the fact that the location of *A Tale of a Tub* lies beyond the central area of London whose activities Jonson had been commissioned by the City to record. It may indeed be the case, as the Oxford editors conjectured, that Jonson located his last comedies outside the central London area precisely in order to avoid offending the city fathers who were now his paymasters, and that, ironically, his work as Chronologer finally put an end to his writing of city comedy.[45] But this employment may also have spurred his enthusiasm for gathering material, in the style of his great mentor William Camden, about contemporary events within a wider geographical area; this scholarly work in turn stimulating Jonson's creativity, and extending, surprisingly, his career as a dramatist. In the character of D'ogenes Scriben of Chalcot, 'the great writer' in *A Tale of a Tub* who zealously collects local records and who tries unsuccessfully to collaborate with In-and-In Medley, the *architectonicus professor*, in the composition of the play's concluding wedding masque, Jonson may be glancing humorously (as we shall see) at his own present condition.[46]

A Tale of a Tub was for many years assumed to have been a very early work of Jonson's, to which he gave the finishing touches in his final years; Herford and Simpson accordingly placed the play at the very head of the dramatic canon in the Oxford *Ben Jonson*. The Oxford editors' assumptions about the dating and nature of the work were convincingly refuted in 1984 by Anne Barton, whose argument that the play, in its sophisticated handling of apparently naive material, is essentially a product of Jonson's late maturity is now widely accepted.[47] *A Tale of a Tub* presents a series of comic wooings and cross-wooings that occur on St Valentine's Day in and around the villages of Tottenham, St Pancras, Finsbury, Kentish Town, Hampstead, Canonbury, and St John's Wood in what were at that time the rural fringes of London. In the play's prologue Jonson presents the piece with characteristic insouciance as a simple and harmless farce.

> No state affair, nor any politic club
> Pretend we in our tale, here, of a tub,
> But acts of clowns and constables today
> Stuff out the scenes of our ridiculous play.
> A cooper's wit, or some such busy spark,
> Illumining the High Constable and his clerk
> And all the neighbourhood, from old records
> Of antique proverbs, drawn from Whitsun-lords,
> And their authorities at wakes and ales,

With country precedents and old wives' tales,
We bring you now, to show what different things
The cotes of clowns are from the courts of kings.

Despite this final disclaimer, *A Tale of a Tub* in its earliest format had been seen by one complainant as presenting all too clear a parallel between the cotes of clowns and the courts of kings, as the play's final licence for performance by the Master of the Revels, Sir Henry Herbert, reveals:

R[eceived]. for allowing The Tale of the Tubb, Vitru Hoop's parte wholly struck out, and the motion of the tubb, by commande from my lorde chamberlin; exceptions being taken against it by Inigo Jones, surveyor of the kings works, as a personal injury unto him. May 7, 1633,—2*l*.0.0.[48]

The relationship between Jones and Jonson had seldom been tranquil, but had deteriorated steadily since Charles's accession, as Jonson sensed Jones's growing dominance and his own waning power at court. Their two final masquing collaborations, *Love's Triumph Through Callipolis* (9 January 1631) and *Chloridia* (22 February 1631), had nevertheless been marked by fresh energy and invention, both masques showing the guiding influence of Henrietta Maria, and ingeniously incorporating new structural elements derived from French *ballets de cour* as they depicted the royal marriage as a harmonious and richly symbolic union.[49] Yet the publication of these masques had also reignited the long-running quarrel between these two brilliant but egotistical collaborators. Jones had been wounded to find that his own name came second to Jonson's on the title page of *Love's Triumph* and *Chloridia* ('The inventors: Ben Jonson, Inigo Jones'). Jonson's irritation at his collaborator's wish to monopolize credit for the masques must have been evident in the original version of *A Tale of a Tub* to which Jones—satirically depicted here as 'Vitruvius Hoop'—objected. Traces of the spat remain in the revised version of the play, where D'ogenes Scriben, invited to write the final wedding masque with In-and-In Medley, remarks that any collaboration with this man is impossible:

He'll do't alone, sir; he will join with no man,
Though he be a joiner. In design, he calls it,
He must be sole inventor. In-and-In
Draws with no other in's project, he'll tell you;
It cannot else be feasible, or conduce... (5.2.35–9)[50]

Jonson's anger extended into a series of heavily sarcastic poems directed against the King's Surveyor: 'An Expostulation with Inigo Jones', 'To Inigo, Marquis Would-be: A Corollary', and 'To a Friend: An Epigram of Him' (*CWBJ*, vol. 6). The circulation of these poems soon began however to cause difficulty for Jonson at court, as his friend and neighbour James Howell warned him tactfully at the conclusion of a friendly letter in 1631: 'I heard you censured lately at court, that you have lighted too foul upon Sir Inigo, and that you write with a porcupine's quill, dipped in too much gall. Excuse me that I am so free with you, it is because I am in no common way of friendship' (Letter (i)). Evidently Jonson chose to ignore this warning, and continued to circulate copies of 'An Expostulation' amongst his friends. Howell was driven to write again, this time more firmly:

> ... your ink was too thick with gall, else it could not have so bespattered and shaken the reputation of a royal architect; for reputation, you know, is like a fair structure long time a-rearing but quickly ruined. If your spirit will not let you retract, yet you shall do well to repress any more copies of the satire; for to deal plainly with you, you have lost some ground at court by it, and as I hear from a good hand, the King, who hath so great a judgement in poetry as in all other things, is not well pleased therewith. (Letter (j))

The reputation that was most bespattered and shaken in this episode—as Howell's letter may indeed imply—was not that of the royal architect (who was much in favour at this moment, and at the end of that year began to receive a supplementary annual payment of £20 for his work at the Queen's Surveyor) but that of the royal poet, who received no further commissions to write court masques.[51] Jonson's evident desire to continue the feud with Jones may help to explain why *A Tale of a Tub* was 'not likte' when presented at court on 14 January 1634.[52]

Jonson was nevertheless to write two more entertainments in the 1630s for his patron William Cavendish, Earl of Newcastle, that show no diminishment either of his artistry or of his capacity to maintain his grudge with Inigo Jones. The first of these was presented before the King at Welbeck Abbey, Nottinghamshire, on 21 May 1633, as he journeyed north to Scotland for his coronation; the second, at Bolsover Castle, Derbyshire, on 30 July 1634, when Charles, now accompanied by Henrietta Maria, stayed for six nights with Cavendish during part of the couple's summer progress.[53] Cavendish, who was angling at the time for court employment, spent immense sums on his entertainment of the King on both these occasions (£20,000, according to the possibly inflated reckonings of his second wife Margaret), attracting the eloquent disapproval of Edward Hyde.[54] Jonson himself did not travel north this time to supervise arrangements for either entertainment, but was well familiar with the locations from earlier visits, and seems likely (as his subsequent correspondence with Cavendish implies, Letter 19) to have discussed details of their staging with Cavendish's chaplain Robert Payne. Through the comical characters of Humphrey Fitzale, the herald and antiquary of Derby, and ABC Accidence, schoolmaster of Mansfield, in *The King's Entertainment at Welbeck,* Jonson invokes local traditions of Robin Hood, Sherwood Forest, and the wonders of the Peak that he had first encountered in this region on his journey by foot to Scotland in 1618.

In *The King and Queen's Entertainment at Bolsover*—now with Charles and Henrietta as his captive audience, and at a safe distance from possible interference by the Lord Chamberlain or the Master of the Revels—Jonson boldly resumed his quarrel with Inigo Jones, Surveyor of the King's Works, unmistakeably figured in the pompous character of 'a surveyor, your Colonel Vitruvius'.

Do you know what this is now? A supervisor! A hard word, but it may be softened and brought in, to signify something. And overseer! One that over-see-eth you. A busy man! And yet I must seem busier than I am, as the poet sings, but which of them I will not now trouble myself to tell you. (36–40)

The 'poet' in question happens to be Chaucer, writing in the prologue to *The Canterbury Tales* about the Man of Law (who always 'seemed bisier than he was'): Jones's knowledge of English poetry, Jonson implies, is as imperfect as is his command of Latin. But then a competence in poetry, as he bitterly complains later in the entertainment, will get you nowhere at court.

Oh, that rhyme is a shrewd disease and makes all things suspected it would persuade. Leave it, pretty Cupids, leave it. Rhyme will undo you and hinder your growth and reputation in court more than anything beside you have either mentioned or feared. If you dabble in poetry once, it is done of your being believed or understood here. (134–8)

Jonson is here reprising a theme from the 'Expostulation':

> Oh, to make boards to speak! There is a task!
> Painting and carpentry are the soul of masque.
> Pack with your peddling poetry to the stage:

> This is the money-get, mechanic age! (49–52)[55]

Jonson knew very well that in his long, highly productive, highly tempestuous collaboration with Jones, he himself (along with 'peddling poetry') had finally been defeated. But he also knew very well how, within this quarrel, to put in the last word.

§§

'Your son and contiguous neighbour', was how James Howell had signed, as usual, one of his letters to Jonson, warning of the dangers of his continuing squabbles with Inigo. There were many young men in England who now regarded themselves as Jonson's sons, and the tribe of Ben was beginning to swell to biblical proportions.[56] Reassuring though it no doubt was to have so many youthful followers, Jonson must have been keenly aware of the growing gap in age between himself and so many of these disciples. As he passed his sixtieth year in 1633, the principal members of the Great Tew circle (for example) were all still in their early twenties. In late July or August 1629, Lucius Cary's close friend Sir Henry Morison had died unexpectedly at Carmarthen of smallpox, on or near his twenty-first birthday. In his moving and intricate Ode 'To the Immortal Memory and Friendship of That Noble Pair, Sir Lucius Cary and Sir H. Morison' (*The Underwood*, 70) Jonson questions the value of living to any great age, and of measuring life 'by the space, | Not by the act'. He imagines a worthless octogenarian:

> Here's one outlived his peers,
> And told forth four-score years;
> He vexèd time, and busied the whole state;
> Troubled both foes and friends;
> But ever to no ends:
> What did this stirrer but die late?
> How well at twenty had he fall'n or stood!
> For three of his four-score he did no good.
> (*The Underwood*, 70.25–32)

'What did this stirrer but die late?' The Ode is in part a poem of consolation offered to Lucius Cary, the surviving member of 'that noble pair', but is also in part a meditation by Jonson on his own condition, and on the doubtful blessings of *dying late*. The poem reaches its equipoise and (for the ageing poet, faintly troubling) conclusion in its famous central stanza.

> It is not growing like a tree
> In bulk, doth make man better be;
> Or standing long an oak, three hundred year,
> To fall a log at last, dry, bald, and sere:
> A lily of a day
> Is fairer far, in May,
> Although it fall, and die that night;
> It was the plant and flower of light.
> In small proportions we just beauty see:
> And in short measures life may perfect be. (65–74)

A further shock was in store when on 1 May 1633 the still-youthful Venetia Digby was found unexpectedly dead in her bed, having suffered a cerebral haemorrhage. Kenelm Digby, deeply in love with his wife and given to experimentalism, had been attempting to preserve her health and beauty through the addition to her diet of edible snails and viper wine. Devastated by her death, he now commissioned a deathbed portrait from Van Dyck (Plate 23), which was executed the following day, and a series of elegiac poems by Jonson which was eventually published under the title 'Eupheme', as *The Underwood*, 84. The most recent editor of the poems suggests that in constructing this sequence Jonson may have included verses he had already presented to Venetia in her lifetime, and that he continued to add supplementary verses over a period of years, extending perhaps to May 1636. In this plausible reading, Jonson's concluding words to one section of the sequence, 'Vowed by a faithful servant and client of your family, with his latest breath expiring it', might well have reference to his own condition during the final months of his life.[57] 'Some suspected that she was poisoned,' Aubrey later reported of Venetia. 'When her head was opened there was found but little brain, which her husband imputed to her drinking viper wine; but spiteful women would say 'twas a viper husband who was jealous of her that she would steal a leap.'[58] Other equally defamatory rumours about Venetia's own behaviour during the period she had believed Kenelm to be dead had been circulating in her lifetime. Jonson's title for the poetic sequence, 'Eupheme'— the Greek word is his invention, and means 'fair fame'—is designed, like the sequence itself, to extinguish any lingering suspicions about the reputations of both Kenelm and Venetia. In this series of adulatory commemorative poems Jonson is acting (one might say) as Venetia's panegyrical biographer, carrying her fame to what he elsewhere calls 'remembrance with posterity'. Kenelm himself, 'to avoid envy and scandal', says Aubrey,

retired into Gresham College at London, where he diverted himself with his chemistry, and the professors' good conversation. He wore there a long mourning cloak, a high crowned hat, his beard unshorn, looked like a hermit, as signs of sorrow for his beloved wife, to whose memory he erected a sumptuous monument, now quite destroyed by the great conflagration. He stayed at the College two or three years.[59]

Before long Kenelm himself, as Jonson's literary executor, would help to promote Jonson's own fair fame in the years following his death.

Jonson's thoughts during his final years continued to return to the region in the north of England through which he had made his memorable journey by foot nearly twenty years earlier. And if Lucius Cary's lines in a poem written after Jonson's death are to be taken literally, he was also contemplating an actual return: 'Not long before his death our woods he meant | To visit, and descend from Thames to Trent.'[60] In the prologue to *The Sad Shepherd*, however, the pastoral drama that was to be left unfinished at Jonson's death—and that might well have warranted a nostalgic visit to the region of Sherwood Forest, where the play is set—the dramatist wryly admits that if the piece fails to please, 'We think we therefore shall not leave the town' (40); for a journey beyond the metropolis (he recognizes) is now entirely beyond his capacities. In this charming fragment Jonson draws inventively on dramatic elements which he seems to have used in his earlier now-lost pastoral *The May-lord*, and on tales of Robin Hood, Friar Tuck, Little John, and Maid Marian that he might well have gathered on his earlier visit to this region.[61] The prologue once again suggests Jonson's careful retrospection over a long dramatic career, stretching back over three reigns, and a gentler accommodation with the audiences against whom he had so long railed.

> He that hath feasted you these forty years
> And fitted fables for your finer ears,
> Although at first he scarce could hit the bore—
> Yet you with patience heark'ning more and more,
> At length have grown up to him and made known
> The working of his pen is now your own ... (1–6)

'The working of his pen is now your own': Jonson's audiences have now 'grown up to him', and are now habituated to his methods. The reference to 'forty years' glances back to 1597, the year in which Jonson received his first payment for work as a dramatist, suggesting that the prologue was written in 1637, in the final months of his life.[62]

Ben Jonson, 'the most famous, accurate, and learned poet of our age', died on 16 August 1637, and, as the Garter Knight Sir Edward Walker reported, was buried the following day. It was the height of summer, and many of Jonson's friends and admirers would have left the metropolis, yet the crowd that assembled at his house in Westminster to accompany the body to the Abbey included 'all or the greatest part of the nobility and gentry then in town'.[63] Jonson's death was evidently seen as a major public event: the passing of the dominant literary figure of the age. Shakespeare's death in April 1616 had been quite a different affair; he had been buried quietly in the chancel of his parish church in Stratford-upon-Avon, having earned this modest place of honour as much from his status as a wealthy and respectable citizen of the town as from his literary distinction; no contemporary writer noted the immediate fact of his death. Jonson's fame in 1637 was otherwise. He had not sought to endear himself to a large public, habitually preferring the judgement of a few discerning friends: 'A man should seek great glory, and not broad,' as he had once written to John Donne (*Epigrams*, 96.12). Yet by the time of his death, as throughout much of his life, he had acquired the status of a celebrity; and a reputation that would undergo even stranger transformations in the years to come.

Remembrance with Posterity

'Posterity pays every man his honour,' declares the historian Cremutius Cordus in *Sejanus* (3.456) as his books are taken away to be burnt, voicing a sentiment that the play's author would also have endorsed. When his own work was threatened by hostile audiences or ignorant authorities, Jonson believed that posterity ultimately would put the record straight. 'I appeal to posterity that will hereafter read and judge my writings, though now neglected,' Jonson wrote in 1605 to Thomas Howard, Earl of Suffolk, from the prison to which he had been dispatched for co-authoring the satirical comedy of *Eastward Ho!* (Letter 2). His writings were not at all neglected at that moment, as it happened, but were attracting rather too much attention, which indeed was why he now found himself in gaol; but posterity, he believed, would have a proper sense of their value. Posterity would be grateful to William Herbert, Earl of Pembroke, for his 'great and singular faculty of judgement' in admiring the tragedy of *Catiline* when it had failed in the theatre, so Jonson wrote in the dedication to that play, and for supporting its author through a difficult period of his life. Thanking Pembroke once more for his protection in the dedication to the *Epigrams*, 'I return you the honour' (he declared) 'of leading forth so many good and great names to their remembrance with posterity.'

Jonson was a writer who looked persistently to the future, to what he variously called 'after-ages' or 'after-state' or 'after-times' or 'after-life' (in the secular rather than the celestial sense of that phrase, to signify a person's reputation in the period following their death), compounds which he seems to have invented or of which he was an early user.[1] Here is how the figure of

Heroic Virtue in *The Masque of Queens*, dressed 'in the furniture of Perseus', invokes that last phrase while describing the House of Fame,

> ... whose columns be
> Men-making poets, and those well-made men
> Whose strife it was to have the happiest pen
> *Renown them to an after-life*, and not
> With pride to scorn the muse, and die forgot ... (344–8, italics added)

Jonson and Inigo Jones had modelled this 'glorious and magnificent build-ing' of the House of Fame—whose friezes, 'both below and above, were filled with several-coloured lights, like emeralds, rubies, sapphires, carbuncles, etc., the reflex of which, with other lights placed in the concave, upon the masquers' habits, was full of glory' (322, 581–3)—on the account they had found in Chaucer's *Hous of Fame* (1419ff.),where the figures of the great poets of the past (Homer, Virgil, Ovid, Lucan, and others 'that written olde gestes', 1515) form the structural pillars of the memorial temple. These poets, phys-ically represented in Jones's and Jonson's presentation, are in a double sense the 'pillars' of the House, as creators of the reputations of others ('Men-making poets') and supreme artists in their own right.

The after-life of the greatest writers, Jonson imagined, was likely to be more glorious than the reputation they possessed within their lifetimes. Virgil would 'live hereafter more admired than now', as the character of Horace is allowed prophetically to remark in *Poetaster* (5.1.138). Shakespeare's reputa-tion in the years to come, as Jonson himself boldly predicted in his memorial poem in the 1623 Folio, would exceed the reputation he enjoyed while still alive. Jonson clearly hoped that the same would be true of himself, and that he too would 'live hereafter more admired than now'. That would have been an entirely reasonable expectation in the closing years of his life, given the celebrity he had achieved within Britain by that time. But Jonson's posthumous reputation was to follow instead a more eccentric path, with a steadily rising curve throughout the century following his death, followed by a steep descent from the early Romantic period. The decline in Jonson's reputation coincided significantly with the eighteenth-century discovery of Shakespeare's powers, the emergence of Shakespearian scholarship, and the rise of popular sentiment for Shakespeare's work. By the nineteenth century Jonson's star, which had seemed so luminous 200 years earlier, had been virtually eclipsed by that of his old rival. Fame, whose uncertainty Jonson had always recognized, had proved to be an erratic friend.[2]

§§

'It is a well-becoming and very worthy work you are about, not to suffer Mr Jonson to go so silently to his grave, and not so suddenly,' wrote James Howell to Brian Duppa in the months following Jonson's death. Duppa, now Dean of Christ Church, had begun to organize a volume of verses entitled *Jonsonus Virbius, Or, The Memory of Ben Jonson Revived by the Friends of the Muses*, which was eventually published early in 1638.[3] Containing thirty-three poems (six of them in Latin and one in Greek), *Jonsonus Virbius* was an academic collection of much the same kind as *Obsequies to the Memory of Edward King*, the volume that appeared from Cambridge University later that same year in memory of Milton's friend Edward King, who had drowned on 10 August 1637, just six days before Jonson's death; though *Jonsonus Virbius* contained no single poem approaching the quality of *Lycidas*.[4] The title of Duppa's volume was said to have been proposed by Lucius Cary, a leading contributor to the collection. *Virbius* (meaning literally 'twice a man') was the name given to Theseus' son Hippolytus who was torn to pieces on the sea-shore by his own stampeding horses after rejecting the advances of his stepmother Phaedra, and then skilfully restored to life through the ministrations of Aesculapius, god of medicine, at the request of the goddess Diana. Jonson, so the title optimistically implies, will be given new life in a similar fashion through these donnish tributes.[5] Yet despite the variable quality of this collection, their combined verdict is striking. The contributors, largely Royalist and Laudian in their sympathies, lament the passing of 'Great Jonson, king of English poetry', 'Wit's most triumphant monarch', the 'Poet of princes, prince of poets': significant analogies in the late 1630s.[6] Jonson is hailed as 'our poet first in merit as in love'; as England's 'rare archpoet'; as 'Father of poets'; as 'Mirror of poets! Mirror of the age!' He is

> The muses' fairest light in no dark time,
> The wonder of a learned age, the line
> Which none can pass, the most proportioned wit
> To nature, the best judge of what was fit;
> The deepest, plainest, highest, clearest pen;

The voice most echoed by consenting men,
The soul which answered best to all well said
By others, and which most requital made;
Tuned to the highest key of ancient Rome,
Returning all her music with his own,
And yet who to himself owed all his art.
    Here lies Ben Jonson. Every age will look
    With sorrow here, with wonder on his book.

So wrote Sidney Godolphin, a friend of Hobbes and member of the Great
Tew circle, in perhaps the most accomplished tribute in the collection. Even
allowing for the element of hyperbole that such collections inspire, the agreed
judgement of these verses is clear: English poetry is now bereft, for the
greatest poet of the age has departed. As the political crisis throughout the
country deepened, the memorial volume seemed to lament the passing not
just of an individual poet, but of a way of life that he and his writings
represented.

On hearing that Duppa was preparing *Jonsonus Virbius* for publication,
Sir Kenelm Digby wrote from London to congratulate him, adding that
he too was working to preserve Ben Jonson's memory: 'I will as soon as
I can do the like to the world, by making it share with me in those excellent
pieces (alas, that many of them are but pieces!) which he hath left behind
him, and which I keep religiously by me to that end.' Shortly before his
death Jonson had presented Digby with 'true and perfect copies' of several
of his writings 'not before printed', which Digby was soon to sell to
the publisher Thomas Walkley for £40, and which Walkley would eventually
publish in Jonson's Second Folio in 1640–1 in the collection known as
The Underwood.[7] On the title page of this collection was a motto from
Martial: *cinera gloria sera venit*. Martial is urging his friend Faustinus to
publish:

> Ante fores stantem dubitas admittere Famam
> Teque piget curae praemia ferre tuae?
> Post te victurae per te quoque vivere chartae
> Incipient: cinera gloria sera venit. (1.25.5–8)

Do you hesitate to admit Fame that stands before your doors, and shrink from
winning the reward of your care? Let writings that will live after you by your aid also
begin to live now; *to the ashes of the dead, glory comes too late.*

432

Fame bestowed posthumously, so these lines suggest, is never as sweet as that which is acquired during the poet's lifetime. Whether this melancholy motto was chosen by Digby or Jonson himself remains unclear, though it sounds like a possible rallying-cry that Digby might have put to his friend in his closing years, urging him to publish these poems before his death. Why Jonson refused to do so, and why he spoke of *The Underwood* in his note 'To the Reader' as containing 'lesser poems of later growth' is equally unclear, for the collection includes some of his finest poems, such as 'An Execration upon Vulcan', 'A Speech According to Horace', 'An Epistle Answering to One that Asked to be Sealed of the Tribe of Ben', and the Cary/Morison Ode (*The Underwood*, 43, 44, 47, 70). There is some indication, as already noted in relation to his epigram to Venetia Digby, *The Underwood*, 78 (412 above), that at this stage of his life Jonson derived more pleasure from seeing his verses circulate in manuscript amongst judicious friends than from print publication. It is possible, too, that he hesitated over the wisdom of publishing poems written in the closing years of his life which openly confessed his sickness and poverty and asked persistently for financial help, along with other poems bewailing the growing troubles in the land.

The Underwood is a large and somewhat disparate collection, less orderly and homogeneous than Jonson's two earlier poetic gatherings, the *Epigrams* and *The Forest*, and it contains a central group of poems (*The Underwood*, 38, 39, 40, and 41) whose authorship has been much contested; at least one of these poems is now thought not to be by Jonson at all.[8] Yet there are some signs that Jonson or Digby had begun to give an architectural shape to the collection. *The Underwood* opens with a sequence of 'Poems of Devotion' (which continue the mood of the final collection in *The Forest*, 'To Heaven') and proceeds to the humorous sequence of love poems 'A Celebration of Charis in Ten Lyric Pieces' (*The Underwood*, 2), which is seemingly balanced by the graver series of poems in memory of Venetia Digby towards the end of the collection, 'Eupheme...Consisting of These Ten Pieces' (*The Underwood*, 84). After the Charis poems come a group of pastoral and amorous verses, a succession of verse epistles, odes, and epigrams, and the spirited longer poems that (in more senses than one) stand at the centre of the collection, 'An Execration upon Vulcan', 'A Speech According to Horace', the 'Tribe of Ben' epistle (*The Underwood*, 43, 44, 47). The second half of the collection presents poems written during Charles's reign, and concludes with a series of classical translations, some on the subject of old age and love. One of the finest of the latter group was a favourite of Jonson's that he had recited to Drummond while in Scotland. Its Latin text Jonson had found in a sixteenth-century edition of Petronius, though the poem is not in fact by him.

> Doing a filthy pleasure is, and short;
> And done, we straight repent us of the sport:
> Let us not then rush blindly on unto it,
> Like lustful beasts, that only know to do it.
> For lust will languish, and that heat decay;
> But thus, thus keeping endless holiday,
> Let us together closely lie and kiss;
> There is no labour, nor no shame in this:
> This hath pleased, doth please, and long will please; never
> Can this decay, but is beginning ever.

With characteristic dexterity, Jonson in that final couplet varies the regular pentameter measure with an extrametrical foot and faintly acrobatic rhyme that subtly suggest the prolongation, the seemingly endless quality, of the experience being described. It is often in such small shifts and surprises, occurring within lines that appear to be moving with the simplicity and directness of everyday speech, that the pleasure of Jonson's verse consists.

§§

Jonson's literary dominance during the latter years of his life and the century following his death is evident in the analogies that his admirers and imitators invoked. For Robert Herrick, Jonson was an object of devotion for those of the 'old religion'.

> When I a verse shall make
> Know I have prayed thee,
> For old religion's sake,
> Saint Ben to aid me.
>
> Make the way smooth for me,
> When I, thy Herrick,
> Honouring thee, on my knee,
> Offer my lyric.

434

> Candles I'll give to thee,
> And a new altar,
> And thou, Saint Ben, shalt be
> Writ in my psalter.[9]

Others figured Jonson (as he had figured himself) as an Old Testament patriarch, the father of a tribe of aspiring writers: of the sons of Ben and more remotely, as the years passed, of the sons of sons of Ben. In panegyrical and dramatic writing throughout the century, Jonson would often return, like Hamlet's father, as a ghost, to prompt or rebuke his progeny.[10] Jonson's practice (so these analogies imply) was transmitted genetically from one generation of writers to the next, or through the operation of memory—as Jonson had imagined the power of the dead Shakespeare who, as his example was recalled, might 'with rage | Or influence chide or cheer the drooping stage'—and through the kind of diligent study, of conscious imitation and self-modelling, that he himself had so strongly commended.[11] For Jonson was not merely a saint or patriarch or ghost: he was also (it was repeatedly insisted) a teacher, whose writings were 'models' or 'lectures' to which aspiring writers should attend with due care.

> They came disciples to attend his preachers,
> But went away confirmed judicious teachers.
> Who sat at others' works like judges stern
> At Jonson's acts were pupils set to learn.
> Who read him true must know much more
> Than his wise tutor ever taught before.[12]

And numerous writers throughout the seventeenth century did indeed set out to be Ben Jonson's students, modelling their work directly or indirectly on his practice. They included dramatists who had known and followed the master in his lifetime, such as Richard Brome and William Cartwright, and those who came later in the century, such as Thomas Shadwell, who imitated his style and imperious manner in a way that a contemporary such as John Dryden could find worthy of ridicule; or (with a greater flair and independence) William Wycherley; and William Congreve, whose letters contain some acute criticism of Jonson's plays, and whose own comedies freely imitate Jonsonian characters, phrases, turns of plot, and details of stagecraft.

Shakespeare, on the other hand, was not remembered throughout the seventeenth century primarily as a teacher, for Shakespeare's example, as subsequent writers found to their cost, proved literally inimitable. Shakespeare was not a model but a true original, a divine freak, and as such (it was ultimately realized) worthy of even greater veneration than the sainted Ben. John Dryden, Jonson's most acute and attentive critic in the decades following his death, suggested this difference memorably in his 'Essay of Dramatic Poesy' in 1668.

If I would compare him with Shakespeare, I must acknowledge him the more correct poet, but Shakespeare the greater wit. Shakespeare was the Homer, or father of our dramatic poets; Jonson was the Virgil, the pattern of elaborate writing; I admire him, but I love Shakespeare.[13]

As *originality* was increasingly promoted throughout the eighteenth century as the hallmark of genius, so Jonson's reputation began quite rapidly to decline, the imagined contrast between Shakespeare's art and that of Jonson serving to reinforce an eighteenth-century aesthetic theory that would be of growing importance throughout the Romantic period. Edward Young's *Conjectures on Original Composition* (1759) show the way the wind was blowing.

Jonson in the serious drama is as much an imitator as Shakespeare is an original. He was very learned, as Samson was very strong, to his own hurt. Blind to the nature of tragedy, he pulled down all antiquity on his head, and buried himself under it; we see nothing of Jonson, nor indeed of his admired (but also murdered) ancients, for what shone in the historian is a cloud on the poet, and *Catiline* might have been a good play if Sallust had never writ.[14]

Modelling one's style on that of another writer with such close attention as to become that 'very he, or so like him as the copy may be mistaken for the principal' (*Discoveries*, 1754–5) no longer seemed, with such preconceptions in mind, such an attractive notion, and the glamour of being regarded in turn as 'the pattern of elaborate writing' began in turn quite dramatically to fall away. Jonson's learning, previously regarded with awe and respect, could in this new perspective be alternatively seen as his principal weakness. Jonson gained his creative knowledge merely from books, Edward Young maintained, while Shakespeare, 'whatever other learning he wanted, was master of two books, unknown to many of the profoundly read, though books which the last conflagration alone can destroy: the book of nature, and that of man'.

This contrast between the scholarly Jonson and the unschooled Shakespeare—the one, trapped beneath the weight of his own laborious learning, the other, drawing his inspiration freely from direct observation of man and nature—was based on a double misunderstanding. To begin with, the learning that Jonson showed in his creative work, while always impressive, was not always as formidable as it appeared, being often derived from Renaissance encyclopedias and *florilegia*, or collections of handy quotations. Yet he chose at times to wear that learning ostentatiously as a kind of protective armour, as in the quarto edition of *Sejanus*, where the text is heavily peppered with marginal annotations vouching for the veracity of the version of history he is presenting. Jonson was trying strenuously here to deflect the accusation that he was playing fast and loose with ancient history in order to reflect upon the present regime; the notes to *Sejanus* are a way of insisting, somewhat disingenuously, that the play contained nothing 'original' or dangerous to the state. Shakespeare's learning, on the other hand, may be lightly worn but was by no means as slight as eighteenth-century commentators imagined. Shakespeare's grammar school education at Stratford and his subsequent reading were altogether more extensive than once was realized, and the plots of his plays are significantly more dependent on source materials than are those of Jonson.[15]

Other aspects of Jonson's art began to trouble readers in the eighteenth century. His plays were seen by some as too dependent upon the weapons of satire and ridicule, qualities esteemed in Renaissance theory and practice but more severely regarded in the age of sensibility, which prized instead the more benevolent, more forgiving, more amiable style that was now associated, through a somewhat selective reading of the canon, with the plays of Shakespeare, and thus (by an easy transition from criticism to biography) with Shakespeare's own personality, believed to be more generous and 'gentle' than that of the supposedly surly Ben Jonson.[16] Jonson's plays were being seen moreover as more localized and topical in reference than those of Shakespeare, and hence more difficult to understand. This criticism of Jonson's plays is not heard until well into the eighteenth century. While Shakespeare's plays were freely adapted for performance at the Restoration, those of Jonson seem, so far as the evidence discloses, to have been performed in something approaching their original state throughout that period (in 'his works you find little to retrench or alter', Dryden had confidently declared) and well into the 1720s.[17] Yet from that decade forward they are repeatedly adapted in an attempt to make them palatable for contemporary audiences. David Garrick, an enthusiastic promoter of Jonson's work, adapted *Every Man In His Humour* for performance in 1752 and *The Alchemist* in 1763; Francis Gentleman adapted *Sejanus* (1752) and *The Alchemist* (1770). Garrick spent three years in his rewriting of *Every Man In His Humour*, judging that 'The language and characters of Ben Jonson (and particularly of the comedy in question) are much more difficult than those of any other writer.' The 'distance of 150 years from the time of writing', so the Advertisement to the 1752 edition of this adaptation declared, 'had occasioned some of the humour to be too obsolete and dangerous to be ventured in the representation at present'.[18] 'Obsolete', 'antiquated': other observers were in strong agreement with this judgement.[19] The theatre historian Thomas Davies, having watched a performance of *Epicene* in 1752, believed that 'the frequent allusions to forgotten customs and characters render it impossible to be ever revived with any probability of success'.[20]

Yet for all these supposed difficulties, Jonson's writings were not attracting the degree of scholarly attention that was now being directed to the works of Shakespeare, who was fast emerging at this moment as England's (if not Europe's) supreme literary genius.[21] In 1716–17 a six-volume edition of Jonson's *Works* had been prepared and published by a syndicate of book-sellers, and in 1756 Peter Whalley produced an illustrated and (lightly) annotated edition of his *Works* in seven volumes. William Gifford's nine-volume edition of 1816 was a more ambitious effort, fired by a passionate enthusiasm for the subject of his labours and an unremitting scorn for those Shakespearians whose blinkered devotion had led them to cast Ben Jonson, through an adverse contrastive judgement, 'a victim to his fame'. In a cantankerous prefatory essay ironically entitled 'Proofs of Ben Jonson's Malignity, from the Commentators on Shakespeare', Gifford squared up against the leading Shakespearian scholars of the age—foremost amongst them the great Edmond Malone, recently deceased—ridiculing their attempts to portray Jonson as an envious and persistent detractor of Shakespeare and his work. The powerful biographical mythology that had developed throughout the eighteenth century, as Gifford was keenly aware, had contributed materially to the current neglect of Jonson's work, and the adoration of Shakespeare. Gifford's indignation was in large measure justi-fied. The notion of Jonson's envy towards Shakespeare was based on a limited understanding of the man and his works. Jonson had repeatedly expressed his affection and admiration for his friend and rival, 'the author, my beloved, Master William Shakespeare'. Yet he needed also space to breathe, and wanted room to measure, with a professional eye, the full dimensions and occasional limitations of Shakespeare's genius: 'for I loved the man, and do honour his memory, on this side idolatry, as much as any.' These words Bernard Shaw would remember many years later when he coined a new word to describe the uncritical devotion to Shakespeare and all his works: *bardolatry.*[22]

Gifford's edition provided the scholarly foundation for subsequent minor editions of Jonson which appeared at intervals throughout the nineteenth century.[23] It also provided a potential opportunity for a much overdue reappraisal of the entire Jonsonian canon, which was then known to the reading public only in part, through selective anthologizing and infrequent theatrical performance.[24] Yet Gifford could hardly stem the swelling tide of popular admiration for Shakespeare, nor did he succeed in restoring the respect and affection for Jonson that had been so strongly in evidence during the decades following the poet's death. Part of the problem lay in Gifford's own embattled character, and the belligerence of his writing. Hazlitt, an unrepentant lover of Shakespeare, remained unconvinced by Gifford's championing of Jonson, wryly noting that the Tory editor of the *Quarterly Review* had chosen to study an author 'most congenial to his own turn of mind', dry and austere.[25] Jonson was to find more sympathetic readers in the nineteenth century such as Samuel Coleridge, and lively admirers of his work, such as Charles Dickens, but the tribe had dwindled perceptibly in number. The larger reappraisal of Jonson's writing and reputation was still to come.

§§

The slow recovery of Jonson's reputation in modern times has built upon the monumental labours of his twentieth-century editors, C. H. Herford and Percy and Evelyn Simpson, and been aided by an ever-growing body of scholarship and criticism and a changed appreciation of his plays' theatrical potential. The Oxford *Ben Jonson* grew out of preliminary textual and biographical forays that Charles Herford and Percy Simpson had conducted in the last two decades of the nineteenth century, and commenced formally with their signing of a contract with Oxford University Press in 1902. The edition was completed half a century later—Herford having died in 1931, and

Evelyn Simpson having joined her husband as co-editor a few years later—when the eleventh and final volume was published in 1952. 'Although an editor today would handle the presentation of the text differently,' wrote Percy Simpson's obituarist in 1962, 'the edition remains one of the great editions of its age. Its commentary is a masterpiece of wide, profound, and exact scholarship.'[26]

Editorial devotion is one (but only one) of the several factors that may aid the recovery of a writer's reputation. It is to be hoped that the new *Cambridge Edition of the Works of Ben Jonson*, prepared by an international team with the help of electronic technology over a shorter period of time, will play its part in the current revival of interest in Jonson's work. It may make more easily achievable the kind of total immersion in his writings that T. S. Eliot recommended, and that James Joyce sought to gain when he read Jonson's works from beginning to end—Jonson being one of only four authors to whom Joyce accorded such close and detailed attention.[27] And it may help to bring some of Jonson's less well-known writings as well as the perennial favourites to the attention of a wider range of readers and lovers of the theatre.

But Jonson's gradual return to public favour has been effected too by other means, and in large measure by the writers and artists who have been touched in some way by his work: by the poets who have admired his verse, from Yeats and Eliot to Thom Gunn and Geoffrey Hill; by dramatists such as Peter Barnes, who was moved by the anarchic energies of Jonson's plays, which he adapted for modern performance and emulated in his own writing. It has been boosted by the brilliance of individual actors from Donald Wolfit to Michael Gambon, and by the memorable productions of theatrical directors from Frank Hauser to Nicholas Hytner, and by the collective talents of the Royal Shakespeare Company, playing his works in repertoire with those of Shakespeare at the Swan theatre at Stratford-upon-Avon.

'His life was of humanity the sphere', wrote Jonson of his friend Sir Henry Morison, who died at an early age in 1629 (*The Underwood*, 70.52), and the same tribute might in turn be paid to Jonson himself, for whom *humanity* in its several senses—the absorption of classical learning and literature, the alertness to contemporary life, the amused and steady attention to 'manners and men' (*Epigrams*, 128.2)—was a constantly significant term.[28] He set out ambitiously to excel in all branches of humanistic knowledge: as a poet, historian, philologist, and rhetorician, as well as a writer for the stage, where he created a kind of comedy more technically perfect in design, more sharply contemporary in subject matter, than that of his greatest rival. 'He made the poets of Greece and Rome', said Oscar Wilde, 'terribly modern.'[29] He has earned in return what he hoped for: remembrance with posterity.

Notes

Chapter 1

1. John Aubrey, *Brief Lives*, ed. Andrew Clark, 2 vols. (Oxford, 1898), 2.13, 1.136, 1.280, 1.148, 1.208–9. When the floor of Westminster Abbey was repaved early in the nineteenth century, the blue marble stone was removed from Jonson's grave and replaced by a triangular stone bearing the same inscription. The original stone, rediscovered around 1846, was set into the wall of the Abbey just to the north of the grave.

2. *Brief Lives*, 1.284, 1.181. On Aubrey's place in seventeenth-century intellectual life in England, see Michael Hunter, *John Aubrey and the Realm of Learning* (London, 1975); and Kate Bennett's forthcoming Oxford edition of his Lives. Aubrey's archaeological interests are described by David Tylden-Wright, *John Aubrey: A Life* (London, 1991). On the contemporary passion for anatomical investigation, see Jonathan Sawday's *The Body Emblazoned: Dissection and the Human Body in Renaissance Culture* (London, 1995). The *OED*'s first citation of the word 'biography' is from Dryden's *Life of Plutarch* (1683), but the word was in common usage twenty years earlier: see Donald Stauffer, *English Biography before 1700* (Cambridge, Mass., 1930), 218–19.

3. Peter Cunningham, *A Handbook of London* (London, 1850), 'Westminster Abbey'. Thornton S. Graves, 'Jonson in the Jest Books', in *The Manly Anniversary Studies in Language and Literature* (Chicago, 1923), 127–39, and Frances Teague, 'Ben Jonson's Poverty', *Biography*, 2 (1979), 260–5, sceptically review a variety of similar dubious anecdotes.

4. Joseph Quincy Adams, 'The Bones of Ben Jonson', *Studies in Philology*, 16 (1919), 289–302, drawing freely on Francis T. Buckland, *Curiosities of Natural History*, 4th series (London, 1900), 229, 238–48.

5. T. S. Eliot, 'Ben Jonson', *Times Literary Supplement*, 13 November 1919, 637–8 (reviewing G. Gregory Smith's *Ben Jonson*); repr. in Eliot's *Selected Essays* (London, 1958), 147–60.

6. G. Gregory Smith, *Ben Jonson*, English Men of Letters (London, 1919), 1.

7. H&S, 1.119, 120. Herford's life of Jonson in this edition is based on the biographical essay he had written for Leslie Stephen's *Dictionary of National Biography*, published in 1891. The present account draws here and there on earlier essays of mine exploring the problems of Jonsonian biography, and especially 'Gathering and Losing the Self: Jonson and Biography', ch. 3 of *Jonson's Magic Houses* (Oxford, 1997); 'Life into Text', *Essays in Criticism*, 41 (1991), 253–61; and 'Biographical Uncertainty', *Essays in Criticism*, 54 (2004), 305–22. Charles G. Salas's introduction to his edited collection, *The Life & The Works: Art and Biography*, Getty Research Institute (Los Angeles, 2007), suggestively surveys this general territory.

8. See in particular Anne Barton's pioneering study *Ben Jonson: Dramatist* (Cambridge, 1984); and the chronological arrangement of *The Cambridge Edition of the Works of Ben Jonson*.

9. See *Jonson's Magic Houses*, ch. 9, 'The Story of Charis'.

10. Martin Butler, 'The Dates of Three Poems by Ben Jonson', *Huntington Library Quarterly*, 55 (1992), 279–94. See also Ch. 18, 394–5 below.

11. William Camden, *Remains Concerning Britain*, ed. R. D. Dunn (Toronto, 1984), 183.

12. Coleridge speaks of Wordsworth's 'Immortality Ode' as 'intended for such readers only as had been accustomed to watch the flux and reflux of their inmost nature, to venture at times into the twilight realms of consciousness', and of Shakespeare's *Venus and Adonis* displaying 'the flux and reflux of the mind in all its subtlest thoughts and feelings': *Biographia Literaria*, vol. 7 of *The Collected Works of S. T. Coleridge*, ed. James Engell and W. J. Bate (Princeton, 1983), vii(2). 21. On Woolf, memory, and sensation, see especially her *Moments of Being*, ed. Jeanne Schulkind (London, 1976), 64. *The Essays of Michael, Lord of Montaigne*, trans. John Florio (1603), 3 vols. (London, 1906), vol. 2, ch. 1, 'Of the Inconstancy of our Actions'. 'Distinguo' = 'I make a distinction', a term used in debating, as a speaker rejects or modifies a proposition that has just been asserted.

13. A. C. Swinburne, *A Study of Ben Jonson* (London, 1889), 130.

14. Ann Moss, *Printed Commonplace-Books and the Structuring of Renaissance Thought* (Oxford, 1996).

15. Ben Jonson, *Discoveries: A Critical Edition*, ed. Maurice Castelain (Paris, n.d. [1906]), p. vii.

16. Seneca the Elder, *Controversiae* ('Declamations'), trans. M. Winterbottom, Loeb Classical Library (Cambridge, Mass., 1974), bk. 1, preface, 2–5.

17. Ian Donaldson, '"The Fripperie of Wit": Jonson and Plagiarism', in Pauline Kewes (ed.), *Plagiarism in Early Modern England* (Basingstoke, 2003), 119–33.

18. On Horace's fatness, see Suetonius, 'Horace', *The Lives of Illustrious Men*, trans. J. C. Rolfe, Loeb Classical Library, 2 vols. (Cambridge, Mass., 1914).

19. Henry Chettle, *England's Mourning Garment* (1603), D2ᵛ–D3; Edward Herbert, 'Upon his Friend Master Ben Jonson and his Translation', in *Q. Horatius Flaccus: His Art of Poetry. Englished by Ben Jonson* (1640), sig. A7; *CWBJ*, Literary Record, Electronic Edition.

20. For a possible link between Jonson's use of these dramatic figures and his friend Thomas Hobbes's discussion of the role of delegation in ch. 16 of *Leviathan* ('Of Persons, Authors, and Things Personated'), see Ian Donaldson, 'Shakespeare, Jonson, and the Invention of the Author', British Academy Shakespeare Lecture 2006, *Proceedings of the British Academy*, 151 (Oxford, 2007), 319–38, at 333–4.

21. See Ch. 12 below, and Edmund Wilson, 'Morose Ben Jonson', in *The Triple Thinkers* (Oxford, 1938). For a more extended response to Wilson's analysis, see Donaldson, *Jonson's Magic Houses*, 31–3.

Chapter 2

1. Jonson's deep knowledge of the city is explored by Fran C. Chalfant, *Ben Jonson's London: A Jacobean Placename Dictionary* (Athens, Ga., 1978). The link between Jonson and Dickens is suggested by Evelyn Simpson, 'Jonson and Dickens: A Study in the Comic Genius of London', *Review of English Studies*, 29 (1943), 85–91, and Richard Dutton, 'Jonson and *David Copperfield*: Dickens and *Bartholomew Fair*', *English Language Notes*, 15 (1979), 227–32.

2. John Norden, *Speculum Britanniae: The First Part* (London, 1593), 9. On the growth of London at this time, see especially A. L. Beier, *Masterless Men: The Vagrancy Problem in England 1560–1640* (London, 1985), Jeremy Boulton, *Neighbourhood and Society: A London*

Suburb in the Seventeenth Century (Cambridge, 1987); Penelope Corfield, 'Urban Development in England and Wales in the Sixteenth and Seventeenth Centuries', in D. C. Coleman and A. H. Johns (eds.), *Trade, Government, and Economy in Pre-Industrial England* (London, 1976); Roger Finlay, *Population and Metropolis: The Demography of London 1580–1650* (Cambridge, 1981); D. M. Palliser, *The Age of Elizabeth: England under the Late Tudors* (London, 1983), ch. 7, 'London and the Towns'; J. F. Merritt (ed.), *Imagining Early Modern London* (Cambridge, 2001). The classic study of Jonson's work in relation to the rise of capitalism is L. C. Knights's *Drama and Society in the Age of Jonson* (London, 1937), an analysis deeply coloured by the work of R. H. Tawney. On the book's limitations, see Don E. Wayne, '*Drama and Society in the Age of Jonson*: An Alternative View', *Renaissance Drama*, NS 13 (1982), 103–29.

3. Boswell observed several parallels between Johnson and Jonson, noting their common love of regulated socializing—Samuel insisted on writing the rules of his Club 'like his namesake, Old Ben' (*Life of Johnson*, ed. R. W. Chapman, corr. J. D. Fleeman (Oxford, 1970), 1261)—and, on the Scottish journey, leading his friend deliberately to a site visited by his predecessor: 'I would by no means lose the pleasure of seeing my friend at Hawthornden, of seeing *Sam Johnson* at the very spot where *Ben Johnson* visited the learned and poetical Drummond'; *The Journal of a Tour of the Hebrides*, ed. Peter Levi (Harmondsworth, 1984), 409.

4. Jonson measures his weight again in his 'Epistle to Mr Arthur Squibb', *The Underwood*, 54. Cf. the poetic exchange with Sir William Burlase (*The Underwood*, 52), and the lines sent to Drummond on leaving Hawthornden, 50–1 below. Jonson probably put on further weight later in life: see Ch. 19 (and n. 1) below.

5. Jonson must have drafted some at least of his projected works while staying with Drummond, who at Jonson's departure noted that 'if he died by the way, he promised to send me his papers of this country, hewn as they were' (*Informations*, 517–18).

6. Seneca, *Epist.* 30.11; cf. *Discoveries*, 95–100. The notion of intellectual 'discovery' recurs throughout this commonplace book: e.g. 163, 170, 1504, etc.

7. William Camden, *Britain*, trans. Philemon Holland (London, 1610), 'The Author to the Reader'. John Aubrey's *Perambulation of the County of Surrey*, conducted in 1673 as part of John Ogilby's 'Geographical and Historical' description of England and Wales, belongs to the same chorographical tradition. On Cotton, see Kevin Sharpe, *Sir Robert Cotton 1586–1631* (Oxford, 1979); his expedition with Camden in 1599 is discussed by David McKitterick, 'From Camden to Cambridge: Robert Cotton's Roman Inscriptions, and their Subsequent Treatment', in C. J. Wright (ed.), *Sir Robert Cotton as Collector: Essays on an Early Stuart Courtier and his Legacy* (London, 1997), 105–28. On Loch Lomond and Edinburgh borough law: *Informations*, 313–14, Jonson to Drummond, 10 May 1619 (Letter 14, *CWBJ*), Drummond to Jonson, 1 July 1619 (Letter (f), *CWBJ*).

8. On this general topic, see Anne Barton, *Ben Jonson: Dramatist* (Cambridge, 1984), ch. 14; J. B. Bamborough, 'The Rusticity of Ben Jonson', in Ian Donaldson (ed.), *Jonson and Shakespeare* (London, 1983), ch. 9; Leah Marcus, *The Politics of Mirth: Jonson, Herrick, Milton, Marvell, and the Defense of Old Holiday Customs* (Chicago, 1986).

9. Camden, *Britannia* (London, 1600), 367, *Britain*, trans. Holland, 421. Virgil, *Eclogues*, 1, in *Virgil, Eclogues, Georgics, Aeneid*, trans. H. Rushton Fairclough, The Loeb Classical Library (Cambridge, Mass., 1965), vol. 1. In his 'Ode Allegorike' addressed to Hugh Holland in 1603 (*CWBJ*, vol. 2) Jonson had provided a panoramic vision of a Britain

(including the northernmost parts of Scotland) that he had not yet fully traversed. Jenny Wormald analyses James's reasons for encouraging the name 'Britain' (or 'Britannia'): 'James VI, James I, and the identity of Britain', in Brendan Bradshaw and John Morrill (eds.), *The British Problem c.1534–1707: State Formation in the Atlantic Archipelago* (Houndmills, 1996), 148–71. Cotton and his patron Northampton prudently followed James's lead: see Kevin Sharpe, 'Introduction: Re-writing Sir Robert Cotton', in Wright (ed.), *Sir Robert Cotton as Collector*, 18.

10. On the political importance at this time of the Gentlemen of the Bedchamber, see Neil Cuddy, 'The Bedchamber of James I, 1603–1625', in David Starkey et al. (eds.), *The English Court from the Wars of the Roses to the Civil War* (Harlow, 1987), ch. 6. See also David Riggs, *Ben Jonson: A Life* (Cambridge, Mass., 1989), 122–6; James Knowles, 'Jonson in Scotland: Jonson's Mid-Jacobean Crisis', in Takashi Kozuka and J. R. Mulryne (eds.), *Shakespeare, Marlowe, Jonson: New Directions in Biography* (Aldershot, 2006), 259–77. John Aubrey reported that Aytoun 'was acquainted with all the wits of his time in England', and that Aytoun and Jonson shared a close acquaintance with Thomas Hobbes, who drew on their combined learning when writing the epistle dedicatory for his translation of Thucydides: John Aubrey, *Brief Lives*, ed. A. Clark, 2 vols. (Oxford, 1898), 1.365. See Ch. 19 below.

11. For an account of the progress, see David Masson's introduction to *The Register of the Privy Council of Scotland*, 11: *1616–1619* (Edinburgh, 1894), pp. viii–xliii. James's words are quoted in Caroline Bingham, *James I of England* (London, 1981), 161–4. On the general background see especially Gordon Donaldson, 'The Scottish Church 1567–1625', in Alan G. R. Smith (ed.), *The Reign of James VI and I* (London, 1973), 40–56; Jennifer Brown, 'Scottish Politics 1567–1625', ibid. 22–39; Jenny Wormald, 'James VI and I: Two Kings or One?', *History*, 68 (1983), 187–209.

12. *Informations*, 257–8. Variants on this witticism are noted by Charles Stanhope (second Baron Stanhope, 1595–1675) in the margins of his personal copy of Jonson's 1640 Folio. One (characteristically confused) note on p. 378 of the Folio reads: 'When Ben Jonson was goinge to Norwich & back againe upon aduenture & came to putt out mony unto Sr Frauncis Bacon upon adventure Mr Atturney told him hee used his feet in uerse soe well that hee would not wish him to use them in any thinge else' (James M. Osborn, 'Ben Jonson and the Eccentric Lord Stanhope', *Times Literary Supplement*, 4 January 1957, 16). Stanhope may have muddled Jonson's journey with that of Will Kemp, who did indeed go to Norwich, and have conflated Bacon's dictum with a memory of Jonson wagering on his chances of completing the walk to Scotland (putting out money 'upon adventure': cf. *OED*, 'Adventure', 7). Bacon described himself as 'no good footman', Aubrey, *Brief Lives*, ed. Clark, 1.75.

13. *CWBJ*, vol. 4, and Michael Strachan, *The Life and Adventures of Thomas Coryate* (London, 1962). Cf. *Bartholomew Fair*, 3.5.230–2.

14. *Kemp's Nine Days' Wonder: Performed in a Dance from London to Norwich*, ed. Alexander Dyce, Camden Society (London, 1890); Sidney Lee, 'William Kemp', *DNB* (1891); David Wiles, *Shakespeare's Clown: Actor and Text in the Elizabethan Playhouse* (Cambridge, 1987), ch. 3.

15. Robert Carey, *Memoirs* (Edinburgh, 1808), 20. Samuel Rowlands refers to the Bristol and Antwerp expeditions in verses prefixed to John Taylor's *The Sculler* (London, 1612). Jonson's Puntarvolo discusses similar 'returns' with his notary for his projected trip to Constantinople ('I am to receive five for one, according to the proportion of the sums put forth') in *Every Man Out of His Humour*, 4.3.35–6.

16. *CSPD James I, 1611–1618*, 92.472.

17. On the same day that he heard of Jonson's projected journey, Carleton was informed by another correspondent that the English party was 'much caressed in Scotland'. There was much coming and going between Edinburgh and London at this time: see *The Register of the Privy Council of Scotland*, vol. ii, pp. xx–xxii.

18. The author of this masque, we are told, has recently journeyed to the moon and found a new world there. Did he walk or ride 'upon the poet's horse for a wager'? Because 'one of our greatest poets—I know not how good a one—went to Edinburgh o'foot, and came back. Marry, he has been restive, they say, ever since, for we have had nothing from him; he has set out nothing, I am sure.' And a herald replies: 'Like enough, perhaps he has not all in. When he has all in, he will set out, I warrant you, at least those from whom he had it' (147, 140–4). *Set out* means both to publish or put into print, and to lay out money, as in a wager. Having *all in* means having material in hand, ready to publish, and also, having one's due accounts paid. The double sense is that since his return from Scotland Jonson (i) appears to have written nothing, and (ii) has not been paid his winnings.

19. James Loxley's preliminary account of this discovery, 'My Gossip's Foot Voyage', was published in *The Times Literary Supplement* for 11 September 2009, 13–15. He is now preparing a full edition of the manuscript in collaboration with Julie Sanders which will appear in the Electronic Edition of the *CWBJ* in 2012, and be followed by a print edition with supplementary essays, published by Cambridge University Press. I am most grateful to Dr Loxley for generously providing me with a transcription of the manuscript and sharing his early thoughts on its interpretation; and to both editors for allowing me to quote selectively from it here.

20. Amongst the several possible candidates who have emerged from Loxley's early researches the most plausible appears to be Thomas Aldersey (1600–75), who was admitted as a pensioner at Queen's College, Cambridge, in Michaelmas 1619. He would have been conveniently between school and university in the summer of 1618, and available to accompany Jonson on the walk. The Aldersey family were known as supporters of the reformed faith, while Jonson had converted to Catholicism in 1598. This would not in itself have been a bar to his standing godfather to a Protestant child. Such cross-faith relationships were not unknown in the period. Jonson had his own children baptized in Anglican churches during his and his wife's Catholic years, and double baptism was in any case a common practice amongst Catholic families at this time (John Morrill, personal information; cf. John Bossy, *The English Catholic Community 1570–1850* (London, 1975), 133–4).

21. On Jonson's later connections with Cavendish, see Ch. 18 below. Lynn Hulse believes the two men had probably first met around 1614 ('William Cavendish, First Duke of Newcastle upon Tyne', *ODNB*). Some sense of the likely dating of the Foot Voyage MS—apparently a copy of a journal maintained on the journey itself—is given by its reference to 'Sir William Candish now Lord Mansfield'. William Cavendish became Viscount Mansfield on 29 October 1620. The copy is thus being made more than two years after the journey itself.

22. Andrew Foster, 'Richard Neile', *ODNB*. Neile's defence of royal rights and prerogatives during the Addled Parliament debates in 1614 had angered many of Jonson's parliamentary friends, such as Sir Thomas Roe: see Ch. 16 below.

23. *Discoveries*, 1432–3, 1436–7. Contrast *Discoveries*, 605–6, on Bacon's style: 'He never forced his language, nor went out of the highway of speaking.'

24. Sir Robert Carey, *Account of the Death of Queen Elizabeth and of his Ride to King James at Edinburgh, 1603*, in *An English Garner: Stuart Tracts 1603–1693*, introd. C. H. Firth (Westminster, 1903). On Carey's ride, see also Ch. 10 below.

25. William Taylor, 'The King's Mails, 1603–1625', *Scottish Historical Review*, 42 (1963), 143–7.

26. Gillian Beer, *Arguing with the Past: Essays in Narrative from Woolf to Sidney* (London, 1989), 105.

27. A possible consequence of this theory is that the journal has finished up amongst the Aldersey family papers not because the diarist was a member of that family, but because a member of that family was in some way involved in the wager, and retained the verifying documentation.

28. *Kemp's Nine Days' Wonder*, ed. Dyce, 17.

29. Thus in his poem 'To Sir Robert Wroth' Jonson speaks of 'The mowed meadows, with the fleecèd sheep, | And feasts that either shearers keep': *The Forest*, 3.39–40.

30. On Jonson's alleged poverty, see Ch. 19 below.

31. The diarist mistakenly records his departure date as 5 November, though it is 'the Monday seven-night after' another event occurring on Saturday 26 September.

32. As John Taylor records, *The Pennyless Pilgrimage* (London, 1618), 58; Masson, *Register of the Privy Council of Scotland*, 11 (1894), p. clxvii.

33. Masson, *Register of the Privy Council*, 11 (1894), pp. clxii–lxxv. On the significance of these terms, see 90 below.

34. Sir Anthony Weldon (attrib.), *A Perfect Description of Scotland* (London, 1649).

35. Letter 14, *CWBJ*, Inigo Jones in his verses 'To his False Friend Mr Ben Jonson' complains of the frequency with which Jonson related 'the tedious story' of his journey to Scotland: *CWBJ*, Literary Record, Electronic Edition.

36. Jennifer Brady, 'Jonson's "To King James": Plain Speaking in the *Epigrammes* and the *Conversations*', *Studies in Philology*, 82 (1985), 380–98. See also Knowles, 'Jonson in Scotland', in Kozuka and Mulryne (eds.), *Shakespeare, Marlowe, Jonson*, 259–77.

37. Taylor, *The Pennyless Pilgrimage*, 58–9. See also Bernard Capp, *The World of John Taylor the Water-Poet 1578–1653* (Oxford, 1994). Gervase Markham experienced a similar difficulty in collecting payment for his sponsored walk in 1624 from London to Berwick without use of bridge or boat (as Dr Gavin Alexander informs me).

38. Robert H. MacDonald describes Drummond's collection in *The Library of Drummond of Hawthornden* (Edinburgh, 1971). MacDonald's account of Drummond's character importantly corrects the general bias of David Masson's *Drummond of Hawthornden* (London, 1873). For Drummond's interest in burning-glasses, see also Ch. 18 below.

39. C. L. Stainer's attempted dismissal of the document as a forgery (*Jonson and Drummond their Conversations: A Few Remarks on an 18th Century Forgery* (Oxford, 1925)) has been decisively rejected by Percy Simpson, 'The Genuineness of the Drummond "Conversations"', *Review of English Studies*, 2 (1926), 42–50, Francis Paget Hett, *The Memoirs of Sir Robert Sibbald (1641–1722)* (Oxford, 1932), and Harold Love, *Attributing Authorship: An Introduction* (Cambridge, 2002), 42–50. For further discussion of the transmission and status of the various texts of *Informations*, see the Textual Essay accompanying my

edition of the work, *CWBJ*, Electronic Edition. For the suggestion that Drummond's original manuscript was destroyed at Penicuik, see Mark Bland, 'Further Information: Drummond's *Democritie, A Labyrinth of Delight*, and his "Certain Informations and Manners of Ben Jonson"', *Text*, 16 (2003), 1–40.

40. Leicester had been suspected of poisoning his first wife so that he might marry Elizabeth. According to a contemporary report, he later tried to poison his second wife's lover, Christopher Blount; she suspected a plot, and allegedly poisoned Leicester himself. See P. Bliss's note to Anthony à Wood's *Athenae Oxonienses* (London, 1691–2), 2.74–5. For more recent speculation, see Chris Skidmore. *Edward VI: The Lost King of England* (London, 2007).

41. Ian Donaldson, *Jonson's Magic Houses: Essays in Interpretation* (Oxford, 1997), ch. 2; Ian Donaldson, 'Looking Sideways: Jonson, Shakespeare, and the Myths of Envy', in Kozuka and Mulryne (eds.), *Shakespeare, Marlowe, Jonson*, 241–57.

42. Drummond's own titles for these notes are preserved in the surviving outer sheet of his now-vanished manuscript: 'Informations & Manners [of Ben Jonson *deleted*] to W. D: 1619' and 'Informations be Ben Johnston | to W. D. when he cam to Scotland upon foot 1619': Hawthornden MSS, vol. 11, MS 2061. fo 140, National Library of Scotland.

43. Masson, *Drummond of Hawthornden*, 67. R. D. S. Jack has well documented Drummond's Petrarchan (and Spenserian) tastes in *Scottish Literature's Debt to Italy* (Edinburgh, 1986), 13–21.

44. For Drummond's preferences, see his *Character of Several Authors*, written between 1612 and 1616 and included in the 1711 folio edition of his works.

45. 'A more learned man [than Buchanan]…this country has not brought forth,' declared Drummond: Masson, *Drummond of Hawthornden*, 34–5. Despite Jonson's disparaging remarks about Buchanan (*Informations*, 442–3), Drummond presented Jonson with a copy of Buchanan's *Rerum Scoticarum Historia*: see David McPherson's and Henry Woudhuysen's accounts of this now unlocated work, Jonson's Library, *CWBJ*, Electronic Edition.

46. 'Memoirs of Ben Jonson', in *The Works of Ben Jonson*, ed. William Gifford, 9 vols. (London, 1816), 1.

47. *The Works of the British Poets with Lives of the Authors*, by Ezekiel Sanford, 3: *Shakespeare and Jonson* (Philadelphia, 1819), 253–8.

48. John Butt, *Pope, Dickens, and Others: Essays and Addresses* (Edinburgh, 1969), 51–2.

49. *William Drummond of Hawthornden: Poems and Prose*, ed. Robert H. MacDonald (Edinburgh, 1976), introduction, p. xi.

50. 'Vindicative' is used again in *Cynthia's Revels* (Q), 5.11.123. Is Drummond's final judgement of Jonson's character entirely independent, or does it partly record Jonson's self-criticism? The phrase 'given rather to lose a friend than a jest' was a favourite of Jonson's, appearing with slight variations in *Every Man Out of His Humour*, Induction, 321 (where the scurrilous Carlo Buffone 'will sooner lose his soul than a jest') and in *Poetaster*, 4.3.110–11 (where Tucca maliciously remarks of Horace—a quasi-portrait of Jonson himself—that 'he will sooner lose his best friend than his least jest').

51. Drummond's intended bride, Euphemia Cunningham, died unexpectedly of fever in 1616. Recent scholarship has suggested that Drummond was writing 'funeral' poems for a deceased mistress at least a year before Euphemia's death: see MacDonald, *The Library of Drummond of Hawthornden*, 11, 27.

Chapter 3
1. William Camden, *Britain*, trans. Holland (London, 1610), 16.
2. C. L. Johnstone, *History of the Johnstones 1191–1909* (Edinburgh, 1909). See also C. L. Johnstone's *History of the Johnstones: Supplement* (Glasgow, 1925), ch. 3.
3. Camden, *Britain*, 18.
4. See Sir William Fraser KCB, LLD, *The Annandale Family Book of the Johnstones, Earls and Marquises of Annandale*, 2 vols. (Edinburgh, 1894).
5. William Camden, *Annales, or the History of the Most Renowned and Victorious Princess Elizabeth, Late Queen of England*, trans. R. N. Gent, 3rd edn. (1635), 121.
6. On the events related here, see Jasper Ridley, *Henry VIII* (London, 1984), ch. 26; William Croft Dickinson, *Scotland from Earliest Times to 1603*, vol. 1 of *A New History of Scotland*, 2nd edn. revised (London, 1965), ch. 30; Gordon Donaldson, *Scotland: James V—James VII*, vol. 3 of *The Edinburgh History of Scotland*, corr. edn. (Edinburgh, 1976), chs. 2–3; *Letters and Papers Foreign and Domestic of the Reign of Henry VIII*, 17 (1900).
7. *Letters and Papers*, 625–6.
8. ibid. 1209.
9. Eamon Duffy, *Fires of Faith: Catholic England under Mary Tudor* (New Haven, 2009); Gina Alexander, 'Bonner and the Marian Persecutions', *History*, 60 (1975), 374–91; T. M. Parker, *The English Reformation to 1558* (London, 1950), ch. 9; Carolly Erikson, *Bloody Mary* (London, 1978); David Loades, *Mary Tudor: A Life* (Oxford, 1989); H. F. M. Prescott, *Mary Tudor* (London, 1952).
10. J. A. Symonds, *Ben Jonson* (London, 1886), 2–3.

Chapter 4
1. Thomas Fuller, 'Westminster', *History of the Worthies of England*, (1662), 243. Mark Eccles, 'Jonson's Marriage', *Review of English Studies*, 12 (1936), 262.
2. C. H. Herford believed that Jonson was born in 1572 (H&S, 1.1), but the Simpsons later opted for a birthdate between October 1572 and May 1573 (H&S, 11.583). Mark Eccles placed Jonson's birth between May 1572 and May 1573: 'Brief Lives', *Studies in Philology*, 79 (1982), 77. For a decisive review of the evidence in favour of 11 June 1572, see W. D. Briggs, 'The Birth-Date of Ben Jonson', *Modern Language Notes*, 33 (1918), 137–45; and Rosalind Miles, *Ben Jonson: His Life and Works* (London, 1986), appendix.
3. For recordings of birthdates in bibles, see David Cressy, *Birth, Marriage, and Death: Ritual, Religion, and the Life-Cycle in Tudor and Stuart England* (Oxford, 1997), 38.
4. Keith Thomas, *Religion and the Decline of Magic* (Harmondsworth, 1971), 343; and, on the status of astrology more generally in this period, 335–458.
5. ibid. 385–6.
6. See R. H. MacDonald, *The Library of Drummond of Hawthornden* (Edinburgh, 1971), 78, 80 (facing fig. 25), 159 (cat. 183), 225 (cat. 1366), etc.
7. Bodleian, Ashmole MS 174, fo. 75. See also R. T. Peterson, *Sir Kenelm Digby: The Ornament of England 1603–1665* (London, 1956), 328 n. 1.
8. 'Born on the day he died, the eleven of June, | And that day bravely fought at Scanderoon. | It's rare that one and the same day should be | His day of Birth, of Death, of Victory!': Dr Richard Farrar, 1665. Anthony à Wood in *Athenae Oxonienes*, 2 vols. (London, 1692), 2.239, skews this symmetry even further by citing a pamphlet alleging that the Battle of

Scandaroon actually took place on 16 June, not 11 June. Sir Thomas Browne discusses the phenomenon of dying on the day of one's birth in *A Letter to a Friend* in *Religio Medici and Other Works*, ed. L. C. Martin (Oxford, 1964), 182–3. Thomas Dekker detected a similar circularity in the life of Queen Elizabeth, who 'came in with the fall of the leaf, and went away in the spring: her life (which was dedicated to virginity) both beginning and closing up a miraculous maiden circle: for she was born upon a Lady Eve and died upon a Lady Eve': *The Plague Pamphlets of Thomas Dekker*, ed. F. P. Wilson (Oxford, 1925), 17.

9. Jonson remembers Spenser's poem more extensively in *The Underwood*, 75, his epithalamion for the wedding of Jerome Weston and Frances Stuart on 25 June 1632, acknowledging that by this date the sun has 'passed thy summer standing' (line 1). 'Divine Spenser's sun was no sooner set, but in Jonson a new one rose,' Digby had declared, linking the two poets in a significant metaphor in his essay on Spenser, written for Thomas May (Peterson, *Sir Kenelm Digby*, 92). On this conjunction see also Ch. 19 below, 412.

10. John Brand, *Observations on the Popular Antiquities of Great Britain*, rev. Sir Henry Ellis, 3 vols. (London, 1849), 1.294, quoting *Festa Anglo Romana*; A. Kent Hieatt, *Short Time's Endless Monument* (Port Washington, NY, 1972), 20 n. 2; 91. On the various rituals and beliefs relating to this period of the year, see E. O. James, *Seasonal Feasts and Festivals* (New York, 1961), 314–16; A. D. Hope, *A Midsummer Eve's Dream* (Canberra, 1970); Ronald Hutton, *The Stations of the Sun: A History of the Ritual Year in Britain* (Oxford, 1996), ch. 30, 'The Midsummer Fires'.

11. Hutton, *The Stations of the Sun*, 313–16.

12. 'The Faeries' Farewell', *The Poems of Richard Corbett*, ed. J. A. W. Bennett and H. R. Trevor-Roper (Oxford, 1955), 50. In *The Masque of Queens* (1609) Jonson was to note the details of 'a vulgar fable of a witch' that 'was a tale when I went to school'.

13. Fuller, 'Westminster', 243.

14. J. B. Bamborough, 'The Early Life of Ben Jonson', *The Times Literary Supplement*, 8 April 1960.

15. See below, Ch. 10, 213.

16. W. David Kay, *Ben Jonson: A Literary Life* (1995), 2.

17. Thomas Mason (ed.), *A Register of Baptisms, Marriages, and Burials in the Parish of St Martin in the Fields... from 1550 to 1619* (1898), Publications of the Harleian Society, xxv, 15, 178, 17, 92, 177. Margareta Brett, baptized 16 June 1585 and Anthony Brett, baptized 31 October 1591 (pp. 18, 22) may have been Jonson's siblings, as well as (perhaps) Sara Brett (buried 15 July 1581), Alicia Breet (buried 25 September 1589), and Rebecca Breet, buried 24 April 1595 (pp. 124, 133, 140). My findings tally broadly with Kay's, but there is a measure of guesswork in all of these identifications.

18. *Athenae Oxonienses*, 1.517.

19. On Hartshorn Lane, see the London County Council *Survey of London*, ed. Sir George Gater and Walter H. Godfrey, 18: *The Strand* (The Parish of St Martin-in-the-Fields, Part II) (1937), 21–7, and (for a slightly later period) Ann Cowper-Coles, '"A Place Much Clogged and Pestered with Carts": Hartshorn Lane and Angel Court, *c.*1614–*c.*1720', *London Topographical Record*, 27 (1995), 149–77. On the neighbourhood more generally, see Edward H. Sugden, *A Topographical Dictionary to the Works of Shakespeare and his Fellow Dramatists* (Manchester, 1925); Fran C. Chalfant, *Ben Jonson's London* (Athens, Ga., 1978); E. B. Chancellor, *Annals of the Strand* (1912); Sir Walter Besant and G. E. Mitton, *The Strand District* (1903).

20. From an inspection of 1677, cit. Cowper-Coles, '"A Place Much Clogged and Pestered with Carts"', 166; John Stow, *A Survey of the Cities of London and Westminster*, corr. John Strype (1720), 76.

21. Gater and Godfrey, *The Strand*, 22.

22. Cowper-Coles describes the sewerage works ('"A Place Much Clogged and Pestered with Carts"', 165), and cites (159) a landlady in the lane who in 1675 had cause to complain of a neighbour's 'continually carrying of dung and running of horse piss from his stable through a door and a passage which he hath lately made through a brick wall which was built for separation ... by means whereof some of the tenants have left their dwellings to her great detriment'.

23. ibid. 152, 156–7; Emrys Jones, 'The First West End Comedy', *Proceedings of the British Academy*, 68 (1982), 215–58. In 1613 Henry Howard, Earl of Northampton—Jonson's 'mortal enemy' (*Informations*, 250)—was to purchase property in Hartshorn Lane as part of the endowment of Trinity Hospital, Greenwich. The resident lessee at the time of Howard's purchase was curiously named Sir Robert Brett; he may conceivably have been a relative of Jonson's stepfather.

24. 'Stirrings' at Charing Cross are keenly anticipated by Doll the courtesan in Dekker's *Northward Ho!*, 1.2. On the area at this time, see J. Holden MacMichael, *The Story of Charing Cross and its Immediate Neighbourhood* (London, 1906).

25. Fuller, 'Westminster', 243; John McMaster, *A Short History of the Royal Parish of St Martin-in-the-Field* (London, 1916), 262; Hezekiah Woodward, *A Light of Grammar* (1641), quoted by Foster Watson, *The English Grammar Schools to 1600: Their Curriculum and Practice* (London, 1908; repr. 1968), 160. Jonson's dislike of corporal punishment is also evident in his reference to 'jerking [i.e. whipping] pedants' in *Poetaster*, 5.3.365, and to John Owen, 'a poor pedantic schoolmaster, sweeping his living from the posteriors of little children', *Informations*, 166–7.

26. Dedication in the Huntington copy of the quarto edition of *Cynthia's Revels*. It is sometimes supposed that the 'friend' was the lawyer John Hoskyns, but as the Oxford editors note, this rests on a strained interpretation of an anecdote by Aubrey: H&S, 1.3 n. 1; 'Hoskyns', John Aubrey, *Brief Lives*, ed. A. Clark (Oxford, 1898), 1.418.

27. On the school, see R. Ackermann, *The History of the Colleges of Winchester, Eton, and Westminster* (London, 1816); John D. Carleton, *Westminster School: A History* (rev. edn. 1965; 1st published London, 1938); John Field, *The King's Nurseries: The Story of Westminster School* (London, 1987); John Sargeaunt, *Annals of Westminster School* (London, 1898); Lawrence E. Tanner, *Westminster School: Its Buildings and their Associations* (London, 1923) and *Westminster School: A History* (London, 1934); Foster Watson, *The Old Grammar Schools* (Cambridge, 1916).

28. 'Plump' in a now obsolete sense of that word (*OED* †1): 'Blunt (in manners); not "sharp" in intellect; dull, clownish, blockish, rude'. See Neil Rhodes, *The Power of Eloquence and English Renaissance Literature* (New York, 1992), section 4.

29. Miles, *Ben Jonson: His Life and Works*, 13.

30. Field, *The King's Nurseries*, 23.

31. *The Life of Edward Earl of Clarendon* (London, 1759), 1.16.

32. Field, *The King's Nurseries*, 27.

33. Camden, *Britannia*, trans. Philemon Holland (1610), 'The Author to the Reader'. Cf. Jonson's *Epigrams*, 9 ('To All To Whom I Write'), *The Underwood*, 84.8, etc., and his recurrent insistence that he celebrates the 'good' as well as the 'great': e.g. *Epigrams*, Dedication, 19. On Camden more generally, see W. H. Herendeen, *William Camden: A Life in Context* (Woodbridge, 2007); F. J. Levy, 'The Making of Camden's *Britannia*', *Bibliothèque d'humanisme et Renaissance*, 26 (1964), 70–97; Graham Parry, *The Trophies of Time: English Antiquarians of the Seventeenth Century* (Oxford, 1995), ch. 1; Stuart Piggott, 'William Camden and the Britannia', *Proceedings of the British Academy*, 37 (1951), 199–217; D. R. Woolf, *The Idea of History in Early Stuart England* (Toronto, 1990).

34. Camden, *Certaine Poemes, or Poesies, Epigrammes, Rythmes, and Epitaphs of the English Nation in Former Times* appended to *Remaines concerning Britaine* (1605), 8. On Holland, see especially L. I. Guiney, *Recusant Poets* (London, 1938), 361ff.

35. T. W. Baldwin, *William Shakspere's Small Latine and Lesse Greeke*, 2 vols. (Urbana, Ill., 1944), provides a detailed account of the curriculum; see in particular ch. xvi. See also Watson, *The English Grammar Schools*.

36. 'He would many times exceed in drink (Canary was his beloved liquor) then he would tumble home to bed, and, when he had thoroughly perspired, then to study': Aubrey, *Brief Lives*, ed. Clark, 2.12.

37. Douglas Duncan, *Ben Jonson and the Lucianic Tradition* (Cambridge, 1979).

38. Camden, *Certain Poemes*, appended to *Remaines*, 7.

39. The paradox here is that Camden's own verses were mainly in Latin. See *Poems by William Camden*, ed. G. B. Johnston, with notes and translations from the Latin, *Studies in Philology*, 72 (1975). On the early development of English literary studies, see in particular Foster Watson, *The Beginnings of the Teaching of Modern Subjects in England* (London, 1909/1971), ch. 1, 'The Teaching of English'; Robert Crawford, *Devolving English Literature* (Oxford, 1992).

40. Watson, *The English Grammar Schools*, 497.

41. Camden, *Annales*, 2.27.

42. Jonson was a boy of 14 at the time of Sir Philip Sidney's death, but there are one or two hints in his work that he may have glimpsed him during his lifetime: see e.g. *Epigrams*, 104.1–2; *Informations*, 173–5. For Jonson's meeting with Heinsius, see Ch. 14 below.

43. It is difficult to assess the likely degree of involvement of a day boy such as Jonson in the Latin play, which was primarily reserved for the school boarders. At the very least he would have been a sharp observer of these activities. Nowell was also celebrated as the inventor of bottled beer, which Jonson was humorously to present as one of the 'enormities' of *Bartholomew Fair*.

44. The accounts are printed in appendix A of Tanner's *Westminster School: A History*.

45. Carleton, *Westminster School*, 3.

46. *CWBJ*, Jonson's Library, Electronic Edition.

47. *Terence*, trans. John Sargeaunt, The Loeb Classical Library, 2 vols. (London, 1912), 1.6–7.

48. The court performance may not have taken place: see Helen Ostovich's introduction to the play, *CWBJ*. In 1632 such a reference to the relative merits of the popular and the monarchical voice has obvious political implications; as in certain of Jonson's poems from this period, e.g. *The Underwood*, 64 and 72.

49. Terence was a particular target of puritan criticism: Baldwin, *Shakspere's Small Latine*, 1.111. See also Jonas Barish, *The Antitheatrical Prejudice* (Berkeley, 1981). On Terence's otherwise high reputation in the period, see William West, *Theatres and Encyclopedias in Early Modern Europe* (Cambridge, 2002), ch. 2.

Chapter 5

1. William Kerrigan, 'Ben Jonson Full of Shame and Scorn', *Studies in the Literary Imagination*, 6 (1973), 199–217, esp. 210–12.
2. Izaak Walton informed John Aubrey that George Morley (Bishop of Winchester from 1662 until 1684) knew Jonson 'very well, and says he was in the 6°—that is the uppermost form in Westminster School'. But Morley was twenty-five years Jonson's junior, and never at Westminster with him. He got to know Jonson only in the late 1620s, and his testimony needs to be treated with caution. H&S originally believed that Jonson was taken directly from Westminster School 'about 1589' to work with his stepfather, but later revised this date to 'probably' 1588 (1.6; 11.571). Both of these dates present difficulties, however, in relation to Jonson's apprenticeship as a bricklayer: see n. 10 below.
3. Thomas Fuller, *History of the Worthies of England* (London, 1662), 243. C. H. Herford dismissed the story as a piece of latter-day myth-making, but did not seriously test its provenance (H&S, 1.4–5 n. 1). Samuel Schoenbaum is equally sceptical about Fuller's reliability as a witness: 'Shakespeare and Jonson: Fact and Myth', in David Galloway (ed.), *The Elizabethan Theatre*, 5 (Hamden, Conn., 1970), 1–19. On Fuller's exceptional powers of memory, see however Ian Donaldson, 'National Biography and the Arts of Memory', in Peter France and William St Clair (eds.), *Mapping Biography* (Oxford, 2002), 67–82; and more generally on Fuller, William Addison, *Worthy Dr Fuller* (London, 1951), Dean B. Lyman, *The Great Tom Fuller* (Berkeley, 1935). For descriptions of James's Cambridge visit, see John Nicholls, *Progresses of James I* (London, 1828), 3.49–50, and Thomas Baker, *History of the College of St John the Evangelist, Cambridge*, ed. John E. B. Mayor, 2 vols. (London, 1869), 1.201–2. J. Bass Mullinger considers the evidence of Jonson's 'ditty' and provenance of books in the college library: 'Was Ben Jonson ever a Member of our College?', *The Eagle* (St John's College, Cambridge), 25 (June 1904), 1–4.
4. Preface to Greene's *Menaphon* (1590), in *The Works of Thomas Nashe*, ed. R. B. McKerrow, with corrections and additions by F. P. Wilson, 5 vols. (Oxford, 1958), 3.317. On Nashe's time at St John's, see Charles Nicholl, *A Cup of News: The Life of Thomas Nashe* (London, 1984), ch. 3.
5. Baker, *History of the College of St John*, 1.180. See also J. Bass Mullinger, *St John's College* (London, 1901), 72ff.; Edward Miller, *Portrait of the College of Saint John the Evangelist, Cambridge* (Cambridge, 1961), ch. 2.
6. *A Catalogue of the Library of Tomas Baker*, ed. Frans Korsten (Cambridge, 2010), item 1476, p. 143; 'Ben Jonson', *Biographia Britannica*, 6 vols. (1747–66), 4.2777, n. [F].
7. Baker, *History of the College of St John*, 184.
8. So Nicholas Oldisworth, 'A Letter to Ben Jonson' (*c.*1629), lines 55–6: 'Lie level to our view, so we shall see | Our third and richest university': *CWBJ*, Literary Record, Electronic Edition. For the dating of Jonson's honorary degree, see Ch. 17 below.
9. Fuller, *Worthies*, 243. John Aubrey, reversing the chronological sequence of Fuller's story, believed that while Jonson worked with his stepfather 'particularly on the garden-wall of Lincoln's Inn next to Chancery Lane', a passing lawyer happened to overhear him declaiming some lines from Homer, and 'finding him to have a wit extraordinary', was

moved to provide 'some Exhibition to maintaine him, at Trinity College in Cambridge'. No evidence of Jonson's association with Trinity has been found, however, and the story is queried by Aubrey himself in the margin of his manuscript. William Oldys, in a hand-written note on his copy of Gerard Langbaine's *An Account of the English Dramatic Poets* (1691), now in the British Library, has written beside Fuller's story concerning Jonson's work at Lincoln's Inn, quoted by Langbaine: 'in the square whose chapel stands, not far from the old gate which leads into Chancery Lane.'

10. Mark Eccles, 'Jonson's Marriage', *Review of English Studies*, 12 (1936), 257–72. In his later dating of these events, 'Ben Jonson: "Citizen and Bricklayer"', *Notes & Queries*, 35 (1988), 445–6, Eccles argues persuasively that since Jonson must have been a freeman by the time of his marriage to Anne Lewis on 14 November 1594, his seven-year apprenticeship must have begun by late 1587.

11. Anthony à Wood, *Athenae Oxonienses*, 2 vols. (1691–2), 1.518; John Taylor, 'A Funeral Elegy', *CWBJ*, Literary Record, Electronic Edition.

12. Fuller, *Worthies*, 243; *The Return From Parnassus*, Part 2, lines 293–8, in *Three Parnassus Plays*, ed. J. B. Leishman (London, 1949); *The Poems of Sir John Davies*, ed. Robert Krueger (Oxford, 1975), 181; *CWBJ*, Literary Record, Electronic Edition. Dekker's Tucca rails at 'Horace', alias Jonson, as a 'foul-fisted mortar-treader', and his Welshman, Sir Rees ap Vaughan, wonders why Horace has abandoned the 'honest trade of building symneys and laying down bricks for a worse handicraftness, to make nothing but rails': *Satiromastix* (1601), ed. Penniman, 4.2.67, 194–6. Thomas Middleton's reference in the *Masque of Heroes, Or The Inner Temple Masque* (207) to 'one o' the silenced bricklayers' may also perhaps be aimed at Jonson: see Jerzy Limon, *Notes & Queries*, 41 (1994), 512; Thomas Middleton, *The Collected Works*, ed. Gary Taylor and John Lavagnino (Oxford, 2007), 13–27.

13. See Mary Edmond, 'Pembroke's Men', *Review of English Studies*, 25 (1974), 129–36; Eccles, 'Ben Jonson: "Citizen and Bricklayer"'; Kay, *Ben Jonson: A Literary Life*, 12–15, and '"Rare Ben": The Bricklayer of Westminster and his Family' (unpublished typescript); David Kathman, 'Grocers, Goldsmiths, and Drapers: Freemen and Apprentices in the Elizabe-than Theater', *Shakespeare Quarterly*, 55 (2004), 1–49. I am grateful to Professor Kay and Dr Kathman for generously sharing their findings with me ahead of publication.

14. David Kathman's discovery: see 'Grocers, Goldsmiths, and Drapers', 20.

15. *CWBJ*, Life Records, 83, Electronic Edition, and Ch. 19 below. I thank Dr Ian Gadd, for advice on Scottish guild terminology and practices.

16. George Unwin, *The Gilds and Companies of London*, 2nd edn. (London, 1928); George Bell, *A Short History of the Worshipful Company of Tylers and Bricklayers of the City of London* (London, 1938); F. W. Fairholt (ed.), *Lord Mayors' Pageants*: Parts 1 & 2 of the Percy Society's *Early English Poetry, Ballads, and Popular Literature of the Middle Ages*, 10 (London, 1844); David M. Bergeron, *English Civic Pageantry, 1558–1642* (London, 1971); Jean Robertson and D. J. Gordon (eds.), *A Calendar of Dramatic Records of the Livery Companies of London*, The Malone Society Collections 3 (London, 1954); Gabriel Heaton and James Knowles, '"Entertainment Perfect": Ben Jonson and Corporate Hospitality', *Review of English Studies*, NS 54 (2003), 587–600.

17. Robertson and Gordon (eds.), *A Calendar of Dramatic Records*, 61–8; Bergeron, *English Civic Pageantry*, 246. Thomas Lowe, who was installed as Lord Mayor in the autumn of 1604, had been apprenticed to the prosperous haberdasher and Member of Parliament

Thomas Aldersey. In his researches for the 'Foot-Voyage into Scotland', found amongst the Aldersey family papers in the Cheshire and Chester archives (and discussed in Ch. 2 above), James Loxley has traced Lowe's connection with the Aldersey family, and wondered whether this connection might have been responsible for Jonson's selection over Munday for this commission. Alternatively, the commission might have brought Jonson into contact with the Aldersey family for the first time. For a fuller review of these possibilities, see James Loxley's and Julie Sanders's edition of this manuscript, *CWBJ*, Electronic Edition.

18. R. H. Tawney and Eileen Power (eds.), *Tudor Economic Documents*, 3 vols. (London, 1924), 1.342; Kay, '"Rare Ben"', n. 22.
19. See in particular Geoffrey Parker, *The Dutch Revolt* (Harmondsworth, 1977), Wallace T. MacCaffrey, *Elizabeth I: War and Politics 1588–1603* (Princeton, 1992), ch. 13, and the same author's *Elizabeth I* (London, 1993), ch. 20; and Abraham B. Feldman, 'Playwrights and Pike-Trailers in the Low Countries', *Notes & Queries* (May 1953), 184–7.
20. See 47 above.
21. Elizabeth herself was less pleased by the conduct of the Sidney brothers, whom she suspected of having had too close an association with their uncle Leicester. Robert was forced to endure long exile in the Low Countries, his repeated requests to return to England being persistently rejected until the final years of Elizabeth's reign. The family's strong Protestant ideology and association with the Essex circle would keep them perpetually at a distance from royal favour. See G. F. J. Levy, 'Sir Philip Sidney Reconsidered', in his *Tudor Historical Thought* (London, 1957), and Millicent V. Hay, *The Life of Sir Robert Sidney, Earl of Leicester (1563–1626)* (London, 1984), 44–6. On Sidney's posthumous reputation, see Gavin Alexander, *Writing after Sidney: The Literary Response to Sir Philip Sidney 1586–1640* (Oxford, 2006).
22. *The Commentaries of Sir Francis Vere*, published by William Dillingham, DD (Cambridge, 1657), 17–18.
23. Livy tells of the three Horatii brothers who fought the three Curiatii brothers in single combat on behalf of the Romans and Albans, and of the victorious survivor, Horatius, displaying his triple *spolia*, thereby provoking further tragedy (1.24–6).
24. Shakespeare's Antony challenges Octavius Caesar to combat of this kind, 'that he and Caesar might | Determine this great war in single fight', *Antony and Cleopatra*, 4.4.36–7, 3.13.25–6. Hamlet's father seemingly encounters Fortinbras in similar fashion, *Hamlet*, 1.1.60–1. On the infrequency of the custom in early modern times, see V. G. Kiernan, *The Duel in European History: Honour and the Reign of Aristocracy* (Oxford, 1988), 58–9. See also Markku Peltonen, *The Duel in Early Modern England: Civility, Politeness, and Honour* (Cambridge, 2003), and Bacon's account of the practice, 'The Charge Touching Duels', in *Francis Bacon*, ed. Brian Vickers, The Oxford Authors (Oxford, 1996), 309.
25. G. B. Harrison, *The Life and Death of Robert Devereux, Earl of Essex* (London, 1937), 62–3.
26. Julie Sanders, *Ben Jonson's Theatrical Republics* (Houndmills, 1998), introduction.
27. [Owen Felltham], *A Brief Character of the Low Countries* (London, 1671), 1, 4.

Chapter 6

1. This account of the early playhouses draws on E. K. Chambers, *The Elizabethan Stage*, 4 vols. (Oxford, 1923); G. E. Bentley, *The Jacobean and Caroline Stage*, 7 vols. (Oxford, 1941–68); Glynne Wickham, Herbert Berry, and William Ingram, *English Professional*

NOTES TO PAGES 101–104

Theatre 1530–1660 (Cambridge, 2000); Andrew Gurr, *Playgoing in Shakespeare's London* (Cambridge, 1987) and *The Shakespearean Playing Companies* (Oxford, 1996); J. Leeds Barroll, Richard Hosley, Alexander Leggatt, and Alvin Kernan, *The Revels History of Drama in English*, 3: *1576–1613* (London, 1975); and Herbert Berry (ed.), *The First Public Playhouse: The Theatre in Shoreditch, 1576–1598* (Montreal, 1979).

2. An even earlier public amphitheatre, the Red Lion, built in Whitechapel in 1567, may also have followed this design: see Wickham, Berry, and Ingram, *English Professional Theatre*, 290–4; Gurr, *Playgoing in Shakespeare's London*, 13.

3. E. H. Sugden, *A Topographical Dictionary to the Works of Shakespeare and his Fellow Dramatists* (Manchester, 1925); Fran Chalfont, *Ben Jonson's London: A Jacobean Placename Dictionary* (Athens, Ga., 1978). The name 'Curtain' (or 'Green Curtain') denoted a plot of grassy land (not a theatrical property): see Bentley, *The Jacobean and Caroline Stage*, 6.131.

4. Wickham, Berry, and Ingram, *English Professional Theatre*, 345–6, 410; Barroll et al., *Revels History*, 3.39–40.

5. John Aubrey, *Brief Lives*, ed. A. Clark (Oxford, 1898), 2.12.

6. Fredson Bowers ('Jonson and Dekker', *TLS*, 12 September 1936, p. 729) speculates on the possibility of Jonson's having played the part of Christopher Sly in *The Taming of the Shrew* for the Chamberlain's Men at the Curtain theatre between October and December 1597: a conjecture based entirely on Dekker's reference to Horace (alias Jonson) as 'a sly knave', *Satiromastix*, 1.2.436.

7. See Ch. 9 below. She may possibly have been the 'Ann Lewis', daughter of William, who was baptized at St Mildred Poultry with St Mary Colechurch on 17 January 1571: see Tom Cain, 'Mary and Bedford Jonson', *Ben Jonson Journal*, 14.1 (2007), 78–87, at 85 n. 4.

8. Sugden, *A Topographical Dictionary*; Mark Eccles, 'Jonson's Marriage', *Review of English Studies*, 12 (1936), 257–72, at 261.

9. John Field, *A Godly Exhortation by Occasion of the Late Judgement of God, Showed at Paris-garden* (London, 1583).

10. In the Induction to *Bartholomew Fair*, written for another venue on the Bankside that doubled as a bear-pit, Jonson would refer again to the powerful stench of the tormented animals that lingered in the open auditorium.

11. See Siobhan Keenan, *Travelling Players in Shakespeare's England* (Basingstoke, 2002), Alan B. Somerset, '"How chances it they travel?" Provincial Touring, Playing Places, and the King's Men', *Shakespeare Survey*, 47 (1994), 45–60; G. E. Bentley, *The Profession of Player in Shakespeare's Time, 1590–1642* (Princeton, 1971), ch. 7; Gurr, *The Shakespearian Playing Companies*, ch. 3.

12. On Thespis and his cart, see also Jonson's translation of Horace's *Ars Poetica*, 311–15, and (more disparagingly) *Discoveries*, 2675–7.

13. F. T. Bowers, 'Ben Jonson the Actor', *Studies in Philology*, 34 (1937), 396–7.

14. On Pembroke's Men, see Gurr, *The Shakespearian Playing Companies*, ch. 15, and on Shakespeare's possible association with the company, pp. 270–1. Mary Edmond, 'Pembroke's Men', *Review of English Studies*, NS 25 (1974), 129–36, argues the case for Jonson's membership of the company in the early 1590s; but the 'Mr Johnson' mentioned in the actor Simon Jewell's will in August 1592, on whom this argument turns, is now thought to be an older actor, William Johnson, a member of the Queen's Men, and not the future dramatist. See Scott McMillan, 'Simon Jewell and the Queen's Men', *Review of English Studies*, NS 27 (1976), 174–7; David George, 'Shakespeare and Pembroke's Men',

Shakespeare Quarterly, 32 (1981), 305–23; Karl Wentersdorf, *Theatre Research International*, 5 (1979), 45–68.

15. Aubrey, 'William Shakespeare', in *Brief Lives*, ed. Clark, 2.226.

16. Gurr, *The Shakespearian Playing Companies*, 100–2.

17. *Epigrams*, 49, 68, 100. The word also occurs in the commendatory verses of 'Cygnus' (probably Jonson's friend Hugh Holland) prefixed to the quarto edition of *Sejanus*, and in Henry Fitzgeffrey's gibe at the dramatist John Webster, 'Crabbed (Websterio), The Playwright, Cart-wright': 'Notes From Blackfriars', in *Satires and Satirical Epigrams*, 1617.

18. G. E. Bentley, *The Profession of Dramatist in Shakespeare's Time, 1590–1642* (Princeton, 1971/1986), ch. 5, pp. 108–9; *Henslowe's Diaries*, ed. W. W. Greg, 2 vols. (London, 1904–8), 2.126–7.

19. See Robert S. Miola's introduction to his edition of the play, *CWBJ*.

20. Hugh Craig's lexical tests on *The Case Is Altered* raise some doubts however as to whether the play was written entirely by Jonson: see 'The 1602 Additions to *The Spanish Tragedy*', in Hugh Craig and Arthur F. Kinney (eds.), *Shakespeare, Computers, and the Mystery of Authorship* (Cambridge, 2009), ch. 8, esp. 175–6. J. M. Nosworthy suggests the play is another version of *Hot Anger Soon Cold*, written in collaboration with Porter and Chettle: '*The Case Is Altered*', *Journal of English and Germanic Philology*, 51 (1952), 61–70. Frank L. Huntley believes Jonson rewrote an older play written by his enemies in the *poetamachia*, in order to strike back at them and at Anthony Munday: 'Ben Jonson and Anthony Munday, or, *The Case Is Altered* Altered Again', *Philological Quarterly*, 41 (1962), 205–14.

21. See Thompson Cooper, 'Edmund Plowden', *DNB* (1895), and for further possible explanations of the phrase, H&S, 9.305–6.

22. 'Centre attractive': *The Magnetic Lady*, Induction, 108–9.

23. *CWBJ*, 1,553.

24. Chambers, *The Elizabethan Stage*, 3.455. This letter seems to have been the precipitating event. On 28 July, however—the very day that their own edict was issued—the Privy Council had received a petition from the Lord Mayor and aldermen of London and Lords of Council at Westminster, asking for plays and playing throughout the metropolis to be suppressed. William Ingram, who has studied this episode in close detail, believes it unlikely that the petition had any effect on the Privy Council's action. Requests of this kind were regularly dispatched at this time of year by the city fathers, frustrated by their lack of control over theatres which lay beyond their jurisdiction, and were just as regularly ignored. There would in any case scarcely have been time for the petition even to have reached the Privy Council on 29 July, let alone swayed their debates. See Glynne Wickham, 'The Privy Council Order of 1597 for the Destruction of London's Theatres', in David Galloway (ed.), *The Elizabethan Theatre* (Toronto, 1969), 21–44; William Ingram, *A London Life in the Brazen Age: Francis Langley 1548–1602* (Cambridge, Mass., 1978), ch. 11; and (for a more recent view, slightly modifying each of these earlier positions) Wickham, Berry, and Ingram (eds.), *English Professional Theatre*, 102–5.

25. From the court transcript, *CWBJ*, Life Records, 10, 11, Electronic Edition. See also my account of *The Isle of Dogs* in *CWBJ*, 1,101–9.

26. *Nashe's Lenten Stuff* (1599), in *The Works of Thomas Nashe*, ed. R. B. McKerrow, with corrections and supplementary notes by F. P. Wilson, 5 vols. (Oxford, 1966), 3.153–4.

27. Francis Meres, *Palladis Tamia*, in G. Gregory Smith (ed.), *Elizabethan Critical Essays*, 2 vols. (Oxford, 1904), 2.324; *The Second Part of the Return From Parnassus*, 5.3.2062–8, in

The Three Parnassus Plays (1598–1601), ed. J. B. Leishman (London, 1949). Despite the bishops' stern edict that all of Nashe's books be destroyed and none 'be ever printed hereafter' (Edward Arber, *A Transcript of the Registers of the Company of Stationers of London 1554–1640*, 6 vols. (London, 1876), 3.677), *Summer's Last Will and Testament* was published the following year: W. W. Greg, *A Companion to Arber* (Oxford, 1967), 49–50.

28. *CWBJ*, Life Records, 11, Electronic Edition.

29. Alan Haynes, *The Elizabethan Secret Services* (Stroud, 2004; 1st published 1992), 60–1.

30. *Henslowe's Diary*, ed. R. A. Foakes, 2nd edn. (Cambridge, 2002), 240.

31. Demolition work began on the Theatre late in 1598 as it had become clear that its lease could not be renewed, not because of the edict. See Wickham, Berry, and Ingram, *English Professional Theatre*, 103.

32. *Henslowe's Diary*, ed. Foakes, 239–40; Wickham, 'The Privy Council Order'.

33. William Empson, 'The English Dog', ch. 7 of *The Structure of Complex Words* (London, 1952); Vincent Carretta, *The Snarling Muse: Verbal and Visual Satire from Pope to Churchill* (Philadelphia, 1983); *The Works of Thomas Nashe*, ed. R. B. McKerrow, 5 vols. (London, 1910), 3.255; *The Roaring Girl*, ed. Coppélia Kahn, in *Thomas Middleton: The Collected Works*, ed. Gary Taylor and John Lavagnino (Oxford, 2007). Middleton's *Micro-cynicon. Six Snarling Satires* (1599) was one of the works condemned in the Bishops' Ban on satire in June 1599.

34. Charles Nicholl, *A Cup of News: The Life of Thomas Nashe* (London, 1984), 247–9.

35. E. K. Chambers, *The Elizabethan Stage*, 3.455; Alice-Lyle Scoufos, *Shakespeare's Typological Satire: A Study of the Falstaff–Oldcastle Problem* (Athens, Oh., 1979); Nicholl, *A Cup of News*, 249–56; Gary Taylor, 'The Fortunes of Oldcastle', *Shakespeare Studies*, 38 (1985), 85–100; Gary Taylor, 'William Shakespeare, Richard James, and the House of Cobham', *Review of English Studies*, NS 38 (1987), 334–54; Richard Dutton, *Mastering the Revels: The Regulation and Censorship of English Renaissance Drama* (Basingstoke, 1991), ch. 4.

36. R. B. Wernham, *The Return of the Armadas: The Last Years of the Elizabethan War against Spain 1595–1603* (Oxford, 1994), 160–1; Paul E. J. Hammer, *The Polarization of Elizabethan Politics: The Political Career of Robert Devereux, 2nd Earl of Essex, 1585–1597* (Cambridge, 1999); Wallace T. MacCaffrey, *Elizabeth I: War and Politics 1588–1603* (Princeton, 1992); Thomas Birch, *Memoirs of the Reign of Queen Elizabeth from 1581 till her Death*, 2 vols. (1754), 2.344ff.; Walter Bourchier Devereux, *Lives and Letters of the Devereux, Earls of Essex*, 2 vols. (1853), 1, chs. xiv–xv.

37. Pliny, *Natural History*, trans. H. Rackham, 10 vols. (Cambridge, Mass., 1950), 6.37.

38. Arnobius of Sicca, *The Case against the Pagans*, trans. George E. McCracken, 2 vols. (New York, 1949), vol. 2.

39. David Hancock, *The Mastiffs: The Big Game Hunters. Their History, Development, and Future* (Ducklington, 2001), 69–74.

40. F. J. Burgoyne, *Collotype Facsimile of an Elizabethan Manuscript Preserved at Alnwick Castle* (London, 1904); *The Works of Thomas Nashe*, ed. McKerrow, 5.29 n. 4; Peter Beal, *Index of English Literary Manuscripts*, 4 vols. in 10 (London, 1980–97), 1.1.18.

41. Burgoyne (ed.), *Collotype Facsimile...at Alnwick*, introduction; [Archbishop Tenison], *Baconiana. Or Certain Genuine Remains of Sir Francis Bacon, Baron of Verulam, and Viscount of St Albans* (London, 1679), 60; James Spedding, *The Life and Letters of Francis Bacon*, 14 vols. (London, 1874), 14.429. The Latin translation of Bacon's *Essays* was published in 1625. Antony à Wood believed Jonson 'did with Dr Hacket (afterwards Bishop of Lichfield) translate into Latin the Lord Bacon's *Essays or Counsels Civil and*

Moral': *Athenae Oxonienses*, 2 vols. (London, 1691–2), 1.509 (mis-pagination). For a more detailed account of Jonson's probable role in this translation, see my entry on *Sermones fideles*, *CWBJ*, Dubia, Electronic Edition.

42. See Ch. 17 below.

43. The role of the secretariat has been examined by Paul E. J. Hammer in two studies, 'The Uses of Scholarship: The Secretariat of Robert Devereux, Second Earl of Essex, *c.*1585–1601', *English Historical Review*, 109 (1994), 26–51; and 'The Earl of Essex, Fulke Greville, and the Employment of Scholars', *Studies in Philology*, 91 (1994), 167ff. On Essex's liberality towards poets and 'men of genius and learning', see Birch, *Memoirs of the Reign of Queen Elizabeth*, 2.487–8.

44. See Martin Butler, '"Servant, not Slave": Ben Jonson at the Jacobean Court', Chatterton Lecture on Poetry, *Proceedings of the British Academy*, 90 (1996), 65–93, especially 76–9.

45. Malcolm Smuts, 'Court-Centred Politics and the Uses of Roman Historians, *c.*1590–1630', in Kevin Sharpe and Peter Lake (eds.), *Culture and Politics in Early Stuart England* (Basingstoke, 1994), 21–43; J. H. M. Salmon, 'Stoicism and Roman Examples: Seneca and Tacitus in Jacobean England', *Journal of the History of Ideas*, 50 (1989), 199–225; Ronald Mellor, *Tacitus* (New York, 1993); Kenneth Schelhase, *Tacitus in the Renaissance* (Chicago, 1976).

Chapter 7

1. Andrew Gurr, *The Shakespearian Playing Companies* (Oxford, 1996), 26–7. On this general topic see also Gertrude Marian Sibley, *The Lost Plays and Masques 1500–1642* (Ithaca, NY, 1933) and C. J. Sisson, *The Lost Plays of Shakespeare's Age* (Cambridge, 1936), Ian Donaldson, lost plays entries, *CWBJ*, and Roslyn L. Knutson and David McInnis, *Lost Plays Database*, www.lostplays.org.

2. Lukas Erne, *Shakespeare as Literary Dramatist* (Cambridge, 2003).

3. *The English Traveller*, 1631, 'To the Reader', in *The Dramatic Works of Thomas Heywood*, 6 vols. (London, 1874), 4.5.

4. Gurr remarks that 'Little beside Jonson's *Isle of Dogs* is known to have disappeared from his long *oeuvre*' (*The Shakespearian Playing Companies*, 26). This is not quite right. In 1618–19 Jonson assured William Drummond 'That the half of his comedies were not in print' (*Informations*, 306). While *Bartholomew Fair* and *The Devil is an Ass*—both subsequently to appear in the Second Folio in 1641—would have been amongst Jonson's unpublished comedies at this date, the group must have included a significant number of other comedies that have failed to survive.

5. David Cressy, *Literacy and the Social Order: Reading and Writing in Tudor and Stuart England* (Cambridge, 1980); Lawrence Stone, 'Literacy and Education in England 1640–1900', *Past and Present*, 42 (1969), 69–139; R. S. Schofield, 'The Measurement of Literacy in Pre-industrial Society', in Jack Goody (ed.), *Literacy in Traditional Societies* (Cambridge, 1968); Keith Thomas, *Religion and the Decline of Magic* (Harmondsworth, 1971), 4–5.

6. See G. E. Bentley, *The Profession of Dramatist in Shakespeare's Time, 1590–1642* (Princeton, 1971), ch. 2, 'The Status of Dramatists'. Sir Thomas Bodley famously instructed his librarian not to bother collecting playbooks for his new library in Oxford (*Letters of Sir Thomas Bodley to Thomas James, Keeper of the Bodleian Library*, ed. G. W. Wheeler (Oxford, 1926), 219–20), but his attitude may have reflected particular needs and constraints at Oxford, rather than the characteristic tastes of contemporary collectors: see

Heidi Brayman Hackel, ' "Rowme" of its Own: Printed Drama in Early Libraries', ch. 7 in John D. Cox and David Scott Kastan (eds.), *A New History of Early English Drama* (New York, 1997), 113–30.

7. Joseph Loewenstein, 'The Script in the Marketplace', in Stephen Greenblatt (ed.), *Representing the English Renaissance* (Berkeley, 1988), 265–78, and the same author's *Jonson and Possessive Authorship* (Cambridge, 2002). See also Ian Donaldson, 'Shakespeare, Jonson, and the Invention of the Author', *Proceedings of the British Academy: 2006 Lectures*, 151 (2007), 319–38.

8. See the robust remarks on Day, Dekker, and Marston, *Informations*, 36, 117.

9. *CWBJ*, Life Records, 8, Electronic Edition. The evidence for this conclusion is not wholly persuasive. For interpretation, see Alwin Thaler, 'Bengemenes Johnsones Share', *Modern Language Review*, 16 (1921), 61–5, and W. W. Greg's reply, 'Bengemenes Johnsones Share', *Modern Language Review*, 16 (1921), 323.

10. *Henslowe's Diary*, ed. R. A. Foakes, 2nd edn. (Cambridge, 2002), 73; cf. 85.

11. ibid. 96; Neil Carson, *A Companion to Henslowe's Diary* (Cambridge, 1988), 49.

12. 'Ben Jonson and the Modern Stage', a debate between Irving Wardle, Peter Barnes, Terry Hands, Jonathan Hammond, and Colin Blakeley, *Gambit*, 6.22 (1972), 5–30, at 17. Cf. Ian Donaldson, 'Jonson and Anger', in Claude Rawson (ed.), *English Satire and the Satiric Tradition* (Oxford, 1984), 56–71.

13. Carson, *A Companion*, 62.

14. Francis Meres, *Palladis Tamis*, in G. Gregory Smith (ed.), *Elizabethan Critical Essays*, 2 vols. (Oxford, 1904), 2.319–20. John Weever's praise of the 'embuskined Jonson' similarly implies that Jonson was known as a writer of tragedy at this time: *Epigrams in the Oldest Cut and Newest Fashion*, 1599, in D. H. Craig (ed.), *Ben Jonson: The Critical Heritage 1599–1798* (London, 1990), 45.

15. *Henslowe's Diary*, ed. Foakes, 123–4.

16. ibid. 124.

17. *CSPD, Eliz.* 286.61. David Kay suggests that it was not in fact *Every Man In His Humour* but *Every Man Out of his Humour* 'which established Jonson as the leading humour satirist and began the literary reputation which encouraged him to leave the Globe for the Blackfriars', but Jonson himself evidently did not share (or wish publicly to advertise) this view of his theatrical progress. See Kay's 'The Shaping of Ben Jonson's Career: A Re-examination of Facts and Problems', *Modern Philology*, 67 (1970), 224–35, at 225. 'Then he undertook again to write a play,' comments John Aubrey with characteristic vagueness, after discussing Jonson's work at the Curtain, 'and did hit it admirably well, viz. *Every Man...*, which was his first good one': John Aubrey, *Brief Lives*, ed. A. Clark (Oxford, 1898), 1.12.

18. *The Works of Mr William Shakespeare*, ed. Nicholas Rowe, 6 vols. (London, 1709), 1.xii–xiii. On the reliability of Rowe's testimony as a biographer, see S. Schoenbaum, *Shakespeare's Lives* (Oxford, 1970), 129–35; on the mythologizing of Shakespeare's and Jonson's characters, see Ian Donaldson, 'Looking Sideways: Jonson, Shakespeare, and the Myths of Envy', in Takashi Kozuka and J. R. Mulryne (eds.), *Shakespeare, Marlowe, Jonson: New Directions in Biography* (Aldershot, 2006), 241–57; on the supposedly 'gentle' Shakespeare, see Katherine Duncan-Jones, *Ungentle Shakespeare: Scenes from his Life* (London, 2001). Rowe's story runs contrary moreover to the company's normal methods of selecting new plays for performance: see Andrew Gurr, *The Shakespeare Company 1594–1642* (Cambridge, 2004), 144 n. 35.

19. For the impact of Jonson's dramatic practice on the company's repertoire, see Gurr, *The Shakespeare Company*, 140–4.

20. Gabriele Bernhard Jackson argues that Burghley is glanced at in Cob's reference to 'some fishmonger's son' at 3.1.169–71 (Q): see her edition of *Every Man In His Humour* (F) in the Yale Ben Jonson series (New Haven, 1969), 200–1.

21. A. L. Beier, *Masterless Men: The Vagrancy Problem in England 1560–1640* (London, 1985), Paul Slack, *Poverty and Policy in Tudor and Stuart England* (London, 1988), 127, cit. Robert Miola (ed.), *Every Man In His Humour*, The Revels Plays (Manchester, 2000), 70; Paul A. Jorgensen, *Shakespeare's Military World* (Berkeley, 1956), 209–12. In the very month that *Every Man In His Humour* was performed, a Proclamation was issued 'against idle vagabonds, wandering about many parts of the realm, especially about London and the court, being able men, and exacting money on pretence of service in the wars, whereas many never did serve, and those who did are provided for in their several counties': 9 September 1598, *CSPD, Elizabeth, 1598–1601*, 93.

22. I owe this suggestion to Martin Butler. Another Spaniard of this name whom Jonson may possibly have remembered was Francisco de Mendoza y Bobadilla, Bishop of Burgos *c*.1550, humanist and scholar, friend of Erasmus and Vives.

23. See 95–7, above, and Donaldson, *Jonson's Magic Houses* (Oxford, 1997), 139–40. Bobadilla's scheme may also refers to the more recent fate of John Barrose, 'a Burgonian by nation and a fencer by profession, that lately was come over and had challenged all the fencers of England' and was hanged in July 1598 for killing an officer of the City who had arrested him for debt: G. B. Harrison, *A Second Elizabethan Journal* (London, 1931), 289–90, entry for 10 July 1598; Stow, *Annales* (1631), 787.

24. The title page of the first quarto edition of *2 Henry IV*, published in the same year in which *Every Man In His Humour* was performed, announces 'the humours of Sir John Falstaff and swaggering Pistol'. Falstaff's followers are termed 'irregular humorists' in the cast of characters in the 1623 First Folio. For the significance of this term in relation to Falstaff's eighteenth-century reputation, see Stuart M. Tave, *The Amiable Humorist* (Chicago, 1969). On the humours more generally, see Gail Kern Paster, *Humoring the Body: Emotions and the Shakespearean Stage* (Chicago, 2004).

25. Donaldson, 'Looking Sideways' (n. 17 above), 249–52.

26. Joseph Quincy Adams, *A Life of William Shakespeare* (London, 1923), 274–6.

27. G. B. Harrison, *A Second Elizabethan Journal*, 286, entry for 23 June 1598; citing Salisbury Papers, 8.219 and 224–31.

28. Vincentio Saviolo, *His Practice* (1595), in James L. Jackson (ed.), *Three Elizabethan Fencing Manuals*, facsimile reprint (Delmar, NY, 1972), 381–5. On the status and problems of duelling in this period see Lawrence Stone, 'The Duel', in *The Crisis of the Aristocracy* (Oxford, 1965), 242–50; V. G. Kiernan, *The Duel in European History: Honour and the Reign of Aristocracy* (Oxford, 1988), 58–9, and Markku Peltonen, *The Rise and Fall of the English Duel* (Cambridge, 2002).

29. T. W. Baldwin, *The Organization and Personnel of the Shakespearean Company* (Princeton, 1927), 157; *Memoirs of Edward Alleyn*, ed. J. Payne Collier, Shakespeare Society (London, 1841), 51. The letter is dated 26 September 1598.

30. See above, 127–8. David Kathman, 'Grocers, Goldsmiths, and Drapers: Freemen and Apprentices in the Elizabethan Theater', *Shakespeare Quarterly*, 55 (2004), 1–49, at 5.

31. *Middlesex County Records (Old Series)*, ed. John Cordy Jeaffreson (London, 1972; reproduced from the original edition of 1886), 1.xlv–xlvii.

32. *Middlesex County Records*, ed. Jeaffreson, 1.xxxix–xl.

33. See Egerton Castle, *Schools and Masters of Fence from the Middle Ages to the Eighteenth Century* (London, 1885), and Stone, *The Crisis of the Aristocracy*, 242–50. The short sword continued to have its champions. In 1599 George Silver in a treatise entitled *Paradoxes of Defence* scornfully dismissed the claims that Vincentio Saviolo had made for the now fashionable rapier, and claimed to have 'proved the true grounds of fight to be in the short ancient weapons, and that the short sword hath advantage of the long sword or rapier': see Jackson (ed.), *Three Elizabethan Fencing Manuals*, 489.

34. Cressy, *Literacy and the Social Order*, 16–17; J. A. Sharpe, *Crime in Early Modern England 1550–1750* (Harlow, 1984), 67; J. H. Baker, *An Introduction to English Legal History*, 4th edn. (London, 2002), 513–15.

35. G. E. Bentley, *Shakespeare and Jonson: Their Reputations in the Seventeenth Century Compared* (Chicago, 1965), 2.59.

36. The identification of the priest who visited Jonson in prison with Father Wright was first made by Theodore A. Stroud in 'Ben Jonson and Father Thomas Wright', *English Literary History*, 14 (1947), 274–82. The present account draws also on Stroud's 'Father Thomas Wright: A Test Case for Toleration', *Biographical Studies*, 1 (1951–2), 189–219; Arnold Pritchard, *Catholic Loyalism in Elizabethan England* (London, 1979); Peter Milward's biographical entry in the *ODNB*; and the informative introductions to two modern editions of Wright's *The Passions of the Mind in General*: by Thomas O. Sloan (Urbana, Ill., 1971), and by William Webster Newbold, for The Renaissance Imagination 15 (New York, 1986).

37. An English text of the tract—attributed to a different Father Wright until Stroud's persuasive identification of its true authorship—is given in John Strype, *Annals of the Reformation*, 7 vols. (Oxford, 1874), 3.2, 583–97.

38. Letter of 17 October 1598, Salisbury papers, 8.394, cit. Newbold (ed.), *Passions of the Mind*, introduction, 8–9. On the degree of Wright's liberty at the time of Jonson's imprisonment, see Newbold (ed.), *Passions of the Mind*, 62, and Stroud, 'Ben Jonson and Father Thomas Wright', 280–1.

39. W. K. Jordan, *The Development of Religious Toleration in England from the Beginning of the Reformation to the Death of Queen Elizabeth* (London, 1932), 194.

40. Salisbury papers, 8.394; Dana F. Sutton (ed.), *Unpublished Works by William Alabaster (1568–1640)* (Salzburg, 1997), 118; Henry Foley SJ, *Records of the English Province of the Society of Jesus*, 7 vols. (London, 1877), 1.66–9. On Alabaster, see also Louise Imogen Guiney, *Recusant Poets, with a Selection from their Work: Saint Thomas More to Ben Jonson* (London, 1938); G. M. Story and Helen Gardner (eds.), *The Sonnets of William Alabaster* (Oxford, 1959); Molly Murray, '"Now I ame a Catholique": William Alabaster and the Early Modern Catholic Conversion Narrative', ch. 7 in Ronald Corthell, Frances E. Dolan, Christopher Highley, and Arthur F. Moretti (eds.), *Catholic Culture in Early Modern England* (Notre Dame, Ind., 2007); Francis J. Bremer, *ODNB* (Oxford, 2004); and, on his devotional verse, A. D. Cousins, *The Catholic Religious Poets from Southwell to Crashaw: A Critical History* (London, 1991), ch. 3.

41. Robert E. Knoll, *Ben Jonson's Plays: An Introduction* (Lincoln, Nebr., 1964), 154–60.

42. Ian Donaldson, 'Jonson's Italy: *Volpone* and Fr. Thomas Wright', *Notes & Queries*, 217 (1972), 450–2.

43. William Alabaster's account of his conversion, 'Seven Motives', which he attempted to convey to Essex, does not survive, though two replies to his apology do (as does a later narrative of his conversion: see Sutton, *Unpublished Works by William Alabaster*). Jonson's *Motives*, listed in Antony à Wood's *Athenae Oxonienses*, 2 vols. (London, 1692), 2.509, was published in 1622, a dozen years after Jonson's conversion back to the Church of England in 1610, and is likely therefore to have concentrated primarily on his reasons for ultimately rejecting the Catholic faith, though it might also have revealed the reasons for his earlier attraction to Rome (see Donaldson, 'Motives', *CWBJ*, *Dubia*, Electronic Edition).

44. E. Pearlman, 'Ben Jonson: An Anatomy', *English Literary Renaissance*, 9 (1979), 364–93, at 369; David Kay, *Ben Jonson: A Literary Life* (Houndmills, 1995), 28; David Riggs, *Ben Jonson: A Life* (Cambridge, Mass., 1989), 52.

45. Wright, *Passions of the Mind*, ed. Newbold, 141.

46. See Chs. 11 and 14 below. Throughout his *English Grammar*, written in the 1620s, Jonson quotes extensively from Bishop John Jewel's *Reply to M. Harding's Answer* (1565), a vigorous piece of anti-Catholic polemic that he had obviously read with close attention. David Norbrook suggests that in converting to Catholicism Jonson may have been influenced by the example of the Belgian scholar Justus Lipsius, whose writings he much admired: *Poetry and Politics in the English Renaissance* (London, 1984), 176. This is possible, though their personal circumstances were very different. Lipsius had been born a Catholic and educated initially in Jesuit seminaries, later converting to Lutheranism. Under pressure to declare his faith in 1591, he wavered for some time before re-embracing Catholicism.

47. The Sacrament of Penance was enshrined in 1551 by the Council of Trent (Sess. 14, c. 1), which cited amongst other texts John 20: 23: 'Whose soever sins ye remit, they are remitted unto them; and whose soever sins ye retain, they are retained.' The Catholic case for absolution in Jonson's day is typically laid out in John Heigham's *Treatise of Auricular Confession, Wherein is Evidently Shown the Authority and Power of Catholic Priests for the Forgiving and Remitting of Sins Against the Protestants' Bare and Only Preaching of Absolution Unto the People* (Saint-Omer, 1622). James P. Crowley suggests that Jonson could well have been absolved by Father Wright without undergoing conversion: '"He took his religion by trust": The Matter of Ben Jonson's Conversion', *Renaissance and Reformation/Renaissance et Réforme*, 12 (1998), 53–70. Jonson might still have perceived the continuing benefits of the Sacrament of Penance made accessible through a formal change of religion.

48. Michael C. Questier, *Conversion, Politics, and Religion in England, 1580–1625* (Cambridge, 1996).

49. Samuel Johnson, 'Dryden', in *The Lives of the English Poets*, ed. George Birkbeck Hill, 3 vols. (Oxford, 1905), 1.377.

50. Leanda de Lisle, *After Elizabeth: The Rise of James of Scotland and the Struggle for the Throne of England* (New York, 2005).

Chapter 8

1. *Henslowe's Diary*, ed. R. A. Foakes, 2nd edn. (Cambridge, 2002), 100. This could have been a scenario newly devised by Jonson that Chapman was now asked to work up, or the

play for which Jonson had been paid the previous December that Chapman was now expected to complete (see 127 above).

2. *CWBJ*, Life Records, 23, Electronic Edition. Leslie Hotson's discovery of the document reporting this action, brought by one Robert Browne, is described by W. G. Bell, *A Short History of the Worshipful Company of Tylers and Bricklayers of the City of London* (1938), 21–2. H&S mistakenly assume the action was brought in January 1599, a slip corrected by Mark Eccles, 'Ben Jonson, "Citizen and Bricklayer"', *Notes & Queries* (December 1988), 445–6. On the possible identity of Robert Browne, see Mark Eccles, 'Elizabethan Actors I: A–D', *Notes & Queries* (March 1991), 41.

3. W. H. Stevenson and H. E. Salter, *The Early History of St John's College, Oxford* (Oxford, 1939), 325.

4. William Drummond to Ben Jonson, 1 July 1619: Letter (f), *CWBJ*. Rosemary Freeman, *English Emblem Books* (London, 1948), 50–1; Michael Bath, *Speaking Pictures: English Emblem Books and Renaissance Culture* (London, 1994), 16–20; Jane Dunn, *Elizabeth and Mary: Cousins, Rivals, Queens* (London, 2003), 408–10.

5. John Manning, *The Emblem* (London, 2002), 59. On Palmer's work, see also John Manning in B. F. Scholz, Michael Bath, and David Weston (eds.), *The European Emblem* (Leiden 1990), 85–106.

6. Wesley Trimpi, *Ben Jonson's Poems: A Triumph of the Plain Style* (Stanford, Calif., 1961). T. S. Eliot, 'Ben Jonson', in *Selected Essays* (London, 1958), 148. Eliot is for once echoing a Victorian verdict: 'Jonson has not dug sufficiently deep', wrote H. A. Taine, 'and his constructions are incomplete; he has built on the surface, and he has built but a single story': *History of English Literature*, trans. Henry Van Laun (Edinburgh, 1873), 2.12.

7. The precise nature of Palmer's sufferings remains obscure. While it is likely he was persecuted on account of his religion, this was not the reason that he was deprived of his Oxford posts, as Herford and Simpson believed (11.124). He was removed on financial, not religious, grounds, an inheritance from his father having rendered him ineligible for further tenure under the college statutes. See Stevenson and Salter, *The Early History of St John's College, Oxford*, 324–5, 422–5.

8. Thomas Wright was later to say, under examination by Lord Chief Justice Popham, Attorney-General Coke, and Roger Wilbraham following Essex's abortive rising of 1601, that 'he thought the Earl of Essex was a Catholic, but concealed it from policy, that so both Puritans and Protestants might be drawn to take his part. Also said that if the Earl were King, it would be a glorious kingdom, and would be the better for them, for he would not be so inhuman as not to free us all, meaning the prisoners in the Tower': *CSPD, Elizabeth I: 1598–1601*, 569.

9. Mark Bland, '"As far from all reuolt": Sir John Salusbury, Christ Church MS 184 and Ben Jonson's First Ode', *English Manuscript Studies*, 8 (2000), 43–78.

10. On one occasion 'when the Queen was offended at him' (so Drummond reported Jonson saying in 1618–19), Essex had adopted as his *imprese* 'a diamond with its own ashes with which it is cut; about it the word, *dum formas minuis*' (*Informations*, 460–2). The motto accompanying this emblem on Essex's tournament shield can be translated 'while you fashion it, you diminish it', and may be read either as a protest or as a diplomatic surrender. For Essex's interest in *imprese*, see P. J. Hammer, *The Polarization of Elizabethan Politics: The Political Career of Robert Devereux, 2nd Earl of Essex, 1585–1597* (Cambridge, 1999), ch. 6, and A. R. Young, 'The English Tournament Imprese', in P. M. Daly

(ed.), *The English Emblem and the Continental Tradition* (New York, 1988), 61–81, and A. R. Young, *The English Tournament Imprese* (New York, 1988). In a scene in Jonson's *Poetaster* (5.3) that possibly glances at Essex's practice, the magistrate Lupus mistakenly suspects that an emblem devised by Horace must libel the emperor Augustus Caesar, failing to observe that the bird depicted is a vulture, not an imperial eagle.

11. See Ch. 6, above.

12. This account of the relationship between the two poets draws in part on my study 'Perishing and Surviving: The Poetry of Donne and Jonson', *Essays in Criticism*, 51 (2000), 68–85.

13. Text from *John Donne: The Complete English Poems*, ed. A. J. Smith (Harmondsworth, 1971); see also *John Donne: The Satires, Epigrams, and Verse Letters*, ed. W. Milgate (Oxford, 1967).

14. I follow James P. Bednarz's brilliant and largely persuasive account of Jonson's strategies during this period in *Shakespeare and the Poets' War* (New York, 2001), while resisting the more speculative notion of a personal antagonism between the two men. On the genre of comical satire, see in particular Alvin Kernan's *The Cankered Muse: Satire of the English Renaissance* (Hamden, Conn., 1976). Helen Ostovich traces the numerous genetic elements of *Every Man Out of his Humour* in her introduction to the Revels edition of the play (Manchester, 2001).

15. For the bishops' ban, see Edward Arber (ed.), *A Transcript of the Registers of the Company of Stationers of London 1554–1640 AD*, 6 vols. (London, 1876), 3.677; W. W. Greg, *A Companion to Arber* (Oxford, 1967), 49–50. Oscar James Campbell, *Comicall Satyre and Shakespeare's 'Troilus and Cressida'* (San Marino, Calif., 1938), believed the ban gave rise to the new genre of comical satire. The basic causes for the bishops' concern are variously interpreted by Richard A. McCabe, 'Elizabethan Satire and the Bishops' Ban of 1599', *Yearbook of English Studies*, 11 (1981), 188–93 and Lynda E. Boose, 'The 1599 Bishops' Ban, Elizabethan Pornography, and the Sexualization of the Jacobean Stage', in Richard Burt and John Michael Archer (eds.), *Enclosure Acts: Sexuality, Property, and Culture in Early Modern England* (Ithaca, NY, 1994), 185–200.

16. See Bernard Beckerman, *Shakespeare at the Globe 1599–1609* (New York, 1962); Andrew Gurr, *The Shakespearean Stage 1574–1642* (Cambridge, 1970), 94–7; Richard Hosley, 'The First Globe Playhouse (1599)', in J. Leeds Barroll, Alexander Leggatt, Richard Hosley, and Alvin Kernan (eds.), *The Revels History of Drama in English*, 3: *1576–1613* (London, 1975), 175–96; J. R. Mulryne and Margaret Shewring (eds.), *Shakespeare's Globe Rebuilt* (Cambridge, 1997); James Shapiro, *1599: A Year in the Life of William Shakespeare* (London, 2005).

17. Cf. *The New Inn*, 1.3.128, 'Where I imagine all the world's a play.' E. R. Curtius explores the ancestry of these theatrical metaphors in *European Literature and the Latin Middle Ages*, trans. Willard R. Trask (London, 1953), 138–44. Jonson's borrowings from John of Salisbury are noted by Margaret Clayton, 'Ben Jonson, "In Travaile with Expression of Another": His Use of John of Salisbury's *Policratus* in *Timber*', *Review of English Studies*, 30 (1979), 397–408. The Latin motto and the image of Hercules supporting the Globe are mentioned by Edmond Malone in 1790, probably drawing on an anecdote by the antiquary William Oldys recorded by George Steevens in his 1778 edition of Shakespeare: see Ernest Schanzer, 'Hercules and his Load', *Review of English Studies*, 19 (1968), 51–3, and

Richard Dutton, 'The Sign of the Globe', *Shakespeare Survey*, 41 (1989), 35–43. Curtius (*European Literature*, 141) believes this motto to have been derived from John of Salisbury.

18. Helen Ostovich, ' "To Behold the Scene Full": Seeing and Judging in *Every Man Out of his Humour*', in Martin Butler (ed.), *Re-Presenting Ben Jonson: Text, History, Performance* (Houndmills, 1999), 76–92. See also J. W. Saunders, 'Staging at the Globe, 1599–1613', *Shakespeare Quarterly*, 2 (1960), 401–25.

19. From the play's initial description of characters. Cf. Jonson's description of himself in relation to the court, 'Thy servant, but not slave', *Cynthia's Revels*, Dedication.

20. Whether *As You Like It* was indeed performed at the Globe theatre after *Every Man Out of his Humour*, as often assumed, remains however uncertain: see Juliet Dusinberre's discussion of this question in her edition of *As You Like It* in the Arden Shakespeare, 3rd series (London, 2006), and especially her appendix 3, 'Ben Jonson, *As You Like It*, and "The War of the Theatres"'. *As You Like It* may have been performed at court early in 1599, but did not appear in print until 1623. The close verbal parallels in the passages examined here appear to suggest that the surviving text follows, and responds to, Jonson's play.

21. The notion of a falling-out between the two dramatists, precipitated by Jonson himself, is evident in Nicholas Rowe's life of Shakespeare prefixed to his edition of *The Works of Mr William Shakespeare*, 6 vols. (London, 1709). By the mid-nineteenth century, the story of this supposed quarrel had become for some readers the interpretative key to unlock the entire oeuvre of both men: see for example Robert Cartwright's *Shakespeare and Jonson: Dramatic, versus Wit-Combats* (London, 1864). More recently, the narrative of the quarrel has been reworked by Katherine Duncan-Jones in her *Ungentle Shakespeare: Scenes from his Life* (London, 2001) and James P. Bednarz in *Shakespeare & the Poets' War* (n. 14 above).

22. *Pierce Penniless his Supplication to the Devil*, in *Thomas Nashe: Selected Works*, ed. Stanley Wells (London, 1964), 35–6.

23. The grant was made to Shakespeare's father John, evidently with William's financial and other assistance. See E. K. Chambers, *William Shakespeare: A Study of the Facts and Problems*, 2 vols. (Oxford, 1930), 2.19–32; C. W. Scott-Giles, *Shakespeare's Heraldry* (London, 1950), ch. 2; Samuel Schoenbaum, *William Shakespeare: A Compact Documentary Life* (Oxford, 1977), 229–32; Park Honan, *Shakespeare: A Life* (Oxford, 1998), 228–9; Duncan-Jones, *Ungentle Shakespeare*, ch. 4.

24. Lawrence Stone, *The Crisis of the Aristocracy 1558–1641* (Oxford, 1965); Wyman H. Herendeen, *William Camden: A Life in Context* (Woodbridge, 2007), ch. 7. On 10 December 1606 Dethick was at last induced to resign the office of Garter Herald on other grounds, having been formally replaced by William Segar as early as January 1604: see Sir Anthony Wagner, *Heralds of England: A History of the Office and College of Arms* (London, 1967), ch. 7, and Anthony R. J. S. Adolph, 'Sir William Dethick', *ODNB*.

25. Jonson possessed a copy of Ralph Brooke's *A Discovery of Certain Errors Published in Print in the Much Commended Britannia* (1594), and may possibly also have owned a copy of *A Discovery of Errors in the . . . Catalogue of Nobility published by Ralph Brooke*, the response to Brooke made by Camden's deputy, Augustine Vincent, in 1622. See David McPherson and Henry Woodhuysen, *CWBJ*, Jonson's Library, Electronic Edition; H&S, 1.262; *The New Inn*, 2.6.28.

26. Duncan-Jones, *Ungentle Shakespeare*, 82.

27. *London Session Records 1605–1685*, ed. Dom Hugh Bowler, Camden Record Society 34 (1934), 6–8.

28. J. A. Symonds ingeniously connected Jonson's 'three spindles' with the shield of the Annandale Johnstones, 'a saltire and a chief, the latter charged with three cushions': *Ben Jonson* (London, 1886), 2–3. His researches are further elaborated by Herford and Simpson with the assistance of F. P. Barnard: *Ben Jonson*, 1.174. For Jonson's wider interest in these matters, see Arthur Huntington Nason, *Heralds and Heraldry in Ben Jonson's Plays, Masques, and Entertainments* (London, 1907; repr. New York, 1968).

29. The significance of this *impresa* is examined by L. A. Beaurline, *Jonson and Elizabethan Comedy* (San Marino, Calif., 1978), 'Epilogue'.

30. *The Arte of English Poesie*, ed. Edward Arber (Westminster, 1895), 118–19.

31. In *Poetaster* 1.2 it is the highly disreputable character of Tucca who ridicules the idea of players applying for arms, and who is answered roundly by Ovid.

32. For Jonson's defence of the original 1599 ending of the play, see appendix A in Randall Martin's *CWBJ* edition of the play. The scene is analysed by Helen M. Ostovich, '"So Sudden and Strange a Cure": A Rudimentary Masque in *Every Man Out of his Humour*', *English Literary Renaissance*, 22 (1993), 315–32.

33. The rumours about a possible physiological impediment which prevented Elizabeth from marrying and bearing children were strenuously denied by Burghley in a memorandum of 1579 during negotiations concerning her possible marriage to François of Valois, duc d'Alençon: see Alison Weir, *Elizabeth the Queen* (London, 1998), ch. 2; Conyers Read, *Lord Burghley and Queen Elizabeth* (London, 1960), 210.

34. The evidence for the court performance of *Cynthia's Revels* is inconclusive. On 6 January 1601 the Children of the Chapel were paid £5 to perform at court 'a show with music and special songs prepared for the purpose', and on 22 February they were paid £10 to present a 'play' at night. E. K. Chambers (*The Elizabethan Stage*, 4 vols. (Oxford, 1923), 3.363–4; 4.113, 166) argues plausibly that *Cynthia's Revels* was the 'show' performed on the earlier date, and is followed by the Oxford editors (H&S, 9.188). Leslie Hotson has objected that the payment of £5 would have been modest for such an occasion (*The First Night of 'Twelfth Night'* (London, 1954), 18). Yet a performance of *Cynthia's Revels* at court just three days after Essex's trial and three days before his execution—with Cynthia's reference to Actaeon's 'fatal doom' (5.5.104) inserted at the last moment as a stern reminder of his downfall—would have made for uncomfortable viewing, to say the least, and the January date of court performance remains the more likely. My account of Essex's rising draws on the following: *CSPD, Elizabeth I, 1598–1601*, 545–602; *A Declaration of the Practices & Treasons attempted and committed by Robert late Earl of Essex and his Complices* (London, 1601); 'The Tryal of Robert Earl of Essex, and Henry Earl of Southampton, at Westminster the 19th of February 1600, and in the 43 Year of the Reign of Queen Elizabeth', in *A Compleat Collection of State-Tryals, and Proceedings*, 4 vols. (London, 1719), 1.164–73; E. M. Tenison, *Elizabethan England*, 13 vols. (Royal Leamington Spa, 1933–61), vol. 11, part 10 ('Essex' Great Fall'); Mervyn James, *Society, Politics, and Culture: Studies in Early Modern England* (Cambridge, 1986), ch. 9; Paul E. J. Hammer, 'Robert Devereux, Second Earl of Essex', *ODNB*; Paul E. J. Hammer, 'Shakespeare's *Richard II*, the Play of 7 February 1601, and the Essex Rising', *Shakespeare Quarterly*, 59 (2008), 1–35; Leeds Barroll,

'A New History for Shakespeare and his Time', *Shakespeare Quarterly*, 39 (1988), 441–64; Jonathan Bate, *Soul of the Age: The Life, Mind, and World of William Shakespeare* (London, 2008), ch. 14. Bate and Hammer have both convincingly rejected Blair Worden's suggestion that the play of Richard II performed at the Globe on 7 February 1601 might have been a dramatization of John Hayward's controversial history of the reign of Henry IV: *London Review of Books*, 10 July 2003.

35. Hester Lees-Jeffries, 'A New Allusion by Jonson to Spenser and Essex?', *Notes & Queries*, NS 50 (2003), 63–5, and (more extensively) *England's Helicon: Fountains in Early Modern Literature and Culture* (Oxford, 2007), ch. 12.

36. The play's lack of success at court may be inferred from the motto Jonson chose for the quarto title page, *Quod non dant procures, dabit histrio* ('you can get from a stage-player what no great man will give you': Juvenal, *Satires*, 7.90) and from Dekker's reference in *Satiromastix* to the plays of 'Horace' being 'misliked at court' (ed. Penniman, 5.2.376).

37. I follow Tom Cain in his Revels edition of *Poetaster* (Manchester, 1995), 28–9, and Gabriele Bernhard Jackson in her *CWBJ* edition in believing Histrio's reference to 'this winter' (3.4.326) more probably points to the final weeks of 1601 than to the winter of 1600–1.

38. The comparison of *Poetaster* with *The Dunciad* is made by Isaac Disraeli, *The Calamities and Quarrels of Authors*, ed. Benjamin Disraeli (London, 1859), 476–7. For Pope's vivid recall and re-enactment of a crucial episode in *Poetaster*, see Paul Baines and Pat Rogers, 'Ben Jonson's Crispinus and the Poisoning of Edmund Curll', *Review of English Studies*, NS 60 (2008), 78–95.

39. Tom Cain '"Satyres, that girde and fart at the time": *Poetaster* and the Essex Rebellion', in Julie Sanders with Kate Chedgzoy and Susan Wiseman (eds.), *Refashioning Ben Jonson: Gender, Politics, and the Jonsonian Canon* (Houndmills, 1998), 48–70.

40. Cain, '"Satyres, that girde and fart"', 54; *CSPD, Elizabeth I*, vol. 5: *1598–1601*, 578; John Aubrey, *Brief Lives*, ed. A. Clark (Oxford, 1898), 2.159; and, for another episode possibly involving Popham and Essex, n. 8 above.

41. The best recent studies of this phenomenon are by Bednarz, *The Poets' War* (see n. 14 above), and Matthew Steggle, *Wars of the Theatres: The Poetics of Personation in the Age of Jonson* (Victoria, BC, 1998). For earlier scholarship, see in particular David Bevington, *Tudor Drama and Politics: A Critical Approach to Topical Meaning* (Cambridge, Mass., 1968), Josiah H. Penniman, *The War of the Theatres* (Boston, 1897), and R. A. Small, *The Stage-Quarrel between Ben Jonson and the So-Called Poetasters* (1899).

42. *Henslowe's Diary*, ed. Foakes, 2nd edn. (Cambridge, 2002), 124.

43. Roslyn Lander Knutson, *Playing Companies and Commerce in Shakespeare's Time* (Cambridge, 2001), doubts that Marston was in fact the author of *Histriomastix*.

44. On this point, see in particular Knutson, *Playing Companies and Commerce*.

45. W.I. [John Weever], *The Whipping of the Satyr* (1601); Nicholas Breton, *No Whipping, Nor Tripping, But a Kind Friendly Snipping* (1601); *Return from Parnassus*, Part 2, lines 1769–73, in *The Three Parnassus Plays* (1598–1601), ed. J. B. Leishman (London, 1949), 337. Shakespeare's so-called 'purge' of Jonson has been variously interpreted. David Riggs, *Ben Jonson: A Life* (Cambridge, Mass., 1989, 84–5) and *Poetaster*, ed. Cain, introduction, 36–8, suggest that Shakespeare satirizes Jonson through the character of Malvolio in the Middle Temple performance of *Twelfth Night* in February 1602, while James Bednarz argues that Ajax in *Troilus and Cressida* is intended as a satirical portrait of Jonson: *Shakespeare and the Poets' War*, ch. 1.

Chapter 9

1. The lines are repeated in Jonson's 'Ode: To Himself' ('Where dost thou careless lie'), *The Underwood*, 23.35–6, and were later admired by Yeats ('While I, from that reed-throated whisperer', *Collected Poems* (London, 1933), 143).

2. *The State of England Anno Dom. 1600 by Thomas Wilson*, ed. F. J. Fisher, Camden Miscellany 16 (1936).

3. *Correspondence of King James VI of Scotland with Sir Robert Cecil and Others in England During the Reign of Queen Elizabeth*, ed. John Bruce, Camden Society 78 (Westminster, 1861); Leanda de Lisle, *After Elizabeth: The Rise of James of Scotland and the Struggle for the Throne of England* (New York, 2005), 64–6, 75.

4. *Discoveries*, 1–5, drawing on Seneca, *To Helvia, On Consolation*, 5.4, *On Providence*, 3.3, 4.5–6, *To Marcia, On Consolation*, 9.5, *On Tranquillity of Mind*, 11.8. For Jonson's interest in Stoical writings, see in particular Robert C. Evans, *Habits of Mind: Evidence and Effects of Ben Jonson's Reading* (Lewisburg, Pa., 1995), especially chs. 2 and 6; Isabel Rivers, *The Poetry of Conservatism, 1600–1745: A Study of Poets and Political Affairs from Jonson to Pope* (Cambridge, 1973), 21–72; Adriana McCrea, *Constant Minds: Political Virtue and the Lipsian Paradigm in England, 1584–1650* (Toronto, 1997), ch. 4, 'A Neostoic Scout: Ben Jonson and the Poetics of Constancy'; and J. H. M. Salmon, 'Stoicism and Roman Example: Seneca and Tacitus in Jacobean England', *Journal of the History of Ideas*, 50 (1989), 199–225.

5. Tom Cain, 'Mary and Bedford Jonson: A Note', *Ben Jonson Journal*, 14.1 (2007), 78–87. No record of Mary's burial has been found. The children of Catholic parents in this period were commonly baptized in Protestant churches to ensure their legitimacy, and to avoid ecclesiastical penalties for clandestine baptism and (following a statute of 1606) an additional £100 fine. They were also commonly buried in Protestant churchyards. See John Bossy, *The English Catholic Community 1570–1850* (London, 1975), 133–4, 140–3.

6. F. P. Wilson, *The Plague in Shakespeare's London* (Oxford, 1927), ch. 3.

7. ibid. 61–4; Paul Slack, *The Impact of the Plague in Tudor and Stuart England* (London, 1985), 203, 33.

8. This aspect of Jonson's character has been suggestively explored by Anne Barton, *Ben Jonson: Dramatist* (Cambridge, 1984). For Donne's vision of his wife and child, see Izaak Walton, 'Life of Dr John Donne', in *Lives* (London, 1927), 39–41.

9. This coincidence is elaborated by Barton, *Ben Jonson: Dramatist*, and David Riggs, *Ben Jonson: A Life* (Cambridge, Mass., 1989). It is by no means certain, however, that the surviving 'Additions' to *The Spanish Tragedy*, the fourth of which (Hieronimo's encounter with a painter who has also lost a son) deals extensively with the idea of paternal grief, are in fact those that Jonson was commissioned to write. Shakespeare may rather be the author of these passages: see Hugh Craig's analysis, *CWBJ*, Dubia, Electronic Edition. On *Richard Crookback*, see *CWBJ*, vol.2.

10. Kathryn Walls, *Notes & Queries*, NS 24 (1977), 136.

11. Mark Eccles, 'Jonson's Marriage', *Review of English Studies*, 12 (1936), 257–72, at 267–8.

12. Cain, 'Mary and Bedford Jonson: A Note' (n. 5 above). In a similar fashion, the Countess had permitted John Donne to call his daughter 'Lucy' and agreed to stand godmother to this child on 8 August 1608: R. C. Bald, *John Donne: A Life* (Oxford, 1970), 176. Jonson's relationship with the Countess of Bedford is less closely documented, but it is tempting to suspect biographical reference in Lady Tailbush's dismissive remark in *The Devil Is an Ass*

(performed around October 1616): 'Some old lady | That keeps a poet has devised these scandals' (4.3.47–8). Though Lucy, Countess of Bedford (baptized 1581) was not 'old' by modern standards in 1616, she had suffered serious illness, and might well have been so described by the forthright Lady Tailbush.

13. *The Diary of John Manningham of the Middle Temple, 1602–3*, ed. Robert Parker Sorlien (Hanover, NH, 1976), 187, 380–1. Sorlien's dating of this entry to 1602 is corrected by Eccles to 1603: 'Jonson's Marriage', 268 (an amendment confirmed by H&S, 11.576–7).

14. *The History, Genealogy, and Alliances of the English and American House of Townshend*, compiled by James C. Townshend et al., rev. Margaret Townshend (New York, 1909; Internet Archive); John Fletcher, verses prefixed to *The Faithful Shepherdess* (c.1610; a play for which Jonson also wrote commendatory verses), *The Works of Francis Beaumont and John Fletcher*, ed. Arnold Glover and A. R. Waller (New York, 1969), 2.320.

15. Letter 1, *CWBJ*. For the redating of this letter, see Mark Bland, 'Jonson, *Biathanatos* and the Interpretation of Manuscript Evidence', *Studies in Bibliography*, 51 (1998), 154–82.

16. I follow Tom Cain's dating: *Sejanus*, introduction, *CWBJ*.

17. This copy of the quarto, formerly owned by T. J. Wise, is now in the possession of the British Library (Ashley 3464).

18. James M. Osborn, 'Ben Jonson and the Eccentric Lord Stanhope', *Times Literary Supplement*, 4 January 1957, 16. In 1616 Jonson was granted by James an annual pension of 100 marks (£66 13s. 4d.), which Charles in 1630 increased to £100 (see 322 and 405 below). Possibly Stanhope is confusing these various annuities; possibly (again) Aubigny may have had a hand in securing Jonson his original pension in 1616. But the further possibility remains that Stanhope's repeated assertions are correct, and that Aubigny did indeed generously provide for Jonson throughout his lifetime.

19. This account of Esmé Stuart and his family draws on ch. 2 of my *Jonson's Magic Houses: Essays in Interpretation* (Oxford, 1997), and the following principal sources: Eileen Cassavetti, *The Lion and the Lilies: The Stuarts and France* (London, 1977); Lady Elizabeth Cust, *Some Account of the Stuarts of Aubigny in France [1422–1672]*, privately printed (1891); Sir William Fraser, *The Lennox*, 2 vols. (Edinburgh, 1874); Sir Robert Gordon of Gordonstoun, *A Genealogical History of the Earldom of Sutherland from its Origins to the Year 1630* (Edinburgh, 1813); David Mysie, *Memoirs of the Affairs of Scotland 1577–1603*, ed. J. Dennistoun, privately printed at the Bannatyne Club, 39 (Edinburgh, 1830); Andrew Stuart, *Genealogical History of the Stewarts from the Earliest Period of their Authentic History to the Present Times* (London, 1798), William Forbes-Leith SJ, *Narratives of Scottish Catholics under Mary Stuart and James VI* (Edinburgh, 1885).

20. P. M. Handover, *Arbella Stuart: Royal Lady of Hardwick and Cousin to King James* (London, 1957), 239. The original building was destroyed in the Great Fire of 1666; the present building dates from 1672.

21. Christopher Devlin, *The Life of Robert Southwell, Poet and Martyr* (New York, 1956), 131ff. Mark Eccles believed that Jonson stayed with Aubigny during a later period, from 1613 and 1618 ('Jonson's Marriage', *Review of English Studies*, 12 (1936), 257–72), and his views were accepted by Riggs, *Ben Jonson: A Life*, 191, 192, 204, 369–70n. The Oxford editors were less convinced, but finally wondered if Jonson could have had two separate periods of residence with Aubigny, 'a shorter one about 1604 and a longer in 1613–18', H&S, 11.576–7. A single five-year period of residence from 1603, during Jonson's Catholic years, seems however more likely, when (as argued more fully below) Aubigny appears to have served as a

protector during Jonson's troubles over *Sejanus, Eastward Ho!*, the Gunpowder Plot, and summonses from the Consistory Courts. The later dating favoured by Eccles fails to explain the gratitude Jonson expresses to Aubigny in *Epigrams*, 127, almost certainly written before 1612.

22. Letter of 15 May 1579 from the Bishop of Ross in Paris to Cardinal de Como in Rome: Forbes-Leith, *Narratives of Scottish Catholics*, 134–6.

23. Forbes-Leith, *Narratives of the Scottish Catholics*, 183 n. 2; Cust, *Some Account of the Stuarts of Aubigny*, 94. Harriet and Mary were married to the Earls of Huntley and of Mar, respectively; Gabriela entered a convent.

24. Neil Cuddy, 'The Revival of the Entourage: The Bedchamber of James I, 1603–1625', in David Starkey et al. (eds.), *The English Court: From the Wars of the Roses to the Civil War* (London, 1987), 173–225; Neil Cuddy, 'Reinventing a Monarchy: The Changing Structure and Political Function of the Stuart Court, 1603–88', in Eveline Cruickshanks (ed.), *The Stuart Court* (Stroud, 2009), 59–85. The restructuring of the royal household had been a central purpose of Esmé Stuart senior's visit to Scotland: Forbes-Leith, *Narratives of Scottish Catholics*, 134–6.

25. Aubigny was an exporter of beer. *CSPD, James I, 1603–1610* (London, 1857), 33, 141, 644; *1611–1618* (1858), 196.

26. Tom Cain proposes a performance of the play in the week of 9 to 16 May: introduction to *Sejanus, CWBJ*. This is entirely possible, though the window is narrow: Aubigny would have arrived in London on 7 May, and the theatres were to close on 17 May. (On the latter date, the Lord Chamberlain's Men received their new Royal Patent allowing them now to be known as the King's Men and to play at the Globe and elsewhere 'when the infection of the plague shall decrease': Glynne Wickham, Herbert Berry, and William Ingram (eds.), *English Professional Theatre 1530–1660* (Cambridge, 2000), 123.) E. K. Chambers believed the 1603 performance referred to in the Folio title page 'may have been at Court in the autumn or winter of 1603'—an unlikely hypothesis, for reasons Cain adduces: *The Elizabethan Stage* (London, 1923), 3.367. 2.210. On the interpretative difficulties arising from these uncertainties over dating, see Richard Dutton, *Mastering the Revels: The Regulation and Censorship of English Renaissance Drama* (Houndmills, 1991), 10–12.

27. On Jonson and Tacitus, see Ch. 6 n. 45 above, and Fritz Levy, 'The Theatre and the Court in the 1590s', in John Guy (ed.), *The Reign of Elizabeth I: Court and Culture in the Last Decade* (Cambridge, 1995), 274–300; Daniel Boughner, 'Jonson's Use of Lipsius in *Sejanus*', *Modern Language Notes*, 73 (1958), 247–55.

28. See David Womersley, 'Sir Henry Savile's Translation of Tacitus and the Political Interpretation of Elizabethan Texts', *Review of English Studies*, 41 (1991), 313–42.

29. *CSPD, Elizabeth*, vol. 275, 449. On Hayward, see Margaret Dowling, 'Sir John Hayward's Troubles over his *Life of Henry IV*', *The Library*, 4th series, 11 (1931), 212–24; S. L. Goldberg, 'John Hayward: Politic Historian', *Review of English Studies*, 6 (1955), 233–44; Edwin Benjamin, 'Sir John Hayward and Tacitus', *Review of English Studies*, 8 (1957), 275–6; *The First and Second Parts of John Hayward's The Life and Raigne of King Henrie IIII*, ed. John J. Manning, Camden 4th series, 42 (London, 1991); John J. Manning, 'John Hayward', *ODNB*. On the parallel between Richard II and Elizabeth, see Ch. 8 n. 34.

30. Donaldson, 'Jonson, Shakespeare, and the Destruction of the Book', ch. 12 in *Jonson's Magic Houses*; Joseph F. Loewenstein, 'Personal Material: Jonson and Book-Burning', ch. 6 in

Martin Butler (ed.), *Re-Presenting Ben Jonson: Text, History, Performance* (Houndmills, 1999).

31. Linda Levy Peck, *Northampton: Patronage and Policy at the Court of James I* (London, 1982), Linda Levy Peck, 'The Mental World of a Jacobean Grandee', in Peck (ed.), *The Mental World of the Jacobean Court* (1991), 148–321; Pauline Croft, 'Henry Howard, Earl of Northampton (1540–1614)', *ODNB*. 'His Majesty's earwig': Pauline Croft, 'The Reputation of Robert Cecil: Libels, Political Opinion, and Popular Awareness in the Early Seventeenth Century', *Transactions of the Royal Historical Society*, 6th series, 1 (1991), 43–69, at 46.

32. Proposing these dates, Tom Cain also identifies the St George's Day brawl with Howard's induction to the Order of the Garter in 1605: introduction to *Sejanus, CWBJ*.

33. The quarto text (as Jonson made clear) removed those parts of the play 'wherein a second pen'—now generally thought to be his friend George Chapman—'had good share' ('To the Readers', 31–3). It may also however have removed those parts which had been reckoned dangerous.

34. If Cain's dating of the first performance of *Sejanus* at mid-May 1603 is accepted, the play would have preceded the trial of Ralegh in November of that year. Philip Ayres, assuming a later date of performance, suggests that Ralegh's trial (in which Northampton had been involved) is glanced at in the trial of Silius in Jonson's play: *Sejanus*, ed. Ayres, Revels Plays (Manchester, 1990), introduction, 16–22. Jonson's attitude to Ralegh, who 'esteemed more of fame than conscience' (*Informations*, 148), was sharply qualified.

35. As Daniel C. Boughner has shown, Jonson read Machiavelli's work with care in the original Italian as well as in the Latin translation of Sylvester Telius: *The Devil's Disciple: Ben Jonson's Debt to Machiavelli* (New York, 1968). John Jowett's reading of *Sejanus* as a 'Catholic' play ('"Fall before this Booke": The 1605 Quarto of *Sejanus*', *TEXT: Transactions of the Society for Textual Scholarship*, 4 (1988), 279–95) has now been extended by Peter Lake, 'From *Leicester his Commonwealth* to *Sejanus his Fall*: Ben Jonson and the Politics of Roman (Catholic) Virtue', in Ethan Shagan (ed.), *Catholics and the 'Protestant Nation'* (Manchester, 2005), 128–61.

Chapter 10

1. *Correspondence of King James VI of Scotland with Sir Robert Cecil and Others in England during the Reign of Queen Elizabeth*, ed. John Bruce, introduction, pp. viii–ix; John Nichols, *The Progresses, Processions, and Magnificent Festivities of King James the First*, 4 vols. (London, 1828), 1.25, 34–5; *Memoirs of Robert Carey, Earl of Monmouth*, ed. G. H. Powell (London, 1907), 72–8; David Harris Willson, *King James VI & I* (London, 1956), ch. 9; Leanda de Lisle, *After Elizabeth: The Rise of James of Scotland and the Struggle for the Throne of Scotland* (New York, 2005). On Carey's ride to Scotland, see also Ch. 2 above, 38–9.

2. P. M. Handover, *The Second Cecil: The Rise to Power 1563–1604 of Sir Robert Cecil, Later First Earl of Salisbury* (London, 1959), ch. 30; Linda Levy Peck, *Northampton: Patronage and Policy at the Court of James I* (London, 1982); D. C. Andersson, *Lord Henry Howard (1540–1614): An Elizabethan Life* (Cambridge, 2009); Pauline Croft, 'Robert Cecil and the Early Jacobean Court' and Linda Levy Peck, 'The Mentality of a Jacobean Grandee', both in L. L Peck (ed.), *The Mental World of the Jacobean Court* (Cambridge, 1991), 134–47, 148–68. 'Though you are but a little man': Lord Burghley to Cecil, 4 April 1603, Cecil MSS 99/88, cit. Pauline Croft, 'Can a Bureaucrat be a Favourite? Robert Cecil and the Strategies of

Power', in J. H. Elliott and L. W. B. Brackliss (eds.), *The World of the Favourite* (New Haven, 1999), 85; 'thrice-honoured': Jonson to Cecil, Letter 3, *CWBJ*; 'trinity of knaves': *Letters of King James VI & I*, ed. G. P. V. Akrigg (Berkeley, 1984), 257.

3. Henry Chettle, *England's Mourning Garment* (1603), *CWBJ*, Literary Record, Electronic Edition.

4. *The Diary of Lady Anne Clifford*, with an introduction by V. Sackville-West (London, 1923), 9.

5. Leeds Barroll, *Anna of Denmark, Queen of England: A Cultural Biography* (Philadelphia, 2001), 62–5. Jonson praises the virtues of Sir Thomas Egerton (later Baron Ellesmere)—the patron of John Donne—in *Epigrams*, 74, *The Underwood*, 31 and 32, and *Discoveries*, 913.

6. The tensions between Dekker and Jonson are further evident in the publishing history of their two volumes in 1604: see Martin Butler's textual essay, *CWBJ*, Electronic Edition. Stephen Harrison's volume, *The Arches of Triumph Erected in Honour of the High and Mighty Prince James*, was published in June 1604 with engravings by William Kip of all seven arches erected for this occasion. See also Richmond Barbour, *Before Orientalism: London's Theatre of the East 1576–1626* (Cambridge, 2003), 70–80, and Kevin Sharpe, *Image Wars: Promoting Kings and Commonwealths in England 1603–1660* (New Haven, 2010), 93–9.

7. Howard Erskine-Hill, *The Augustan Idea in English Literature* (London, 1983). James himself was keen on the imperial analogy, and was the first English monarch to portray himself on his coinage as a Roman emperor: see Jonathan Goldberg, *James I and the Politics of Literature* (Stanford, Calif., 1989), 33–54.

8. Florus, *On the Quality of Life*, 9; cf. *Epigrams*, 79.1; *Every Man In His Humour* (F), 5.5.38–40, *Discoveries*, 1728–9, *The New Inn*, epilogue, 23–4.

9. Jonson, *Epigrams*, 5, 35, 51.

10. The identification is probable though not certain. Daniel's masque, originally scheduled for performance on Twelfth Night (6 January) 1604, was actually performed two nights later, on 8 January. Roe's poem reflecting on the event is dated 6 January. The only event performed that night, a Scottish sword-dance, is unlikely to have been the cause of the trouble. See Jonson's report of the incident to Drummond, *Informations*, 113–16, and the careful analysis by Martin Butler, *The Stuart Court Masque and Political Culture* (Cambridge, 2008), ch. 2; as well as Joseph Loewenstein, 'Printing and "The Multitudinous Presse": The Contentious Texts of Jonson's Masques', in Jennifer Brady and W. H. Herendeen (eds.), *Ben Jonson's 1616 Folio* (Newark, NJ, 1991), 168–91.

11. 'To Ben Jonson, 6 January 1603' (= 1604), 7–12. The poem was attributed for a time to Donne, and was printed in the 1633 edition of his works. The attribution to Roe was made by Herbert J. C. Grierson in his edition of *The Poems of John Donne*, 2 vols. (Oxford, 1912), 2.cxxix–cxxxv; the text is at 1.414–15. Jonson may perhaps recall this episode in Lovel's speech in *The New Inn*, 4.4.184–7: 'I am kept out a masque, sometime thrust out, | Made wait a day, two, three, for a great word | Which, when it comes forth, is all frown and forehead; | What laughter should this breed rather than anger.'

12. Jonson, *Epigrams*, 27, 32, 33; Alvaro Ribeiro, 'Sir John Roe: Ben Jonson's Friend', *Review of English Studies*, NS 24 (1973), 153–64. Ribeiro's examination of evidence relating to Roe's and the Gunpowder Plotters (pp. 161–4) makes untenable B. N. De Luna's thesis that he was implicated in the final stages of the conspiracy: *Jonson's Romish Plot: A Study of 'Catiline' and its Historical Context* (Oxford, 1967): see n. 38 below.

13. John Harley, *William Byrd, Gentleman of the Chapel Royal* (Aldershot, 1997), especially 67–81, 126–31; W. B. Squire, 'William Byrd', *DNB*.

14. The question of Anne's Catholicism is cautiously reviewed by Leeds Barroll in *Anna of Denmark*, appendix, 162–72. See also Forbes-Leith, *Narratives of the Scottish Catholics*, 263–7, 272–3, and Albert J. Loomie, 'King James I's Catholic Consort', *Huntington Library Quarterly*, 34 (1971), 303–16. It is possible Anne was persuaded to accept Catholicism by Lady Henrietta Stuart (the sister of Jonson's patron Esmé Stuart), whom James had married to the Catholic Earl of Huntley: see Caroline Bingham, *James I of England* (London, 1981), 55–6. On James's religious position, see Kenneth Fincham and Peter Lake, 'The Ecclesiastical Policies of James I and Charles I', in Kenneth Fincham (ed.), *The Early Stuart Church, 1603–1642* (Basingstoke, 1993), 23–49; and W. B. Patterson, *King James VI and I and the Reunion of Christendom* (Cambridge, 1997)

15. Leeds Barroll's analysis and plausible conjecture: *Anna of Denmark*, ch. 3. David Norbrook suggests, perhaps with justice, that Jonson was favoured over Samuel Daniel because 'Daniel's hostility to pomp and ceremony was too deep-rooted to make him a very effective court poet', arguing that Jonson was less opposed to conspicuous spending on the court masques: *Poetry and Politics in the English Renaissance* (London, 1984), ch. 7, at 178–9. On Jonson's attitude to masquing expenditures, see Ch. 15 below, 280–1.

16. Though Inigo Jones was the first English architect to be honoured by a biography—written by his pupil John Webb in 1665, two years after his death—information about his early life is remarkably sparse. Christopher Wren is reported as saying that as a young man Inigo was apprenticed to a joiner in St Paul's churchyard. Wren's information that Jones was a Catholic no longer seems probable, however: John Newman, 'Inigo Jones', *ODNB*. On Jones and his work, see Stephen Orgel and Roy Strong, *Inigo Jones: The Theatre of the Stuart Court*, 2 vols. (Berkeley, 1973); Christy Anderson, *Inigo Jones and the Classical Tradition* (Cambridge, 2007); H. M. Colvin, *A Biographical Dictionary of British Architects*, 3rd edn. (New Haven, 1995), 554–8; J. A. Gotch, *Inigo Jones* (London, 1928); John Peacock, *The Stage Designs of Inigo Jones: The European Context* (Cambridge, 1995).

17. *Blackness*, 4; E. K. Chambers, *The Elizabethan Stage*, 4 vols. (Oxford, 1923), 1.206. Martin Butler doubts that this was a common practice: *The Stuart Court Masque and Political Culture*, 84–5. On the cost of *The Masque of Blackness*, see Orgel and Strong, *Inigo Jones*, 1.89.

18. See in particular D. J. Gordon, 'Poet and Architect: The Intellectual Setting of the Quarrel between Ben Jonson and Inigo Jones', in *The Renaissance Imagination: Essays and Lectures by D. J. Gordon*, ed. Stephen Orgel (Berkeley, 1975), 77–101; Orgel and Strong, *Inigo Jones*, 1, ch. 1, 'The Poetics of Spectacle'; Allan H. Gilbert, *The Symbolic Persons in the Masques of Ben Jonson* (Durham, NC, 1948). The quotations in this paragraph are from *Hymenaei*.

19. Dudley Carleton to Ralph Winwood, January 1605: *CWBJ*, Masque Archive, Electronic Edition. On the perspective line of the King's chair, see Allardyce Nicoll, *Stuart Masques and the Renaissance Stage* (London, 1937), 34, Stephen Orgel, *The Jonsonian Masque* (Cambridge, 1965), 66.

20. Barroll, *Anna of Denmark*, 104–8; Lindley (ed.), *Blackness* and *Beauty*, *CWBJ*; D. J. Gordon, 'The Imagery of Ben Jonson's *Masques of Blacknesse and Beautie*', in Gordon, *The Renaissance Imagination*, ed. Orgel, 134–56. Martin Butler, *The Stuart Court Masque and Political Culture* (Cambridge, 2008), 110–15, examines the masque's deeper political sub-text.

21. Lawrence Stone, *The Crisis of the Aristocracy* (Oxford, 1965), 74–82. On the Gentlemen of the Bedchamber, see Ch. 9 n. 22 above.

22. J. S. Brewer (ed.), *The Court of King James*, 2 vols. (London, 1839), 1.320–1; Jenny Wormald, 'The Union of 1603', in Roger A. Mason (ed.), *Scots and Britons: Scottish Political Thought and the Union of 1603* (Cambridge, 1994), 17–40; 21. The young Anne Clifford offered a similar comment on the Scottish lack of hygiene while visiting Theobalds in 1603: 'we all saw a great change between the fashion of the Court as it is now and of that in the Queen's time, for we were all lousy by sitting in the chamber of Sir Thomas Erskine': *Diary*, 5–6.

23. Jonson was not philosophically opposed to the idea of knighthoods, and in the *Epigrams* balances his satirical portraits of unworthy knights—Sir Luckless Woo-All, Sir Voluptuous Beast, Sir Cod the Perfumed, Sir Annual Tilter—against more numerous poems of praise to those who deserve the honour: Sir John Roe, Sir Henry Cary, Sir Henry Goodyere, Sir Horace Vere, Sir John Radcliffe, Sir Henry Savile, Sir Thomas Roe, Sir Edward Herbert, Sir Henry Neville, Sir Thomas Overbury, Sir William Jephson, Sir Ralph Sheldon, Sir William Uvedale. In *The Speeches at Prince Henry's Barriers* (1610) the character of Chivalry would welcome the return of knighthood 'like a flood | Upon these lists' (399–400). For the later rumour that Jonson himself was soon to be knighted, see 367 above.

24. The term 'East End' develops in the nineteenth century, but the east/west axis of metropolitan growth, and consequent social demarcations, were of growing significance in this period. See M. J. Power, 'East and West in Early Modern London', in E. W. Ives, R. J. Knecht, and J. J. Scarisbrick (eds.), *Wealth and Power in Tudor England: Essays Presented to S. T. Bindoff* (London, 1978), 167–85; Vanessa Harding, 'City, Capital, and Metropolis: The Changing Shape of Seventeenth-Century London', in J. F. Merritt (ed.), *Imagining Early Modern London: Perceptions and Portrayals of the City from Stow to Strype, 1598–1720* (Cambridge, 2001), 117–43; and Emrys Jones, 'The First West End Comedy', *Proceedings of the British Academy 1982*, 68 (Oxford, 1983), 215–58.

25. W. W. Greg (*Modern Language Review*, 23 (1928), 76; *The Library*, 4th series, 9 (1929), 303–4) and E. K. Chambers (*The Elizabethan Stage* (1923), 3.255) believed the problems of the play had been occasioned by its publication, not by its original staging. For persuasive arguments to the contrary, see however R. E. Brettle ('*Eastward Ho*, 1605, by Chapman, Jonson, and Marston', *The Library*, 4th series, 9 (1929), 287–301), and J. Q. Adams ('*Eastward Hoe* and its Satire against the Scots', *Studies in Philology*, 28 (1931), 157–9), along with Richard Dutton, *Mastering the Revels: The Regulation and Censorship of English Renaissance Drama* (Houndmills, 1991), 174, and Suzanne Gossett and David Kay's introduction to *Eastward Ho!*, *CWBJ*. It seems likely that the authors or the company, anticipating the difficulties that would prevent future performance of the play, sold the text on to the stationers Aspley and Thorpe, who in turn gave it to George Eld to print.

26. British Library Ashley 371. For closer analysis, see Brettle, '*Eastward Ho*, 1605'; Gossett and Kay, *Eastward Ho!*, Textual Essay, *CWBJ*, Electronic Edition.

27. W. A. Shaw, *The Knights of England*, 2 vols. (London, 1906), 2.128; John Nichols, *The Progresses, Processions, and Magnificent Festivities of King James the First*, 4 vols. (London, 1828), 1.245–6, 601; 2.44n.; David Harris Willson, 'King James I and Anglo-Scottish Unity', in W. A. Aiken and B. D. Henning (eds.), *Conflict in Stuart England* (London, 1970), 41–56, at 47.

28. Bertram Dobell, *The Athenaeum*, 3830 (23 March 1901), 369–70; 3831 (30 March 1901), 403–4; 3832 (6 April 1901), 433–4; 3833 (13 April 1901), 465–7. The manuscript book was purchased by the New York collector W. A. White in the same year, and subsequently acquired by the Folger Shakespeare Library. The book as a whole has been edited by A. R. Braunmuller, *A Seventeenth-Century Letter-Book: A Facsimile Edition of Folger MS. V. a.321* (Newark, NJ, 1983); the ten letters written from prison by Jonson and Chapman I have edited as Letters 2–9 and (a)–(c) in *CWBJ*.

29. George Chapman, Letter (a), 'To His Most Gracious Majesty'. While the precise distribution of authorial responsibility for the various scenes of *Eastward Ho!* has been the subject of much speculation, it seems probable, as Chapman says, that neither he nor Jonson had written the most offensive passages in the play. Improvisation or mimicry on the part of the players might well have aggravated an already sensitive situation.

30. See Chapman's Letter (c) to Suffolk (*CWBJ*), and his grateful words to 'Oraculous Salisbury' and 'Most noble Suffolk' in verses prefixed to the quarto edition of *Sejanus* in 1605, '*In* Sejanum', 147, 151. For Salisbury's payment to Murray, see Ben Jonson, George Chapman, and John Marston, *Eastward Ho!*, ed. C. G. Petter, The New Mermaids (London, 1973), 32, note to 2.2.75.

31. On the significance of the presence on this occasion of those two politically like-minded figures, Camden and Selden, see Blair Worden, 'Ben Jonson among the Historians', in Kevin Sharpe and Peter Lake (eds.), *Culture and Politics in Early Stuart England* (Houndmills, 1994), 67–90. Cf. G. J. Toomer, *John Selden: A Life in Scholarship*, 2 vols. (Oxford, 2009), 1.13: 'it is remarkable to find such a close association between Selden and Jonson at this date (1605, when Selden, aged 20, was still a student of barely a year's standing at the Inner Temple). This early friendship helps to explain Selden's entry into the London literary milieu, since Jonson was familiar with (if not always friendly with) almost all contemporary poets and playwrights.'

32. Sir John Harington, *Nugae Antiquae*, 3 vols. (London, 1779), 2.275.

33. Neil Cuddy, 'Anglo-Scottish Union and the Court of James I, 1603–1625', *Transactions of the Royal Historical Society*, 5th series, 39 (1989), 107–124. See also Cuddy's further studies on these matters, cited in n. 24 of ch. 9. The appointment of Philip Herbert in June 1603 finally broke the Scottish monopoly, but was balanced by the appointment of yet another Scotsman, James Hay.

34. Albert J. Loomie SJ, *Guy Fawkes in Spain: The 'Spanish Treason' in Spanish Documents*, Bulletin of the Institute of Historical Research Special Supplement No. 9 (London, 1971), appendix, 62–3.

35. Cuddie, 'Anglo-Scottish Union', 113–14, *CSPV*, 10 (1603–7), 165, 168.

36. James F. Larkin and Paul L. Hughes (eds.), *Stuart Royal Proclamations*, 1: *Royal Proclamations of King James I, 1603–1625* (Oxford, 1973), 70–3; Raleigh Trevelyan, *Sir Walter Raleigh* (London, 2002), 356–69; Robert Lacey, *Sir Walter Ralegh* (London, 1973), ch. 37; de Lisle, *After Elizabeth*, 207ff., 273. The projected date of the Bye Plot coup was initially 25 June, then 20 June, then 24 June. 'Na Na, gud faith' etc.: James's alleged words are of doubtful authenticity, being reported by the convicted Bye Plot conspirator Anthony Copley: see Mark Nicholls, 'The Gunpowder Plot', *ODNB*.

37. Thomas Birch, *The Court and Times of James I* (London, 1848), 1.37; Jenny Wormald, 'Gunpowder, Treason, and Scots', *Journal of British Studies*, 24 (1985), 141–86, at 161; Bruce Galloway, *The Union of England and Scotland 1603–1608* (Edinburgh, 1986), 80.

38. *CWBJ*, Life Records, 29, Electronic Edition. This document from the State Papers 14/216, part 2, no. 132, was first published by J. L. Hotson, *I, William Shakespeare, do appoint Thomas Russell Esquire* (London, 1937), 186–7. The unidentified guest is sometimes thought to have been Jonson's friend Sir John Roe (see e.g. Alan Haynes, *The Gunpowder Plot* (Stroud, 1996), 71), but Roe was absent from England at this time, taking a brave stand in an otherwise doomed engagement in the Low Countries which Jonson commemorates in *Epigrams*, 66 ('To Sir Henry Cary'), in which Roe received a serious head wound. See Ribeiro, 'Sir John Roe: Ben Jonson's Friend' (n. 12 above), 161–4.

39. On this last conjecture, see De Luna, *Jonson's Romish Plot*, ch. 4; Francis Edwards SJ, *The Real Story of the Gunpowder Plot* (London, 1969), 155; Paul Durst, *Intended Treason* (London, 1970), 85.

40. On Cecil's relations with English Catholics, see Brian Magee, *The English Recusants* (London, 1938), ch. 3; Handover, *The Second Cecil*, ch. 29; Dennis Flynn, 'Donne's *Ignatius his Conclave* and Other Libels on Robert Cecil', *John Donne Journal*, 6 (1987), 163–83.

41. The notion that Cecil masterminded the Plot developed early (see e.g. Godfrey Goodman, Bishop of Gloucester, *The Court of King James I*, ed. John Brewer (London, 1839), 102) and was set out at length by Father John Gerard SJ, *What Was the Gunpowder Plot?* (1897). S. R. Gardiner countered this reading magisterially in *What Gunpowder Plot Was* (1897); Father Gerard rejoined with *The Gunpowder Plot and the Gunpowder Plotters, in reply to Professor Gardiner* (1897). Francis Edwards SJ, *The Real Story of the Gunpowder Plot?* (London, 1969) sympathetically revisits the anti-Cecilian version of events, as does Antonia Fraser's *The Gunpowder Plot: Terror and Faith in 1605* (London, 1996). For more a sceptical reading, see e.g. Mark Nicholls, *Investigating Gunpowder Plot* (Manchester, 1991) and 'The Gunpowder Plot', *ODNB*. Father Edwards responds to Mark Nicholls in *Recusant History*, 21 (1992–3), 305–46. The trial of the conspirators and of Father Garnet and James's own narrative of events are reported in *A Complete Collection of State Trials*, compiled T. B. Howell, 34 vols. (London, 1809–28), 2.161–357.

42. *State Trials*, ed. Howell, 2.201.

43. James's letter is reproduced by Fraser, *The Gunpowder Plot*, following p. 252.

44. Extract from the lost Register of the Privy Council, BL Add. MS 11402, fo. 108; *CWBJ*, Life Records, 30, Electronic Edition.

45. Letter 9, *CWBJ*.

46. *CSPV 1603–7*, 295; Paul Arblaster, 'George Blackwell', *ODNB*. Robert Persons wrote in similar vein that 'due detestation of so rash and heinous an attempt, Catholics, no less than Protestants, do willingly admit', *The Judgement of a Catholic Englishman Concerning Triplici nodo, Triplex cuneus* (1608).

47. See Ch. 9 above, 191, and n. 32. Cain's theory is not without its difficulties. Jonson's Privy Council warrant does not summon him to answer questions about his own writings, or even about his own role in relation to the Plot, but authorizes him merely to escort a priest before the commission. It is unlikely Jonson's tragedy would have been seen by the Council as a matter of pressing consequence on a day of acute national emergency. Yet the charges concerning *Sejanus* and *Eastward Ho!*, even if already resolved, might still have been a powerful factor in securing Jonson's collaboration at this moment.

48. Richard Broughton, *English Protestants' Plea and Petition for English Priests and Papists* (London, 1621), vol. 218 of English Recusant Literature 1558–1640, ed. D. M. Rogers

(Ilkley, 1974), 59; [Peter Walsh?], *The Advocate of Conscience Liberty, or An Apology for Toleration Rightly Stated* (London, 1673), 227; Francis Teague, 'Jonson and the Gunpowder Plot', *Ben Jonson Journal*, 5 (1998), 249–52.

49. Patrick Martin and John Finnis, 'A Gunpowder Priest?', *Times Literary Supplement*, 4 November 2005, 12–13. On the dating of Strange's gift to Jonson of a copy of the Vulgate Bible (1600, not 1605), see Mark Bland, *TLS*, 9 December 2005. Further details on Strange are from Henry Foley SJ, *Records of the English Province of the Society of Jesus*, 7 vols. (London, 1877), vol. 7, part 2, 980–1, 987.

Chapter 11

1. On Henry Howard's role, see Peck, 'The Mentality of a Jacobean Grandee' (Ch. 10 n. 2 above), 167. A further wedding between Frances Howard's sister Catharine and Robert Cecil's son and heir William would shortly follow, to consolidate the alliance. Though James's guiding hand was behind the occasion, *Hymenaei* was not a royal masque, and was paid for by friends of the bride and groom: Orgel and Strong, *Inigo Jones, The Theatre of the Stuart Court* (Ch. 10 n. 16, above), 1.105. For more detailed explication of the masque and its background, see in particular D. J. Gordon, '*Hymenaei*: Ben Jonson's Masque of Union', in his *The Renaissance Imagination*, ed. Stephen Orgel (Berkeley, 1975), 157–84; Martin Butler, *The Stuart Court Masque and Political Culture* (Ch. 10 n. 10, above), 115–20, and ch. 6; David Lindley, *The Trials of Frances Howard: Fact and Fiction at the Court of King James* (London, 1996), ch. 1; and Lindley's edition of the masque, *CWBJ*.
2. David Harris Willson, *King James VI and I* (London, 1956), ch. 6.
3. For Cotton's Roman altar, see David McKitterick, 'From Camden to Cambridge: Sir Robert Cotton's Roman Inscriptions and their Subsequent Treatment', in C. J. Wright (ed.), *Sir Robert Cotton as Collector: Essays on an Early Stuart Courtier and his Legacy* (London, 1997), 116–17. John Pory's comments on the masque are in a letter to Cotton of 7 January 1606, BL Cotton MS Julius C. iii, fos. 301–2, *CWBJ*, Masque Archive, Electronic Edition.
4. Galloway, *The Union of England Scotland 1603–1608* (Ch. 10 n 36, above); Cuddy, 'Anglo-Scottish Union and the Court of James I' (Ch. 10 n. 32, above); Conrad Russell, 'The Anglo-Scottish Union 1603–1643: A Success?', in Anthony Fletcher and Peter Roberts (eds.), *Religion, Culture, and Society in Early Modern Britain: Essays in Honour of Patrick Collinson* (Cambridge, 1994), ch. 10. On Cecil's relationship with Katherine, Countess of Suffolk, see Pauline Croft, 'The Reputation of Robert Cecil: Libels, Political Opinion, and Popular Awareness in the Early Seventeenth Century', *Transactions of the Royal Historical Society*, 6th series, 1 (1991), 43–69, at 58–61.
5. *CSPV 1603–1607*, 303; G. B. Harrison, *A Jacobean Journal 1603–1606* (London, 1941), 262–5; Francis W. X. Fincham, 'Notes from the Ecclesiastical Court Records at Somerset House', *Transactions of the Royal Historical Society*, 4th series, 4 (1921), 103–39, at 109–10; *CWBJ*, Life Records, 31, 32, Electronic Edition.
6. David Mathew, *Catholicism in England* (London, 1955), 71; Michael L. Carrafiello, *Robert Parsons and English Catholicism 1580–1610* (Selinsgrove, Pa., c.1998), ch. 8. On the Oath of Allegiance, see Ch. 13 below.
7. Michael C. Questier, *Conversion, Politics, and Religion in England, 1580–1625* (Cambridge, 1996), 172–3.
8. On the seriousness of this charge, see Ch. 7 above, 141, and n. 39.

9. A. W. R. E. Okines, 'Why Was There So Little Government Reaction to Gunpowder Plot?', *Journal of Ecclesiastical History*, 55 (2004), 275–92, at 282.

10. Fincham, 'Notes from the Ecclesiastical Court Records', III.

11. Tucca on Horace, *Satiromastix*, 5.2.217–19: 'you nasty tortoise, you and your itchy poetry break out like Christmas, but once a year.'

12. Mosca's suggestion oddly recalls Jonson's own suggestion in *Epigrams*, 60, that 'An obelisk or column' be erected in London in honour of Monteagle's actions; see Ch. 10 above.

13. 'Let me have a good ground. No matter for the pen, the plot shall carry it', says Antonio in *The Case Is Altered*, and Onion replies, 'Indeed, that's right; you are in print already for the best plotter' (1.1.83–4). (The character of Antonio is modelled on Anthony Munday; Jonson is alluding here to Meres's description of Munday in *Palladis Tamia*, which was 'in print' late in 1598: G. Gregory Smith (ed.), *Elizabethan Critical Essays*, 2 vols. (Oxford, 1904), 2.320. These lines form part of a late addition to the original text of *The Case Is Altered*, and carry a touch of irony.) In *Discoveries* Jonson again treats the word 'plot' as an established term of art: 'The fable or plot of a poem defined' (marginal note to line 1902). 'Counter-plot' is not recorded by *OED* before 1611.

14. These qualities are well chartered by William W. E. Slights, *Ben Jonson and the Art of Secrecy* (Toronto, 1994).

15. Coleridge, *Literary Remains* (1836), quoted in Jonas A. Barish (ed.), *'Volpone': A Casebook* (London, 1972), 52; W. B. Yeats, *On the Boiler* (Dublin, 1939), 33. Yeats writes again of the ending of *Volpone* in a letter of 1921, *The Letters of W. B. Yeats*, ed. Allan Wade (London, 1954), 665.

16. See in particular S. L. Goldberg, 'Folly into Crime: The Catastrophe of *Volpone*', *Modern Language Quarterly*, 20 (1959), 233–42; Stephen Greenblatt, 'The False Ending in *Volpone*', *Journal of English and Germanic Philology*, 75 (1976), 90–104; Ian Donaldson, 'Unknown Ends: *Volpone*', ch. 7 in *Jonson's Magic Houses* (Oxford, 1997); and John Creaser's defence of the closing movement of the play in the introduction to his edition of *Volpone* for the London Medieval and Renaissance Series (London, 1978).

17. *Volpone* may have been played in Oxford by the King's Men in July 1606 and was certainly performed there on 7 September 1607 during a period of plague in London. Alan Nelson finds no record of the play's performance in Cambridge, and is inclined to doubt that one occurred: *Cambridge*, Records of Early English Drama, 2 vols. (Toronto, 1989), 2.984–6. The commendatory poems of Edmund Bolton and E.S. prefixed to the 1607 quarto clearly suggest, however, that the play was performed with success in both cities (though probably not on college or university premises).

18. Richard Dutton, *Ben Jonson: Authority: Criticism* (London, 1996) and *Ben Jonson, 'Volpone', and the Gunpowder Plot* (Cambridge, 2008).

19. Speed Hill, 'Biography, Autobiography, and *Volpone*', *Studies in English Literature 1500–1900*, 12 (1972), 309–38. Alvin B. Kernan in his Yale edition of *Volpone* (New Haven, 1962) sees similarities between Jonson's own career and that of Scoto of Mantua (note to 2.1.36). These are sceptically regarded by John Creaser (see n. 16 above), in his note to the same passage. Jonson was sometimes thought to have taken the wealthy founder of Charterhouse, Thomas Sutton, as his model for Volpone: see Ch. 16 (and n. 15) below.

20. On the Venetian setting of the play, see in particular R. B. Parker, 'Jonson's Venice', in J. R. Mulryne and Margaret Shewring (eds.), *Theatre of the English and Italian Renaissance*

(New York, 1991), 95–112. Julie Sanders explores the political significance of this location in *Ben Jonson's Theatrical Republics* (Houndmills, 1998), ch. 3.

21. The case for Wotton is made by J. D. Rea in his edition of *Volpone*, Yale Studies in English (New Haven, 1919); that for Sherley by S. C. Chew, *The Crescent and the Rose: Islam and England during the Renaissance* (Oxford, 1937), 239; that for Cecil, by James Tulip, 'Comedy as Equivocation: An Approach to the Reference of *Volpone*', *Southern Review* (Adelaide), 5 (1972), 91–100, and 'The Contexts of *Volpone*', in *Imperfect Apprehensions: Essays in English Literature in Honour of G. A. Wilkes* (Sydney, 1996), 74–87.

22. Richard Dutton, *Ben Jonson, 'Volpone', and the Gunpowder Plot* (Cambridge, 2008). Cecil's lack of an ancient lineage would not in itself have been a matter of concern to Jonson, who mocks such prejudices in 'A Speech According to Horace' (*The Underwood*, 44) and in Sempronia's dismissive assessment of Cicero, 'the new man', in *Catiline*, 2.1.115-42.

Chapter 12

1. The probable dates of these plays are taken from G. K. Hunter, *English Drama 1586–1642: The Age of Shakespeare*, Oxford History of English Literature (Oxford, 1997), appendix: Chronology.

2. John Aubrey, *Brief Lives*, ed. A. Clark (Oxford 1898), 2.15. Later in the century Jeremy Collier was interestingly to exempt Ben Jonson from the accusations of blasphemy and immodesty that he levelled at other dramatists of the period. While Shakespeare was at times guilty of 'smut' and 'misbehaviour', Collier maintained, 'Ben Jonson is much more reserved in his plays, and declares plainly for modesty in his *Discoveries*': *A Short View of the Immorality and Profaneness of the English Stage* (1698), 50–1. In a similar way Jonson defended his *Epigrams* as 'my chaste book', *Epigrams*, 49.6.

3. Barbara A. Mowat, 'Q2 Othello and the 1606 "Acte to restraine Abuses of Players"', in Christa Jansohn and Bodo Plachta (eds.), *Varienten—Variants—Variantes* (Tübingen, 2005), 91–106. On the general effects of this Act, see Richard Dutton, *Mastering the Revels: The Regulation and Censorship of English Renaissance Drama* (Houndmills, 1991).

4. Anthony à Wood, *Athenae Oxonienses*, 2 vols. (London, 1691), 2.54. For more on these connections, see Ch. 17 below.

5. For further details of Jonson's income, see Ch. 19 below.

6. For Jonson's renewal of his membership of the Company, see above, 89.

7. G. E. Bentley, *The Profession of Dramatist in Shakespeare's Time, 1590–1642* (Princeton, 1986), 288–9; David Bevington, 'Actors, Companies, and Playhouses', *CWBJ*, 1.cxvi–cxxx. See also Andrew Gurr, *The Shakespearian Playing Companies* (Oxford, 1996); Gurr, *The Shakespearian Company, 1594–1642* (Cambridge, 2004); and Peter Thomson, *Shakespeare's Professional Career* (Cambridge, 1992).

8. For a suggestive account of the tensions stemming from these various attachments, see Peter Womack, *Ben Jonson* (Oxford, 1986).

9. The accounts of this occasion assembled by the Company's Clerk, Richard Langley, are to be found in C. M. Clode's *Memorials of the Merchant Taylors* (London, 1885), 147–82, and his *Early History of the Guild of Merchant Taylors of the Fraternity of St John the Baptist*, 2 vols. (London, 1888), 1, ch. 16. See *CWBJ*, Masque Archive, Electronic Edition.

10. Clode, *Early History*, 1.280.

11. ibid. 1.290.

12. I am grateful to Dr David Lockie for first drawing my attention to the three songs from the Hatfield House archive that he suspected might be by Jonson, and to my pupil Dr Gabriel Heaton for brilliantly confirming this conjecture in his Cambridge doctoral dissertation 'Performing Gifts: The Manuscript Circulation of Elizabethan and Early Stuart Royal Entertainments' (2003), now published in revised format as *Writing and Reading Royal Entertainments from George Gascoigne to Ben Jonson* (Oxford, 2010). Dr Heaton and Dr James Knowles—who had independently been researching this occasion as part of his larger study of Jonson's private and civic entertainments—have together reconstructed this occasion in '"Entertainment Perfect": Ben Jonson and Corporate Entertainment', *Review of English Studies*, 54 (2003), 587–600.

13. John Stow and Edmund Howes, *The Annales, or General Chronicle of England* (London, 1615), 891; Clode, *Memorials*, 182. John Bull composed a keyboard piece that bears some resemblance to the English national anthem, but the words of the anthem were certainly not written by Jonson, and probably date from the mid-eighteenth century. Some of the words in the national anthem happen (ironically) to resemble those in the prayer appointed to be read in the churches on the anniversary of the Gunpowder Plot: 'Scatter our enemies...assuage their malice, and confound their devices'. See Percy Scholes, *Oxford Companion to Music* (London, 1970), 409–11.

14. Clode, *Early History*, 1.283.

15. The entertainment was presented that same day; a note on Robert Singleton's bill for materials for costumes for this occasion in the Hatfield House papers speaks of 'the shewe in the librarie mad the 6th of Maye 1608': Katherine Craik, personal information. The bill is partly transcribed in Orgel and Strong, *Inigo Jones: The Theatre of the Stuart Court*, 1.122–3; and more fully in *CWBJ*, Masque Archive, Electronic Edition. I am indebted to James Knowles's pioneering work on these entertainments, and especially here to his essay '"To raise a house of better fame": Jonson's Cecilian Entertainments', in Pauline Croft (ed.), *Patronage, Culture, and Power: The Early Cecils* (New Haven, 2002); and to Gabriel Heaton for his detailed analysis of Jonson's work for Robert Cecil, *Writing and Reading Royal Entertainments*. See also Scott McMillin, 'Jonson's Early Entertainments: New Information from Hatfield House', *Renaissance Drama*, NS 1 (1968), 156–9.

16. *Epigrams*, 65.12; Knowles, '"To raise a house"'.

17. For Cecil's building ambitions, see Lawrence Stone, *Family and Fortune: Studies in Aristocratic Finance in the Sixteenth and Seventeenth Centuries* (Oxford, 1973), 92–5.

18. Orgel and Strong, *Inigo Jones*, 1.122–5.

19. Stone, *Family and Fortune*, 97. See also Stone's 'Inigo Jones and the New Exchange', *Archaeological Journal*, 114 (1959), 108–11.

20. Wilson had a close financial interest in the development of the New Exchange (see A. F. Pollard, rev. Sean Kelsey, *ODNB*). In 1601–2 he had worked as an agent for Cecil in Italy, reporting on Catholic plots against England and Ireland. Neither of these activities would have endeared him to Jonson.

21. For details, see James Knowles, 'Jonson's *Entertainment at Britain's Burse*', in Martin Butler (ed.), *Re-Presenting Ben Jonson: Text, History, Performance* (Houndmills, 1999), ch. 7.

22. See Cheryl Lynn Ross, 'The Plague of *The Alchemist*', *Renaissance Quarterly*, 41 (1988), 439–58; F. P. Wilson, *The Plague in Shakespeare's London* (Oxford, 1927); Paul Slack, *The Impact of the Plague in Tudor and Stuart England* (London, 1985); J. Leeds Barroll, *Politics, Plague, and Shakespeare's Theater: The Stuart Years* (Ithaca, NY, 1991).

23. Wilson, *The Plague in Shakespeare's London*, 187. This figure is queried by Barroll, *Politics, Plague, and Shakespeare's Theater*, 97–100, but there seems in general to have been some flexibility in the way the companies responded to these orders: see Andrew Gurr, *The Shakespearian Playing Companies* (Oxford, 1996), 87–93, and especially 90 n. 35.

24. From a series of detailed references within the play it is possible to deduce that its action is occurring on a precise day, 1 November 1610, heightening the sense of immediacy. Despite the Oxford editors' doubts (H&S, 10.94), this date is precisely calculated—see Ian Donaldson, *Jonson's Magic Houses* (Oxford, 1997), ch. 6, at 93–4. The plague deaths in London in the liberties and the city that week totalled 58 (Wilson, *The Plague in Shakespeare's London*, 187), so the theatres would still have been closed at that time. The calculations within the play are those found in the quarto (1612) and folio (1616) texts. It is possible that when the play was performed in London earlier in 1610 a different set of figures was used in order to suggest a greater coincidence between the date depicted within the play and the date of performance.

25. R. L. Smallwood, '"Here, in the Friars": Immediacy and Theatricality in *The Alchemist*', *Review of English Studies*, 32 (1980), 142–60.

26. Keith Thomas, *Religion and the Decline of Magic* (Harmondsworth, 1971), 770–1.

27. Thomas, *Religion and the Decline of Magic*, 792; *The Alchemist*, ed. C. M. Hathaway, Yale Studies in English (New Haven, 1903), 38–9.

28. Julian Roberts and Andrew G. Watson, *John Dee's Library Catalogue* (London, 1990), 57, 169; Julian Roberts, 'John Dee', *ODNB*. Frances Yates believed that Jonson's Subtle (as well as Shakespeare's Prospero) was modelled on Dee, adding that 'There is an undoubted satirical allusion to Dee's *Monas hieroglyphica* in Jonson's play, and Dee's mathematical preface is parodied throughout': *The Occult Philosophy in the Elizabethan Age* (London, 2001), 188–9. See also Deborah E. Harkness, *John Dee's Conversations with Angels: Cabal, Alchemy, and the End of Nature* (Cambridge, 1999).

29. E. M. Butler, *The Myth of the Magus* (Cambridge, 1993); Owen Davies, *Cunning-Folk: Popular Magic in English History* (London, 2003).

30. Thomas, *Religion and the Decline of Magic*, 756; *The Alchemist*, 3.4.121–6; Lauren Kassall, *Medicine and Magic in Elizabethan London: Simon Forman: Astrologer, Alchemist, and Physician* (Oxford, 2005), 189; Kassall, 'Simon Forman', *ODNB*. Susan Cerasano finds a direct allusion to Forman's astrological chart, 'Ephemerides', drawn up for Philip Henslowe, in *The Alchemist*, 4.6.46–50: 'Philip Henslowe, Simon Forman, and the Theatrical Community of the 1590s', *Shakespeare Quarterly*, 44 (1993), 145–58.

31. See Ch. 15 below. Jonson refers to Forman's skill with love-potions in *Epicene*, 4.1.110–11, and to his attempts to raise the Devil in *The Devil Is an Ass*, 1.2.2.

32. See David Lindley's introduction to the masque, *CWBJ*; *CWBJ*, Masque Archive, Electronic Edition; Orgel and Strong, *Inigo Jones: The Theatre of the Stuart Court*, 1.131ff.

33. This case is set out by Stephen Orgel, 'Jonson and the Amazons', in Elizabeth D. Harvey and Katharine Eisaman Maus (eds.), *Soliciting Interpretation: Literary Theory and Seventeenth-Century English Poetry* (Chicago, 1990), 119–39, and in 'Marginal Jonson', in Orgel, *The Authentic Shakespeare and Other Problems of the Early Modern Stage* (London, 2002), ch. 13. For a careful reassessment of gender relations in the masque, see Butler, *The Stuart Masque and Political Culture*, ch. 5.

34. *Demonology, in Form of a Dialogue, Divided into Three Books* (Edinburgh, 1597), in *Minor Works of King James VI and I*, ed. James Craigie, Scottish Text Society (Edinburgh, 1982), preface, p. xix.
35. ibid. 30.
36. See H&S, 10.504, and Lindley's *CWBJ* edition, note to 250 and Jonson's marginal note 37. On Scott, see David Wootton, *ODNB*.
37. *The Discovery of Witchcraft*, ed. Montague Summers (London, 1930), bk. 13, ch. 7, and bk. 13, ch. 15. If the 'excellent philosopher' here is indeed Cardano, this reference to his writings (so Ian Maclean and Nancy Siraisi kindly inform me) cannot be traced.
38. Lindley, introduction, *The Masque of Queens, CWBJ*; Butler, *The Stuart Court Masque and Political Culture*, 141–2.

Chapter 13

1. Raymond Williams, *Keywords: A Vocabulary of Culture and Society* (1976), 66.
2. Conal Condren, *The Language of Politics in Seventeenth-Century England* (Basingstoke, 1994), 106. On the significance of the concept in this period, see especially Alexandra Shepard and Phil Withington (eds.), *Communities in Early Modern England: Networks, Place, Rhetoric* (Manchester, 2000); Phil Withington, *The Politics of Commonwealth: Citizens and Freemen in Early Modern England* (Cambridge, 2005); Claude J. Summers and Ted-Larry Pebworth (eds.), *Literary Circles and Cultural Communities in Renaissance England* (Columbia, Mo., 2000), and Benedict Anderson's classic study, *Imagined Communities: Reflections on the Origin and Spread of Nationalism*, revised and extended edition (London, 1991).
3. On the Oath of Allegiance and on the state of the Catholic community at this time, see John Bossy's 'The English Catholic Community 1603–1625', in Alan G. R. Smith (ed.), *The Reign of James VI and I* (London, 1973), 91–105, and *The English Catholic Community 1570–1850* (London, 1975); James Broderick SJ, *The Life and Work of Blessed Robert Francis Cardinal Bellarmine SJ* (London, 1928), ch. 23, and *Robert Bellarmine Saint and Scholar* (London, 1961), ch. 10; John Hungerford Pollen SJ, *The Institution of the Archpriest Blackwell* (London, 1916); Paul Arblaster, 'George Blackwell', *ODNB*; Stefania Tutino, *Law and Conscience: Catholicism in Early Modern England* (Aldershot, 2007), 117–59; Rebecca Lemon, *Treason by Words: Literature, Law, and Rebellion in Shakespeare's England* (Ithaca, NY, 2006); *A Large Examination Taken at Lambeth, According to His Majesty's Direction, of M. George Blackwell* (London, 1607; 1975). Documents in the controversy include [King James I,] *Triplici nodo, triplex cuneus, Or, An Apology for the Oath of Allegiance against the Two Breves of Pope Paulus Quintus and the Late Letter of Cardinal Bellarmine to George Blackwell the Priest*, in *The Works of the Most High and Mighty Prince James* (London, 1616); [King James I,] *An Apology for the Oath of Allegiance* (London, 1609); William Barlow, Bishop of Lincoln, *An Answer to a Catholic Englishman* (London, 1609); Robert Persons, *The Judgement of a Catholic Englishman Living in Banishment for his Religion* (1608), introduced by William T. Costello SJ, facsimile reprint (Gainesville, Fla., 1957); Robert Parsons, *A Discussion of the Answer of Mr William Barlow* (London, 1612); Thomas Fitzherbert, *A Supplement to the Discussion of M. D. Barlow's Answer to the Judgement of a Catholic Englishman* (1613).
4. Wright himself had subscribed to the Oath: see Hugh Aveling, *Northern Catholics: The Catholic Recusants of the North Riding of Yorkshire 1558–1790* (London, 1966), 251.

5. Emrys Jones, 'The First West End Comedy', British Academy Shakespeare Lecture 1982, *Proceedings of the British Academy*, 68 (1982), 215–58. On the significance of the play's location, see also Leo Salingar, *Dramatic Form in Shakespeare and the Jacobeans* (Cambridge, 1986), ch. 10.

6. Ray L. Heffner, Jr., 'Unifying Symbols in the Comedy of Ben Jonson', in W. K. Wimsatt, Jr. (ed.), *English Stage Comedy*, English Institute Essays (New York, 1954), 74–97.

7. 'Of Dramatic Poesy: An Essay', in John Dryden, *Of Dramatic Poesy and Other Critical Essays*, ed. George Watson, 2 vols. (London, 1962), 1.71.

8. Lady Arbella, who had been courted by Stephano Janiculo, claimant to the Romanian throne of Moldavia, was offended by an ambiguous reference in the play by La Foole at 5.1.19–20 to 'the Prince of Moldavia and . . . his mistress, Mistress Epicene' (by 'his' La Foole in fact means Sir John Daw's). References by the Venetian Ambassador appear to suggest that the play was temporarily suppressed as a result of Lady Arbella's interventions (*CSPV* 1607–10, 426–7). Jonson announces that his second prologue was 'Occasioned by some person's impertinent exception'.

9. *The Lives of Philip Howard, Earl of Arundel and of Anne Dacres his Wife*, ed. the Duke of Norfolk, EM (London, 1857), 216–17.

10. Richard Dutton's introduction to his Revels edition of *Epicene* (New York, 2002) proposes a more extensive 'Catholic' context for the play.

11. [W. R. Chetwood,] *The British Theatre: Containing the Lives of the English Dramatic Poets* (Dublin, 1750), 26.

12. See Ch. 1 n. 21 and Ch. 7 and n. 18 above, and Katherine Duncan-Jones, *Ungentle Shakespeare: Scenes from his Life* (London, 2001).

13. Daniel C. Boughner, *The Devil's Disciple: Ben Jonson's Debt to Machiavelli* (New York, 1968); Julie Sanders, *Ben Jonson's Theatrical Republics* (Houndmills, 1998), ch. 2.

14. Sir Politic Would-be's 'known patriots, | Sound lovers of their country' (*Volpone*, 4.1.95–6) is the *OED*'s first example of this sense of the word 'patriot'. Jonson writes ironically of 'those grave and wiser patriots' in the Epistle prefixed to the 1607 quarto of *Volpone*, and had earlier used the word in this sense in *Sejanus*, 4.290 (Arruntius to Lepidus: 'What are thy arts—good patriot teach me them'). Cicero in *Catiline* speaks of 'good Petreius, who's a worthy patriot' (4.6.17), and the word is used in this positive sense throughout *Discoveries* (386, 663–4, etc.). In earlier usage the word meant simply 'fellow-countryman' or 'compatriot'. In early modern usage, words such as 'commonwealth' and 'nation' often referred to smaller social units than they customarily do today (as in the phrase 'city commonwealth', or 'Fools, they are the only nation', in *Volpone*, 1.2.66).

15. 'Samuel Butler', in *Aubrey's Brief Lives*, ed. Oliver Lawson Dick (Harmondsworth, 1962), 146. This etymology is not endorsed by the *OED* or by the best modern authority on this topic, Peter Clark, *British Clubs and Societies 1580–1800: The Origins of an Associational World* (Oxford, 2000).

16. I. A. Shapiro's account of 'The "Mermaid Club"', *Modern Language Review*, 45 (1950), 6–17, needs now to be supplemented by Mark Bland's study of 'Francis Beaumont's Verse Letters to Ben Jonson and "The Mermaid Club"', *English Manuscript Studies*, 12 (2005), 139–79. See also Michael Strachan, 'The Mermaid Tavern Club: A New Discovery', *History Today*, 17 (1967), 533–8; Kenneth Rogers, *The Mermaid and Mitre Taverns in Old London* (London, 1928); Michelle O'Callaghan, 'Patrons of the Mermaid Tavern', *ODNB*. Thomas Fuller's account of Shakespeare's and Jonson's 'wit-combats' appears in

The History of the Worthies of England (1662), 'Warwickshire', 126, and is closely echoed by Thomas Carlyle, *Historical Sketches of Notable Persons and Events in the Reign of James I and Charles I* (London, 1898), 76. See S. Schoenbaum, *Shakespeare's Lives* (Oxford, 1970), 94–5, 294–8; Ian Donaldson, *Jonson's Magic Houses* (Oxford, 1997), ch. 2. Shakespeare's only proven association with the Mermaid was when its landlord, William Johnson, acted as one of his co-purchasers of a house in Blackfriars in 1613: see S. Schoenbaum, *William Shakespeare: A Compact Documentary Life* (Oxford, 1977), 273–4.

17. John Aubrey, *Brief Lives*, ed. A. Clark, 2 vols. (Oxford, 1898), 1.418. On Hoskyns, see David Colclough, *Freedom of Speech in Early Stuart England* (Cambridge, 2005).

18. Sir Philip Sidney, *An Apology for Poetry*, ed. Geoffrey Shepherd (London, 1965), 108–9.

19. Stanley Fish, 'Author-Readers: Jonson's Community of the Same', *Representations*, 7 (1984), 26–58, reprinted in Stephen Greenblatt (ed.), *Representing the English Renaissance* (Berkeley, 1988), 231–63; quotation at 260.

20. Edward, Earl of Clarendon, *The History of the Rebellion and Civil Wars in England*, ed. W. Dunn Macray, 6 vols. (Oxford, 1888; repr. 1958), 1. §§ 120, 121; Michael G. Brennan, *Literary Patronage in the English Renaissance: The Pembroke Family* (London, 1988); Victor Stater, 'William Herbert, Third Earl of Pembroke', *ODNB*; Dick Taylor, Jr., 'The Third Earl of Pembroke as a Patron of Poetry', *Tulane Studies in English*, 5 (1955), 41–67, and 'Clarendon and Ben Jonson as Witnesses for the Earl of Pembroke's Character', in Josephine W. Bennett, Oscar Cargill, and Vernon Hall, Jr. (eds.), *Studies in the English Renaissance Drama* (New York, 1959), 322–44; Donaldson, *Jonson's Magic Houses*, ch. 11.

21. Martin Butler, 'Jonson's Folio and the Politics of Patronage', *Criticism*, 35 (1993), 379–81.

22. Martin Butler, '"Servant, but not Slave": Ben Jonson at the Jacobean Court', *Proceedings of the British Academy*, 90 (Oxford, 1996), 65–93, at 76–7. Blair Worden similarly notes that 'The men most earnestly praised by Jonson are carefully chosen. He favours political failures or half-failures, whose antique virtue the court cannot accommodate': 'Ben Jonson among the Historians', in Kevin Sharpe and Peter Lake (eds.), *Culture and Politics in Early Stuart England* (Houndmills, 1994), 67–90, at 87.

23. See Ch. 9, above. On Savile and his friend Henry Cuffe, hanged at Tyburn for his role in the rebellion, see G. H. Martin and J. R. L. Highfield, *A History of Merton College, Oxford* (Oxford, 1997), ch. 8; R. D. Goulding, 'Sir Henry Savile', *ODNB*; Paul E. J. Hammer, 'The Uses of Scholarship: The Secretariat of Robert Devereux, Second Earl of Essex, *c.*1585–1601', *English Historical Review*, 109 (1994), 26–51; David Womersley, 'Sir Henry Savile's Translation of Tacitus and the Political Interpretation of Elizabethan Texts', *Review of English Studies*, 42 (1991), 313–42.

24. Sergeant Yelverton at Essex's trial in 1601 declared that this rebellion 'is more manifest than the sedition of Catiline to the city of Rome, and consequently England is in no less danger; for as Catiline entertained the most seditious persons about all Rome to join with him in his conspiracy, so the Earl of Essex had none but Papists, Recusants, and atheists for his adjutors and abetters in their capital rebellion against the whole estate of England': *A Compleat Collection of State-Tryals, and Proceedings*, 4 vols. (London, 1719), 1.165. Sir Edward Coke pursued the same analogy: G. B. Harrison, *The Life and Death of Robert Devereux Earl of Essex* (London, 1937), 299. Like Sallust, Catiline too had been charged with extortion after his return from a period as a provincial governor in Africa. See M. C. Howatson, *The Oxford Companion to Classical Literature*, 2nd edn. (Oxford, 1997); D. C. Earl, *The Political Thought of Sallust* (Cambridge, 1961).

25. Alan Harding, 'Neville, Henry (1562–1615) of Billingbear, Berks and Mayfield, Suss', in P. W. Hasler (ed.), *The House of Commons 1558–1603* (London, 1981), 122–4; M. Greengrass, 'Sir Henry Neville', *ODNB*; Annabel Patterson, *Reading between the Lines* (London, 1993), 182, 199–200; Clayton Roberts, *Schemes and Undertakings: A Study of English Politics in the Seventeenth Century* (Columbus, Oh., 1985), ch. 1; Maija Jansson, *Proceedings in Parliament 1614* (House of Commons) (Philadelphia, 1988). Brenda James and W. D. Rubinstein advance Neville's claims as the 'real' William Shakespeare: *Truth Will Out: Unmasking the Real Shakespeare* (Harlow, 2005).

26. For John Roe, see Ch. 9 and n. 12, above; for William Roe's lawsuit, see *CWBJ*, Life Records, 39, Electronic Edition, and H&S, 1.223–31; on Thomas Roe, who had written commendatory poems on both *Sejanus* and *Volpone*, see Michael Strachan, *Sir Thomas Roe 1581–1644: A Life* (Salisbury, 1989), and Richmond Barbour, *Before Orientalism: London's Theatre of the East 1576–1626* (Cambridge, 2003).

Chapter 14

1. 'Proofs of Holy Writ', *The Sussex Edition of the Works in Prose and Verse of Rudyard Kipling*, 30, *Uncollected Prose*, 2, 339–56; first published in *Strand Magazine* for 7 April 1934. David Norton describes the genesis of this story in *Kipling Journal*, 63 (1989), 18–27.

2. Opinion on this matter amongst learned Catholics had however been shifting. Cardinal William Allen had long been concerned about the advantages that Protestants enjoyed over Catholics in questions of faith because of their ready access to an English Bible, and had secured financial support for Gregory Martin's translation of the New Testament, published in 1582, to which he also provided many of the doctrinal notes: Eamon Duffy, 'William Allen', *ODNB*. This translation was one of many taken into account by the translators of the King James Bible.

3. Sir Thomas Overbury, *Observations upon the Provinces United and on the State of France* (1650), 76–7.

4. Roland Mousnier, *L'Assassinat d'Henri IV: 14 mai 1610* (Paris, 1964; repr. 2008); Maurice Lee, Jr., *James I and Henri IV: An Essay in English Foreign Policy 1603–1610* (Urbana, Ill., 1970), 169–71; Mark Greengrass, *France in the Age of Henri IV: The Struggle for Stability*, 2nd edn. (London, 1987; 1st edn. 1984), 251–4; Michel Cassan, *La Grande Peur de 1610* (Paris, 2010); Alistair Horne, *Seven Ages of Paris* (London, 2002), 99–101; Jean Castarède, *1610: L'Assassinat d'Henri IV: un tournant pour Europe?* (Chaintreaux, c.2009).

5. John Field, *The King's Nurseries: The Story of Westminster School* (London, 1987), 31. J. F. Larkin and P. L. Hughes (eds.), *Stuart Royal Proclamations*, 1: *James I 1603–1625* (Oxford, 1973), 245–50.

6. Thomas Fuller, *The Church History of Britain*, ed. J. S. Brewer, 6 vols. (Oxford, 1845), 5.386–97 (book 10, century 17), at 387. Chelsea College was funded initially from the New River scheme, which took water from the River Lea to the city and suburbs of London. The College failed partly because of the death of Prince Henry, who had backed the project, partly because the Provost, Matthew Sutcliffe, was too 'morose and testy' (in Fuller's judgement) to win many supporters, and partly because many churchmen and members of the universities were suspicious of the scheme. See also Wyman H. Herendeen, *William Camden: A Life in Context* (Woodbridge, 2007), 425, 516. Richard Smith helped to establish, with papal approval, the College of Arras in Paris in 1611, to counter the

Protestant teachings of Chelsea College (Joseph Bergin, 'Richard Smith', *ODNB*). Father Thomas Wright, who resided at the College of Arras for a time, seems to have been associated with an attempt to establish a College of Writers in Rome with similar aims (Theodore Stroud, 'Father Thomas Wright: A Test for Toleration', *Biographical Studies*, 1 (1951–2), 189–219, at 208–9).

7. One reason for the Roman Church to withhold the chalice during the eucharist at this time was the structure of the service, which needed to be restarted from scratch if an enthusiastic communicant such as Jonson drained its entire contents. In the Anglican Church the service would recommence with new wine after a few brief words of consecration. In a private communion (such as James had been commending at this time) these risks were minimized. Possibly Jonson was the sole communicant on this occasion (John Morrill, personal communication).

8. Roy Strong, *Henry Prince of Wales and England's Lost Renaissance* (London, 2000), 54, quoting Georges Ascoli, *La Grande-Brétagne devant l'opinion française au XVIIe siècle* (Paris, 1930), 27. On Prince Henry's deep admiration of Henri IV and Maurice of Nassau, see Strong, *Henry Prince of Wales*, 50–1.

9. Cit. Strong, *Henry Prince of Wales*, 44.

10. On the Clèves/Juliers crisis, see Mousnier, *L'Assassinat d'Henri IV*, 139–46, Maurice Lee, *James I and Henri IV*, ch. 7.

11. Sir Charles Cornwallis, *A Discourse of the Most Illustrious Prince Henry, Late Prince of Wales* (1641), 9. For the unpopular mechanism by which funds were raised for Henry's investiture, through the levy of a feudal aid, see Frederick C. Dietz, *English Public Finance 1485–1641*, 2 vols. (New York, 1962; 1st edn. 1932), 2: *1558–1641*, 122–3.

12. Strong, *Henry Prince of Wales*, 122. On relations between Henry and Cecil at this time, see Martin Butler, *The Stuart Court Masque and Political Culture* (Cambridge, 2008), 176. *Oberon* was designed in part to honour the French Ambassador Extraordinary, the Marshal de Laverdin, who was expected to arrive in England with a revised version of the treaty between France and England that Henri IV had been negotiating with James at the time of his assassination; but the Queen Regent, Marie de Médicis, not wanting attention drawn to the new treaty, deliberately delayed Laverdin's departure from Paris to prevent his attending the masque.

13. See Tessa Grant, 'White Bears in *Mucedorus, The Winter's Tale*, and *Oberon, the Fairy Prince*', *Notes & Queries*, 246 (2001), 311–13; Barbara Ravelhofer, '"Beasts of recreacion": Henslowe's White Bears', *English Literary Renaissance*, 32 (2002), 287–323. The risks and difficulties of bringing real bears into close proximity with a courtly audience at Whitehall would however have been considerable: see Lindley's note to *Oberon*, 213–14, *CWBJ*.

14. Dietz, *English Public Finance*, 149, and chs. 7–8; Menna Prestwick, *Cranfield: Politics and Profits under the Early Stuarts: The Career of Lionel Cranfield, Earl of Middlesex* (Oxford, 1966), chs. 3–4.

15. *The Alchemist*, presented by the King's Men some time before mid-July 1610, is likely to have been substantially completed by the time of Jonson's re-conversion.

16. *The Diary of Samuel Pepys*, ed. R. C. Latham and W. Matthews, 11 vols. (London, 1971), 8.575; Gerard Langbaine, *An Account of the English Dramatick Poets* (London, 1691), 288; R. G. Noyes, *Ben Jonson on the English Stage 1660–1776* (1935; repr. New York, 1966), ch. 8, '*Catiline*', 302.

17. G. E. Bentley, *Shakespeare and Jonson: Their Reputations in the Seventeenth Century Compared*, 2 vols. (Chicago, 1945; repr. 1965, 2 vols. in 1), 1.112. Bentley's methodology has been challenged by Alfred Harbage, *Modern Language Notes*, 60 (1945), 414–17, W. W. Greg, 'Shakespeare and Jonson', *Review of English Studies*, 22 (1946), 58, and David L. Frost, *The School of Shakespeare: The Influence of Shakespeare on English Drama 1600–1642* (Cambridge, 1968), especially 19–22.

18. B. N. De Luna, *Jonson's Romish Plot: A Study of* Catiline *and its Historical Context* (Oxford, 1967), 33. For a more extended version of the present argument, see my 'Talking with Ghosts: Ben Jonson and the English Civil War', *Ben Jonson Journal*, 17 (2010), 1–18. Susan Wiseman traces the impact of *Catiline* in mid-century in '"The Eccho of Uncertaintie": Jonson, Classical Drama, and the English Civil War', in Julie Sanders with Kate Chedgzoy and Susan Wiseman (eds.), *Refashioning Ben Jonson: Gender, Politics, and the Jonsonian Canon* (Houndmills, 1998), 208–29. See also Andrew Lynn's Cambridge Ph.D. dissertation (2000) 'The Impact of Ben Jonson, 1637–1700'.

19. Robert Sidney's poetry has been identified and edited from autograph by P. J. Croft, *The Poems of Robert Sidney* (Oxford, 1984). The family's musical talents have been explored by Gavin Alexander, 'The Musical Sidneys', *John Donne Journal*, 25 (2006), 65–105, and the remarkable library at Penshurst by Germaine Warkentin (e.g. 'The Library of the Sidney Family', *Sidney Newsletter and Journal*, 15 (1997), 3–13) and Joseph L. Black, who together with William Bowen are now preparing a book-length edition of the seventeenth-century manuscript collection at Penshurst. Jonson had dedicated *The Alchemist* to Lady Mary Wroth, whom he praised as 'The lady most deserving her name and blood' ('Wroth' being alternatively spelled 'Worth'). Later he addressed her in a sonnet (*The Underwood*, 28), an uncharacteristic form for Jonson that he adopted here in recognition of her own skills as a sonneteer. For his assistance in the circulation of her writing, see Michael G. Brennan, 'Creating Female Authorship in the Early Seventeenth Century: Ben Jonson and Lady Mary Wroth', in George L. Justice and Nathan Tinker (eds.), *Women's Writing and the Circulation of Ideas: Manuscript Publication in England, 1550–1800* (Cambridge, 2002), 73–94. On Mary's sister Philip Sidney, see Lisle Cecil John, 'Ben Jonson's Epigram CXIV to Mistress Philip Sidney', *Journal of English and Germanic Philology*, 45 (1946), 214–17.

20. This was the identification of William A. Shaw, editor of *Report on the Manuscripts of Lord De L'Isle and Dudley Preserved at Penshurst Place, Kent*, 4: *Sidney Papers, 1608–1611* (London, 1942), 279. The name is transcribed as 'Jonson' in *Domestic Politics and Family Absence: The Correspondence (1588–1621) of Robert Sidney, First Earl of Leicester, and Barbara Gamage Sidney, Countess of Leicester*, ed. Margaret P. Hannay, Noel J. Kinnamon, and Michael G. Brennan (Aldershot, 2005), Letter 213, p. 165. Shaw misreads the date of this letter as 21 July, as these editors point out.

21. Michael G. Brennan and Noel J. Kinnamon, 'Robert Sidney, "Mr Johnson", and the Education of William Sidney at Penshurst', *Notes & Queries*, 248 (2003), 430–7.

22. Shaw (ed.), *Report on the Manuscripts of Lord De L'Isle*, 4.134, 164; L. C. John, 'Ben Jonson's "To Sir William Sidney, on his Birthday"', *Modern Language Review*, 52 (1957), 168–76; A. Miller, '"These forc'd ioyes": Imitation, Celebration, and Exhortation in Ben Jonson's Ode to Sir William Sidney', *Studies in Philology*, 86 (1989), 168–76.

23. J. C. A. Rathmell finds a possible clue to a later dating in lines 45–7: 'And though thy walls be of the country stone, | They're reared with no man's ruin, no man's groan; | There's none that dwell about them wish them down', noting that Lord Lisle's correspondence

refers to the building of a new orchard wall with stone from a local quarry in May 1612 ('Jonson, Lord Lisle, and Penshurst', *English Literary Renaissance*, 1 (1971), 250–60, at 252–3). Yet there is no indication that this is the piece of work to which Jonson's line refers, or that stone walls did not exist at Penshurst before 1612. The poem has attracted much good commentary; see in particular Don E. Wayne, *Penshurst: The Semiotics of Place and the Poetics of History* (London, 1984), Alastair Fowler (ed.), *The Country House Poem* (Edinburgh, 1994), G. R. Hibbard, 'The Country House Poem of the Seventeenth Century', *Journal of the Warburg and Courtauld Institute*, 19 (1956), 159–74, Raymond Williams, *The Country and the City* (London, 1973), 27–34.

24. Suetonius, *Vita Virgili*, 5. The commemoration of a celebrated tree (whether still existent or not) had become a commonplace of classical poetry, as the opening of Cicero's *De Legibus*, 'On the Laws', suggests.

25. *The Works of Ben Jonson*, ed. William Gifford and Francis Cunningham, 3 vols. (London, 1903), 3.263.

26. John Rathmell's pioneering account, 'Jonson, Lord Lisle, and Penshurst' (n. 23 above), has now been supplemented by the studies of other scholars, including Germaine Warkentin, Margaret Hannay, Martin Elsky, Craig Muldrew, Susie West, and Joseph Black, working on the Sidney papers and financial issues in the period. Some of their findings were presented at a conference at Penshurst Place in July 2003, 'The Textures of Life at Penshurst Place, 1552–1743', convened by Germaine Warkentin and Susie West, sponsored by the Paul Mellon Centre for the Studies in British Art and Cambridge University's Centre for Research in the Arts, Social Sciences, and Humanities (CRASSH).

27. The last phrase means 'fodder for horses'. Noel J. Kinnamon and Michael G. Brennan, *Domestic Politics and Family Absence: The Correspondence (1588–1621) of Robert Sidney... and Barbara Gamage Sidney* (Aldershot, 2005), 133–4: Letter 167, Lord Lisle to his wife, 10 November 1607.

28. See Daniel Lysons, *The Environs of London* (London, 1796), 29–39. Theobalds however had now passed into King James's hands; Jonson therefore prudently (and characteristically) makes any specific identification impossible.

29. Juvenal, *Satires*, 5.24ff., Martial, 3.60.1–2, 9.

30. I am grateful to Martin Butler and Michael Brennan for their guidance and advice about this puzzling text, which I have also attempted to analyse in *CWBJ*, vol. 5. For the relationship of *The May-lord* to Jonson's unfinished pastoral *The Sad Shepherd*, see Anne Barton's introduction to that work, *CWBJ*. See also I. A. Shapiro, 'Jonson's *The May-lord*', *Harvard Library Bulletin*, 23 (1975), 258–63.

31. 'Beaumont wrote that elegy on the death of the Countess of Rutland, and in effect her husband wanted the half of his—in his travels', *Informations*, 164–5.

32. *Sir Thomas Overbury*, 1622, D4(3). John Considine (*ODNB*, 'Overbury') doubts the veracity of this story, whose very oddity could on the other hand suggest that in broad outline it may be true; Jonson is unlikely to have made up a story that reflects so badly on himself.

33. A further motive for Jonson's return to London might have been the sickness and death of 'Benjamin Johnson sonne to Benjamin', who was buried at St Anne's, Blackfriars on 18 November: see Eccles, 'Jonson's Marriage', 267 (citing Collier's identification). This is probably the 'Beniamin Johnson sonne to Beniamin' who was christened at this same church on 20 February 1608, and by now would have been 3½ years old.

The birth of another Benjamin, son of Benjamin Johnson, is recorded in April 1610 at St Martin-in-the-Fields (see 181 above). It is not clear whether either or both of these boys was the son of our Ben Jonson, or whether the later born of the pair was still alive in 1611.

34. On the connection with Salusbury and Essex, see Ch. 8 above, 149. The general structure of *The Forest* is described by Alastair Fowler, 'The Silva Tradition in Jonson's *The Forrest*', in Maynard Mack and George deForest Lord (eds.), *Poetic Traditions of the English Renaissance* (New Haven, 1982), 163–80. David Norbrook examines the gap between Jonson's presentation of Sir Robert Wroth and the reality of his social position: *Poetry and Politics in the English Renaissance* (London, 1984), ch. 7.

35. Robert Burton, *The Anatomy of Melancholy*, 3 vols. (London, 1927), 3.373 (part 3, section 4, subsection 2: heading).

36. The only evidence as to Jonson's likely departure date and length of his travels comes in a letter of 23 April/3 March from Jean Beaulieu in Paris to William Trumbull in Brussels which speaks of Jonson's 'having spent some twelve months travel in this country'. Literally understood, this would mean that Jonson and Ralegh had left England in the spring of 1612. They were certainly in Paris for the Featley/Smith debate in early September 1612, and Drummond dates their more flamboyant exploits to 1613 (*Informations*, 226).

37. John Aubrey, *Brief Lives*, ed. A. Clark (Oxford, 1898), 2.185–94. For the comment by Ralegh's Oxford tutor, see *DNB*. Oldys in his MS notes to Langbaine's *An Account of the English Dramatic Poets* (Oxford, 1691; now in the British Library) gives a further account of the relationship between Ralegh and Jonson. The year after travelling with Jonson, Wat Ralegh quarrelled with a certain Mr Knowles, and a duel was narrowly averted: see William A. Shaw and G. Dyfnallt Owen (eds.), *Report on the Manuscripts of the Right Honourable Viscount De L'Isle, V.C., Preserved at Penshurst Place, Kent*, 5: *Sidney Papers, 1611–1626* (London, 1962), 209; Henry Wotton to Ralph Winwood, 11/21 May 1615, *The Life and Letters of Sir Henry Wotton*, 2 vols. (Oxford, 1907), 2.79.

38. *Brief Lives*, ed. Clark, 2.192.

39. On this episode, see B. S. Centerwall, 'A Reconsideration of Ben Jonson's Contribution to Sir Walter Ralegh's *The History of the World* (1614)', *Ben Jonson Journal*, 7 (2000), 539–54; Charles G. Salas, 'Ralegh and the Punic Wars', *Journal of the History of Ideas*, 57 (1996), 195–215; and Katherine Craik, *CWBJ*, Dubia, Electronic Edition.

40. John Stoye, *English Travellers Abroad 1605–1667: Their Influence in English Society and Politics*, rev. edn. (New Haven, 1989), 39ff. See also Edward Chaney, *The Evolution of the Grand Tour: Anglo-Italian Cultural Relations since the Renaissance* (London, 1998); Daniel Carey, *Continental Travel and Journeys beyond Europe in the Early Modern Period: An Overlooked Connection*, The Annual Hakluyt Society Lecture 2008 (London, 2009); Andrew Hadfield, *Literature, Travel, and Colonial Writing in the English Renaissance 1545–1625* (Oxford, 1998).

41. See Michael G. Brennan's introduction to his edition of *The Travel Diary (1611–1612) of an English Catholic, Sir Charles Somerset* (Leeds, 1993); Michael G. Brennan, *English Civil War Travellers and the Origins of the Western European Grand Tour*, The Hakluyt Society Annual Lecture 2001 (London, 2002); Antoni Maczak, *Travel in Early Modern Europe*, trans. Ursula Phillips (Cambridge, 1995; first published in Polish: Warsaw, 1980), ch. 12, 'Catholics, Protestants, and Relics'; John Lough, *France Observed in the Seventeenth Century by British Travellers* (Boston, 1985).

42. Sir Walter Ralegh, *Instructions to his Son and to Posterity* (1609). The reports of Jonson's drunken behaviour on these travels are confirmed by Archdeacon Plume: *CWBJ*, Life Records, Early Lives, Electronic Edition.

43. Thomas Coryate, *Crudities*, 2 vols. (London, 1611), 1.176–82; quotations at 178. A few years later, the Earl of Bristol and his wife caused grave offence in Madrid by failing to stand for the sacrament of the altar as it passed by their window during the Corpus Christi festival: Glyn Redworth, *The Prince and the Infanta: The Cultural Politics of the Spanish Match* (New Haven, 2003), 52.

44. Henry Constable, a religious controversialist who had converted to Catholicism, was now living in Paris as a friend of Cardinal Duperron. Jonson praises his 'ambrosiac muse' in *The Underwood*, 27.27. On Pory, see *Letters of John Chamberlain*, ed. McClure, 1.377–8, and William S. Powell, *John Pory 1572–1636: The Life and Letters of a Man of Many Parts*, with microfiche supplement, *Letters and Other Minor Writings* (Chapel Hill, NC, 1977), 36–41; Kevin Sharpe, *The Personal Rule of Charles I* (New Haven, 1992), 684–7.

45. *The Sum and Substance of a Disputation Between Mr Dan Featley, Opponent, and D. Smith, the Younger, Respondent . . . at Paris, September 4 1612* in Featley's *The Grand Sacrilege of the Church of Rome* (1630), 285ff. Powell, *John Pory*, 39, regards this as a publication jointly organized by Jonson and Pory in 1630 to draw attention to 'the kind of man' Smith was, and diminish his political power; in 1631 Smith left England permanently for Paris. The Catholic view of the debate is represented in *The Conference Mentioned by Doctor Featley in the End of his Sacrilege, with some notes added upon the occasion of the minister's relation*, by S.E. (Douai, 1632), and *The Relection of a Conference Touching the Real Presence, or, A Bachelor's Censure of a Master's Apology for Doctor Featley*, by L. I. B. of Art, of Oxford (Douai, 1635); W. D. Briggs, 'On Certain Incidents in Ben Jonson's Life', *Modern Philology* (1913), 1–10, and Rocco Coronato, 'Was it just an Anecdote? Ben Jonson and the Eucharist, Paris 1612', *Ben Jonson Journal*, 4 (1997), 35–46.

46. The first volume of Duperron's collected writings (Paris, 1620, 1622) contains his 'Traité du sacrament de l'Eucharistie'.

47. Jacques Duperron, translator, *Partie du premier et quatriesme livre de l'Aenéide de Virgile* (Paris, 1611). Drummond's dismissive remark that Jonson 'neither doth understand French nor Italian' (*Informations*, 53) needs to be understood as the exaggerated comment of one who himself spoke both languages with fluency; Jonson may have had trouble in keeping up. Yet Jonson certainly passed judgement on works translated from French before he had mastered the language; confessing that he had praised Sylvester's translation of Du Bartas 'ere he understood to confer': *Informations*, 20–1.

48. Powell, *John Pory*, 36–7; John Chamberlain to Dudley Carleton, *The Letters of John Chamberlain*, ed. McClure, 1.326. Duperron's 'Réplique à la Réponse du Roy de la Grande-Bretagne' is in the second volume of his 1620/1622 collected works. Casaubon's *Responsio ad epistolam Cardinalis Perronii* was published in 1612.

49. *The Trumbull Papers*, Sotheby's sale catalogue (London, 1989), 57.

50. BL, Add. MS 72250; *CWBJ*, Life Records, 45, 46, Electronic Edition; Sonia P. Anderson, 'The Elder William Trumbull: A Biographical Sketch', *British Library Journal*, 19.2 (1993), 115–32, and her *ODNB* entry, 2004.

51. *CWBJ*, Masque Archive, Electronic Edition.

52. Anderson, 'The Elder William Trumbull', 119.

53. On 26 March/3 April the business agent John Brownlowe in Antwerp informed Trumbull that he had honoured one of Jonson's and Ralegh's bills of exchange: *CWBJ*, Life Records, 47.

54. David McPherson, 'Ben Jonson Meets Daniel Heinsius, 1613', *English Language Notes*, 44 (1976), 105–9. If Jonson and Ralegh were in Antwerp in April 1613, it is not likely that they were in Leiden (which is north of Antwerp) in March, as McPherson proposes—unless it is assumed that the transaction in Antwerp with the bills of exchange took place on the return journey.

55. Paul R. Sellin, *Daniel Heinsius and Stuart England, with a Short-Title Checklist of the Works of Daniel Heinsius* (Leiden, 1968).

56. James M. Osborn, 'Ben Jonson and the Eccentric Lord Stanhope', *Times Literary Supplement*, 4 January 1957, 16: *CWBJ*, Life Records, 44.

57. *Informations*, 463. The motto is taken from Silius Italicus, *Punica*, 6.332–5. It was later adopted for the Nova Scotia baronets created by Charles 1 in 1625.

Chapter 15

1. *The History of the World*, bk. 5, ch. 6.

2. See M. Corbett and R. Lightbown, *The Comely Frontispiece* (London, 1969), 132–3, and A. H. Gilbert, who argues for Jonson's probable collaboration in the design of the frontispiece: *The Symbolic Persons in the Masques of Ben Jonson* (Durham, NC, 1948), 121–2. For an illuminating reading of the poem in its historical contexts, see Annabel Patterson, *Censorship and Interpretation: The Conditions of Writing and Reading in Early Modern England* (Madison, 1984), 134–9.

3. 'An Expostulation with Inigo Jones', 35–41, *CWBJ*, vol. 6; Stephen Orgel and Roy Strong (eds.), *Inigo Jones: The Theatre of the Stuart Court*, 2 vols. (Berkeley, 1973), 2.451.

4. In *Epigrams*, 98.10 Jonson counsels Sir Thomas Roe to 'study conscience more than thou wouldst fame', advice that is repeated by the Chorus after Act 2 in *Catiline*, 378.

5. This account of the Overbury affair draws on two outstanding recent studies, David Lindley's *The Trials of Frances Howard: Fact and Fiction at the Court of King James* (London, 1996), and Alastair Bellany's *The Politics of Court Scandal in Early Modern England: News Culture and the Overbury Affair, 1603–1660* (Cambridge, 2002), as well as on John Considine's *ODNB* entry on Overbury (Oxford, 2004), Beatrice White, *Cast of Ravens: The Strange Case of Sir Thomas Overbury* (London, 1965), and Anne Somerset, *Unnatural Murder: Poison at the Court of James I* (London, 1997). Lindley's study brilliantly re-examines Frances Howard's popular reputation both in her own time and in recent scholarship. Bellany's equally original account explores the case in relation to the transmission of news and scandal in early modern England.

6. The significance of this episode is examined by Martin Butler, *The Stuart Court Masque and Political Culture* (Cambridge, 2008), ch. 7.

7. James Spedding (ed.), *The Life and Letters of Francis Bacon*, 7 vols. (London, 1861–74), 5.312.

8. *The Diary of John Manningham of the Middle Temple, 1602–3*, ed. Robert Parker Sorlien (Hanover, NH, 1976), 236.

9. Lawrence Stone, *The Road to Divorce: England 1530–1987* (Oxford, 1992), 191; Stone, *The Family, Sex, and Marriage in England 1500–1800* (Oxford, 1977), 37, and 691n. on the long-standing custom of female juries testing the virginity of wives in cases of alleged non-consummation. Attempts have at times been made to link this episode in *Epicene* quite

implausibly to the Essex divorce case: see Ian Donaldson, *Jonson's Magic Houses* (Oxford, 1997), ch. 8.

10. The possibility of collusion between the contesting parties on this central question cannot be ruled out: see Lindley, *The Trials of Frances Howard*, ch. 3.

11. Bellany, *The Politics of Court Scandal*, 57.

12. John Chamberlain, *Letters*, ed. McClure, 1.495–500.

13. *The Letters of John Chamberlain*, ed. N. E. McClure, 2 vols. (Philadelphia, 1939), 1.499; John Nichols, *The Progresses, Processions, and Magnificent Festivities of King James the First*, 4 vols. (London, 1828), 2.732–3. Two songs only survive from Middleton's *Masque of Cupids*; they are edited and annotated by John Jowett with an introduction by M. T. Jones-Davies and Ton Hoenselaars in *Thomas Middleton: The Collected Works*, ed. Gary Taylor and John Lavagnino (Oxford, 2007). *A Challenge at Tilt* and *The Irish Masque* have been edited by David Lindley for *CWBJ*; *The Masque of Flowers* by E. A. J. Honigmann in *A Book of Masques: In Honour of Allardyce Nicoll* (Cambridge, 1967); and *The Somerset Masque* by Walter R. Davis, in *The Works of Thomas Campion* (New York, 1969).

14. John More, *CWBJ*, Masque Archive, Electronic Edition; Butler, *The Stuart Court Masque and Political Culture*, 216–17. Many friends of Essex (so the Agent of Savoy reported) nevertheless refused to participate in the masque (Lindley, introduction to *A Challenge at Tilt*, *CWBJ*).

15. For this speculation, see Lindley, *The Trials of Frances Howard*, 128–9; and for closer analysis of the political context, David Lindley, 'Embarrassing Ben: The Masques for Frances Howard', *English Literary Renaissance*, 16 (1986), 343–59, J. M. Smith, 'Effaced History: Facing the Colonial Contexts of Ben Jonson's *Irish Masque at Court*', *ELH: English Literary History*, 6 (1998), 297–31, and Butler, *The Stuart Masque and Political Culture*, 121–2.

16. On the Addled Parliament (convened 5 April 1614 and dissolved on 7 June) see Ch. 16 below. No legislation was passed, though Maija Jannson argues for the constitutional importance of its debates: *Proceedings in Parliament, 1614, House of Commons* (Philadelphia, 1988).

17. See Bellany, *The Politics of Court Scandal*, 59, and Andrew Thrush, 'The French Marriage and the Origins of the 1614 Parliament', in Clucas and Davies (eds.), *The Crisis of 1614 and the Addled Parliament*, 25–35.

18. Suffolk's appointment as Lord Treasurer was to prove disastrous for the country, and lead to his removal from office in the summer of 1618. It may nevertheless have prompted Jonson's lines 'Since men have left to do praiseworthy things', *Epigrams*, 67. H&S believed this poem was written in 1605 after Suffolk had helped to rescue Jonson and Chapman from imprisonment following the *Eastward Ho!* affair; a dating also preferred by Martin Butler, '"Servant, but not Slave": Ben Jonson at the Jacobean Court', *Proceedings of the British Academy*, 90 (Oxford, 1996), 65–93, at 92. The later dating, first proposed by Peter Whalley, is favoured by Donaldson, *Ben Jonson: Poems* (Oxford, 1975) and Colin Burrow, *CWBJ*, despite the traditional belief that no poem in the *Epigrams* is to be dated later than 1612.

19. Roger Lockyer, *Buckingham: The Life and Political Career of George Villiers, First Duke of Buckingham, 1592–1628* (London, 1981), ch. 1; Goodman quotation on p. 20.

20. John Chamberlain to Sir Dudley Carleton, 1 December 1614, *Letters*, ed. McClure, 1.561.

21. *CSPV*, 15 (1617–1619), 113–14; *CWBJ*, Masque Archive, Electronic Edition.

22. *Discoveries*, 1334–5, following Vives, *De Ratione*, 1.86; *Cynthia's Revels* (F), 5.4.508.

23. Lyndy Abraham, *A Dictionary of Alchemical Imagery* (Cambridge, 1998), 'Mercurius', 124–8, quotation at 124.

24. According to one persistent but unverifiable rumour, Winwood had received a tip from William Trumbull concerning the Countess's role in Overbury's murder following a deathbed confession by a runaway apothecary's boy in the Netherlands: Bellany, *The Politics of Court Scandal*, 72 n. 222.

25. Even in confinement Somerset managed, astonishingly, to negotiate further additions to his extensive art collection: A. R. Braunmuller, 'Robert Carr, Earl of Somerset, as Collector and Patron', in Linda Levy Peck (ed.), *The Mental World of the Jacobean Court* (Cambridge, 1991), 230–50; cf. Lindley, *The Trials of Frances Howard*, 191 and n. 156, and Somerset, *Unnatural Murder* (n. 5 above), 357.

26. For the dating of this work (thought incorrectly by H&S to have been presented at court a year earlier), see Martin Butler's introduction to the masque, *CWBJ*. There is some irony in a masque that celebrates the return of true Justice being performed in such a triumphalist style while the Somerset trials were still *sub judice*.

27. Jonson's estimation of Spenser's work has been re-evaluated since the discovery some years ago of Jonson's extensively annotated personal copy of the 1617 Folio of *The Faerie Queene, The Shepheard's Calendar, Together with Other Works of England's Arch-Poet, Edm. Spenser*: see James A. Riddell and Stanley Stewart, *Jonson's Spenser: Evidence and Historical Criticism* (Duquesne, Pa., 1995).

28. Though Jonson's appointment was not that of Poet Laureate, it was at times later confused with that post; see Edmund Kemper Broadus, *The Laureateship: A Study of the Office of Poet Laureate in England with Some Account of the Poets* (Oxford, 1921). Jonson's patents of appointment of 1616 and 1630 are reproduced as appendices 2 and 3 in this study. For Charles Stanhope's (perhaps confused) belief that Esmé Stuart gave Jonson an annuity of £100 per annum, see Ch. 9 n. 18 above.

29. Nicholas Rowe, *Some Account of the Life of Mr William Shakespeare* (1709), introd. Samuel H. Monk (Ann Arbor, 1948), p. xxxv.

30. There is, on the contrary, some evidence to connect him with events in London during these years: see Park Honan, *Shakespeare: A Life* (Oxford, 1998), ch. 18. The quotation is from Henry James, introduction to *The Tempest* (1907) in *Henry James: Literary Criticism*, ed. Leon Edel, 2 vols. (New York, c.1984), 1: *English Writers*. Edward Bond's play *Bingo* (1973) pictures a meeting (melancholic, rather than merry) between Shakespeare and Jonson in Stratford during the final year of Shakespeare's life.

31. 'The Vision of Ben Jonson, On the Muses of his Friend, M. Drayton', 94, from *The Battle of Agincourt*, 1627; *CWBJ*, vol. 6.

32. Samuel Schoenbaum, *Shakespeare's Lives* (Oxford, 1970), 120–2; Schoenbaum, *William Shakespeare: A Compact Documentary Life* (Oxford, 1977), 296–7; Park Honan, *Shakespeare: A Life* (Oxford, 1998), 406–7.

33. On Jonson's attitude to publication, see in particular Joseph Loewenstein, 'The Script in the Marketplace', in Stephen Greenblatt (ed.), *Representing the English Renaissance* (Berkeley, 1988), 265–78, and the same author's more extended studies, *Jonson and Possessive Authorship* (Cambridge, 2002); and *The Author's Due: Printing and the Prehistory of Copyright* (Chicago, 2002). The present argument draws on my 2006 British Academy Shakespeare Lecture,

'Shakespeare, Jonson, and the Invention of the Author', *Proceedings of the British Academy 2006*, 151 (Oxford, 2007), 319–38.

34. Lukas Erne, *Shakespeare as Literary Dramatist* (Cambridge, 2003); the passage quoted is from page 86. Erne (ch. 2) corrects Douglas Brooks's mistaken assertion (*From Playhouse to Printing House: Drama and Authorship in Early Modern England* (Cambridge, 2000), 71 and *passim*) that the quarto title page of *2 Henry IV* in 1600 was the first to attribute authorship to Shakespeare; it was in fact the sixth such attribution. Peter W. M. Blayney speculates that peaks in publication of playbooks between December 1593 and May 1595 and May 1600 to October 1601 may suggest a deliberate policy of 'publicity' or 'advertising' of plays for the theatre: 'The Publication of Playbooks', ch. 21 in John D. Cox and David Scott Kastan (eds.), *A New History of Early English Drama* (New York, 1987), 383–422, at 386.

35. Jonson would have been in France by the time the entry was placed, and by the time he got back Stepneth was no longer alive. The possibility of the volume having been published cannot however be ruled out entirely. William Drummond noted 'Ben Jonsons epigrams' amongst the 'books read by me anno 1612', while some verses by 'R.C.' in *The Time's Whistle* seem to suggest that the *Epigrams* had appeared as a separate 'book' or 'pamphlet' (*CWBJ*, Literary Record, Electronic Edition). Other verses by Henry Parrot from *The Mastiff, or Young Whelp of the Old Dog: Epigrams and Satires*, published in 1615, seem also to imply familiarity with at least one poem in the collection: see Donaldson, *Jonson's Magic Houses*, 210 n. 24. Jonson himself frequently refers moreover to the *Epigrams* as though they constituted a separately published 'book': e.g. *Epigrams*, title page, 1, 2, 3, 49.6, 77.2, 83.2, etc.

36. Mark Bland, 'William Stansby and the Production of the Workes of Beniamin Jonson, 1615–16', *The Library*, 6th series, 20 (1998), 1–33; James A. Riddell, 'The Concluding Pages of the Jonson Folio of 1616', *Studies in Bibliography*, 47 (1994), 147–54, and Riddell, 'Addendum: The Printing of the Plays in the Jonson Folio of 1616', *Studies in Bibliography*, 50 (1996), 408–9; Kevin J. Donovan, 'The Final Quires of the Jonson 1616 Workes: Headline Evidence', *Studies in Bibliography*, 40 (1987), 106–20; Jennifer Brady and W. H. Herendeen (eds.), *Ben Jonson's 1616 Folio* (Newark, Del., 1991) (and in particular Donovan's essay in this volume, 'Jonson's Texts in the First Folio', 23–37); and David L. Gants, 'The Printing, Proofing, and Press-Correction of Jonson's Folio *Workes*', in Martin Butler (ed.), *Re-Presenting Ben Jonson: Text, History, Performance* (Houndmills, 1999), 39–58. There is no evidence to support the notion, once canvassed by H&S (1.64), that Jonson intended to publish his Folio in 1612 or 1613, or F. G. Fleay's theory that it was to be dedicated to Prince Henry, whose death in November 1613 thwarted this plan: see W. D. Briggs, 'On Certain Incidents in Ben Jonson's Life', *Modern Philology*, 11 (1913), 1–10, and W. W. Greg, 'Some Notes on Ben Jonson's Works', *Review of English Studies*, 2 (1926), 129–45, at 137.

37. Thus the early pages of *Poetaster* in the 1616 Folio mistakenly carry the running heads of *Cynthia's Revels*, an error deliberately perpetuated in the Oxford *Ben Jonson*. The Oxford editors' assumptions about the authority of the 1616 Folio received an early challenge from (amongst others) Johan Gerritsen, 'Review of *Ben Jonson: Commentary*', *English Studies*, 38 (1957), 120–6, and 'Stansby and Jonson Produce a Folio', *English Studies*, 40 (1959), 52–5, and have been reviewed in detail by the editors of the *Cambridge Edition of the Works of*

Ben Jonson: see the introductory essays to volume 1 of the *CWBJ* Print Edition, and textual discussions in Butler (ed.), *Re-Presenting Ben Jonson*.

38. *Wit's Recreations* (1640), epigrams, 269, 270.

39. See Corbett and Lightbown, *The Comely Frontispiece* (n. 2 above), 145–52; Ian Donaldson, 'Collecting Ben Jonson', in Andrew Nash (ed.), *The Culture of Collected Editions* (Houndmills, 2003), 19–31.

40. William West, *Theatres and Encyclopaedias in Early Modern Europe* (Cambridge, 2003).

41. The 1616 Folio is clearly intended as a mid-career gathering of Jonson's works. The *Epigrams* in the Folio are described as a first book: Jonson evidently anticipated compiling a second collection. For John Selden's hopes to see a 'splendid second edition' of Jonson's works, see below, 333. No further volume of epigrams was however to appear, and Jonson's Second Folio was not to be published until after his death.

42. On Sir Francis Stuart, see Martin Butler, 'Sir Francis Stewart: Jonson's Overlooked Patron', *Ben Jonson Journal*, 2 (1995), 101–27; for the libel troubles of *Epicene*, see Ch. 13 n. 8 above.

43. Broadus, *The Laureateship* (n. 28 above), 47–50, G. J. Toomer, *John Selden: A Life in Scholarship*, 2 vols. (Oxford, 2009), 1.14.

44. *CWBJ*, Literary Record, Electronic Edition.

45. *Epigrams*, 131.14.

Chapter 16

1. On the Oxford editors' mistaken belief that copy for the Folio went to press in 1612 or 1613 (H&S, 9.15), see Ch. 15 n. 36, above. The Folio in any case includes texts composed later than *Bartholomew Fair*, such as *The Golden Age Restored*, performed in 1616.

2. T. S. Eliot, 'Ben Jonson', in *Selected Essays* (London, 1958), 147–60, at 155.

3. *Informations*, 58–61. For a guess at the possible nature of this work, see Freda Townsend, *Apologie for Bartholomew Fayre* (New York, 1947).

4. Donne to Goodere, letter of 17 July 1613; R. C. Bald, *John Donne: A Life* (Oxford, 1970), 196–7. Jones was actually travelling in Europe with Thomas Howard, Earl of Arundel, for over a year in 1613–14. It is unclear why Jonson had wished to satirize him at this moment, and why Holland was distressed on Jones's behalf.

5. Selden's letter to Jonson on this question is dated 28 February 1616, but it would be surprising if the two men had not consulted on this question while the play was in composition. The possibility of their doing so in 1613 is suggested by the survival of the name 'Inigo Lanthorn' in one manuscript of Selden's *Table-Talk* (see n. 6 below). A full scholarly edition of the letter by Jason P. Rosenblatt and Winfried Schleiner is provided in an appendix to Rosenblatt's monograph *Renaissance England's Chief Rabbi: John Selden* (Oxford, 2006); the exchange between the two men is further discussed on 61–6. See also *CWBJ*, Electronic Edition, G. J. Toomer, *John Selden: A Life in Scholarship*, 2 vols. (Oxford, 2009), 1.13–14; and on cross-dressing in the early modern theatre, Stephen Orgel, *Impersonations: The Performance of Gender in Shakespeare's England* (Cambridge, 1996).

6. *Table-Talk: Being the Discourses of John Selden Esq.* (London, 1689), ed. Edward Arber, English Reprints (London, 1868), 103–4, following Harleian MS 690 (which reads 'Inigo Lanthorne', where Harleian MS 1315 has 'Rabbi Busy').

7. Jonson's 'Epistle to Master John Selden' (later reprinted as *The Underwood*, 14) was prefixed to Selden's *Titles of Honour* in 1614. Jonson spoke of Selden's work with deepest admiration during his time in Scotland: *Informations*, 101–3, 483–5.

8. Frederick C. Dietz, *English Public Finance 1485–1641*, 2 vols. (New York, 1962; 1st edn. 1932), 2: *1558–1641*, 101.

9. See Dietz, *English Public Finance*, vol. 2; Thomas L. Moir, *The Addled Parliament of 1614* (Oxford, 1958); Maija Jansson, *Proceedings in Parliament 1614 (House of Commons)* (Philadelphia, 1988); Stephen Clucas and Rosalind Davies (eds.), *The Crisis of 1614 and the Addled Parliament* (Aldershot, 2003); and Menna Prestwich, *Cranfield: Politics and Profits under the Early Stuarts. The Career of Lionel Cranfield, Earl of Middlesex* (Oxford, 1966).

10. Jonson's continuing admiration for Hoskyns is evident in his later transcription of a long passage from Hoskyns's *Directions for Speech and Style* in his commonplace book, *Discoveries*, 1508–1623. On Hoskyns, see David Colclough, '"The Muses Recreation": John Hoskyns and the Manuscript Culture of the Seventeenth Century', *Huntington Library Quarterly*, 61 (1998), 369–400; Colclough, '"Better Becoming a Senate of Venice"? The "Addled Parliament" and Jacobean Debates on Freedom of Speech', in Clucas and Davies (eds.), *The Crisis of 1614*, 51–61; Colclough, *Freedom of Speech in Early Stuart England* (Cambridge, 2005); and Wilfrid Prest, 'John Hoskins', *ODNB*.

11. Jansson, *Proceedings in Parliament 1614*, p. xv.

12. *A Counterblast to Tobacco* (London, 1604), in *Minor Prose Works of King James VI and I*, ed. James Craigie and Alexander Law, Scottish Text Society (Edinburgh, 1982), 85, 'To the Reader'; John Creaser, note to *Bartholomew Fair*, 2.6.17, *CWBJ*, and introduction, on the political context of the play.

13. The first version of *The King's Majesty's Declaration to his Subjects Concerning Lawful Sports to be Used* was issued in 1617 with respect to Lancashire; it was reissued the following year with apparent application to the whole of England. See Craigie and Law's edition of the work, *Minor Prose Works of King James VI and I* (n. 12 above), and Leah S. Marcus, *The Politics of Mirth: Jonson, Herrick, Milton, Marvell, and the Defense of Old Holiday Pastimes* (Chicago, 1986).

14. Hugh Trevor-Roper, 'Thomas Sutton', *ODNB* (Oxford, 2004).

15. John Aubrey, *Brief Lives*, ed. A. Clark (Oxford, 1898), 2.246. The similarities between Sutton and Volpone were probably largely coincidental; for a careful examination of the evidence, see Robert C. Evans, *Jonson and the Contexts of his Time* (Lewisburg, Pa., 1994), ch. 3. For further evidence of Jonson's connections with Charterhouse, see my headnotes to Letters 12 and 13, *CWBJ*.

16. Prestwich, *Cranfield* (n. 9 above), 93–8, 101; Michael J. Braddick, 'Lionel Cranfield', *ODNB*. Jonson later received instalments of his pension from Cranfield, when the latter was serving as Lord Treasurer: N. W. Bawcutt, 'New Jonson Documents'. *Review of English Studies*, 47 (1996), 50–2.

17. Prestwich, *Cranfield*, 59, 66, 72.

18. Astrid Friis, *Alderman Cockayne's Project and the Cloth Trade: The Commercial Policy of England in its Main Aspects 1603–1625* (Copenhagen, 1927), ch. 4; Prestwich, *Cranfield*, ch. 4; Evans, *Jonson and the Contexts of his Time*, ch. 4; Rosalind Davies, 'Intervention in the Cloth Trade: Richard Hakluyt, the New Draperies, and the Cockayne Project of 1614', in Clucas and Davies (eds.), *The Crisis of 1614*, ch. 9; Vivienne Aldous, 'William Cockayne', *ODNB*.

19. *CSPD James 1611–1618*, xc.147; William Robert Scott, *The Constitution and Finance of English, Scottish, and Irish Joint-Stock Companies to 1720* (Cambridge, 1912), 144.
20. 8 June 1616, *Letters*, ed. McClure, 2.8.
21. N. W. Bawcutt, 'Ben Jonson's Drunken Hamburgians: An Entertainment for King James', *Notes & Queries*, 242 (1997), 92–4, citing PRO SP 14/87, item 57.
22. The drunken Hamburgians might also have been intended to represent disgruntled members of the old Merchant Adventurers' Company resident in that city, who had refused to take an oath imposed upon them by the new company, and had complained to the Privy Council: see Friis, *Alderman Cockayne's Project*, 284–6. On Sir Noel de Caron, see Ole Peter Grell, *Dutch Calvinists in Early Stuart London: The Dutch Church in Austin Friars 1603–1642* (Leiden, 1989), 48, 155; A. G. H. Bachrach, *Sir Constantine Huygens and Britain: 1596–1687* (Leiden, 1962), 117–19; Roberta Anderson, 'Sir Noel de Caron', *ODNB*. Though Caron had been granted the title of ambassador and was received in this capacity at court, his status was not recognized by the Spanish.
23. Grell, *Dutch Calvinists in Early Stuart London*, 149.
24. Taylor's writings about money have been of interest to economic historians of the early modern period. Deborah Valenze describes him as 'perhaps the single most important influence on popular literature regarding money in the late seventeenth and early eighteenth centuries, functioning as a pathway between early modern and modern attitudes to money': *The Social Life of Money in the English Past* (Cambridge, 2006), 73.
25. Dietz, *English Public Finance*, ch. 8; Scott, *Constitution and Finance*, ch. 7. Writing to Sir Ralph Winwood from Venice on 11 October 1616, Sir Henry Wotton describes and commends a couple of new inventions that would help in draining the Lincolnshire fens: *The Life and Letters of Sir Henry Wotton*, 2 vols. (Oxford, 1907), 2.105–6.
26. The case for Ker is proposed by Marcus, *The Politics of Mirth*, 100, and that for Argyll by Evans, *Jonson and the Contexts of his Time*, ch. 4. It is tempting to wonder whether some revision has occurred in Act 2 scene 4 of the play, where Merecraft is proposing possible titles to Fitzdottrel to designate his dukedom. When Fitzdottrel rejects the title 'Gloucester', Merecraft responds, 'What say you to this then?', and the stage direction reads, 'He whispers him of a place'. Fitzdottrel replies: 'No, a noble house | Pretends to that. I will do no man wrong.' Might another county have been audibly named at this moment in an earlier text of the play, identifying a particular 'noble house' and present holder of the title? ('The crucial word "whisper" ' writes Annabel Patterson in relation to a passage in Jonson's *The Underwood*, 'is a sure sign of the hermeneutics of censorship': *Censorship and Interpretation: The Conditions of Writing and Reading in Early Modern England* (Madison, 1984), 142.)
27. Craig Muldrew, *The Economy of Obligation: The Culture of Credit and Social Relations in Early Modern England* (Houndmills, 1998), 98–103; Valenze, *The Social Life of Money* (n. 23 above), 34.
28. Muldrew, *The Economy of Obligation*, ch. 1.
29. Christina Larner, 'James VI and I and Witchcraft', in Alan G. R. Smith (ed.), *The Reign of James VI and I* (London, 1973), ch. 4; Philip C. Almond, *Demonic Possession and Exorcism in Early Modern England: Contemporary Texts and their Cultural Contexts* (Cambridge, 2004).
30. G. L. Kittredge, 'King James I and *The Devil is an Ass*', *Modern Philology*, 9 (1911), 195–209.

Chapter 17

1. *CWBJ*, Life Records, 62, Electronic Edition.
2. John Aubrey, *Brief Lives*, ed. A. Clark (Oxford, 1898), 2.12. On the house, see also 405 below. Aubrey also records a report that Jonson 'lived without Temple Bar, at a comb-maker's shop, about the Elephant and Castle' (2.12): i.e. just outside the city limits, at the west end of Fleet Street.
3. *CWBJ*, Life Records, 69, Electronic Edition; Bodleian MS.Eng. hist. e.1, fo. 63ᵛ; J. P. Collier, *Memoirs of the Principal Actors in the Plays of Shakespeare*, Shakespeare Society (London, 1846), p. xxiv. Mark Eccles judged it 'unlikely' but 'not impossible' that this record indicated a second marriage by Jonson: 'Jonson's Marriage', *Review of English Studies*, 12 (1936), 257–72, at 272. The Simpsons required 'fuller evidence to accept this marriage' (H&S, 11.576).
4. *Athenae Oxonienses*, 2 vols. (London, 1691–2), 2.518.
5. 'Wm then Lord Chamberlayne and Earl of Pemb. Made him Mr of Arts wᵗʰ his Letter,' notes George Chapman in his 'Invective Written against Master Ben Jonson', *The Poems of George Chapman*, ed. P. B. Bartlett (New York, 1941/1962), 478. For the University's record of this event, see *CWBJ*, Life Records, 60, Electronic Edition. Pembroke's letter of commendation is not included in the Register.
6. In the corresponding passage in *EMI* (Q), 1.1.11–13, Lorenzo senior says of his son, 'He is a scholar, if a man may trust | The liberal voice of double-tongued report, | Of dear account in all our academies.'
7. See Ch. 5 above, 85. During this visit Jonson might have seen George Ruggle's Latin comedy *Ignoramus*, with which Robert C. Evans believes he was familiar, which was performed at that time at Trinity College before an audience of 2,000 people: *Jonson and the Contexts of his Time* (Lewisburg, Pa., 1994), ch. 4.
8. Thomas Baker, *History of the College of St John the Evangelist*, 2 vols. (Cambridge, 1869), 1.202. The visit is also described by John Nichols, *Progresses of King James the First* (1828), 3.43ff.
9. 'A Certain Poem, As it was presented in Latin by divines and others before His Majesty in Cambridge by way of interlude, stiled *Liber novus de adventu regis ad Cantabrigian*, faithfully done into English, with some liberal additions', 139–44, in *The Poems of Richard Corbett*, ed. J. A. W. Bennett and H. R. Trevor-Roper (Oxford, 1955), 17.
10. James Loxley, *Royalism and Poetry in the English Civil Wars: The Drawn Sword* (Houndmills, 1997), 20, 51, acknowledging information from John Gouws. By the time of Jonson's arrival at the College the lavish annual celebrations of the Westminster/Christ Church connection had in fact become something of an embarrassment. In 1611 the Dean and Chapter decreed 'that the entertainment of the new Westminster Scholars be utterly taken away for ever, because it has grown to an intolerable excess': an order that was to be repeated, without much effect, over subsequent years. See Henry L. Thompson, *Christ Church*, University of Oxford College Histories (London, 1900), 59–61.
11. *Athenae Oxonienses*, 2.511.
12. Aubrey, *Brief Lives*, ed. Clark, 1.183–8.
13. Bennett and Trevor-Roper (eds.), *The Poems of Richard Corbett*, p. xviii.
14. A copy of Jonson's poem written on a vellum funerary placard, together with other epitaphs by Richard Corbett and John Selden, designed originally to hang in St Mary's church, Twickenham, is now in the Beinecke Library at Yale.

15. Thompson, *Christ Church*, 49; Nicholas W. Cranfield, 'Richard Corbett', *ODNB*.
16. This debt is implicitly acknowledged in 'A New Year's Gift, to my Lord Duke of Buckingham', in *Poems*, ed. Bennett and Trevor Roper, 71–2. Corbett's attachment to Buckingham prompted popular criticism that he was 'a parasite, a sycophant, [and] a foist': Thomas Cogswell, *The Blessed Revolution: English Politics and the Coming of War, 1621–1624* (Cambridge, 1989), 46–7.
17. John Newman, 'The Architectural Setting', ch. 3 of Nicholas Tyacke (ed.), *Seventeenth-Century Oxford* (Oxford, 1997), volume 4 of *The History of the University of Oxford*.
18. Orgel and Strong, *Inigo Jones*, 2.823–9; John R. Elliott Jr., 'Drama', ch. 12 in Tyacke (ed.), *Seventeenth-Century Oxford*.
19. Other poets soon to enter the College from Westminster School included John Donne the younger (son of the Dean of St Paul's), Jasper Mayne, and William Cartwright. Mayne and Cartwright, along with their contemporary Thomas Randolph (who had headed for Trinity College, Cambridge) were amongst the 'sons of Ben'. See Joe Lee Davis, *The Sons of Ben: Jonsonian Comedy in Caroline England* (Detroit, 1967).
20. Antony à Wood, *The History and Antiquities of the University of Oxford*, ed. John Gutch, 2 vols. (Oxford, 1796), 2.339. Evidence for Jonson's possible hand in the revision of *Technogamia* is examined by David McInnis in *CWBJ*, Dubia, Electronic Edition. Holyday later wrote commendatory verses for John Benson's 1640 edition of Jonson's translation of Horace's *Ars Poetica*. In his translation of Juvenal and Persius, published in 1673, Holyday thanks Jonson, his 'dear friend, the patriarch of poets', for the loan of 'an ancient manuscript written partly in the Saxon character' (H&S, 1.251; *CWBJ*, Jonson's Library, Electronic Edition). On Goffe's work, see in particular G. K. Hunter, *English Drama 1586–1642: The Age of Shakespeare*, Oxford History of English Literature (Oxford, 1997), 423–5.
21. John Nichols, *Progresses*, 1.548; Orgel and Strong, *Inigo Jones*, 2.824.
22. Antony à Wood, *Athenae Oxonienses*, 4 vols. (London, 1815), 2.652–3. See also J. B. Bamborough, 'Robert Burton', *ODNB*. At the time of his death Burton owned quarto editions of two of Jonson's masques, *Hymenaei* and *The Fortunate Isles*, both now in the Bodleian Library.
23. On Duppa, see Loxley, *Royalism and Poetry*; Ian Green in *ODNB*; Raymond A. Anselment, 'The Oxford University Poets and Caroline Panegyric', *John Donne Journal*, 3 (1984), 181–201; *The Correspondence of Bishop Brian Duppa and Sir Justinian Isham 1650–1660*, Publications of the Northamptonshire Record Society (Lamport, 1951).
24. *Correspondence*, 21–2, responding to Duppa's letter of 22 October 1650 (amending the printed text which reads, presumably in error, 'Though this hath already come to moe maturity...').
25. George Vertue studied Holland's work with close attention, as is evident from the annotations in his personal copy of *Heroologica Anglica*, now in Cambridge University Library, Keynes.D.5.19. See Ian Donaldson, 'National Biography and the Arts of Memory', in Peter France and William St Clair (eds.), *Mapping Lives: The Uses of Biography* (Oxford, 2002), 67–82, at 73–4; Keith Thomas, *Changing Concepts of National Biography: The Oxford DNB in Historical Perspective*, The Leslie Stephen Lecture 2004 (Cambridge, 2005). Jonson's interest in memorializing coincided with that of his friend Robert Cotton, working in another medium, of funerary monuments: see David Howarth, 'Sir Robert Cotton and the Commemoration of Famous Men', *British Library Journal*, 18 (1992), 1–28.

26. The district is brilliantly evoked by Charles Nicholl in *The Lodger: Shakespeare on Silver Street* (London, 2007).

27. Jonson's library has been studied by a number of scholars including H&S (1.250–71; 11.593–603), David McPherson, 'Ben Jonson's Library and Marginalia: An Annotated Catalogue', *Studies in Philology*, 71, Texts and Studies (1974), Robert C. Evans, *Habits of Mind: Evidence and Effects of Ben Jonson's Reading* (Lewisburg, Pa., 1995), and Henry Woudhuysen, Jonson's Library, *CWBJ*, Electronic Edition.

28. McPherson, 'Ben Jonson's Library and Marginalia', 6.

29. Graham Parry, *The Trophies of Time: English Antiquarians of the Seventeenth Century* (Oxford, 1995), ch. 3.

30. Kevin Sharpe, 'Introduction: Re-writing Sir Robert Cotton', in C. J. Wright (ed.), *Sir Robert Cotton as Collector: Essays on an Early Stuart Courtier and his Legacy*, The British Library (London, 1997), 1–39, at 12; Kevin Sharpe, 'The Library of Sir Robert Cotton', ch. 2 of his *Sir Robert Cotton 1586–1631: History and Politics in Early Modern England* (Oxford, 1979), 58.

31. Colin G. C. Tite, *The Manuscript Library of Sir Robert Cotton*, The Panizzi Lectures 1993, The British Library (London, 1994); Frances A. Yates, *Theatre of the World* (London, 1969), ch. 1, quotation at 11; William H. Sherman, *John Dee: The Politics of Reading and Writing in the English Renaissance* (Amherst, Mass., 1995).

32. *CWBJ*, Letter 1. On the context and dating of this letter, see Mark Bland, 'Jonson, *Biathanatos* and the Interpretation of Manuscript Evidence', *Studies in Bibliography*, 51 (1998), 154–82.

33. Tite, *The Manuscript Library of Sir Robert Cotton*, 15. Requests from Jonson and Donne for loans from Cotton's library are on record: Hilton Kelliher, 'British Post-Mediaeval Verse in the Cotton Collection: A Handlist', in Wright (ed.), *Sir Robert Cotton as Collector*, 307–90, at 308.

34. Tite, *The Manuscript Collection of Sir Robert Cotton*, 79. The visitor, Richard Lapthorne, reports also seeing portraits of Henry Spelman, George Buchanan, and John Wycliffe.

35. Elizabeth's failure to endorse the Society's proposal may have been partly due to pressure from the universities; James's rejection seems to have been motivated by political nervousness. See [Rupert Bruce-Mitford,] *The Society of Antiquaries of London* (London, 1951), 11; Joan Evans, *A History of the Society of Antiquaries* (Oxford, 1956). The Society was reconstituted in the early eighteenth century, and finally gained its charter from George II in 1751.

36. Sharpe, *Sir Robert Cotton*, ch. 2.

37. G. J. Toomer, *John Selden: A Life in Scholarship*, 2 vols. (Oxford, 2009), 1. ch. 8; Parry, *The Trophies of Time* (n. 29 above), ch. 4; John Aitkin, MD, *The Lives of John Selden, Esq. and Archbishop Usher* (London, 1812), 25; D. R. Woolf, *The Idea of History in Early Stuart England* (Toronto, *c.*1990), 200–42.

38. Mark Bland, '"Invisible Dangers": Censorship and the Subversion of Authority in Early Modern England', *Papers of the Bibliographical Society of America*, 90 (1996), 151–93.

39. John Selden, *Vindiciae secundum integritatem existimationis suae, per convitium de scriptione Maris Clausi* (London, 1653), 16–19, at 17.

40. Toomer, *John Selden*, 1.306–7.

41. Though John Chamberlain in 1624 described the Apollo Room as having been 'lately built' (*Letters*, ed. McClure, 2.566), John Buxton (*Modern Language Review*, 48 (1953), 52–4) has

shown that this statement is unreliable, and that Drayton's ode of 1619, 'The Sacrifice to Apollo' (in *Works*, ed. J. W. Hebel (Oxford, 1961), 2.357–8), must derive from the *Leges Convivales*, rather than (as Percy Simpson had assumed, *Modern Language Review*, 24 (1939), 367–73; H&S, 11.294–300) the other way about. On the verses over the door, see K. A. Esdaile, *Essays and Studies*, 29 (1943), 93–100.

42. *CWBJ*, vol. 5.

43. On these early efforts, see Ian Donaldson, 'The Idea of an Academy', 2009 Annual Lecture, *Proceedings of the Australian Academy of the Humanities 2009* (Canberra, 2010), 139–54; J. P. Mahaffy, 'On the Origins of Learned Academies in Modern Europe', *Proceedings of the Royal Irish Academy*, 30 (1913), 429–44; [Sir Humphrey Gilbert,] *Queene Elizabethes achedemy* ['The eretion of an Achedemy in London for educacion of her Maiesties Wardes, and others the youth of nobility and gentlemen', BL Lansdowne MS98, art 1, fo. 2], ed. F. J. Furnivall, Early English Text Society (London, 1869); Raffaello Morghen, *The Accademia Nazionale dei Lincei in the Life and Culture of United Italy on the 368th Anniversary of its Foundation (1871–1971)* (Rome, 1990).

44. On Bolton and his proposed academy, see D. R. Woolf, 'Edmund Mary Bolton', *ODNB*; Joan Evans, *A History of the Society of Antiquaries* (n. 34 above), 16–20; Wyman H. Herendeen, *William Camden: A Life in Context* (Woodbridge, 2007); and Ethel M. Portal, 'The Academ Roial of King James I', *Proceedings of the British Academy 1915–16*, 189–208. Portal confesses she has been unable to trace one of Bolton's manuscripts of 1626, which contains the list of eighty-four foundation Essential members, including Ben Jonson, and relies therefore on a description of it read to the Society of Antiquaries some seventy years previously; Joseph Hunter, 'An Account of the Scheme for Erecting a Royal Academy in the Reign of James the First', *Archaeologia, Or Miscellaneous Tracts Relating to Antiquity*, 32 (1847), 132–49.

45. Edmund Bolton, *Hypercritica, Or, A Rule of Judgement for Writing or Reading our Histories* in *The Art of English Poesy, &c.* (London, 1815), 251. In a Rawlinson MS variant to an earlier section of *Hypercritica* (246–7), Jonson's name is included amongst those who were said to have 'the most proper graces' in English language and style.

46. Richard Drayton, 'The Strange Late Birth of the British Academy', in Martin Daunton (ed.), *The Organization of Knowledge in Victorian Britain* (Oxford, 2005); Sir Frederic G. Kenyon, *The British Academy: The First Fifty Years* (Oxford, 1952); *The British Academy 1902–2002: Some Historical Documents and Notes*, The British Academy (London, 2002).

47. BL Harl. MS. 389, fo. 118; *CWBJ*, Life Records, 66, Electronic Edition.

48. The warrant for the reversion is dated 5 October 1621: *CWBJ*, Life Records, 65, Electronic Edition. W. W. Greg speaks erroneously of this being 'a sub-reversion of the Mastership of the Revels, which he was able to transfer to his son, though neither lived to enjoy it': *English Literary Autographs*, 4 vols. (Oxford, 1932), 1. section XXIII. The paradox of Jonson as poacher nearly turned gamekeeper is examined by Richard Dutton in *Mastering the Revels: The Regulation and Censorship of English Renaissance Drama* (Houndmills, 1991). In what may perhaps be an amused memory of the granting of this warrant, Jonson has Compass in *The Magnetic Lady* receiving the reversion of the Surveyorship of Projects General on the death of Thinwit (4.6.15–20).

49. John Chamberlain, *Letters*, ed. McClure, 2.407–8.

50. Jonson elsewhere complained 'that half the preachers of England were plain ignorant, for that either in their sermons they flatter, or strive to show their own eloquence',

Informations, 290–1. James listened with great attention to preachers, who were in fact often critical of him and his policies. See Peter E. McCullough, *Sermons at Court: Politics and Religion in Elizabethan and Jacobean Preaching* (Cambridge, 1998), ch. 3.

51. Aubrey, *Brief Lives*, ed. Clark, 2.12.

52. James Howell, *Epistolae Ho-Elianae* (1645), section 5, xvii, 22–3; Letter (k), *CWBJ*, Electronic Edition. Howell wrote most of these letters in order to make money, many years after the events which they purport to describe; they do not represent immediate (or in all cases, trustworthy) reportage. (Why would he have written to Jonson when he could more simply have stepped next door?) They may nevertheless often refer to events which Howell recalls having actually occurred.

53. 'Invective Written against Master Ben Jonson', in *Poems*, ed. Bartlett, 374–8, esp. lines 119–20 ('Burn things unborn, and that way generate things,' etc.); *CWBJ*, Literary Record, Electronic Edition; R. B. Sharpe, 'Jonson's "Execration" and Chapman's "Invective": Their Place in their Authors' Rivalry', *Studies in Philology*, 42 (1945), 555–63. Mark Bland takes Jonson's mention of his 'desk' in line 85 of the poem to mean that the fire was not extensive: 'Ben Jonson and the Legacies of the Past', *Huntington Library Quarterly*, 67 (2004), 371–400, at 392. Marcus Nevitt on the other hand imagines 'the wholesale destruction of Ben Jonson's library' in the fire; 'the loss must have been immense': 'Ben Jonson and the Serial Publication of News', *Media History*, 11 (2005), 53–68, at 53.

54. See n. 5 above for Chapman's marginal note at this point in the manuscript.

55. An early version of the translation was published by John Benson in 1640, and a later version, revised in the light of Daniel Heinsius' 1610 edition of Horace, appeared in the final volume of Jonson's Second Folio in 1641. Both versions have been edited by Colin Burrow in *CWBJ*: the revised version in the Print Edition and the early version in the Electronic Edition.

56. Derek Britton has convincingly refuted the Oxford editors' belief that Jonson did not commence his revision of the *Grammar* until his final years, and suggests that by 1624 at least 40% of this work was completed: 'The Dating of Ben Jonson's *English Grammar*', *Notes & Queries*, 247 (2002) 331–4, and *CWBJ* Introduction to *The English Grammar*. The Third Folio of Jonson's *Works*, published in 1692, presents an intelligent revision of *The English Grammar* by an unknown scholar. Jonson was also pursuing other linguistic interests around this time, as his correspondence with Joseph Webbe in 1628 testifies (BL Sloane MS 1466). Another letter from a number of signatories, including Jonson, Cotton, Andrewes, Selden, Farnaby, and Spillman (BL Sloane MS 1466, fo. 16), was probably written around the same time, supporting Caleb Morley of Balliol College, Oxford, in his project for 'a speedie & certain Course for ye attaining & retaining of languages & other partes of good literature purposed for ye generall ease & benefit of ye studious in either kinde'. For discussion, see *CWBJ*, Electronic Edition; W. D. Briggs, *Modern Philology* (1913), and Robert C. Evans, *Jonson and the Contexts of his Time* (Lewisburg, Pa., 1994), ch. 7.

57. On Barclay and *Argenis*, see Marc Fumaroli, 'A Scottish Voltaire: John Barclay and the Character of Nations', *The Times Literary Supplement*, 19 August 1996, 16–17; Nicola Royan, 'John Barclay', *ODNB*; Paul Salzman, *English Prose Fiction 1558–1700: A Critical History* (Oxford, 1985), 148–55. On 11 May 1622 John Chamberlain had informed Sir Dudley Carleton that Jonson was undertaking this translation at James's behest: *Letters*, ed. McClure, 2.436.

58. The passage just cited is from this translation (116); Salzman, *English Prose Fiction*, 153.
59. The Oxford editors at first believed the fire occurred 'probably in or about the month of October, 1623', but later accepted Fleay's dating, 'say, in November': H&S, 1.261, 11.73. The Stationers' Register entry for the Shakespeare First Folio is 8 November 1623. On the timing of these events and the larger significance of the fire, see Ian Donaldson, *Jonson's Magic Houses* (Oxford, 1997), ch. 12, and on Jonson's poem to Shakespeare's memory, ch. 1. On the Folio, see in particular Peter W. M. Blayney, *The First Folio of Shakespeare*, Folger Shakespeare Library (Washington, DC, 1991); W. W. Greg, *Shakespeare's First Folio* (Oxford, 1935); Charlton Hinman, *The Printing and Proof-Reading of the First Folio of Shakespeare*, 2 vols. (Oxford, 1963) and *The First Folio of Shakespeare*, The Norton Facsimile (New York, 1968), introduction.
60. On Heminges and Condell see Mary Edmond's entries for both men in *ODNB*; Mark Eccles, 'Elizabethan Actors, 1: A–D', *Notes & Queries* (March 1991), 44–5, and 'Elizabethan Actors, 2: E–J', *Notes & Queries*, 236 (1991), 457–9; and J. A. Riddell, 'Some Actors in Ben Jonson's Plays', *Shakespeare Studies*, 5 (1969), 285–98.
61. Anne Barton, *Ben Jonson: Dramatist* (Cambridge, 1984), ch. 12.
62. And cf. *The New Inn*, Dedication, 2–5, 'if thou canst but spell and join my sense, there is more hope of thee than of a hundred fastidious impertinents who were there present the first day, yet never made piece of their prospect the right way'.
63. Cf. 'When we do give, Alfonso, to the light | A work of ours, we part with our own right': 'To the Same' [Alfonso Ferrabosco], *Epigrams*, 131.1–2; 'When I suffered it to go abroad, I departed with my right', *Queens*, 569–70.
64. Jonson elsewhere compares the critic's role with that of the magistrate: cf. 'To the Learned Critic', *Epigrams*, 17, and the dedication to William Herbert, Earl of Pembroke, prefixed to the quarto edition of *Catiline*, 10–11. For a more detailed account of parallels between Jonsonian phraseology and the address 'To the Great Variety of Readers' and (more fleetingly) in the dedication 'To the Most Noble and Incomparable Pair of Brethren', see my analysis in Dubia, *CWBJ*, Electronic Edition.
65. Quintilian, *Institutio Oratoria*, 3.7.10.
66. *CWBJ*, Life Records, 70, Electronic Edition.
67. Sir George Buc, *The Third University of England*, in John Ward, *The Lives of the Professors of Gresham College* (London, 1740), p. ix (from the appendix to Edmond Howes's continuation of John Stow's *Annals*, 1615, 980). See also Christopher Hill, *Intellectual Origins of the English Revolution* (London, 1972), ch. 1; Richard Chartres and David Vermont, *A Brief History of Gresham College 1597–1997* (London, 1998).
68. C. J. Sisson, 'Ben Jonson of Gresham College', *The Times Literary Supplement*, 21 September 1951, 604: largely repeated and endorsed by the Oxford editors, H&S, 11.582–5. George Burke Johnston, 'Ben Jonson of Gresham College', *The Times Literary Supplement*, 28 December 1951, 837, suggests that the bilingual presentation (Latin and English) of *The English Grammar* indicates its origins as Gresham lectures. But it had long been the custom to present grammars (as well as other texts) in Latin to ensure their wider readership. Bacon prepared a Latin translation of *The Advancement of Learning* so the work could be 'a citizen of the world, as English books are not', while Jonson was translating Bacon's *Essays* into Latin with the same aim.
69. Ward, *Lives of the Professors*, p. viii.
70. I am grateful to Mark Bland for this information.

71. Ward, *Lives of the Professors*, 308–10.

72. Paul R. Sellin points out that one such invitation in *Discoveries* to come to the next lecture to learn more is taken straight from Heinsius: *Daniel Heinsius and Stuart England, with a Short-Title Checklist of the Works of Daniel Heinsius* (Leiden, 1968), 152–3.

73. Thus one episode in *Discoveries*, 229, is dated 1630, while another extended passage at 1752–62 draws upon Buchler's *Institutio Poetica*, published in 1633.

74. Thomas Sprat, *The History of the Royal Society* (London, 1667); Thomas Birch, *The History of the Royal Society of London*, 4 vols. (London, 1756–7), reprinted with an introduction by A. Rupert Hall (London, 1968); Charles Richard Weld, *A History of the Royal Society with Memoirs of the Presidents*, 2 vols. (London, 1848); Michael Hunter, *Establishing the New Science: The Experience of the Early Royal Society* (Woodbridge, 1989).

75. *Discoveries*, 668–72, 1481–505. 'For no perfect discovery can be made upon a flat or level,' writes Jonson at one point in *Discoveries* (1504–5), echoing Bacon's words in *The Advancement of Learning* (ed. Arthur Johnston (Oxford, 1974), 34): 'For no perfect discovery can be made upon a flat or level: neither is it possible to discover the more remote and deeper parts of any science, if you stand but upon the level of the same science, and ascend not to a higher science.' For Bacon's influence on the Royal Society, see Sprat, *The History of the Royal Society*, 35–6.

76. See Ch. 6 above, and n. 41.

77. Writing (in Latin) to Count Gondimar, 6 June 1621: *The Works of Francis Bacon*, ed. J. Spedding, R. L. Ellis, and D. D. Heath, 14 vols. (London, 1857–74), 14.285.

78. The passage nicely illustrates the interpretative difficulties of *Discoveries*, for it is actually a translation (made by Thomas Hobbes) of part of a letter by the Venetian patriot Friar Fulgenzio Micanza to the first Earl of Devonshire, reflecting on Bacon's fall. The first-person 'I' is strictly speaking Micanza, not Jonson; but that Jonson cared to transcribe the passage suggests that he probably shared its sentiment.

79. Jonson is recalling Bacon's own confident statement at the conclusion of the second book of *The Advancement of Learning* 'that this third period of time' under James's rule 'will far surpass that of the Grecian and Roman learning': ed. Arthur Johnston (Oxford, 1974), 200.

80. Suetonius, *Divus Augustus*, 28; Samuel Johnson, 'Life of Dryden', in *Lives of the English Poets*, ed. J. P. Hardy (Oxford, 1972), 200.

81. 'A Proclamation Declaring His Majesty's Further Pleasure for the Matter of Buildings', 12 March 1619, no. 186 (pp. 428–31) in *Stuart Royal Proclamations*, ed. James F. Larkin and Paul L. Hughes (Oxford), 1973, reinforcing a proclamation of 1 March 1605 (Larkin and Hughes, no. 51).

Chapter 18

1. Fletcher is not known to have written any masques; Drummond may have intended to write 'Beaumont' (author of *The Masque of the Inner Temple and Gray's Inn*, 1613). The identification of *The Masque of the Twelve Months* as the unnamed masque presented at the Banqueting House on 6 January and 8 February 1619 was made by Martin Butler, who has confirmed Chapman's authorship and edited the text: 'Chapman's *Masque of the Twelve Months* (1619) [*With Text*]', *English Literary Renaissance*, 37 (2007), 360–400.

2. *CWBJ*, Masque Archive, Electronic Edition. Martin Butler analyses the reasons for the masque's failure in 'Ben Jonson and the Limits of Courtly Panegyric', in Kevin Sharpe and

Peter Lake (eds.), *Culture and Politics in Early Stuart England* (Houndmills, 1994), 91–115, and *The Stuart Court Masque and Political Culture*, 230–5.

3. On the particular allusiveness of this passage, see Ch. 2 n. 18 above.

4. Paul R. Sellin's suggestion that *News from the New World Discovered in the Moon* 'saw at least ten performances, probably twelve' during the season (*English Studies*, 61 (1980), 491–7, at 497)—a record that would imply that the masque enjoyed quite unprecedented popularity—rests on some probable misidentifications of contemporary references. See Martin Butler, 'Jonson's *News from the New World*, the "Running Masque," and the season of 1619–20', *Medieval and Renaissance Drama in England*, 6 (1993), 153–78. On this group of late Jacobean masques—*The Masque of Augurs*, performed 6 January and 5 May 1622; *Time Vindicated To Himself and to His Honours*, performed 19 January 1624; *Neptune's Triumph for the Return of Albion*, written 1624; *The Masque of Owls*, performed 19 August 1624; *The Fortunate Isles and their Union*, performed 9 January 162—see in particular Sara Pearl, 'Sounding to Present Occasions: Jonson's Masques of 1620–5', in David Lindley (ed.), *The Court Masque* (Manchester, 1984), 60–77; and Butler, *The Stuart Court Masque and Political Culture*, ch. 8.

5. On Jonson and the telescope, see Fig. 8 above, *Britain's Burse*, 145–9, and *Love Freed from Folly and Ignorance*, 157–65. Hans Lippershey and Zacharias Janssen, spectacle-makers of Middleburgh in Holland, had been amongst the first to experiment with the possibilities of the telescope: Michael White, *Galileo Antichrist: A Biography* (London, 2007), ch. 8; David Whitehouse, *Renaissance Genius: Galileo Galilei and his Legacy to Modern Science* (New York, 2009), chs. 3 and 4. See also John North, 'Thomas Harriot and the First Telescopic Observation of Sunspots', in John W. Shirley (ed.), *Thomas Harriot: Renaissance Scientist* (Oxford, 1974), ch. 7.

6. *The Life and Letters of Henry Wotton*, ed. Logan Pearsall Smith, 2 vols. (Oxford, 1907), 1.485–7.

7. *Sidereus Nuncius* (*The Starry Messenger*), in *Discoveries and Opinions of Galileo*, translated with an introduction and notes by Stillman Drake (New York, 1957), 21–58, at 31.

8. Robert Burton, *The Anatomy of Melancholy* (1621), part 2, section 2, mem. 3; part 1, section 2, mem. 1, subs. 2; Marjorie Hope Nicolson, *Science and Imagination* (Ithaca, NY, 1956) and *Voyages to the Moon* (New York, 1960). Cf. Donne, 'She baits not at the moon, not cares to try | Whether in that new world men live and die': 'Of the Progress of the Soul: The Second Anniversary', 195–6, in John Donne, *The Epithalamions, Anniversaries, and Epicedes*, ed. Wesley Milgate (Oxford, 1978).

9. 'A Letter Sent from Doctor Corbett to Master Aylesbury, December 9, 1618', lines 53–4, in *The Poems of Richard Corbett*, ed. J. A. W. Bennett and Hugh Trevor-Roper (Oxford, 1955), 63–5; 'Burton to Gunter writes, and Burton hears from Gunter,' lines 41–2. See also John W. Shirley, *Thomas Harriot: A Biography* (Oxford, 1983), 417.

10. 'The First Anniversary: An Anatomy of the World', 205–13, in Donne, The *Epithalamions*, ed. Milgate. On this debate, see Victor Harris, *All Coherence Gone* (Chicago, 1949); M. Macklem, *The Anatomy of the World* (Minneapolis, 1958). Jonson voiced his reservations about Donne's First and Second Anniversaries in *Informations*, 31–3.

11. On the significance of this phrase, see Derek Britton, 'The Dating of Ben Jonson's *English Grammar*', *Notes & Queries*, 247 (2002) 331–4. On early modern classifications of the stages of human life, see John Burrow, *The Ages of Man* (Oxford, 1986). On Jonson's late period, see in particular Anne Barton, *Ben Jonson: Dramatist* (Cambridge, 1982); David Norbrook,

Poetry and Politics in the English Renaissance (London, 1984), ch. 9; Martin Butler, 'Late Jonson', in Jonathan Hope and Gordon McMullan (eds.), *The Politics of Tragicomedy: Shakespeare and After* (London, 1992), 166–88; and Julie Sanders, *Ben Jonson's Theatrical Republics* (Houndmills, 1998). On the larger question of late-career creativity, see Edward Said, *On Late Style: Music and Literature against the Grain* (New York, 2006).

12. The statement of Neander in 'An Essay of Dramatic Poesy', in John Dryden, *Of Dramatic Poesy and Other Critical Essays*, ed. George Watson, 2 vols. (London, 1972), 1.69.

13. Writing from Venice on 27 November 1618: *The Life and Letters of Sir Henry Wotton*, ed. Logan Pearsall Smith, 2 vols. (Oxford, 1907), 2.160–1.

14. See Peter H. Wilson's *Europe's Tragedy: A New History of the Thirty Years War* (London, 2010); Roger Lockyer, *Buckingham: The Life and Political Career of George Villiers, First Duke of Buckingham 1592–1628* (London, 1981); Ronald G. Asch, 'Elizabeth, Princess (1596–1662)', *ODNB*; and Rosalind K. Marshall, *The Winter Queen: The Life of Elizabeth of Bohemia 1596–1662* (Edinburgh, 1998).

15. Parliament was due to meet on 16 January 1621. The masque was repeated on Shrove Tuesday, 11 February 1621. For the establishment of this dating and a masterly account of the masque's political agenda, see Martin Butler, 'Ben Jonson's *Pan's Anniversary* and the Politics of Early Stuart Pastoral', *English Literary Renaissance*, 22 (1992), 369–404. On the behaviour of the 1621 Parliament, see S. L. Adams, 'Foreign Policy and the Parliaments of 1621 and 1624', in Kevin Sharpe (ed.), *Faction and Parliament: Essays on Early Stuart History* (Oxford, 1978), 139–71.

16. For all Jonson's skill in imaginatively supporting royal policy in *Pan's Anniversary*, the masque's pro-Spanish tendencies did not much please the French Ambassador Extraordinary, the Marquis of Cadenet, with whom James was attempting at that moment to negotiate. See Butler, 'Ben Jonson's *Pan's Anniversary*', 387–92.

17. Lockyer, *Buckingham*, 99.

18. *CWBJ*, Masque Archive, Electronic Edition.

19. William Empson, *The Structure of Complex Words* (London, 1952), ch. 7.

20. Lockyer, *Buckingham*, 108–11; David Harris Willson, *King James VI and I* (London, 1963), ch. 21.

21. Dale B. J. Randall, *Jonson's Gypsies Unmasked* (Durham, NC, 1975) offers a detailed interpretation of the masque.

22. For the context of this poem, see Ch. 1 above.

23. For detailed accounts of the expedition to Madrid (and differing explanations of its likely motivation), see Thomas Cogswell, *The Blessed Revolution: English Politics and the Coming of War, 1621–1624* (Cambridge, 1989), and Glyn Redworth, *The Prince and the Infanta: The Cultural Politics of the Spanish Match* (New Haven, 2003).

24. *CSPV* 1623–1625, 564: Zuane Pesaro to the Doge and Senate, 24 January 1625.

25. John Chamberlain to Sir Dudley Carleton, 17 January 1624, *Letters*, ed. McClure, 2.538–9. *Neptune's Triumph* was ultimately performed in a reworked format in 1625 as *The Fortunate Isles and their Union*. For a nuanced account of the difficulties which the original masque encountered and its subsequent transformation, see Butler, *The Stuart Court Masque and Political Culture*, ch. 8.

26. John Chamberlain to Sir Dudley Carleton, 14 May 1625, *Letters*, ed. McClure, 2.616.

27. James Knowles, 'Royal Entry (1625–6; Lost)', *CWBJ*, vol. 5; Ole Peter Grell, *Dutch Calvinists in Early Stuart London: The Dutch Church in Austin Friars, 1603–42* (Leiden,

1989), 91–2; Christopher Wordsworth, *The Manner of the Coronation of King Charles the First of England 2 February 1626*, Henry Bradshaw Society 2 (London, 1892).

28. See D. F. McKenzie's pioneering account, '*The Staple of News* and the Late Plays', in William Blissett, Julian Patrick, and R. W. Van Fossen (eds.), *A Celebration of Ben Jonson* (Toronto, 1973), 83–128, at 124–5.

29. On the contemporary popularity of the word 'new' see Christopher Hill, *Intellectual Origins of the English Revolution* (London, 1972), 110.

30. The plural form had recently come to be treated as a singular noun: 'When news is printed, | It leaves, sir, to be news', declares Cymbal in 1.5.48–9. See *OED*, News, 2b.

31. Cogswell, *The Blessed Revolution*, 20ff.

32. Joad Raymond, *The Invention of the Newspaper: English Newsbooks 1641–1649* (Oxford, 1996), ch. 1; McKenzie, '*The Staple of News* and the Late Plays'; Pearl, 'Sounding to Present Occasions', 61; Mark Z. Muggli, 'Ben Jonson and the Business of News', *Studies in English Literature, 1500–1900*, 32 (1992), 323–40; Jeremy Black, *The English Press 1621–1861* (Stroud, 2001).

33. Muggli, 'Ben Jonson and the Business of News', 326–7.

34. David Masson, *Drummond of Hawthornden: The Story of his Life and Writings* (London, 1873), ch. 8, at 161. The idea of the burning glass as a weapon of wholesale destruction continues to haunt the modern imagination, as evidenced in Charles Morgan's play *The Burning Glass*, 1953.

35. L. E. Harris, *The Two Netherlanders: Humphrey Bradley and Cornelius Drebbel* (Leiden, 1961), ch. 14; H. A. M. Snelders, 'Cornelis Drebbel', *ODNB*. Jonson refers to Drebbel's perpetual motion machine in *Epigrams*, 97.2, *Epicene*, 5.3.47–8, and *Britain's Burse*, 308. Henry Briggs was probably the brother of Jonson's friend Richard Briggs, Headmaster of Norfolk School, to whom Jonson presented a copy of Thomas Farnaby's edition of Martial in 1623. Henry Briggs had moved from London in 1620 to take up the new Savilian chair of Geometry in Oxford, but continued to work with colleagues at Gresham College such as Henry Gellibrand and Edmund Gunter. He and Jonson are likely to have been acquainted. Napier, who died in 1617, would have been well known to William Drummond, many of whose experimental interests he shared.

36. I differ reluctantly here from the view proposed by the late D. F. McKenzie, '*The Staple of News* and the Late Plays', 120–1. Pennyboy Junior's wish also to establish an academy (Intermean 4.18) may similarly mirror, but need not therefore mock, Edmund Bolton's proposal to establish an Academ Roial, with which Jonson's name had been associated (see Ch. 17 above). Cf. *The New Inn*, 1.5.56ff.

37. Kevin Sharpe, *The Personal Rule of Charles I* (New Haven, 1992), 9–23. Cf. the figure of Bat Burst, the 'broken citizen' of *The New Inn*.

Chapter 19

1. In *The Underwood*, 54, Jonson refers to a current wager that he weighs 'Full twenty stone, of which I lack two pound' (see Ch. 2 and n. 4). As neither of these poems is firmly datable it is difficult to assess any possible fluctuations in his weight around this time. In *The Magnetic Lady*, 2.3, Doctor Rut offers a detailed account of the swelling disease of dropsy (today known as oedema, often involving renal failure and a build-up of bodily fluid), which Jonson may possibly have been researching in relation to his own condition.

2. A stroke could have affected Jonson's facial nerves, causing palsy (or paralysis) and the lopsided appearance which Aubrey notes ('one eye lower than t'other': caption, Frontispiece). Poliomyelitis might similarly have restricted Jonson's mobility, but in the circumstances seems a less likely diagnosis. I am grateful to Dr Nicholas Alfieri MBBS for these suggestions. The quoted phrase is from Jonson's Letter 17, addressed to Cavendish in December 1631. 'Disease, the enemy, and his engineers, | Want, and the rest of his concealed compeers, | Have cast a trench about me, now, five years,' Jonson writes in 'An Epistle Mendicant', *The Underwood*, 71.4–6, a poem against whose title in the 1640–1 Folio a marginal date of '1631' is given, suggesting 1626 as a possible (though less likely) date for the onset of the illness.

3. *The Life of Edward Earl of Clarendon . . . Written by Himself* (Oxford, 1759), 16.

4. Anne Barton, *Ben Jonson: Dramatist* (Cambridge, 1984), 315–17; David Kay, *Ben Jonson: A Literary Life* (London, 1995), 168–9. For the full text of the poem (BL MS Sloane 826, fos. 192^v–193^v) see *CWBJ*, Dubia, Electronic Edition. A collection of the poems celebrating Buckingham's death was assembled by F. W. Fairholt, *Poems and Songs Relating to Buckingham and his Assassination*, Percy Society (London, 1850). On the assassination and its consequences, see Lockyer, *Buckingham*, chs. 10 and 11; 'The Examination of Benjamin Jonson', in W. Douglas Hamilton (ed.), *Original Papers Illustrative of the Life and Writings of John Milton*, Camden Society 75 (London, 1859), 72–3; *CWBJ*, Life Records, 76, Electronic Edition; Alastair Bellany, ' "Rayling Rymes and Vaunting Verse": Libellous Politics in Early Modern England', ch. 11 in Kevin Sharpe and Peter Lake (eds.), *Culture and Politics in Early Stuart England* (Houndmills, 1994).

5. On 14 November John Pory reported to Joseph Mead that Townley 'is got safe over to the Hague where some say he will print an apology for the fact': [Thomas Birch,] *The Court and Times of Charles I*, 2 vols. (London, 1848), 1.427. Townley later wrote verses responding to Alexander Gil's attack on *The Magnetic Lady*, and a verse tribute to Jonson for Benson's 1640 octavo edition of Jonson's translation of Horace's *Ars Poetica*. For his eulogy to Camden, see Wyman H. Herendeen, *William Camden: A Life in Context* (Woodbridge, 2007), 493–4. Townley was evidently at odds politically with his Christ Church colleague Richard Corbett, a lavish defender of Buckingham, his patron. See V. L. Pearl and M. L. Pearl, 'Richard Corbett's "Against the Opposing of the Duke in Parliament, 1628" and the Anonymous Rejoinder, "An Answere to the Same, Lyne for Lyne": The Earliest Dated Manuscript Copies', *Review of English Studies*, 42 (1991), 32–9.

6. Both Cotton and Selden were on hostile terms at this time with Heath, who may possibly have ordered a search to be made of Cotton's house during which the verses were discovered. Jonson, as a regular visitor to Cotton's house, might then have been suspected of having written them, and been called in for questioning. But this is guesswork. On Cotton's and Selden's relationship with Heath at this time, see Kevin Sharpe, *Sir Robert Cotton* (Oxford, 1979), 145, and G. J. Toomer, *John Selden: A Life in Scholarship* (Oxford, 2009), 1.327–8; for Townley's reply to Gil, H&S, 1.243.

7. L. E. Tanner, 'Literary Links with Westminster Abbey', *Transactions of the Royal Society of Literature*, 18 (1940), 27–8, cit. H&S, 11.576.

8. This record was discovered by Mark Bland, whose explanation of Jonson's presence on this occasion I follow here: 'Jonson, *Biathanatos* and the Interpretation of Manuscript Evidence', *Studies in Bibliography*, 51 (1998), 154–82 at 169 and n. 34; *CWBJ*, Life Records, 84, Electronic Edition.

9. *CWBJ*, Life Records, 83.

10. Gary Taylor, 'Thomas Middleton: Lives and Afterlives', in Gary Taylor and John Lavagnino (eds.), *Thomas Middleton: The Collected Works* (Oxford, 2007), 45.

11. Jonson may have known that Chaucer enjoyed a similar gift from the crown throughout his lifetime: Edmund Kemper Broadus, *The Laureateship: A Study of the Office of Poet Laureate in England with Some Account of the Poets* (Oxford, 1921), 42 n.2.

12. N. W. Bawcutt, 'New Jonson Documents', *Review of English Studies*, 47 (1996), 50–2, at 52.

13. The court acted 'at His Majesty's pleasure signified unto them by the Right Honourable the Earl of Dorset for and in the behalf of Benjamin Jonson, the City's Chronologer': *CWBJ*, Life Records, 87, Electronic Edition. In *The Underwood*, 13, Jonson thanks Dorset for 'Great and good turns' and 'noblest benefits' that he has bestowed upon him in times of need. It is tempting to think that *The Underwood*, 13 might have been written in response to the restoration of his pension, though its title, 'An Epistle to Sir Edward Sackville, now Earl of Dorset', suggests an earlier date of composition, and an earlier set of favours (Sackville became fourth Earl of Dorset in March 1624). Dorset may possibly be the addressee of Jonson's 'An Ode' ('High-spirited friend'), *The Underwood*, 26 (see Ian Donaldson (ed.), *Ben Jonson*, Oxford Authors (Oxford, 1985), 689, and Girolamo Lando's characterization of Dorset, who 'belongs to a great house, is of high spirit and universally esteemed, being considered one of the most active and generous persons of the kingdom': to the Doge and Senate, 19 March 1621: *CSPV*, 16 (1619–1621), 606.

14. *CWBJ*, Life Records, 64.

15. On 1 June 1621 he assigned £36 to John Hull: H&S, 1.236–7. On 26 April 1623 he assigned £20 to his 'verie loving ffrend Nicholas Harman esquier', former financial secretary to Richard Martin and now secretary in the Wards to Lionel Cranfield: Bawcutt, 'New Jonson Documents'.

16. See Frances Teague, 'Ben Jonson's Poverty', *Biography*, 2 (1979), 260–5.

17. *CWBJ*, Life Records, 72, 88, Electronic Edition.

18. *CWBJ*, Letter (i), Electronic Edition. A *regalo* is a choice feast, and a *musaeum* is a home of the muses, a place dedicated to learning.

19. Erasmus, *De Conscribendis Epistolis*, 172: vol. 24 of *The Collected Works of Erasmus*, ed. Craig Thompson (Toronto, 1978), cit. Heather Wolfe, *Elizabeth Cary, Lady Falkland: Life and Letters* (Cambridge, 2001), 43.

20. Letters 16.1, 17.31, 19.1. On Cavendish, see Ch. 2 above; Geoffrey Trease, *Portrait of a Cavalier: William Cavendish, First Duke of Newcastle* (London, 1979); Lynn Hulse, *ODNB*; Barton, *Ben Jonson: Dramatist*, ch. 14; *The Cavendish Circle*, ed. Timothy Raylor, special issue of *The Seventeenth Century*, 9 (1994) (especially Nick Rowe, '"My Best Patron": William Cavendish and Jonson's Caroline Dramas', 197–212, and Cedric C. Brown, 'Courtesies of Place and Arts of Diplomacy in Ben Jonson's Last Two Entertainments for Royalty', 147–71); *The Correspondence of Thomas Hobbes*, ed. Noel Malcolm, 1: *1622–1659* (Oxford, 1994).

21. Gerard Langbaine, *An Account of the English Dramatic Poets* (Oxford, 1691), 386.

22. John Aubrey, *Brief Lives*, ed. A. Clark (Oxford, 1898), 1.365, 25–6. Hobbes's account 'Of Persons, Authors, and things personated' in ch. 16 of *Leviathan* may perhaps have been influenced by his contact with Jonson: see my 'Shakespeare, Jonson, and the Invention of the Author', 2006 Shakespeare Lecture, *Proceedings of the British Academy*, 151 (2007), 319–38, at 333–4. On Hobbes as Fitz-Ale, see A. P. Martinich, *Hobbes: A Biography* (Cambridge, 1999), 88.

23. Edward Hyde, Earl of Clarendon, *History of the Rebellion and Civil Wars in England*, ed. W. Dunn Macray, 6 vols. (Oxford, 1888), 3.178–9, 180. The best account of the Great Tew circle is still that of Hugh Trevor-Roper in *Catholics, Anglicans, and Puritans: Seventeenth-Century Essays* (London, 1989), ch. 4. See also B. H. G. Wormald, *Clarendon, Politics, History, and Religion* (Cambridge, 1951), part 3; J. A. R. Marriott, *The Life and Times of Lucius Cary, Viscount Falkland* (London, 1907); K. B. Murdock, *The Sun at Noon: Three Biographical Sketches* (New York, 1939); Kurt Weber, *Lucius Cary, 2nd Viscount Falkland* (New York, 1940); J. C. Hayward, 'New Directions in Studies of the Falkland Circle', *Seventeenth Century*, 2 (1987), 19–48;; Paul G. Stanwood, 'Community and Social Order in the Great Tew Circle', in Claude J. Summers and Ted-Larry Pebworth (eds.), *Literary Circles and Cultural Communities in Renaissance England* (Columbia, Mo., 2000), 173–86.

24. Lady Falkland's translation was seized and burned on the instructions of Archbishop Abbot when it arrived in England, despite its dedication to Henrietta Maria. Lucius Cary maintained a high regard for 'the great, eloquent, and judicious Cardinal Perron', while differing from his religious views: Weber, *Lucius Cary*, 241–2.

25. 'Brawls': Hyde's comment on Hales, but generally true of the group: *Clarendon: Selections From the History of the Rebellion and The Life By Himself*, ed. G. Huehns (London, 1955), 40. Financial support: ibid. 64.

26. G. D. Boyle, *Characters of the Great Rebellion* (London, 1889), 294.

27. *Brief Lives*, ed. Clark, 1.225.

28. From Digby's essay on Spenser, written for Thomas May: BL Harley MS 4153, fo. 4.

29. On the significance of these patrons, see Robert C. Evans, *Jonson and the Contexts of his Time* (Lewisburg, Pa., 1994), ch. 8; Kevin Sharpe, *The Personal Rule of Charles I* (New Haven, 1991); R. T. Peterson, *Sir Kenelm Digby: The Ornament of England 1603–1665* (London, 1956); and E. W. Bligh, *Sir Kenelm Digby and his Venetia* (London, 1932). On the coexistence throughout the seventeenth century of print and manuscript circulation, see Harold Love, *Scribal Publication in Seventeenth-Century England* (Oxford, 1993). The importance to Jonson of manuscript circulation has been brilliantly established by the work of Colin Burrow: see his introduction to the poems in *CWBJ*, Electronic Edition.

30. 'Decaying': 'The Country's Censure on Ben Jonson's *The New Inn*', 1; 'declining wit': Owen Felltham, 'An Answer to the Ode of "Come, leave the loathed stage, &c."', 3: *CWBJ*, Electronic Edition.

31. Barton, *Ben Jonson: Dramatist*, ch. 12. John Caird's 1987 RSC production of the play was at the Swan theatre, with John Carlisle as Lord Lovel and Fiona Shaw as Lady Frampul: see Margaret Shewring and Ronnie Mulryne, *This Golden Round* (Stratford-upon-Avon, 1989), Lois Potter, 'The Swan Song of the Stage Historian', in Martin Butler (ed.), *Re-Presenting Ben Jonson: Text, History, Performance* (Houndmills, 1999), ch. 10, and Julie Sanders's introduction to the play in *CWBJ*.

32. The passage is based on Seneca's *De Constantia*, 4.2–3.

33. Barton, *Ben Jonson: Dramatist*, ch. 14. The precise nature of this nostalgia has prompted debate. Martin Butler, observing that 'in the 1630s the memory of Elizabeth could be appropriated in the service of more than one ideology', argues that Jonson's habit of retrospection in the late plays does not reflect adversely on the current style of Caroline rule: 'Stuart Politics in Jonson's *Tale of a Tub*', *Modern Language Review*, 85 (1990), 12–28; at 17. Julie Sanders detects a more critical and subversive political attitude informing the late plays: *Ben Jonson's Theatrical Republics* (Houndmills, 1998), especially chs. 9 and 10.

34. Jonson robustly defends Weston against the criticism of 'the envious' in *The Underwood*, 73, and speaks of him admiringly in *The Underwood*, 71, 75.97ff., 77; 78.27–8. The popular verdict on Weston went otherwise: 'He died unlamented of any, bitterly mentioned by most who never pretended to love him, and severely censured and complained of by those who expected most from him, and deserved best of him,' wrote Edward Hyde, Earl of Clarendon, *The History of the Rebellion and the Civil Wars in England* (Oxford, 1702), 1.43. On Jonson's loyal poems addressed to Charles and Henrietta Maria in the early 1630s, see James Loxley, *Royalism and Poetry in the English Civil Wars: The Drawn Sword* (Houndmills, 1997), especially 31–2.

35. BL Harley MS 7000, fo. 336. Pory had presumably been aware that Jonson was alive on 13 January 1631, when he had sent a report on the orders for *Love's Triumph through Callipolis* to Puckering: *CWBJ*, Masque Archive, Electronic Edition.

36. *CWBJ*, Electronic Edition.

37. Langbaine, *An Account of the English Dramatick Poets*, 292.

38. The figure returns throughout the play (4.8.51; 4 Chorus, 1–3; 5.10.81; 5.10.81) and is used by Jonson elsewhere in relation to the narrative skills of the historian ('To Sir Henry Savile', *Epigrams*, 95.14–16). On the central metaphors of the play, see Helen Ostovich, 'The Appropriation of Pleasure in *The Magnetic Lady*', *Studies in English Literature 1500–1900*, 34 (1994), 425–42.

39. On the significance of Jonson's emblem, see L. A. Beaurline, *Jonson and Elizabethan Comedy* (San Marino, Calif., 1978), appendix. On the circle, see Allan H. Gilbert, *The Symbolic Persons in the Masques of Ben Jonson* (Durham, NC, 1948), 'perfectio', 189–92, and Thomas M. Greene, 'Jonson and the Centred Self', *Studies in English Literature 1500–1900*, 10 (1970), 325–48.

40. In the epilogue written for court performance, Jonson remarks of the King: 'He knows our weakness and the poet's faults, | Where he doth stand upright, go firm, or halts, | And he will doom him. To which voice he stands, | And prefers that 'fore all the people's hands' (6–9). The lines refer both to Jonson's physical and creative capacities, may suggest his readiness to attend a performance at court, and stand respectfully in the royal presence.

41. See Peter Happé's introduction to his Revels Plays edition of *The Magnetic Lady* (Manchester, 2000), 32–4, and Helen Ostovich's introduction to her edition, *CWBJ*. On Briggs, see Ch. 18 n. 35 above.

42. Ostovich, introduction to *The Magnetic Lady*, *CWBJ*.

43. Julie Maxwell, 'Ben Jonson among the Vicars: Cliché, Ecclesiastical Politics, and the Invention of "Parish Comedy"', *Ben Jonson Journal*, 9 (2002), 37–68, at 49; Martin Butler, 'Ecclesiastical Censorship of Early Stuart Drama: The Case of Jonson's *The Magnetic Lady*', *Modern Philology*, 89 (1992), 469–81. Jonson appears to have been on friendly terms with John Grant, who had presented him with a copy of a book once owned by his father (Aldo Manuzio the younger's *De Quaestis per Epistolam Libri III* (Venice, 1576), now in the Cambridge University Library) with the inscription 'Ex dono Amici iuxta et erudite. [?] [?] D. Joanis Grant' ('the gift of my close and erudite friend, the Reverend John Grant'). See Fig. 43, and Jonson's Library, *CWBJ*, Electronic Edition.

44. Maxwell, 'Ben Jonson among the Vicars'; Butler, 'Ecclesiastical Censorship'; Sanders, *Ben Jonson's Theatrical Republics*, ch. 10.

45. H&S, 1.93–4. Whatever work Jonson completed in the capacity of City Chronologer does not survive. Two manuscript books of Middleton's were however extant as late as the

eighteenth century and are described by William Oldys in his annotations (now in the British Library) to Langbaine's *Account of the English Dramatic Poets*. One of these books, 'Annales', recorded civic events, being evidently related to Middleton's duties as Chronologer; the other, 'Middleton's Farrago', contained notes on various non-civic, political, and social topics of the day (see C. H. Herford, 'Thomas Middleton', *DNB*, 1894).

46. Diogenes the Cynic philosopher lived in poverty in a tub, scorning any further needs: a comically distorted version of Jonson himself in his final years. In his letter to Cavendish already quoted (409), Jonson had seen his own pet fox as another Diogenes, living reluctantly in a tub and cynically bewailing his master's impoverished state.

47. Barton, *Ben Jonson: Dramatist*, ch. 15; Peter Happé, introduction to *A Tale of a Tub*, *CWBJ*.

48. N. W. Bawcutt, *The Control and Censorship of Caroline Drama: The Records of Sir Henry Herbert, Master of the Revels, 1623–73* (Oxford, 1996), 179; Richard Dutton, *Mastering the Revels: The Regulation and Censorship of English Renaissance Drama* (Houndmills, 1991), 134–5.

49. Karen Britland, *Drama at the Courts of Queen Henrietta Maria* (Cambridge, 2006).

50. In the printed text of *Love's Triumph* (1–10) Jonson makes it clear that Charles's commission for the masque had come equally to himself and Jones, and that 'after some debate of cogitation with ourselves' they had jointly composed it.

51. John Newman, 'Inigo Jones', *ODNB*.

52. Bawcutt, *The Control and Censorship of Caroline Drama*, 186.

53. On these two entertainments, see Cedric C. Brown, 'Courtesies of Place and Arts of Diplomacy in Ben Jonson's Last Two Entertainments for Royalty', *Seventeenth Century*, 9 (1994), 147–71; Leah Marcus, *The Politics of Mirth: Jonson, Herrick, Milton, Marvell, and the Defense of Old Holiday Pastimes* (Chicago, 1986); and James Knowles's introductions to both entertainments, *CWBJ*. On Charles's journey to Scotland, see Sharpe, *The Personal Rule of Charles I*, 778–83.

54. Margaret Cavendish, Duchess of Newcastle, *The Life of William Cavendish, Duke of Newcastle*, ed. C. H. Firth (London, 1906), 103–4; Edward Hyde, Earl of Clarendon, *The History of the Rebellion and Civil Wars in England*, ed. W. Dunn Macray, 6 vols. (Oxford, 1888), 1.167; Brown, 'Courtesies of Place', 151.

55. Jonson also mounts a more searching critique of Jones's intellectual priorities and abilities in this entertainment, as D. J. Gordon demonstrates in the concluding section of his 'Poet and Architect: The Intellectual Setting of the Quarrel between Ben Jonson and Inigo Jones', in *The Renaissance Imagination: Essays and Lectures by D. J. Gordon*, ed. Stephen Orgel (Berkeley, 1975), 77–101.

56. See Joe Lee Davis, *The Sons of Ben: Jonsonian Comedy in Caroline England* (Detroit, 1967); Ian Donaldson, 'Fathers and Sons: Jonson, Dryden, and *Mac Flecknoe*', ch. 10 in *Jonson's Magic Houses* (Oxford, 1997); Martin Butler, 'The Sons of Ben', *ODNB*.

57. See Colin Burrow's detailed discussion of probable composition dates for this sequence and its variant texts, *CWBJ*.

58. *Brief Lives*, ed. Clark, 1.231.

59. ibid. 1.226–7.

60. *Jonsonus Virbius*, *CWBJ*, Literary Record, Electronic Edition.

61. See Anne Barton's introduction to *The Sad Shepherd*, *CWBJ*; and Stephen Knight's ' "Meere English flocks": Ben Jonson's *The Sad Shepherd* and the Robin Hood Tradition',

in Helen Phillips (ed.), *Robin Hood: Medieval and Post-Medieval* (London, 2005), 129–44; and, on Francis Waldron's eighteenth-century redaction of Jonson's play, Tom Lockwood, 'Francis Godolphin Waldron and Ben Jonson's *The Sad Shepherd*', *The Library*, 3 (2002), 390–412.

62. Eugene Giddens, n. to *The Sad Shepherd*, Prologue, 1, *CWBJ*.

63. *Notes & Queries*, 1st series, 6, 405; Wayne H. Phelps, *Notes & Queries*, NS 27 (1980), 146–9.

Chapter 20

1. 'After-times': *Epigrams*, 56.11 and 95.20; 'after-ages', *Catiline*, 3.3.259; 'after-state', *Epigrams*, 51.8. 'After-times' is also used by Shakespeare in *2 Henry IV*, 4.2.51 ('Much too shallow | To sound the bottom of the after-times': unrecorded by *OED*). 'After-life' is first found in the 1598 dedication to Marlowe's *Hero and Leander*: 'the impression of the man, that hath been dear unto us, living an after-life in our memory, there putteth us in mind of farther obsequies due unto the deceased.'

2. There is at present no complete study of Jonson's after-life, though its initial phase has been studied by G. E. Bentley, *Shakespeare and Jonson: Their Reputations in the Seventeenth Century Compared*, 2 vols. (Chicago, 1945), Hugh Craig, *Ben Jonson: The Critical Heritage* (London, 1990)—now revised and enlarged in the *CWBJ*, Literary Record, Electronic Edition—and Andrew Lynn, 'The Impact of Ben Jonson, 1637–1700', unpublished Ph.D. dissertation, Cambridge University (2000). For critiques of Bentley's methodology, see Ch. 14 n. 17 above. Gunnar Sorelius has examined Jonson's impact on Restoration drama in *'The Giant Race before the Flood': Pre-Restoration Drama on the Stage and in the Criticism of the Restoration* (Uppsala, 1966), and Robert Gale Noyes has written on *Ben Jonson on the English Stage 1660–1776* (Cambridge, Mass., 1935; reissued New York, 1966). Tom Lockwood has analysed the way in which Jonson was treated by his editors and remembered by poets and critics in the eighteenth and early nineteenth centuries: *Ben Jonson in the Romantic Age* (Oxford, 2005).

3. For *Jonsonus Virbius*, see *CWBJ*, Electronic Edition, Literary Record. The volume was printed in London by Elizabeth Purslowe and licensed for publication on 23 January 1638. Andrew Lynn analyses the collection in detail and traces its connections with Laudian Oxford and the Great Tew circle: 'The Impact of Ben Jonson, 1637–1700', unpublished Ph.D. dissertation, Cambridge University (2000), ch. 1. For Howell's letter, see *CWBJ*, Electronic Edition.

4. The volume in memory of King may have been compiled in emulation of *Jonsonus Virbius*: see Gordon Campbell, and Thomas N. Corns, *John Milton: Life, Work, and Thought* (Oxford, 2008), 97–8.

5. John Aubrey, *Brief Lives*, ed. A. Clark (Oxford, 1898), 1.151; Ian Donaldson, *Jonson's Magic Houses* (Oxford, 1997), ch. 1.

6. James Loxley, *Royalism and Poetry in the English Civil Wars: The Drawn Sword* (Houndmills, 1997), 38–9.

7. The phrases quoted are from the court record of a subsequent legal dispute between Walkley and the rival publisher John Benson concerning the publication of these works. See Frank Marcham, 'Thomas Walkley and the Ben Jonson "Workes" of 1640', *The Library*, 4th series, 11 (1930–1), 225–9, and Colin Burrow's textual essay on The Poems, *CWBJ*, Electronic Edition. On the composition and publication history of Jonson's

Second Folio, 1640–1, see the textual essays by David Gants, John Creaser, and Peter Happé, *CWBJ*, Electronic Edition.

8. *The Underwood*, 39, is now reckoned to be by Donne, and the remaining poems in the group probably by Jonson, though written in a style imitating that of Donne. For discussion, see Colin Burrow's headnote to *The Underwood*, 38, *CWBJ*.

9. *Herrick's Poetical Works*, ed. L. C. Martin (Oxford, 1956), 212–13.

10. 'The happy fields hold not a happier ghost,' wrote Lucius Cary in his eclogue in *Jonsonus Virbius* (146). William Cavendish, Barten Holyday, Samuel Sheppard, Andrew Marvell, and Charles Sackville, Lord Dorset, all employ the same analogy, often imagining Jonson however as a vexed rather than a happy ghost. See Ian Donaldson, 'Talking with Ghosts: Ben Jonson and the English Civil War', *Ben Jonson Journal*, 17 (2010), 1–18.

11. See *Discoveries*, 1752–62, and Ch. 1 above.

12. George Stutvile, Literary Record, *CWBJ*, Electronic Edition.

13. Spoken by Neander in 'An Essay of Dramatic Poesy' in John Dryden, *Of Dramatic Poesy and Other Essays*, ed. George Watson, 2 vols. (London, 1962), 1.70.

14. Edward Young, *Conjectures on Original Composition* ed. Edith J. Morley (Manchester, 1918), 35.

15. T. W. Baldwin, *Shakspere's Small Latine and Lesse Greeke*, 2 vols. (Urbana, Ill., 1944); Emrys Jones, *The Origins of Shakespeare* (Oxford, 1977). For the eighteenth-century view that Jonson—a keen detector in his lifetime of acts of plagiarism in others—was himself a plagiarist, see my essay ' "The Fripperie of Wit": Jonson and Plagiarism', in Paulina Kewes (ed.), *Plagiarism in Early Modern England* (Houndmills, 2003), ch. 8.

16. See Stuart M. Tave, *The Amiable Humorist: A Study in the Comic Theory and Criticism of the Eighteenth and Early Nineteenth Centuries* (Chicago, 1960); Donaldson, *Jonson's Magic Houses*, chs. 2 and 11.

17. Noyes, *Ben Jonson on the English Stage 1660–1776*, 28.

18. ibid. 253; *The Plays of David Garrick*, ed. H. W. Pedicord and F. L. Bergman, 7 vols. (Carbondale, Ill., 1980–2), 6: *Garrick's Alterations of Others, 1751–1756* (1982), 53.

19. Noyes, *Ben Jonson on the English Stage, 1660–1776*, 29, 33.

20. *Dramatic Miscellanies*, 2 vols. (London, 1784), 2.101–2.

21. On this large reorientation of scholarly admiration and attention, see R. W. Babcock, *The Genesis of Shakespeare Idolatry, 1766–1799* (Chapel Hill, NC, 1931); Jonathan Bate, *Shakespearean Constitutions* (Oxford, 1989); Howard Felperin, *The Uses of the Canon* (Oxford, 1991), ch. 1; Margreta de Grazia, *Shakespeare Verbatim* (Oxford, 1991); Michael Dobson, *The Making of the National Poet: Shakespeare, Adaptation and Authorship, 1660–1769* (Oxford, 1992); Simon Jarvis, *Scholars and Gentlemen: Shakespearian Textual Criticism and Representations of Scholarly Labour, 1725–1765* (Oxford, 1995); and Lockwood, *Ben Jonson in the Romantic Age* (n. 2 above).

22. Preface to *Three Plays for Puritans*, *The Bodley Head Bernard Shaw Collected Plays with their Prefaces*, ed. Dan H. Laurence, 7 vols. (London, 1971), 2.40–1.

23. These include Ezekiel Sanford's edition of 1819, Barry Cornwall's of 1838, and Robert Bell's 1856 edition of the poems. Gifford's own edition was reprinted by Francis Cunningham in three volumes in 1870 and, with additional editorial commentary, in nine volumes in 1875.

24. For an acute analysis of the strengths and limitations of Gifford's edition, see Lockwood, *Ben Jonson in the Romantic Age*, ch. 4.

25. William Hazlitt, 'On Shakespeare and Ben Jonson', in *The Complete Works of William Hazlitt*, ed. P. P. Howe, after the edition of A. R. Waller and Arnold Glover, 21 vols. (London, 1930–4), 6, 30–49. See also Hazlitt's 'Mr Gifford' in *The Spirit of the Age*, 11.
26. Helen Gardner in the *DNB*.
27. See Ch. 1 above; T. S. Eliot, *Selected Essays* (London, 1958), 148; J. B. Bamborough, 'Joyce and Jonson', *A Review of English Literature*, 2 (1961), 45–50.
28. See 64–5 above.
29. *The Artist as Critic: Critical Writings of Oscar Wilde*, ed. Richard Ellmann (New York, 1969), 34–5.

Index